CW00794767

# HIGHWAYS AND BYWAYS

IN

# GALLOWAY AND CARRICK

*Loch Neldricken and The Merrick.*

# Highways and Byways

IN

# Galloway and Carrick

BY THE REV. C. H. DICK
WITH ILLUSTRATIONS BY
HUGH THOMSON

ISBN 1 872350 38 0

First published 1916
Pocket edition 1924
Revised 1938

Special C. H. Dick Memorial edition 2001

Published & reset in
Scotland's National Book Town
by
G.C. Book Publishers Ltd
17 North Main Street
Wigtown
Scotland DG8 9HL
tel/fax 01988 402499
web: http://www.gcbooks.demon.co.uk
email: sales@gcbooks.demon.co.uk

Printed and bound in Great Britain by
Antony Rowe Ltd., Chippenham, Wiltshire

C. H. Dick

The new Pocket Edition of
*Highways & Byways in Galloway & Carrick* by C. H. Dick
Introduction by Julia Muir-Watt

I was once advised by a connoisseur that, if anyone should
wish to purchase only one Galloway book for a library, *Highways
and Byways in Galloway and Carrick* by the Reverend C.H.Dick
should be that book, and that its accuracy was such that it should
satisfy, even at the distance of over eighty years, any
topographical or historical query one might have. By coincidence,
only some weeks later, I received a copy of the leather-bound
pocket edition as a gift: the worn condition of that volume is now
testament to the way in which I rapidly learnt to verify the
prediction. My library may now have expanded from that single
Galloway volume, but C.H.Dick's book is the first and invariable
resort before any expedition, and the demand for a new edition
such as this one is proof that, for many others also, Dick is
foundation-writ.

The "Highways and Byways" series was begun in 1897 by
Macmillan, and its final volume was published as late as 1948. The
series was launched at a time when the motor-car was opening up
the countryside to tourists, and there was a ready market for guide-
books to less accessible areas and landmarks, with explanations
for the visitor of the historical, literary, architectural or folkloric
features of note. The writers invited to contribute to the series
were known experts on the counties in question, and included
some well-known writers, like E.V. Lucas, or, like C.H.Dick, those
who were less widely known, but who had already published
articles on the area. In Dick's own case, these included articles in
*Chambers's Journal*, *The Glasgow Herald*, *The Scottish Field*
and *The Scottish Review*, and comprised a fund of previous
expertise about the area which explains in part how it was possible
for authors to adhere to Macmillan's rather strict timetable of one

or one and a half years to complete both physical exploration and text. The Galloway and Carrick volume was one of only four to cover Scotland: by the early 1930's the only other Scottish volume was Andrew and John Lang's volume covering the Borders. This was eventually remedied , late on in the series, by the addition of two volumes written by Seton Gordon on the West and Central Highlands.

The series was also notable for the distinction of the illustrators chosen and the generous number of illustrations per volume. In this case, Hugh Thomson, one of the most sought-after topographical artists of the time, was commissioned to complete the illustrations and over one hundred pencil drawings appear in the text. Thomson was born in Coleraine, Northern Ireland, in 1860, moved to London in 1883, and began as illustrator, particularly of eighteenth and early nineteenth century subjects, for *The English Illustrated Magazine* from 1884. Macmillan then commissioned him to illustrate the English classics, such as the Pickwick Papers, Silas Marner and all the Jane Austen novels. His co-operation with the equally well-known American artist, Joseph Pennell, on the earliest volumes in the "Highways and Byways" series (Devon and Cornwall, 1897, North Wales, 1898, and Yorkshhire, 1899) marked the beginning of an involvement in the series which was to last until his death in 1920 (after finishing work on the illustrations for the Gloucestershire volume) and his artistic progression away from figure drawing to landscape and topographical studies.

It was an interesting feature of Macmillan's method in producing these books that the artists and writers did not collaborate, and indeed that the artist often received a separate and prior commission to visit the counties and complete the sketches before the writer had been selected, or at least before the text was completed. We know that Thomson was at work on the illustrations for the Galloway and Carrick volume in mid-August 1914, since he was mobbed by a jingoistic crowd while sketching at the Maxwellton bridge and mistaken for a German spy. C.H.Dick, who was by this time consolidating his previous articles into a continuous text for Macmillan's, wrote in the artist's defence to the *Stranraer Free Press* pointing out to a nervous public that anyone seen sketching might simply be illustrating his forthcoming book. The whole incident may account for some humorous description in the book, of the prevailing atmosphere of war hysteria :

"In the early months of the war the province was racked with the fearful joy of an airplane scare. There were strong suspicions, amounting almost to imperturbable conviction, that the enemy had a base in the Minigaff hills. Over-strained eyes saw hostile planes above Glentrool, and there were even rumours of hydroplanes disporting themselves over the lochs. It was reported in Newton Stewart one forenoon that a discovery of 'fifteen hundred tins' of petrol had been made; by the afternoon, the quantity had reached 'fifteen hundred tons'! Schoolboys neglected the works of Mr. Henty and Captain Brereton for more immediate thrills, and Mr. Buchan wrote *The Thirty-Nine Steps*".

Thomson usually spent anything from two to six months in an area he was sketching, and despite the annoyance of the Maxwellton incident and his first inclination to leave in disgust, he fortunately determined to finish the Galloway and Carrick sketches. In the early volumes of the series, Thomson's drawings were finished in pen-and-ink from his initial quick pencil sketches made on the spot, but the publisher eventually suggested that the first sketches would be of a standard quite suitable for publication. The original sketches, now highly sought after, as indeed are Thomson's published works, are on a much larger scale than the printed versions, since line blocks were used in their reproduction , a photographic process which enabled reduction without loss of detail.

Macmillan's choice of author for the Galloway and Carrick volume was particularly happy, and yet, for a writer whose name is now so closely associated with the literature of the province, his own biography has proved – as anyone will know who has tried – particularly difficult to trace. One gets the impression that he has been almost deliberately self-effacing. It is only due to his close friendship with his more famous contemporary and school-friend, John Buchan, that as much detail as survives has been preserved, and it is only thanks to his parishioners on the Shetlands that I finally managed to established his correct date of death □.

Charles Hill Dick was son of Rev. G. H. Dick , minister of Eglinton Street United Presbyterian Church in Glasgow; his mother's, Jessie Imbrie Mearns', father was Rev. Peter Mearns, of Coldstream West United Presbyterian Church. His great great grandfather and grand-uncle were respectively ministers of the Secession Church and of the United Secession church; an uncle was a vicar in England, and a cousin Congregational minister and Secretary of the London Congregational Union. With such a clerical and dissenting background, the choice of profession in the ministry must have seemed virtually inevitable. He was educated at Albert Road and Hutcheson's College, where he made the formative friendship of his lifetime, with his contemporary, John Buchan, whose charismatic personality, even at the time, gathered round him an admiring circle of classmates. Buchan's recent biographer, Andrew Lownie, makes it clear from his extensive references to the Dick-Buchan correspondence that the friendship continued throughout their lives, despite the physical distance which separated them in later years, and that Buchan confided in Dick on most of the important political, personal and literary events of his life. They went on to Glasgow University together, where Dick graduated in Arts in 1898 and in Divinity in 1901. During their university years, it may be that both became acquainted with Galloway, as well as Buchan's native Borders, on extensive walking tours taken during the vacations. Dick was also an impassioned angler, and in 1895, edited *The Compleat Angler* and lives of Izaak Walton and Charles Cotton, both in Scott's Library. In his last year at university, Dick edited the *Glasgow University Magazine* and had already begun contributing to *The Gentleman's Magazine*, *The Glasgow Herald*, and other periodicals, to which he eventually submitted the articles which became embodied in the "Highways and Byways" volume.

Dick's clerical career began in Glasgow, at Claremont Church, and included various locum charges at St. Andrew's, but he seems to have begun deliberately distancing himself from city appointments, and after being ordained at Bellshill East in 1906, he took on the charge of St. Mary's United Presbyterian Church at Moffat, in 1910. It was from here that he was enabled to consolidate his knowledge of the Galloway countryside, which he had already become acquainted with during a brief assistantship at Stranraer St. Ninian's in 1904/5 and which, on the evidence of his own testimony in the book, he had already begun to explore on cycling tours in the year 1909 (p.287). By the outbreak of the First World War , the popularity of his illustrated talks on his Dumfriesshire and Galloway tours, and other wider forays he had made - into the Russian steppes, for example - was such that they could raise funds for the war effort. Dick first served as a war-time teacher at Moffat Academy, and then enlisted as a private in the R.A.S.C. and was due for a commission when the Armistice was declared.

In the summer of 1919, he accepted a call to Greyfriars Church, Port of Spain, West Indies, returning only in 1924, on grounds of his health, after spending part of 1923 in Standard Oil's field in Eastern Venezuela. Pursuing what was an evident bent for the remote, however, he was immediately inducted at Uyeasound by the Presbytery of Shetland, beginning a career on the islands which lasted for the next 21 years, until his death. John Buchan visited him at Unst, giving an address from Dick's pulpit at Uyeasound in 1926. Dick moved to Cunningsburgh, despite the reluctance of the congregation at Uyeasound, and there presided over some stormy sessions relating to the reunification of the United Free Church with the Church of Scotland. He was in fact himself to participate prominently in the newly reunified church, when he acted as chaplain to John Buchan, chosen as Lord High Commissioner to the General Assembly of the Church of Scotland in 1933 and 1934. He also visited Buchan, when, as Lord Tweedsmuir, the latter became Governor-General of Canada in 1935. Dick's final posting was to the parish of Delting, also on the Shetlands, where in 1940 he undertook the charge of a mission station at Mossbank and Firth. There he married Catriona McRae, schoolmistress of Firth, and subsequently, of Skeld. It was at Skeld Schoolhouse that he died in March 1952.

Although the book is constructed as a circular journey from Maxwellton, along the Galloway coast, up into Carrick and back down to the Stewartry of Kirkcudbright via the Glenkens, it is clear that the writer had covered sections of the tour on different occasions: he refers to visiting the Moors of Wigtownshire in 1909, Stranraer in 1911, and S.R. Crockett's country near Loch Ken, in 1916. On page 28, he explains that: " I had made journeys along separate parts of the Galloway coast and had been so much delighted with what I had seen that I resolved to make a tour along the whole of it, from Maxwelltown, that is, and then up the coast of the Firth of Clyde". In earlier volumes of "Highways and Byways" in fact, such itineraries were marked in red on the fold-out map at the back of the book. The journey more or less coincides with the boundaries of the old province of Galloway, when the Stewartry of Kirkcudbright extended to Maxwellton and Carrick was part of Galloway.

The origin of the series in the coming of the motor-car had its irony, at least in the case of the Galloway and Carrick volume, since C.H.Dick not only carried out the entire tour on a bicycle, but makes it clear that the appreciation of the Galloway countryside would be dulled, if not destroyed, by the speed with which one travelled it. Speaking of the road from Carsphairn, he writes: "In the case of such roads as these the bicycle is the most rapid means of travel that one should permit oneself. One really ought to walk." It is clear that he disapproves of the roads, which – built to accommodate the new cars – were "modern, good and dull", when one can choose to take those which are "old, precipitous and delightful". (p. 344). He refers several times to the "serious" or "sentimental" traveller, the reverse of one who "lodges at a hotel, plays golf, pays his bill and goes away, and does not know that he has been in Galloway".

This then, is a demanding sort of travelling, and a demanding sort of travel-book, interested much more in by-ways than highways, and one which requires us to reverse our sense of priorities, so that the significance of places depends not on their populousness and connection with the greater world, but on a richness of association – historical , literary, folkloric, personal – which may leave little trace, except to the discerning eye. "The space allotted to places in this book", he declares, "is usually in inverse proportion to their size and commercial prominence". I cannot resist quoting a passage relating to St. John's Town of Dalry in the Glenkens, both because it demonstrates this cultivated taste for the apparently obscure, and because it is vintage C.H.Dick:

"I have tried to be sparing of superlatives in previous chapters, remembering that I had still to deal with Dalry and that if I could not hope to rise to the lyrical eloquence that it deserves, I must at least refrain from squandering prematurely the language at my command….How best to approach the village presents no problem to one who has never been there before – it is simply a question of convenience; but for the devotee it is one of propriety…."

It is the density of historical and other references which populate Dick's landscapes and townscapes. Facts deftly drawn from architectural history (the Inventory of Ancient Monuments for Wigtownshire was newly published in 1911) , Covenanting history, folklore, literary associations,  etymology and place-names, smuggling, shipbuilding, all contribute to give texture and depth to what is immediately before our eyes, and enable us, as it were, to see into another dimension. Added to that is Dick's awareness and profound knowledge of the distinguished tradition of travel-writing in and about Galloway which preceded his own. The list of authors he refers to includes Lord Cockburn, Thomas Pennant, Malcolm Harper, the Statistical Account of Scotland, Bishop Pococke, Daniel Defoe, George Borrow, Robert Louis Stevenson, John McDiarmid, and John Keats.

The sheer pleasure of reading C.H.Dick and the fact that the book has aged so well in its eighty-five year existence are due, however, not to the accuracy of the facts he adduces, but also, and mostly, to the delights of his style, to his powers of description and to the flashes of a rather quizzical sense of humour, which make one feel , by the end of the book, as if one has known the author for years. One thinks, for example, of his visit to Carsethorn, where he stayed at the Steamboat Inn: "all men know that no steamboat ever comes to Carsethorn. This was enough to put one in a good humour with the place.." Or one thinks of his account of the extraordinary courtship of John Livingstone, the eminent Presbyterian minister of Stranraer; Dick concludes the lengthy quotation from Livingstone's own account of his struggles with chastity, with the aside: "The story baffles comment; but one is glad to know it ended well".

If the evidence of re-issues is anything to go by, Dick's book found the audience it required and deserved: first published in 1916 in blue cloth with large block lettering on the front ( also including the illustrator's name) and a dust jacket printed in blue on cream paper, it was reissued in 1919, and in 1927. It was brought out in a pocket edition on thin paper in 1924, including an edition in publisher's trade leather with a slip-case. In 1937, the publishers asked for a revision, and the Second Pocket Edition, with a new preface, one new chapter, and new appendices appeared in 1938. All three thousand copies of this new edition were sold by 1946. GC Books of Wigtown reprinted in 1994, and I am happy to say, a further printing is now required.

☐ My thanks to Mr. Robert Jarmson of Cunningsburgh, Shetland, for providing me with CH Dick's date of death of 20th March 1952, and to Shetland Archives for their help tracing his obituary. His date of death is incorrect in my article on C.H.Dick in *Dumfries and Galloway – A Literary Guide*, Dumfries and Galloway Libraries, 2000.

☐ "John Buchan : Presbyterian Cavalier", Andrew Lownie,

*In the Galloway Highlands.*

# PREFACE TO THE SECOND EDITION

THE chief reason for issuing a second edition instead of another reprint is that the introduction of a Hydro-Electric Scheme into Galloway has given occasion for recasting some pages in Chapters XXX, XXXI, and XXXII, making some minor adjustments, and adding an appendix on the subject. Altered conditions arising from other causes and fresh knowledge have demanded revision of a large number of short passages, and some other additions have been made, including the whole of Chapter XXXVI and the Note on the Galloway Church Window.

When this book was first published, I was indebted to the writer of a review in *The Montrose Standard* for pointing out an inaccuracy on page 31. This was remedied before the first reprint was issued, and at the same time some minute emendations were made here and there. This new preface gives an opportunity of referring to some other matters.

The writer of the *Montrose Standard* review thought that, instead of ignoring the tradition that the Lady Dervorgilla built the old bridge on the Nith at Dumfries, I should have mentioned it, stating that it was baseless. This allusion will satisfy other readers who may have thought likewise. Here I may say that the reason for the unfinished state of Mr. Thomson's drawing on page 2 is that, while he was making it in August 1914, he was arrested by the police on suspicion of being a German agent.

A reviewer in *Nature* remarked on the omission of the loop of the Greek P on the right of the upper limb of the cross in the drawing of the " Peter " stone on page 239. The monument appears, however, to belong to the time when the Greek P was giving place in western Christendom to the Roman R. The otherwise admirably executed design has been corrected, and two letters required to complete the inscription have been added. The rough surface of the stone might easily cause such details to escape the artist's notice. I have also revised the drawing of the Kirkmadrine crosses on page 320 to make clear the Chi-Rho monogram in its later form.[1]

At this point I should like to supplement the account given of these crosses on pages 318–322 by quoting the authoritative opinion of Professor R. G. Collingwood that the Latinus stone in the museum at Whithorn is earlier. Discoursing on the Kirkmadrine monuments to the Cumberland and Westmorland Antiquarian and Archæological Society in June 1937, he described the Latinus stone as " hardly different from an ordinary Roman tombstone of the fourth century ", and attributed it to the early days of Ninian's Church. It was the oldest existing monument of Celtic Christianity,[2] the only man-made work of which one could say, " Perhaps this was actually seen and

---

[1] A modern example of the use of the Chi-Rho monogram in its earlier form may be seen on the Carsphairn memorial of the men from that parish who fell in the war of 1914–18.

[2] On the same occasion Professor Collingwood indicated the order in which the Celtic Churches were founded. There were four groups of Christian Churches which arose in the Celtic world just about the time when the Roman Empire failed any longer to hold these regions. Of these four the oldest was the church of Galloway. It was actually before the Romans finally left Britain that S. Ninian, who was a British prince by origin and had been educated in Rome, came and settled at Whithorn about the year 400 and began to evangelize Galloway, which had been outside the temporal power of the Roman Empire. This was the event which really founded the Celtic Church. It was exactly a generation later that the evangelization of Ireland began, for S. Patrick was consecrated bishop in 432, thirty-five years after the foundation of Candida Casa. The Welsh Church was still younger, for S. Illtud, who was its real founder, belonged more to the early sixth century than the late fifth, and S. David, its patron, belonged wholly to the sixth. Lastly, the Scottish Church, beginning with the foundation of Iona in 563, did not begin to develop until quite late in that century. Thus the four great branches of the Celtic Church appeared in this order : Galloway, Ireland, Wales and Iona.

touched by one of the great founder saints." Like the Whithorn tombstone, the Kirkmadrine monuments were rough stone pillars or narrow, upright slabs bearing inscriptions in a more or less Roman style. Unlike the Whithorn stone, they had a Chi-Rho monogram in a circle at the top, and the inscription came below it. The Whithorn stone had no Chi-Rho monogram; it was a tombstone pure and simple. These Kirkmadrine stones were a combination of tombstone and christened menhir, and were thus half-way between the Whithorn stone and the memorial crosses of the Anglian age. All of them belonged to the same school of design, and this was not a school that they could trace at Whithorn. In all three the Chi-Rho monogram in its circle was conceived and executed in very much the same way, and in all three there was one identical detail: the word ET was invariably written as a monogram with the cross-bar of the T joined to the middle stroke of the E. This monogram was not found in Roman inscriptions nor in the post-Roman inscriptions of Cornwall or Wales, nor had he found it in their Gallic and Spanish contemporaries. It seemed a peculiarity of these three stones and entitled them to speak of a distinct Kirkmadrine school with a tradition of its own. His general conclusion from these three stones was that the community at Kirkmadrine, founded perhaps as early as the time of Ninian himself, lasted there for at least four hundred years of continuous life and continuous tradition—continuous in its tradition of both worship and workmanship—and they could carry the story on for three other centuries at least if they took into account the other carved stones there. The significance of Professor Collingwood's inference in relation to the facile opinion that S. Ninian's work was soon extinguished by a pagan revival is obvious. It does not seem an extravagant supposition that the Church at Kirkmadrine, as at Whithorn, owed its origin to the only evangelist of the period whose name has come down to us in connexion with Galloway.

I was greatly obliged to Sir Herbert Maxwell for sending me some notes of his on the progress of Mary, Queen of Scots, through the south-western shires in 1563. These are based on a document preserved in the General Register House, Edinburgh. Use has been made of them on pages 154 and 236. The document shews that on the 10th of August the Queen visited the shrine of S. Ninian—the last sovereign to do so. It also implicitly justifies the name of Queen Mary's Bridge on the Penkill Burn near

Newton Stewart. The bridge had come to be associated in popular tradition with Queen Mary's flight from the battle-field of Langside. It is, however, well established that she came south by Sanquhar and Dumfries in 1568, and I was so sceptical about her having given ground for connecting her name with the bridge that in the first edition Mr. Thomson's drawing on page 155 was entitled "Bridge on the Penkill"; but now the popular name is given.

The chief aid in revising the footnotes on place-names has been Sir Herbert Maxwell's *The Place-Names of Galloway : Their Origin and Meaning Considered* (1930), a work that is the fruit of more than forty years of study subsequent to the publication of his 1887 volume on the subject, and is full of interest and charm, whether for the resident in Galloway or for the visitor. Some of his interpretations have not commanded the assent of a younger generation of scholars, but he did most valuable work as a pioneer in a difficult field and had, of course, the great advantage of minute local knowledge. I have been glad to avail myself also of the investigations of Professor William J. Watson in his monumental work, *The History of the Celtic Place-Names of Scotland*. Much thanks is due to the Carnegie Trustees and the Royal Celtic Society for facilitating the publication of these works.

Other books on Galloway deserving honourable mention are *The Merrick and the Neighbouring Hills : Tramps by Hill, Stream, and Loch* by Mr. John McBain and *Galloway : The Spell of its Hills and Glens* by Mr. Andrew McCormick. The latter volume contains a valuable chapter on "The Geology of the Merrick Region" by Mr. R. J. A. Eckford of His Majesty's Geological Survey. Along with this may be mentioned a very minute and exhaustive account of "The Loch Doon 'Granite' Area" by Mr. Charles Irving Gardiner, M.A., F.G.S., and Professor Sidney Hugh Reynolds, M.A., Sc.D., F.G.S. (read April 22nd, 1931), in *The Quarterly Journal of the Geological Society of London*. A similar monograph by these writers on the Cairnsmore of Fleet granite appeared in *The Geological Magazine* for July 1937.

In recent fiction set in Galloway scenes there are Miss H. M. Anderson's *Kelston of Kells*, Mr. R. W. McKenna's stories of the Covenanting period, and Mr. John Buchan's *Castle Gay*. Miss E. M. C. Balfour-Browne's *Solway Tides and Other Tales* and

" *If All Tales* . . ." belong rather to the Western Border; but one of the stories in the latter volume is set on and around Heston island. Mr. Freeman Wills Crofts in *Sir John Magill's Last Journey* makes a good use of Castle Douglas railway station. Miss Sayers' *The Five Red Herrings* has delighted a wider public than the artists of Kirkcudbright. A famous Gallovidian, Paul Jones, is the leading figure in Mr. John Herries McCulloch's *The Splendid Renegade*. Lord Sands used some Galloway material in four of the stories in *Kinlochmoidart's Dirk and Other Tales*— " The Beadle in Barbary," " The Bride of Baldoon," " The Laird of Kittlecummer," and " The Mochrum Elder."

As was to be expected of the author of *Adventures in a Coracle*, Mr. J. W. Herries did not neglect the possibilities of the Solway Firth for his favourite kind of navigation, and in his later work, *I Came, I Saw*, allows us to see him making his solitary cruise on his flimsy craft from Auldgirth on the Nith to the estuary of the Urr.

It should be stated that the page-headings give the names of the parishes.

Some readers may have noticed omissions. In dealing, however, with such an extent of country and such a variety of interests in a volume that was originally the longest in the series and that cannot be swelled indefinitely one cannot be minutely exhaustive and must sometimes be content, after leading the traveller so far, to leave him to make some discoveries for himself.

C. H. D.

The Manse,
    Cunningsburgh, Shetland.
        *January 22nd,* 1938.

# PREFACE TO THE FIRST EDITION

As the title announces, this book has for its subject Galloway and Carrick, a district which has remained unknown to the world longer than any other part of Scotland with the possible exception of the island of Rockall. For an illustration of the former neglect of the province of Galloway I would cite *The Scottish Tourist*, a guide-book published in Edinburgh in 1825 for the benefit of travellers who were induced to visit Scotland by the poems of Burns and Scott, but "above all" by the writings of "The Author of *Waverley*". This work is more remarkable for what it omits than for what it contains, and the most conspicuous omission is that of any allusion to Galloway. Both Burns and Scott were far from being oblivious of the province. The references to Galloway places and persons in the former are too numerous to notice here. *The Heart of Midlothian* derived some of its leading figures from the parish of Irongray; the coast of The Stewartry of Kirkcudbright provided the scenery, and more than the scenery, of *Guy Mannering*; the sad story on which *The Bride of Lammermoor* was founded belongs to the annals of Wigtonshire; and it was to the castle on the island in Lochinvar that "the lost bride of Netherby" was brought. The publishers of *The Scottish Tourist* "respectfully solicited corrections and suggestions for the improvement of future editions of the Work"; but when the fourth edition appeared, there was still nothing of Galloway, and the map of Scotland accompanying it is bounded on the south by a line running through Ayr, S. Mary's Loch, and Jedburgh!

Much more recent signs of ignorance could be recorded. I

remember using at school a text-book in geography which in
its account of the mountains of the south of Scotland mentioned
the Lead Hills, the Muirfoot Hills, and others, including " a low
ridge called the Haughshaw Hills " between the Firth of Clyde
and the Clyde basin ; but two considerable ranges in Galloway,
one of them distinguished by the highest peak on the mainland
south of the Grampians, appear to have had less reality for the
geographer than the mountains of Lyonnesse. It is not necessary
to enter into the reasons for this neglect. I hope that the following pages will do something to shew its folly. The credit of
making Galloway known more widely in recent years is due
mainly to Mr. S. R. Crockett's series of tales and romances
which began with *The Stickit Minister* and *The Raiders*.

The title indicates also that this is a book of the road.
It deals with highways and byways—

> The highways paced of men that toil or play,
> The byways known of none but lonely feet—

and the wide, uninhabited wildernesses where there is no road
but what a man makes for himself. It is not a guide-book in
form ; yet I should be both surprised and sorry if any traveller
did not find in it all the guidance that he needed. As for those
people who have the good fortune to be natives of the country
and can dispense with my descriptions, I hope that they will be
pleased with the quotations from former travellers. " Two
hundred years ago, it may be," says Mr. Birrell in one of his
essays, an itinerist " came through our village, passed by the
wall of our homestead, climbed our familiar hill, and went on
his way ; it is perhaps but two lines and a half he can afford
to give us, but what lines they are ! "

The plan of such a book as this excludes a formal history of
the country ; but I have inserted notes on the more important
phases in what seemed to be appropriate settings. For a connected narrative the reader will turn to *A History of Dumfries
and Galloway* by Sir Herbert Maxwell, or to the still useful
work of the Rev. William Mackenzie, *The History of Galloway*,
published in 1841. Some account of the more prominent
archæological subjects has been given, mainly from the recently
issued *Fourth Report and Inventory of Monuments and
Constructions in Galloway: Vol. I., County of Wigtown*, and
the *Fifth Report and Inventory of Monuments and Construc-*

*tions in Galloway*: *Vol. II., Stewartry of Kirkcudbright* of the Royal Commission on the Ancient and Historical Monuments and Constructions of Scotland. These volumes are referred to in the text as " the *Inventory* ". The principal sources of the translations of place-names are Sir Herbert Maxwell's *Studies in the Topography of Galloway* and *Scottish Land-Names*, and the Rev. James B. Johnston's *Place-Names of Scotland*. I am also indebted to Mr. Johnston for invaluable personal help and for revising the proofs of the foot-notes on place-names. I have not relied on books for epitaphs, but have either photographed or copied them afresh, and have been surprised to find how much need there was to do so.

It should be stated here that the Galloway of to-day consists of The Stewartry of Kirkcudbright and The Shire of Wigton. These have also been known respectively as Lower and Upper Galloway. Before 1186, Carrick, the southern division of Ayrshire, was included in the lordship. Apart from Carrick, the province sometimes extended over a wider area than its present.

The Stewartry was governed through a steward, who was sometimes called the Steward of Galloway ; The Shire through a sheriff, who was usually styled the Sheriff of Galloway. The latter office was hereditary. The province as a whole was the land of the Stranger Gaels. " During the latter years of Kenneth's reign (A.D. 844–860)," says Dr. Skene, " a people appear in close association with the Norwegian pirates, and joining in their plundering expeditions, who are termed Gallgaidhel. This name is formed by the combination of the two words ' Gall ', a stranger, a foreigner, and ' Gaidhel ', the national name of the Gaelic race. It was certainly first applied to the people of Galloway, and the proper name of this province, Galwethia, is formed from Galwyddel, the Welsh equivalent of Gallgaidhel. It seems to have been applied to them as a Gaelic race under the rule of ' Galls ', or foreigners, Galloway being for centuries a province of the Anglic kingdom of Northumbria, and the term ' Gall ' having been applied to the Saxons before it was almost exclusively appropriated to the Norwegian and Danish pirates." According to another view, represented in *The Encyclopædia Britannica*, the name was occasioned by the alliance into which the Picts of Galloway entered with the invading Northmen. The history of the Pictish lords is outlined in the chapter on

Kirkcudbright, and that of the Douglas line in connexion with Thrieve Castle.

It is vain to inquire

> What aspect bore the Man who roved or fled,
> First of his tribe, to this dark dell—who first
> In this pellucid Current slaked his thirst ?
> What hopes came with him ? what designs were spread
> Along his path ?  His unprotected bed
> What dreams encompassed ?  Was the intruder nursed
> In hideous usages, and rites accursed,
> That thinned the living and disturbed the dead ?

The earliest reference to the inhabitants of these parts occurs in the *Agricola* of Tacitus in connexion with a campaign waged about A.D. 81.  In the following century, Ptolemy calls the people of the country west of the Nith Νοονάνται (Latin, *Novantae*), a word formed from Νοονίος (Latin, *Novius*), the name of the river.[1]  It was probably in the same way that Bede at a later period called them *Niduari*.[2]  Pausanias,[3] writing about A.D. 175, states that Antoninus deprived the Brigantes of most of their territory because they had begun a war of aggression against the province of Genunia, which was subject to Rome, and it has been supposed that Galloway corresponds to that district ; but this identification is very doubtful.[4]  We are on surer ground in connecting the inhabitants of Galloway with the *Attacotti* of Ammianus Marcellinus [5] and the *Atticoti* of Jerome [6] in the fourth century. Ammianus speaks of *Picti, Saxonesque et Scotti et Attacotti* as sources of constant distress to the Britons of the Roman province.  Though the country of the *Attacotti* is not known

---

[1] *See* Note on Ptolemy's Place-Names, page 524.

[2] *Vita S. Cuthberti*, xi.

[3] ΠΕΡΙΗΓΗΣΙΣ 'ΕΛΛΑΔΟΣ, viii., 43, 4.

[4] "Genunia is unknown, but it has been conjectured to be Vinonia (Vinovia), now Binchester, near Bishop Auckland in the county of Durham, where there are remains of Roman walls and other antiquities."—Sir James G. Frazer's *Pausanias's Description of Greece*.

[5] *Rerum Gestarum*, xxvi., 4, 5.  Cp. xxvii., 8, 5.

[6] *Adversus Jovinianum*, ii, 7: *Quid loquar de caeteris nationibus, quum ipse adolescentulus in Gallia viderim Atticotos, gentem Britannicam, humanis vesci carnibus : & quum per silvas porcorum greges & armentorum pecudumque reperiant, pastorum nates & feminarum, & papillas solere abscindere, & has solas ciborum delicias arbitrari ?* See also the *Epistulae*, lxix, 3.

with certainty, "it seems probable", says Mr. C. J. Elton,[1]
"that they inhabited the wilder parts of Galloway." The
*Notitia Dignitatum*, an official gazette of the Empire compiled
about the end of the fourth century, mentions several
regiments of *Atecotti* as serving principally in Gaul and Spain.
Two of these regiments were enrolled among the Honorians.[2]
For a hundred and fifty years after the Roman power had
faded away, we learn nothing of this people; but towards
the end of the sixth century, when the kingdoms of
Bernicia, Deira, Strathclyde, and Dalriada were in conflict,
Galloway, says Mr. Hume Brown, "played a part of its own".
"Of its inhabitants we have only vague and contradictory
accounts; but they are usually spoken of as the 'Picts of Galloway', though their connection with the other Picts has not been
clearly made out."

The Anglic rule seems to have been established about the
opening of the sixth century and ended about 793, when the
Northmen attacked Northumbria. The first Scandinavian
settlements in Galloway were made in the latter half of the ninth
century, and the invaders maintained their supremacy until
the reign of Malcolm Canmore. The Norse suzerainty does not
appear to have precluded the existence of native lords. Even so
late as 1124 the inhabitants of Galloway were still reckoned a
distinct race, for David the First on coming to the throne in
that year addressed a proclamation to "all good men of my
whole kingdom—Scottish, English, Anglo-Norman, and Gallovidians". At the Battle of Northallerton, in 1138, the Gallovidians fought in the van of the Scottish Army in accordance
with a privilege which is supposed to have been conferred upon
them by Kenneth MacAlpin, who had won his crown with their
help in 844. They drove the English from their position; but
the other divisions of the army held back, whether from jealousy
or from some other cause, and the battle was lost to Scotland.
Justice was administered in Galloway under Celtic Law until the
death of Alan, the last of the Pictish lords. In 1324, Robert
the First gave a charter of "Liberties of new granted to the
inhabitants of Galloway" confirming "perpetuallie to our cap-
tanes and subjects in Galloway anent anie thing that sall be
said against them, be the sergents of Galloway that they sall
have ane gude and true assise of country men, and that they

[1] *Origins of English History.*    [2] *Ibid.*

sall not be oblissed to make purgation nor acquaintance conforme
to the auld law of Galloway". Gaelic was spoken in the
province until the end of the sixteenth century at least in the
hill districts.

Certain animals bearing the name of the province sometimes
arouse the inquiries of visitors. " Know we not Galloway
nags ? " says Pistol in the second part of *King Henry the
Fourth*. King Robert is said to have been mounted on one
when he met Sir Henry de Bohun on the field of Bannockburn—
the breed was well adapted for rapid manœuvring. William
Lithgow, the author of *The Totall Discourse of the Rare
Adventures and painfull Peregrinations of long nineteene
Yeares*, whose observations were made in 1628, says, " This
Country aboundeth in Bestiall, especially in little Horses, which
for metall and Riding, may rather be tearmed bastard Barbs,
then Gallowedian Nagges." Defoe notes about 1725 that
" the People of *Galloway* . . . . have the best Breed of strong,
low, punch Horses in *Britain*, if not in Europe, which are from
thence called *Galloways*.[1] These Horses, which are very much
bought up in *England*, are remarkable for being good natural
Pacers, strong, easy Goers, hardy, gentle, well-broken, and,
above all, not apt to tire." The breed had become scarce by
the eighteenth century, and when the second Earl of Stair was
abroad as an Ambassador, he is said to have selected a pair of
Galloway nags sometimes as a gift for persons of distinction.
The scarcity is explained thus by a writer in *The Statistical
Account* of 1845 : " A small breed of horses, from twelve to
fourteen hands high, was formerly common, and held in high
estimation in Galloway. There being little occasion to employ
them in the draught, they travelled quickly and safely, in a
rugged and mountainous country. The ancient breed is now
almost lost. Horses of greater weight became necessary, as
those every way fitted for predatory excursions ceased to be of
peculiar value for the operose processes of agriculture. Their

[1] *En ninguno de los puestos, o territorios de Escocia son las lanas
tan finas, y de tan buena raça los cavallos, puesto que pequeños, los del
pays les llaman* Galoway-nages ; *de suerte que ocasiona la prerogativa
desta tierra en esta especie el comun termino entre los Ingleses, que
hairendo de alabar la generosidad, partes, o servicio bueno de un
cavallo, le llaman* Galoway, *como por exemplo en España Xerezano, o
Cordoves.—Descripcion de Galoway por Ivan Maclelano in* Flæu's
*Nveve Atlas* (Amsterdam, 1662).

colour is generally a light bay or brown, with black legs ; their heads were unusually small, and their whole form indicated a capability of enduring great fatigue." Galloway nags would be classed correctly, no doubt, under " the northern, or dun, type, represented by the dun ponies of Norway (*Equus caballus typicus*), the closely allied Celtic pony (*E. c. celticus*) of Iceland, the Hebrides, &c., and the wild pony of Mongolia (*E. c. przewalskii*), with which the now extinct tarpan of the Russian steppes appears to have been identical ". MacKerlie refers to the belief that they were introduced from Scandinavia by the Northmen.

" The native sheep of Galloway ", says a writer in *The Statistical Account*, " was a small handsome white-faced breed with very fine wool. . . . This breed has long ago disappeared." Lithgow thought that the wool of the country was " nothing inferiour to that in Biscai of Spaine ; providing they had skill to fine, Spin, Weave, and labour it as they should. Nay, the Calabrian silke had never a better luster, and softer gripe, then I have seene and touched this growing wooll there on Sheepes backes ; the Mutton whereof excelleth in sweetnesse." The Scottish black-faced is the only breed that thrives to-day on the mountains.

Galloway cattle are hornless and have rough, glossy, black coats. There is also a White-Belted Galloway breed representing an ancient stock. The native cattle are valued for beef. Large numbers of Ayrshire cattle have been brought into the province for dairy-farming.

The Galloway pippin is referred to in the chapter on Wigton.

I close the preface with another quotation from Lithgow. " I found heere in Galloway, in diverse Rode-way Innes, as good Cheare, Hospitality, and Serviceable attendance, as though I had beene ingrafted in Lombardy or Naples." The modern traveller may count on a similar experience.

C. H. D.

S. MARY'S MANSE, MOFFAT.
*January 25th*, 1916.

P.S.—I have to thank the proprietors of *Chambers's Journal*, *The Glasgow Herald*, *The Scottish Field*, and *The Scottish Review* (Messrs. Thomas Nelson & Sons) for permission to reprint certain sections of the following chapters.

*Portling.*

*Kirkmadrine.*

# CONTENTS

## CHAPTER I

The Old Bridge on the Nith—Richard Franck—Witch-burning
—" I'm banish't! I'm banish't!"—The Brigend of
Dumfries—" Maxwellton braes "—The Mote of Troqueer
—Lincluden—*Ca' the Yowes to the Knowes*—Pennant's
notes—The Convent—The College—The tomb of the
Duchess of Touraine—The Lincluden Border Ordinances
—Royal guests in 1460—Their linen, wine, and postages
—James the Fourth and his *largesse*—The last provost
and his descendants—Terregles Queir—Terregles House.

## CHAPTER II

The grave of Helen Walker, the prototype of Jeanie Deans—
The crime and condemnation of Isobel Walker—Helen's
exertions on her behalf—Helen's history and character
—Scott's inscription on the tombstone—A Covenanters'
grave—John Welsh, minister of Irongray—The Communion Stones of Irongray.

## CHAPTER III

The road from Maxwelltown to New Abbey—Sweetheart
Abbey—Notes on the Abbey Church—Edward the First
at Sweetheart Abbey—The Archbishop of Canterbury
fords the Solway to meet him—The monks prepare for
the Reformation—Inscription in the churchyard—Views
of the Abbey Church—The Abbot's Tower—Kirkconnell
Tower.

## CHAPTER IV

## CHAPTER V

## CHAPTER VI

## CHAPTER VII

# CHAPTER VIII

# CHAPTER IX

# CHAPTER X

# CHAPTER XI

## CHAPTER XII

## CHAPTER XIII

## CHAPTER XIV

## CHAPTER XV

## CHAPTER XVI

## CHAPTER XVII

## CHAPTER XVIII

## CHAPTER XIX

## CHAPTER XX

# CHAPTER XXV

# CHAPTER XXVI

# CHAPTER XXVII

# CHAPTER XXVIII

## CHAPTER XXXIII

## CHAPTER XXXIV

## CHAPTER XXXV

*Small Cannon in front of Monreith House.*

*Palnackie.*

# LIST OF ILLUSTRATIONS

*Auchencairn.*

# HIGHWAYS AND BYWAYS

### IN

# GALLOWAY AND CARRICK

# HIGHWAYS AND BYWAYS

IN

# GALLOWAY AND CARRICK

## CHAPTER I

### MAXWELLTOWN AND LINCLUDEN

The Old Bridge on the Nith—Richard Franck—Witch-burning—"I'm
banish't! I'm banish't!"—The Brigend of Dumfries—
" Maxwellton braes "—The Mote of Troqueer—Lincluden—*Ca'
the Yowes to the Knowes*—Pennant's notes—The Convent—
The College—The tomb of the Duchess of Touraine—The
Lincluden Border Ordinances—Royal Guests in 1460—Their
linen, wine, and postages—James the Fourth and his *largesse*—
The last provost and his descendants—Terregles Queir—
Terregles House.

THE motor-car, the landau, and the caravan have their several
uses and joys ; but none of them can be driven along the Old
Bridge on the Nith. I exulted, therefore, in my humble bicycle,
for there seemed to be a sentimental propriety in entering the
Province of Galloway by this ancient structure. No man, indeed,
may hope to ride up the flight of steps leading to it ; but after
a brief portage one may mount and glide smoothly along.

The massive piers and narrow arches give an unusual impression of solidity. Looking at the bridge end-wise, you might take
it for a buttressed causeway. Built originally of nine arches,
it consists now of only six.[1] When the new bridge a little

[1] *The Encyclopædia Britannica*, by an odd inadvertence, gives the
present number as three (1916) and has continued to do so in the
twelfth, thirteenth and fourteenth editions !

farther up the river was opened in 1794, the eastmost arch was taken away. Later, as the river was confined more and more by extensions of the embankment, two others became stranded high and dry, and with their removal and the addition of the steps that were needed to give access, the bridge took its present form. The recesses in what is now the middle indicate the place where the fortified gatehouse stood. Serious damage has been caused by floods on several occasions; but this has always been repaired.

The earliest reference to the bridge occurs in 1426, when

*The Old Bridge on the Nith and Maxwelltown.*

Margaret Duchess of Touraine, Countess of Douglas, and Lady of Galloway and Annandale, confirmed a grant of the customs and tolls of the bridge to " God Almighty, the Blessed Virgin Mary, S. Francis, and the Warden and Friars-Minors of Dumfries ". One wonders if, as she crossed the river, the friars threw open the gate without demanding toll, or if she insisted on paying like other people.

We have next the Papal Relaxation of 1431–2, where mention is made of " the building of the bridge which has been begun recently over the river Nith near the burgh of Drumfres by the burgesses and inhabitants of these parts ".

It is stated in the Duchess's charter that the bridge custom

was one which " our ancestors and we were wont to receive
at the end of the bridge of Drumfres ". The Duchess was
a daughter of Robert the Third. The Old Bridge was
probably preceded by a wooden one, the property of the
Crown.[1]

" Here ", says Richard Franck,[2] a soldier who had fought
under Cromwell and came to Scotland on a fishing tour about
1656, " you may observe a large and spacious bridg, that directly
leads into the country of Galloway, where thrice in a week you
shall rarely fail to see their maid-maukins dance corantos in
tubs." Had he been here on a certain April afternoon in 1659
and looked down at the open space on the left bank of the river,
he would have seen a less diverting spectacle, the strangling and
burning of nine women who had been found guilty on the
charge of various acts of witchcraft[3]; and if he had stood here
on a certain day a few years later, he would have heard a child
who was being carried along in a basket wailing out, " I'm
banish't ! I'm banish't ! "—an incident of another form of
suffering. The Rev. John Blackader, minister of the parish
of Troqueer[4], of which Maxwelltown forms a part, had been
ejected by the Glasgow Act of 1662 ; [5] and from a son who was
ten years old we get a story of the Persecution as it appeared
to a child : " A party of the King's life guard of horse, called
Blew-benders, came from Dumfries to Troqueer to search for
and apprehend my father, but found him not, for what occasion
I know not : whether he stayed beyond the set day for transporting himself and numerous family of small children ten miles
from his parish church ; or because he was of the number of

---

[1] For further details see *The Growth of a Scottish Burgh ; A Study
in the Early History of Dumfries* by G. W. Shirley.

[2] *Northern Memoirs.*

[3] The sentence was that they should be taken " to the ordinar
place of execution for the burghe of Dumfreis, and ther, betuing two
and four hours of the afternoon, to be strangled at staikes till
they be dead, and thereftter ther bodyes to be burned to ashes, and
all ther moveable goods to be esheite" .

[4] The name is probably the same as Traquair, green farm.—
Johnston.

[5] The Act ordained that every minister who had not obtained
presentation from the lawful patron and collation from the bishop
must now do so. Nearly three hundred ministers preferred to risk
expulsion from their charges. The majority of the Privy Council
are said to have been drunk when they passed the Act.

those who refused to observe the 29th of May.[1]  So soon as the
above party entered the close, and came into the house, with
cursing, swearing, and damning, we, that were the children,
were frightened out of our little wits and ran up stairs, and I
among them ; who, when I heard them all roaring in the room
below, like so many breathing devils, I had the childish curiosity
to get down upon my belly, and peep through a hole in the floor
above them, to see what monsters of creatures they were ; and
it seems they were monsters indeed for cruelty ; for one of them
perceiving what I was doing, immediately drew his sword, and
thrust it up, with all his force, where I was peeping, so that the
mark of the point was scarce an inch from the hole, though no
thanks to the murdering ruffian, who designed to run it up
through my eye.   Immediately after, we were forced to pack up,
bag and baggatch, and to remove to Glencairn, ten miles from
Troqueer.   We who were the children were put into cadgers'
creels, where one of us cried out coming throw the Brigend of
Dumfries, ' I'm banish't, I'm banish't.'   One happened to
ask, ' Who has banish't ye my bairn ? ' he answered, ' Byte
the sheep[2] has banish't me.' " [3]

After Blackader had settled at Glencairn, he decided to remove
his family to Edinburgh and went thither to seek a lodging.
On the day of his departure, Sir James Turner received instructions from the Bishop of Galloway to apprehend him.   When the
soldiers came to his house at Glencairn, there ensued another

---

[1]  " In this session [1661] the parliament hade made ane act, that
the 29th day of May should be a solemn holy day, both because it
was the birth-day of the king, and also the day of his restauration.
This was a great offence to all the children of the church of
Scotland, who used to be very zealous for the observation of the
Lord's Sabbath, but very much also for the preservation of
Christian liberty for all other dayes, nor could they apprehend
the obligation upon the nation, either upon the account of the
king's birth or restauration, to be so great as to bind those that
refused to keep Christmas for Christ's birth-day, or Pasch for
his resurrection day, to doe that for Charles they scrupled to doe
for their Saviour."—*The Secret and True History of the Church of
Scotland from the Restoration to the Year* 1678 by James Kirkton.
[2]  Sir James Turner, who commanded the military at Dumfries,
was known among the Covenanters as Bloody Bite-the-sheep.
Dalzell of Binns was The Muscovy Beast.   He had been a general
in the Russian Army and had fought against the Turks and Tatars.
He commanded the troops who suppressed the Pentland Rising.
[3]  *Memoirs of the Rev. John Blackader* by Andrew Crichton.

experience of terror for the children. "These rascally ruffians besett our house round, about two o'clock in the morning," says his son, "then gave the cry, 'Damn'd whigs, open the door.' Upon which we all got up, young and old, excepting my sister, with the nurse and the child at her breast. When they came in, the fire was gone out: they roared out again, 'Light a candle immediately, and on with a fire quickly, or els we'l roast nurse and bairn and all in the fire, and make a braw bleeze.'" The soldiers searched the house for Blackader, breaking down furniture and running their swords through beds, while the boy, trembling in his night-shirt, was compelled to hold the candle. "So soon as I was relieved of my office, I begins to think, if possible, of making my escape, rather than to be burnt quick, as I thought and they threatened. I goes to the door, where there was a sentry on every side, standing with their swords drawn: for watches were set round to prevent escape. I approached nearer and nearer, by small degrees, making as if I were playing myself. At last, I gets out there, making still as if I were playing, till I came to the gate of the house; then, with all the little speed I had, (looking behind me, now and then, to see if they were pursuing after me), I ran the length of half a mile in the dark night, naked to the shirt. I got to a neighbouring toune, called the Brigend of Mennihyvie; where thinking to creep into some house to save my life, I found all the doors shut, and the people sleeping. Upon which I went to the cross of the toune, and got up to the uppermost step of it; and there I sat me down, and fell fast asleep till the morning. Between five and six, a door opens, and an old woman comes out; and seeing a white thing upon the cross, comes near it; and when she found it was a little boy, cryes out, 'Jesus, save us!—what art thou?' With that I awaked, and answered her, 'I am Mr. Blackader's son.' 'O my puir bairn! what brought thee here?' I answers, 'There's a hantle of fearful men, with red coats, has brunt all our house, my breether and sister, and all the family.' 'O puir thing,' (says she,) 'come in and lye down in my warm bed:'—which I did; and it was the sweetest bed that I ever met with."

The Brigend of Dumfries referred to in the foregoing narrative is the town at the west end of the Old Bridge. It was erected into a burgh of barony in 1810 and into a parish *quoad sacra* in 1834, and was given the name of Maxwelltown in honour of the lord superior. The "Maxwellton braes" of the song, *Annie Laurie*, are not to be seen here ; but are in the Dumfriesshire parish of Glencairn. The song itself, however, in its earliest form may belong to Galloway, for it has been attributed to William Douglas, laird of Fingland, a small estate near Dalry. It consisted of two verses. Lady John Scott re-wrote the second and added the third.

The original version was :

> Maxwelton banks are bonnie
>   Whare early fa's the dew ;
> Whare me and Annie Laurie
>   Made up the promise true ;
> Made up the promise true,
>   And never forget will I ;
> And for bonnie Annie Laurie
>   I'l lay down my head and die.

> She's backit like a Peacock,
>   She's breastit like a Swan,
> She's jimp about the middle,
>   Her waist ye may weill span ;
> Her waist ye may weill span,
>   And she has a rolling eye,
> And for bonnie Annie Laurie
>   I'l lay down my head and die.

The lady of the song was Anne, daughter of Robert Laurie of Maxwellton, who was created a baronet of Nova Scotia in 1685. She was born on the 16th of December, 1682, and became the wife of Alexander Ferguson of Craigdarroch, who was elected a member of Parliament in 1717.

The parish of Troqueer possesses a significant monument in the mote at the south end of Maxwelltown. There were four motes in the immediate neighbourhood of the ancient burgh of Dumfries—at Troqueer and Lincluden on the west bank of the Nith, and at Townhead and Castledykes on the east. They commanded the fords and the approaches to the burgh, and it is possible that they were designed to strengthen it as a Norman outpost against the wild Celts of Galloway.

The Troqueer Mote is unusually large. Its neighbour at Lincluden, about two miles up the river, is comparatively small. The sides are terraced, and may have been fortified with palisades. It is now covered with living trees, and one can spend delightful hours lying on the grassy slope under their shade, looking at the beautiful chancel of the Collegiate Church, and listening to the murmur of the Cluden and the Nith.  Burns often walked the mile or two to Lincluden when he lived in Dumfries.  His poem, *The Vision of Libertie* speaks of " yon roofless tower " and tells how—

> The burn, adown its hazelly path,
>     Was rushing by the ruin'd wa',
> Hasting to join the sweeping Nith,
>     Whose roarings seem'd to rise and fa'.

Another of his poems deserves quotation in full :

### CA' THE YOWES TO THE KNOWES

#### *Chorus*

> Ca' the yowes to the knowes,
> Ca' them whare the heather grows,
> Ca' them whare the burnie rowes,
>     My bonnie dearie.

> Hark the mavis' evening sang
> Sounding Clouden's woods amang !
> Then a faulding let us gang,
>     My bonnie dearie.
>
> > Ca' the yowes, etc.

> We'll gae down by Clouden side,
> Thro' the hazels spreading wide,
> O'er the waves that sweetly glide,
>     To the moon sae clearly.
>
> > Ca' the yowes, etc.

> Yonder Clouden's silent towers,
> Where at moonshine midnight hours,
> O'er the dewy bending flowers,
>     Fairies dance sae cheerie.
>
> > Ca' the yowes, etc.

> Ghaist nor bogle shalt thou fear ;
> Thou'rt to love and heaven sae dear, .
> Nocht of ill may come thee near,
>     My bonnie dearie.
>
> > Ca' the yowes, etc.

> Fair and lovely as thou art,
> Thou hast stown my very heart ;
> I can die—but canna part,
>     My bonnie dearie.

*Chorus*

> Ca' the yowes to the knowes,
> Ca' them whare the heather grows,
> Ca' them whare the burnie rowes,
> 　　My bonnie dearie.

When I first saw the ruin under the strong sunshine and blue
sky of a morning in spring, it proved to be much more beautiful

*Lincluden College.*

than I had expected, and I was not surprised later by the enthusiasm of the *Inventory* in describing it as " probably the richest
example of · Decorated work in Scotland ". Any published
photographs that I had seen had not been happily conceived ;
everything had been sacrificed to the desire to bring the Cluden
Burn into the picture—I suppose, because Burns had written
about it. The best view disclosed itself as I sought to take a
photograph of the mote-hill, when the sunshine lit up the
weather-worn walls and the beautiful window traceries while

the leafless trees on the right cast long, straggling shadows on the grass. A thin iron railing protecting the ruin from the successors of a former generation of the schoolboys of Maxwell-town and Dumfries who scrambled unchidden on the walls and over the window-sills is harmless from the pictorial point of view. When these boys are old enough to be lovers, they will be glad of the care bestowed none too soon upon this pleasant goal of lovers' walks.

Thomas Pennant, who made tours in Scotland in 1769 and 1772, saw little of Galloway, like many another visitor from the south. He came, however, to Lincluden and was much pleased with the carved stone-work. What he says of its history may serve as a summary. " This religious house is seated on a pleasant bank, and in a rich country : and was founded and filled with *Benedictine* nuns, in the time of *Malcolm* IV. by *Uthred*, father to *Roland*, Lord of *Galloway*. These were expelled by the Earl of *Douglas* (known by the titles of *Archibald* the black, or *grim*, and the terrible) probably as *Major* insinuates, on account of the impurity of their lives, for the Earl was a man in piety singular through his life, and most religious according to those times. He fixed in their places a provostry, with twelve beads-men, and changed the name to that of the college."

In establishing the convent, Uchtred was following the example of his father, Fergus, who founded the priories of Whithorn and S. Mary's Isle and the abbeys of Dundrennan, Soulseat, and Tongland. It must have been between 1160 and 1164 that the foundation took place. The remains of the convent buildings shew that they were of the style of the Transition period when Norman architecture was being succeeded by Early English.

Of the history of the convent for considerably more than two centuries, the only incident recorded is that the Prioress Alianore swore fealty to Edward the First at Berwick in 1296. The peace was broken in a high-handed fashion by Archibald the Grim, the third Earl of Douglas and the first of the line to rule over the whole of Galloway. It is not clear whether his expulsion of the nuns was interested persecution or well-deserved discipline. The historian who claims that Douglas was moved simply by " an eye for religion, and a special care for the pure and sincere worship of God " admits that he did thereby " greatly increase his revenues, and enlarge his dominions ".

On the other hand, it is scarcely credible that Douglas should have pressed a groundless charge against the nuns in so grave a matter as their vows of chastity. The explanation of the

*The Duchess of Touraine's Tomb.*

incident seems to be that "irregularities" had occurred, and that Douglas, instead of insisting that the culprits should be brought before an ecclesiastical court, used the occasion for enriching himself.

In place of the convent he founded the College or Provostry

of Lincluden, partly in order to silence criticism and partly to glorify the house of Douglas. The latter motive appears in the remarkable number of shields used in the chancel decorations. The masses were to be offered for the exclusive benefit of the Douglas family, and the principal offices were allotted to Douglases and their friends. The community consisted at first of twelve canons or secular priests with a provost, and was enlarged some years later to include eight prebendaries, twenty-four bedesmen, and a chaplain.

The remains of the convent and the college exhibit side by side the styles of the twelfth and fourteenth centuries, the earlier built with a simple massiveness, the later with rich decoration.[1] Enough of the ornamentation of the chancel has survived the ravages of weather and of profane hands to enable one to picture the beauty of its prime. The tomb of Margaret, daughter of Robert the Third and wife of Archibald fourth Earl of Douglas and Duke of Touraine, appears to have been built at the same time as the chancel and while the Duchess was yet alive. The epitaph speaks of her as *regis Scocie filia* as if her father were reigning, and there is no indication of when she died. Her title as Duchess of Touraine is not given.[2] This is the inscription :—

alaide : de : dieu

Hic : iacet : dña : margareta : regis : scocie : filia : quoda
comitissa : de : douglas : dña : galwidie : et : vallis
anadi . .

The badly-defaced fragments of the effigy of the Duchess have been restored to their position on the ledge above the

---

[1] For a detailed description see the *Inventory*.

[2] " The absence of any heraldic device or emblem referable to the duchy of Touraine on the tomb seems to point to its completion prior to 1424. Princess Margaret, in a letter dated 1447, addressed to Charles the Seventh of France, claimed her terce out of the duchy of Touraine, to which, however, the French king replied that as the duchy had reverted to the crown upon the death of the first duke, and owing to a report of the second duke's death, he had bestowed the duchy upon Louis of Anjou, king of Sicily. The omission of the title, Duchess of Touraine, from the epitaph on the back of the tomb is thus explained."—The *Inventory*.

actual tomb[1] and under the deeply-recessed, arched canopy.
Pennant makes the extraordinary statement that " her bones,
till lately, were scattered about in a most indecent manner by
some wretches who broke open the repository in search of
treasure ".

The college buildings were used sometimes for other purposes
than those of the religious life. A convention summoned by
William eighth Earl of Douglas, as Warden of the Western
Border, to revise the laws relating to Border warfare met
here in 1448. When " the whole Lords, Freeholders, and eldest
Borderers, that best knowledge had " were assembled, statutes
were made under the following heads : 1 Intercommoning
with Englishmen, 2 Of him that passeth from his company,
3 That all men fight on foot, 4 Arraying the host, 5 Taking
another man's horse, 6 Taking of prisoners, 7 Rieving of other
men's prisoners, 8 Contention for a prisoner, 9 Ransoming
officers, 10 Proportioning of ransom, 11 Takers or concealers
of traytors, 12 Beacons to be sustained, 13 Pursuit on firing
the beacons, 14 Prisoners not to pass without safe conduct,
15 Suffering prisoners to escape, 16 Parting of goods, 17 Desert-
ing, 18 Rieving of prisoners or goods. These are known as
the Lincluden Border Ordinances.[2]  The text of some of them
follows :

*Intercommoning with Englishmen :* " It is founded and
ordained by the law of Marches, that no manner of person,
man nor woman, of any degree, shall intercommon with any
English man or woman either in Scotland or in England,
except the prisoners shall come in Scotland, without the special
licence of the warden or his deputy asked and obtained in
time of warfare, under the pain of treason."

*Taking of prisoners :* " When it shall happen us to win any

---

[1] The blazonings on nine shields carved on the lower part of the
tomb, so far as they can be deciphered, are as follows :—(1) A
saltire and chief (Annandale), (2) a lion rampant crowned (Galloway),
(3) three stars (Murray of Bothwell), (4) a man's heart with three
stars in chief (Douglas), (5) (too much wasted for identification),
(6) seemingly vair or bars *nebulé* or wavy, for Drummond (the coat
of the Princess Margaret's mother), (7) a fess chequy (Stewart),
(8) (uncharged or completely effaced), (9) five pallets (Atholl).—The
*Inventory.*

[2] Harleian MSS., vol. 4700, British Museum. See MacDowall's
*Chronicles of Lincluden,* Appendix C.

field, whoever he be that arrests any prisoner, and then follows off the field, and he will swear, when he comes home, that he did that for safety of his prisoner's life, that condition shall be of no avail; and whoever he be that slays his fellow's prisoner, after he be arrested, shall pay his ransom to his taker, if he be of power; and if he be not of power, he shall die therefore.

" Also it is found statute and use of Marche, that it is lawful to any man to take as many prisoners as he may, both on foot and horse, so that he lead them with the strength of Scotsmen; and to take a token of his prisoner with him, that he may be sufficiently known, and to leave his token with his prisoner. And so many as he takes in suchlike manner to be his prisoners; and the determination thereof to be decided by the warden or his deputy, if there be any complaints."

*Pursuit on firing the beacons :* " Whoever he be, an host of Englishmen coming in the country, the bails being burned, that follows not the host on horse or on foot, ever till the Englishmen be passed off Scotland, and that they have sufficient witnesses thereof, all their goods shall be escheat, and their bodies at the warden's will, unless they have lawful excuse for them."

The majority of the places where bale-fires were to be kept in readiness are in Annandale and Nithsdale. The " Criffel " named is believed to stand for Cruffel in Sanquhar parish. We learn from other sources that when it was necessary to call the men of Galloway to arms, fires were lit on Bengairn, Cairnsmore of Fleet, and the Knock of Luce.

In 1460, the Provost of Lincluden found himself called upon to entertain some royal guests. First came Margaret of Anjou, the Queen of Henry the Sixth, and her son Edward, a child of eight years, refugees from England after the Lancastrian defeat at Northampton. The English Queen was a niece of the King of France who had made the fourth Earl of Douglas Duke of Touraine, and when she resolved to seek the hospitality of Galloway, must have known that although the Douglas power was broken, there were still Douglases at Lincluden. When she reached Scotland, news was flying through the country that the King, James the Second, had been killed through the bursting of a cannon at Roxburgh Castle. The newly widowed Queen, Mary of Gueldres, received a message from Queen

Margaret, and after the King's funeral came to Lincluden to welcome her to Scotland. Her little son, James the Third, came with her, and also some of the great men of the kingdom, who conferred with Queen Margaret's English lords, promising assistance to the Lancastrian cause on the condition that Berwick should be restored to the Scots.

While his guests were considering matters of high politics, the provost was addressing himself to the problem of how to entertain them. He applied for certain requisites to the bailies of Dumfries, as we learn from the *memorandum* of a claim of theirs for 15s. for a bed-cover and a pair of sheets lost *apud Lynclouding* at the time when the Queen was there with the Queen of England. The accounts of William, Abbot of Dundrennan, the Chamberlain of Galloway, include items of expenditure in connexion with the same occasion : £13 10s. for three pipes of the white wine of Poitou sent to "Lincloudane", 5s. for ten pints to fill out the said pipes, 32s. for their carriage to the College, 30s. for three bolls of salt, and 12s. 2d. for two servants riding with letters *de collegio de Lyncloudane versus Kirkcubrycht et le Rynnys*.

James the Fourth made frequent journeys to the shrine of S. Ninian at Whithorn and travelled sometimes by way of Lincluden. The Lord High Treasurer's Accounts for August, 1505, include payments of 42s. "in Linclowden, to the piparis to part amang thaim, be the Kingis command", and 14s. "to the masons of Linclowden, of drinksilvir". In May of the following year there were payments of 18s. "to the menstrales in Linclowden", 9s. "to the masons and werkmen thair", and 6s. "to ane priest in Linclowden, be the Kingis command"; and 40s. were given "to Schir Andro Makbrek to dispone in Linclowden".

There are one or two strange tales to be told in later chapters about the transference of church lands to lay proprietors at the Reformation. The process in the case of Lincluden College was marked by the attempt of the provost to secure his own interests at the expense of the prebendars. The last provost was a son of the Laird of Drumlanrig in Dumfriesshire. He was created Earl of Queensberry and built Drumlanrig Castle. His grandson, the third Earl, was made Duke of Queensberry in 1684, and his great-grandson, the second Duke, was an active supporter of the Union of the Parliaments.

Besides Lincluden College, there is another old ecclesiastical building in the same parish, the Queir[1] or Choir of Terregles[2] Church.    One can reach it from Lincluden along three or four miles of byways.  It is " an interesting example of the late

*Doorway in Terregles Queir.*

Gothic architecture which accompanied the revival of Episcopacy in Scotland under King James the Sixth towards the

[1] Permission to see the interior can be obtained from the factor of the Terregles estate in Dumfries.

[2] " 1350, Travereglys, *i.e.,* G. *treamhar eaglais* (Welsh *eglwys*), ' farm by the church '; also 1461, Tarriculis, Torrekillis."— Johnston.

beginning of the seventeenth century ".[1] A stone above the doorway bears the date, 1583, the year in which the church was rebuilt by the fourth Lord Herries. The Queir was restored by Captain Maxwell of Terregles in 1875, and is used as a mortuary chapel. The exterior buttresses were added then, the mullions and tracery of the two-light windows renewed, and the interior reconstructed. There are two old monuments within. The one shews a figure in profile with sixteenth-century costume. The left hand grips the hilt of the sword ; the right points to a tablet bearing the letters I H S on the left breast. The inscription is distributed over the rest of the stone and runs : HEIR LVIS EDWARD MAXWEL LAIRD OF LAMINGTOWN DEPAIRTIT SEPT. XXIX 1568 AND MARGRAT BAILIE HERETRIX OF LAMINGTOVNE HIS SPOUS. Two shields at the upper end exhibit respectively the arms of Maxwell and Baillie.

The other monument consists of two panels, the one presenting a male, and the other a female figure in the attitude of prayer, and is surmounted by an angel. The legends are GLORIE BE TO GOD, cut on a label above the angel, and, in two lines below it, COME YE BLESSED OF YE LORD RESAIF ZOVR INHERITANCE. Of two shields, the one bears the initials S R M for Sir Robert Maxwell of Spottis ; the other, D E G, for Dame Elizabeth Gordon, his spouse.

A pair of stalls which belonged to Lincluden College, but are now preserved in the Queir, " are of special interest seeing that mediæval church furniture in Scotland is exceedingly rare ; but another feature of even greater rarity is a fragment of mediæval painting upon two of the boards which formed part of the infilling of the upper framework. The painting, which is much faded, has represented a figure of the Blessed Virgin Mary crowned, and clad in a robe of which the upper part is blue, while the turnover at the hand is brown. The crown and bordering of the dress are yellow." [1]

Terregles House is modern. The following note in the *Memoirs* of Lord Herries belongs to the year 1568 and concerns an earlier building : " The Lord Herreis hous of Terreglis, the Regent gave full orders to throw it doune. But the Laird of Drumlanrig, whoe was the Lord Herreis uncle, and much in favour with the Regent, told that the Lord Herreis wold take it for a favour, if he wold ease him of pains, for he was

[1] The *Inventory*.

resolved to throw it doune himselfe, and build it in another place. The Regent sware, he scorned to be a barrowman to his old walls! And so it was safe." [1]

Lord Herries had supported the Reformation and been accounted by John Knox "a man stout and zealous in God's cause", but reverted to the Roman Catholic side, became one of Queen Mary's chief advisers, led her cavalry at Langside, and escorted her on her journey to England. His great-grandson, John, became third Earl of Nithsdale. The fifth Earl joined the Jacobite rising of 1715, was made a prisoner at Preston, and was confined in the Tower of London. On the night preceding the day fixed for his execution, his wife contrived, with the help of two Jacobite ladies, to disguise him as a woman, and he escaped to France. The Earl and Countess lived thereafter in Rome at the court of the Pretender.

[1] *Historical Memoirs of the Reign of Mary Queen of Scots, and a Portion of the Reign of King James the Sixth* by Lord Herries, printed by the Abbotsford Club in 1836.

*A Galloway Loch.*

# CHAPTER II

The grave of Helen Walker, the prototype of Jeanie Deans—The
crime and condemnation of Isobel Walker—Helen's exertions
on her behalf—Helen's history and character—Scott's inscription on the tombstone—A Covenanters' grave—John Welsh,
minister of Irongray—The Communion Stones of Irongray.

" My father and I went off a long walk ", says Stevenson in a
letter written at Dumfries in 1873, " through a country most
beautifully wooded and various, under a range of hills. You
should have seen one place where the wood suddenly fell away
in front of us down a long, steep hill between a double row of
trees, with one small fair-haired child framed in shadow in the
foreground ; and when we got to the foot, there was the little
kirk and kirkyard of Irongray,[1] among broken fields and woods
by the side of the bright, rapid river." Here is the grave of
Helen Walker, the prototype of Jeanie Deans, with a stone
erected, and an inscription composed by Sir Walter Scott.

In the year 1736 there were living at Cluden a widow and her
two daughters, Helen and Isobel Walker, who supported the
home by labouring in the fields. On the 18th of October the
Cluden Water was in flood, and the dead body of a male infant,
with a white and blue kerchief tied tightly round the neck, was

---

[1] *Earrann*, landquarter, *graigh* or *graidh*, a herd or stud of
horses. " This ", says Sir Herbert Maxwell, " is the very district
of the once famous Galloway nags." Pont gives " Arngra." The
Rev. S. Dunlop, minister of the parish, states that the pronunciation is " Arngra." He estimates the percentage of Celtic
place-names in the parish at about forty-four, and of Old English
or Norse at forty-two, the remainder consisting of modern names.
Along the Cairn Valley the Saxon names predominate ; nearer
the hills, the Celtic. Irongray was well within the Celtic fringe.

found stranded on the Dumfriesshire bank. Isobel Walker was suspected of having given birth to the child. She denied all knowledge of either its birth or its death, and the ordeal by touch was applied. When the dead infant was laid on her knees, she lost her nerve and began to make statements such as that " the child was none of hers; that she had thrown the child which she had borne into the Water of Cluden, and that it was not a ripe child ". At the trial several witnesses deponed to the state-ments which they had heard her make, and the kerchief was recognized as her property. After the jury had considered their verdict, " They all in one voice find it proven that the pannel Isobel Walker time and place lybelled did bring forth a child which was thereafter found dead or amissing and not found And that the said pannel dureing the whole time of her preg-nancy did conceal her being with child and did not call for help and assistance in the time of the birth ." Isobel Walker was accordingly sentenced to be hanged on the 14th of June and was removed to her cell in the Tolbooth of Dumfries, where, it is said, Waugh, who was the father of her child, talked with her at night through the window-bars.

Before the trial, her sister, Helen, had been pressed to appear as a witness and defend the accused with a lie ; a single word would save her sister, it was urged, and she would have time to repent afterwards ; but the strength of her sisterly affection could not shake her integrity. So soon as the trial was over she had a petition drawn up on her sister's behalf, borrowed some money, and set out the same evening to walk barefoot to London. She completed the journey in fourteen days—Mrs. Goldie, who communicated the story to Scott, tried in vain to learn any details of her experiences on the way—and inquired for the Duke of Argyll's house. When she arrived at the door, the Duke was about to step into his carriage. Helen presented her petition, dropped on her knees, and urged her plea with natural eloquence. The Duke was moved to use his influence on behalf of the prisoner ; a reprieve was granted until the 15th of August ; and a full remission followed on the 12th of July " with this express condition that she depart the Kingdoms of Great Britain and Ireland within fourty days after she is liberate in virtue of the said Remission never to be seen therein unless she obtain a licence from his Majestie or his Royal succes-sors for that effect ". Either a free pardon or liberty to live in

Britain must have been granted later, for Isobel, who was married to Waugh after she came out of prison, spent the rest of her life in Whitehaven. Miss Goldie told Scott that an old woman who was a distant relative of the Walker family said that " every year Helen received a cheese from her sister, who lived at Whitehaven ", and that a relative of Mrs. Goldie " who happened to be travelling in the North of England, on coming to a small inn, was shown into the parlour by a female servant, who, after cautiously shutting the door, said, ' Sir, I'm Nelly Walker's sister', thus practically showing that she considered her sister as better known by her high conduct than even herself by a different kind of celebrity ".

Elizabeth Grierson, a housekeeper in Dumfries, told John MacDiarmid, the author of *Sketches from Nature*, that when she was a girl she had known Helen Walker, who was often in Elizabeth's home, had nursed her mother, and been " the leading gossip at all the christenings ". Many of her neighbours considered her " pensy ", that is, conceited or proud, an impression caused perhaps by her superior mental and moral calibre. All were agreed about her high character, her religious devotion, her diligent private study of the Bible—" it was observed by her visitors that when she lacked leisure to read continuously, she sometimes glanced at a single verse, and then appeared to ponder the subject deeply "—and her regular attendance at the public worship of the Church. When out-of-doors work could not be obtained, she supported her mother and herself by " footing " stockings. She was constrained sometimes " to dine on dry bread and water rather than pinch her poor old mother ", and consoled herself with the idea that " a blessing flowed from her virtuous abstinence ". She advised Elizabeth Grierson not to follow her example when a lover came her way, but to " winnow the corn when the wind blew in the barn-door ". She had had a sweetheart who, riding on horseback, had overtaken her on the road at a fair time, and when she asked if he would take her up behind him, had answered, " That I will, Helen, if ye can ride an inch behind the tail." She had been so offended by this jest that she had cast her lover from her heart. This incident supports the statement that her deportment was " sedate and dignified in the extreme ". She was always silent regarding the famous event of her life. Mrs. Goldie asked a woman who had lived beside Helen in her later years if she had ever spoken about it, and received the reply, "Na. Helen was a wily body, and whene'er ony o' the neebors asked anything about it, she aye turned the conversation." It was a short time before Helen died that Mrs. Goldie met her. She

*Grave of Helen Walker ("Jeanie Deans") (within railing).*

was then " a little, rather stout-looking woman, who seemed to be between seventy and eighty years of age ; she was almost covered with a tartan plaid, and her cap had over it a black silk hood, tied under the chin, a piece of dress still much in use among elderly women of that rank of life in Scotland ; her eyes were dark, and remarkably lively and intelligent."

Mrs. Goldie's communication to Scott was anonymous, and Scott was at that time the mysterious " author of *Waverley* ". When his identity became known, Miss Goldie sent him further details about Helen Walker and referred to her late mother's desire that a stone should be placed over the grave in Irongray Churchyard, saying that the money could be raised easily in the neighbourhood, and inviting Scott to write an epitaph. Scott not only did this, but had the stone erected at his own expense.

THIS STONE WAS ERECTED
BY THE AUTHOR OF WAVERLEY
TO THE MEMORY
OF

### HELEN WALKER

WHO DIED IN THE YEAR OF GOD 1791
THIS HUMBLE INDIVIDUAL
PRACTISED IN REAL LIFE
THE VIRTUES
WITH WHICH FICTION HAS INVESTED
THE IMAGINARY CHARACTER OF

### JEANIE DEANS

REFUSING THE SLIGHTEST DEPARTURE
FROM VERACITY
EVEN TO SAVE THE LIFE OF A SISTER
SHE NEVERTHELESS SHOWED HER
KINDNESS AND FORTITUDE
IN RESCUING HER
FROM THE SEVERITY OF THE LAW
AT THE EXPENSE OF PERSONAL EXERTIONS
WHICH THE TIME RENDERED AS DIFFICULT
AS THE MOTIVE WAS LAUDABLE

———

RESPECT THE GRAVE OF POVERTY
WHEN COMBINED WITH LOVE OF TRUTH
AND DEAR AFFECTION

The comments of Dr. A. K. H. Boyd, who was minister of Irongray for some years and wrote *The Recreations of a Country Parson* and other popular works, will interest literary purists : " Although, of course, it is treasonable to say so, I confess I think this inscription somewhat cumbrous and awkward. The antithesis is not a good one, between the difficulty of Jeanie's ' personal exertions ' and the laudableness of the motive

which led to them.   And there is something not metaphysically
correct in the combination described in the closing sentence—
the combination of poverty, an outward condition, with truth-
fulness and affection, two inward characteristics. . . . Poverty
might co-exist with, or be associated with, any mental qualities
you please, but assuredly it cannot correctly be said to enter
into *combination* with any."

A little farther up the stream is another grave belonging
to an older century and emblemizing another heroism.   Captain
Bruce had captured six Covenanters on the moor of Lochenkit
in Kirkpatrick-Durham, the next parish, and ordered four
of them to be shot at once.   The other two, Edward Gordon
and Alexander MacCubine, were carried to the Bridge of Urr,
where Sir Robert Grierson of Lagg was administering the
Oath of Abjuration.[1]   Bruce wished to have them tried by jury;
but Lagg refused and took them the next day to Irongray,
where they were " hanged upon an oak tree near the Kirk
of Irongray, at the foot of which they were buried ".   When
MacCubine was asked if he had any message to send to his
wife before he died, he said, " I leave her and the two babes
upon the Lord and to His promise ; ' A Father to the fatherless
and a judge of the widows is God in His holy habitation ' " ;
and when the hangman asked his forgiveness for what he was
about to do, said, " Poor man, I forgive thee and all men.
Thou hast a miserable calling upon earth."   Wodrow says,
" Both died in much composure and cheerfulness."

---

[1] The Oath of Abjuration was directed against " The Declaration
and Testimony of the true Presbyterian, anti-prelatic, anti-erastian,
persecuted party in Scotland " formally read and adopted by
Richard Cameron and others at the Market Cross of Sanquhar on
the 22nd of June, 1680, whereby " although we be for Government
and Governors such as the Word of our God and our Covenant allows,
yet we for ourselves and all that will adhere to us as the representatives
of the true Presbyterian Kirk and Covenanted nation of Scotland . . .
do by thir presents disown Charles Stuart that has been reigning
(or rather tyrannizing as we may say) on the throne of Britain
these years bygone as having any right, title to, or interest in the
said Crown of Scotland for Government, as forfeited several years
since, by his perjury and breach of covenant both to God and His
Kirk and usurpation of His Crown and Royal prerogative therein. . . .   As also, we, being under the standard of the Lord Jesus
Christ, Captain of Salvation, do declare a war with such a tyrant
and usurper. . . ."

The stone lies on the ground and bears the following inscription—

> HERE LYES EDWARD GORDON AND ALEXANDER
> McCUBINE, MARTYRES,
> HANGED WITHOUT
> LAW BY LAGG AND CAP.
> BRUCE FOR ADHEREING
> TO THE WORD OF GOD,
> CHRISTS KINGLY GOVE-
> RMENT IN HIS HOUS:
> AND THE COVENANTED
> WORK OF REFORMATION
> AGAINST TYRANNY,
> PERJURY AND PRELACY
> REV. 12: II. MAR. 3: 1685.

> AS LAGG AND BLOODIE
> BRUCE COMMAN'D,
> WE WERE HUNG UP BY
> HELLISH HAND:
> AND THUS THEIR FURIO-
> US RAGE TO STAY
> WE DYID NEAR KIRK
> OF IRON-GRAY:—
> HERE NOW IN PEACE
> SWEET REST WE TAKE
> ONCE MURDER'D FOR
> RELIGEON'S SAKE.

I should have liked to see the stone in its original simplicity. There may be some justification for the railing surrounding it; but what is to be said of the persons responsible for the tall monument erected on the very edge of the grave and telling of a congregation assembled here to listen to a sermon on the Covenanters, giving the name of the preacher, and referring to the collection made to defray the expense of this superfluous erection?

The martyrdom of Gordon and MacCubine is not the only incident connecting this district with the history of the Covenants. Indeed, no parish in the land is richer in memories of the great struggle. Wodrow states that " the first open opposition to the settlement of the curates I have heard was at Irongray, where Mr. John Welsh was minister ". This Welsh was a

grandson of the more famous John Welsh, minister of Kirkcudbright, who married a daughter of John Knox and, sharing
his father-in-law's zeal as a Reformer, was exiled to France.
The Pentland Rising of 1666 began with an incident at Dalry ;
but Irongray Church was the place where the faithful were convened before marching on Dumfries to capture Sir James
Turner ; and the minister of Irongray was a leader of the rebels,
inflaming their enthusiasm with sermons delivered by the
way and with his exhortations on the field of battle.  He
escaped from the slaughter at Rullion Green and led a hunted
life for many years, preaching among the Covenanters in
Galloway and other parts of Scotland.  The large sum offered
by the Government for his capture shews their estimate of
his influence.  No traitor was found among his followers,
and it does not appear that he fell at any time into the hands
of the persecutors.[1]

He was one of the ministers who officiated at one of the
greatest sacramental occasions in Scottish history, when some
thousands of Covenanters assembled on a high moor about
four miles west of the church of Irongray.  The Communion
Stones still lie among the heather and can be reached by the
Routin' Bridge and the farm of Maxwelltown.  From the
latter point there is an ascent of a mile over the face of a broad,
moorland hill, and when the summit is reached, the scene
of the great conventicle opens out.  One might search long
and vainly for the Communion Stones, were it not for the
polished granite obelisk that flashes like a lighthouse when
the sunshine strikes it.  The inscription on the monument
runs thus : " Erected by voluntary [2] subscription in 1870
to mark the spot where a large number of Covenanters met
in the summer of 1678 to worship God, and where about 3,000
communicants on that occasion celebrated the Sacrament
of the Lord's Supper.  The following ejected ministers officiated :—John Welsh of Irongray, John Blackadder of Troqueer,
John Dickson of Rutherglen, and Samuel Arnot of Tongland
—the adjacent stones being used as the Communion Table.
These stones are significant memorials of those troublous
times, in which our Fathers, at the peril of their lives, contended

---

[1] " January 9th, 1681, dyed  Mr. John Welch peaceably at
London."—Law's *Memorialls.*

[2] Why " voluntary " ?

for the great principles of civil and religious freedom [1]." The
Stones are not protected by any kind of railing, but seem to
have suffered no derangement, such is the reverence in which
they have been held. The communicants sat on the long

*The Routin' Bridge.*

parallel rows while the ministers stood beside a circular heap
to preach and dispense the sacrament. The Stones would
afford sitting room for about a hundred and twenty communicants at a time. Sentinels were placed meanwhile on the near
heights to give the alarm if the dragoons approached.

It is a strange, impressive incident, this gathering of the

[1] Not quite accurate.

thousands from far and near—some from very great distances
—fording rivers, traversing bogs, and risking greater dangers
from their persecutors, to worship God according to their
proscribed rites in loyalty to the principles of the Scottish Reformation.   You can think of them coming through the glens
and over the moors with the Psalmist's words in their minds :—

> He took me from a fearful pit
> and from the miry clay
> And on a rock he set my feet,
> establishing my way,

or

> So they from strength unwearied go
> still forward unto strength,
> Until in Sion they appear
> before the Lord at length,

and perhaps singing the words as they came.   Then you must
imagine the huge concourse inhabiting that solemn moor
for some hours, the stillness as they listened to the preachers,
the silence broken by the jangle of a horse's bit as the sacrament
was being received, the occasional glance towards the watchmen
on the heights, the thousands of voices uplifted in some old
minor psalm-tune that might have seemed the very voice of
the moor itself, according with the dull tones of that bare landscape and of the sky—we are told that " it was a cloudy and
gloomy day, the sky lowering and often threatening showers ".
The clouds did not break, but withheld their moisture, " as
it were to accommodate the work ".   As the people were scat-
tering, there arose a cry that the dragoons were coming.   The
horsemen of Clydesdale, Nithsdale, and Galloway mounted
and formed ; and four or five companies of infantry were made
ready for action.   " All this was done in the twinkling of an
eye, for the people were willing and resolute."   Vedettes and
single horsemen were sent out to discover if the enemy were
near, and reported that there was none visible.   The dragoons
had really spied upon the Covenanters and considered that
they were too strong for attack.   After remaining for three
hours in a position of defence, the multitude separated in groups,
each accompanied by a guard of horsemen and infantry.   Then
the clouds discharged a great rain, so that the streams were
much swollen.   Most of the people had to pass through both
the Cluden and the Cairn.

*New Abbey.*

# CHAPTER III

### NEW ABBEY

The road from Maxwelltown to New Abbey—Sweetheart Abbey—
Notes on the Abbey Church—Edward the First at Sweetheart
Abbey—The Archbishop of Canterbury fords the Solway to
meet him—The monks prepare for the Reformation—Inscription
in the churchyard—Views of the Abbey Church—The Abbot's
Tower—Kirkconnell Tower.

I HAD made journeys along separate parts of the Galloway
coast and had been so much delighted with what I had seen
that I resolved to make a tour along the whole of it, from Maxwelltown, that is, to the Mull of Galloway and then up the coast
of the Firth of Clyde. I did not, of course, bind myself to keep
pedantically to the roads running nearest the shore. On the one
hand, I knew that there would be places nearer the sea than


28

any road, caves haunted in old days by saints and smugglers, for instance, headlands crowned with the remains of Norse and other strongholds, and great cliffs where one might pass an idle hour watching the bird-life; I might even have occasion to embark on the sea now and then and explore parts of the coast in a fisherman's boat ; and, on the other hand, I should make digressions inland to visit old castles, churches, and memorials of vanished races, and, penetrating into the folds of wooded glens, lose the sea altogether. I have no hesitation in granting the precisian that Maxwelltown is not on the coast ; it was, however, the convenient starting-point for such an enterprise.

Of the seven-mile road running over the alluvial plain of the lower part of Nithsdale towards the village of New Abbey, where the coast may be said to begin, I remember two details. One is that from the top of a hill I looked across the strath and saw against the sky at the distance of about four miles a group of buildings crowning a slope of mingled meadows and plantations and including what was plainly a large church with a central tower. I have read a statement somewhere that the highest commendation that an Englishman can give any part of his own country is to say, " It's quite like a foreign place." It is otherwise with us in Scotland. We praise foreign places when we say that they bear a likeness to something in our native land. It is not, therefore, to advertise the charm of the view from this point that I say that it reminded me of the Bavarian plain with one of its abrupt heights covered with the houses, church, and burg of a little town. It was with a kind of disappointment that I learned on referring to the map that I had been looking at the buildings of that munificent foundation, the Crichton Asylum near Dumfries, for I had trusted that it was some ancient place.

I remember also that, on reaching the top of a hill near New Abbey and looking across the glen where the village lies, I became aware of Criffel towering in front. Since it rises from near the level of the sea, it gets the full value of its eighteen hundred and sixty-six feet, and impresses you all the more for the past miles of plain. It was a cloudy afternoon when I stood here, and the hill was all of a beautiful smoke-like blue. Dull as the light was, it fell so that a bit of Loch Kindar, revealed by a break in the wood at the foot of the hill, gleamed like silver.

The wooded valley was full of a windless quiet and looked as restful as Criffel itself.

There had been trees standing along many parts of the road from Maxwelltown ; but all of these were dwarfed by the rows of ancient limes and firs running down the gentle hill to New Abbey. The avenue may have been formed in the days of the monks. The trees are set so close together, and their upper branches are so interwoven, that the light is as dim as in a cathedral. Free-wheeling down the avenue and glancing between the trunks on the left, one gets impressive glimpses of the Abbey Church.

The road crosses the Pow Burn at the foot of the slope and, turning to the left, enters New Abbey. Looking along the

*Loch Kindar and Criffel.*

short, winding street, you realize in another second that this is not like the streets of other villages, for above the farther end are the walls and lofty tower of the great church. Rising in sudden majesty, they took me by surprise very much as Criffel had done a few minutes before.

Sweetheart Abbey, sometimes called New Abbey to distinguish it from the older abbey of Dundrennan,[1] was the latest

[1] The abbeys of Dundrennan, Glenluce, and Sweetheart belonged to the Cistercian Order. Sweetheart Abbey was colonized by monks from Dundrennan.

foundation of its kind in Scotland. The name has handed down to later ages the thirteenth-century love-story of Lady Dervorgilla and her husband, John Baliol. Baliol did not come into the unhappy prominence that was thrust upon his son ; but his memory endures by reason of the great love that he inspired in the noble lady who was his wife. After forty years of wedded felicity, he died in 1269. Dervorgilla then caused his heart to be embalmed and enclosed in a silver-mounted ivory casket, and wherever she went, the relic was taken. When she sat down to a meal, she had it placed beside her and did reverence to it as if her lord himself had been present. As each course was brought from the kitchen, some of it was placed in a silver vessel in front of the casket, and when she rose from meat, the portions were taken out and given to the poor. This, says Andrew of Wyntoun,

> scho cessyt nevyr to do
> Quhill lyvand in this warld wes scho.

She thought ere long of a monastery with a noble church where she could be buried with her husband's embalmed heart resting on her own, and had the building begun in 1273. The reason for the selection of the site was the obvious one, that every considerable district of Galloway except that between the Nith and the Urr had its great religious house already. Here, then, within a loop of the Pow Burn, under the shadow of Criffel, and within a mile or two of the Solway—its waters provided the monks with salmon, and its sands were the scene of profitable salt-works—Dervorgilla saw her beautiful monument rise. The *Chronicon de Lanercost* states that she was at Barnard Castle when she died in 1289. In obedience to her instructions, her husband's heart was placed on her bosom, and the funeral procession began the long journey across part of Yorkshire and through Westmorland and Cumberland into Scotland. When the last stage had been completed, the monks in their white robes and black scapularies opened their gates, Dervorgilla's body was laid near the high altar, and her dream was fulfilled.

Besides the Abbey of the Embalmed Heart, Dervorgilla founded or repaired other religious houses and, in fulfilment of her husband's intention, erected Balliol College in Oxford. It is easy to understand the enthusiasm of the monkish chronicler, Andrew of Wyntoun, when he says :

> This lady
> Dyd all thir dedis devotly.
> A bettyr lady than scho wes nane
> In all the yle off Mare Bretane.

He adds that

> Scho wes rycht plesand off bewté.

The abbey precinct covered about thirty acres and was
bounded by a massive stone wall about four feet wide, an unusual
feature. The north-east and west sections remain, and range
from three to twelve feet in height. The granite boulders of
which the wall is composed are in many cases enormous, and
the average diameter is about four feet. The walls of
the church consist of unhewn granite covered with dressed
freestone. According to tradition, Dervorgilla was not
the only lady associated with the building of the abbey,
for a carved stone in the wall of a house in the village, shewing
the side of a boat surmounted by three heads, commemorates
some maiden ladies who kept a ferry and displayed both their
piety and their muscularity by transporting all the freestone
required from the other side of the Nith.

The architecture is Early English with Decorated additions.
The chancel was probably completed by the end of the thirteenth
century ; but the traceried windows are later. The main piers
and arches of the nave have the character of early fourteenth-
century work. The great window at the west end must have
contained mullions and tracery originally, but has been spoiled
by the introduction of a mass of masonry below the wheel at
the top, no doubt because it was feared that the building was
not sufficiently strong. This and other alterations were probably made in the latter part of the fourteenth century after
the abbey had suffered serious damage from lightning.

A number of carved stones lying in the south transept are
supposed to have formed parts of an altar-tomb. Four of
them are lettered thus :—

> (1) . . . . . (G)ILLA FUDATRIX
> (2)          HUI(US) MONA. . . .
> (3)          STII QUE OBIIT
> (4)          M CC LXXXIIII

The reference is to Dervorgilla, the foundress of the abbey.
1284, of course, was not the year of her death. The *Inventory*

points out that " the style of lettering shows that these fragments probably date from the sixteenth century. It has been suggested that the monument may have been erected by Lord Herries in the sixteenth century, and the fact that his mother was a Douglas is a possible explanation of the three stars in chief on one of the shields."

An escutcheon in the roof of the south transept aisle has

*Sweetheart Abbey from the North-west.*

arms in relief, " two croziers in saltire between a heart in chief and three stars in flanks and base (apparently the arms of Macguffock, subsequently of Rusco)," and an inscription scarcely legible on account of its height. The legend was supposed by Grose to be CHRISTUS MARITUS MEUS, but is understood now to be CHUS TIM O' NID,—" Choose time of need "—a play, perhaps, on " Nith ".

The abbey was the scene of an important event about a quarter of a century after it was founded. When Edward the First made his annual incursion into Scotland in 1300, he overran a part of Galloway and, as he returned, halted at Sweetheart Abbey. It was here that he first heard of and perhaps received the Bull of Pope Boniface the Eighth calling upon him to desist from his oppression of the Scots and claiming for himself the superiority of Scotland on the ground that the country had been won to the Christian faith by the relics of S. Andrew. The Pope had ordered Robert of Winchelsea, the Archbishop of Canterbury, to convey the bull with his own hand to the King, and while Edward was encamped at Sweetheart Abbey, the primate was on the other side of the Solway, waiting for the means of a safe crossing. He sent two messengers to the King " across certain perilous passages of the sea ", to quote his own account, to inform him of his errand and to ask how he could best complete it. He seems to have feared capture by the Scots as well as the dangers of the Solway.

The King did not consider the receipt of the bull a matter of urgency, nor had he any anxiety to see the Archbishop, with whom his relations were already strained. He replied that he had no ship to send and advised the Archbishop to go to Berwick, where the Queen was, adding that he intended to meet her there. As Dr. Neilson suggests, this was very much like telling the Archbishop to " go to Jericho ". The Archbishop has left an account of his adventurous journey to " the new abbey of Duzquer " telling how he " took advantage of an opportunity at ebb tide " and, " guided by some men who were sure to know the way across ", passed on horseback " through four streams within the sea-area—*per quatuor meatus aquarum maritimarum* ". He thought the quicksands and the irregularities of the sea-bottom quite as dangerous as the depth of the water in the channels, and says that he did reach the camp although it was almost more than he had expected. The King was dining when the Archbishop arrived, but did not invite the tired traveller to join him, explaining that he was too busy to speak with him that day, but would hear him on the morrow. It was on the following day that Edward moved across the Nith to Caerlaverock, and it is possible that the docket on the copy of the bull in the English archives indicating that it was served *apud Carlaveroks* is correct. The sequel, foreshadowing the final breach with the Roman

*Sweetheart Abbey from the West End.*

See in the time of Henry the Eighth, belongs to English history.

When the monks saw the Reformation approaching, they

prepared to meet the storm by putting their property under the protection of a powerful family, leasing their estates to the Lords Maxwell and appointing them heritable bailies. So long as the monks remained at the abbey, the Maxwells paid the revenues to them and, when they were driven away, retained the church lands. The departure of the monks was delayed longer here than perhaps anywhere else. It was not until many years after the Reformation that the Privy Council resorted to force to disperse the fraternity.

The last and only well-known name in the list of abbots is that of Gilbert Brown, who belonged to a branch of the family of Carsluith in Kirkmabreck Parish. Reference is made to him more than once in the customary fulminations of the General Assembly of the Church of Scotland against " Jesuits, Seminarie preests, traffiquing Papists, and recepters therof ". Brown was working hard to promote the Roman Catholic reaction in Galloway and the west of Scotland, and his apprehension was demanded by the Assembly in 1594 and 1596. He had a literary duel with John Welsh, minister of Ayr, and wrote *Ane Answere to ane certaine libell or writing, sent by Mr. John Welsche, to ane Catholicke, as ane Answer to ane Objection of the Romane Kirk, whereby they go about to deface the veritie of that onely true religion whilk we professe.* Welsh published in 1602 *A Reply against Mr. Gilbert Browne, priest,* reprinted under the title, *Popery Anatomized.* The abbot is described as the " famous excommunicat, foirfaultit, and perverting papist named Mr. Gilbert Browne, Abbot of New Abbey, quho evir since the reformatioun of religioune had conteinit in ignorance and idolatrie allmost the haill south-west partis of Scotland, and had been continowallie occupyit in practiseing of heresy ". About the end of August, 1605, says Calderwood in his *The Historie of the Kirk of Scotland,* " the Abbot of Newabbey was taikin about Newabbey, by the Lord Cranstoun, not without perrell from the country people, who rose to rescue him out of his hands. He was sent first to Blacknesse, and, after two or three days, was transported to the Castell of Edinburgh, where he was inter- teaned upon the King's expences till his departure out of the countrie." In the following November, " having all his idola- trous relicts, croces, Agnus Deies, &c., restored to him, he was sett at libertie, and permitted to embark at Leith, not without appearance of saying of masse in Edinburgh, the night before his departure; for his masse clothes, chalices, &c., were found by the bailliffes." He died in Paris in 1612.

Lord Cockburn said of the adjoining churchyard that "the unlettered muse" seems never to have entered it. "There is not even an attempt at an inscription in it, beyond names and dates." He had overlooked, however, this epitaph:—

M

W      G

Q.—QUARE LEVIS LAPIS SUB
OPACI TEGMINE SAXI ?
R.—IN VISCERE TELLURIS
AUREA GEMMA LATET.
1660
MEMORIAM
W. GLADSTONE

The lines may be translated thus:

Q.—Wherefore lies the Gladstone
Hidden by the dark stone ?
A.—The bosom of the earth
Conceals the gem of gold.

Walter Gladstone was a minister of the parish.

By leaving the burial-ground at the north-east corner and walking across the meadow towards the old boundary wall, one arrives at a good point for admiring the church. The tower presents itself in a majestic fashion between the gables of the chancel and the north transept.

For the best general view of the church and its surroundings, one must follow the Maxwelltown road for a few hundred yards and turn to the right along a byway leading to the farm-steading of Landis. A lady who deserves the benediction of travellers caused a seat to be placed by the roadside, and here one should spend at least half-an-hour looking at the green valley and the beautiful church with Criffel behind. "I'll tell you, scholar: when I sat last on this primrose bank, and looked down these meadows, I thought of them as Charles the Emperor did of the city of Florence, 'that they were too pleasant to be looked upon, but only on holy-days'."

I came to this point for the first time on an evening at the end of March. It was about the hour of sunset, the sky was overcast, and everything appeared in a grey twilight— the meadows, the clumps of trees, the church in the bottom of the glen, and the high hill behind—and had the thin, ghostly look of an under-exposed negative. It was the season of heather-burning, and the side of Criffel was on fire. A huge stack of smoke was rising and disappearing into haze, and one might have looked to see the tenuous landscape fade away also on the windless air.

A little farther along this byway is the Abbot's Tower. It appears to be a sixteenth-century building and is believed to have been used as a place of retreat by the abbots. The ivy-covered walls remain.

Joining this road at right angles is another byway leading

*Sweetheart Abbey and Criffel.*

to the ancient tower of Kirkconnell, the second oldest inhabited house in Scotland. The older house is Traquair in Peeblesshire. Kirkconnell, therefore, is the oldest in Galloway. The road plunges down almost immediately into the woody depths of the March Glen, and one would be tempted to follow it even if there were no old house at the end. Tall trees hide the greater part of the building ; but the crow-stepped roof of the tower appears above the upper branches.

The property belonged from some unknown time to the Kirkconnells of that ilk. The line ended with an heiress who was married to Aymer, second son of Sir Herbert Maxwell of Caerlaverock, and brother of Herbert, the first baron. The

succeeding line concluded with another heiress in 1827. Miss
Maxwell became the wife of her cousin, Mr. Robert S. J. Witham,
and the family bear the name of Maxwell Witham. The proprietors of Kirkconnell have always adhered to the Roman
Catholic Church. The house includes both an old and a
modern chapel.

James Maxwell, who became owner in 1739, joined in the Re-
bellion of 1745 and had to flee to France, but returned in 1750.
He wrote a *Narrative of Charles Prince of Wales' Expedition to
Scotland in the Year* 1745. It was printed by the Maitland
Club in 1848. A collection of Stewart and Jacobite relics contains miniatures of Charles the First, the Old Pretender, and
Princess Mary of Orange, daughter of James the Seventh. The
family portraits include those of James Maxwell, the author
of the *Narrative*, and his son, Dr. William Maxwell, a friend of
Burns, to whom the poet bequeathed a pair of pistols now in
the Antiquarian Museum in Edinburgh.

The principal approach to Kirkconnell Tower branches off
the road between Maxwelltown and New Abbey. The avenue
is lined with oak trees. Many of these begin to branch out very
near the ground. This is attributed to the cutting of shillelaghs
by the Highlanders at the 'Forty-Five.

*Kirkbean.*

*Carsethorn, the Solway, and the English Coast.*

## CHAPTER IV

### FROM NEW ABBEY TO SATTERNESS

Loch Kindar—The Solway—S. Adamnan's adventure—Carsethorn—
A tradition of Sir Robert Grierson of Lagg—Arbigland, the
birthplace of Paul Jones—Old market-cross of Preston, a
vanished village—Satterness—The lighthouse.

THE road had run almost straight south so far, apart from a few
angles here and there. On leaving New Abbey, it takes the
south-easterly direction for a mile or so and then continues
south once more to Kirkbean. I was not, however, to follow
so direct a course, being sure that I should be troubled with
regrets if I did not have a near view of Loch Kindar.

The byway begins at a very short distance from New Abbey.
I passed almost immediately through a farm-steading and then
over some fields, dismounting to open one or two gates, and came
in sight of a disused granite quarry on the nearest slope of Criffel.
The intervening pasture was traversed by a very narrow, rusty
pair of rails on which the little trucks used to run between
the quarry and a jetty on the Nith, and I saw some derailed
wagons against which cattle were rubbing themselves with great
satisfaction. These relics of the vanished industry were there
in the spring of 1910; but I do not remember seeing them
when I returned in the following year.

The loch is visible from the point where you are likely to

conclude that the track is going to be of no further use. The steep side of Criffel rises from the south-western shore, and there are plantations at the north and south ends—the trees that frame the water when you get the first glimpse of it from the hill above New Abbey. The two islands have an antiquarian interest. The one was a crannog or lake-dwelling and consists of stones resting on oaken piles. The other was the site of the ancient church of the parish, and there are some remains of the building. An island seems an inconvenient situation for a church ; but there was a causeway from the shore. Standing on the margin of the secluded loch, with no dwelling-place in sight, one is slow to imagine the scene when

> Within that little lonely isle
> There stood a consecrated Pile ;
> Where tapers burned, and mass was sung,
> For them whose timid Spirits clung
> To mortal succour, though the tomb
> Had fixed, for ever fixed, their doom !

It is scarcely necessary to point out that the parish must have been known by another name than " New Abbey " before the time of Dervorgilla. The older name, " Loch Kindar ", taken from the site of the church, occurs in various forms. The redundant form, " Lochkendeloch ", appears in a charter granted by Roland, Lord of Galloway, near the end of the twelfth century. Dervorgilla granted the church of " Loch Kindur " to the monks of Sweetheart Abbey. The name occurs as " Lochkinderloch " in a rent-roll of the abbey in 1570. It is called " Lockindeloch *alias* New Abbey " and " Lochindoloch *alias* New Abbey " in the reigns of James the Sixth and Charles the First. The name is traced to Cendaeladh, a king who died A.D. 580. I carried away a pleasant vision of blue water dancing and fringing shore and islands with spume, sea-gulls and duck floating on the surface, cattle standing in the shallows, and green Criffel hung against the sky.

I had not travelled far along the road before the bright Solway appeared. I saw also dim mountains on the other side, the hills of Cumberland. These mean little to Galloway, but the Solway much—the ancient highway of evangelists, pirates, smugglers, and flotillas of war. Respectable historians have connected " Solway " with *Selgovæ*, the name given by the Romans to a British tribe inhabiting Dumfriesshire. Dr.

George Neilson—*maxima cum laude*—has traced it to *Sulwath*, the name of a ford at the mouth of the Sark.[1] *Sulwath* is "The Muddy Ford". "Solway Sands (*Sulwey sandis*)" came to be used of the extreme eastern end of the Firth, the Firth itself being regarded still as part of the Irish Sea. Caerlaverock Castle is spoken of in 1300 as looking towards *la mer de Irlande*. It is only since the seventeenth century[2] that "Solway" has been extended gradually over the Firth as a whole. The Salmon Fisheries (Scotland) Act of 1868 fixed the limit dividing the Solway Firth from the sea to be "a straight line drawn from the Mull of Galloway to Hodbarrow point, in the parish of Millom, in the county of Cumberland".

S. Ninian, S. Cuthbert, and S. Adamnan all sailed on the Solway in the course of their evangelistic labours. The first does not seem to have had any adventures; but both of the other missionaries had. S. Adamnan's experience is worthy of quotation: "The people of Erin besought Adamnan to go in quest of the captives in Saxonland. He went to demand the surrender of the prisoners and put in at Tracht Romra.[3] The strand is long, and the flood rapid, so much so that if the best horse in Saxonland mounted by the best rider were to start from the edge when the tide begins to flow, he would have to swim before he brought his rider ashore. . . . Now, the Saxons were unwilling to let Adamnan land. 'Push your curraghs on the shore,' said Adamnan to his people, 'for both their land and their sea are obedient to God, and nothing can be done

---

[1] *Annals of the Solway until A.D.* 1307. "*Sol* is a term, common to Anglo-Saxon and the Norse languages, for mud. Anglo-Saxon, *wæth*—Norse, *vad* or *vath*, a frequent suffix in Icelandic local names —is a word for ford." Earliest mention, *Sulewade*, Patent Rolls, 1218.

[2] *Cruzanla, o la atraviessan, las corrientes de los seis rios, Orr, De o Dee, Ken, Cree, Bladna, y Luss, que todos páran en el mar de Hibernia.—Descripcion de Galoway por Ivan Maclelano*, in Blaeu's *Atlas* (Amsterdam, 1662). For other instances see Dr. Neilson's *Annals of the Solway until A.D.* 1307.

[3] ."Doubtless *Tracht* is the same word as Old Welsh *Traeth*, glossed by Giraldus Cambrensis (*Itinerarium Cambriae*, i. cap. 6) as *tractus maris*, and by his editor in Camden's *Anglica Normannica*, as a wide stretch of sand." "Mr. Cadwallader J. Bates, Historian of Northumberland, has kindly offered me the very ingenious suggestion that 'Tracht Romra' may be interpreted 'the shore of the strong tide.' He quotes O'Reilly's *Irish-English Dictionary*, 1817, for 'Romhara, a spring tide, a full sea.' The explanation seems entirely rational and happy."—Neilson. See note, page 51.

save with His permission.' The clergy did as he bade them. Adamnan drew a circle with his crozier round about the curraghs, and God made the strand firm underneath and built up the sea in a high wall around them. Thus the place where they were became an island, and the sea receded from it and did them no hurt. On seeing this very great miracle, the Saxons trembled for fear of Adamnan and gave him all that he asked." Thus does the hagiographer turn to purposes of edification the common incident of being stranded on a sand-bank as the tide goes out! I shall tell later how I came near sharing the experience of S. Adamnan in Rough Firth and how Lord Cockburn was exasperated in the estuary of the Dee.

Soon after my first glimpse of the Solway, I saw Carsethorn. Some travellers might think the inducements to go thither pathetically slight. I was adhering, however, to my plan of following the coast-line closely. Carsethorn, moreover, is the first village in Galloway that fronts the Solway. Another point was that it has received the most cursory notice in such works as Mr. Harper's *Rambles in Galloway* and the Stewartry guide-book, where it is merely mentioned as being visible from the road. It seemed a poor thing to leave it at that, to explore the rest of Galloway and know nothing more of Carsethorn than just the memory of a distant jumble of whitewashed cottages standing against the shining Firth, and I was the more willing to be there that the afternoon was wearing on, and the map told me that I should find an inn, and an inn suggested the thought of tea.

I left the main road at the little village of Kirkbean and reached Carsethorn in a few minutes. I was glad that I had made the digression, for a powerful west wind was blowing that day and, while I was at the inn, it brought up dense clouds that dulled the aspect of the Solway, hid the Cumberland hills, and discharged themselves in heavy showers. The weather was so threatening that I decided to pass the night here if I could get a room; but the modest look of the house made me fear that the landlord would advise me to proceed on my travels. My request, however, was accorded with alacrity, and there was allotted to me an excellent bedroom looking, I was glad to notice, seawards. When I went out to survey the exterior of my lodging more leisurely than I had done on my arrival, I was much diverted at its name, for I learned from the sign-

board that it was called *The Steamboat Inn*, and all men know
that no steamboat ever comes to Carsethorn. This was enough
to put one in a good humour with the place, and my satisfaction
only increased with the landlady's ambitious endeavours for
my entertainment.

I learned later that the name of the inn was not a joke, but
that it had some historical justification. The Carse Bay was

*The Nith Estuary from Carsethorn.*

the scene of a considerable shipping trade before the day of
railways. The channel ran much nearer the shore than it does
now, and steamboats came within actual hail of the village.
More than that, when *The Statistical Account* was written in
1844, a wooden pier had been erected recently for the Liverpool
steam-packet, which made two voyages weekly in summer and
one in winter and conveyed the fat stock from the neighbouring
farms to a better market than could be found nearer home.

When I strolled along the sea-front before sunset, the rain

had ceased, the tide was out, and there was a colossal rainbow
bestriding the channels and the gleaming sands of the empty
Firth. Beyond the arc was its reflection on the clouds,
making the phenomenon called a double rainbow. The atmospheric appearances are among the memorable incidents of
a residence on the Solway shore.

Before going to bed I threw up the window and looked out
on darkness, seeing nothing but points of light—the stars, for
the sky had cleared, and a little constellation low down made by
the lamps of Silloth. The full tide was washing quietly against
the shingly beach within a short stone-throw of my window ;
but the darkness was too deep for the water to be seen. Looking
out upon the night, I recalled the tale of a small vessel sailing
up the Firth amid darkness and storm about the end of the
year 1733. There had come a lull in the tempest, the black clouds
parted, and the moonlight broke through, revealing to the eyes
of the seamen the crests of the tossing waves and also what
they took to be a sail a mile or two behind them. As they watched,
however, it seemed to be overhauling them rapidly in spite of
the strong north-east wind. The clouds obscured the moon
once more and left them wondering. When the light shone forth
again, it shewed a great State-coach, drawn by six black horses,
with outriders, coachmen, footmen, torch-bearers, and followers,
driving over the waves. The skipper, steeling himself to hail
the apparition, ran forwards and cried, " Where bound ? and
where from ? " The answer came, " To tryst with Lagg !
Dumfries ! from Hell ! " Such is the legend of the passing
of the soul of Sir Robert Grierson. He had been notorious
as a persecutor of the Covenanters.

The village itself does not provide matter for a long discourse.
There is a short row of mean hovels at the south end running
inland ; a little nearer the centre of the village, a double row
of dwellings occupied formerly by coastguardsmen ; and along
the sea-front, a terrace of two-storey houses with fanlights over
the doors and gardens in front ; and elsewhere straggling
groups of cottages. The look-out house of the old coastguard
now contains a village library. Most of the inhabitants are
labourers on the farms of Kirkbean Parish or fishermen.

While I was talking to a man on the beach in the morning, I
heard him use a word from the Norse tongue. We were watching
two fishermen wading shorewards through the channels. Each

of them had a long pole over his shoulder with a net attached. I asked the man beside me what kind of nets those were, and he said they were "haf-nets". Now, *haf* is Old Norse for "sea". Another Old Norse word that survives in place-names in these parts is *rak*. Its meaning is a stripe or streak. The best-known instance of the word is the Skager Rack of Denmark. The sand-banks between Silloth and Satterness were known in the sixteenth century as "the Longrake sande". There is a "rack" between The Scaur and Rough Island and

*Gamekeeper's Cottage at Arbigland (Paul Jones's Birthplace).*

another between Heston and the mainland. The Norsemen called a low group of rocks a *scar*, and so we have the Big Scar and the Little Scar between Burrow Head and the Mull of Galloway. *Nes* for "headland" is very frequent, and *fjall* for "hill", as in "the Fell of Barhullion", "Eschoncan Fell", and "Criffel".[1]

A Norse origin has been attributed to "Arbigland", the name of an estate about a mile and a half south of Carsethorn, where Paul Jones was born. The road running directly thither from Kirkbean climbs to the summit of a tree-covered

---

[1] *Mons Crefel*, c. 1330; Pont, Crafel. N. *Kraka fjall*, crow's hill; L.Sc. craw fell; and Icel. *kryfja* (to split), split fell, have been suggested.

ridge and descends the other side through a dark wood to the entrance of the Arbigland grounds, where one turns to the right for the gamekeeper's cottage where John Paul, known better as Paul Jones, was born, the son of a gardener, in 1747. The boy looked beyond the garden, he heard the call of the sea, and was allowed to cross the Solway to Whitehaven at the age of twelve and become apprentice to a merchant trading with America.

*Old Market-cross at East Preston Farmhouse.*

He rose to be a captain when he was twenty-one, adopted the name of Jones as a mark of regard for an American family of that name who shewed him much kindness in his youth, and came to look upon America as his home. His strong love of liberty led him to sympathize with the revolted Colonies, and he entered the navy of his adopted country as a lieutenant in 1775. He advanced rapidly in the service and was entrusted with the most important commands. He regarded the British Navy as " the best regulated of any in the world ", and laboured to bring that of the States to a similar efficiency. Americans look upon him as " the father " of their Navy—" the name of no other man is so associated with our flag as is his," says Mr. Brady, the American author of one of the biographies. Jones's was a brilliant, adventurous, and indomitable spirit, and his exploits, although achieved under the flags of the United States and Russia, shed lustre on the land of his birth. It is, no doubt, the old calumny, that he was " a pirate ", that has hindered him from being counted among the greatest of Scotsmen. In the midst of his strenuous career he was never forgetful of his early home. He saw his family in 1771 for the

*Satterness.*

last time, but continued to send them frequent remittances of money, caused a stone to be erected over his father's grave in Kirkbean Churchyard, and left all his property to his two sisters and their children.

When Paul Jones was a boy, there were three villages in the parish, " Kirkbean, Preston,' and Salterness ". Preston[1] has disappeared ; but its old market-cross was unearthed in the course of digging operations about the middle of the last century and has been re-erected beside East Preston farmhouse. It is made of freestone, measures six feet and four inches in height, and two feet and two inches across the arms, and bears no

[1] Priest's dwelling

inscription or carving of any kind.  A zig-zag course along the emptiest of byways leads one from Arbigland to its present site.

From this point a perfectly straight road a little over a mile in length runs over marshy flats to Satterness, and on this open, wind-swept space one may see many land and sea birds.  The naturalist who wrote under the pen-name, " Mabie Moss ", noted in 1909 that sheldrakes were a rapidly increasing

*Satterness Lighthouse.*

species here, and spoke of this neighbourhood as the headquarters of these birds in Galloway.  He had seen so many as a hundred of them at more than one nesting-place, and in an old wood full of rabbit-holes, some miles away from Satterness, a flock of about a hundred pairs.  The rabbit-warrens close to Satterness were haunted by jackdaws in great numbers until some years ago ; but almost all of them have gone, and their places have been taken by the stock-dove.  This bird has come into the district recently and seems to find it congenial.  The writer whom I have quoted remarks, " It does sound a little bit strange to hear a pigeon cooing from a rabbit-hole ! "

No sooner had I reached Satterness than I went down to the shore, set up my camera, and turned it on the lighthouse. A man whom I took to be the keeper swept down upon me from a cottage and asked if it would " improve it " if he ascended to the top. I understood him to mean that if he posed himself gracefully on the balcony, I should have a more lively and pleasing picture. I therefore pressed the shutter without delay and replied that if he were about to ascend, I should be glad to go with him.

The tide was full, and there was a strong wind, so that waves were breaking into foam all along the shore. There was also bright sunshine making the white cottages facing the sea and the white lighthouse on the beach as dazzling as the crests of the waves. I looked down from the balcony to the little roofs, the broad stretch of sandy shore, and a few lady bathers and children in the water. Behind the village, the flats of Kirkbean extended towards the skirt of Criffel on the right, and far on the left were the rugged cliffs of Colvend surmounted by green slopes.

A motor-car ran into the village and stopped. The man beside me shouted into my ear, striving to make himself heard above the wind, and I gathered that on some days so many as four or five cars would arrive with bathers ; " and no wonder ", the voice seemed to say, for there is " no danger here ", but a gentle incline of firm sand and plenty of it. There is, however, danger in the outgoing tides of the Solway.

There is nothing of the modern upstart about this watering-place. Writing in 1795, the author of the old *Statistical Account* says that this village " is now chiefly inhabited by persons who keep furnished rooms, to accommodate such as, during the season, come to it for the benefit of sea bathing ". The author of the later *Account* of 1844 thought that " owing to the great demand for bathing quarters, and the eagerness with which rich and genteel families occupy very indifferent cottages at Saturness during the summer months, it cannot be doubted that building a number of neat, comfortable cottages there would be an excellent speculation ".

The original form of the name is " Salternes ". It occurs as " Salterness " in the old *Statistical Account* and in the

colloquial form of " Saturness " in the new *Account*. " Satterness "[1] is more philologically accurate. The salt-work of
Salternes was granted by Roland, Lord of Galloway, to the
monks of Holme Cultram on the other side of the Solway.

The lighthouse is the oldest in Galloway. The tower was
erected as a landmark for vessels sailing in the Firth. The
writer of the old *Account* says that " a part of it was built
many years ago, by some merchants in Dumfries, then carrying
on a considerable trade with Virginia ", that it had been raised
to " its present height " afterwards, and that it would be still
more useful " were lights placed in it ". This seems to have
been done before the eighteenth century closed.

[1] What fate is deserved by the " over-wise person or persons "
referred to by Dr. Neilson who, " giving way, perhaps, to baseless
anterior philological fancies," have " improved " the name into
" Southerness " ?

[Note on *Tracht Romra* by Mr. Johnston: "*Tracht* must be Erse
or Gaelic as *Romra* or *Romhava* is. The Old Welsh is cognate, but
the word here clearly is G. *traigh*, genitive *tragad*, 'sea-beach', and
*Tracht* must represent an old genitive." See note on page 42.]

*The Scaur.*

*Cliffs of Colvend.*

## CHAPTER V

### FROM SATTERNESS TO THE SCAUR

The ghost of the three cross-roads—The Castle of Wraiths—Allan
Cunningham and the lass of Preston Mill—The Southwick
coast—The old church of Southwick—The site of S. Laurence's
Chapel and Fairgirth—The coast near Douglas Hall—Ship-
wrecks on the Barnhourie Sands—Douglas Hall—Portling—
Port o' Warren and a smuggling tale—The White Loch of
Colvend—The Scaur, or Kippford—The path to Rockcliffe—A
voyage to Heston.

ON the way from Satterness to the main road I passed the
only very old building in the parish of which any part remains,
the Castle of Wraiths[1]. The name in its English meaning is
appropriate in a parish six miles long and boasting of a ghost
to every mile. Mr. Samuel Arnott, who has discoursed so
pleasantly on the history of Kirkbean Parish in various periodicals, collected all that could be gathered about these ghosts
in a communication to the Dumfriesshire and Galloway Natural
History and Antiquarian Society. One of the ghosts "is
said to have haunted what is known as ' the three cross-roads '
near Arbigland, a lonely spot where, on a wild night, the dread

[1] Gaelic *rath*, a circular earthen fort.

feeling which was in those days felt in the deep darkness caused by the surrounding trees must have been intensified by the sound of the wind through their branches and the roar of the waves of the boisterous Solway. The ghost was generally supposed to be that of a young man, and the tale is a romantic one, which, in the hands of an accomplished novelist, would form a thrilling narrative. As is pretty well known, Arbigland at one time belonged to a family of the name of Craik. Its then representative had a daughter who, it is said, had become attached to a young man named Dunn, who was in her father's employment as a groom or horse-breaker. One day a shot was heard, and soon after the lifeless body of Dunn was found near where the ghost was said afterwards to appear. In the eyes of the law the sad occurrence was considered a case of suicide; but popular belief took an opposite view and attributed it to the murderous act of one of Miss Craik's brothers, who had discovered the attachment between his sister and Dunn and in his anger at the discovery had taken the young man's life. It is said that Miss Craik was of the latter opinion, and that she left Arbigland and went to reside in England, never returning to the place so full to her of tragedy. . . . With the prevailing opinion regarding this ghastly tale, it is little wonder that the apparition of the unfortunate man was said to frequent the lonely spot where he met his death. It was hardly to be expected, however, that a haunted place like this should be deserted by the white ladies who are so familiar in ghost stories and whose affection for Kirkbean seems somewhat remarkable, and one of my informants speaks of a white lady who was said to appear here also. The weight of authority (if I am justified in using such a phrase in this connexion) is, however, almost exclusively in favour of the tradition that the apparition was that of Dunn."

The Castle of Wraiths belonged to the barony of Preston and was the property of the Regent Morton. James the Sixth is said to have stayed here sometimes when he was under the Regent's care. There is a tradition that he once visited a house in the neighbourhood belonging to a poor but proud family when the larder was practically empty and " the only thing they had to present was a dish of flounders; but they managed to produce two courses by giving first the brown side and then the white side of the flounder, upon which James remarked,

' Oddsfish, man ! thae's fine fish, but I think the white anes
are the best ! ' "

The property changed hands several times. On the 13th
of May, 1742, Mary and Willielma Maxwell, daughters and
heirs-portioners of the deceased William Maxwell of Preston,
had sasine. Mary was married in 1761 to William Earl of
Sutherland, and had two daughters, one of whom became
Countess of Sutherland in her own right. She was married
in 1785 to George Granville Leveson Gower, who became
Marquess of Stafford and was created Duke of Sutherland in
1833. Willielma, the other daughter of William Maxwell,
became the wife of John Viscount Glenorchy, about 1761,
and built the church in Edinburgh known as Lady Glenorchy's.

If the reader has followed my route so far, whether with or
without the help of the map, it will be obvious that the two miles
of the main road between Kirkbean and Mainsriddle[1] have been
left untraversed. My reason for pausing over this is that about
half-way along this section is the home of " the lovely lass of
Preston Mill ", the subject of one of Allan Cunningham's poems.
Cunningham is not a widely-read author in these days ; but
no one who is acquainted with " A wet sheet and a flowing
sea " needs plead total ignorance of his works. He was
born in 1784 in the parish of Keir in Dumfriesshire and was
not, therefore, a native of Galloway ; he was, however, the
author of the greater part of Cromek's *Remains of Nithsdale
and Galloway Song*. He led Cromek to believe that his verses
were examples of old ballad literature collected among the
peasantry of the south-west, but imposed upon few people
besides Cromek, if even upon him. His prose works included
*Lives of the Most Eminent British Painters, Sculptors and
Architects*, the *Life, Journals and Correspondence of Sir David
Wilkie*, and several novels, in one of which Paul Jones appears.
It was while he was practising his trade of stonemason at Arbigland that he met Jean Walker, the lass of Preston Mill, whom
he married.[2]

From Maxwelltown to Mainsriddle the highway runs in a
series of long, straight stretches, but after Mainsriddle is full

[1] Riddell's farm-steading.
[2] The *Encyclopædia Britannica* gives the following account of his
sons, who may be claimed for Galloway : " Joseph Davey Cunningham (1812–1851) entered the Bengal Engineers, and is known by his

of variety and pleasing surprises. It dips down to the woody
depths of the Southwick Glen, where the banks are glorious with
daffodils in spring, and attacks and gradually surmounts the
steep hill on the other side, passing one or two small groups of
pretty, flower-decked cottages. It is now on the top of the long,
high bank by which the land falls abruptly to the sea, and continues to disport itself along the heights with ever-recurring
winds and dips and rises, as if intoxicated with joy of the country
through which it runs. The bank below is covered with mixed
wood and undergrowth, through which one looks down to grassy
flats where the Southwick Burn makes a languid, circuitous
progress towards the sea. A little farther on, it is the sheen of
the sea itself that is visible below the woody tangle. On the
right there rises close at hand a series of moorland fells. The
largest of them, the Bainloch Hill, made me think of the Drei
Zinnen in Tirol with the points flattened down. Darkness
was falling, moorburn was going on, and the broad summit
was covered with flames and smoke as if the hill were actually
consuming away.

On the following morning, brilliant sunshine fell on cliffs
and fells, on wooded slopes and gleaming beach, and I could
not but return to this part of the coast from The Scaur, where
I had spent the night. I scrambled down among the trees to
the shore, where the conspicuous rock called Lot's Wife rises,
with the Bainloch Burn descending behind it in a pretty cascade.
There are large rocks here clad with ivy, and a wealth of ferns
and wild flowers wherever they can find root. I was reminded
of the idyll of Theocritus in which he speaks of the wind whispering in the pine tree and the music of the water pouring over
the high face of the rock.

I returned to the road and came soon to the beginning of a
descent where the hedge of trees on the left ceased, giving an

*History of the Sikhs* (1849). Sir Alexander Cunningham (1814–
1893) also entered the Bengal Engineers, attaining the rank of
major-general; he was director general of the Indian Archæological
Survey (1870–1885), and wrote an *Ancient Geography of India* (1871)
and *Coins of Medieval India* (1894). Peter Cunningham (1816–
1869) published several topographical and biographical studies, of
which the most important are his *Handbook of London* (1849) and
*The Life of Drummond of Hawthornden* (1833). Francis Cunningham
(1820–1875) joined the Indian Army, and published editions of Ben
Jonson (1871), Marlowe (1870), and Massinger (1871)."

open view of Sandyhills Bay and the cliffs of Colvend.[1]  Before
going on to Sandyhills, however, I took the first turn to the right,
pushing my bicycle up a steep byway towards the old church
of Southwick Parish.  It was about noon, the day was warm,
and I thought that the worshippers who used to toil up here on
Sundays must have wished that their Zion was not set on so
high a hill.  Few ruins in Galloway are so entirely neglected.
Almost every inch is covered with ivy, and dilapidation is going
on rapidly.  Before photographing one of the east lights, I
had to spend a long time in cutting and tearing the ivy away,
and I congratulate myself that I have arrested its action at this
point.  The east lights give the only evidence of the architectural character of the church.  Unhewn granite has been
used for the walls ; but the windows are framed with red freestone with a round top in the Early English Gothic style.  " It
is to be noted ", says the *Inventory*, " that the arch-heads are
hewn out of single stones, and the jambs have no check for
leaded glass."  Scarcely anything is recorded of the history
of the church.  Edward the First made an offering of money,
with his devotions, to " Our Lady of Southwick " in 1300.
Since 1612 Colvend and Southwick have been united.  In 1891,
however, arrangements were made for erecting a new church
farther east, and Southwick is a parish once more *quoad sacra*.

When I had descended to the main road and come to Sandyhills, where there are an old mill, some cottages, and a few two-
storey granite houses for summer visitors, and sometimes a
caravan or two halted near the beach, I turned again to the
right to reach the site of S. Laurence's Chapel at Fairgirth[2]
farmhouse.  I had seen no literature dealing with it, and went to
investigate.  The tenant's wife kindly assisted me, shewing me
a bit of low garden-wall about three feet wide and saying,
" That was never made for a garden-wall ! "  This opinion,
however, is open to question.  She drew back some of the ivy
on the top and revealed a dressed and moulded piece of freestone, saying that she thought it was the top of a head-stone and
that there were one or two more of such stones among the ivy.  I
noticed, however, that the stone was not shaped with the symmetry
usual in head-stones.  I learned also that when the garden was

---

[1] Pronounced " Co'en ".  Gaelic *cul bheinn*, back of the hill, or
G. and Irish *cabhan*, a hollow.  Really old forms are lacking.

[2] Old Norse *faer garðr*, sheep-fold ; but quite possibly "fair garden."

being dug over some years ago, a large dressed stone had been found in the middle and left in its place, and that when alterations were made on the farm-offices on the north side of the house, human bones were discovered.

The door of the farmhouse is framed in granite blocks with a single circular moulding. On both sides the moulding is intermitted with a plain block at the top, inserted apparently to increase the height of the entrance. In the older part of the house there is a granite newel stair of two storeys leading to an attic with an ambry in the north wall. A *Description of the Stewartrie of Kirkcudbright* drawn up in the time of James the Fifth and included in the Sibbald collection of manuscripts gives a list of nine of the most important houses in The Stewartry, and of these Fairgirth is one.

It may be remembered that the cliffs of Colvend have been mentioned twice already. I saw them first from the balcony of the lighthouse at Satterness and nearer from the road below the Bainloch Hill. I was now to walk along the foot of them and see them towering heavenwards, and I may say at once that I consider Sandyhills, Douglas Hall, and the neighbouring coast one of the most delectable parts of seaboard Galloway. Read what the Rev. James Little, minister of Colvend and Southwick, wrote in *The Statistical Account* in 1796: " The sea coast here along the frith is remarkably bold and rocky, forming high and tremendous precipices, from which the tide ebbs, leaving dry a large tract of flat sand, from whence, at low water, may be viewed some picturesque and magnificent scenes : High and pointed spires, at the bases of which are passages through them in form of rude arches ; spacious and regular amphitheatres, and mouths of caverns running up under ground into the land, farther than any human being hath ever adventured to explore. In the crevices of the rock, but generally where the precipice is overhanging, or most inaccessible, is found the marine plant *samphire*, well known as a preserve or pickle ; to the dangerous expedients for gathering which, as alluded to of old by Shakespeare, the people here are, at this day, no strangers." The account of the parish given by Mr. Little's successor, the Rev. Andrew MacCulloch, is so very brief that I suspect that he thought putting pen to paper a great trouble ; but if he has little to say about the parochial history, antiquities, industries, and economy, it is plain that the scenery and the sensational incidents and possibilities of the coast appealed to him. Much his longest paragraph relates to the " Coves or Caves ", and is as follows : " There are a number of these along the ' wild shores of caverned Colvend '. The principal of these is called the Piper's cove, from a legend that a piper undertook to explore it. He carried his pipes with him, and continued to play under ground till he reached Barnbarrach, about four

*The Needle's Eye and Cliffs near Douglas Hall.*

miles distant from its mouth. The sound then ceased, and nothing was ever heard again of the unfortunate minstrel. It is found, however, to be only a hundred and twenty yards in length. There is a well in the middle, twenty-two feet deep. There are a number of fissures in the rocks along the shore. Close by the Piper's cove, already mentioned, there is a rude natural arch, about forty feet in height, called the Needle's Eye. Another arch, bearing the same name, and lying more to the eastward, is more regularly formed though not so high."

He singles out two other features for notice. "There is a well called the Murderers' Well, near the Southwick Needle's Eye. According to tradition, it was named from the following circumstance : A set of border reivers came to levy blackmail on the peaceable inhabitants of Colvend. The parishioners rallied, and seizing the leaders of the foray, threw them down this rock to the well below." The other detail is a sand-bank : "The Barnhourie sand-bank, so fatal to vessels, especially to those who are strangers to the coast, runs from the mouth of the Urr to the Nith. Nearer to the English side is another bank called the Robin Rig."

A contributor to *The Gallovidian* has told the stories of two of the ships that have been wrecked on the Barnhourie bank. The *William Levitt* "brought a cargo of timber from the S. Lawrence River to Allonby and Greenock. Having discharged her Allonby portion, she was being towed round to Greenock when the tow-rope broke, and the weather being bad, she drifted on to Barnhourie bank and rapidly became a total wreck." The *Forest Queen*, having been sold to a Norwegian company, "left Dublin to be delivered to her new owners. On the night previous to her sailing, her crew had spent a jolly night among the public-houses. In consequence of this drinking bout the captain's navigation was at fault, and mistaking the Ross for Pladda light, he, carrying full sail, passed Heston and the mouth of the Urr, and thinking he was running up the Firth of Clyde, never learned his fatal mistake until his ship struck on Barnhourie Sands. In a few days the vessel was settled firmly and deeply in the sands and was afterwards sold for a few pounds." The figureheads of these two ships stood for many years in the yard of Messrs. Wilson & Sons, shipping agents, in the Station Road, Dalbeattie.

After hearing about Douglas Hall and being impressed by its high-sounding name, you will be surprised to find how little a place it is. Two or three cottages and a shop or two among trees between the road and the shore are all that there is of it, and you have passed through it before you have realized that you are there. If its name is famous, this is because it lies on the byway leading to the sands that stretch along the

base of those precipices with their caverns and natural arches
which aroused the enthusiasm of the writer of the old *Account*.

Of Portling[1] there is nothing to be said save that at the top
of the shore there are rows of stakes for drying the nets belonging
to a salmon fishery, and that it is overhung by some granite
houses like those at Sandyhills.  If one walk along the high
ground from Portling to Port o' Warren,[2] one's breath will be
taken away by the abrupt discovery of the single fisherman's
cottage in the depths of the rocky recess.  Port o' Warren is
connected with the following tale of woe which was communicated
by Joseph Train to the author of *The History of Galloway* :

"By the Act 12 Geo. III., salt was allowed to be imported
into the Isle of Man from Great Britain duty free, for the purpose
of curing herrings ; but the boon was turned to the disadvantage
of the British Government by the smuggling back into Britain,
large quantities of such duty-free salt.  A young man of Ramsay,
who was on the eve of being married to a respectable girl of that
neighbourhood, contrary to the advice of her relations, resolved to
run a few bags of fishery salt into some creek of the Solway, where
he knew he would meet a ready market, and thereby raise a
small sum to assist him in defraying the expense of his wedding.

"In this ill-omened enterprise he was accompanied by the
bride's brother only.  They had passed the shores of Barn-
houry, and were steering up the Solway Frith, near Balcary
bay, where the Prince Ernest Augustus Cutter, commanded
by Sir John R——, lay at anchor, when they were suddenly
surprised by a voice, ordering them through a trumpet to
'*lay to.*'  The poor Manxmen from not understanding the
English language distinctly, disregarding the order, kept on
their way towards Port O'Warren, a noted landing place ;
but they had not proceeded many yards, till a ball from the
cutter deprived the bridegroom of life.  Panic-struck by such
an instantaneous calamity, the surviving lad ran the boat
ashore at the nearest point of Colvend, and took to flight lest
he should fall into the fangs of the seaguard, as he saw the
cruiser bearing down upon him under a press of sail.  The
corpse, being of little value as a prize, was thrown on the beach
by the sailors ; but the crazy Scout, with a few bushels of salt
on board, was taken in tow and carried away to the custom-
house of Kirkcudbright.

[1] *Port luing*, ship's port.          [2] *Port a' gharrain*, horse port.

" Near the lonely spot where the bleeding corpse lay on the strand, several shipwrecked mariners had previously found a

*Port o' Warren.*

resting place, and there the smuggler was likewise buried by pitying strangers, till under a warrant from the sheriff, the body was raised and re-interred in the neighbouring church-yard of Colvend.

"Meanwhile the surviving smuggler made his way home to Ramsay, with intelligence of the calamity just related. The father of the deceased had been by the temporary suppression of the illicit trade of the island, which took place at the revestment, reduced from a state of affluence to dependence for support on the last survivor of a numerous family, the account of whose death filled his heart with sorrow. Unable as he was to encounter the dangers of the sea, even for a short distance, he resolved nevertheless on removing the remains of his unfortunate son from Scotland to the family burying place in the Church-yard of Kirk Christ Lezayre.

"The survivor of the former unfortunate voyage, with some other relations, agreed to assist in this frenetic undertaking, and what was more singular still, the distracted bride could not be dissuaded from appearing as chief mourner in the funeral group.

"Permission was obtained to remove the body from the church-yard of Colvend, and the mournful party embarked with it for Ramsay; but ere they had reached the Isle of Heston, a hurricane arose and a foaming breaker engulphed the fragile bark, near the spot from whence the fatal shot was fired, that brought so many relations to a tragical end, and caused lasting grief to a wide circle of surviving friends.

"Sir John R——, the commander of the cutter, was arraigned for the murder of the Manxman, before the High Court of Justiciary at Edinburgh, and acquitted of the charge. On the lonely shore of Colvend, a little below the farmhouse of Glenstocken, the Manxman's first grave is yet pointed out by the neighbouring peasants, and all the concomitant circumstances connected with it as here related, are feelingly told to the enquiring stranger."

Rather less than two miles from Port o' Warren and just before the coast-line recedes into the estuary of the Urr is the Castle Hill Point, and near it a memorial of another ship-wreck, a cairn with a slab bearing this inscription : " The schooner Elbe, Capt. Samuel Wilson, after providentially landing her crew here, backed off the rocks and sank off Rascarrel, December 7th, 1867." The *Inventory* notices a promontory fort here, with the unusual feature of a stone wall about ten feet thick for the main line of defence.

Immediately after leaving Sandyhills, the road passes the
Colvend golf-course, and this reminds me that I have not
yet told the reader that there is no such place as Colvend.
There is a parish of this name, and a Colvend post-office, but
no town or village. The clachan beside the post-office is called
Lochend, a name derived from the White Loch of Colvend,
the wood-girt sheet of water visible from the road. The
cliffs that overhang the sea are only a few minutes' walk distant,
and to pass from their ruggedness to the beauty of this inland
water is like turning

> Abruptly into some sequestered nook,
> Still as a sheltered place when winds blow loud.

"The other evening," wrote Mr. W. H. Armistead, a naturalist who lived in Kippford, "I walked over to the White
Loch. . . . Leaving the road and crossing a green field bright
with hyacinths and cuckoo flowers, I plunged into a wood of
birches bordering the loch. The sun shone brightly low in the
west. It would have been difficult to choose a time when the
magic of spring was more strikingly exhibited. Beneath
the birches ran a small stream over golden gravel. All around
flamed clusters of marsh marigold, and the horizontal rays
of the sun lit up the broad green leaves of irises till they were
fringed with gold. Overhead the delicate and intricate tracery
of birch branches against a sky of purest blue, with here and
there a white drifting cloud, made a restful contrast to the
flaming sunlit colours at my feet. As I looked eastward, the
quiet waters of the loch could be seen through a thick cluster
of last year's tall feathery reeds (*Arundo phragmites*), and
behind, a rugged hill with patches of white and yellow, black
thorn and gorse, against a rich brown background, the effect
being greatly enhanced by the bright green of freshly opened
leaves, and the magic touch of sunlight pouring in golden streams
from the summit of Screel. Swallows were flitting over the water,
coots and waterhens were splashing in the reeds; from the
far shore came the persistent note of the cuckoo. The wild
sweet song of the thrush was heard in a thicket near at hand,
and almost overhead sounded the gentle cooing of wood pigeons."

The Scaur[1], or Kippford[2], is a village of seamen. Some of

---

[1] The rock or cliff.      [2] The ford of the tree-trunk, from
Gaelic and Irish *ceap*, gen. *cip*; or from Dan. *kippe*, a low alehouse.

them are employed on the schooners that pass up the Urr[1] to Dalbeattie to exchange cargoes of manure for granite. There is scarcely any fishing industry; but one man does a business in mussels, which he sends to fisheries elsewhere. Shipbuilding was carried on here in the earlier, and to a slight extent even in the later, part of the nineteenth century. The product consisted of brigs and schooners designed mainly for the coasting trade. The last vessel built here was the *Balcary*

*The Scaur, or Kippford, and the Valley of the Urr.*

*Lass*, of two hundred and forty tons burden. She was launched in 1884 and made two successful voyages, but was lost thereafter in a gale off the coast of Newfoundland. The only work done now is the repairing of wooden vessels. An important industry is in the hands of the women, that of letting rooms and catering for the many visitors who come hither for a quiet holiday.

The Scaur consists chiefly of one irregular row of cottages

[1] *Ur* is the Basque word for water.

including one or two hotels and boarding-houses all facing the little estuary of the Urr. On the other side is a peninsula running into Rough Firth; and behind that, the hills called Screel[1] and Bengairn[2] present a sharp edge against the western sky. The mud banks that are left bare when the tide goes out have no likeness to the clean, hard sand to be found in so many parts of the Solway, but are soft, sticky, and perhaps dangerous. It is all the more delightful to watch the rising tide submerging them, the stranded schooners gradually righting themselves, and the yachtsmen busying themselves with their gaily-painted craft. Then is the time, too, to follow the path to Rockcliffe, not so much for the sake of Rockcliffe itself—a quiet group of houses for visitors spread round a shallow, sandy bay—but for the inland and sea-ward views to be had as one ascends to the higher parts of the track. If you look back after a few hundred yards, you have at your feet the roofs of The Scaur and the estuary itself in a setting of heathery knolls and, for a background, a series of wooded, gibbous hills and the meadows lying along the Water of Urr. On the south there is the long peninsula between Rough Firth and Orchardton Bay, a very paradise of wildfowl; in the midst of the Firth, Rough Island, approachable on foot at low water; and beyond Almorness[3] Point, Heston Island about three miles away on the edge of the outer Firth of Solway. Near Rockcliffe there are plantations, and the medley of green islands, peninsulas and shining waters is beautifully framed among pines.

One of the seamen at The Scaur carries the monthly " lighthouse letter " from Heston. His boat visits the island almost every day in summer, two or three times a week in winter if wind and weather are favourable, and sometimes not for two or three weeks.

We left The Scaur at a quarter past three in the afternoon. There was a contrary wind, so that we had to tack all the way, and it was not until a quarter to six that the boat was moored at the jetty on the Heston shore. On climbing to the higher part of the island, I saw a magnificent panorama of the mainland, a far-extended chain of broken, rocky hills, sharp peaks, and elevated plateaux. Screel and Bengairn were the most pro-

---

[1] Hill of the screaming, from Gaelic *sgreadail*.
[2] Hill of the cairn.
[3] Pronounced Ámmerness.

minent, because the nearest, hills. Seen thus from the south, they closely resemble their aspect from the north, but with increased grandeur. As the tide was receding, I could not stay here long, and hurried down to the cave which S. R. Crockett magnified and elaborated into " The Great Cave of Isle Rathan "[1] in *The Raiders*. For anyone who had allowed his expectations to be formed by Crockett's story, the cave would be a great disappointment. It is plain that it was a mere pretext for the drawing of the most soul-satisfying cave of which Crockett had ever dreamed.

I found in the only dwelling-house on the island an aged lighthouse-keeper, who was about to retire from his office. He told me that he paid £24 as rent for the island and received £25 as lighthouse-keeper. He supplemented the £1 of balance by sheep-farming. There are some slender remains of an old building beside the keeper's house. These may represent MacDouall's castle on " the island of Estholm ".[2] After the fall of the Douglases, Heston became the property of the monks of Dundrennan Abbey. There was on the shore what was known as " the monks' pool " for confining salmon.

When we left the island, the tide was running out fast, and the wind that would have been so useful now had fallen away to the gentlest puffs, so that we were as much delayed as on the outward voyage. When we came abreast of Rough Island, there was very little water, and presently we were aground in the middle of the bay. There was imminent risk of being stranded until the return of the tide, and the boatman hastily stepped overboard and began to push the boat towards deeper water. We found the channel of the Urr, and the boatman took the oars. I held the rudder, keeping our craft close to the mud-bank, where the strength of the current was least. It was now a night of the deepest darkness ; but the lights of The Scaur were shining, and the heather and whins on the scrubby knolls behind the village were blazing as Bainloch Hill had done the night before. So profound was the gloom that the world was almost blotted out, and those points and splashes of red might have belonged to either earth or sky.

[1] " Rathan " is an old name for Heston.
[2] See page 324.

*Heston Island from the coast road near Auchencairn.*

## CHAPTER VI

### FROM THE SCAUR TO KIRKCUDBRIGHT

The Round Tower of Orchardton—A possible source of *Guy Mannering*—Palnackie—Auchencairn—Messrs. Clark, Crain, and Quirk—The Rerwick coast—Brandy-holes—Smugglers' routes—The racketing spirit of Ringcroft of Stocking—Stone fires—Dundrennan Abbey—Flight of Queen Mary from Langside—Hutton's tradition of her visit to Dundrennan—Port Mary.

A CHILD living at The Scaur and looking towards Bengairn, especially about the time of sunset, might well think that fairyland lay that way. The streak of gold across the estuary, the shadowed mystery of the country beyond, and then the feathered sides of the hill—all of this would make him think that if he climbed up among those distant trees to the sky-line, he would behold a vision splendid.

Whether one has fairyland in view or the more prosaic places lying along the foot of the hills, it is plain that one must pass the barrier of the Urr. So far as I could learn, the nearest bridge was at Dalbeattie, four miles away, and I had no wish to make the *détour* of over eight miles. If I continued my journey by crossing the Urr at The Scaur, I should be doing what few travellers had ever done before, what few would

do again, and should land on a wild and desolate coast.  My
bicycle, therefore, was bestowed in the bow of a rowing-boat,
and in a few minutes I lifted it out on a muddy bank on
the farther side, wheeled it over a bog, and found an ancient
byway running down one side of the peninsula and up the
other after skirting what is called the Castle Hill.  Only in the
shaded parts did this track preserve the character of a road.
Wherever it was open to the sky, it was a narrow ribbon of green

*Round Tower of Orchardton.*

sward winding among bracken.  On consulting the map, I saw
that it was an endless byway beginning and ending in Palnackie[1] with a course of about five miles.  Summer visitors
do not come to Palnackie ; but if they did, I am sure that this
would be one of their favourite walks.  I had the road all to
myself as I travelled onwards looking for the Round Tower of
Orchardton.

This old battlemented tower, weather-worn, but scarcely

[1] Probably Gaelic *poll an cnaic*, stream at the fissure.—Johnston.

deserving to be called a ruin, stands on a green slope in one of
the quietest corners of the world. A surviving fragment of a
mediæval keep, it is something less than impressive, but is
unique among Galloway buildings, and is associated with *Guy
Mannering* as the scene of one of the traditions on which the
romance is believed to have been based. The plan is circular,
but in other respects resembles that of the smaller castles of the
fifteenth century. The entrance is at the top of an outside
stair. The first-floor apartment appears to have been used as
a chapel, for wrought in the sill of an ambry is a piscina with a
drain. A corbel carved on the north side of the doorway about
three feet above the level of the floor may have been used as a
lamp-stand. The small gabled cape-house and the projecting
parapet supported on moulded corbels redeem the otherwise
plain exterior from insignificance. The lands of Orchardton
are said to have come into the possession of Alexander Carnys,
Provost of Lincluden College, who died in 1422, and John
Cairnis is said to have erected a residence on them in the middle
of the fifteenth century.

Whether the following story had anything to do with the
plot of *Guy Mannering* or not, it is interesting enough in itself.
After the Battle of Culloden, some of the rebels who had escaped
capture contrived to reach the Galloway coast, hoping to find
a ship. They fell into the hands of the military and were brought
before the Commissary of Dumfriesshire, John Goldie of Craigmuie in Balmaclellan Parish, the father-in-law of Mrs. Goldie,
who sent the narrative of Helen Walker to Sir Walter
Scott, and whose daughter wrote an unpublished volume of
family recollections containing a version of the story. The
Commissary had no alternative but to order the captured
rebels to military execution; but as they were being led away,
he noticed one of them trying to tear a document, and ordered
the officer guarding him to seize it. On reading it, he said,
" Why, young man, you were attempting to destroy yourself.
This paper is your commission from the King of France as an
officer in his army; and I now detain you as a prisoner of war
instead of sending you off to be shot as a rebel." A rumour
arose in Dumfries that the prisoner was the long-lost heir of the
house of Orchardton. An old nurse who had been in the service
of the late Sir Robert Maxwell of Orchardton obtained admit-
tance to the prison, and after some talk with the youth confirmed

the idea. Sir Robert had been educated at the Jesuit College at Douay and had sent his son to the same institution in 1739. He died in the following year, and his brother, who took over the management of the estate, gave instructions that his nephew should be trained for the priesthood, designing thereby to secure the succession for himself. Young Maxwell was unwilling to become a priest and ran away from college. On being brought back he ran away again, enlisted in a French infantry regiment, and fought at Dettingen and Fontenoy. He bore an ensign's commission in the French force sent to aid Prince Charles Edward in 1745 and was wounded at Culloden. His uncle, meanwhile, had died, and his cousin, Sir Thomas, was in possession of Orchardton. Young Maxwell returned to France on being set at liberty, but in 1754 came back to Scotland, took the formula against Popery, and began a law plea against his cousin. He alleged that as a minor he had not been in a position to make a free choice of his religion, and that it was with a sinister intention that his uncle had destined him for the Roman Catholic priesthood. The Court of Session decided the case in his favour. Sir Thomas appealed to the House of Lords and died before a decision was given. Sir Thomas left no family, and the pursuer succeeded as heir at law. Sir Robert Maxwell, who had thus come at last to his own, built a good house on the property and married a daughter of Robert Maclellan of Barscobe. According to Miss Goldie's account, he was " the ornament and delight of the country, uniting all the gentlemanly dignity of the old school with the bland and graceful gaiety of foreign manners ". He became a shareholder in Douglas, Heron, and Company's Ayr Bank, which stopped payment in 1773. Sir Robert had to leave Orchardton and live thereafter on a small pittance. He died in 1786 and had no heir.

It sometimes happens that one who is a serious traveller, and not a mere tourist in the restricted sense of one who commits himself to the programmes which railway and steamboat companies dictate or recommend mainly for the reason that they have trains and steamers going to such and such places, will discover in the course of his independent wanderings surprising and memorable effects in places that are hardly named in guide-books and not at all in railway time-tables, scenes that he would be sorry to have missed. As a small instance there might

be mentioned the odd incident, when you are going along a quiet
country road among fields and woods, of seeing suddenly in
front of you a ship's rigging rising towards the clouds beyond a
wayside cottage or two.  Palnackie, where you may have this
sensation, is a small village about a mile north of the Tower of
Orchardton, and might be thought worth visiting for such a
reason as this, unless, indeed, in the case of people who revel in
harbours and quays of every kind.  The port of Palnackie
was once the scene of a considerable trade, and when the new
*Statistical Account* was written, the accommodation was insufficient for the vessels arriving there.  Now you may see but a

*Auchencairn.*

single ship, and sometimes none at all.  The decline of this and
some other ports has followed, of course, upon the introduction of
the railway into Galloway.  There is still a slender import trade.
The principal export is granite from the Craignair quarries
near Dalbeattie.

What Mr. Crockett has described as " the little, bright, rose-
bowered, garden-circled, seaside village of Auchencairn[1]" is
about four miles to the south of Palnackie.  One detail Mr.
Crockett has omitted from his summary description : the
village, like Dalry, runs down the steep side of a hill.  The main

[1] Gaelic *achadh-an-cairn*, field of the cairn.

street, as in the case of that other more famous village, is bordered with bright cottages, but is not so wide, and, instead of running down into the depths of a green glen, conducts you to the margin of the shallow bay of Auchencairn. In one's recollection of the place the steepness of this principal street comes first, then the white walls of the cottages with their clambering roses and other creepers, and finally the road that sweeps round from the foot of the village and runs along the edge of the bay. As you cycle along here, you have before you for some minutes a fine view across the water to Heston Island. Then the road enters a thick wood that lies along the shore, and you would hardly suspect that you were near the sea at all but for an occasional gleam of shining water beyond the screen of leaves on the left.

Within the great bay of Auchencairn is the secondary one of Balcary, and just opposite the middle of it stands Balcary House, to which this road leads. The origin of the house is more interesting, so far as I am aware, than anything in its later history, for it was built not by the landlord of the estate, nor by a respectable tenant, but by an important company of smugglers. If the names of Messrs Clark, Crain, and Quirk were fictitious, one at least was happily chosen. If the names were real, there can be no doubt as to whose was the brain of the enterprise. While Clark and Crain may have supplied some of the capital, you can imagine how they would learn the wisdom of deferring to the judgment of the subtle Quirk. When the company was in a close corner, everything depended on Quirk. I have no doubt that it was Quirk who designed the underground cellars at Balcary House for the reception of contraband from The Isle of Man. If you lived at Balcary House, you would often picture that lean figure with the eager face pacing up and down the shore on a dark night as he looked for a long-expected lugger that did not come, and muttering maledictions across the waters at the deplorable Clark and the unspeakable Crain.

Between Auchencairn and Dundrennan[1] the road makes an ascent of three miles to a point rather more than four hundred feet above the sea, and after a descent of a mile and a half reaches the latter village. Abundance of time should be allowed for the journey, for one ought really to travel considerably more than four and a half miles between Auchencairn and

1 Gaelic *dùn draighneanan*, hill of the thorn-bushes.

Dundrennan. There are one or two tempting byways to be trodden, and such digressions usually add enormously to the expenditure of time.

I am not sure that it will be worth the trouble for many people to follow the side road to the farmhouse of Rascarrel [1] and the beach just beyond. The rugged character of the coast can be seen here, also a natural bridge over a little chasm, and a large, beautiful cave. The coast, however, is much grander between the bays of Barlocco and Orroland [2]. A narrow road leaves the highway near the summit, passes a place called the Dons Knowe—formerly the home of a smuggling fraternity —and continues through the pastures of Barlocco farm, where there are many bramble bushes bearing huge, luscious berries. At the west end of Barlocco Bay there begins a series of great cliffs, and beneath them is a shore of an extraordinary roughness. It is rent here and there by deep chasms running into the cliff behind and making narrow caves. Standing near the edge, one can hear the restless water surging and gurgling in the depths and then see it dash up in spray at the cave's mouth. It is better not to go very near, as the sides are formed of conglomerate, and the embedded stones are apt to give way under one's feet. I should say that on account of the chasms it would be almost impossible to make one's way along this shore without a ladder. The great caves of Barlocco might be reached with less difficulty from Orroland Bay ; but much the best method would be to take a boat.

These caves were used by smugglers. Secret cellars also were often constructed near the shore for hiding contraband. About fifty years ago some workmen discovered a store of brandy on Barcheskie Hill. They took some friends in Dundrennan into their confidence, and with their help the stuff was transported to more convenient hiding-places near the abbey. One of those who shared in the find concealed his barrel in a field on his farm. Some rumour of the incident went abroad, and the excise authorities at Dumfries came to Dundrennan to make a search. Since coming into possession of the liquor, the farmer had made a daily journey to his cask, and a well-beaten track was the result. The only way in which he could keep the secret was to plough the field, and ploughed it was—a year earlier than the lease conditions required !

[1] Pronounced " Roscarrel."      [2] Debatable ground.

The smugglers had not only natural caves and artificial brandy-holes, but also routes of their own into the interior and favourite inns by the way. From Barlocco, Orroland, Port Mary, and Abbey Burnfoot four branches converged on a main line running northwards across the wild moorland spread below Bengairn. About five miles from Burnfoot the

*The Coast near Abbey Burnfoot.*

road passed one of their inns called Fell Croft. The site is now occupied by a shooting-lodge. Thereafter the road crossed the Dee below Dildawn and went through Clachanpluck and New Galloway. "From Heston, Balcary, and Auchencairn Bay generally, the track led through the vale of Rerwick[1]

---

[1] "1562, Rerryk. Possibly 'reaver's, robber's dwelling,'; Old English *redfere-wic.*"—Johnston.

and over the Barchain Moor to what was once a clachan near
the present Buittle Church and onwards by Corsock to join
the main track to Clydesdale and the north."[1]

Ringcroft of Stocking in this parish of Rerwick was the scene
in 1695 of some racketing-spirit manifestations which are referred
to in *The Encyclopædia Britannica* article on that subject. The
record was given by Alexander Telfair, minister of the parish,
who was ordained in 1689, and the title of his pamphlet is
*A True Relation of an Apparition, Expressions, and Actings of
a Spirit, which infested the House of Andrew Mackie, in Ring-Croft
of Stocking, in the Paroch of Rerrick, in the Stewarty of Kirkcudbright, in Scotland, 1695. By Mr. Alexander Telfair, Minister
of that Paroch; and attested by many other Persons who were also
Eye and Ear Witnesses*.[2] Mr. Andrew Lang, the writer of the
*Encyclopædia* article, remarks that Telfair was " a good chronicler " and that he shews " unusual regard for securing signed
evidence ".

The trouble began in February, 1695, when Andrew Mackie
found that some young beasts were " still loosed " during the
night in a mysterious manner. He tried the effect of removing
them to another place, and " the first night thereafter,
one of them was bound with a hair-tedder to the balk of the
house, so strait that the feet of the beast only touched the ground,
but could not move no way else, yet it sustained no hurt ". On
another night when the family were all asleep, a large basket
of peats was placed in the middle of the floor of the house and
set on fire. The smoke awakened the family, and so the house
was saved from being burned. All this time nothing was either
seen or heard. Stone-throwing began on the 7th of March.
It went on all over the house; but it could not be discovered
whence the stones came. It occurred at intervals by day and
night, but principally at night. It became more serious on
Sunday, the 11th of March, especially " in time of prayer ",
and the stones were directed chiefly at the person praying.
Andrew Mackie went to church and told the minister about it
after the service. The minister called at the house on the

[1] *Smuggling in the Solway and around the Galloway Sea-board*
by Dr. Maxwell Wood.
[2] Defective editions have appeared. A reprint of the original
quarto pamphlet will be found in C. K. Sharpe's edition of Law's
*Memorialls*.

following Tuesday, stayed for a considerable time, prayed twice, and saw nothing of the trouble. "Then I came out with a resolution to leave the house, and as I was standing speaking to some men at the barn end, I saw two little stones drop down on the croft at a little distance from me, and then immediately some came crying out of the house that it was become as ill as ever within; whereupon I went into the house again, and as I was at prayer, it threw several stones at me, but they did no hurt, being very small; and after there was no more trouble till the eighteenth day of March, and then it began as before and threw more frequently greater stones, whose strokes were sorer where they hit, and thus it continued to the 21st." Besides the throwing of stones there was beating with staves, gripping of people by the hair, dragging of them up and down the house by their clothes. The bar of the door and other objects would move through the house as if someone were carrying them while it was plain that no one was doing so. One night "it lifted the cloaths off the children as they were sleeping in bed and beat them on the hipps as if it had been with one's hand, so that all that were in the house heard it." While prayers were being offered, it whistled, groaned, and cried "Bo, bo" and "Kick, cuck." On the 20th of April "it continued throwing stones, whisling and whisting, with all its former words. When it hit any person and said, 'Take you that till you get more,' that person was sure immediately of an other; but when it said, 'Take you that,' the person got no more for a while."

On the evening of the 26th it was in a communicative mood, and Andrew Mackie, who was sleeping, was awakened by the other people in the house. He heard it say, "Thou shalt be troubled till Tuesday". He asked, "Who gave thee a commission?" It answered, "God gave me a commission, and I am sent to warn the land to repent, for a judgement is to come if the land do not quickly repent." It commanded him to reveal this upon his peril, and added that if the land did not repent, it would go to its father and get a commission to return with a hundred worse than itself and would trouble every family in the land. On the night of Wednesday, the 1st of May, "it fired a little sheep-house; the sheep were got out safe, but the sheep-house was wholly burnt. Since there hath not been any trouble about the house by night nor by day."

The minister relates that one night " as I was once at prayer, leaning on a bedside, I felt something pressing up my arme ; I casting my eyes thither, perceived a little white hand and arm, from the elbow down, but presently it evanished.  It is to be observed that, notwithstanding of all that was felt and heard, from the first to the last of this matter, there was never any thing seen, except that hand I saw ; and a friend of the said Andrew Mackie's said, he saw as it were a young man, red faced, with yellow hair, looking in at the window ; and other two or three persons, with the said Andrew his children, saw, at several times, as it were a young boy about the age of fourteen years, with gray cloths, and a bonnet on his head, but presently disappeared ; as also what the three children saw sitting at the fire-side."   What the children saw at the fireside throws no light on the matter, as it proved to be a four-footed stool set on end with a blanket cast over it.

Telfair's relation is attested " as to what they particularly saw, heard, and felt " by the ministers of Kells, Borgue, Cross-michael, Parton, and Kelton, and others whose testimony would be expected to carry conviction.

Rerwick was the subject of a communication to the Dumfries and Galloway Natural History and Antiquarian Society in the session of 1896-7, when it was stated that " within living memory " " a stone fire " had been laid in a farm-house by a tenant who was leaving.  " It was at one time a common custom for a farmer who was evicted, or who was leaving his farm under a sense of grievance, to fill up the fireplace in every room with broken bottles and small stones and to lay on his successor a curse which should never be lifted until these fires burned. When the stone fire had been laid and the curse said, the doors were locked and the tenant made his way out by the window, the curse alighting on the first person who entered thereafter. It was a custom also in such cases to sow a part of the farm with sand and to curse the succeeding tenant until the sand should grow.  This form of cursing was carried out in the parish perhaps seventy years ago, and tradition said that the incoming tenant did not thrive ; but this was probably due more to the ill-will of his neighbours than to the curse of his predecessor."

Such practices seem incongruous in the neighbourhood of the beautiful Abbey of Dundrennan.  It lies in a deep glen, and, whatever its spiritual influence may have done or failed to do, its buildings do not dominate the countryside. The process of dilapidation had gone far before landlords were aroused from their apathy and the remains placed in the care of the Commissioners of Woods and Forests. The nave has disappeared; but large parts of the walls of the transepts and choir still stand, also the *façade* of the chapter-house and some vaults.

*The North Transept, Dundrennan Abbey.*

Old trees tower up even higher than the walls with an air of guardianship.

Lord Cockburn found the abbey in a pitiable condition in 1839. " Though greatly abridged," he wrote, " it is still a beautiful and interesting mass. But every other feeling is superseded by one's horror and indignation at the state in which it is kept. . . . Not a trace of it will be discoverable in fifty years." An improvement had been effected by 1844, and he wrote, " I have revisited Dundrennan Abbey and claim the principal merit of its being in the state it now is. The objurgation which I have recorded in 1839 was freely administered verbally. This roused Thomas Maitland, now of Dundrennan, and he roused Lord Selkirk and others; and the result is that the Commissioners of Woods and Forests have cleaned out the rubbish and drained the ground and made some judicious repairs and cleared away the abominable offices of the manse and enclosed the whole." Such is the care now bestowed upon the ruin that you may not use a stand camera within the precinct without permission from His Majesty's Office of Works in Edinburgh.

There are many ancient carved stones[1] here, of which the most important and interesting are known as the Abbot's Monument, the Cellarer's Monument, and the Nun's Monument. Of the last, the *Inventory* points out that the effigy is more probably that of " a widow under vows. The inscription seems to show that she was lady of Orchardton . . . this would account for her burial in the abbey church, a circumstance that would be difficult to explain in the case of a nun." Several gravestones of abbots were exposed recently in the floor of the chapter-house, and within a semi-circular arched recess in the north wall of the aisle of the north transept are the remains of what is said to be the effigy of Alan, the last of the Pictish Lords of Galloway.

Little is known of the history of the abbey between its beginning in or about the year 1140 and the visit of Queen Mary in 1568. The foundation is attributed to Fergus, Lord of Galloway. Fordun claims it for David the First. There is a theory that it was founded by both conjointly; but this is merely an attempt to reconcile conflicting statements.

Abbeys were falling on evil days when Queen Mary came this way on her flight to England after the Battle of Langside. The old Galloway tradition is that she rode south through The Glenkens to a place called Queenshill, which was believed to have received its name from her having rested there, and that she then went on in the direction of Tongland and crossed the Dee by an ancient wooden bridge about a mile above that place. Mr. Hume Brown's statement that " she fled south by way of Dumfries to Dundrennan " serves as a summary of the account given in the *Memoirs* of Lord Herries, who says : " So soone

---

[1] A full description is given in the *Inventory*.

as the Queen saw the day lost, she was carried from the field by the Lords Herreis,[1] Fleming, and Livistoune. Prettie George Dowglas and William the Fundlin escapt also with the Queen. She rode all night, and did not halt untill she came to the

*The Chapter-House, Dundrennan Abbey.*

Sanquhir. From thence she went to Terregles, the Lord Herreis hous, where she rested some few dayes, and then, against her friends advyce, she resolved to goe to England, and commit

[1] Not the writer of the account.

herselfe to the protection of Queen Elisabeth ; in hopes, by her assistance, to be repossessed in her kingdome. So she imbarked at a creek neer Dundrennen, in Galloway, and carried the Lord Herreis to attend her with his counsel ; and landed at Cockermouth, in Cumberland. Heer she stayed, and sent the Lord Herreis to Londone in hopes to be receaved with honor."

It is usually stated that the Queen spent her last night on Scottish soil under the shelter of Dundrennan Abbey. If this were so, the " some few dayes " of Herries's account must be an exaggeration. The battle was fought on the 13th of May, and if the Queen rode that night to Sanquhar and halted there, she could not reach Terregles until the 14th. It was on the 16th that she crossed the Solway, and if she passed the previous night at Dundrennan, she cannot have remained for two whole days at Terregles.

If she was at Dundrennan on the night of the 15th, the question arises, Did she spend it in the abbey or in some other house ? Mackenzie quotes from Hutton's *History of Dundrennan* a tradition with which he says that he agrees. Hutton's statement is as follows : " An impression has long been erroneously cherished that her last sad sojourn on the shores of a country which she never revisited except in dreams . . . . was passed under the roof of the Abbey. The monks, no doubt, bore her true fealty, but they perhaps dreaded the vengeance of her pursuers in the shape of fine or confiscation ; and, from whatever motive, a lodging was provided in a private house, which at the period alluded to was occupied by the ancestor of the late Mrs. Anderson of Stroquhan. In the family the Queen observed a fine little boy who attracted her attention to such a degree that she requested he might be allowed to sleep with her during that night ; and it was his lot to share the caresses of Majesty and beauty united, unconscious as he might be of the honour thus acquired. After great personal fatigue and distress of mind, the unfortunate Mary passed a comfortable night, as was observed from her looks when the monks waited upon her in the morning ; but before departing for the creek from which she embarked she acknowledged her sense of the kindness received by leaving behind a valuable ring and rich damask tablecloth, which formed part of her slender luggage, both of which bore the royal arms. These relics, after remaining for years in the family, were gifted by the grandmother of the lady whose name we have mentioned to a house of considerable distinction in this county, where in all probability they still remain.   The above anecdote, so far as we know, never appeared in print before, and the reader may rest assured that it is not hazarded on slight authority."

Is this pure fiction, or has it some basis of fact ?   A fugitive queen may very well carry valuable rings with her ; but it is scarcely likely that Mary thought about tablecloths before beginning her flight from the battle-field of Langside.   There is also an annoying vagueness about the history of the relics.

On the 16th the Queen, accompanied by Lord Herries and some other persons, went down the glen to what has since been called Port Mary, embarked on an open fishing-boat, and sailed across to Workington, where she landed the same day ; and no doubt the sentimental traveller, before continuing his journey to Kirkcudbright, will follow her route to the margin of the sea and look upon the place where the unhappy queen said farewell to Scotland—a longer farewell than she dreamed.

*Port Mary.*

*Kirkcudbright.*

# CHAPTER VII

### KIRKCUDBRIGHT

Lord Cockburn's description—Houses in High Street—The Tolbooth —Loch Fergus Castle—Outline history of the Pictish Lords of Galloway—Castledykes—Kirkcudbright Castle—The Lords Kirkcudbright—Tombstones in S. Cuthbert's Churchyard—The Caird of Barullion—Black Morrow—The port of Kirkcudbright —Invasions and rumours of invasion—Royal visitors—Travellers' descriptions—Glimpses of old-world Kirkcudbright from the burgh records—Tongland—The old fort near Torrs Point.

SEA and land breezes blow by turns through the quiet old streets of Kirkcudbright,[1] and ancient trees embower the town. Woods, indeed, fill the whole valley, softening the outlines of shore and sky. In the midst is the estuary of the Dee, an expanse of shining water when the tide is in, an expanse of shining mud when it has receded; so that one may say that there are two Kirkcudbrights: the Kirkcudbright of the flood, when the brimming waters besiege it on two sides, giving it a claim to Lord Cockburn's description, "The Venice of Scotland"—at

[1] Church of S. Cudberct, *i.e.*, S. Cuthbert: pronounced "Kirkóobry".

a high spring-tide, reinforced by a southerly wind, the waters will overflow the river-front and threaten the houses and shops in S. Cuthbert Street—and the Kirkcudbright of the ebb, when, to quote Lord Cockburn again, it looks like " a town surrounded by a lake of bird-lime ".

Lord Cockburn's description is so good so far as it goes that I must set it down here, for *Circuit Journeys* is not in every private library : " To-day I went to Tongueland Hill to have

*S. Mary Street, Kirkcudbright.*

another view of Kirkcudbright. I doubt if there be a more picturesque country town in Scotland. Small, clean, silent, and respectable, it seems (subject, however, to one enormous deduction) the type of a place to which decent characters and moderate purses would retire for quiet comfort. The deduction arises from the dismal swamps of deep, sleechy mud, by which it is nearly surrounded at low tide. It is a dreadful composition. And what fields, and streaks, and gullies of it ! The tide rises at an average about twenty or twenty-five feet, and often a great deal more—sometimes thirty-five. This great flow fills up all the bays, making a brim-full sea for three miles above the town, and for six or eight below it. It is then a world of waters. But when the sea, ashamed of its advancement, shrinks back, what a change ! It becomes a world of sleech. It is worse than even at Chepstow, where the abomination, though deeper, does not cover so extensive a surface. I believe that painters don't dislike this substance, which they don't require to touch. It is not unpicturesque, of a leaden grey colour, very shiny, in the sun even silvery in appearance ; utterly solitary, except to flocks of long-billed and long red-legged sea birds, and to occasionally a heavy fisherman working at a stranded boat in huge boots ; with its dull plains interspersed with odd streaks and pools of shallow water, it has hues and objects enough to afford subjects for many pictures. But, Lord, how horrible it is in real life ! Think of being surrounded by a dirty substance, impossible to be touched, and most dangerous to be gone upon. A town surrounded by a lake of bird-lime ! " I believe that the insistent antipathy of these remarks on the " sleech " is to be explained in part by a personal experience of it. A lifelong inhabitant of the burgh told me that Lord Cockburn had once been stranded on a mud-bank. Since it was " most dangerous to be gone upon ", he had found it " horrible in real life " until the rising tide floated him off.

The older streets of the town are full of houses standing end to end with closes here and there that give glimpses of the gardens behind. They are plainly fashioned dwellings, but some have ornamental doorways, and most of them a little fanlight above the entrance. *The Selkirk Arms*, an old hotel of a character happily not rare in Galloway, has its front in High Street at the south-east end and is, therefore, close to the line of the vanished wall of the town. Behind the houses here are large gardens held formerly under a " watch and ward " superiority duty ; that is, the due exacted from the tenants was that they should watch and defend the wall in time of alarms and danger. The due is represented now by small money payments, in one case by sixpence, the grand total of seven-and-six being collected every fifteen years. Beside *The Selkirk Arms* is the Old Bank House occupied in former days by the agent of the Bank of Scotland and now the residence of the sheriff. It gets an odd look from the slightly convex curves occurring on the front, where the principal windows are, as if these had hoped to be bow

windows and had received an untimely check in this aspiration.
Paul Jones, who included that of a Freemason among his *rôles*,
was present at the laying of the foundation of this house ; and
at the other end of this part of High Street—the street has two
parts at right angles to each other—is the old Tolbooth where
he was once a prisoner. He had been arrested at the instance
of the friends of a sailor whose death he was said to have caused
in the West Indies. He was liberated on bail, and there is no
record of further proceedings against him. His innocence
was attested in an affidavit sworn at the Mansion House, London,
on the 30th of January, 1773, by James Eastment, who stated
that " Mungo Maxwell, in good health, came on board his vessel,
the Barcelona packet, then lying in Great Rockley Bay, in the
island of Tobago, about the middle of June, 1770, and in his
capacity of carpenter. He was in perfect health for some days
after he came on board, after which he was afflicted with fever
and lowness of spirits. This continued for four or five days,
when he died on the passage from Tobago to Antigua. He never
heard Maxwell complain of having received any ill-usage from
John Paul, and he believed that his death was occasioned by
fever and lowness of spirits."

The beginning of the building of the Tolbooth is attributed
to the end of the sixteenth century, and its completion to the
middle of the seventeenth. The tower owes its pleasing effect
largely to the projecting parapet. This is supported by small
corbels connected by miniature arches. At each of the angles
there is a pyramidal pinnacle. The little spire is said to have
been built of stones brought from Dundrennan Abbey. The
market cross of the burgh used to stand in High Street, but
was removed in the last century to the platform at the head
of the outside stair of the Tolbooth. It bears the date 1610.
The old iron " jougs " that closed on the neck of the culprit
who was condemned to be exhibited at the cross are now fixed
to the north-west angle of the building. Of the two bells in
the tower, the larger bears the legend—SOLI DEO GLORIA
MICHAEL BVRGERHVYS ME FECIT ANNO 1646, and the smaller,
—QUIRIN DE VISSER ME FECIT 1724 KIRKUDBRIGHT.[1] The

---

[1] The Museum in S. Mary Street includes what is known as
S. Ninian's Bell. Symson says in 1684, " There is at present a
Bell at the Church of Penigham with this Inscription in Saxon
letters *Campana Sancti Niniani de Penygham M.* dedicat as it

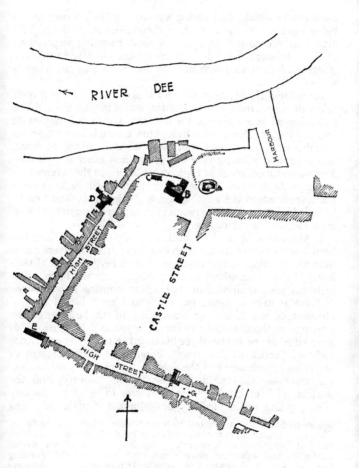

*Plan of old Kirkcudbright.*

A, Greyfriars Church; B, Kirkcudbright Castle; C, Auchengool House; D, Broughton House; E, The Tolbooth; F, Claverhouse's Lodging; G, Socket-stones of the "Muckle Yett."

(Reproduced from the *Inventory* with the permission of the Controller of His Majesty's Stationery Office.)

clock has two dials, each facing a section of High Street, and is lighted every evening at dusk, a cheerful detail in the nightly aspect of the town. One of the most haunting impressions of Kirkcudbright, indeed, is given by the old street with the illuminated clock-face overhung by the moon and the evening star.

Broughton House, near the north-east end of High Street, takes its name from the Broughton estate in The Shire. The site belonged at one time to the Murrays, who owned that estate and Cally near Gatehouse. Broughton House is larger than its neighbours, has a paved court and an iron railing in front, and is painted white, giving a very brilliant effect in sunshine. Two domestic buildings in High Street belong to the seventeenth century—Auchengool House, which is believed to have been the town house of the MacCullochs of Auchengool ; and Claverhouse's Lodging, where the rooms in the upper storey are panelled from the floor to the ceiling.

In the course of the long history of Kirkcudbright there has been a succession of three castles that have arisen to overshadow humbler dwellings. The first was that of Fergus, Lord of Galloway, built on an island in Loch Fergus near the town. The loch has been drained, but the island remains as a mound. Nothing is known of the parentage and early life of Fergus. He emerges into history on succeeding to the lordship of the province on the death of two chiefs, Ulgric and Dovenald, who were killed at the Battle of the Standard in 1138. The province included Carrick at that time. Fergus was strong enough to assert his independence of the Scottish Crown. The mountains, the morasses, the trackless forests of his country, and the warlike spirit of his people enabled him to resist successfully two invading armies led by Malcolm the Fourth. A third

seems to Saint Ninian in the thousand year after the birth of Christ." According to the account given by the Museum authorities, the bell hung in the old church of Penninghame Parish for several centuries, and when the church was transferred to the growing town of Newton Stewart, was recast. It now bears the following words in large raised letters : " Kirk Bell of Penningham 1750 " and the motto, " Awake thou that Sleepest and Christ Shall give thee Life ". When the present church was built about 1838, it was provided with a new bell, and the old one was hung in the church which was erected at that time at Bargrennan. It was in use there for sixty years. It became cracked and was then placed in the Museum.

invasion on a more formidable scale, however, broke down his opposition. Forts were erected in Galloway—" most probably ", says Dr. Neilson, " those Motes which are so curiously

*The Tolbooth and High Street, Kirkcudbright.*

important in the archæological remains of the south-west ", and " the plantation of these forts was accompanied by the settlement of Anglo-Norman families, at once garrisons and colonists." Fergus resigned the lordship in 1160, retired to Holyrood Abbey, and died in the following year. He married an illegitimate daughter of Henry of England, and is an ancestor of the British royal family. His liberality as a founder of churches and monasteries is comparable to that of David the First.

His daughter, Affrica, was married to Olaf, King of Man. His sons, Uchtred and Gilbert, divided his dominion between them in accordance with Celtic law. When William the Lion became a prisoner in England, they threw off their allegiance, made war on the Anglo-Norman garrisons in their midst and wrecked the forts, and the Gallovidians shewed their racial hatred by slaughtering " all the Englishmen and French " who fell into their hands.

A quarrel arose between the two lords in the same year. Uchtred was captured by his brother and died in consequence of monstrous mutilations inflicted upon him by Gilbert's orders. While the Scottish King was still a prisoner at Falaise, Gilbert sought to strengthen himself by becoming a vassal of Henry the Second, offering him an annual tribute, with a view to the ultimate assertion of absolute independence. His proposals were declined; and when William recovered his liberty, he invaded Galloway and punished Gilbert by exacting a fine. One of the articles of the Treaty of Falaise was that William and his nobles should do homage to the English King for the realm of Scotland, and accordingly Gilbert accompanied William to the English court in 1176, did homage to Henry without any reservation in favour of the King of Scotland, promised Henry the payment of a thousand pounds, and gave his son, Duncan, into his hands as a pledge for his good behaviour. Gilbert was now less dependent on the Scottish Crown than ever; his wild Celts made frequent raids into the more civilized country on the east of the Nith[1]; and for the rest of the period of his

---

[1] About 1259 " Galuvet ", that is, "Gallovidian ", was synonymous with " thief " in the usage of the people of Dumfries. An instance occurs in connexion with the inquest on the body of Adam, the miller. " They say that the above-named Richard and Adam *molendinarius* (the miller) met on Sunday next after the feast of S. Michael at the church of the said saint, and Adam in the cemetery there defamed Richard, calling him a thief, viz., ' Galuvet ', and said that he would make Richard clear out of the town. It chanced on the following Thursday that Richard walked in the street, while

rule Galloway was a source of serious disturbance to the central government. Meanwhile, William was in the humiliating position of requiring to ask permission from a superior before taking punitive measures against the Lord of Galloway, and it suited Henry's policy that William's sway over some of his subjects should be of a nominal kind. The royal castles and burghs of Ayr, Lanark, and Dumfries were all founded in William's reign. The leading motive appears to have been that their sites were on or near the Celtic fringe.[1]

Gilbert died in 1185, and the lordship was claimed by Roland, Uchtred's son, who had spent the previous ten years at the Scottish court, had married the daughter of Richard de Moreville, the Hereditary Constable, and become " a Scoto-Norman more than a Galwegian ". His title was upheld by the King; but Gilbert's son, Duncan, had a strong party in his favour, and the consequence was that Galloway was convulsed by a fierce war, in which Roland was victorious. Henry called him to order for his forcible seizure of the lordship and marched at the head of an army towards Galloway in support of Duncan.

When he had reached Carlisle, the King of Scotland intervened, and an arrangement was made at that city whereby Roland became Lord of Galloway, that is, of the area represented by The Stewartry of Kirkcudbright and Wigtonshire, while Carrick was handed over to Duncan as an earldom. A condition of this agreement was that Roland should swear fealty to the King of England. Roland became Constable of Scotland in right of his wife, the daughter of Richard Moreville. He is remembered as the founder of Glenluce Abbey. His death occurred in 1200.

Adam stood in the door of a house. A woman said to him ' Withdraw yourself; here is Richard '. Adam said, ' I will not; I have as sharp a knife as he ', and then entered the house and drew a knife to disembowel Richard, who in defending himself drew a sword and struck Adam with the flat. Then Adam twisted (*circuivit*) his arm round the sword, and Richard snatching it away, wounded him mortally. Then Richard said, ' I have not killed thee; thou thyself didst it '. The barons jurors concur *in omnibus* with the burgesses jurors. They all say that Richard is faithful, but Adam was a thief and defamer."—Bain's *Calendar of Documents Relating to Scotland.*

[1] " Dumfries : Its Burghal Origin " by George Neilson, LL.D., in *The Transactions of the Dumfriesshire and Galloway Natural History and Antiquarian Society* (1913–14).

His eldest son, Alan, long known as Alan the Great, succeeded him as Lord of Galloway and Constable of Scotland. He assisted King John in his invasion of Ireland in 1211 and was rewarded with a valuable grant of lands in Antrim and elsewhere. He owned large estates in the counties of Northampton and Leicester, and was one of the great barons who extorted the *Magna Carta* from the sovereign. Later, he became Chancellor of the Kingdom of Scotland. He possessed a fleet and made several descents on the coasts of Ireland, The Isle of Man, and the Western Isles, enriching himself with plunder ; and Olaf, King of Man, found it necessary to appeal to Haco, King of Norway, for protection. It is said that when Alan received news of this request, he pointed out that the sea was as navigable between Scotland and Norway as between Norway and Scotland and expressed the hope that he might prove that Norwegian harbours were as accessible as those of Galloway ; but he did not live to carry out his threat. He died in 1234, the last in the male line of the Pictish Lords of Galloway, and was buried in Dundrennan Abbey. He left three daughters, who were all married to Anglo-Norman lords—Helena to Roger de Quenci, Earl of Winchester ; Dervorgilla to John Baliol of Barnard Castle ; and Christian to William de Fortibus, Earl of Albemarle. The Gallovidians resented the introduction of these alien lords, among whom Alan's territory thus fell to be divided, and requested that the lordship should be assumed by the Crown. When this was refused, they rebelled in support of Alan's illegitimate son, Thomas, and in vindication of the ancient Brehon law that no female could inherit land or exercise government. The rebellion was suppressed, and feudal institutions were introduced. In later centuries another line of Lords of Galloway were to prove a source of serious trouble to the Scottish Monarchy.

It is not known when the castle in Loch Fergus was superseded by the building that stood on the left bank of the Dee a little below the town. The site is called Castledykes. The fosse can still be seen ; and the foundations of two circular towers with traces of a portcullis gateway between them were discovered in 1912, and also a fragment of circular walling on the west. According to the *Inventory*, the towers " have been of exceptional size, each measuring about thirty-five feet in diameter over walls of undetermined thickness." The castle came into the hands of Dervorgilla's son, John Baliol, the successor of the Lords of Galloway, and was the residence of Edward the First during his stay in Kirkcudbright in the year 1300. It was a stronghold of the Douglases while they held the lordship, and had a visit from King James the Second when he broke their power in 1455. It was in this year that the town was made a royal burgh. The castle became Crown property and was a temporary residence of James the Fourth in 1508. In the following year that sovereign presented it along with some lands to the magistrates of the burgh for the common good of the inhabitants.

The third castle, that of the Maclellans or Lords Kirkcudbright, is within the town, and its walls remain almost intact. It was built by Sir Thomas Maclellan of Bombie, an estate lying on the east of the burgh. The escutcheon above the main door bears the date 1582. Sir Thomas died in 1597, and was buried in an aisle of the old parish church of Greyfriars. The monument above the vault is " an interesting example of the admixture of late Gothic work with the classical forms of the early Renaissance " and bears the following legend:

> H DOMINUS SITUS EST T MCLELLANVS ET VXOR
> D GRISSELL MAXWEL MARMOR VTRVMQVE TEGIT
> HIS GENITVS R D KIRKCVDBRIVS ECCE SEPVLCHRVM
> POSVIT HOC CHARI PATRIS HONORE SVI
> ILLE OBIIT ANN DOM                          1597[1]

His eldest son, Robert, was knighted by James the Sixth and made a baronet by Charles the First in 1629 and a peer in 1633 with the title of Lord Kirkcudbright. His nephew, Thomas, the second Lord Kirkcudbright, was prominently concerned in public affairs, supporting Presbyterianism against Episcopacy and the Monarchy against the Commonwealth. In 1640 he became colonel of the South Regiment, a cavalry force raised chiefly in Galloway and forming part of the army which the Earl of Leven led to victory over the English at Newburn. In 1644 he attended Parliament and succeeded the Earl of Nithsdale as Steward of Kirkcudbright. In the following year he distinguished himself at the Battle of Philiphaugh, where he commanded a regiment recruited in Galloway at his own

---

[1] " Here is laid Sir T. Maclellan and his wife Lady Grissel Maxwell. The marble covers them both. Their son Robert, Lord Kirkcudbright, behold, placed this tomb in honour of his beloved father. He died A.D. 1597."

expense. Parliament voted a sum of fifteen thousand merks—which was never paid—for distribution among his men in recognition of their conspicuous gallantry.

When he died in 1647, the succession passed to his cousin, John Maclellan of Borgue, who had similar political and ecclesiastical sympathies and ruined the family fortunes thereby.

*The Maclellan Monument, Greyfriars Church.*

He raised a regiment in Galloway and maintained it during the Civil War. He was one of the deputies sent from the Convention of Estates to negotiate with Oliver Cromwell at Berwick in 1648. After the execution of Charles the First and the proclamation of Charles the Second, his regiment, which had been sent to oppose the troops of the English Parliament in Ireland, was nearly cut to pieces in an engagement in Ulster. His estates were unable to support the heavy burdens incurred, and the remnants of his fortune were dissipated through his opposition to the appointment of an Episcopal minister to the parish of Kirkcudbright in 1663. The only recognition of his services to the Royalist cause was a place in the retinue of Charles at the Restoration. He died in 1665. His successors did not restore the fortunes of the family. Its representative at the beginning of the eighteenth century kept an ale-house in Kirkcudbright, and a later head of the house sold gloves in Edinburgh, and when the Scottish Peers met to elect their representatives in the House of Lords, used to supply them with those articles. The title is now dormant.

Besides old castles, houses, and municipal buildings, there is another class of memorials of the past in which Kirkcudbright is rich. Some of the martyrs' graves referred to in this book lie far from beaten tracks ; but in S. Cuthbert's Churchyard there are two within a few hundred yards of a railway station. The story of the Covenanters who were surprised by Claverhouse and his dragoons on Auchencloy Hill is given in connexion with Carsphairn. The two men who were made prisoners in that affair were brought to Kirkcudbright, where after undergoing a trial they were hanged and beheaded. Their grave is at the east side of the churchyard, and the stone bears this epitaph :

HOUNTURE 1684   WILLIAM ROBERT SMITH

THIS MONUMENT SHALL SHEW POSTERITY
TWO HEADLES MARTYRES UNDER IT DOTH LY
BY BLOODY GRHAME WERE TAKEN AND SURPRISED
BROUGHT TO THIS TOUNE AND AFTERWARD WERE SAIZ'D
BY UNJUST LAW WERE SENTENCED TO DIE
THEM FIRST THEY HANG'D THEN HEADED CRUELY
CAPTANS DOUGLAS BRUCE GRHAME OF CLEVERHOUS
WERE THESE THAT CAUSED THEM BE HANDLED THUS
AND WHEN THEY WERE UNTO THE GIBBET COME
TO STOPE THEIR SPEECH THEY DID BEAT UP THE DRUM
AND ALL BECAUS THAT THEY WOULD NOT COMPLY
WITH INDULGENCE AND BLOODY PRELACIE
IN FACE OF CRUEL BRUCE DOUGLAS AND GRHAME
THEY DID MANTAINE THAT CHRIST WAS LORD SUPREAM
AND BOLDLY OUNED BOTH THE COVENANTS
AT KIRKCUDBRIGHT THUS ENDED THESE TWO SANTS

On the west side of the churchyard there is another martyr's grave, that of John Hallume, a youth of eighteen years. He was walking along a road in the next parish of Tongland when he saw a party of dragoons at a little distance. Anxious to

*The Castle, Kirkcudbright.*

avoid them, he stepped aside from the road, but had been observed, was pursued and wounded, first with shot and then

with a sword-cut on the head, while as yet no question had
been asked of him. He was taken to Kirkcudbright, where
the Abjuration Oath was put. On his refusing to take it,
an assize consisting of the soldiers was called, and he was condemned and executed. The epitaph covers the two sides of the
stone:

HERE LYES IOHN
HALLUME    WHO
WAS     WOUNDED
IN  HIS  TAKEING
AND  BY  UNJUST
LAW  SENTENCED
TO   BE  HANGED
ALL  THIS  DONE
BY        CAPTANE

MEMENTO MORI
(Skull and
cross-bones)

DOUGLAS         FOR
HIS     ADHERENCE
TO      SCOTLANDS
REFORMATION
COVENANTS NATION
ALL  AND  SOLEMN
LEAGUE     1685

Other monuments belonging to the seventeenth century are
described fully in the *Inventory*. I shall merely give some of the
inscriptions. A table stone not far from the south side of the
churchyard bears the date, 1626, the carelessly-spelt words,
HIC IACET ANDRES CARSANE MARCATOR VIVENS MORINS ET
SESVRGENS IN CHIRTO, and the verses:

IN FAITH IN CHRIST I LIVED AND DIED
IN HOPE HAVE LAID MY BODE DOVN
MY SAVL IS ASCENDIT TO ADORE
HIR SAVIOVR IN CELESTIAL GLORE
WITH QVHOM SHE SAL CVM AND RECAL
THESE CORPS AGANE OVT OF THIR GRAVE
AND THEN INIOY TRIVMPHANTLIE
DEVINE DELIGHT PERPETVALI.

The elaborate Ewart monument near the entrance has the
following legends:

WELCOM SOFT BED MY SWEIT REPOSE
AND  SO  FOR  CHRIST  FROM  HENCE  AROSE
WELCOM   SWEIT   SLEIP  FROM   THE   I  WAKE
OF    ENDLES    JOYES    FOR    TO   PARTAKE
WELCOM    FAIR    NIGHT    THY    FAIREST    MORRO
DRIVES    FROM    MINE    EYES    ETERNAL    SORRO
WELCOM  SOFT  BED  SWEIT  SLEIP  FAIR  NIGHT  TO  ME
THRISE  WELCOM  CHRIST  WHO  HES  SANCTIFIED  YOW  THR[1]

---

[1] These lines are attributed to Samuel Rutherford, minister of
Anwoth.

I : E : OBIIT · 15 · KAL · FEB · AN · DOM · 1642 · ÆTAT · 24

IOAN HEWART KIRKCVB CONSVL
HOC STRVXIT MONVMENTVM[1]

1644    REPENT IN TYM YOVRE LIVES AMEND    I E   H E
         THAT IN CHRIST IESVS YEA MAY END

MORS SVA SCEPTRA TENET TOTI COMMVNIA MVNDO
PROPERAT CVRSV VITA CITA TE.   VIVE MEMOR LETHI.[2]

INCLVSVS LAPIDE HOC QVIESCIT EHEV
EHEV FLOS IVVENVM ANDREAS HAVARTUS
NVPER KIRKCVBRIÆ IVBAR CORVSCVM
NVNC NOVAE SOLYMAE IVBAR CORVSCANS
QVOD MORTALE FVIT PATER SEPVLCHRO
HVIC DEDIT LACHRYMIS TERENS SENECTAM HIS
MOLE SVB HAC LAPIDVM IVVENEM TE MAESTVS HVMAVI
QVI ME DEBVERAS CONTVMVLASSE SENEM[3]

I GOE TO GRAVE AS TO MY BED TO SLEEP AND RYSE AGAIN
I LIVED IN CHRYST I DIED IN CHRYST I MVST NOT
    HEIR REMANE

       OVR TYME RVNNES FAST AS WE MAY SIE
       WHICH BEING SPENT THEN MVST WE DIE

No professions or ascriptions of religious piety have been carved on the tombstone of William Marshall, the famous Galloway gypsy. It stands near the grave of John Hallume and has this unadorned announcement :

The Remains of
WILLIAM MARSHALL
*Tinker,* who died
28th Novr 1792
*at the advanced age of*
120 Years

Two ram's horns and two tablespoons crossed are carved on the other side.

[1] " John Hewart, Magistrate of Kirkcudbright, erected this monument."
[2] " Death holds his sceptre over the whole world alike. Life speeds thee swiftly on its course. Live mindful of death."
[3] " Shut in by this stone rests, alas ! alas ! the flower of the youths, Andrew Hewart, lately a bright star of Kirkcudbright, now a shining star of the New Jerusalem. What was mortal his father consigned to this tomb, wearing out his old age with these tears. Under this pile of stones I have buried in sorrow thee, a youth, who ought rather to have buried me, an old man."

"The Caird of Barullion" was the high-sounding *sobriquet* of this notorious—one might almost say, distinguished—member of his class. *Caird* means "gypsy", and "Barhullion"[1] is the name of a hill in a wild moorland country much haunted by the gang whom he led. "King of the Gypsies of the Western Lowlands" was the title he claimed, and "Billy Marshall" the more familiar nomenclature. "He was born in the parish of Kirkmichael about the year 1671;" says Sir Walter Scott in a note to *Guy Mannering*, "and as he died at Kirkcudbright, 23rd November, 1792, he must then have been in the one hundred and twentieth year of his age. It cannot be said that this unusually long lease of existence was noted by any peculiar excellence of conduct or habits of life. Willie had been pressed or enlisted in the army seven times; and had deserted as often; besides three times running away from the naval service. He had been seventeen times lawfully married; and besides such a reasonably large share of matrimonial comforts, was, after his hundredth year, the avowed father of four children by less legitimate affections." There was published in *Blackwood's Magazine* for August, 1817, a letter by Mr. James Murray MacCulloch of Ardwall, who wrote as "one of an old family in the Stewartry of Galloway with whom Billy was intimate for nearly a whole century". He states that "he visited regularly twice a year my great-grandfather, grandfather, and father, and partook, I daresay, of their hospitality, but he made a grateful and ample return; for during all the days of Billy's natural life . . . the *washings* could have been safely left out all night without anything from a sheet or a tablecloth down to a dishclout being in any danger". He adds that "for a great part of his long life he reigned with sovereign sway over a numerous and powerful gang of gypsey tinkers who took their range over Carrick in Ayrshire, the Carrick mountains, and over the stewartry and shire of Galloway; and now and then by way of improving themselves and seeing more of the world they crossed at Donaghadee and visited the counties of Down and Derry". In 1723 Billy attained a transitory prominence as a leader of the Levellers.[2]

Scott tells this story about him: "In his youth he occasionally took an evening walk on the highway with the purpose of assisting

[1] May be either *barr chuillinn*, hill of the holly, or *barr chuilleann*, hill of the whelps.—Maxwell.       [2] See page 507.

travellers by relieving them of the weight of their purses.  On
one occasion the Caird of Barullion robbed the Laird of Bargally
at a place between Carsphairn and Dalmellington.  His purpose
was not achieved without a severe struggle, in which the Gipsy
lost his bonnet, and was obliged to escape leaving it on the road.
A respectable farmer happened to be the next passenger, and
seeing the bonnet, alighted, took it up, and rather imprudently
put it on his own head.  At this instant, Bargally came up with
some assistants, and recognising the bonnet, charged the farmer
of Bantoberick with having robbed him, and took him into custody.  There being some likeness between the parties, Bargally
persisted in his charge, and though the respectability of the
farmer's character was proved or admitted, his trial before the
Circuit Court came on accordingly.  The fatal bonnet lay on the
table of the court : Bargally swore that it was the identical
article worn by the man who robbed him ; and he and others
likewise deponed that they had found the accused on the spot
where the crime was committed, with the bonnet on his head.
The case looked gloomy for the prisoner, and the opinion of the
judge seemed unfavourable.  But there was a person in court
who knew well both who did, and who did not, commit the crime.
This was the Caird of Barullion, who, thrusting himself up to the
bar, near the place where Bargally was standing, suddenly
seized on the bonnet, put it on his head, and looking the Laird
full in the face, asked him, with a voice which attracted the attention of the Court and crowded audience—' Look at me, sir,
and tell me by the oath you have sworn—Am not *I* the man who
robbed you between Carsphairn and Dalmellington ? '  Bargally
replied in great astonishment, ' By Heaven ! you are the very
man.'  ' You see what sort of memory this gentleman has,'
said the voluntary pleader ;  ' he swears to the bonnet, whatever
features are under it.  If you yourself, my Lord, will put it on
your head, he will be willing to swear that your Lordship was the
party who robbed him between Carsphairn and Dalmellington ! '
The tenant of Bantoberick was unanimously acquitted, and
thus Willie Marshal ingeniously contrived to save an innocent
man from danger, without incurring any himself, since Bargally's
evidence must have seemed to every one too fluctuating to be
relied upon."

An old Kirkcudbright tradition relates to an alien belonging
to a much earlier period, but also classed—inaccurately—as a

gypsy—a runaway from some vessel which had put in at The Manxman's Lake. He was called Blackimore, Black Morrow, or Black Murray, had his abode near the town in what is still known as the Black Morrow Wood, and used to cross the Dee in a small boat to the opposite coast of Borgue, where he committed many depredations. This obscure figure comes into connexion with the history of the Maclellan family in the way shewn as follows by Sir George Mackenzie, the seventeenth-century lawyer : A crest sometimes " represents some valiant Act done by the Bearer, thus *M'clelland* of *Bombie* did, and now the Lord *Kirkcudbright*, does bear a naked Arm, supporting on the point of a sword a *Mores* head ; because *Bombie* being forfeited, his Son kill'd a *More*, who came in with some Sarazens to infest *Galloway ;* to the Killer of whom the King had promised the Forfeiture of *Bombie ;* and thereupon was restored to his Fathers land, as his Evidents yet testifie."[1] One would like to know what terror thrust this Saracen upon his hunted life on this northern coast, what he thought of its dank woods and heathy crags, how he prayed in his loneliness, and if a vision of burning sands came to him at the end.

The number of inscriptions in the churchyard telling of men " lost at sea " or dying in Colonial or foreign ports points to the old maritime importance of Kirkcudbright. Few, if any, recent epitaphs are of this class ; but up till about 1830 Kirkcudbright was visited regularly by so many as sixty vessels, some of them bringing timber from distant ports such as those of Canada, Nova Scotia, and the Baltic Sea, and great raft-like accumulations of logs were then moored in the river. The shipping business has disappeared almost entirely since the coming of the railway and is represented now by a few steamers and schooners carrying foodstuffs from Glasgow and Liverpool. It is long also since *The Countess of Galloway* stopped her coasting voyages in these parts. The older inhabitants still speak of the long strings of carts that awaited her arrival and distributed her cargo all over The Stewartry, even to the remotest places of The Glenkens.

Not only honest shipping, but sometimes smuggling craft furrowed the water of the bay. Scott tells a story of the Dutch

---

[1] See Mr. David Macritchie's *Scottish Gypsies under the Stewarts* for an interesting discussion of the terms, *Moor, Saracen,* and *Gypsy* in connexion with this tradition.

skipper, Yawkins, the prototype of Dirk Hatteraick. " On one occasion he was landing his cargo at the Manxman's Lake near Kirkcudbright when two revenue cutters (the Pigmy and the Dwarf) hove in sight at once on different tacks, the one coming round by the Isles of Fleet, the other between the point of Raeberry and the Muckle Ross. The dauntless free-trader instantly weighed anchor and bore down right between the luggers, so close that he tossed his hat on the deck of the one and his wig on that of the other, hoisted a cask to his maintop

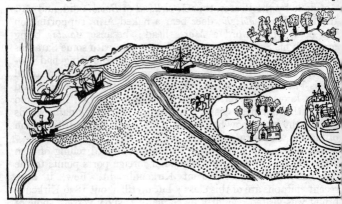

*Kirkcudbright in* 1566.

(The original drawing is in the British Museum. It illustrates a report by an English officer on the defences of the Western Marches. Block kindly lent by Mr. J. Robison.)

to show his occupation, and bore away under an extraordinary pressure of canvass without receiving injury."

Many more famous people than Captain Yawkins have sailed into or out of the bay. If Blind Harry is to be believed for once, it was at Kirkcudbright that Sir William Wallace embarked for France after the battle of Falkirk in 1298. Two years later an English fleet of thirty ships arrived here in support of Edward the First's invasion of Galloway, and the port was used for bringing in horses from Ireland and sending wheat to be ground at Dublin, Whitehaven, and Workington. In 1507 a Manx fleet under Thomas, Earl of Derby, raided the Galloway coast and nearly destroyed Kirkcudbright, whereupon Cutlar MacCulloch retaliated by raising a Galloway fleet and terrifying the inhabitants of The Isle of Man by repeated descents. This was the port at which the Duke of Albany arrived from Brest in 1523 with " a fleet of eighty-seven small vessels and a force of four thousand foot, to which were added five hundred men at arms, a thousand hagbutteers, six hundred horse, of which one hundred were barbed, and a fine camp of artillery ". Kirkcudbright might have been the scene in 1588 of a still more formidable landing. Lord Maxwell, the principal supporter of the Roman Catholic party in the south of Scotland, was in Spain when the Armada was being prepared, and advised Philip that the Galloway ports should be used. He arrived at Kirkcudbright in April, 1588, mustered his kinsmen and tenants, and fortified the royal castles of Lochmaben, Dumfries, Thrieve, and Langholm and his own stronghold of Caerlaverock, intending to co-operate with the Spanish forces ; but his rising was suppressed long before the Armada was seen off the Lizard. In 1690 King William's fleet lay wind-bound here for many days. Kirkcudbright was considered seriously in connexion with at least one of the projected Jacobite invasions. In 1778, during the war with America, Captain Paul Jones, commanding *The Ranger* frigate, sailed into the bay with the intention of kidnapping the Earl of Selkirk, whose house stood on the peninsula called S. Mary's Isle near the town. The Earl was away from home ; but the seamen declined to depart without some plunder. With Jones's authority, but much against his inclination, the silver plate was demanded from the Countess, who surrendered it at once. Jones bought it at a high valuation with a view to returning it to its owners ; but it was not until 1784 that it actually reached their hands. The burgh records of Kirkcudbright contain little that bears on the general history of the country ; but on working through them I found that in 1797, when the air was full of rumours of Napoleon's designs against Britain, a meeting of the town council was called to consider whether, in the then alarming state of the country, it might not be necessary to have one or more men stationed at or near the mouth of the harbour to keep a constant look-out and report on the appearance of any of the enemy's ships, and that it was decided to place men on the headlands at the mouth of the bay to watch the coast both day and night.

It was not only from the sea that Kirkcudbright was exposed to alarms and attacks. At least twice in its history it saw an English army. Edward the First's invasion of 1300 has been referred to already. He entered Galloway on the 17th of July by way of Lochrutton and Hills Castle, where he spent a night, reached Kirkcudbright on the 19th, and remained here for ten days. The Gallovidians regarded him with favour as the patron of Thomas, the son of Alan; were impressed by the size and equipment of his army—one of the strongest ever led against Scotland; and did not seriously oppose his advance. It was otherwise in 1548, when an English force under Sir Thomas Carleton captured Dumfries and attacked Kirkcudbright, but met with such an effectual resistance that they had to retire and content themselves with lifting cattle, sheep, and horses. A force of "Galloway folks from beyond the Water of Dee" came upon the invaders and compelled them to leave the sheep behind. A little later, when Annandale and Nithsdale had come under the rule of the English, and The Stewartry was overrun by their troops, Kirkcudbright fell into their hands for a time.

There have been a few royal visitors who came on peaceful errands. James the Fourth, travelling to Whithorn, came this way in 1501 and 1509. James the Sixth was here in 1587 and presented the burgh with a small silver gun to be shot for by the Incorporated Trades "to encourage them in the use of fire-arms". This gun has been shot for in recent times on such important occasions as the Coronation of His Majesty King George the Sixth.

Some visitors have recorded their impressions of the burgh. Boece described it in 1526 as "ane rich toun and full of merchandise". Andrew Symson's description belongs to the latter half of the seventeenth century. "Kirkcudburgh", he says, "is the headburgh of the Stewartry being about twenty four miles from Dumfreis Westward, and about sixteen miles eastward from Vigton. It is a burgh royal, having a weekly mercat much frequented, together with some other annual faires. It is situated in a very pleasant place, in a flexure of the river of Dee, more than a large mile from the mouth of that river. It hath an excellent natural harbour, to which ships of a very great burthen may at full sea come, and ly safely from all stormes, just at the side of the Kirk wall."

An anonymous work entitled *A Journey through Scotland In Familiar Letters from a Gentleman Here, to his Friend Abroad*

*Being the Third Volume, Which Compleats Great Britain. By
the Author of The Journey thro' England* was published in 1723.
Bibliographers have traced the authorship to John Macky,
a secret agent of the British Government in the Revolution
period, who should be more widely known both in England and
in Scotland if only for the excellence of his observations on
the latter country, as where he says, "The Scots have made
a greater Figure Abroad, than any other Nation in *Europe ;*
this hath been generally ascribed to the Barrenness of their
Country, as not being able to maintain its Inhabitants : But
this is a vulgar Error, for it's entirely owing to the Fineness
of their Education. A Gentleman in *Scotland*, that hath
Four or Five Sons, gives them equal Education. The eldest
Son, though often not the finest Gentleman, succeeds to the
Estate ; and the others being bred above Trades, go to seek
their Fortune in Foreign Countries, and are thereby lost to
their own : " and "Since their Kings came to be Kings of
*England*, they were always govern'd as a distant Province,
under the Direction of a Secretary of State. Although they
had Parliaments of their own, those were generally influenced
by an *English* Ministry, till now, by the *Union*, they represent
themselves in the Parliament of *Great Britain* : and yet the
Number seems too few, for so numerous a Nobility, and so
populous and large a Country."

Macky's account of Kirkcudbright is the fullest that has
come down to us from any period before the end of the eighteenth century, when Heron wrote. He had sailed over from
The Isle of Man. "I arriv'd here", he says, "on Saturday
Night, at a good Inn ; but the Room where I lay, I believe,
had not been washed in a hundred Years. Next Day I expected,
as in *England*, a piece of good Beef or a Pudding to Dinner ;
but my Landlord told me, that they never dress Dinner on a
*Sunday*, so that I must either take up with Bread and Butter,
a fresh Egg, or fast till after the Evening Sermon, when they
never fail of a hot Supper. Certainly no Nation on Earth
observes the Sabbath with that Strictness of Devotion and
Resignation to the Will of God : They all pray in their Families
before they go to Church, and between Sermons they fast ;
after Sermon every Body retires to his own Home, and reads
some Book of Devotion till Supper, (which is generally very
good on *Sundays*), after which they sing Psalms till they go

to Bed "—a picture suggesting an odd mixture of piety and the flesh-pots of Egypt.

Macky was struck with the situation of the town, " a perfect Amphitheatre, like the Town of *Trent* on the Confines of *Italy*, and like it not surrounded with high Mountains, but a rocky stony Crust, which in this Country they call Crags. . . . In the middle of this craggy Country lies this little Town, which consists of a tolerable Street, the Houses all built with Stone, but not at all after the Manner of *England ;* even the Manners, Dress, and Countenance of the People, differ very much from the *English*. The common People wear all Bonnets instead of Hats ; and though some of the Townsmen have Hats, they wear them only on *Sundays*, and extraordinary Occasions. There is nothing of the Gaiety of the *English*, but a sedate Gravity in every Face, without the Stiffness of the Spaniards : and I take this to be owing to their Praying and frequent long Graces, which gives their Looks a religious Cast." The Dee he thought " the prettiest navigable River " that he had seen in Britain.

Defoe, who wrote about the same time, says, " Though its Situation is extremely convenient for carrying on a very advantageous Commerce, we saw nothing but a Harbour without Ships, a Port without Trade, and a Fishery without Nets. This is owing partly to the Poverty, and partly to the Disposition, of the Inhabitants, who are indeed, a sober, grave, religious Sort of People, but have no Notion of acquiring Wealth by Trade ; for they strictly obey the Scriptures in the very Letter of the Text, by *being content with such Things as they have.*"

Robert Heron discourses on Kirkcudbright for about fourteen pages of his *Observations made in a Journey through the Western Counties of Scotland in the Autumn of* M.DCC.XCII, but does not provoke quotation. More interest attaches to the visits of his friend, Robert Burns, who was sometimes the guest of Lord Daer at S. Mary's Isle. Another poet, John Keats, made a walking tour through Galloway in July, 1818, and says in one of his letters, " Kirkcudbright County is very beautiful, very wild, with craggy hills, somewhat in the Westmoreland fashion. We have come down from Dumfries to the sea-coast part of it. . . . Yesterday was passed in Kirkcudbright, the country is very rich, very fine, and with a little of Devon."

The burgh records give more intimate glimpses of old-world

Kirkcudbright than the notes of travellers usually afford and shew the great variety of matters coming within the cognizance of the Town Council. For instance, a minute dated the last day of July, 1697, tells of the judgment passed by the magistrates and council on a highly unpopular character, Janet Corbie. The accusations brought against her were that she had been in the habit of abusing her neighbours with scandalous expressions, on account of which she had been fined more than once already; that her conduct in this respect shewed no signs of improvement; that she had been endeavouring to dissuade Elspeth MacEwen, then in prison as a witch, from confessing her crime and " said that people sinned their souls wha said she was a Wutch "; that she abused the Lord's Day constantly, stealing her neighbours' goods " sic as onyons and bowcale " (no doubt, when they were in church) and carrying her booty into the country, where she sold it; and that she was a person who lived by " pickery and steeling ". Besides all this—not to condescend on too many particulars—there were " several other things " to confirm the opinion that Janet Corbie had been suffered to live in the place far too long and that her presence could be tolerated no more. The magistrates and council, therefore, ordained that the said Janet should remain in the Tolbooth until the following Monday morning at ten o'clock and then be taken forth by the officers and with tuck of drum be " transported over the Ferry-boat " and so expelled for all time coming from " the society or conversation of all guid Christians and indwellers in the place ". Any person holding communication with her was to be liable to a fine of forty pounds.

The disturbers of the peace of Kirkcudbright were not confined to one class. The minutes describe how Lady Auchlane had come " in the dark cluds and silence of the nicht " to the house of Jean Kirk and taken away a pot which did not belong to her. She had given this pot to her son, the Laird of Auchlane, and he was put into prison until he should find caution for its restoration.

The town-clerk and several country gentlemen from S. Mary's Isle, Orroland, and other estates in the neighbourhood assaulted a messenger-at-arms on a market-day and paraded the streets with drawn swords, and when Bailie Meek, with much boldness, called on them to surrender themselves as prisoners, " they all came in ane furious maner and did assasinat and fall upon the said bailyie by cutting and wounding his heid with drawn swords (some whereof was bruk upon his head) as also cutt the jaylour's heid and persewed the assistants with drawen swords."

David Corrie, a jailor, having been brought before the council to explain how a prisoner, Thomas Anderson, had been allowed to make his escape the previous night, met the situation with an air of bewildered innocence. He stated that Hellen Anderson, the prisoner's daughter, and two other persons had been in the jail (making a friendly call, apparently, on the prisoner); that he had gone to the jail at eight o'clock at night, locking the outer door behind him, and entered the place where the prisoner was, carrying two candles for Anderson's use. Anderson had lighted one of the candles, gone out of the prison into the court house along with his daughter, and shut the door behind him. Hellen Anderson had returned in less than two minutes without her father and, when she was asked where he was, answered that he was standing at the door. Thereupon, Corrie, awaking, it would seem, to a sense of his responsibility, had gone out immediately and found " nothing but darkness ". As his eyes became accustomed to the gloom, however, he had perceived that the outer door was standing partly open and, going down, found a key in it, " with which he supposes the prisoner had opened the door and made his escape ". This key he had secured with admirable promptitude and now produced declaring that he knew no more of the matter and adding that, when he had locked the outer door behind him, he had put the key into his pocket. The council compared the false key with the true and found that they corresponded exactly. A close inspection of the latter discovered " something like dried Clay " adhering to it, whence they concluded that the prisoner or his friends had had it in their hands and taken an impression on " some sort of paist ". Considering the jailor's careless conduct, by which he had given the prisoner " full liberty to have made the Jaylor himself a prisoner and to use what freedom he pleased The Magistrates and Councell Do . . . Dismiss the Jaylor from his office and Declare him Incapable of any Trust in the Toun in time coming, without prejudice always to the Toun in sueing the Jaylor and his Cau$^r$ for what Damages they may Incurr by the prisoners Escape."

The prison is referred to in another minute containing a representation from the Deputy Steward that two smugglers, " Samuel Campbell and James Crosbie in Claycroft were Incarscerate within the Tolbooth . . . for the Crimes of violently Resisting and Assulting James Ramsay and other officers of Execise and Attacking them with fire Arms and other offensive Arms in order to preventing their Seizing a parcel of Uncustomed Goods or to Rescue them after they were Lawfully Seized ", that these crimes are punishable with death, and that " the prison of this Burgh is altogether insufficient for the safe Keeping of any prisoners, especially those above mentioned incarscerate for the Crime of so high a Nature ".

On the 26th of June, 1750, John Newall, being called before the council, accepted the office of executioner for the town and county of all corporal and capital punishments inflicted by the magistrates, sheriff, and justices of the peace. In particular, he became bound to execute the capital sentence on Henry Greig, *alias* John Wilson, on the approaching 6th of July. The page of the minutes-book registering the agreement is signed with Newall's initials witnessed by two of the bailies.

Greig belonged to a gang of gypsies or tinkers who had made themselves a general nuisance. On the 31st of May Henry Greig, Margaret Stewart, and Anne Gibson, a daughter of Billy Marshall, were imprisoned. Their agent admitted some of the charges brought against them and stated that " in order to save the Court from further trouble they were willing to subject themselves to transportation to any of His Majesty's plantations, never to return ". The proposal was accepted in respect of the women ; but there was to be no mercy for Greig, who was accordingly found guilty of " theft, robbery, and house-breaking " and condemned to be taken " from the Tolbooth of Kirkcudbright to the ordinary place of execution of the burgh and there between the hours of two and four o'clock of the afternoon to be hanged by the neck on a gibbet until he should be dead ".

In 1726 a complaint was made to the council about the intolerable grievance caused to the merchant burgesses by the malpractices of itinerant merchants who were in the habit of selling their goods freely through the burgh, and it was enacted that in future no " forreign Pedlar Chapman Travelur Traffiquer

or Merchant " should expose his goods for sale except in the
public market-place and at the lawful market hours.

In 1761 the magistrates and council took into consideration
the great number of people in the burgh who sold ale, brandy,
and other kinds of spirits " without keeping proper accommodation for either man or horse " and at the same time followed
no other occupation. They regarded this as a great nuisance,
since it tended to " discourage industry and promote idleness " ;
but to avoid rash measures for remedying the evil, they recommend " every member of the Councill to prepare and bring in
his thoughts on this subject against next Councill day And also
on the Nusance of people keeping cattle who have no visible
way to subsist them ". At the next meeting it was represented
that many of those who sold ale had no other way to support
themselves and their families, and the majority of the council
were of the opinion that they could not well reduce the number
of such people. It was considered that the retailers of spirits
were a much greater nuisance. The council, therefore, " unanimously Enact Statute and ordain That whoever shall be con-
victed of Retailing of forreign Spirits, who are not duly Licenced
for that purpose, and not prosecuted by the proper officers,
shall upon such conviction before the Baillies of the Burrow
at the instance of the pro^r fiscal or any Licenced dealer in
Spirits be fined in terms of the act of parliament."

On the 2nd of June, 1768, the magistrates and council approve
of the action of the provost in giving ten guineas in their name
to " a fund to repair the high road from Rhoanhouse of Kelton
by Tongland Bridge to Kirk of Twynholm so as to Join at both
places to the Great Military Road from Sark to Portpatrick ".

On the 2nd of November, 1789, " It being Represented That
it is impossible to furnish the two Companies of Soldiers
presently lying here with quarters without distressing the
Inhabitants beyond what they can bear The Council request
the Magistrates to write the Commander in Chief for Scotland
desiring that he will remove one of the Companies within three
weeks otherways after that period Billets will only be issued
for one of the Companies."

The parish was greatly excited in 1761 by the appointment of
Thomas Blacklock as its minister. Blacklock was a friend of
Burns, who says in a well-known letter, " I had taken the last
farewell of my few friends ; my chest was on the road to

Greenock ; I had composed the last song I should ever measure
in Caledonia, *The gloomy night is gathering fast,* when a letter
from Dr. Blacklock to a friend of mine overthrew all my schemes
by opening new prospects to my poetic ambition ". " This
morning," says Dr. Samuel Johnson in a letter dated 1773, " I
saw at breakfast Dr. Blacklock, the blind poet, who does not
remember to have seen light, and is read to by a poor scholar
in Latin, Greek, and French. He was originally a poor scholar
himself. I looked on him with reverence." The parishioners
of Kirkcudbright were unwilling to have a blind man as their
minister, and opposed the settlement with all the vehemence
that the Scottish people are wont to shew in their ecclesiastical
affairs. Their anxiety was so great as to lead to a step which
must surely have few parallels. The appointment was made by
the Crown, and among other opposition measures the council,
" encouraged by your Lordship's honour, piety, and tender
regard for the welfare of the Christian Church ", appeal to the
Bishop of London to use his influence in high places on their
behalf. They state as the ground of their opposition that Mr.
Blacklock is, by reason of his stone-blindness, " unfit in many,
if not in all respects, for Discharging the most important of all
dutys, That of a minister of Jesus Christ, in any parish at all,
and more so in a Royal Burrow, to which a large parish is an-
nexed. The extreamitys thereof are about five miles distant
from the parish church and minister's residence and where there
are about 1500 souls or thereabout." The ordination took place
in 1762 ; but Blacklock found it advisable to arrange for the
appointment of an ordained assistant within two or three years
and retired to Edinburgh. Besides the works published during
his life, he wrote a long lampoon on his leading opponents in
Kirkcudbright. It was entitled *Pistapolis : An Hyperpindaric
Ode with Notes by Scriblerus Redivivus. Written in 1765.* It
was published *sub cura* Mr. Frank Miller in *The Scottish Historical
Review* for January, 1907.

In consequence of Blacklock's settlement, the elders of the
kirk were about " to cease acting as such ", and it was " more
than probable that some of the Inhabitants of the Toun may
not resort to Church for publick worship as formerly ". The
council, therefore, requested the session-clerk and kirk-treasurer
to keep the account-book and cash as heretofore and resolved
that " one of them along with one of Mr. Garthshore's

elders[1] in the Toun shall attend at the east and west gates of the Church to Collect the poors money every day of publick worship and that every Munday they call at the houses of such Inhabitants as have not been at Church for their Charity to the poor ".

After these extracts from the musty folios of the town council records, it is pleasant to return to the open air and advise the reader about some little journeys in the neighbourhood. I strongly recommend the walk to Tongland by the path on the left side of the river. In about a mile it brings one opposite the house and woody grounds of Cumstoun.[2] Here the Tarff joins the Dee, and on the wide banks of sand and mud sea and land birds feed and fight, filling the air with screaming or plaintive notes. A patient watcher may behold here the grave and gay incidents of bird-life—an infuriated drake driving a flock of gulls away from his young family or a duckling falling a victim to the ravenous assault of a gull. At Tongland Bridge and for a mile upstream, the Dee was formerly at its grandest, a deep, dark, foam-flecked flood between precipitous, thickly-wooded banks; but the dam and power-station have changed the scene.

*The Statistical Account* of the parish of Tongland was written by the minister, the Rev. Dugald Stewart Williamson, a keen naturalist ; and had not the exigencies of space forbidden, I should have quoted a good deal of the very readable pages in which he discourses on the missel-thrushes that built in the manse garden, the wagtails, the sheldrakes, the cuckoos, the rooks ; on otters, salmon, and trout, and the ways in which they are taken. Of other beasts and birds seen in the neighbourhood he mentions the fox, the badger, the polecat, the weasel, the stoat, the bittern, the king-fisher, the heron, the cormorant, the curlew, the lapwing, the dorhawk, the corncrake, the tern, the white owl, the golden plover, the water-hen, the stock dove, the fieldfare, the starling, the golden-crested wren, the corn-bunting, the snow-bunting, the speckled diver, the long-tailed " titmouse ", the little grebe, the bullfinch, and all the kinds of game birds with the exception of the ptarmigan.[3]

---

[1] George Garthshore was Blacklock's predecessor as minister of the parish.

[2] The tradition that Alexander Montgomerie, the sixteenth-century poet, lived for a time at Cumstoun Castle, and that his poem, *The Cherrie and the Slae*, refers to the river Dee lacks evidence.

[3] There is a collection of the local *fauna* in the Kirkcudbright Museum.

On the right bank of the river there are some remains of the Premonstratensian Abbey of Tongland founded by Fergus. The most famous person associated with it in later times was

*The Dee at Tongland.*

the Lombard, John Damian, who was Abbot in the reign of James the Fourth. He was a believer in the possibility of human flight, and fitting himself with wings made of birds' feathers, tested his theory by launching himself from the battlements of Stirling Castle. He had the good fortune to fall on a dunghill and escaped with a broken thigh. His failure was satirized by William Dunbar in *The Fenziet Freir of Tungland*; but perhaps his spirit was joyfully aware of airships and airplanes patrolling the Galloway coast in 1915!

If I may lapse once more into personal impressions, I must record that the most delightful of all the journeys which I made around Kirkcudbright was to the old fort between the farm-house of Drummore[1] and Torrs Point. It is very rarely that from a height above a sea-shore one can see so much of the land. The fort looks down upon all its immediate neighbourhood, and commands such an extent of country as I should have thought incredible from a cursory glance at the map. Down at my feet were The Manxman's Lake and the estuary with their wooded shores. Barstobrick Hill, which makes the sky-line as you look northwards from the town, was now sunk to a mere hummock in the middle distance. Filling the horizon throughout the huge semi-circle beginning with the Mull of Galloway and ending near Dumfries were series of blue and grey hills, some distant, but clear, and others just perceptible—Cairnharrow, Cairnsmore of Fleet, the hills north of Newton Stewart, Merrick and its neighbours, Cairnsmore of Carsphairn and the Cumnock Hills, Queensberry in Dumfriesshire, and Criffel near New Abbey—an immense prospect containing here and there groups of squares like those on a chess-board, but really great fields where men would soon be reaping corn; plantations contracted to the appearance of small shrubberies; brown patches the size of a finger-nail that were wide moors with scores of sheep; and streams like faint silver threads.

The Stewartry has been the birthplace of some famous artists, the brothers John, James and Thomas Faed; while others, attracted by the country, have had their studios in Kirkcudbright and its neighbourhood. The most eminent of these are Mr. George Henry and Mr. Edward A. Hornel, who made Broughton House his home.

---

[1] Gaelic *druim mór*, great ridge.

*The Murray Arms Hotel, Gatehouse-of-Fleet.*

# CHAPTER VIII

### BORGUE AND GATEHOUSE-OF-FLEET

The old ferry at Kirkcudbright—The road to Borgue—Senwick
Churchyard — The Frenchman's Rock — Borgue — The old
church of Girthon—Gatehouse-of-Fleet—The Fleet canalized—
The glen of Fleet—Castramont—Rusco Castle—Anwoth and
Samuel Rutherford—Archbishop Ussher's visit—Mrs. Cousin's
verses—Epitaphs on the Gordon monument—John Bell of
Whiteside, the martyr—The old road to Creetown.

PEOPLE travelling on foot from Kirkcudbright to the parish
of Borgue[1] crossed the Dee by a ferry-boat until 1868. Mr.
Harper gives the following incidents of the ferry traffic in his
*Rambles in Galloway* : " William Ireland of Barbey, steward-
substitute of Kirkcudbright, was drowned when crossing in
the ferry-boat in his carriage in 1845. Towards the end of the
eighteenth century the Provost of the burgh of Kirkcudbright
went in an afternoon into the parish of Twynholm, where he
had a property. He returned after nightfall to the ferry on

---

[1] " Old Norse, Swedish, and Danish *borg*, Old English *burg, burh*, a
fort, ' shelter place', a ' burgh '."—Johnston.

the Twynholm side of the river and hailed 'the boat.' The boatman answered by asking him if he had a horse. Carriages in those days were few and far between. He made the inquiry to guide him as to taking the 'big boat' or the 'wee boat.' Not liking the prospect of pulling the small boat, it might be, across an ebbing tide, *plus* a spate, for the small fare of a 'bawbee,' the boatman told the Provost (not recognised) to wait 'till he got a neebour.' The Provost did wait, 'nursing his wrath to keep it warm.' Another passenger having cast up, the Provost and he were taken over. On the Provost landing, he went direct to the burgh officer and ordered him to apprehend the boatman and put him into the Tolbooth, to which place the Provost went to see the boatman shut up. On this being done, he, on bended knee, implored the Provost to pardon and liberate him, whereupon his honour told the boatman to wait 'till he got a neebour'."

When the iron bridge spanning the Dee at the point where the ferry-boat used to cross was erected, a section of it was designed to swing back in order to allow of the passage of the ships that used to go up the stream to Tongland. It is scarcely ever opened now, however, and the wheels must be very rusty.

The way to Borgue appeals to the *connoisseur* in roads. If one were to make a list of the pleasantest roads in Galloway, this would be one. Running along the tree-clad bank of the estuary of the Dee and following closely the gentle windings of the shore, it keeps you ever between the dark wood and the shining water. The pity is that there is not more of it, for one could travel happily on it for a whole day.

Just at the point where it veers away from the estuary towards the village of Borgue there is the beginning of Senwick Wood. The wood holds close by the shore of Kirkcudbright Bay for a mile or two farther south, and in the midst of it is the churchyard of the old parish of Senwick[1] with some slight remains of the church and manse, all on a steep slope falling away to the edge of the bay and surrounded by tall trees. Here lie the dead of bygone centuries with few sounds heard about their resting-place save the whispering of the wind in the leaves and the washing of the water on the pebbly beach.

There is a rock in the bay called The Frenchman's Rock, and the name is connected with an incident in the history of

---

[1] Norse, *sandr vik*, sandy bay.

Senwick Church. The tradition is that a gang of French pirates had landed here and carried off the silver plate. Guilty of both sacrilege and robbery, they met what was regarded as a just doom before they had sailed far from the scene of their crime. A storm arose, the ship struck on the rock, and all were drowned.

*Borgue Church.*

The parish of Senwick was merged in that of Borgue in 1618.

The road running southwards past Senwick Wood ends on the shore of Ross Bay under the slope of the Meikle Ross or " Great Headland ". The cliffs fronting the sea on the south side of the promontory are very steep and are surmounted by some remains of ancient forts. The name of the Little Ross

Island immediately to the east points to a time when it formed part of the mainland. In the early years of the nineteenth century it was possible to walk over to the island at low tide. The lighthouse was built by Thomas Stevenson, the father of Robert Louis.

It may be said of Borgue that no other parish in Galloway has so quiet a village for its centre. There is no hotel, nor is there a public house in the parish. In the middle of the village—if, indeed, one may speak of the middle of a place that ends before it has really begun—there is a " Coffee House ". A cheap and clean lodging may be had here, and the range of beverages supplied is not confined strictly to coffee. Borgue is proud of its Academy, an institution founded by a native of the parish, Thomas Rainy, who left this country about the middle of the eighteenth century and made a fortune in the Island of Dominica ; of its handsome church standing on a little hill—one of its ministers, the Rev. Samuel Smith, was the author of a well-known book, *A General View of the Agriculture of Galloway*, published in 1810 ; of its great wealth of flowers and famous honey ; and although it is not mentioned by name, it is plainly the principal scene of Stevenson's *The Master of Ballantrae*. The village on the Carrick coast supplied the author of that romance with no more than a musical name. The story belongs to " Solwayside ", and it was on " the Muckle Ross " that the excellent Mackellar once saw the smoke of a beacon fire.

Close to the Academy there is a monument erected in honour of William Nicholson, the author of *The Brownie of Blednoch* and other poems, who was born in this parish in 1783 and died in 1849. The poem on which his reputation chiefly rests will be quoted in a later chapter.[1] Nicholson was buried in the churchyard of Kirkandrews, about two miles west of Borgue village. There was formerly a separate parish of Kirkandrews ; but in 1657 it became, like Senwick, a part of Borgue. In the same churchyard there is the grave of a martyr, " Robert M'Whae who was barbarously shot to death by Grier of Lagg in the Paroch of Tongland for his adherence to Scotlands Reformation Covenants National and Solemn League 1685 ". The stone bearing this inscription is not the original one, but a facsimile.

[1] See page 281.

As one goes north towards Gatehouse-of-Fleet, one sees
on the right hand the remains of Plunton Castle, which is

*Old Church of Girthon and a Covenanter's Tombstone.*

said to be the scene of that dull work, *The Doom of Devorgoil*,
and just before reaching the farm of Lennox Plunton on the

left, a gate opening upon a byway to the old church of Girthon Parish. The digression should be made if only for the pleasure of going along a road that is scarcely used at all.

Girthon[1] Church is very old and is classed as belonging to either the Norman or the First Pointed Period. It ceased to be used as a place of worship in 1817, when the present church was built in Gatehouse. Near the entrance is the grave of Robert Lennox, a Covenanter. The inscription, which runs as follows :

> WITHIN THIS TOMB
> LYES THE CORPS OF
> ROBERT LENNOX SOME
> TIME IN IRELANDTOUN
> WHO WAS SHOT TO
> DEATH BY GRIER OF
> LAGG IN THE PAROCH
> OF TOUNGLAND FOR
> HIS ADHERENCE TO
> SCOTLANDS REFORMATION
> COVENANTS NATIONAL
> AND SOLEMN LEAGUE
> 1685

is attributed to " Old Mortality ". The lettering is smaller than in the case of the stone in Glentrool, but is in the same style.[2] At the end of the " Introduction " to *Old Mortality*, Scott gives a curious anecdote about the old man, who was working " in the churchyard of Girthon ". The farmhouse of Girthon Kirk, just outside the churchyard, was formerly the manse, and was occupied at one time by the Rev. John MacNaught, in whose case Scott was concerned as an advocate in 1793.

There are one or two nooks in Gatehouse where an artist might sit down to compose a picture, little *culs-de-sac* at right angles to the streets ; but it would be the splendour of the overshadowing trees rather than any beauty in the houses that would attract him. Apart from such corners, the village is of a deplorable dullness. The main street, perfectly straight and full of houses of an almost uniform plainness, does not harmonize with the noble curves of the great trees or with the gentle outlines of the hills. The secondary streets running

---

[1] " Icel. *garðr*, Middle English *garth, girth*, ' yard, garden', with suffixed Norse article."—Johnston.

[2] Mr. Thomson's drawing on page 119 shews the ligatures.

parallel with it are plainer still and dingy besides, for Gatehouse has been a place of factories, and the humbler dwelling-houses have been built after the manner of industrial towns. This, however, is all that can be said against the village : that it is a dull stone in a glorious setting.

*The Angel Hotel* [1] commends itself to me on account of its

*Gatehouse-of-Fleet.*

open view to the south-west. The windows of the upper storeys clear the roofs of the cottages on the same side of the street. Straight in front and at the distance of about a third of a mile,

---

[1] *The Murray Arms Hotel* boasts of a room in which Burns is said to have committed *Scots wha ha'e* to writing. The verses had been composed during a walk over the moors from Kenmure Castle.

there is the woody height where the walls of Cardiness Castle, a severe note amid the surrounding softness, overtop the trees. Below it on the left is the gleaming streak of the canalized Water of Fleet[1] with the little Fleet Bay beyond it and, farther off, the faint line of the Wigtonshire coast. A little more to the left, meadows and a stretch of woodland border the bay. This view is the subject of Mr. John Faed's[2] picture hanging in the town hall, with the difference that the artist has included the village in the foreground.

I strolled round one evening to the northern edge of the village and was confronted with another pleasing vision presented by the glen of Fleet. The river wound between banks shaggy with willows, elders, and young beech-trees, skirting meadows where cattle grazed. Running back towards the north was a soft fairyland of wooded hillsides, pastures dotted with single trees, and the shadowed sides of fir and larch plantations breaking the high moorland spaces and standing clear-cut against the cold light of the sky. Three or four miles away, the hills of Castramont and Culreoch stood full in the sunshine, while the details of the glen itself made a tangle of streaks and masses of shadow and of sunlit patches. The scene was full of the spirit of pastoral evening peace, and I should never visit Gatehouse without coming towards sunset to look at the "intermingled pomp of vale and hill."

The name of the village seems to mean the house on the *gait* or road. This certainly was the significance of the place in 1642, when the earliest known allusion occurs. " In that year," says Mr. Alexander Bryson, a diligent student of the history of the Gatehouse district, " a rebellion raged in Ireland, and the English Parliament, wishing to keep in closer touch with the army there, established a line of posts between Carlisle and Portpatrick. The local appointments were—' Andrew McMinn, from Dumfries to the Steps of Orr, twelve mile ; Ninian Muir, betwix the Steps of Orr and Gatehouse-of-Fleet, twelf mile ; George Bell, from thence to Pethhouse, eleven mile ; John Baillie, from thence to the Kirk of Glenluce, thirteen mile ; and John Kaig, from that to the Port.' These men were looked upon as the ' only ones fit for that employment, as being innkeepers and of approved honesty '." The next notice belongs to 1661,

---

[1] Icelandic *fljót*, a stream.
[2] The Faed family belong to the Gatehouse district.

when Richard Murray of Broughton procured an Act of Parliament enabling him to rebuild a bridge over the Fleet and to levy pontages to meet the cost and keep the structure in repair. " I claim ", says Mr. Bryson, " that this bridge built by Richard Murray still stands and is probably that portion nearest the sea. This, the original bridge, was about eleven feet wide, which, with parapet walls off, would give a roadway of about nine feet. This would be ample at a time when no wheeled vehicles were in use for farm work. However, after a time it was found insufficient, and another bridge, five feet wide, was added. So we have now three bridges in one."

Gatehouse continued to be " the house on the road " long after Murray's bridge was built, and it was not until considerably more than a century later that there was much of a village here. Heron says that there were people living in 1792 who remembered the time when there was only one house. James Murray of Broughton and Cally, who built Cally House, was responsible for the uprising of Gatehouse as a place of cotton factories towards the end of the eighteenth century. When Heron made his journey through Galloway, he found the new industries attracting the people like a freshly discovered gold district. " The ploughman forsakes his plough, the schoolmaster lays down his birch, the tanner deserts his tan-pits, the apothecary turns from the composition of pills and the mixing of unguents ; and all earnestly commence spinners of cotton-yarn or weavers of cotton-cloth." There were six cotton mills, a muslin factory, a soapery, a brewery, a tannery, a branch of the Paisley Bank, and, later, a shipbuilding and repairing yard. " The principal firms in cotton manufactures ", says Mr. Bryson, " were Messrs. Birtwhistle and Messrs. Thomas Scott and Company, and it was the latter firm whose name and illustration of the mill appear on the trade token known as the Gatehouse halfpenny, a coin which holds the unique position of being the only trade token issued in the south-west of Scotland, the nearest approach being the Edinburgh halfpenny payable at Dumfries." A bobbin mill survived into the early years of this century.

Besides the erection of the grim buildings where the cotton, leather, soap, and other goods were made, the industries of Gatehouse led to two alterations in the neighbouring country. As the Fleet ran too low to drive the mills, a water-supply had to be obtained from Loch Whinyeon, three miles away. Its effluent ran towards the Dee ; but the outlet was stopped, a tunnel cut through a hill, and the water conveyed by an aqueduct to the factories.

The story of the canalization of the Fleet given in *The Statistical Account* of Girthon Parish in 1844 by Dr. Alexander Murray, the author of *The Literary History of Galloway*, is interesting enough to be quoted : " In order to facilitate the navigation to Gatehouse, and to reclaim a considerable portion of land which at high water was covered by the sea, Mr. Murray of Broughton has constructed a canal which, besides gaining the two objects in question, has greatly shortened the distance between the Fleet Bay and the town. Of this canal, which was begun on the 17th of June, 1824, and opened on the 3rd of October following, the length is fourteen hundred yards. The cost was calculated by an eminent engineer at about £5000, and the time required for constructing it to be two summers. But Alexander Craig, Esq., then Mr. Murray's factor, whose ingenuity is well known, setting his local knowledge in opposition to the science of the engineer, cut a narrow trough along the centre of the projected line of the canal, and of nearly the depth to which it was to be excavated, into which he forced the water of the Fleet. The result corresponded with Mr. Craig's anticipations ; for, in the course of only two days, the river formed a channel for itself of the exact width and depth required ; and the total expense instead of being £5000, was greatly under the half of that sum—being only £2204 3s. 5d. ! Nor is this all : no repairs have since been necessary to maintain or secure the banks of the canal so rapidly and singularly formed. There is another remarkable circumstance in connection with the construction of this work. A rock on each side of its banks, directly opposite each other, and nearly level with the bottom, jutted out ; and on these rocks the pins of a swing bridge have been erected, which affords great convenience to the neighbourhood, and has enabled Mr. Murray to remove the parish road from his domain. Thirty-six acres intervened between the line of the canal and the bed of the river, of which fifteen belonged to Anwoth ; and the quantity of land reclaimed is no less than a hundred and seventy acres, now forming one of the most fertile and productive farms in Girthon."

On the Cally estate there are some remains of an old castle, including an arched fireplace ten feet wide and three deep in

the north gable ; but there are no features to decide the date.
There is also a well-preserved mote in a park about half a mile
north-east of Cally House. When Lord Cockburn was here
in 1839, he wrote, " The *place*, with its wood, its well-kept home
ground, its varied surface, its distant, bounding hills, and its
obvious extensive idea of a great and beautiful domain, is one
of the finest in Scotland. As to the house—granite and marble
though it be—and though its portico be designed by Papworth
and admired by Playfair, I was disappointed ", and he gave
his reasons ; but after another visit in 1844 he wrote, " I retract
much of what I have formerly said of that house. It is not too
small ; and, indeed, being in just proportions, size is not very
material. . . . On the whole, it is a beautiful portico ; and
Papworth's taste may be observed in all the internal details."
On the earlier occasion he wished that he had " the two busts
of Napoleon and Washington ". He thought Gatehouse " clean
and comfortable, but too visibly the village at the Great Man's
Gate ". Cally House is now a hotel, open in the summer months.

The northward view referred to earlier in this chapter left
me doubting whether I should explore the glen or be content
with the delicate beauty of that evening impression ; but when a
fine, sunny morning found me with no definite plans for the day,
I yielded to the invitation of the tree-embowered road entering
Gatehouse on the eastern side of the valley. After passing the
Castramont woods and one or two farmhouses, it climbs up to
the moors of the Little Water of Fleet and ends within a few
miles. One has here, therefore, the real seclusion of the byway
that stops, in contrast to the publicity of the highway, where
every passing pedestrian, cyclist, and motorist reminds one of
the openness of the road before and behind and of all the world's
travelling and trafficking. For the former half, indeed, this is
little more than a private approach to Castramont House, and
then come three lonely, uphill, moorland miles and the end,
where one lies down on the heather, surrounded by black moss-
haggs and tiny rills tinkling among granite stones, while the
air is tremulous with the cries of moorfowl and sheep.

The Latin look of the name, " Castramont ", led some antiquarians to suppose that there had been a Roman camp here,
and they thought that they had found one. MacKerlie, for
instance, says, " That a Roman camp did exist at Castramont,
or Castramen, is certain, and a very fine and large one it is

believed to have been ", and he proceeds to give its measurements, but Mr. Coles refers to " this so-called ' Roman camp ' ", and remarks that it " has been the fruitful source of much of that theorizing on matters of archæology which a generation back

*Rusco Castle.*

passed for scientific research ". It is only recently that the name has taken its present form. Sir Herbert Maxwell thought that it might be *carse* and the Erse *tromán*, " the carse of the elder trees ". There appears to have been some kind of ancient fortification here; but serious antiquarians hesitate to say "how much of the appearance of the ground is due to it, and how much to the levelling when the present mansion-house was built".

Rusco [1] Castle on the other side of the glen has some points of architectural interest. "The projecting parapet is supported by a double row of moulded corbels placed chequer-wise. On the exterior an unusual feature is to be seen in the splayed and weathered projections of stone over the lintels of the large win-

*Old Church of Anwoth.*

dows. Their purpose has obviously been to throw the rain off the walls at these points. The entrance doorway is somewhat unusual in form. The arch-head is almost straight, formed of joggled arch-stones and rounded at the angles. Above is a moulded panel containing two shields placed one over the other : the upper shield bears the royal arms of Scotland carved in

[1] Gaelic *riasgach*, marshy land.

relief beneath a crown with supporters. . . . . [and] in the sinister corner a figure ' four ' presented in the early Arabic form of numeral." The charge on the lower shield is almost entirely obliterated. The castle belonged to the Gordons of Lochinvar throughout the sixteenth and the earlier half of the seventeenth centuries.

I believe that a considerable number of visitors come to Gatehouse, and I am certain that I have seen advertisements of " apartments to let ". It may be news to some of these visitors and to some readers of this book that there are travellers who halt at Gatehouse for no other reason than that it is near a little ruined church where a certain man exercised a Christian ministry nearly three hundred years ago. A footpath begins at the south-west end of the village, undulates over some scrubby heights, and brings you down within a mile into one of the quietest nooks in Galloway. The old church is so thickly covered with ivy that it does not stand out sharply from the neighbouring trees and background of green slopes, but suggests a humility and a reticence that are in keeping with its finest associations. It was not because the minister of Anwoth was previously Professor of Latin in Edinburgh University, nor afterwards Professor of Divinity in S. Andrew's, that he made Anwoth known to the world, but because whether he trod the lonely hill-tracks of Galloway on his pastoral errands or ministered in his sanctuary or, driven from his charge by Episcopal tyranny, lived in banishment at Aberdeen—

> *Quod Chebar et Patmos divinis vatibus olim*
> *Huic fuerant sancto claustra Abredaea viro—*

or sat a grave counsellor in the Westminster Assembly of Divines, or bore the many griefs of his private life, his spiritual affections were incandescent and provided the driving force for a mind the extraordinary keenness and erudition of which were revealed when it was brought to bear upon the theological disputations of the day.[1]

Narrowness of sympathy is often the penalty of intensity,

---

[1] " The discussion of Predestination by Samuel Rutherford . . . is justly famed as a masterpiece of profound thought, recondite learning, and metaphysical argumentation, not unworthy of Calvin and Beza themselves."—*The Theology of the Reformed Church in its Fundamental Principles* by William Hastie, D.D.

and it was so with Samuel Rutherford. His controversial methods are not admirable ; but it was an age when men were willing to give their lives for some refinement of dogma or policy and it was thought that words ought to cut like swords. In *Lex Rex, a Dispute for the Just Prerogative of King and People*—a work which had the distinction of being burned by the common hangman—he expressed the best political convictions of his time.[1]

It is not for his controversial writings that he is remembered to-day, but for his letters and, in a less degree, his sermons. The former are a sort of spiritual *Jar of Honey from Mount Hybla*, expressing the ravishing joys of an intense mystical experience and revealing an apostolic eagerness for the welfare of his correspondents. His indulgence in erotic imagery when he is dealing with spiritual relations and affections offends modern minds that are in fundamental sympathy with him ; in spite of their blemishes, however, the letters hold an enduring place in devotional literature.[2]

A pleasant story is told of a visit which Rutherford received from Archbishop Ussher, the prelate who was of so catholic a spirit as to assure the leaders of the Ulster Presbyterians that " it would break his heart if their successful ministry in Ulster were interrupted ". He was travelling from England to his Irish diocese by way of the Galloway coast. Passing near Anwoth on a Saturday afternoon, he resolved to adopt the guise of a poor wayfarer and seek a lodging for the night at the manse. He was kindly received. In the evening Rutherford retired

---

[1] Livingstone says in his *Memorable Characteristics*, " It is reported that when King Charles the First saw it, he said that book would hardly ever get ane answer."

[2] "It is not easy to find any one in Church history with whom to compare this remarkable man (though I have sometimes thought of Bernard of Clairvaux), a man of power, I may say of genius, fresh, bold, penetrating, to whom no subject came amiss, teeming with intellectual energy, distinguished for his learning, but never cumbered by it, the greatest scholastic of our Presbyterian Church, and yet we are told, the plain and faithful teacher, the fiercest of Church leaders and the most devout of saints, equally at home among the tomes of Aquinas, and writing letters to a poor congregation. . . . He is one of our highest names. And it was not only his countrymen that thought thus of him ; he was twice over invited to occupy a chair in the Low Countries."—*The Theology and Theologians of Scotland* by James Walker, D.D.

F

to his study to prepare for the services of the next day, and Mrs. Rutherford, following the custom of the household, gathered the family about her for the purpose of catechizing them on Christian doctrine. The lowly stranger was included in the circle. Mrs. Rutherford questioned him on the number of the Commandments. He answered that there were eleven. Later in the evening Mrs. Rutherford expressed to her husband her regret that their visitor was deplorably backward in religious knowledge, mentioning that he did not even know the number of the Commandments.

On the Sunday morning Rutherford rose early to go to pray in the church. He was surprised to find his guest already there [1] and to hear him praying aloud. From the tenor of the prayer it was plain that the stranger must have a cure of souls. When the suppliant rose from his knees, Rutherford assured him that he believed he was not the obscure traveller that he seemed. Ussher was not unwilling to make his real character known. He agreed to Rutherford's request that he should conduct the service in the church that day and used for once the Presbyterian form of worship. When he announced the text of his sermon, it was " A new commandment I give unto you, that ye love one another." This explained the stranger's heresy. " There ", Rutherford whispered to his wife, " is the eleventh Commandment." The truth of this story has been doubted ; but it has no inherent improbability.

The popular hymn beginning, "The sands of time are sinking ", consists of a selection of verses from Mrs. Cousin's poem [2] based on the last words and other characteristic sayings of Rutherford. Some of the verses are not found in hymn-books on account of their unsuitability for common worship, but deserve quotation here.

[1] According to another version this meeting took place on a foot-path called Rutherford's Walk. The path ran among trees between the church and the old house known as Bush o' Bield, which Rutherford occupied. The house was removed in 1826.

[2] Anne Ross Cousin, *née* Cundell, was the wife of the Rev. William Cousin, minister of the Free Church, Melrose. " Her most popular hymn, ' The sands of time are sinking ', was first published in *The Christian Treasury* for 1857, and gives its title to the collected edition of her poems published in 1876, as *Immanuel's Land and other Pieces by A. R. C.*"—*A Dictionary of Hymnology* edited by John Julian.

Oft in my sea-beat prison
  My Lord and I held tryst ;
For Anwoth was not Heaven,
  E'en preaching was not Christ.
And aye my murkiest stormcloud
  Was by a rainbow spanned,
Caught from the glory dwelling
  In Immanuel's land.

But that He built a Heaven
  Of His surpassing love,
A little new Jerusalem
  Like to the one above :
" Lord, take me o'er the water,"
  Had been my loud demand ;
" Take me to love's own country,
  Unto Immanuel's land."

But flow'rs need night's cool darkness,
  The moonlight and the dew ;
So Christ from one who loved Him
  His shining oft withdrew :
And then for cause of absence
  My troubled soul I scanned ;
But glory, shadeless, shineth
  In Immanuel's land.

The little birds of Anwoth,
  I used to count them blest ;
Now beside happier altars
  I go to build my nest :
O'er these there broods no silence,
  No graves around them stand ;
For glory, deathless, dwelleth
  In Immanuel's land.

Fair Anwoth by the Solway,
  To me thou still art dear !
E'en from the verge of Heaven
  I drop for thee a tear.
Oh ! if one soul from Anwoth
  Meet me at God's right hand,
My Heaven will be two Heavens
  In Immanuel's land.

The oblong monument near the east end of the church [1] bears the epitaphs of three members of the Gordon family. The first

[1] " There is preserved at Anwoth the bell of the parish church, which is a fine example of a small mediæval bell, probably of late fourteenth-century date. It is 10⅝ inches in diameter, and is

is that of MARIOVNE MVRE, GOODWIFE OF CVLLINDACH, DE-
PAIRTED THIS LIFE ANNO 1612.

> WALKING WITH GOD IN PVRITIE OF LIFE
> IN CHRIST I DIED AND ENDIT AL MY STRYFE,
> FOR IN MY SAVLE CHRIST HEIR DID DWEL BY GRACE.
> NOW DWELIS MY SAVLE IN GLORIE OF HIS FACE.
> THAIRFOIR MY BODIE SAL NOT HEIR REMAINE
> BOT TO FUL GLORIE SVIRLIE RYSE AGAINE.

The second concerns MARGRAT MAKCLELLANE, GOODWIFE OF
ARDWEL, DEPAIRTED THIS LIFE 2 APPRILE 162–, AETATIS
SVA 31.

> DVMBE SENSLES STATVE OF SOME PAINTED STONES
> WHAT MEANES THY BOAST THY CAPTIVE IS BOT CLAY
> THOW GAINES NOTHING BOT SOME FEW LIFLES BONES
> HIR CHOYSEST PAIRT HIR SOVLE TRIVMPHIS FOR AY.
> THEN GAZENG FREINDIS DO NOT HIR DEATH DEPLORE,
> ZOW LOSE A WHILE, SCHE GAINES FOR EWERMORE.

The third relates to CHRISTEN MAKCADDAM, LADY CARDYNES,
DEPAIRTED 16 IVNY 1628 AETATIS SVAE 33.

> ZE GAIZERS ON THIS TROPHEE OF A TOMBE
> SEND OVT ONE GRONE FOR WANT OF HIR WHOIS LYFE
> TWYSE BORNE ON EARTH AND NOW IS IN EARTHIS WOMBE
> LIVED LONG A VIRGINE NOW A SPOTLES WIFE.
> CHVRCH KEEPIS HIR GODLIE LIFE THIS TOMBE HIR CORPS
> AND EARTH HIR FAMOVS NAME.
> WHO THEN DOES LOSE HIR HVSBAND NO SINCE HEAVEN
> HIR SAVLE DOES GAINE.

In the churchyard, near the south-west corner of the church,
is the grave of John Bell, the proprietor of Whiteside in Anwoth,
who suffered many things for the Covenant. He was a hunted
fugitive for several years and had several narrow escapes from
his persecutors. At last in February, 1685, Grierson of Lagg
learned that he was hiding on Kirkconnel Moor with four
other Covenanters and came upon him with a troop of horse.
Promise of quarter was given, the fugitives surrendered, and

inscribed on the shoulder † M (crown) A (crown) R (crown)
I : A."—The *Inventory*. The church was built in 1627; but a
cross-slab unearthed in the churchyard about twenty years ago
and now placed close to the interior of the north wall suggests
that the site is one of considerable antiquity.

were immediately shot. The inscription on the stone runs thus :

OF     WHITESYDE    WHO    WAS    BARBOUROUSLY    SHOT    TO

THIS MONUMENT SHALL TELL POSTERITY
THAT BLESSED BELL OF WHITESYDE HERE DOTH LY.
WHO AT COMMAND OF BLOODY LAG WAS SHOT,
A MURTHER STRANGE WHICH SHOULD NOT BE FORGOT.
DOUGLAS OF MORTON DID HIM QUARTERS GIVE,
YET CRUEL LAG WOULD NOT LET HIM SURVIVE
THIS MARTYRE SOUGHT SOME TIME TO RECOMEND,
HIS SOUL TO GOD BEFOR HIS DAYES DID END.
THE TYRANT SAID WHAT DEV'L YE'VE PRAY'D ENOUGH
THIS LONG SEVEN YEARE ON MOUNTANS AND IN CLEUGH
SO INSTANTLY CAUS'D HIM WITH OTHER FOUR,
BE SHOT TO DEATH UPON KIRCONNEL MOOR.
SO THUS DID END THE LIVES OF THESE DEARE SANTS
FOR THERE ADHERENCE TO THE COVENANTS.

*(Left margin, reading upward: HERE LYES JOHN BELL. Right margin, reading downward: DEATH IN THE PAROCH. Bottom margin, inverted:)* OF TONGLAND AT THE COMMAND OF GRIER OF LAG ANNO 1685

Anyone who is curious to see by what sort of route people travelled through Galloway in the eighteenth century ought to go from Anwoth to Creetown by the Corse o' Slakes.[1] The road climbs up steeply to high, open moors and follows in parts the line of the old military road constructed about 1760. Before that time the road through Galloway was almost impassable for carriages. The reform is said to be due to the first Marquess of Downshire, who " being on his way from Ireland to London, was overtaken on the Corse of Slakes by a storm, when he and those who were with him, owing to the badness of the road, found it impossible to proceed and had to remain in their carriages during the night. When he reached London, he stated the circumstance to the Government, who sent military parties from various quarters to make a new road. In 1800 the line of this road was changed in many places, and the road itself much improved."

Bishop Pococke, who visited Galloway in 1760, says that after reaching " Ferrytown," that is, Creetown, " we turned to the east and came among disagreeable mountains, travelled over a hill to a vale, and over two more to that pleasant romantic country through which the river Flete runs into the bay, and came to the inn called Gatehouse of Flete."

---

[1] L.Sc. The crossing of the passes.

# CHAPTER IX

## FROM GATEHOUSE-OF-FLEET TO NEWTON STEWART

The road—Ardwall—The wicked Laird of Cardiness—*The Beech Tree's Petition*—Early records of the MacCullochs—Sir Alexander MacCulloch of Myrton—Sir Godfrey MacCulloch—Younger sons—The country of *Guy Mannering*—Dirk Hatteraick's Cave—How to find it—Cassencarie—Antiquities in the parishes of Anwoth and Kirkmabreck.

SOME time ago a distinguished writer entered a plea for " an austere regimen in scenery " as being " healthful and strengthening to the taste ". In such a landscape as will provide this regimen it may be said that there will be no striking stage effects and no garden-like prettiness. Rather will the scenery be of the rugged, spacious order of the upland parts of the south-western counties. In the rocky, ice-worn, treeless heights of Galloway ; in its brown, swelling moorlands drained by deep, narrow, ink-black, unkindly-looking burns ; in its wide, barren glens with tempestuous streams swirling and breaking among their multitudinous granite boulders, may be found a fine tonic prescription for the jaded *connoisseur* in landscape. No more austere kind of scenery, indeed, than that of the Galloway Highlands could well be conceived, unless it be the deserts of Turkestan, or the icefields of the Antarctic.

This grim background gives an especial piquancy to the more gracious scenery of the Stewartry coast-lands—the transition is so sharp. Between New Galloway station and Creetown the railway crosses one of the most desert tracts of moorland in Scotland, and I have seen travellers to whom such scenery is distasteful shudder at the recollection. A little more than half-way along this section of the line is the station for Gatehouse-of-Fleet, a mere alighting-place for passengers. There is no vestige

of a village here, nothing but surrounding miles of moor
and bog and granite crags. It is from this point that the
transition just referred to is made most abruptly, for a swift
descent of about six miles down the valley of the Water of Fleet
brings one into the midst of the pastoral and woodland prettiness
of the Gatehouse neighbourhood.

Even before there was a Road Board, the highway from Gatehouse to Newton Stewart was good, and Sir Herbert Maxwell
could tell of a friend who cycled from London to Monreith
and held that the section of the road from Dumfries onwards
was the best in the whole route. The scenic attractions of the
part between Gatehouse and Newton Stewart are also great.
The wooded heights on the right ; on the left, the wide prospects
across Fleet Bay to the Isles of Fleet, and across Wigton Bay
to the coast of The Machars, or, farther still, to The Isle of Man ;
the striking rock scenery at Ravenshall ; the cave of the smuggler,
Dirk Hatteraick, near the foot of the Kirkdale[1] Glen ; here a
closely wooded tract where, through the leafy veil on the
left, one can just detect the shimmering waters of the Solway ;
there another opener stretch presenting one again with a broad
vista ; the ruined castles of Cardiness, Barholm, and Carsluith,
with their old-world stories, in turn engage and divert the mind
and eye.

Within a mile and a half of Gatehouse the road passes the
grounds of the Ardwall estate. The intervening part of the way
is shaded by many great old trees, especially where it skirts
the high knoll crowned by the castle of Cardiness. At this
point one catches a glimpse through the trees around Ardwall
of its pale yellow rough-cast front, its gleaming windows and
steep roof, and with another bend one has reached the lodge
and the beginning of the short avenue.

Perhaps there is no other house in Galloway so delightful
as Ardwall ; certainly there is none more delightfully situated.
Standing among trees on a little plateau from which the ground
slopes away on three sides, it has on the remaining one a dense
tract of woodland screening the house from the road. In his
essay on *The Ideal House*, Stevenson, who has been quoted
already at the beginning of this chapter, has postulated that
" the house must be within hail of either a little river or the

---

[1] Pronounced " Kirdle "; Norse for " valley with the church."
" Glen " is tautologous. Kirkdale was formerly a parish.

sea ". Here you have both ; for the little river of Fleet and the
Skyre Burn[1] are near, and from the garden you could throw a
stone over the wall into the salt water of Fleet Bay. Another
amenity of Ardwall is the unusual proximity of sea and woodland.
Immense trees grow right down to the top of the beach, and
at a high tide their branches almost overhang the waves. The
pungent odours of the sea contend with the delicate scents
of the forest, and the cooing of wood-pigeons is interrupted
by sea-birds' cries.

The house was built of whinstone quarried from the beach.
The walls are rough-cast, and the windows and corners faced with
freestone. The old part, dating from the Georgian period,
is flanked by modern wings, adding dignity and grace to the
original structure. Ascending a long flight of whinstone steps
leading above the level of the basement, one looks into the
hall, and is confronted by two narrow, graceful archways, with
a stair rising to the upper storeys from that on the left, and a
second stair leading down to the basement from the other.
An old-fashioned feature of the former stair is that, where it
takes a bend half-way up, the separate under sides of the steps
become visible through the right arch. A very old clock is
enclosed in the column between the archways, with its dial
between the capital and the cornice of the hall.

The front windows command a view of a great park where
stalwart trees stand at intervals. Through a break in the foliage
may be seen at a little distance the severe outline of the tall ruin
of Cardiness Castle, softened usually, and made mysterious-
looking, by the haze from the sea. Out of the south window
one looks across a greensward to such towering masses of foliage
as shut out the whole landscape in that direction. But, as
Stevenson said, " a great prospect is desirable ", and among
its many attractions Ardwall has this. By ascending to the
attic storey one rises above the level of the surrounding
tree-tops, and can look down the Bay of Fleet, and past the
Isles of Fleet and the irregular coast of the parish of Borgue,
into the wide, dim distances of the shining Solway. The isles
may be reached by riding over the sands when the tide is out.
Ardwall Isle has some excavations—Norse graves originally,

[1] Burn of the cliff. " A Skyreburn warning " is a proverbial
phrase occasioned by the suddenness with which the burn comes
down in flood.

it is believed, but used later by smugglers for concealing contra-band.

The story of how Cardiness came into the hands of the Mac-

*Cardiness Castle.*

Cullochs is related thus in *The Hereditary Sheriffs* : " A Border ruffian, having built up his house by violence and rapine, took to himself a wife to perpetuate his name. His spouse presented him with nine daughters in succession, each new comer more unwelcome than the last. After a long pause his wife was again as ladies like to be who love their lords. Just before her lying-in, he burst into her bower and brutally declared that, unless she produced a son, he would drown her and her whole progeny in the Black Loch. So capable was he thought of acting on his threat that great was the joy of the whole countryside, as of the old rascal himself, when a boy was actually born. It was midwinter, and the laird, in jovial mood, ordered a feast to be prepared on the frozen surface of the loch. The neighbours were bidden, and on a bright Sunday they and his house-hold assembled on the ice, the lady and her precious babe being carried thither. The glass went merrily round, fun was at its highest, when suddenly the ice collapsed; wife, son, and the whole bevy of daughters save one, who was ill and had been left at home, sank fathom deep in the dark waters, the devil claiming the wicked laird as his own.

"The little heiress, on growing to womanhood, gave her hand to a MacCulloch, carrying to that family the lands and tower, which thenceforth had the name of Cardoness, ' the castle of ill-luck.' "

Until recently there stood in the park a famous tree. Its threatened destruction in 1800 led to the writing of Thomas Campbell's lines, *The Beech Tree's Petition*,[1] often confused, by the way, with Southey's verses beginning, " Oh ! woodman, spare that tree ". " The Poet's Beech " grew in what was then the Ardwall garden. On account of the hurtful effect of the wide-spreading branches the gardener sought permission from Mr. MacCulloch to cut it down, and this was granted. A few days later, however, a party of visitors, including Miss Campbell, sister of the poet, were being taken through the garden, when, on their remarking upon the beauty of the beech tree, Mr. MacCulloch told them that it was about to be removed. They remonstrated upon this drastic measure, and Miss Campbell promptly sent her brother an account of the tree, informing him of its imminent fate, and invoking the aid of his eloquence on its behalf. In response to this appeal Campbell wrote

[1] The Oxford edition of Campbell's works mistakenly indicates that Ardwall is in Dumfriesshire.

### THE BEECH TREE'S PETITION.

Oh ! leave this barren spot to me !
Spare, woodman, spare the Beechen Tree !
Though bush or flow'ret never grow
My dark, unwarming shade below,
Nor summer bud perfume the dew
Of rosy blush, or yellow hue—
Nor fruits of autumn blossom-born,
My green and glassy leaves adorn—
Nor murm'ring tribes from me derive
Th' ambrosial amber of the hive—
Yet leave this barren spot to me ;
Spare, woodman, spare the Beechen Tree.

Thrice twenty summers I have seen
The sky grow bright, the forest green ;
And many a wintry wind have stood
In bloomless, fruitless solitude,
Since childhood, in my rustling bower,
First spent its sweet and sportive hour ;
Since youthful lovers in my shade
Their vows of truth and rapture made—
And on my trunk's surviving frame,
Carv'd many a long-forgotten name.
Oh ! by the sighs of gentle sound
First breathed upon this sacred ground—
By all that love hath whisper'd here,
Or beauty heard with ravished ear,
As love's own altar honour me—
Spare, woodman, spare the Beechen Tree.

It was decided ultimately that the garden, instead of the tree, should be removed, and it has occupied since then a site a little farther to the south.

Copies of Campbell's verses were printed at the time for private circulation, with a note by Mr. MacCulloch narrating the circumstances of their inspiration, and concluding with the following injunction : " Although the tree cannot be so lasting as the fame of him who composed its poetic, pathetic, and beautiful prayer, nevertheless the present owner hereby fervently solicits his successors to let their tenderness and taste be marked by giving a life-rent lease to this magnificent plant ; or to spare this little spot until the ruthless hand of time, which spareth not either *man* or *things*, may terminate the existence of the ' Beechen Tree.' "

Thereafter the tree had never been threatened with the axe,

but it has been laid low at last by " the ruthless hand of time ". Signs of decay had appeared recently—the tree was about a hundred and seventy years old—and the moderate gale of the 12th of November, 1909, was sufficient to blow it down. The trunk was only fourteen feet high, but above it the tree divided into " many large and fairly equal-sized branches bearing a vast crown of smaller branches and twigs ". At the height of four and one-third feet from the ground the girth of the trunk was fourteen feet and six inches. There will be general agreement in the opinion that it is better that it should have been " blown down than remain a decayed trunk, for in view of 'The Petition' it would never have been cut down even when dead, and a dead tree is a melancholy sight ".

Another accident was the cause of the curious shape of an enormous fir-tree standing on one side of the avenue. The top was blown off in 1839. The tree then put forth a great shoot on either hand. The girth of the shoots is little less than that of the trunk itself, and, as they sought and presently achieved the perpendicular direction, the shape of the tree resembles closely that of a chandelier.

The early records of the MacCullochs, who are represented by Lady Ardwall, are, as in the case of all of the very old families, slight and intermittent, but give evidence of a spirited, warlike, and sometimes unscrupulous race. Tradition states what is equally beyond proof and disproof, that they are descended from Ulgric, a Galloway lord, who fell at the Battle of the Standard in 1138. During the War of Independence they are found siding with the English king. In this, of course, they were with the rest of the Galloway families, among whom Bruce was unpopular on account of the murder of the Red Comyn.

Cardiness Castle seems to have been built about 1450 by Gilbert MacCulloch, who was succeeded by James, his son. James was outlawed in 1471, no doubt for sufficient reasons, if his earlier deeds were in keeping with his later record. In 1480, for instance, the Court ordered him, as the result of a suit brought against him by the Vicar of Cally, " to pay six cwt. of bere (barley) of the measure of Galloway for his wrongous occupation of the lands of Marybute and Marytown, and [the finding] to be published because it stood as a redding of the marches "; and again, three years later, Agnes Spot was successful in a lawsuit against him " for the wrongous occupation of the lands of Kirkcok ".

Ninian MacCulloch, the next of kin to James, seems to have been of a similar disposition. After James's death it appeared to him a poor thing that a widow should hold her lawful share of the property, and in consequence of his acts of spoliation and violence he was made to compound to Elizabeth Lennox in 1508 for " reiving from her 1,500 sows, wedders, and younger sheep, for taking rents which were by right due to her, and for breaking in her barn doors ".

Sir Alexander MacCulloch of Myrton, who received the wardship of Cardiness during the minority of Thomas, the son of Ninian, was a more pleasantly distinguished member of the clan. He was a friend of James the Fourth, and in 1505 held the office of Keeper of the Palace at Linlithgow. He was custodian also of the King's falcons, made journeys to Orkney for the purpose of getting hawks for the royal falconry, and received moneys from the Exchequer for the expenses thus incurred. The King visited him at Myrton when on a journey to the shrine of S. Ninian at Whithorn, and, in recognition of the hospitality then received, created Myrton a barony. Sir Alexander, however, appears also in another character than that of the valued official and friend of the king ; for, " having a feud with the Adairs of Garthland, he attacked them and starved them into submission at Dunskey Castle, and later in the same year he fell upon his clansman, MacCulloch of Ardwell (Wigtonshire), and drove him from his own house, which he gutted, plundered, and then burnt." For these doings he obtained, with perhaps little difficulty, the royal pardon. He fell at his sovereign's side at Flodden.

The old line of the MacCullochs ended with Sir Godfrey, who was executed in 1697. The estates had been mismanaged before his day and were heavily encumbered, Cardiness Castle had passed into the hands of the Gordons early in the century, and Sir Godfrey succeeded to " little more than a few doubtful rights ". There was an old feud between the Gordons and the MacCullochs, and it was this that led to his ruin. He went on a certain day in the autumn of 1690 to Bush o' Bield, the residence of William Gordon, to secure the release of some cattle that had been impounded. He sent a servant to the house to ask Gordon to speak with one who had business with him. When Gordon appeared at the door with a gun in his hand, Sir Godfrey fired at him, breaking his thigh-bone and inflicting other wounds, whereof he died in a few hours. When Sir Godfrey learned that the shot had been fatal, he fled abroad, making his home in England. After six years he ventured to return to Scotland, and one Sunday he was in a church in Edinburgh. A man from Galloway recognized him and shouted, " Steik the door ; there's a murderer in the house ! " Sir Godfrey was arrested, tried, and condemned to be beheaded. He was the last criminal to be executed by means of The Maiden, an instrument which may be seen in the Antiquarian Museum in Edinburgh.

An old tradition records a variant version of Sir Godfrey's end. He was cutting a drain through the mote-hill on which the old tower of Myrton stands when a little man in a green coat appeared and informed him that he was interfering with a fairies' dwelling-place. He promised Sir Godfrey that if he would give up his plan, he would meet some day with a great reward ; otherwise, he would be visited with the fairies' displeasure. Sir Godfrey yielded, and the promise was made good on the day appointed for his execution, for the little man in the green coat came riding along on a white horse, lifted Sir Godfrey out of the cart, and bore him off to no man knows where.

Until the time of Mr. Walter MacCulloch, who died unmarried in 1892, Ardwall had passed from father to son for many generations, save in three instances, when it went to a brother. Mr. Walter MacCulloch was succeeded by his niece, the wife of Sheriff Jameson, who, on being raised to the bench in 1905, took the title of Lord Ardwall.

One cannot survey the records of any old family without being struck by the varied destinies of men—especially of younger sons—offshoots of one stock, going forth from one home into multifarious vocations and all the countries of the earth. For instance, of the sons of David MacCulloch, who succeeded in 1696, one was a colonel in the army, and died abroad ; another was a surgeon, and was slain on a ship that was boarded by a Barbary corsair in the Mediterranean ; James was a captain in the mercantile marine ; Robert a merchant in Jamaica ; and John, after living in The Isle of Man, spent his later years in Brittany. The sons of David MacCulloch, whose tenure began in 1740, were Edward, the eldest, who was engaged in the East India Company's Military Service until his father's death ; David and Alexander, who were merchants in Bengal and Jamaica respectively ; Robert, who entered the Navy Pay Office in London, and John, who died in America. Of the sons of James Murray MacCulloch, who became proprietor in 1796, David, the eldest, was a merchant in Bombay ; Walter was a Writer to the Signet ; James died in Jamaica ; Alexander conducted a business in Canton ; and Edward died in Ceylon.

In the seventeenth century the MacCullochs were allied by marriage with two noble families. Marion, a granddaughter of William MacCulloch, to whom Ardwall was granted in 1587, became by her second marriage wife of the fifth Viscount Kenmure ; and in the next generation Agnes, wife of William Maclellan of Borness, was the mother of William, who became sixth Lord Kirkcudbright. More interest attaches at the present day, however, to the association of the family with Sir Walter Scott. Sir Walter's brother, Thomas, a Writer to the Signet, married Elizabeth, daughter of Edward Mac-Culloch mentioned above. Sir Walter relates in the *Tales of a Grandfather* an incident derived, he tells us, from the recollections of Mrs. MacCulloch of Ardwall. Her father was Robert Corsane[1] in Dumfries, a strong supporter of King George's government. When the Jacobite forces came to Dumfries, this lady was a child of six, and she remembered being carried out of her father's house in the arms of a Highland officer— the Jacobites intended to burn the building. The child asked the officer to shew her " the Pretender ". This he agreed to do on condition that in future she should call him " the Prince ".

The coast between Gatehouse and Creetown is the country of *Guy Mannering*. Gatehouse is identified with " Kipple-ringan," Barholm Castle with " Ellangowan ", Cassencary with ' Woodbourne ", and Creetown with " Port-an-Ferry ". I recommend to schoolboys and active persons of greater age a visit to Dirk Hatteraick's Cave. I had tried to find it more than once, but had only wasted much time. I made a firm resolve, therefore, not to seek it again unless I could secure a guide to

---

[1] Scott calls him " the provost of Dumfries, a gentleman of family named Corsan ". Robert Rae, who assumed his mother's name, Corsane, on acquiring a certain property, was a member of the Dumfries Town Council for many years, but was never provost. See " Mr. Peter Rae, V.D.M., Printer," by G. W. Shirley in *The Records of the Glasgow Bibliographical Society*, Vol. I.

take me to its very mouth. The cave is not easy to enter. It
begins with a narrow slit in the rock shaped like an isosceles
triangle, the floor is somewhere about twenty feet below, and
you look down from the opening into deep darkness. A very
steep slope of *débris* fallen from the cliff overhead runs down to

*Barholm Castle.*

the bottom of the descent. For the first yard or so you can
keep yourself erect, but must then stretch yourself on the earth
and slide or wriggle down the chimney until you are able to rise
without knocking your head against the rock. With a few more
downward steps you are standing on the large, loose stones of
the floor.

I turned on my electric lamp and examined the cave from

end to end. I estimate the length at about forty feet. I do not think the breadth is greater than six at any point. The roof is very irregular and varies in height from about seven to twelve feet. I caught the sound of running water, and on going to the inner end found a little stream pouring over the rock from some invisible entrance. It ran down the bottom of the cave and then disappeared about half-way along. I looked afterwards for the continuation of the stream on the beach, but did not find it. Where the stream did not run, the stones were kept wet by the drip from the roof. There is, however, scarcely any drip along the left side, and here there are tiers of large, square pigeon-holes built of stone and lime. Buried in the bowels of the earth and remote from the influences of rain, sun, and wind, they look as fresh as when they were made.

The tiers fall away to two at one point, and the rock-wall recedes into a little shallow cavern where one or two men could lie in comfort if they had provided themselves with some kind of bedding. It is very likely that the recess was used as a sleeping apartment. The cave, however, is not to be recommended as a health resort, and I should not advise any tramp of my acquaintance to seek a lodging here. The place is very damp, and as the air of the upper world reaches its midday warmth, is filled with a dense mist that floats out very slowly by the chimney and does not cease, I suppose, until the evening. When I entered the cave at a quarter-past ten in the forenoon, there was none of this mist; but by one o'clock the light of my lamp would hardly penetrate more than a yard. I do not wonder that Dirk Hatteraick had " a short, dry cough ". My reason for staying so long was that I was taking flashlight photographs. This, of course, did nothing to improve the atmosphere. I do not think I ever felt the charm of light and of fresh air so much as when I emerged from the cave, looked out on the bright Solway, and was met by a breeze from the sea.

Before leaving the cave, however, I must give the reader this from *Galloway Glimpses :* " At the top, and quite close to the rock-ceiling of the cave, it is stated that there is a crevice which admits a man's recumbent body sideways and leads to yet another cave on the western side. Many people who have been in the principal cave and thought they had fully explored it have never seen this high crevice nor had any suspicion that there was another cave entering only from the top of the in-

terior wall of the principal one. In the event of this latter being
besieged and taken, this second cave would prove a useful
refuge, not likely to be easily discovered." It will be observed
that the writer had not seen it, and I never heard of anyone who
had. One would need to take a ladder with one in order to
settle the question.

I have said that it is not easy to enter the cave. It is less
easy to leave it. Looking up out of the dark to the little patch
of daylight at the entrance, you might quote the lines from
*Titus Andronicus* which Scott placed at the head of a chapter
in *Guy Mannering*:

> Why dost not comfort me, and help me out
> From this unhallow'd and blood-stained hole?

When you are working your way through the narrowest part,
you must search with your feet for little crevices in the rock-face
in order to give yourself a thrust upwards. It is necessary
to take care that the dampness of the rock does not cause
your foot to slip at the critical moment, for if it does,
you will slide down ignominiously into the cave and, like
Sisyphus, have to begin all over again.

This cave does not correspond with the one in *Guy Mannering*
in any particular. It is visible from the foot of the cliffs; the
other was concealed " behind a large, black rock ". It is
high above sea-level; in the case of the other, " the aperture
to the sea was filled with water when the tide was in ". You
slip into this cave feet foremost; that cave was entered " in
a creeping posture ". The bottom of this cave consists of large
stones lying at all angles; the bottom of the other is " covered
with the purest sand " in Chapter xxxiv. and consists of " un-
even rocks " in Chapter liv. If Scott had seen this cave, he
certainly did not attempt to describe it. His descriptions of the
scenery, on the other hand, apply to the Ravenshall coast.

I shall now give infallible instructions for finding Dirk Hatteraick's Cave. Coming from Gatehouse-of-Fleet, you arrive
at the bridge over the Kirkdale[1] Glen after a little more than six
miles. (1) Leave the right-hand side of the road at the east end

---

[1] Patrick Hannay, the poet and soldier, who died in 1629 (?),
" was probably the third son of Alexander Hannay of Kirkdale "—
*Dictionary of National Biography*. A collective edition of his poems
was published in 1622. The title-page reads thus : " *The Nightingale.
Sheretine and Mariana. A happy Husband. Eligies on the death*

of the bridge, descend the bank, and pass under the east arch.
Follow a path leading down the glen to the sea. The path
crosses the burn once by a wooden foot-bridge so that (2) when
you come to the beach, you are on the west side of the burn.
Cross the burn by one of the innumerable series of natural
stepping-stones, and continue eastwards along the beach for a
short distance, say, one or two hundred yards. (3) Turn your
back to the sea, survey the coast, and note two details—the
one, a cottage on the left beyond the Kirkdale Burn ; the other,
the extreme point of the beach within view on the right. About
half-way between the cottage and the extreme point, some
rocks stand up from the beach near the foot of the cliff.
Immediately beyond these rocks the cliff recedes into a gully,
with two or three trees at the bottom. The entrance to the
cave is more than halfway up the gully.

Cassencary, the reputed original of " Woodbourne ", is a
charming old house near the pleasant village of Creetown. It
was the great collection of books here which aroused the enthusiasm of Dominie Sampson. There is a different library in
the house now, but it also is " prodigious " both in size and in
the range of its contents. Cassencary was the home of Mrs.
Caird, whose name was well known to readers of novels and the
monthly reviews in the early years of this century.

A little-known road coming down the Moneypool Burn from
Gatehouse Station to Creetown was not overlooked by Miss
Dorothy L. Sayers, who made an exact use of these highways
and byways in *The Five Red Herrings*.

In the parishes of Anwoth and Kirkmabreck[1] there are numerous objects of antiquarian interest—rock sculptures at Lower

*of Queen Anne. Songs and Sonnets* by Patrick Hañāy gent. Per
Ardua ad Alta London printed for Nathaniel Butter. 1622." and has
an elaborate border with two bars of music in the upper part and
the author's portrait below. The book is very scarce, and it is
said by a writer in *The Statistical Account* that about 1835 a copy
was sold in London for £42 10s. 6d. A reprint was issued in 1875
by the Hunterian Society. There is prefixed to *Songs and Sonnets*
an epistle dedicatory addressed to a soldier under whom Hannay
had served on the Continent, " Sir Andrew Gray, Knight, Colonell
of a foot regiment and General of the Artillerie to . . . Prince
Fredericke King of Bohemia." See Saintsbury's *Minor Poets of
the Caroline Period.*

[1] No clue to the dedication; may commemorate Brioc or Brieuc.

Laggan[1] cottage, Trusty's Hill[2], High Auchenlarie[3], Cardiness House, Mossyard, and Cairnharrow[4]; cairns at Cauldside, High Auchenlarie, Cairnholy, Larg[5] Moor, and Bagbie; stone circles at High Auchenlarie, Glenquicken, and Claughreid; standing-stones at Newtown and Bagbie; cross-slabs at Cardiness House and Kirkclaugh; motes at Polchree, Boreland, and Kirkclaugh; and a vitrified fort on Trusty's Hill.

[1] Gaelic *lagan*, a hollow.
[2] " Drust's hill " ; there was a Pictish King Drust in the sixth century. *Cp*. Bardrestan (Urr), Bardristan (Kirkmabreck), Bartrostan (Penninghame), and Trostan (Carsphairn, Dalry, Monigaff, and New Abbey).
[3] Gaelic *achadh na làira*, the field of the threshing-floor.
[4] Gaelic *carn gharbh* (where the first *h* eclipses the *g*), rough cairn.—Johnston.
[5] Gaelic *learg*, the side or slope of a hill.

*Dirk Hatteraick's Cave*

*The Road near the Murray Monument.*

# CHAPTER X

### NEWTON STEWART TO THE DUNGEON

The Cree at Newton Stewart—The founding of the town—Monigaff
—Carved stones at the old church—Roads near Newton Stewart
—The Cree Valley—A loch that is "nonsense"—A bridge
where there is no road—Glentrool—Robert the Bruce—Battle
with the English—King Robert and the beggar woman—Another battle—The martyrs' grave at Caldons—The Gairland
Burn—Moraines—Loch Valley—The Jarkness Rig—The Murder
Hole—Loch Enoch—Scythe sand—The " clints " of Craignairny—Sheep in peril—Wild goats—Bruce monument.

THE river Cree[1] is the boundary between The Stewartry
and The Shire. It is shallow at Newton Stewart and has a
shingly bed, and so could be forded easily unless in time of
flood. The convenience of the crossing accounts in part for the
rise of the town. A ford gave a place the same kind of importance
that a bridge does, and it is not surprising to learn that the
first building in Newton Stewart was the Ford-house.

I think this must be the place to which Defoe refers in the
following passage : " Proceeding from *Lower Galloway* hither,"
that is, from The Stewartry to Whithorn, " we had like to have
been driven down the Stream of a River, though a Countryman

---

[1] Erse *crich*, Gaelic *crioch*, a boundary.

went before for our Guide ; for the Water swelled upon us as we
passed, and the Stream was very strong, so that we were obliged
to turn our Horses Heads to the Current, and sloping over, edged

*Newton Stewart from near the Railway Station.*

near the Shore by degrees ; whereas, if our Horses had stood
directly cross the Stream, they could not have kept their
Feet."

The ford and ferry-boat were replaced by a bridge in 1745.

It lasted until 1810, when it was ruined by a flood. The present bridge, made of granite from the Monigaff[1] moors, was begun in 1813. The only other architectural detail of Newton Stewart that does not look quite modern, apart from a few cottages, is the town hall with its odd, cupola-roofed tower.

The beginning of the town was made by William Stewart, third son of the second Earl of Galloway and proprietor of the Castle Stewart estate. He built a few houses as the nucleus of a village and called the place Newton Stewart. The charter making it a burgh of barony is dated the 1st of July, 1677. Later, the estate was purchased by William Douglas,[2] a manufacturer, who erected cotton and other mills at the cost of £20,000, and changed the name of his new centre of industry to Newton Douglas. The mills, however, failed, and the name failed with them.

The town is faced by the villages of Creebridge and Monigaff on the left bank of the river. The great mass of Cairnsmore rises behind them to the height of over two thousand three hundred feet. The railway station is the best point for a general view. The screen of hills rising behind the town in the depths is very grand. Bishop Pococke thought it " much like the face of Switzerland ".

The church and village of Monigaff are very old. MacKerlie states that " Moniegov appears to have been a free parsonage early in the thirteenth century ". Symson says, the parish " hath in it a litle town, or burgh of baronrie, depending on the Laird of Larg, situate upon the Eastside of the river of Cree, neer the brink thereof. It hath a very considerable Market every Saturday, frequented by the Moormen of Carrick, Monygaffe, and other moor places, who buy there great quantities of meal and malt, brought thither out of the parishes of Whitherne, Glaston, Sorbie, Mochram, Kirkinner, &c." There stands within the walls of the old church an ancient, elaborately carved stone with a Celtic cross surmounted by a bird and two panels of Celtic ornament below. It has been supposed that the bird represents the chough, the favourite bird of S. Columba. Two other sides of the stone bear faint traces of a design. The block had long served as a lintel in the Old Market House of

[1] The prefix is obviously *monadh* [money], a moor, which agrees with the prevailing character of this vast parish.—Maxwell.

[2] See page 495.

Monigaff, and was discovered when that house was taken down.
"Two Ancient Carved Stones" is the title of an article by Dr.
Norman MacKie in the ninth number of *The Gallovidian*. One
of them is in the churchyard—the MacClurg stone, and the
other in a wall of the old church—the memorial erected by

*The MacClurg Stone in Monigaff Churchyard.*

Patrick MacKie of Cumloden in honour of Uchtred MacDowall,
who was a brother or other near relative of his wife. The
MacClurg stone is connected with the story of the three youths
of Craigencaillie who assisted King Robert the Bruce at the
battle of Moss Raploch.[1] In course of time the representatives
of the three young men appear to have adopted two ravens as

[1] See page 471.

their coat of arms. Here we see " a shield on which are two
ravens hanging pale-ways with an arrow through their necks
fess-ways, in base a crescent ; the helm and mantling are such
as appear above and around the shield of a gentleman ; the
crest is a raven transfixed by an arrow, with the motto OMNIA

*Carved Stones in Monigaff Old Church.*

PRO BONO. The reason why the birds look towards the left
of the shield instead of the right, as is usual in heraldry, and also
why the N's are turned the wrong way, is that the sculptor
probably got a seal to copy and carried out his task by carving
directly from the seal instead of first taking an impression.
The arms are those of MacClurg ", and the inscription relates
to members of the MacClurg family. The other stone is about

four hundred years old. "The shield has on it the arms of McDowall impaled with those of Gordon; the supporters are the lions of McDowall. The arms of McDowall are a crowned silver lion rampant on an azure shield, and were the armorial bearings of the line of the ancient Lords of Galloway, from whom the McDowalls claim descent. The boars' heads of Gordon are familiar to all." The inscription is 𝕳𝖎𝖈 𝕵𝖆𝖈𝖊𝖙 𝕻𝖆𝖙𝖗𝖎𝖈𝖎𝖚𝖘 𝕸'𝕽𝖊 𝖉𝖊 𝕮𝖆𝖑𝖔𝖉𝖆 𝖒𝖊 𝕱𝖎𝖊𝖗𝖎 𝕱𝖊𝖈𝖎𝖙.

Having more urgent matters in view, I must briefly recommend a ramble to Garlies Castle on the north side of Cumloden[1] deer-forest, a walk through Bargaly[2] Glen to Talnotry,[3] and still more the road that runs to New Galloway, passing Murray's Monument.[4] Queen Mary and her suite took this road with eighteen saddle horses and six baggage mules on the 13th. of August, 1563, after her visit to the shrine of S. Ninian and on her way, as her French equerry records, *soupper et coucher a Quinemur chez Mons de Locquenar*—that is, at Kenmure, the residence of Sir John Gordon of Lochinvar. She crossed the Penkill[5] at Monigaff by what is known as Queen Mary's Bridge and forded the Black Water of Dee at Clatteringshaws.

For the beginning of one of the greatest journeys in Galloway you have nine miles of gradual ascent up the beautiful valley

[1] Gaelic *cam lodan*, curving pool.       [2] Pronounced "Bargawly," Aulay's dwelling.

[3] An interesting discovery was made at Talnotry in 1912. "The wife of a cottar occupying a solitary house noticed a metal object drop out of a peat which she was putting on the fire, which led to an examination of the other peats, and finally of the place from which they had been dug." A number of objects found "seem to have been lying on the glacial clay at the bottom of the peat deposit. The hoard, as recovered, consisted of a pair of silver pins with flat circular heads pierced at one side for a chain to be worn between them, a pair of oval loops of silver wire ending in hooks, a plain finger-ring of gold, a globular head of a pin of bronze ornamented with filagreework, a belt tag of silver with a panel of niellowork representing a nondescript animal, a leaden weight with a brass top beautifully ornamented with interlaced work, a broken cross of thin bronze, three spindle-whorls of stone, a circular piece of jet, an agate in its rough natural state, and a part of a cake of some substance like beeswax. Besides these there were a number of coins of Burgred, King of Mercia (833–874), Northumbrian styeas, one French coin of about the period of Charlemagne, and one Cufic coin."—*The Glasgow Herald*. "Talnotry" or "Dunnottrie" is Uthred's dwelling.

[4] Murray was a shepherd's son who entered the ministry and became Professor of Oriental Languages in Edinburgh University in 1812.

[5] Originally *poll cill*, the church burn.

of the Cree. The aromatic woods, the game-coverts, the phalanxes of tall trees marshalled along the roadside, the

*Queen Mary's Bridge.*

glimpses of the rapid passages and still stretches of the river, the waterside meadows, the green wall of wooded hills on the

farther side with the white cascade of Cardorcan[1] flashing
down it—in an east wind you can hear the roar of the water—
and the distant mountains that overhang Glentroől and Loch
Dee make this one of the most delightful valleys in Scotland.

A broad part of the river immediately beyond Penninghame
House is called Loch Cree. Everyone will agree with Lord
Cockburn's comment that " Loch Cree, which I have so often
heard complimented, is, as a loch, nonsense. It is no loch. A
loch one hundred yards across ! It is a widening of the River
Cree ; the river being only so much the worse of the widening " ;

*Murray Monument.*

but Lord Cockburn was unaware very likely of the statement
in *The Statistical Account* of 1838 that " the loch was much larger
before the cutting of a rock and deepening of the channel of the
river at the bottom of it about forty years ago. That cutting
gained a quantity of excellent meadow on each side of the water ",
or that Andrew Heron of Bargaly had written of " the Islands
in that Lake ".

Spanning the Water of Minnoch, a tributary of the Cree,
near Bargrennan,[2] is an old structure called popularly The
Roman Bridge, but really of much more recent date than the

---

[1] Pont shews " Garrowdorken " on " Pooldorken Burn." His spell-
ing indicates *ceathramh* [carrow], quarter land, as prefix.—Maxwell.

[2] *Barr grianain*, hill house, hill of the mansion.—Maxwell.

Roman occupation of Britain. According to the *Inventory*
"the type of masonry is not inconsistent with a date in the
seventeenth or even the eighteenth century." In any case,
it is a long time since the bridge fell out of common use. The
nearest public road is somewhere about two miles away, and

*Old Bridge on the Minnoch.*

this old bridge in the heart of a great moor, with no road
running up to it, gives a curious sense of incongruity, as if one
found a windmill in Trafalgar Square. There are still, however,
faint signs of the ancient track that wound across the moor—a
favourite route with the smugglers of the eighteenth century as

they carried their goods on pack-horses from the south-western landing-places towards the centre of Scotland and Edinburgh.

At Bargrennan there is scarcely anything but the church,

*Lower part of Loch Trool.*

manse, school, and post-office. About two hundred yards farther on is the House of the Hill Inn, so called, I suppose, from the fact that an earlier building stood on the top of the hill that rises on the other side of the burn. In another mile or so one turns to the right and begins the approach to Glentrool.

This is the most interesting way to The Dungeon of Buchan. Visitors come to the beautiful shores of Loch Trool[1] thinking that they have done well to travel so far into the wilds and never dreaming of ascending into the mysterious hill-country on the north. Glentrool, indeed, is worth seeing for its own sake. It is narrow, and steep hills rise to great heights on both sides—huge green slopes, broken on the upper levels by precipitous rocks—and along the greater part of the shore of the loch are pine woods. As you approach by the road that winds over the moor from Bargrennan, you enter the shade of the trees and catch glimpses through their tops of the massive Mulldonach[2] and Lamachan mountains on the right, and the colossal Fell of Eschoncan[3] on the left. Presently the road descends nearer to the level of the loch, the impression of grandeur that the surrounding heights make is increased, and there grows upon you the sense of being shut within a mountain prison-house. You are beginning to wonder where the loch can be when your eye is caught by its waters shimmering through the pine woods that stand between you and it. About half-way up the loch, concealed in the depth of the trees that cover the steep lower slope of the Eschoncan Fell, is a shooting lodge[4] belonging to the Earl of Galloway, and, skirting the wooded enclosure, the road here climbs the hill and then twists abruptly downwards to a bridge over the Buchan Burn, which, just before reaching this point, has made a sudden descent in a fine series of waterfalls.

---

[1] " Strool Bay. ' Kirkcolm '. *Sruthair* [sruhar], a stream. The change of final *r* to *l* is rule-right ; so is the insertion of *t* after initial *s*. The word is further disguised when, as sometimes happens, the initial *s* is dropped " as in Trool.—Maxwell.

[2] Duncan's hill.

[3] Pronounced " Skyoncan ". Pont spells it " Eshsheskewachan ". The prefix is *eas*, a waterfall.

[4] The following occurs in the seventeenth-century *Description of the Paroch of Minigaff* by Andrew Heron : " The house is surrounded with pretty groves of Scots Pines black cherries, and other kinds of planting, which make a fine umbello to the house and from the front a walk down to the lake which enters upon a little mole prettily planted in devices with seats and a beautifull litle boat lodg'd ther under a shade for taking pleasure in a fine day upon the water."

If Robert the Bruce cared for fine scenery, he could hardly have found a more delectable retreat than Glentrool.

*Head of Glentrool.*

Here he spent many days hunting deer and wondering what schemes his enemies might be devising against him.

> In Glentruell a quhile he lay,
> And went weill oft to hunt and play,
> For to purchase thame venysoun,
> For than the deir war in sesoun.[1]

News of his place of refuge was brought to the Earl of Pembroke, who was then at Carlisle, and a little army was sent off and led towards Glentrool by way of the Cree Valley.

*The Buchan Falls.*

The King, learning of the advance of the English, sent some of his followers to the summit of the precipitous Mulldonach with orders to collect as many as possible of the loose granite blocks that lay about, and arrange them along the edge that they might hurl them down upon the invaders as they sought to pass. The rest of the King's men were placed in a strong position at the head of the loch, while the King himself selected a point on the side opposite to Mulldonach whence he could command the scene.

The men worked hard amid the darkness of the night, and when the morning sunshine touched the summit of the hill, the King was delighted to see the great gleaming boulders extending, like a ruined wall, along the sky-line. His men

[1] *The Bruce* by John Barbour, Book VII.

also were there, waiting for the moment when his bugle should give the signal for action.

The invaders left their horses at the farm of Borgan,[1] near the meeting of the Cree and Minnoch waters, and advanced over the moor towards the glen. When they came abreast of the loch and proceeded along the slopes on the south side, they could no longer maintain military formation, and it was a thin, straggling band that crept along the foot of Mulldonach. At varying heights there lay a path which was so narrow that men could follow it in single file only. About half-way along the hillside it passed over a steep projection called The Steps of Trool,[2] where there is a sheer fall of about twenty feet to the water. Above this point the hill is almost perpendicular, and here the King intended that disaster should befall the English.

The quiet of the glen was broken suddenly by three blasts from the King's bugle. The echoes were still flying from hill to hill, when down the side of Mulldonach the boulders began to pour, rolling and bounding from one point to another, until they shot into and through the English force, crushing some and carrying others into deep water. Those who had so far escaped looked upwards, and were dismayed to see a second discharge descending swiftly towards them. Only those who were in the rear of the column could escape this demoralizing kind of assault, and they promptly took to flight as Bruce's men came down the hill prepared to complete their work with bow and arrow.

A bit of meadow at the head of the loch bears the name of The Soldiers' Holm, because there, it is said, the slaughtered English were buried.

On another occasion, according to a tradition preserved by Barbour, an English force, led by the Earl of Pembroke, contrived to approach with greater secrecy. Riding by night, and lying under cover by day, they arrived unobserved within a mile of where Bruce was. A woman, dressed as a beggar, was sent to ask charity from the King that she might bring information about the position of his followers. When she came before him, however, her bearing aroused his suspicions. He bade his men seize her, and she, being in fear for her life, con-

---

[1] Diminutive of *borg*, a shelter place. See Borgue.
[2] It was swept away by a waterspout in the last century.

fessed that the English had sent her as a spy, and that Sir
Aymer and Lord Clifford and " the flour of Northumbirland "
were close at hand. The King assembled his three hundred
men at once and set them in battle array. Scarcely had he

*Glentrool.*

done so when the enemy were seen approaching swiftly on
foot, carrying spears, since in that wooded and marshy country
cavalry could operate with little effect. The Scottish King
was foremost in the attack, and led his men with such vigour
and skill that the English were discomfited, although they
numbered about fifteen hundred men. The leaders of the

defeated army fell to quarrelling among themselves over the
causes of their failure, says Barbour—

> Bot Schir Amer, that wes wis,
> Departit thame with mekill pane,
> And went till Ingland hame agane.

A martyrs' monument stands among the trees on the south-
west of the loch, where some Covenanters were surprised at
worship on a Sunday morning in January, 1685. Andrew
Heron says that "that morning Captain Orchar had that expression, that being so angry with the badness of the way, he wished
the devil might make his ribs a broiling iron to his soul if he
should not be revenged on the Whiggs that day, which was the
Sabbath morning he entred the Glen of Troul, and according
to his wish, came upon these poor people, as they were worshiping
God upon his day with a surprizing crueltie". Six men were
killed, and a stone, said to be the first erected by "Old Mortality" in honour of the Covenanters, commemorates their
martyrdom. The inscription covers both sides.

|                                  |                                  |
| -------------------------------- | -------------------------------- |
| HERE LYES                        | CORNET                           |
| IAMES AND ROBERT                 | IAMES DOUGLAS AND                |
| DUNS, THOMAS AND                 | BY THEM MOST IMPIOUS             |
| IOHN STEVENSONS,                 | LY AND CRUELLY                   |
| IAMES MCCLIVE,                   | MURTHERED FOR THEIR              |
| ANDREU MCCALL, WHO               | ADHERENCE TO SCOT                |
| WERE SURPRISED                   | LANDS REFORMATION                |
| AT PRAYER, IN THIS               | COVENANTS NATIONAL               |
| HOUSE, BY COLNELL                | AND SOLEMN LEAGUE                |
| DOUGLAS, LIEVTNANT               | 1 6 8 5                          |
| LIVINGSTON, AND                  |                                  |

One of the persecuted had a remarkable escape. He fled
and was followed by two of the dragoons. Turning towards the
loch, he was hidden from them by a little hill. He slipped into
the water where the shore was steep and stood there with his
head concealed by a clump of heath. His pursuers gave up the
search, crying that the devil had taken him.

A curious story is told of Captain Urquhart or Orchar. He
had dreamed that he would meet his death at a place bearing
a certain name. Coming past the end of the loch on the search
for the Covenanters, he asked by what name the place was known.
Being told "Caldons", he cried out a great oath, drew up his
horse, doubtful whether to advance or to retreat, and at that
moment of hesitation was shot dead from a cottage window.

I have received another version which has not, so far as I am aware, been published hitherto. It introduces Peden, the

*Glenhead of Trool.*

Prophet. Urquhart had been concerned in the arrest of Peden, who told him that he would die among the Chaldaeans. Urquhart had laughed, saying that the Chaldaeans were people in the Bible and that he was never likely to be among them. As

*The Gairland Glen.*

he lay on the ground after the fatal shot was fired, he demanded the name of the place. Hearing it, he muttered, "The prophecy!" and died.

I had difficulty in finding the Covenanters' grave, and shall, therefore, try to give clear directions. Going up Glentrool, you come to a road branching to the right about a quarter of a mile before you are abreast of the foot of the loch. It leads to the farmhouse of Caldons[1]; but you must not follow it so far as that. So soon as you have crossed the Water of Trool by the wooden bridge, begin to go warily, looking for a footpath running from the road into the wood on your right hand. It begins at not more than one hundred and twenty-five paces from the bridge. As you go along it, the silver birches and the oaks and the play of sunlight and shadow among them will make you glad that you came on this errand. In a few minutes you come to a ditch interrupting the path, and if from this point you look through the trees on your left hand, you will see the low, square wall enclosing the monument. A concrete

[1] O. Erse *colldean*, plural of *collde*, an adjective glossing *colurnus* hazelly.—Watson. The English plural added.

path replacing the old stepping-stones will help you over the
boggy ground.

Unless you made this digression, you would miss seeing the
beautiful Water of Trool where it leaves the loch.  There is
more to be said, however, about a burn which comes down to
Loch Trool at the upper end, surging and tumbling down its
narrow bed of boulders in a continuous riot of white from somewhere in cloudland, you would think.  It really has its origin
in an earthly sheet of water, Loch Valley, and its name is The
Gairland Burn.

A tenant of Glentrool Lodge once made a barrier with a
sluice across the outlet so that the burn might be put into good
fishing condition whenever he wished to do so.  Heavy rains

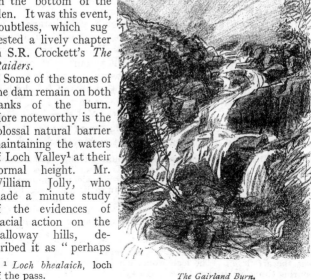

fell, the waters of Loch
Valley rose, broke the
barrier, and came roar-
ing down to Loch Trool.
A huge boulder trans-
ported by the flood lies
on the bottom of the
glen. It was this event,
doubtless, which sug
gested a lively chapter
in S.R. Crockett's *The
Raiders.*

Some of the stones of
the dam remain on both
banks of the burn.
More noteworthy is the
colossal natural barrier
maintaining the waters
of Loch Valley[1] at their
normal height.  Mr.
William Jolly, who
made a minute study
of the evidences of
glacial action on the
Galloway hills, de-
scribed it as " perhaps

[1] *Loch bhealaich,* loch
of the pass.

*The Gairland Burn.*

the grandest geological sight in the district ".  " I know of no more striking example ", he says, " of a lake whose waters are dammed back by moraine *débris* than this—none in which the dam has that assertive, artificial look so demonstrative of deposited glacial remains.  Seen from the west, the view of the mounds is very remarkable, rising in a beautiful series from a considerable distance down the glen up to the water's edge." [1] At the south-west corner of the loch there is an extensive deposit of immense granite blocks carried by the glacier from the Loch Enoch plateau and resting upon one another at every possible angle.  To traverse them is both tedious and adventurous. The foxes and otters of the district have their headquarters here.

On every side the loch is surrounded by rough, heathery slopes.  Only the cries of grouse and whaups are heard.  A few easily-scared sheep feed where they can.  You may pass this way ninety-nine times and never see a fellow-creature.  If on the hundredth occasion you see one, it will likely be the shepherd from The Buchan.  It is as wild a scene as could be imagined, short of Loch Enoch.  When Sir John Foster Fraser was travelling through the Persian wilderness, he could not do better than compare it to " a bit of gaunt Galloway ".

If you ascend the Jarkness Rig and go a little distance down the south slope, bearing to the left, you come to the Long and the Round Loch of Glenhead.  At the beginning of the twentieth century you could fish there assured that yours were probably the only artificial flies that the trout would see in a year; but anglers are more numerous now.  Another reason for climbing the Rig is the northward view.  The lower part of Loch Valley is below your feet, the broken waters of the Mid Burn come down from Loch Neldricken [2] into it, above that burn you see the loch itself, and behind it slopes and crags stretching backwards and

---

[1] " Another remarkable moraine is found at the head of Loch Valley, at the watershed between the Trool and the Dee at Cornarroch Strand.  This is deserving of notice, being composed, for the most part, of confused heaps of granite boulders—as huge a barrier accumulation of rocks as we know. . . .  It lies to the east of Loch Narroch."—" On the Evidences of Glacier Action in Galloway " by William Jolly in *The Transactions of the Edinburgh Geological Society* (1867–8).

[2] Loch Eldrig in Penninghame is loch of the *eileirg*, deer trap. Here we seem to have a diminutive, *eileirgín.*—Watson.  The initial *n* is the article *an*.  The loch would get its name from the neighbouring Craig Neldricken.  See page 536.

*The Murder Hole, Loch Neldricken.*

upwards to the heights where Loch Enoch[1] looks up to the
clouds.

[1] The pronunciation is Ennoch.  The most likely derivation is
from the Gaelic *aonach* in the sense of a lonely mountain ground.
Pont gives *Aingoch*.

If you have sufficient energy, you will go farther into the wilds and see, on passing the west end of Loch Neldricken, the natural feature boldly adopted by the author of *The Raiders* as The

*Loch Enoch, the Loch-in-loch, and Mullwharchar.*

Murder Hole. A part of the loch is encircled by equisetum and grass growing thickly in surrounding shallows. Since Mr. Thomson's drawing was made in 1914 the equisetum has extended within the oval and interfered with its symmetry. The hole is gradually filling with mud. Any attempt to use it for the purpose to which S. R. Crockett devoted it would almost certainly be as fatal for the criminal as for the victim. If you try to wade towards it, you begin to sink almost immediately in the muddy bottom, and it is impossible to reach it without a boat or some substitute. Crockett transferred the name from The Murder Hole at Rowantree. A version of the traditional story is given in Chapter XXIX.

In order to reach Loch Enoch a considerable ascent over rough ground must be made. At the end of it, if you keep rather to the right for the sake of the view of The Merrick, you step out upon great sheets of ice-worn granite,[1] and the loch, with its wide-spread waters and silvery islets, promontories and beaches is before you. From the edge of the farther bays the mountain towers up to the height of two thousand, seven hundred and sixty-four feet above the sea ; on the hither side are The Dungeon and the conical Mullwharchar, fields of rocks ; and on the north a long glen falls away under the shadow of Kirriereoch, Tarriefessock and Shalloch on Minnoch.

There is a peculiar pleasure in reaching Loch Enoch, due partly to the strange beauty of the place, partly to the obstacles that have been overcome. It seems as if you had ascended a long way nearer to the stars since you left Glentrool. From the level at which you stand it is a short climb to the summit of The Merrick ; yet that is the highest hill on the mainland of the south of Scotland. From the ridge on the south side of the loch you look up to The Merrick and Benyellary,[2] but down upon almost everything else. Loch Neldricken is far in the depths, Loch Valley lower still, Loch Trool utterly hidden from sight, lying deep on the other side of the Buchan Hill.

One of the refreshing byways of Galloway is the swim to the island containing the little loch. The distance is short, but the

[1] " Everything round this quadrangular rock-basin exhibits incontestably the severest action of ice, as clearly as the first day the glacier evaporated from its surface. Every cape, peninsula, and island is bare rock *in situ*, worn, rounded, and smoothed to the heart's content of the keenest glacier-hunter. . . . The scooping power of the ice is rather strangely shown in a lakelet on the largest island of the loch, quite rock-bound, and visible from the shore."— ' On the Evidences of Glacier Action in Galloway " by William Jolly in *The Transactions of the Edinburgh Geological Society* (1867–8).
[2] Gaelic *beinn iolaire*, hill of the eagles.

channel is deep, and Mr. McBain remarks that "very few adventurers have been on" the island. He walked over on ice. The water is reputed to be extremely cold in this highest of British lochs; but Mr. Andrew McCormick, author of *Galloway: The Spell of its Hills and Glens*, and his elder boy and I found the water quite genial on the 2nd. of August, 1937. The surface of "the loch-in-loch," as it is called, is about sixteen feet above the level of the water that surrounds the island. On stepping down into the "lochan", I found the bottom mossy, but firm, and inferred that one would not need to dig far down to reach the fundamental rock. Another island is separated from this one by a channel a few inches wide, and it was on this island that we landed first. On both, juniper grows freely among the heath.

The extreme hardness of the silver sand of the beaches caused it to be prized formerly above all other for sharpening scythes. There is a character in *The Raiders* who did a business in scythe sand and got his supplies here. I knew a man who used to carry a sack to this loch occasionally although it was a much longer and more difficult journey than to other places where granite sand could be obtained. The practice was to cut a piece of bog-oak four-square, grease it and dip it into the sand. When the surfaces had been hardened under pressure, the scythe was stroked with this implement and took a very fine edge.[1]

The way to The Cauldron of The Dungeon lies along the rocky edge of Craignairny. If you pass here in spring, the hawk that nests in the "clints" below will come swooping towards you, screaming fiercely, veer away, and come at you again and again until you disappear into the great gully opening on the east between The Dungeon and Craignaw. Crockett calls the gully The Wolf's Slock, but this is inaccurate. The name belongs properly to a narrow passage between two rocks at the head of it.

The "clints" or precipices are sources of trouble to the herds, for the sheep go along narrow ledges in quest of pasture and are sometimes unable to turn. Wild goats, the descendants probably of tame ones, pay an occasional call at The Dungeon and are

---

[1] John Mactaggart's *The Scottish Gallovidian Encyclopædia* contains the following article on Loch Skerrow: "A large, wild loch, to the north of Galloway, famous for its scythe sand. This is found on the beach of the lake and is wrought of grey stones, in the lake by the waters; it is sold in shops during the mowing season at about 2*d*. the Scotch pint."

very unwelcome intruders, for the sheep follow their tracks and reach points from which the goat can return, but the sheep cannot. When a sheep is seen to be in peril, three men go to the rescue if so many are available. One drives a crowbar into the ground at the top of the precipice, a second manages a rope passed round the crowbar, and a third takes an end of the rope, climbs to the sheep, and ties the rope round its horns. It is then dragged up to the top. If it is not noticed, it dies or falls off its ledge sooner or later and is killed on the rocks below.

The importance of the ledges is recognized in some cases by individual place-names. In this parish of Monigaff we find, for instance, The Buckdass of Cairnbaber (Norse *bukkr dass*), which means "the he-goat's ledge"; and in the adjacent parish of Kells there is Greendass, "the green ledge". "Dass", Sir Herbert Maxwell wrote in 1930, "is still used in the hill districts of Galloway to express a shelf or ledge on a cliff. 'Yon sheep's clinted on a dass', I have heard said when the animal had fed along a ledge till it could not turn."

This country is the scene of Lord Tweedsmuir's story, "No-Man's-Land" [1] and also in part of his *The Thirty-Nine Steps*.

Arriving in or leaving Glentrool, we shall notice the monument erected in 1929 in honour of King Robert with this inscription : IN LOYAL REMEMBRANCE OF ROBERT THE BRUCE, KING OF SCOTS, WHOSE VICTORY IN THIS GLEN OVER AN ENGLISH FORCE IN MARCH 1307 OPENED THE CAMPAIGN OF INDEPENDENCE WHICH HE BROUGHT TO A DECISIVE CLOSE AT BANNOCKBURN ON 24TH JUNE 1314.

A correspondent referring to the footnote on page 176 kindly told me that he had seen Loch Enoch water pouring into the Pulskaig glen. This was after heavy rains. The loch can be so flooded as to make the glen a spillway.

---

[1] *The Watcher by the Threshold.*

# CHAPTER XI

### THE CAULDRON OF THE DUNGEON

> The Back Hill of The Bush—The Forest of Buchan—King Robert
> escapes from Sir Aymer de Valence and John of Lorn—He is
> pursued by a bloodhound—Five Highlanders are killed—The
> pursuit fails—Three men with a wether—All are killed—The
> Cooran Lane—The Silver Flow—The truth about the Lochs
> of The Dungeon.

IF, when you reach The Dungeon, the shepherd at The Back
Hill of The Bush is able to give you lodging, it is an immense
advantage. One cannot, by any route, visit and return from
The Dungeon in a single day with any satisfaction. One needs
to live beside it, fish the lochs and streams, scramble on the crags
with a camera, watch The Fingers of The Awful Hand[1] creep
across the moor as the evening sun throws the shadows of the hills
eastwards, talk with the shepherd over a peat-fire at night,
and rise in the morning to see the mist floating along the faces
of The Dungeon and Craignaw.

You are here in the heart of the great Cauldron, on an expanse
of moor and bog drained by many streams. Although it is
almost completely encircled by hills, it gives a wonderful sense
of spaciousness. The loneliness is profound, for the house is
distant about six miles from any road-end. When the daughter

---

[1] John Mactaggart has the following article in *The Scottish Gallovidian Encyclopædia :* " MERRICK. Five large hills or mountains
in Galloway. They lay beside one another and gradually rise, the
one a little higher above the other. In the morning and evening the
shadows of these hills on the level moors below seem like the fingers
of an awful hand. Hence the name Merrick which in Gaelic signifies *fingers*." Mr. Johnston supplies the following note : " Merrick.
' Pronged, branching ' hill-range, from *meur*, a finger, also a branch,
a prong ; *meurach*, ' branched, pronged '."

174

of a shepherd who lived here went to New Galloway to visit her
dressmaker, she stated that she had not seen another woman
for eight months.

Were this
Man's only dwelling, sole appointed seat,
First, last, and single, in the breathing world,
It could not be more quiet.

If you wander about casting into the burns, you have a feeling
of constraint that prevents you from becoming absorbed in
your sport. You are here on a precarious sufferance. Something
in the wilderness is uneasy and resentful at your presence.
It is patient, but has the latent possibility of capricious out-
breaks, and you cannot tell when or how it may strike. Tramping
over the moors, you have now and then the sensation of being
watched by an alien intelligence, and you turn round as if to face
an indefinable threat. Heaven help the man who is taken by
a sudden rush ! You are glad to hear the croak of the raven that
tells you that you are not quite alone. This is the effect of the
place in fine weather. On a sunless day, when the clouds are
low, you feel like a lost soul committed to some chill reach of
Eternity. The insignificance of Time weighs on you. The
Ordovician Period, that saw those granite mountains rend the
Earth's crust while as yet water covered almost the whole of
the lands that men call England and Ireland to-day, might have
been last century. The final dwindling of the latest glacier
might have taken place a week ago. On returning to the cottage
at nightfall, it is as if one were coming back after a tour through
Geological Time to the Kainozoic Period.

A small enclosure provides grazing-ground for a pony, an
important animal at this outpost of the human race. When
the peats have been cut and dried, the pony drags them on a
sledge to the cottage. When the shepherd is bringing a store
of provisions from Dalry, he carries them on his back to the top
of Millfire, lays his burden down, descends for the pony and
sledge, and leads them up to the nick. Many years ago a
shepherd's wife died here in mid-winter. A snowstorm came
on as the funeral party were crossing Millfire, and the body had
to be left on the summit for three days.

At one time the country was densely wooded wherever trees
could grow. Remains of the ancient forest are visible among
moss-haggs on the Loch Enoch plateau, sixteen hundred and fifty

feet above the sea. " The Bush " indicates trees. Other names tell us some of the kinds. " Alder Holm " near the cottage is " the river meadow of the alders ". " Beoch " is " a place of birches "; " Caldons " means " hazelly "; " Loch Goosie ", " lake of the pine wood ". The Sauch Burn is " the burn of the willows ". The Pulskaig,[1] which rises in a steep glen between Loch Enoch and the Gala Lane, is " the stream of the haw-thorns ". About the end of the fourteenth century Lord Kennedy delighted to be known as Range of the Forest of Buchan and had many hunting-lodges. One of them, called Hunt Ha', stood at the foot of Craigtarson, facing The Dungeon. Another was at Garrary, a few miles to the south, and yet another at Polmaddy, on the other side of the hills. Polmaddy is " the stream of the dogs ", and it is said that the food for Lord Kennedy's hounds was prepared there. The ancient sporting interest of the country is commemorated also in the name of a conical hill on the north side of Loch Enoch, Mullwharchar, " the hill of the hunting-horn ". So late as the early part of the eighteenth century, according to a description of the parish of Monigaff written by Andrew Heron of Bargaly, there were found in this mountainous district " very large Red-deer ; and about the top thereof that fine bird called the mountain Patridge, or, by the commonalty, the Tarmachan, about the size of a Red Cock, and its flesh much of the same nature ; feeds, as that bird doth, on the seeds of the bullrush, and makes its protection in the chinks and hollow places of thick stones, from the insults of the eagles, which are in plenty, both the large gray and the black, about that mountain ".

" The tradition runs ", says Sir Herbert Maxwell, " that the last red stag was slain on these hills by the minister of Kirkinner towards the close of the eighteenth century. The ptarmigan disappeared, as an aged hill shepherd informed me in my youth, in that notable year of drought 1826, still remembered as ' the year o' the short corn ' ; but the eagles survived for long after that." Recently the eagles have returned. " Last spring [1906], seventy-one years since the last golden eagles were hatched in Minnigaff, a pair of these noble birds sought out the hereditary haunt of their race and built an eyrie. The female laid but one egg (two is the regulation number), sat upon it

---

[1] The Ordnance Survey map shews the Pulskaig as if coming out of Loch Enoch. Loch Enoch has only one effluent, the Eglin Lane

for some weeks, but abandoned it, when the egg was found to be addled."

It was through the thick woods that once covered this treeless waste that King Robert had one of his narrowest escapes from his enemies. Sir Aymer de Valence was advancing from Carrick with twenty-two men-at-arms and eight hundred Highlanders. Bruce was watching his approach from the heights near Loch Enoch and retiring before him and nearly fell into the clutches of another force ascending from Glentrool under John of Lorn. The King had only three hundred men with him and dared not risk a battle on two sides against greatly superior numbers. He divided his men into three bands, that they might escape through the forest by different routes, and that the enemy might be at a loss to know in which direction he himself had gone. John of Lorn, however, had with him a large bloodhound which had belonged to Bruce. When it was brought to the place where Bruce's army had separated, it promptly took up one of the trails, and John of Lorn followed its lead with all his men. The King, descending probably between The Dungeon and Craignaw, saw that the enemy had chosen to follow his company with a numerous force and caused all his men to scatter that the enemy might be baffled in their attempt to single him out. He kept with himself only one attendant, who was a foster-brother.

The bloodhound, however, followed the trail steadily, and John of Lorn sent on five swift-footed Highlanders to effect the capture. They soon overtook the King. Three of them attacked him, while two sought to kill his attendant. The King promptly slew one of his assailants, and, as the other two drew off for a moment, turned to the help of his man and killed one of those who had set upon him. The two Highlanders, recovering from their momentary discouragement, came at the King again, but he despatched them both, while his attendant slew the only one who was left.

There still remained the bloodhound and John of Lorn and the rest of his men, and the King was now so worn out by his exertions that he felt as if he could maintain the flight no farther.

> The King toward the wod is gane,
> Wery, for-swat, and will of wayn.
> In-till the wod soyn enterit he,
> And held doun toward a vale

> Quhar throu the wod a wattir ran.
> Thiddir in gret hy went he than,
> And begauth to rest hym thair,
> And said he mycht no forthirmar.[1]

His man, however, encouraged him to press on a little farther. A stream, which must have been the Cooran Lane, ran through the wood. The fugitives stepped into it and walked down its channel for a time that they might make the bloodhound lose the trail. They then stepped out on the other bank and lay down to rest in a thicket.

Barbour gives two accounts of the final failure of the pursuit. According to the one, the chase was abandoned when the dog reached the stream and could not find the scent. The other says nothing about the wading ruse, but tells that when the King was exhausted, his companion doubled back on the trail and shot the hound as it passed.

> Bot quhethir his eschaping fell
> As I tald first, or now I tell,
> I wat it weill, without lesyng,
> At that burn eschapit the King.

The King and his foster-brother continued their journey, hoping to find some place where they could get food. They met three men carrying a wether. The men were well armed, and this put the King on his guard. When they saluted him, he inquired whither they were going. They replied that they were seeking the King, as they intended to join themselves to his party. He said that if they would come with him, he would lead them to the King. The spokesman of the party seemed to be somewhat confused at this, and the King's suspicion that the strangers were aware of his identity and wished to secure the reward offered for his person was strengthened. He made them walk in front of him and his companion, and so they travelled until they came to a ruined cottage. Here they stopped, and decided to kill the sheep and cook part of it. The King insisted that two fires should be made, one at

---

[1] *The Bruce* by John Barbour, Book VII. On the credibility of Barbour see the " Introduction " to Mr. W. M. Mackenzie's admirable edition of *The Bruce* and the notes, which shew " how trustworthy " Barbour is in the main, " and, repeatedly, how strikingly and minutely accurate ".

either end of the house, and a leg of mutton was given to him
and his man to be broiled on their fire.

When they had eaten their meal, the King was overcome
with drowsiness and desired his foster-brother to watch while
he slept, as he had no confidence in their neighbours; but it
was not long before the other was asleep also. The three
traitors, seeing this, rose, drew their swords, and in so doing
awakened the King, who sprang to his feet to face them, at the
same time awakening his attendant with a kick. Before the
latter could rise he was slain by the foremost of the assailants,
and so, for the second time that day, the King had to meet
three enemies single-handed; but,

> Throu Goddis grace and his manheid,

he slew them one after another. Alone now, he went on to
Craigencaillie, where his men were appointed to reassemble, and
thereafter won his victory over the English forces at Moss
Raploch.[1]

As one looks round upon those desolate hills and moors,
it is strange to think that they were once traversed by hosts
of armed men, and that some of the incidents leading to the
independence of Scotland took place there.[2] The aspect of the
country has been changed greatly through the disappearance
of the forest. There is an austerity in its grandeur to-day.
The Cooran Lane, indeed, is still the same. In spite of the
character indicated by its name there are parts of its course
where the ruse attributed to King Robert could have been
adopted easily. The term "lane" is applied to those smooth,
deep parts of a stream where the motion is so slow as to be
almost imperceptible, and in the course of this water there
are long sections corresponding to this description. Coming
to the edge of the perpendicular bank, you look down into

---

[1] See page 471.
[2] On the 25th of September, 1307, " the King commands Robert
de Clifford, justiciar of the forest *ultra* Trent, to allow the men of
Galloway to feed their flocks and herds in Englewood forest, whither
they have come to take refuge for fear of Robert de Brus and his
accomplices."—Bain's *Calendar of Documents Relating to Scotland.*
" Bruce issuing from the hills where he had sheltered himself from
the late king, carried fire and sword through Inner Galloway.
One object doubtless was to punish the chief of the Macdougals who
had led his two brothers to die on the gallows of Carlisle in spring."
—Bain's *The Edwards in Scotland.*

*In The Cauldron of The Dungeon.*

astonishing peaty depths sufficient to drown you two or three
times over, and you step back warily over the quaking ground.
But in other places the water courses cheerfully over a stony
channel where it would be easy to walk.

After a long day on the hills it is delightful to take one's rod in the evening and follow the stream for a mile or so below the cottage and then fish upwards. Even so early as midsummer trout of a good size may sometimes be taken in this narrow burn, and all that are caught are of an unusually good quality, due probably to the fact that the Loch Dee trout spawn here.

Lying between the cottage and The Dungeon is a huge bog called The Silver Flow, which must be either crossed or circumvented if one wishes to fish the Dungeon Lochs or ascend to the rock plateau where Loch Enoch lies. It is a very awkward place, and I believe that in wet weather it is really dangerous. Sometimes you must take a flying leap over some watery patch of ooze, landing heavily on a heathery tussock, and making the whole bog quake for yards around. If you miscalculate the distance, you merely clutch the heather with your hands and sink up to the knees in mire. It is a great waste of time to attempt a direct passage between the cottage and the lochs, and much pleasanter to make a circuit over the hard ground on the north.

"The Dry Loch, Round Loch, and Long Loch of the Dungeon are all joined to each other by a small burn." This venerable misstatement held its place in the eighth edition of the Stewartry guide-book. The world, familiar with the confusion and ignorance prevailing at one time as to the sources of the Congo, the Niger, and the Nile, does not know of the darkness in which it has lain hitherto in the matter of the sources of the Dee !

The Dry, the Round, and the Long Loch lie in a straight line from north to south at the foot of The Dungeon and Craignaw. No stream flows southwards from the Dry Loch into the Round Loch. The watershed is between them, and the stream issuing from the Dry Loch runs northwards to Loch Doon. What has misled previous observers is a small trickle entering the Round Loch from the north.

The following statement occurs in the " Introduction " to the second volume of the *Inventory of Monuments and Constructions in Galloway* published in 1914 by the Royal Commission : " With a long meandering course under different names, and through Loch Ken, the waters of the Dee take their rise in Loch Doon on the Ayrshire border, draining the eastern flank of the Kells range."[1]    This is very much as if one were to say that the Tweed flows out of the Devil's Beef-tub or that the Clyde rises in Loch Skene.    The tributaries of the Dee, moreover, drain both the eastern and western flanks of the range.

Mr. Harper quotes the following old rhyme:

> The Slock, Millquharker, and Craignine,
> The Brishie and Craignaw,
> The five best hills for corklit
> John Tamson ever saw.

Symson says, " In the parish of Monnygaffe there is ane excrescence, which is gotten off the Craigs there, which the countrey people make up into balls. . . . This they call Cork lit and make use thereof for litting or dying a kind of purple colour."

The easiest route from The Back Hill of The Bush to Glentrool is by Lochs Narroch and Valley.

[1] " There is a spring of water on Mount Kotilios, from which a certain writer states that the river Lymax rises ; but he must neither have seen the spring himself, nor received his information from one who had."—Pausanias.

*Loch Valley.*

*The Square, Wigton.*

# CHAPTER XII

## WIGTON

The Moss of Cree—The Bishop's Burn—Wigton—Its old buildings—
The castle and the earldom of Wigton—The convent—The
harbour—The martyrs' graves—The story of Margaret Maclachlan and Margaret Wilson—Traditions connected with the
martyrdom—The stone circle of Torhouse—Heraldic panel
at Mochrum Park House—The Old Place of Mochrum.

THE Moss of Cree!—who could read of it in books or notice
how cartographers had written its name in large letters on
their maps without wishing to see it, to wander through it,
to revel in all its wild expanse of peat, heather, and bog-myrtle?
for plainly, since the map shewed " Moss of Cree ", this was
not a mere wayside bit of bog, but a marish tract extensive
enough to be a feature of the countryside. I turned aside
from the Wigton road into a byway veering towards the river
and observed presently on the right hand some peats cut recently
and arranged in little stacks for drying; but after this saw
slender justification for the great name, " Moss of Cree ",
for I continued to cycle amid turnip fields, bean fields, corn
fields, and pastures, and only here and there did I see any
rough moorland. The name, " Moss of Cree ", indeed, applies

now to a much restricted area. Even in Heron's time much
had been done by draining, pumping, manuring, and the
introduction of other earths to make the soil productive of
rich crops, and the process was continued during the last century.
I talked with an old man who pointed to a field of corn and said
that he remembered seeing peats cut at the head of it. I
asked him if he knew anything about a stream called the Bishop's
Burn, and he shewed me where it ran. When I inquired
if he could tell me how it got its name, he said that he did not
know, but gave me what he had learned about a field on the
farther bank, namely, that cattle-drovers used to pass through
it on their way to a ford, that their herds occupied it for hours
sometimes as they waited for the fall of the tide, and that a
woman who lived in a cottage on this side piloted the droves
across the sands.

My question about the Bishop's Burn was not prompted by
a desire for information, but by curiosity as to what the man
might say. I am sorry that I did not give him the tradition, as
it might have pleased him. It is very likely now that he will
die without having heard even the name of that monkish adven-
turer, Wymond *alias* Malcolm MacHeth, or of the valiant Bishop
Gilaldanus, who threw his hatchet at him. Wymond was a
monk of Furness who became Bishop of Man. Soon after his
consecration he declared that he was the son of Angus, Earl of
Moray, who had been killed in the rebellion of 1130. He
renounced his vows, began to call himself Malcolm MacHeth,
married a daughter of Somerled, Lord of the Isles, and with the
assistance of his father-in-law and other chiefs ravaged the northern coasts. He evaded defeat by all the forces sent against him
until he made a descent on the shore of Wigton Bay. Gilaldanus,
the bishop, in the absence of Fergus, Lord of Galloway, advanced
at the head of an army against the invader. The two forces
confronted each other on the banks of the burn. MacHeth
made to lead his followers across and was himself in mid-stream
when Gilaldanus hurled his axe. It struck MacHeth and caused
him to fall. Elated with this success and giving the enemy no
time to recover from their discomfiture, the Gallovidians pressed
their attack and cut down so many men that the burn ran red.
MacHeth escaped by one of the fords of the Cree, but was captured
in the east country and imprisoned in Roxburgh Castle.

This tradition may be true, and yet the burn have obtained its name in another way. One possible source is that the bishops of Galloway had a residence in this parish of Penninghame; another is that the lands of Clary lying along the burn belonged to the Gordons of Lochinvar, one of whom was the famous Alexander Gordon, Bishop of Galloway and titular Archbishop of Athens.

I was traversing this Moss of Cree both for its own sake and

*Wigton Bay from the Square, Wigton.*

in order that I might see the county town. Wigton[1] is spread over the broad top of a considerable hill standing by itself, so that whether one come from Newton Stewart in the north or

[1] Commonly said to be " dwelling on the bay "; O.E. *wic*, O. Norse *vig-r*; but " Wyggeton," 1283, should be " village of *Wiga*."— Johnston.

from Kirkcowan in the north-west or over the moors of Mochrum or by any of the roads passing through or near Kirkinner in the south or by ship over Wigton Bay, one must climb to enter the town.   One looks up to it with a certain respect, not only because its situation is dignified, but also on account of the dust of the martyrs lying in its churchyard.   From all that I had read I had learned to look for an air of solemnity about the place, and this anticipation was fulfilled.   One might say that it had a dull dignity, or if one were content to let phrases go and speak bluntly, one might say that it was dull.   It is clear that Sir Andrew Agnew inclines to this opinion, for has he not said that Wigton " reminds one of an old English cathedral town " ? Yet one could not say bluntly that it was dull without having a slightly uneasy conscience, for, dull though it be, it is not with a trivial and mean dullness, but in a large and almost a grand way.   This qualification comes partly of the antiquity of the town and partly of the spaciousness of the central street, which is not so much a street as a huge square with tennis and bowling greens surrounded with venerable trees in the midst.

When Symson knew Wigton in the seventeenth century, there were some " pretty good houses " three storeys high, and a few of them remain.   The older of the two crosses standing together in the square, a monolith about ten feet high sur-mounted by a square stone carved with dials and a stone pome-granate for a finial, bears the date 1738.   It was restored to a place of honour beside the modern cross after many years of obscurity in a cell of the old prison.   Its neighbour, a tall granite structure, was erected in 1816.

One cannot pass through the town without noticing a two-storey house projecting from the line of the other houses at the west end of the square.   It formed a side of the West Port. So recently as the middle of the eighteenth century the inhabi-tants used to drive their cattle within the Ports every evening, and then the gates were closed until morning.   When fences became common, this was necessary no longer, and the town council resolved to have the Ports removed because " they greatly incommode the carrying the corps of the deceast through the same ", and " the wheeled vehicles of noblemen and gentle-men comeing to the place " could not enter.   The house on the north side of the West Port escaped destruction, perhaps because the removal of the opposite house was sufficient. The clearance was made in 1761.

Nothing remains of the old Tolbooth. Symson says, " The Tolbooth standing neer the middle of the town, is lately beautify'd with a Pyramis erected upon a square platforme, upon the top of the steeple, set round with pylasters, which adds a fine ornament to the town." Its place has been taken by the new Court House and Town Hall[1] at the east end of the square. The older buildings of the Castle and the Friary have disappeared also.

The fact that Wigton gave its name to the whole of western Galloway witnesses to the importance of the Castle. It was one of the strongholds delivered into the hands of Edward the First in 1291. When David the Second created Sir Malcolm Fleming Earl of Wigton in 1342, he gave him the custody of the Castle and jurisdiction over the whole Shire. The charter states that " because the said place of Wigtoun was lookt upon as the principal manor of the whole sheriffdom, the King ordained that the said Malcolm and his heirs should for ever take the name of Earl and be called the Earls of Wigtoun ". The earldom did not descend in the Fleming family beyond the third generation. The first Earl was succeeded by his grandson, Thomas, who was unfit to control the baronage of The Shire and was constrained to surrender his rights and possessions in Wigtonshire to Archibald Douglas, the Grim, in 1371.

The convent of Dominican or Black Friars has left only the slightest traces. Symson, who wrote in 1684, says, " On the South east of this town, there was long since a Friarie, but the very ruines therof are now allmost ruined." He adds, " The greatest quantity of Agrimony that I ever saw in one place, grows about this Friarie." MacKerlie states that a well-known pippin came from the orchard. " Over one hundred years ago," he says, " two trees, then about a century old, remained, from which grafts were sent to all parts." The tree became known in England as the Galloway Pippin. The monks no doubt introduced it.

---

1 " Hung in the steeple of the town hall are three bells, dated respectively 1633, 1777, and 1881. The first . . . bears an inscription which, so far as decipherable, reads : O GOD LET WIGTOUNE FLOURISH BY THY WORD IN CHRIST WHO IS ONLIE OUR HEAD. ANNO 1633."—The *Inventory*.

I had not been accustomed to think of Wigton as a seaport, and was surprised, therefore, on walking down to the lower part of the square, to see an enamelled plate on a wall bearing the legend, "Harbour Road". I should not have wondered at it, however, had I remembered the common derivation of the name of the town. I set off to see the harbour, and after about half a mile came to a pier and a dock on the bank of the Bladnoch[1]—a pier covered with grass and sea-pinks, and a dock occupied by one small rowing-boat. Before the making of the

*Wigton Bay from the Quay, Wigton.*

railway *The Countess of Galloway* used to call here regularly; but now the port is deserted.

If there was little to amuse one about it, it at least gave a splendid view of the other side of Wigton Bay. Just as from the Ravenshall coast I had seen Wigton and its neighbourhood afar off, so now from Wigton I looked across to the miniature presentment of the country through which I had passed a day or two earlier. The great mass of Cairnsmore lay far on the left with its upper half hidden by a cloud. Creetown, indicated by an irregular grey patch among trees, was the first place belonging strictly to the shore of the bay. A minute speck of yellow stood

[1] Pronounced "Blaidnoch"; "Gaelic *bladh* (or *blaidh*)-*an-achaidh*, 'bit of the field'. In Irish *bladh*, *blod*, *blag* is a division, partition."—Johnston.

for Cassencary House. The elevator at the end of the pier at
Kirkmabreck looked like a small target. Carsluith village, the
castle, and the extreme point beyond Dirk Hatteraick's Cave
completed the series of dwarfed details. Behind them all rose
the lower slopes of Cairnharrow and Cambret[1], their summits,
like that of Cairnsmore, covered with clouds.

A narrow, grass-grown embankment protecting one or two
meadows from high tides wound from the pier towards the lower
part of the town. A footpath ran along the top, mounted a
bank, passed through a small plantation, and ended near the
churchyard. A well-worn track runs among the graves to those
of the martyrs, which are enclosed with an iron railing. The
inscriptions are as follows :

(1) A table stone :

HERE LYES MARGRAT WILLSON DOUGHTER TO GILBERT WILLSON IN GLENVERNOCH WHO WAS DROUNED ANNO 1685 AGED 18

LET EARTH AND STONE STILL WITNES BEARE
THEIR LYES A VIRGINE MARTYRE HERE.
MURTHERD FOR OUNING CHRIST SUPREAME,
HEAD OF HIS CHURCH AND NO MORE CRIME.
BUT NOT ABJURING PRESBYTRY,
AND HER NOT OUNING PRELACY
THEY HER CONDEMD BY UNJUST LAW,
OF HEAVEN NOR HELL THEY STOOD NO AW.
WITHIN THE SEA TYD TO A STAKE
SHE SUFFERED FOR CHRIST JESUS SAKE,
THE ACTORS OF THIS CRUEL CRIME
WAS LAGG · STRACHAN WINRAM · AND GRHAME ·
NEITHER YOUNG YEARES NOR YET OLD AGE
COULD STOP THE FURY OF THERE RAGE ·

(2) A small upright stone :

*(On top)*

MEMENTO MORI

*(On front)*

HERE LYES
MARGRAT LACHLANE
WHO WAS BY UN
JUST LAW SENTENC
ED TO DIE BY LAGG
STRACHANE WIN
RAME AND GRHAME
AND TYED TO A
STAKE WITHIN THE
FLOOD FOR HER

---

[1] Gaelic *ceann breac*, brindled or dappled hill.

(*On back*)

(Crossbones and skull)

ADHERENCE
TO   SCOTLANDS   RE
FORMATION COVE
NANTS NATIONAL
AND SOLEMN LEAGUE
AGED   63   1685

HERE LYSE WILLIAM JOHNSTO
JOHN MILROY GEORGE WALKER
WHO WAS WITHOWT SENTE
NCE OF LAW HANGED BY MA
JOR WINRAM FOR THEIR ADHER
ANCE TO SCOTLANDS REFOR
MATION COVENANTS NATIO
NAL AND SOLAM LEAGUE
1685

HERE LYES
MARGRAT LACHLAN
WHO WAS BY UN
JUST LAW SENTENC
ED TO DIE BY LAGG
STRACHANE WIN
RAME AND GRHAME

HERE LY MARGRAT
WILLSON DOUGHTER
TO GILBERT WILLSON
IN GLENVERNOCH
WHO WAS DROUED 18
ANNO 1685 AGED 18

LET EARTH AND STONE STILL WITNES BEARE
TEIR LYES A VIRGINE MARTYRE HERE
MURTERD FOR OWING CHRIST SUPREAME
HEAD OF HIS CHURCH AND NO MORE CRIME
BUT NOT ABJURING PRESBYTRY,
AND HER NOT OWNING PRELACY
TEY HER CONDEM'D BY UNJUST LAW,
OF HEAVEN NOR HELL TEY STOOD NO AW
WITHIN TE SEA TYD TO A STAKE
SHE SUFFERED FOR CHRIST JESUS SAKE &
TE ACTORS OF THIS CRUEL CRIME
WAS LAGG STRACHAN WINRAM AND GRHAME
NEITER YOUNG YEARES NOR YET OLD AGE
COULD STOP TE FURY OF TERE RAGE

(3) A small upright stone:

(*On top*)

MEMENTO MORI

(*On front*)

N

HERE LYSE WILLIAM JOHNSTO
JOHN MILROY GEORGE WALKER
WHO   WAS   WITHOWT   SENTE
NCE OF LAW HANGED BY MA
JOR WINRAM FOR THEIR ADHER
ANCE  TO  SCOTLANDS  REFOR
MATION   COVENANTS   NATIO
NAL  AND  SOLAM  LEAGWE
1685.

The classical passage on the martyrdom of Margaret Wilson and Margaret Maclachlan is in Wodrow's *The History of the Sufferings of the Church of Scotland*. " Upon the 11th of May," he says, " we meet with the barbarous and wicked execution of two excellent women near Wigton, Margaret McLachlan and Margaret Wilson." Margaret Wilson, aged eighteen years, and her sister, Agnes, who was not yet thirteen years old, were the daughters of Gilbert Wilson, tenant of Glenvernoch in the parish of Penninghame,[1] who conformed to Episcopacy. The girls adhered to the Covenants, fell into the hands of the persecutors, and were imprisoned. Later, they left the district and wandered through Carrick, Galloway, and Nithsdale with their brothers and some other Covenanters. On the death of King Charles, there was some slackening of the persecution, and the girls returned to Wigton. " There was an acquaintance of theirs, Patrick Stuart, whom they took to be a friend and well-wisher, but he was really not so, and betrayed them ; being in their company, and seeking an occasion against them, he proposed drinking the king's health ; this they modestly declined : upon which he went out, informed against them, and brought in a party of soldiers, and seized them. As if they had been great malefactors, they were put in the thieves' hole, and after they had been there some time, they were removed to the prison where Margaret McLauchlan was."

Margaret Maclachlan was the widow of a tenant in the parish of Kirkinner, " a country woman of more than ordinary knowledge, discretion, and prudence, and for many years of singular piety and devotion : she would take none of the oaths now pressed upon women as well as men ; neither would she desist from the duties she took to be incumbent upon her, hearing presbyterian ministers when providence gave opportunity, and joining with her Christian friends and acquaintances in prayer, and supplying her relations and acquaintances when in straits, though persecuted. It is a jest to suppose her guilty of rising in arms and rebellion, though indeed it was a part of her indictment, which she got in common form now used." She was very roughly dealt with in prison, and was allowed neither fire nor bed although she was sixty-three years of age.

All the three prisoners were indicted " for rebellion, Bothwell-bridge, Ayr's Moss, and being present at twenty field-conven-

[1] O.E. *peneg hám*, penny holding or land.

ticles ". None of them had ever been within many miles of Bothwell or Ayr's Moss. " Agnes Wilson could be but eight years of age at Ayr's Moss, and her sister but about twelve or thirteen ; and it was impossible they could have any access to those risings : Margaret McLauchlan was as free as they were." When the Abjuration Oath was put to them, they refused it, the assize found them guilty, and the sentence was that " upon the 11th instant, all the three should be tied to stakes fixed within the flood-mark in the water of Blednoch near Wigton, where the sea flows at high water, there to be drowned ". Gilbert Wilson secured the liberation of the younger girl under a bond of a hundred pounds sterling to present her when he was required to do so.

The sentence was executed on Margaret Maclachlan and Margaret Wilson. The narrative must be given as it stands in Wodrow's *History*. " The two women were brought from Wigton, with a numerous crowd of spectators to so extraordinary an execution. Major Windram with some soldiers guarded them to the place of execution. The old woman's stake was a good way in beyond the other, and she was first despatched, in order to terrify the other to a compliance with such oaths and conditions as they required. But in vain ; for she adhered to her principles with an unshaken steadfastness. When the water was overflowing her fellow-martyr, some about Margaret Wilson asked her, what she thought of the other now struggling with the pangs of death. She answered, what do I see but Christ (in one of his members) wrestling there. Think you that we are the sufferers ? no, it is Christ in us, for he sends none a warfare upon their own charges. When Margaret Wilson was at the stake, she sang the 25th Psalm from verse 7th, downward a good way, and read the 8th chapter to the Romans with a great deal of cheerfulness, and then prayed. While at prayer, the water covered her : but before she was quite dead, they pulled her up, and held her out of the water till she was recovered, and able to speak ; and then by major Windram's orders, she was asked, if she would pray for the king. She answered, ' She wished the salvation of all men, and the damnation of none.' One deeply affected with the death of the other and her case, said, ' Dear Margaret, say God save the king, say God save the king.' She answered in the greatest steadiness and composure, ' God save him, if he will, for it is his salvation

I desire.' Whereupon some of her relations near by, desirous
to have her life spared, if possible, called out to major Windram,.
' Sir, she hath said it, she hath said it.' Whereupon the major
came near, and offered her the abjuration, charging her instantly
to swear it, otherwise return to the water. Most deliberately
she refused, and said, ' I will not, I am one of Christ's children,
let me go.' Upon which she was thrust down again into the
water, where she finished her course with joy."

No other event of the Persecution has been the subject of
such vehement controversy. Mark Napier, Sheriff of Dumfries
and author of *Memorials and Letters of Graham of Claverhouse*
(1859-62), contended that the sentence was not carried out, and
wrote a monograph entitled *The Case for the Crown in re the
Wigtown Martyrs proved to be Myths*. His argument is based
on the fact that a reprieve was granted in response to petitions
presented on behalf of the prisoners. Effective replies were
written by the Rev. Archibald Stewart, minister of Glasserton,[1]
and others ; and the only lasting result of the controversy has
been the accumulation of evidence in support of Wodrow.

Local traditions traceable almost to the time of the execution
and illustrating the popular conviction of its actuality have been
collected in *The Hereditary Sheriffs of Galloway*. " A minister
long resident in the district told the author that the name of
the man by whose information the women were arrested is well
known, and his memory execrated still. One of his descendants,
getting into an altercation with a person in the borough, was
thus taunted the other day : ' I wadna like to have had a
forebear who betrayed the martyrs ; I wadna be coomed o'
sic folk '.

" Another informant had communed with a person (Miss
Suzan Heron) whose grandfather had seen the execution ;
whose words were : ' The sands were covered wi' cluds o' folk,
a' gathered into clusters, many offering up prayers for the women
while they were being put down '."

Some rather grotesque stories are told. " A town sergeant,
who had been officiously active—when the women finally
refused Lagg to take the test—pressed down their heads with
his halbert, and cried with savage glee : ' Tak' another drink
o't, my hearties ! ' Hardly had he returned home when he was

[1] *History Vindicated in the Case of the Wigtown Martyrs.* Second
Edition. (1869.)

troubled by an extraordinary thirst : it continued. No amount of drink he could take could allay it. His unnatural craving forced him, when obliged to go abroad, to carry a pitcher on his back. If crossing a stream, he was irresistibly impelled to kneel down and lap water like a dog. Medical skill was of no avail : as the wretch wandered about the country, now turning to curse a group of urchins who followed to mock his sufferings, now sprawling to moisten his tongue in the gutter, even his ribald companions shrank from him with horror, and the people, whose sympathies were with his victims, pointed to him as a man whose eternal sufferings had begun.

" Still more grotesque is the tradition of the ' Cleppie Bells '. A constable who was held to have carried out his orders un-feelingly, as he fastened the women to the stakes, was asked how the poor creatures behaved when the cold wave roared and foamed about their heads. ' Oo,' he replied jocularly, ' they just clepped roun' the stobs like partons, and prayed.' Soon after, Bell's wife was brought to bed, when the howdie exclaimed in horror : ' The bairn is clepped ! ' (i.e. the fingers grew firmly together). Another child was born, and yet another, and as each little wretch in turn was seen to be ' clepped ', the most incredulous were convinced it was a judgment of Providence. We have been gravely assured that within the memory of man a female descendant of the bad constable, on giving birth to a child, was horrified by the exclamation, ' The bairn is clepped ! ' "

The following saying belongs to more recent days. " An old elder in the parish, on being told that historical doubts had been started as to whether the said women had been drowned at all, answered with much simplicity : ' Weel, weel, they that doots the droonin' o' the women wad maybe doot the deein' o' the Lord Jesus Christ '."

Some of the results of the Persecution are illustrated by entries in the kirk-session records of Wigton for the early years of the eighteenth century : " To Jo. Flokart, who suffered ye loss of all he had dureing ye late Persecution for hearing and entertaining minrs. and honest folk in his house, £1, 9s " ; " To James Williamson, a sufferer in the late times, 6s. " ; " To one Isabella Wilson, from Glasgow, a late sufferer, 8s." ; " To John Flockhart, a sufferer in the late times, 18s." There is also " To Mr. James Spark, a Curate, £1, 4s."

Other items reveal the strange variety of matters coming at times within the cognizance of the kirk-session: "To two men who had been taken by the Turks, 4s."; "To John Rutherford, taken by ye French, 10s."; "To a distracted naked man, to help to buy Cloathes, 6s. 6d."; "To Balmeg's daughter, to take her to a 7th sone to be cured of the cruels, 6s."; "To Jo. Robison and Wm. Maxwell, cast away coming from Virginia, 6s."; "To a blewgoun, 2s."; "To Jacob Sobieski, a Polonian, a Protestant, 8s."; "To two men who had been taken by the Pirates, 8s."; "To Jean Lowzier, a French gentlewoman, who had been shipwraked, 12s."; "To Will McKie

*The Standing Stones of Torhouse.*

going to Moffat for health, £3"; "To Robert Guthrie, for keeping out vagrant and sturdy beggars for 5 weeks, 15s."; "To a shilling returned to one who had thrown it in by mistake to ye poor."

A little more than three miles from the martyrs' graves are some much more ancient monuments with no story, the stone-circle of Torhouse and other standing stones in the neighbourhood. The circle "consists of nineteen stones—all natural boulders—and contains within the periphery an arrangement of peculiar character not observed elsewhere: three large blocks of stone in alignment, those at the ends each some two feet and nine inches away from the central stone, on which there

rests in a C-shaped curve a low bank or wall."[1] Symson wrote,
" In the high way betwixt Wigton and Portpatrick, about three
miles Westward of Wigton, is a plaine call'd the Moor, or Standing
Stones of Torhouse in which there is a monument of three
large whin stones, call'd King Galdus's tomb, surrounded, at
about twenty foot distance, with nineteen considerable great
stones, (but none of them so great as the three first mentioned,)
erected in a circumference. In this Moor, and not far from the
tomb, are great heaps of small hand-stones, which the Countrey
people call Cairnes, supposed by them to be the buriall places
of the common souldiers. As also at severall places distant
from the Monument, are here and there great single stones
erected, which are also supposed to be the buriall places of
his Commanders and men of note. But herein I determine
nothing, only I think fit to add, that, at severall places in this
Countrey, there are many great heaps of hand stones, call'd
Cairnes ; and those heaps, or Cairnes, of stones are very seldom
single, but many times there are two of them, and sometimes
moe, not far distant from each other."

What appear to be the remains of other circles are found near
at hand. Three large prostrate boulders about two hundred
yards north-west seem to have their bases on the arc of a circle,
and about a hundred and thirty yards to the east there is a
similar group. There are records and remains of former circles
at other places in The Shire : at Blairbuy in Glasserton Parish,
at Eldrig in Mochrum, at Longcastle in Kirkinner, near
Glenturk in Wigton, and at Glentirrow in Inch. The circle
at Torhouse is the only complete one.[2]

Archæologists describe such circles as sepulchral constructions
of the bronze age without seriously invalidating the thoughts
of the poet :

> Isled and estranged from every mood
> Of all that lived and grew,
> Deep in forgotten Time they stood—
> The Stones of Stanton Drew.

---

[1] The *Inventory*.

[2] According to the *Inventory*, the stone circles in The Stewartry
" number apparently thirteen, though of that number some are very
imperfect." The places where they are found are Cauldside and
High Auchenlarie in Anwoth, Holm of Daltallochan in Carsphairn,
Ernespie in Kelton, Drummore in Kirkcudbright, Glenquicken and
Claughreid in Kirkmabreck, Easthill in Lochrutton, Drannandow
in Monigaff, and Park and Lairdmannoch in Tongland.

> How many ages have gone by
>     Since last a mortal knew
> Who set you there, and when, and why,
>     O Stones of Stanton Drew ?
>
> All sunlit was the Earth I trod,
>     The Heaven was frankest blue ;
> But secret as the thoughts of God
>     The Stones of Stanton Drew.[1]

The Torhouse property adjoins that of Mochrum Park,
a modern home of an old family. The most interesting detail
of Mochrum Park House is a heraldic panel[2] belonging originally to the gatehouse of the Bishop's Palace in Glasgow.
About the middle of the eighteenth century, when the Palace
was being demolished, the stones forming the panel were built
into a tenement in the High Street of Glasgow. They were
removed later to the house of Sir William Dunbar, a descendant
of the famous Archbishop, Gavin Dunbar, who was a son of
Sir John Dunbar of Mochrum by his second wife, Janet, a
daughter of Sir Alexander Stewart of Garlies. He became
Dean of Moray, Prior of Whithorn, Archbishop of Glasgow, and,
in 1528, Lord High Chancellor, and died in 1547.

Mochrum Park is not to be confused with the Old Place of
Mochrum, the former home of the Galloway Dunbars and now
the property of the Marquess of Bute. The Old Place stands
in a lonely situation in the midst of a great expanse of moors
and lochs[3] in the parish of Mochrum about eight miles west of
Wigton. It is described in the *Inventory* as " perhaps the most
remarkable castle " in The Shire and " consists of two independent towers built within a large courtyard and separated by a

---

[1] *New Poems* by William Watson.

[2] " It is formed of two detached portions of stone carved in relief,
on which are three shields bearing arms :—*The upper stone :* (1) A
lion rampant within a royal tressure (for Scotland) : supporters,
two unicorns : encircling the shield, the Collar of the Thistle, and,
beneath, the royal monogram of James the Fifth, no longer legible.
*The lower stone :* (2) Three cushions lozenge-ways within a royal
tressure (Archbishop Dunbar) : beneath the shield a salmon on its
back with a ring in its mouth, and, behind, an archiepiscopal cross :
(3) A chevron chequy between three martlets (that in dexter chief
*ontourné*) : a rose in chief for difference (James Houston, Sub-
dean of Glasgow)." The stones are believed to be the only remains
of the Episcopal Palace of Glasgow.

[3] Drumwalt or Mochrum Loch, the subject of Mr. Thomson's
drawing, is the largest.

space of about thirteen feet, without any apparent means of communication, and joined only by a single wall which probably completed the courtyard on the south side. The west tower, which is the older building, has the usual characteristics of this

*The Old Place of Mochrum.*

period.[1] The entrance is from the courtyard and leads to vaulted room on the ground floor and to a wheel-stair in the south east angle, which gives direct access to the hall on the first floor

[1] The fifteenth century.

to the second floor, to the attics and parapet walk.   The corbels
supporting the stone parapet are of small projection, and there
are no machicolations for the purpose of defence—showing a
departure from the earlier defensive arrangements due to the
anticipation of less strenuous hostilities.   The east tower shows
a further development in this direction.   The staircase, instead of
being formed within the wall, is built in a projecting wing to the
north, while the wall-head supports the ends of the rafters,
and the parapet and walk are abolished.   The form of crow-
steps employed at the gables is particularly worthy of notice

*Drumwalt Loch.*

s being peculiar to Galloway.   They are made up of small
tones covered on the upper surface with a thin stone slab
projecting slightly at the free end."   The west tower is attributed
o the fifteenth, and the east to the sixteenth, century.   Con-
emporary sketches shew that at the end of the eighteenth
entury the castle was roofless and partly ruined.   The work of
estoring it and of making additions was begun by the third
Marquess of Bute, and has been continued by his successor.
  The writer of *The Statistical Account* of 1796 said, " In the
middle of the moor-land appears an old tower or castle, whose
walls are very strong, and almost entire ;  and, being nearly surrounded by lakes, when viewed at a distance it has a most curious
and picturesque appearance, resembling much a large ship at sea."
he plantations formed by the third Marquess have changed the
spect of the neighbourhood, so that this effect appears no longer.

*The Gateway and Ruins of Baldoon Castle.*

# CHAPTER XIII

### KIRKINNER

The Bride of Baldoon and *The Bride of Lammermoor*—Symson's description of the making of shell lime—The name of the parish—Andrew Symson, Episcopal minister and author of *A Large Description of Galloway*—His relations with his parishioners—An account of the sufferers in the Persecution—Kirkinner Church—An ancient Celtic cross—The Vans Agnews of Barnbarroch—The attempted abduction of Miss Vaus of Barnbarroch in 1738.

AFTER crossing the Bladnoch by the bridge about a mile south west of Wigton, I turned along a byway leading down the right bank, for the map shewed that it would bring me shortly to Baldoon.[1] I remembered that the place was associated with *The Bride of Lammermoor*, being indeed the scene of the death of Janet Dalrymple, the daughter of Sir James Dalrymple of Stair, who was created Viscount Stair in 1690. The road ran pleasantly among trees along the river-side until it turned into the trim grounds of the pretty farmhouse of Baldoon. A little beyond the house I saw the beautiful carved-stone gateposts of the old castle, and behind the gateway the ivy-covered remains of the castle itself, whither David Dunbar brought his reluctant bride on the 24th of August, 1669.

[1] Gaelic *baile duine*, townland of the fort.

The only contemporary evidence for the history is contained in an elegy written by Andrew Symson, minister of Kirkinner Parish, wherein Baldoon lies, and gives no suggestion of either murder or madness as playing a part in the course of events. The elegy is not too long for quotation.

ON THE UNEXPECTED DEATH OF THE VERTUOUS LADY, MRS. JANET DALRYMPLE, LADY BALDONE, YOUNGER.

*Nupta Aug.* 12. *Domum ducta Aug.* 24. *Obiit Sept.* 12. *Sepult. Sept.* 30. M.DC.LX.IX.

*Dialogus inter Advenam et Servum Domesticum.*

*Adv.*  What means this sudden unexpected change ?
This mourning company ?  Sure, sure, some strange
And uncouth thing hath happen'd : Phoebus's head
Hath not been resting on the wat'ry bed
Of sea-green Thetis fourty times, since I
In *transitu* did cast my tender eye
Upon this very place, and here did view
A troop of gallants : Iris never knew
The various colours which they did employ
To manifest and represent their joy.
Yea, more ;  methinks I saw this very wall
Adorn'd with emblems hieroglyphicall ;
As first, the glorious sun in lustre shine ;
Next unto it, a young and tender vine
Surround a stately elm, whose tops were crown'd
With wreaths of bay-tree reaching to the ground ;
And to be short, methinks I did espy
A pleasant, harmless, joyfull comedy.
But now (sad change, I'm sure,) they all are clad
In deepest sable, and their faces sad ;
The sun's o'erclouded, and the vine's away,
The elm is drooping, and the wreaths of bay
Are chang'd to cypress, and the comedie
Is metamorphos'd to a tragedie.
I do desire you, Friend, for to unfold
This matter to me.

*Serv. Dom.*  Sir, 'tis truth you've told ;
We did enjoy great mirth, but now, ah me !
Our joyful song's turn'd to an elegie.
A vertuous lady, not long since a bride,
Was to an hopeful plant by marriage ty'd
And brought home hither.  We did all rejoyce
Even for her sake.  But presently our voice
Was turn'd to mourning, for that little time
That she'd enjoy ;  she waned in her prime ;
For Atropus, with her impartial knife,
Soon cut her threed, and therewithall her life.

And for the time, we may it well remember,
It being in unfortunate September,
Just at the equinox ; she was cut down
In th' harvest, and this day she's to be sown,
Where we must leave her till the resurrection ;
'Tis then the saints enjoy their full perfection.


   This, of course, is not great poetry, and I have set it down
simply because, written by one who was both minister of the
parish and an intimate friend of the bridegroom, it shews
that the actual history of David Dunbar and his bride was less
sensational than the popular traditions of later generations
represented it to have been, for it is scarcely conceivable that
Symson should have used the correct sentiments of these common-
place verses as a veil for a story too terrible to be given to the
world by a friend, and there is no reason to suppose that he was
trying to make the best of a difficult situation since he was under
no compulsion to write an elegy at all.
   The foundation of the later versions of the bride's story lies
in the following facts.  Janet, the eldest daughter of Sir James
Dalrymple, known better by his title of Viscount Stair, had been
sought in marriage by Archibald, third Lord Rutherford, who
was poor.  She had plighted her troth ; but the attachment was
opposed resolutely by her parents, who preferred another lover,
David Dunbar, the heir of Sir David Dunbar of Baldoon.  The
mother in particular, a woman capable of an inflexible determination, urged her daughter to depart from her engagement
and agree to become the wife of Dunbar, and is said to have
wrought upon her child's mind by insisting on the Levitical law
contained in the thirtieth chapter of *The Book of Numbers*, that
a woman shall be free of a vow " if her father disallow her in
the day that he heareth ".  The distracted victim of this attack
was unable to stand her ground indefinitely and yielded at last
to her parents' desire.  The marriage took place on the 12th of
August, 1669, at the Kirk of Old Luce, about two miles from
Carscreugh, the home at that time of the Dalrymples.  The bride
rode to church behind one of her younger brothers, who spoke
long afterwards of the extraordinary coldness of her hand when
it had happened to touch his own, a detail given to Sir Walter
Scott by a lady who had it from young Dalrymple himself.
The wedding party remained at Carscreugh until the 24th of
August, when a gay troop of friends accompanied the bridegroom

and bride to Baldoon, where they were entertained with a masque. The bride died nineteen days later.

According to the first of the later versions, the bride stabbed the bridegroom on their wedding night and died a maniac a few days afterwards ; according to the second, the bridegroom stabbed the bride and was " found in a state of idiocy " ; the third introduces the disappointed lover, conceals him in the bridal chamber, and represents him as attacking his successful rival and then escaping into the garden by a window. It seems as if the whole harvest of gruesome variations on the known history were due to the malicious invention of Sir William Hamilton of Whitelaw, a bitter enemy of Lord Stair and his unsuccessful competitor for the position of President of the Court of Session. His scurrilous verses on Lord Stair and his family include a characteristic reading of the unhappy bridal of Baldoon, namely, that the bridegroom suffered violence at the hands of the Devil, to whom the bride had vowed herself in case she should break her engagement with her first lover. Having come to claim his due,

> Nick did Baldoon's posterior right deride
> And, as first substitute, did seize the bride ;
> Whate'er he to his mistress did or said,
> He threw the bridegroom from the nuptial bed,
> Into the chimney did so his rival maul,
> His bruised bones ne'er were cured but by the fall.

The last line alludes to the fact that Dunbar died as the result of a fall from his horse. This occurred in 1682. Dunbar had as his second wife a daughter of Hugh, seventh Earl of Eglinton. His daughter and only child was married to Lord Basil Hamilton and became an ancestress of the S. Mary's Isle family. Lord Rutherford never married, and died in 1685. He was an uncle of David Dunbar ; this fact, however, has no significance for the history.

Lord Basil Hamilton, who married the heiress of Sir David Dunbar, became prominent, not as a figure in a romantic history, but in the more useful part of cattle-breeder. He imported cows from Ireland in order to improve the native stock, and " may be given the credit of taking the initiative in developing what continued for nearly two centuries the principal source of the Galloway farmer's profit." Of the cattle on Sir David Dunbar's estate Symson says, " those of his owne breed,

at four year old, are very large, yea, so large, that in August
or September, 1682, nine and fifty of that sort, which would
have yeilded betwixt five and six pound sterling the peice,
were seiz'd upon in England for Irish cattell; and because the
person to whom they were entrusted, had not witnesses there
ready at the precise hour, to swear that they were seen calved
in Scotland, (though the witness offered to depone that he
liv'd in Scotland, within a mile of the Park where they were
calv'd and bred,) they were, by the sentence of Sir J. L., and
some others, who knew well enough that they were bred in
Scotland, knockt on the head and kill'd; which was, to say
no more, very hard measure, and an act unworthy of persons
of that quality and station, who ordered it to be done."

If you cross the meadows of Baldoon to the shore of the
bay, you will see the place where Symson watched his parishioners making shell lime more than two hundred years ago.
Any reader who thinks that it is impossible for him to take any
interest in the details of this primitive industry will please skip
the following paragraph, for I cannot refrain from transcribing
Symson's account of the matter. The information might be
useful if one were cast away upon a desert island.

"On the bank of this Park, that lyes opposit to the sea,
if there be in the winter time any high tides and storms from
the South East, the sea casts innumerable and incredible
quantities of Cockleshells, which the whole shire makes use
of for lime, and it is the onely lime which this countrey affoords.
The way of making it is thus : Upon an even Area, (the circumference they make less or more, according to the quantity
of shells they intend to burne,) they set erected peits, upon which
they put a layer of shells, a foot thick or more, and then upon
them again lay peits, though not erected as at first, and
then another layer of shells, and so *stratum super stratum*,
till they bring it to an head like a pyramis ; but as they put
on these layers just in the center, they make a tunnell of peits,
like a chimney, hollow in the middest, reaching from the bottom
to the top, (just almost as Evelyn describes the making of
charcoal ;) this done, they take a pan full of burning peits,
and put them down into this tunnel, or chimney, and so close
up all with shells. This fire kindles the whole kilne, and in
twentie-four hours space, or thereby, will so burn the shells
that they will run together in a hard masse ; after this, they

let it cool a litle, and then with an iron spade they bring it
down by degrees, and sprinkling water thereon, with a beater
they beat it, [or berry it, for that's their terme; this word
they also use for threshing, and so call the thresher of their
corne, the berrier] and then put it so beaten into litle heaps,
which they press together with the broad side of their spade,
after which, in a short time, it will dissolve [they call it melting]
into a small white powder, and it is excellent lime. I have
heard good masons say, that, as it is whiter, so also it binds
stones together surer and better than stone lime itself."

You can imagine the smoking piles on that bleak beach

*Kirkinner.*

fanned every now and then into masses of smouldering fire by
the rising and falling wind, and how the glow enduring through
the night would arrest watchers on the other side of the bay.

On leaving Baldoon I did not need to return as I had come,
for I found another byway running past the castle and
joining the main road near the farmhouse of Moor Park. After
about a mile of the main road I reached the village of Kirkinner.
The parish bears the same name.

" The popular tradition respecting the name of the parish
is as follows. In former times, the parish of Kirkinner included
in it what now forms the parish of Kirkcowan. The clergyman
preached two Sundays at the church in the southern part
of the parish, and the next in another place of worship, in

the northern part of it. In those days, the one was distinguished as the Inner Kirk, hence the name Kirkinner; the other was called the Outer Kirk, which in course of time was changed into Kirk-cowan, and now forms the parish of that name." This from the new *Statistical Account* is one of the most shining examples of a popular " derivation " to be found in the literature relating to Galloway. The name is really a memorial of S. Kennera, who was believed to have been one of " the eleven thousand virgins of Cologne ".

Symson's *Description of Galloway* has been referred to or quoted frequently in these pages, and there will be more allusions and quotations in the pages that follow. To the reader who is not familiar with Galloway literature it is very likely that Symson has been a mere name so far. Now that we have reached the parish where he laboured as a minister and, judging it " not altogether excentrical to my profession to comply something with my Genius " as a man of letters, drew up his account of Galloway and wrote a number of pieces of verse, it is time to set forth the slight outline of his history that is now traceable.

His introduction to the parish took place in 1663, the year following that in which his predecessor, George Waugh, had vacated it in consequence of the restoration of lay patronage. From the dedication of his *Tripatriarchicon; or, the Lives of the three Patriarchs, Abraham, Isaac, and Jacob, extracted forth of the Sacred Story, and digested into English verse*, we learn that he had been " a con-disciple at the University "—the University of Edinburgh—with Lord Garlies, son of James, Earl of Galloway, and it is possible that it was through the Earl's patronage that he was presented to the living. In the preface to the same work he gives some account of the beginning of his ministry and of the various phases of his relations with the people of the parish in the course of it—an account full of interest to the student of the times inasmuch as it shews that every Episcopal minister was not the bloodthirsty tyrant that some have supposed him to be, and illustrates the attitude of the better kind of incumbent towards the people. " Though we had not a formal and explicit call," says Symson, speaking for himself and the other Episcopal ministers sent into Galloway to supply the vacant churches, " yet we had it virtually, and upon the matter, for after we had several Lord's days preached in our respective congregations for which we were designed (seven Lord's days I am sure for my own part), our edicts served and duly execute, the representatives of the parish attended on our ordinations, and the generallty of the parish came to our solemn admissions ; and thereafter waited on the ordinances under our administrations, yea, and the very members of the former sessions concurr'd with us, and assisted us in the exercise of discipline, and rectifying such affairs as was incumbent to them, after the old manner."

He proceeds to describe the attitude of the Episcopalian clergy towards those of their parishioners who adhered to Presbyterianism, and here we find the odd spectacle of a Scottish Episcopalian referring to Presbyterians as " dissenters " ; but, of course, from a legal point of view the description was not without some justification in the period between the Restoration and the Revolution. " As for those few that were dissenters," he says, " we us'd all peaceable and Christian methods to gain them ; so that when the commander of the forces, that lay in the Stewartrie of Kirkcudburgh (for there were none of them in our countrey), wrote to us to send him a list of them, we absolutely refused him, and sent two of our number, yet living, to signify the same to him ; upon which account we were complained of as enemies to the government, and obstructers of the settlement of the peace of the countrey." When the various acts and proclamations against the Presbyterians were about to be put into force, " we us'd ", he says, " our outmost endeavours to ward off the blow ; and by our intercession and diligence in that affair, we got the penalty most times mitigated, yea, and many times wholy taken off, for which we got but little thanks many times from both parties ; but there were some faults, such as murders, robberies, forgeries, and crimes of that nature, that we could not plead for ; and when such persons were punished for such and the like misdemeanours (because they assumed to themselves the title of the godly party) we were blamed for all those punishments that lighted upon any of them, which so stirr'd up others to maltreat us at the rate, which in this poem I sometimes do complain of." The general revolt against Episcopacy, however, was gathering strength, so that even peaceable ministers like Symson found their congregations dwindling away. Among Symson's ever faithful hearers was David Dunbar of Baldoon, on whose death he wrote a *Funeral Elegie* containing the following lines :

He was no schismatick, he ne'er withdrew
Himself from th' House of God ; he with a few
(Some two or three) came constantly to pray
For such as had withdrawn themselves away.
Nor did he come by fits ; foul day or fair,
I, being i' th' church, was sure to see him there.
Had he withdrawn, 'tis like these two or three,
Being thus discourag'd, had deserted me.

With so slender a congregation, the minister naturally entertained a peculiarly warm regard for the one constant worshipper !

Symson was not entirely free, meanwhile, from insults and
injuries ; but these proceeded not so much from his own parishioners as from strangers. " I must in the mean time acknowledge, that as my lot was cast in a very pleasant place, so I had
to do with a very well-natur'd people, who, following the example
of the gentry, their landlords, payed me great deference and
respect, for which people, for I hate ingratitude, I shall have a
kindness as long as I breath, so that I was for the most part
free from those male-treatments that many of my brethren
mett with (towards whom my religion obliged me to have a
sympathy). I confess I was not altogether free of my own
troubles, which proceeded much more from strangers than those
of my own parish ; for they in the mean time were so kind to me,
that, when they were advertis'd of any approaching danger,
they have both by day and night advertis'd me thereof, upon
which I have many times retired myself quietly into their
countrey-houses, where I was lodg'd and kindly entertain'd,
and so escaped the danger I might otherwise have been subject
to." In the dedication to his *Tripatriarchicon* he tells of one
of the acts of kindness of the Earl of Galloway : " In the year
1679, when things were come to that hight, that the publick
owning of us was almost look'd upon as a crime, and I for my
own safety was necessitate to retire to a quiet lurking place,
his Lordship accidentaly lighted on me, took me home with
him to his house, and kindly entertained me there."

It is recorded that Symson gave the civil authorities a list
of the disorderly persons, that is, the Presbyterians, in his
parish on the 15th of October, 1684.[1] and that he was inducted
to the parish of Douglas on the 12th of January, 1686, so that
he must have left Kirkinner between these dates. He was

---

[1] In accordance with the requirement of the Act of Parliament
of the 31st of August, 1681.

" outed " from his new parish at the Revolution on the ground that he had been obtruded upon the people " without their consent and lawfull call ". The church at Douglas was ordered to be declared vacant on the 23rd of March, 1692. It was on the 28th of June in the same year that Symson wrote the " Advertisement " to *A Large Description of Galloway*, having just completed this work.

His undertaking it had been occasioned by some inquiries circulated throughout Scotland by Sir Robert Sibbald, His Majesty's Geographer, with a view to the publication of a Scottish atlas. Symson was interested in the project, and drew up his general *Description of Galloway* in 1684 ; but, he tells us in the " Advertisement ", " the troubles, which very shortly thereafter did ensue, occasion'd these Papers to be cast by, yea and almost wholy forgotten for some yeares." Living, however, at " Dalclathick, in Glenartnae " in June, 1692, he had " time and leasure enough " to enlarge, revise, and transcribe his original notes. The completed work was sent to Sir Robert Sibbald and deposited ultimately in the Advocates' Library along with the other papers forming the Sibbald Collection. It was printed for the first time in 1823, and may be found most readily in the appendix to the second volume of Mackenzie's *The History of Galloway*, or in the *Geographical Collections Relating to Scotland made by Walter Macfarlane*, published by the Scottish History Society.

That Symson entertained no exaggerated conception of his powers as a poet is evident from the preface to the *Tripatriarchicon*, for, says he, " it will sufficiently satisfy me, if this pass among the judicious for a tolerably good trotting poem ; for it was never my design, nor did ever my ambition prompt me to it, to set up for a courser, or, with Icarus, to aspire to high flights, foreseeing, that I might so quickly run myself out of breath, or catch a fall, which would have hinder'd me to attain my design'd end, to which, by trotting on, I have at length come."

The Editor's introduction to *A Large Description of Galloway* was followed by a bibliographical addendum contributed by Mr. William Rowand, " Sub Librarian of the Theological Library of the University of Edinburgh ". Symson was not so voluminous an author as Mr. Rowand thought, for the list includes two works, almost deserving the description, " monumental ", the compilation of which is due to Symson's father, who was also a minister of the Church of Scotland. These are the sixth and much enlarged edition of Wilson's *Christian Dictionary*, published in 1655, and a *Lexicon Anglo-Graeco Latinum Novi Testamenti*, which appeared in 1658.

Symson went into business as a printer in Edinburgh, and died in 1712, when he was about seventy-four years of age. He had three sons, one of whom became a canon of Lincoln Cathedral.

In spite of the endeavours which Symson claims to have made to shield his parishioners, many of them suffered the rigours of the Persecution. This is evident from an important document by the minister of the parish, in which he gives an account of these persons. It was embodied in the session records under the date, the 15th of April, 1711, and is reproduced in *The Statistical Account* and elsewhere. The list begins with Margaret Maclachlan, who was drowned at Wigton, and her husband, John Millikin, who " when he lived in Killeal, being frequently quartered on by the soldiers, was obliged to pay to six of them eight shillings Scots to each man, ilk day, for a considerable time, and afterwards was carried prisoner to Dumfries, where he was fined in a considerable sum ".

The following is the most poignant case in the recital : " William Sprot in Clutoch being, about 1685, obliged to leave his own house to shun persecution and went to Portpatrick on his way to Ireland, and then at Portpatrick was apprehended and brought back on his feet betwixt two dragoons, exactly by his own house-door to Wigtoun prison ; his wife being big with child, followed him to the said prison, when she saw him laid on his back, in the cold prison, put in the irons, his ears cut off, his fingers burnt by fiery matches ; and afterwards he was sentenced to be banished to America, and in his voyage thither he died. He was a person eminent for piety. His poor wife for grief miscarried of her child."

Prominent families are represented in the list : " Alexander Vaux of Barwhannie, brother-german to John Vaux of Barnbarroch, and Margaret Maxwell, his lady, (who afterwards became Laird and Lady of Barnbarroch,) from 1666 to 1689, the time of the late happy revolution, were harassed, processed, and fined, though there was nothing could be laid to their charge, but that they would not comply with the times, and did resett godly people and ministers " ; " Mistress May Dunbar, second daughter to Sir David Dunbar of Baldoon, of known piety all her life, was forced to abscond and leave her father's house, and live for some time here and there, frequently in herd's houses, where she could not be accommodated according to her birth and rank.

One day she very providentially and narrowly escaped the enemy's fury at the Caldons, about the year 1685." Perhaps this was the occasion when six Covenanters were shot in Glentrool.[1]

I do not think that anything remains of the church where Symson preached to David Dunbar and his "two or three" fellow-worshippers. I attended the service in the present church on a Sunday and heard a sermon on toleration of which I have no doubt that Symson would have approved. The church was built in 1828. It has mullioned windows, buttresses, a

*Ancient Cross in Kirkinner Churchyard.*

battlemented tower, and crow-stepped gables, and is more handsome than most of the churches in this part of the country. Sir Andrew Agnew says, " Its appearance was enhanced until recently by two magnificent old trees with immense boles and spreading limbs. But they were pronounced to be a danger to the church and have therefore been cut down. One of them

[1] See page 164

was an ash in whose stem one hundred and seventy-eight rings could be distinctly counted. The other was a sycamore which is supposed to have been still older ; and which may possibly have formed a link between Symson's day and our own." There is still a monument in the churchyard forming a link between our own and a much earlier day than Symson's, a wheel-headed cross of Celtic design standing about thirty feet from the south-west corner of the church. It is a cross of a kind that was especially common in Galloway ; there are several similar examples in the museum at Whithorn Priory ; but I do not remember another instance where such a cross stands at the head of a grave to this day. Since it has this exceptional interest, I transcribe the details noted in the *Inventory* : " The extent of the arms is indicated by grooves, and the circular hollows at the points of intersection are pierced with holes four inches in diameter. In the centre is a flat boss measuring five and a half inches in diameter, relieved with four small radial leaf-shaped markings, which have probably formed a cross, and surrounded by a ring. On the back the boss is plain. The head rests upon a thin flat shaft one foot and five inches in breadth, enriched with double-beaded interlacing spirals much worn away. The shaft has been broken across and is now clamped on both faces with iron bands riveted through the stone. The whole height above ground is four feet and two inches, of which two feet represents the diameter of the head."

The red-freestone burial vault with a coat of arms over the entrance is that of the family of Vans Agnew of Barnbarroch, whose mansion house stands among plantations between one and two miles from Kirkinner. The family was Norman originally, and bore the name of Vaus, from Vaux near Bayeux. The name of Agnew was added when the family succeeded to the estate of the Agnews of Sheuchan, and the *Vans* form gradually took the place of *Vaus* or *Waus*, as it was written sometimes. *Andre Vaus de Gallovay, le frère d'armes du Seigneur Archinbald,* according to a French historian, fell at the battle of Poitiers in 1356, fighting against the English. It appears from *The Correspondence of Sir Patrick Waus* that Alexander Vaus held church livings in Galloway so early as the year 1381 and was consecrated bishop of the diocese in 1420. His brother or cousin is said to have married the heiress

of Barnbarroch about 1384. George Vaus, a cousin of Alexander, was also Bishop of Galloway. It was in the time of this
prelate that " the Lords Auditors addressed letters to Andrew
Agnew, Sheriff of Wigtown, ' to take prufe before him, and warn
all parties to be present,' in a case in which George Vaus, now
Bishop of Galloway, sued Sir William Stewart of Garlies and
Lady Euphemia Graham or Vaus, his wife, for ' withholding
the males, farmez, profits, gressums, and other duties, from
Patrick Vaus his nephew, and Lady Euphemia's son.' She
and her second husband had occupied Barnbarroch during
her son's minority and were disinclined to make it over to him
when he came of age. The Lords Auditors, on the sheriff's
report, adjudged that ' they did wrong in the occupation of
the said lands, and shall restore the back rents and duties
so far as Patrick Vaus can prove before the sheriff that they
have retained them '."

Sir Patrick Vaus was the most celebrated member of the
family. He became a Lord of Session with the title of Lord
Barnbarroch in 1589, and was sent to Copenhagen by James
the Sixth to negotiate his marriage with Princess Anne of
Denmark.

A case tried in the sheriff court about 1738 concerned " a
daring attempt by a scamp named M'Cleary to carry off Miss
Vaus of Barnbarroch. The deposition of one of the witnesses,
as taken down on the 29th of November, sufficiently describes
the case.

" ' John Stewart of Phisgill, aged about thirty-three years,
and married, declares as follows :—

" ' I came to the house of Barnbarroch upon a Sabbath day,
the 13th of August last.

" ' About two hours after daylight was gone, I was sitting in
a chamber with Lady Barnbarroch and John Dun, tutor on the
estate. A noise was heard, and presently a servant came and
told that a great number of men with arms had broke into the
house and were then in the kitchen.

" ' I, John Dun, and Lady Barnbarroch ran immediately
downstairs, and there I saw Thomas M'Alexander, a soldier,
holding a cocked pistol in his hands, swearing he would shoot
some one if they did not show him the way upstairs. I also
saw Andrew Mitchell, servant to John M'Clery, holding a pistol
with a drawn hanger in his hand, Robert Dinnan with a pistol,

and one Hannay with a rusty sabre, and several other armed men.

" ' On it being demanded what they wanted, they replied, " Miss Vaus : " and on being told they could not get her, they swore they would go upstairs, upon which they forced by me and broke open the lady's chamber door, and broke it in pieces.

" ' A scuffle ensued, and I, John Stewart, seed M'Alexander and the lady in grips with one another, the lady's head-cloathes torn off her head, and her hair hanging round her face and shoulders. After M'Alexander was disengaged from the lady, he snapped a pistol twice, which was some time afterwards taken from him and a shot found in it.

" ' Meanwhile I saw Hannay seize Miss Elizabeth McDowall, the lady's sister, and saw several of the servants wounded to the effusion of blood.

" ' Before this, Miss Vaus had asked me to lock her into a private cellar, which I did.

" ' M'Clery was now told he could not see her that night, upon which he searched the lady's room, and her bed, and the presses. He then called up his men and placed them sentry over the room, and searched the dining-room and other rooms of the house.

" ' I at the same time saw William M'Beatt in Drumbuie standing on the stairhead with a sabre in his hand, also Simon Guthrie, apprentice to John M'Cailie, wright in Wigtown.

" ' After some communing M'Alexander fired a pistol and they all went off, and the party were lurking about the house. I went out and told them their stay was not agreeable, and they answered they would not go till M'Clery had seen Miss Vaus.

" ' A short time after assistance arrived, which had been sent for, and on this all sallied out to apprehend the party ; but they now ran off, and they could take none but M'Clery, who was brought into Barnbarroch house, and by a warrant of Mr. Heron of that ilk, sent to the Tolbooth of Wigtown.'

" It is to be regretted that the result of the trial, whether adjudicated on by the sheriff or remitted by him to a superior court, is not forthcoming."[1]

[1] *The Hereditary Sheriffs of Galloway.*

# CHAPTER XIV

## SORBIE AND WHITHORN

The Forest—Dowalton Loch—Monuments in the old church of
Sorbie—Garlieston—The Earls of Galloway—Cruggleton Castle
—Cruggleton Church—The Isle of Whithorn—Story of a
smuggler—The Isle of Whithorn Castle—S. Ninian—*Candida
Casa*—Pious pilgrims—Whithorn—The Priory—Ancient monu-
ments—S. Ninian's Cave—The fort at Rispain.

THE changes produced on the face of the earth, whether by
the sudden or slow work of nature or by the artifice of man,
fascinate the imagination—the dislocations, upheavals, and
subsidences wrought by volcanic energy, the basins worn in
living rock by the millennial grinding of the glacier, the attrition
of a gorge, the alteration of a river's course, the march of a peat-
bog, the construction of a lake-dwelling, or the mere clothing of
barren hills or plains with woods where herons and pigeons
nest. This by way of introduction to The Forest and
Dowalton Loch in Sorbie Parish.

Galloway has a tract called The Forest absolutely, forest
in the special sense of woodland, and you pass through it as you
go from Kirkinner to Sorbie village. There is not much of it,
not more than two miles, just enough to let you see that it does
not belie its name, that it is not a mere wood, but The Forest.
On a fine day it will delight you greatly with its sunlit glades
and long vistas and the echoing calls of the birds.

As for its history, it appears that there were no trees here
in the seventeenth century, but that the tradition of an ancient
forest lingered. I thank Andrew Symson—so soon must I
quote him again—for the following sentence : " There is also
in the parish of Sorbie, betwixt the Kirks of Kirkinner and Sorbie,
a large moor, called the Forrest Moor ; but why so called, I

know not, except it be, as the people say, because there was long since a great wood growing therein, though at present there is not one tree growing there, unless two or three bushes may be call'd so." If the older forest was destroyed by a conflagration, one can imagine the spectacle that it would provide for the dwellers on the hills across Wigton Bay, greater than that of the burning lime-kilns on the beach.

The interest of Dowalton Loch grows as one learns about it.

Many an angler, as he drifted over a loch, has wondered what appearance the bottom would present if the water were drained away. At Dowalton, about two miles west of Sorbie village, we see not, indeed, the area of a newly-emptied loch, but its aspect after the passage of many years. Nature has had abundant time to cover the space with vegetation; but the bottom is still of a swampy character.

Five or six of the islands are crannogs or artificial lake-dwellings, one of the most captivating subjects of antiquarian research whether one thinks of the ways in which they have come to light or of the hints that they give about the life of primitive man. It was in 1863 that Sir William Maxwell of Monreith, wishing to expose new land and to drain more thoroughly the extensive meadows and mosses in the western part of the Dowalton valley, cut through the barrier of rock at the east end of the loch. "The water having been partially drawn off," wrote Lord Lovaine, who was then in the neighbourhood, "the bed of the loch exhibits the appearance of an immense sheet of mud, surrounded by beaches of different elevations, covered with large rolled stones and angular blocks of slate. It contains a few small islets, composed apparently of the same materials as the beaches. . . . On visiting the spot, 19th August, 1863, to obtain further information, I observed some timbers standing on an island near the centre of the loch and was told that someone had been there in a boat when it first appeared above water and had found bones, a small granite quern, and piles ; and a spot was pointed out to me at the extremity of one of the little promontories where similar piles were observable, which, on inspection, I found to be true. These piles varied from a foot to eighteen inches in circumference." This was the first discovery of lacustrine dwellings in Scotland.[1]

[1] "In addition to the true crannogs, or timber-built islands, there occur in the Loch of Dowalton and in the White Loch of Raven-

A trench was cut round one of the islands, and thus " a small quantity of ashes was turned up, in which were teeth and burnt bones, a piece of a fine earthenware armlet of a yellow colour, and a large broken earthenware bead, striped blue and white, together with a small metal ornament, apparently gilt ; two other pieces of an armlet of the same material, one striped with blue and white, were also found on the surface."

When a deep cutting was made into the structure, " it proved to be wholly artificial, resting on the soft bottom of the loch ; the uppermost layer was a mass of brushwood about two feet thick ; beneath it large branches and stems of small trees, mostly hazel and birch, mingled with large stones, evidently added to compress the mass ; below that were layers of heather and brushwood, intermingled with stones and soil, the whole resting upon a bed of fern about one foot thick, which appeared in all the structures examined to form the foundation. The whole mass was pinned together by piles and stakes of oak and willow, some of them driven two and a half feet into the bottom of the loch, similar to those above mentioned. The islet was surrounded by an immense number of these, extending to a distance of twenty yards around it ; and masses of stone, which apparently were meant to act as breakwaters, were laid amongst them."

Dr. Munro says of the lowlands of The Shire as a whole that, " though not deeply intersected by river channels, [they] are of an extremely undulating character, consisting of a succession of rounded bosses of rock or hillocks of till, with intervening hollows, many of which are clearly defined as rock-scooped basins. When the great ice-sheet finally disappeared, the country must have been profusely studded with small, shallow lakes. But many of them, owing to the pluvial condition of the climate which subsequently prevailed, have now become entirely obliterated by peat-bogs and other deposits of organic *débris*. When, however, by any chance, portions of these hollows become ex-

---

stone islands to all appearances formed artificially, with masses of large boulders. Excavation on the island in the latter loch established the fact that the base of the construction was a timber platform resting on the peaty bottom. On the level top of this island are the ruins of two parallel rows of rectangular buildings."—The *Inventory*. The White Loch of Ravenstone has been drained. The site is less than a mile west of Ravenstone Castle.

posed, as by the removal of the superficial peat or the artificial drainage of a loch, the rocky bottom is found to have the characteristic glacial polish and markings. Striking instances of these phenomena are at the present time to be seen on the dried bed of Dowalton Loch and that of the partially drained Loch of Dernaglaur, as well as many other places. In the higher districts of Galloway the glacial *striae* (which always indicate the direction of the ice) follow the trend of the valleys, but in the southern and lower parts, as the Rhinns and the Machers,[1] their general direction is from north-east to south-west, a course which appears to have been unaffected by the surface inequalities of the land. But notwithstanding the filling up of so many of these lake basins, there is still no county in Scotland which contains so large a number of lakes and mossy tarns supplying the special conditions of security sought after by the constructors of the lake-dwellings of prehistoric times." [2]

In the old, roofless, ivy-covered church of Sorbie there is a vault in which several of the Earls of Galloway have been buried, and a large slab bearing the following inscription :

Here lyes the Reverend Learned and Zealous Servant of Jesus Christ Master Archibald Haddin, late Minister of the Gospel at Sorbie, who after he had laboured for the space of one and twenty years in the work of the Gospel amongest this people departed this life August the 3 day 1721 aged 45.

> He like a watchman at his post
> With careful diligence and cost
> Of restless pains his station keept
> And oft did wake while others sleept
> The wandring sheep from harm to keep
> And preached and prayed the flock to meet
> In Canaan's pastures where he feeds
> And lives on joys which finite thoughts exceeds.

Another stone erected by Alexander Mackie in memory of his wife, Elizabeth Smith, who died on the 31st of July,

[1] Wigtonshire consists of The Moors, The Machars (the plains), and The Rhinns (the headlands). The Machars is the triangular area between Wigton Bay and Luce Bay. The Rhinns is the peninsula on the south-west. The Moors is the northern part of The Shire.

[2] "The Lake Dwellings of Wigtonshire" by R. Munro, M.A., etc., in *Archæological and Historical Collections relating to Ayrshire and Galloway, Vol. V.*

1816, bears an epitaph which halts both in language and in metre :

> She was—
>> But words are wanting to say what.
> Think what a good wife should be,
>> And she was That.

I went to Garlieston with the intention of spending a night there, but, finding myself the only guest at a comfortable little inn, decided to remain for the rest of a week and explore the

*Garlieston.*

Whithorn country from this point. Garlieston is a pleasant, clean village on a bay. The front row of houses follows the curve. Two bowling-greens occupy part of the ground between the houses and the beach. Before the bowling-greens were laid out there was an open space here providing a field of operations for circuses and itinerant agitators and hucksters. Mr. Alexander A. Cuthbert, who contributed a pleasant chapter

of " Memories of Garliestown " to the thirty-seventh number of
*The Gallovidian*, has told how " on one occasion great havoc
was wrought amongst the stock of a dealer who had spread
out his dishes to the best advantage over an extended area.
A passing horse, led by a long halter, shied at something, and
executed a number of erratic movements among the plates
and bowls. The damage done was considerable, and the
case went into Court. The crockery man was heard in support
of his claim, but he gave such a ravelled account of the circumstances connected with the mishap and introduced so many
irrelevancies that the Sheriff became impatient and was about
to dismiss the case when the poor plaintiff, in an almost de-
spairing effort at a more lucid explanation, exclaimed, ' The
thing's as plain as parritch, my lord. Just for a meenute
suppose yoursel' to be Peter Tamson's horse, an' ye cam' caperin'
by, an' ye kickit up yer auld d—d heels, an' broke my crockery,
wha's to pay me for the damage ? ' If I remember aright, the
crockery man obtained no pecuniary redress, but had to spend
a few hours in a cell for contempt of court."

The burn flowing over the beach near the north end of The
Crescent comes from the area of Dowalton Loch. The harbour,
once the scene of a busy trade, is now almost deserted. An
" excursion " steamer sometimes sails in summer to The Isle
of Man.

The landward street of Garlieston is under the shadow of
the trees in the grounds of Galloway House, long the principal
seat of the Earls of Galloway. The house was built by the
sixth Earl in 1740, and it is said that he chose the site because
nowhere else in The Shire could he have his home surrounded
by such fine trees. A hundred years later, the writer of *The
Statistical Account* says, " In Lord Galloway's pleasure grounds
there are some beautiful specimens of laurel, evergreen oak,
horse-chestnut, and Turkey oak. Some of the laurels rise to
the height of thirty-one feet and are considered among the
finest in Scotland. There is one Turkey oak, planted not more
than fifty years ago, which deserves to be particularly noticed
for its beauty and for the rapidity of its growth. The circumference of its branches is about a hundred and fifty-six feet,
and the girth of its stem measures nine feet, five inches. The
soil here is also peculiarly adapted to the growth of evergreen
shrubs. In his Lordship's garden peaches and figs are suc-

cessfully cultivated on the open wall, even upon south-west
aspects. Here, also, there is a vine which merits notice for
its size and the quantity and quality of its fruit. Its stem
measures thirteen inches in circumference and the spread of
its branches is forty feet. It produces about three hundred
and forty-six bunches, each averaging one and a quarter pounds,
and some of the individual berries are three and a quarter
inches in circumference." Among the more notable trees
to-day are silver firs a hundred feet high, and larches measuring
twelve, and beeches eighteen feet, round the boles. The
trees grow to the edge of the shore, as at Ardwall, and shade
the path running towards Cruggleton Castle.

The Stewarts were originally a Breton family. One of
them came to England in the time of Henry the First, and a
son, Walter fitz Alan, followed David the First into Scotland
and was appointed by him High Steward of the realm. The
office became hereditary, and the family took their name from
it. It was in the person of Alexander, the fourth High Steward,
who was born in 1214, that they first acquired lands in Galloway.
Alexander was appointed one of the Regents of Scotland on
the death of Alexander the Second, led the Scottish contingent
in one of the Crusades, gave valuable services against the
Norsemen in the battle of Largs, and helped to bring The Isle
of Man and the Western Hebrides under the Crown. He
was rewarded with the lands and barony of Garlies, and these
have remained in the hands of his descendants, the Earls
of Galloway, whose chief residence is at Cumloden. Many
members of the family have distinguished themselves in the
Navy and the Army and other branches of public service.
Of the ninth Earl, who died at Galloway House in 1873, Mac-
Kerlie says that " although an Episcopalian and attached to
his own Church, he made no attempt to thrust his creed on
those around him. Instead of this, while he had his own
private chapel, his desire was to do all he could to advance the
interests of the Presbyterian Church as the Church of the people
of Scotland, and particularly of the old race of Gallovidians.
The handsome new parish churches of Minnigaff, Penninghame,
Wigton, and Sorbie remain as records of this, for as the chief
proprietor he had much to do with their erection, the old
churches having become dilapidated from age." A monument
to his memory stands beside the bridge at Newton Stewart.

The site of Cruggleton Castle is on the top of a huge cliff. It is worth while going to see the cliff alone with its sheer fall of two hundred feet to the sea. Of the castle nothing remains but a single fragment of vaulting, a poor little relic of what was once a great fortress. It stands, a clear-cut half-circle against the sky whether seen from the sea or from the land. " Crowgiltone, seated one a rocke, environ'd withe the sea " is mentioned by Timothy Pont, who made a survey and map of Galloway early in the seventeenth century, as one of the " Castells and Gentlemen's Housses of cheiffe notte in the countrey of Galloway ". After passing through the hands of various owners, it came into the possession of the Agnews of Lochnaw in 1642. Symson describes it as " now wholy demolish'd and ruinous ". It appears to have been used as a quarry for less impressive, but more useful buildings.

Cruggleton Castle and Cruggleton Church are in the same latitude. The latter stands in a clump of trees near the road, and the key is kept at a farmhouse a few hundred yards farther south. What I had read about the building led me to apply for the key, and I should advise other travellers to do the same, for this is one of the few examples of early Norman architecture in Galloway. It was probably erected in the twelfth century, and illustrates the Norman type of church with nave and chancel. It appears to have fallen into disuse after the Reformation, and became partially ruined, but towards the end of last century was completely restored by the third Marquess of Bute. The chancel arch seems to have been almost intact. The following details are given in the *Inventory*: " It was an excellent example of early Norman work and had three orders on the west side ; each jamb had two angle shafts which terminated in cushion caps. The in-goings of the jambs and the arch soffit were built of ashlar and finished with a sharp arris at the interior angle next the chancel. An extremely simple impost marked the line from which the chancel arch sprang." There is a single narrow light behind the altar. A few half-buried tombstones rise among the flagstones of the floor.

The meteorological notes in *The Statistical Account* of Sorbie Parish will be of interest both to residents and to travellers. " Our prevailing winds are from the west, south-west, and south ; but in spring and the latter end or autumn, we have often a long period of east wind, which is generally accompanied

by dry weather. The state of the weather is sometimes prog-
nosticated by a cloud resting on Cairnsmoor, a high hill in Kirkcudbrightshire; which, after a long period of dry weather,
affords a pretty sure sign of a change to rain. A dark haze

*Cruggleton Church.*

stretching from the south to the west, and studded with small
white clouds, is remarked as often preceding rain; and an
appearance in the atmosphere, here called the 'weather gaw',
which resembles the rainbow in colour, but is much shorter,
and hangs in a vertical line, is sometimes pointed out as indicating a change."

About a mile south of Cruggleton Church, the road crosses the Kevands[1] Burn and enters Whithorn Parish. I never look at any of the water-courses in the district without recalling a phrase used by the writer of *The Statistical Account*. Most of the contributors to that monumental work wrote in a uniformly dull, conventional manner, and I wish to name as an honourable exception the Rev. Christopher Nicholson, who was minister of the parish in 1839. The phrase he achieved was " innumerable perennial limpid rills "—" Though there are no rivers and few burns, the parish is well watered with innumerable perennial limpid rills." [2] The list of his *elegantiae* is not long, but includes the following departure from crude literalism : " Frost and snow have been of such rare occurrence, and of such short continuance, that the children in Whithorn run the risk of becoming as incredulous about the effect of cold upon water as the Emperor of China."

The Isle of Whithorn deprecates too close a scrutiny of its title to its name. It is only at an exceptionally high tide that the little spur becomes an island. Nor do the inhabitants desire that the name should be justified, for it could only be at their grave inconvenience. There are really two necks in the peninsula, and at an ordinary high tide it is obvious that if the level of the water were raised a few feet, we should have two Isles of Whithorn. Bishop Pococke, who was here in 1760, speaks of a bridge connecting The Isle with the mainland ; but I think that this must be an instance of careless observation. The Prestrie[3] Burn flows into the harbour and is spanned by a bridge ; but the beginning of The Isle is about a hundred yards farther south.

" I came to the isle," says Pococke, " which is a little harbour formed by a pier, within which they have eighteen feet water at high tydes, and a ship of three hundred tuns can come in. They export barley, and import plank and iron from Gotten-

---

[1] Welsh *cefn*, a ridge.
[2] Was he thinking of these lines of Wordsworth ?—

> There is a little unpretending Rill
> Of limpid water, humbler far than aught
> That ever among Men or Naiads sought
> Notice or name !—It quivers down the hill,
> Furrowing its shallow way with dubious will.

[3] Land of the priests.

burgh in Sweden, and send it by boats to Wigtown, as the entrance and harbour there are not good. There is a bridge over to the island, under which the sea passes at high water. The principal houses are on the west side of it, and on the Isle near the bridge is a row of poor houses. This part of the isle is flat, and in high seas the water seems to have come over and divided it from the rising ground beyond it, on which there is a small church. . . . The ground rises higher beyond the church, and the east end of the island has been defended by a fossic, which seemed to be very old, and it is probable that this was the ancient Candida Casa." Although many of the houses have been built or rebuilt since 1760, this account calls for little revision to-day.

The village of The Isle of Whithorn is a place to which visitors come, and I am constrained to set down some little details. The small tower on the highest part of the promontory was built to support a flagstaff used for signalling to ships making the harbour. This was formerly a coastguard station, and there remain on the rocks traces of rings for erecting a tent to shelter the men in their watch in wild weather. It was very likely a coastguardsman who relieved the tedium of life at The Isle by carving the incised compass-table on a rock beside the flagstaff tower. A chart printed in 1818 came into my hands, and I learned from it that there had been a " fish-yard " within the harbour, that is, a certain area confined by a low wall where fish were taken easily as the tide went out. The chart indicates " Stone Dyke for intercepting Fish ". There is an old cottage which used to be known as " the fish-yard house ".

" *The only danger on going in is the reef called the* SCREENS *upon which the tide sets strongly.*" This is a note in a corner of the chart. I had a close view of the Screens one evening when my landlord announced that he was going to fish for " blockans " and invited me to go with him. I had neither a sporting nor a culinary knowledge of the blockan ; but when I remembered that I had read of it in the old account of Galloway written for Sir Robert Sibbald by Dr. Archbald, the invitation was irresistible. Dr. Archbald described the blockan as being " about the bigness of a white salmond-troot, of shape and colour like the lyth, but a dryer fish ". My landlord's preparations suggested that the enterprise was to resemble

I

ordinary fly-fishing; but this promise was not fulfilled. It is true, there was a rod, a line, and a fly; but the line was a short and strong one tied to the rod, and the fly was trolled with a bit of lead to keep it a few inches below the surface. No landing-net was used. With such tackle none was needed. Meanwhile, our boat was rowed along the edge of that reef. As the water surged and lapsed, it gave a glimpse here and there of the terrible teeth. A ship driving upon them must have its bottom stove in or torn out. A danger-signal in the form of a " perch," that is, a tall iron pole supporting a barrel, was set up many years ago. It has suffered a good deal of damage. The barrel is gone, and the wire hawsers, and one stormy day a Dutch barque drifted against the pole and gave it a bend from which it has not recovered.

Mr. Gordon Fraser tells a good story of The Isle of Whithorn Bay in *Lowland Lore*. "Early one morning a richly laden lugger from the Isle of Man was surprised off the Mull of Galloway by the Government cutter under the command of Sir John Reid. The smuggler was running for Cairndoon on the Glasserton shore of Luce Bay, and disregarding the hail and the order to heave to, set every stitch of canvas, and with a freshening south-western breeze sped merrily away followed by the cutter also carrying as much sail as she could stagger under. The wind was increasing, but both vessels held on and made no attempt to shorten sail. An eye-witness describes the rate at which they were going as almost incredible. The lugger stood in for the Glasserton shore, closely followed by the cutter, and as the distance between the two vessels was gradually lessening, it was very apparent that unless something turned up in favour of the smuggler, he would have to heave to, it being thought impossible that she could round the Burrow Head, whose iron coast and jagged cliffs were at the time, on account of the high wind causing an extra rapid tide, more than ordinarily dangerous. But the fearless smugglers' maxim was ' Do or die,' and after being now carried to the giddy pinnacle of a gigantic wave and anon plunged into a yawning chasm of the mighty deep, the dangerous head was rounded. At length it seemed the weary chase was to end in favour of the Revenue cutter, for when the object of its pursuit was off the Isle of Whithorn, it was observed that she was making for the Isle harbour as if giving up her attempts to elude her

pursuer. The cutter, satisfied that her prey was soon to be
in her grasp, shortened sail and followed into the Isle under
easy canvas. But what was her surprise on finding, after she
had leisurely moored, that no lugger was in the harbour!
At the time this incident took place the Isle harbour could be
entered by one route and vessels of small tonnage could clear
by another. No one would have thought the smugglers' large
craft would have attempted to depart by this narrow channel

*The Isle of Whithorn.*

of egress. But owing to the high tide at the time she made
the attempt, she succeeded. The chagrin of Captain Reid
was of no moderate nature when on looking through the port
he had the mortification of seeing his imagined prize standing
away for the English coast with all sail set. When the tide
receded, a few curious seamen at the Isle examined the hazardous
route of the lugger in leaving the harbour, and found a track
made by the keel of the vessel in the shingly bottom about
a hundred yards long. Several large stones had also been

shifted. Carrying so much sail and having great way on,
she had completely forced her passage through the unlikely
channel.''

When Sir John Reid was stationed here as Superintendent
of the Coast Guard, he lived in The Isle of Whithorn Castle.
Symson refers to this building as " a good stone house, on the sea side,
just beside the sea-port of Whitherne, called the Isle of Whitherne." It had been erected in 1674. When I found that I could
have lodgings in so old a house as this, I felt bound to take them.
The *Inventory* gives a very full description and a plan. " The
building is small, but has at one time been a good example of
its type. The plan is of the L-shape, with a comparatively
large staircase in the re-entering angle, practically square. . . .
The main portion facing south is vaulted upon the ground floor.
It has originally been entered by a doorway in the west wall
(now built up), and was no doubt used as a cellar. The main
entrance to the dwelling-house has been at the west side of the
staircase turret. The doorway has been destroyed, and its
place concealed by the erection of an unsightly modern porch.
. . . . A garret is formed in the roof, access to which is gained
by a wooden ' trap ' stair starting at the termination of the stone
stair on the second floor. The two windows in the south wall
lighting the upper floor apartments have been inserted in modern
times. At the corners of the south wing are two angle turrets,
each supported on three corbels at the second floor level. . . .
It is interesting to note that the roof timbers are of home-grown
oak, the slates being fixed to the sarking by means of wooden
pegs."

The southern part of The Machars is associated with no other
historic person so much as with S. Ninian, the first preacher of
the Christian faith in Scotland and the founder of the first
church. His lifetime fell within the latter half of the fourth
century and the early part of the fifth and witnessed, therefore,
the decline and fall of the Roman power in Britain. It is regret-
table that no contemporary biography of so significant a figure
exists. Such a work would have been no doubt, like its successors, a collection of the visions, portents, and miracles dear to the
hagiographer ; but some important facts might have been given
by the way. The earliest allusion to S. Ninian occurs in the
*Historia Ecclesiastica* of Bede, who wrote about three hundred
years after the death of the saint. He records that the

Southern Picts[1] " are said to have forsaken the error of idolatry a long time before ", that is, a long time before 565, " and embraced the true faith as the fruit of the preaching of Ninian, a Briton, a deeply revered bishop, and a man of great sanctity.   He had undergone a course of regular instruction in the faith and the mysteries of the truth at Rome.   His episcopal see, called after S. Martin, the bishop, and famous on account of the church where he rests in the body [2] along with many other saints is now in the hands of the Angles.   The place belongs to the province of the Bernicians and is commonly called The White House.[3]   It received this name because he built the church there of stone, not a common practice among the Britons."   The building presented a marked contrast to the wattled huts of the people.

We come next to Alcuin, that voluminous letter-writer, who lived, like Bede, in the eighth century, and addressed an epistle to the fraternity at Whithorn, dwelling on the noble character of S. Ninian.   It was not until the twelfth century that the earliest remaining biography was compiled.   Its author was Ailred, Abbot of Rievaulx, who visited Galloway as a missionary in 1164 and wrote his *Vita Sancti Niniani* afterwards, basing it, as he says, on an older biography written in " a barbarous tongue ".

The substance of the traditions relating to S. Ninian is that he was a son of a chief and was born on the shore of the Solway ; that he studied at Rome and broke his homeward journey to spend some time with Martin, Bishop of Tours and head of the monastery of Marmoutier ; that he preached the gospel to the Picts of Galloway and built his White House beside the sea ; that, receiving the news of the death of Bishop Martin [4] while

---

[1] The Picts of Galloway were not, of course, the people designated as " Southern Picts " by historians.   The Southern Picts occupied the territory on the south-east of the Grampians, and Bede means that S. Ninian evangelized them besides founding the church in Galloway.

[2] S. Ninian's body was probably buried in the church at The Isle and removed to Whithorn when the church of the monastery was built.

[3] *Ad Candidam Casam.*   For the use of the preposition, cp. *Ad Murum* and *Ad Capræ Caput* in Bede's *Historia Ecclesiastica* (III., 21) and see Miss A. M. Sellar's note in her edition, p. 119. The name, *Candida Casa*, came into common use for the monastery and the diocese.   The bishopric did not include the whole of Galloway, but was limited on the east by the Urr.

[4] S. Martin died about 397.

the church was a-building, he resolved to dedicate it to his memory—Ailred states that Bishop Martin had sent masons to assist in the work—and that he led the Southern Picts to accept the Christian faith.

There has been some difference of opinion about the site of *Candida Casa*; but Ailred's minute description applies, not to Whithorn, but to The Isle. He says that the place was on the coast, ran out into the sea, was bounded by the sea on three sides, and could be approached from the north only. No one but an airman looking down upon the country from a very great

*S. Ninian's Chapel.*

height would think of describing the site of the town of Whithorn in this way. Ailred's language is supported, moreover, by the ruined church at The Isle called S. Ninian's Chapel, a building attributed to the thirteenth century, but the successor almost certainly of *Candida Casa*. Standing beside the rough walls of this little, ancient sanctuary on the sea-washed, wind-swept, green peninsula and looking perhaps on some of the stones of the building erected with apostolic hopefulness more than fifteen centuries ago, one remembers that for the history of Christianity The Isle of Whithorn has a similar significance in Scotland to that of Philippi in Greece or Kiev in Russia.

The fame of S. Ninian was great, and there are numerous

dedications to him in the south and east of Scotland. The tradition that he evangelized Ireland is to be explained perhaps by the fact that the monastery which was soon established at Whithorn was a centre of education attracting Irish students as well as Scottish. Dr. James Mackinnon, whose *Culture in Early Scotland* contains an instructive chapter on S. Ninian, points out that " by one of those singular turns of history, Columba himself was at least indirectly indebted to *Candida Casa*, from the fact that Finnian, the first abbot of the celebrated monastic school of Maghbile, whose disciple he was, enjoyed for several years the benefit of the teaching of Mugentius ", a monk of Whithorn and the author of a Latin prayer which has been preserved. Within a century or two [1] of S. Ninian's death, which is said to have taken place in 432, the foundation had become famous as a home of sacred and secular learning—the university of the period—and was known as *Magnum Monasterium* or *Rosnatense Monasterium* or *Rosnatum Monasterium* or Whithern, which with Irish writers becomes *Futerna*. " Whithern ", of course, is the Saxon equivalent of *Candida Casa* (*hwit erne*) and not, as Camden thought, a translation of Ptolemy's Λουκοπιβία, the name assigned by him to a town west of the Nith. S. Ninian's evangelistic work among the Picts was largely undone by a resurgence of paganism ; but we are not driven to the conclusion that it was extinguished. A fresh impulse was given by the mission of S. Kentigern in the following century, and we learn from Bede that about 730 *Candida Casa* was erected into an episcopal see on account of the increase in the number of the faithful ; but with the waning of the Anglic power in Galloway towards the end of the same century, the bishopric fell into abeyance. The Premonstratensian Priory was founded by Fergus, Lord of Galloway, in the twelfth century ; the bishopric had been revived in 1125 ; and the Priory Church became the cathedral of the diocese. The indefiniteness of the relation of Galloway to the Scottish Crown, shewn already in another connexion,[2] is illustrated by the first bishop's acceptance of

---

[1] Mr. Hume Brown says, " The existence of a monastic school at Whithorn, within a century after Ninian's death, is only a probability."

[2] So late as 1297 Edward the First issued a commission to present the Chancellor of Scotland to a living in Scotland or Galloway—*in dicto regno vel terra Galwediæ.*—Stevenson's *Historical Documents relating to Scotland.*

consecration at York. Obedience to an English primate was
forbidden by the Crown in the case of Scottish bishops.[1]

The royal burgh [2] of Whithorn went to sleep in the year 1581
and has scarcely stirred since that time. For some centuries
before that date the inhabitants never knew when they might
not see some great person in Church or State riding into the
burgh to worship at the shrine ; but in 1581 pious pilgrimages,
which had been forbidden at the Reformation, were made
penal by Act of Parliament to the great loss of Whithorn both in occasions of popular excitement and in revenue.
The burgh slumbers so deeply to-day that it does not even
dream of the kings, queens, nobles, bishops, and abbots who
were once its frequent guests.

Kenneth the Second, who conquered Galloway, is said to have
visited S. Ninian's relics.[3] Mackenzie refers to Carruthers
for the statement about Kenneth the Third, who died in 994,
that "this pious, though guilty, prince visited Whithorn to
pay his devotions at the shrine of S. Ninian ; and thus set
an example which was repeatedly followed by his royal successors". Cardinal Vivian came to Scotland as a papal
legate in the winter of 1176, and passing into Galloway, sailed
from Whithorn to The Isle of Man. King Robert the First
arrived in poor health a few months before he died to plead
at the shrine for his recovery. Margaret of Denmark, the
Queen of James the Third, upon whom the lordship of Galloway
with the customs of Kirkcudbright and Wigton, had been settled
in 1471, made a progress through the district with the King
a few years later to receive the homage of her vassals and seek
the favour of the Saint.

James the Fourth came to Whithorn oftener than any other
sovereign, sometimes more than once a year. His usual routes
were by Ayr, Girvan, Glen App, and Glenluce, or by Dumfries

[1] "When in 1177 a papal legate convened the Scottish bishops,
the Bishop of Galloway refused to attend the meeting on the ground
that he was an English bishop. Although he was suspended in
consequence, his successors maintained his contention, receiving
their consecration from York and acting episcopally within that
province, while taking part in State affairs as Scotsmen."*A History
of the Church in Scotland* by Alex. R. MacEwen, D.D.

[2] In 1511 James the Fourth granted a charter confirming an earlier
one which is believed to have been given by Robert the First.

[3] Bishop Forbes's edition of *Lives of S. Ninian and S. Kentigern.*

and Kirkcudbright ; but when, early in 1507, the Queen had been seriously ill at the birth of a child, and the state of her health, Leslie tells us, grieved the King " sa sair that he wald not be comforted : nouther of man wald receive ony consolatione ", he set off on foot, travelling by Linton, Dolphinton, Crawford, Durisdeer, Penpont, Moniaive, Dalry, Monigaff, and Wigton. The item, " for soling of one pair schone to the King in Penpont, xvj *d* ", in the Lord High Treasurer's Accounts occurs in connexion with this journey.

The accounts shew the sums expended for food and lodging by the way. Thus we find " to the monks of Corsraguell xx *s*.", " to the Freris of Wigtoun, xiiij *s*.", " to the Freris of Drumfreis, xiiij *s*.", " to the monkis of Drumdranan, xx *s*.", " that nycht in Dolphingtoun to the preist for fire, candill, and belcheir, quhair the King lay, xviij *s*.", " in Bigar, quhair the King dynyt, in belcheir, xiiij *s*.", and " in Wigtoun, in belcheir quhar the King lay, xxviij *s*." There is evidence of a picnic on the shore of Loch Ryan on a September day in 1497, for while the King was eating his meal, the horses, which had been turned loose, were consuming the growing oats, and compensation had to be paid to some of the Sheriff's tenants near Innermessan.

After the Queen's recovery from her illness in 1507, both their Majesties went to Whithorn to give thanks. The Queen had a new gown for the occasion, and three pillions were provided for her litter. The charges for the material, lining, stuffing, buckles, trimmings, and making are given—" for vj elne j quartar grene taffeti to the Quene quhen scho raid to Quhithirn ", " for iij elne iij½ quartaris wellus[1] to be ane pilzan to the Quene agane hir passand to Quhithirn ", " for iij elne iij½ quartaris dames[2] to be ane other pilzan for hir ", " for iiij elne half ane quartar chamlot[3] to be ane thrid pilzan ", " for ane steik[4] bukram to lyne the samyn thre pilzans ", " for iiij elne Melan fustian to the thre coddis[5] for the said pilzanis ", " for xxx pund fedderis to stuf the samyn thre coddis ", " for making of the thre pilzans " and " for taggis, bukkilles, and small graith to thaim ".

The King's pilgrimages were not marked by a uniform solemnity, for we read of gifts to singers, pipers, fiddlers, lutanists,

---

[1] Velvet.        [2] Damask.        [3] Camlet.
[4] Roll.        [5] Cushions.

and 'tale-tellers who beguiled his leisure at the halting-places
—" in Linclowden, to the piparis to part amang thaim, be
the Kingis command ", " to the menstrales in Linclowden ",
" to ane fithelar and ane clarschaar[1] in Wigtoun ", " to ane
lutar of Galloway ", " to the foure Italien menstrales ", " to
tua trumpetis that wer at Quhithirn with the King ", " to
ane pipar playit with the schawmis ", " to Wantonnes[2] and hir
marowis that sang to the King ", " to tua tail tellaris " and " to
ane pure man tald talis to the King ". The four Italian minstrels
attended him when he went to Whithorn on foot ; but
they were not accustomed to walking tours, and horses had
to be hired to carry them to Tongland. The King was always
ready for a game or a shooting match by the way, and so we
find " to William Douglas, quhilk he wan fra the King at schuting
with the corsbow, xxviij s.", " to the King to play at the cartis
with the Abbot of Tungland, vj Franch crounis ", and " in
Wigtoun, to the King, quhilk he tynt with David Craufurd
at cors and pile, xlij s." He lost eighteen shillings in a game
of " kyles ", or nine-pins, at Glenluce Abbey to which the
Abbot had invited some of the neighbouring barons. On the
other hand, the note of seriousness is suggested by a payment
" to ane man that gydit the King fra Wigtoun to Quhithirn
before day ". This may mean that he made the journey
fasting.

We have the record of gifts to poor persons met on the way
—" to ane pure man in Dolphingtoun hed ane kow slane ",
" to ane wif that hed hir silvir stollin away ", " to ane dum
cheld that kepit the yet in Lochmabanne ", " to ane pilgryme
of Ingland that Sanct Niniane kythit miracle for ", " to certain
Inglis pilgrymes in Wigtoun " and " to ane Irland freir ".
Finally, there are offerings at churches and chapels and at
Whithorn itself—" to the Kingis offerand to the Haly Croce
of Peblis ", " to the Kingis offerand on the bred in the kirk
of Moffet ", " to the Kingis offerand in our Lady chapell at the
toun end of Drumfreis ", " to the Kingis offerand in Sanct
Medanis kyrk ", " ane relique quhilk the King offerit at Quhithirn, made of the Kingis aun silvir, weyand xxvij½ unce ; for
the fasoun of ilk unce iiij s. ; summa v li. iiij s. Item, for

---

[1] A player on the Irish harp.
[2] " A name given to a singer who impersonated a character of
gaiety and sportiveness."

ij Hary nobles and quik silvir to gilt the samyn, iij *li*. iiij *s*. ",
" the ix day of August, to the Kingis offerand in Quhithirn
at the Rude altair, at the ferter,[1] in the utir kirk, at the reliques
at the hye altair, at the Lady altair, and in the chapell on the
hill[2]; ilk place xiiij *s*., summa iiij *li*. iiij *s*. Item, the x day
of August, Sanct Laurence day, to the Kingis offerand at the
reliques in Quhithirn, xiiij *s*. Item, to Schir Andro Makbrek,

*Whithorn.*

to dispone thare, vi *li*." The King's last visit was in the year
before Flodden.

Archibald Douglas, Earl of Angus—" Bell-the-Cat "—fought

---

[1] The shrine in which the body of the Saint was kept.
[2] " Probably what is termed in the Ordnance Survey Map, Chapel
Outon, which stands on a little eminence of two hundred feet, about
one mile north of Whithern."—Bishop Forbes's edition of *Lives of
S. Ninian and S. Kentigern*.

in that battle and rode off the field with only six attendants.
Both his sons had been killed, and he was so stricken with grief

*Norman Doorway in the Priory Church.*

that he retired to Whithorn for consolation and died there before
the end of the year.

Visits of James the Fifth occurred in 1526 and 1533, and of Queen
Mary in 1563. In humbler rank we find in the " will of Robert

Ardean, 22 Oct. 1540, 32 Hen. viii ", in *Lancashire and Cheshire Wills,* published by the Chetham Society : " Also I will that one be hyryt to go for me. . . . Seynt Truyons[1] in Scotlande, and offer me a bende placke whyche ys in my purs." [2]

*The Pend leading into the Priory.*

In those days the buildings of the priory had an imposing appearance, rising above the lowly cottages of the burgh. Now

[1] The Saint's name appears in a variety of forms such as Ringan, Ringen, Dingan, Trinyon. *Cp.* Killantringan (Ninian's church) in the parishes of Portpatrick, Leswalt, and Ballantrae ; S. Ringan's Well in Kelton, and Chipperdingan in Kirkmaiden, which has the same meaning.

[2] Forbes.

the conventual church is screened behind the two-storey houses
erected after the Napoleonic wars. The Rev. Christopher
Nicholson, who wrote in 1839, says, " The burgh of Whithorn
consists chiefly of one street, running from north to south,
which is very irregular being inconveniently narrow at both
extremities, and uselessly wide in the middle. The town-house
and gaol were removed about twenty years ago from the middle
of the street, where they formerly stood, and are now erected
upon the west side of the street, about the centre of the town,
and ornamented with a steeple." Besides the town-house and
jail, there was at one time a row of shops or booths in the middle
of the street called, like a similar range in the High Street
of Edinburgh, the Luckenbooths. Although the street may be
now " uselessly wide ", it has acquired a certain dignity through
the removal of that old row.

The only part of the priory buildings visible from the street
is the archway called The Pend.[1] It is surmounted by a shield
bearing the Royal Arms of Scotland.[2] Passing through it,
one sees the walls of the nave.

Near the south-west angle is a famous Norman doorway, the
richest piece of old architecture remaining in Galloway. The
account in the *Inventory* is as follows : " It is four feet wide
and eight feet, three inches, from the ground to the soffit of
the arch-head, containing four orders of engaged shafts in the
jambs, and the same number of orders in the arches. Three
of the latter are enriched with characteristic chevron ornament,
while the second order has flower and interlaced designs irregularly arranged. The mouldings of the bases, caps, and abaci

---

[1] " The arch . . . . is modern, not older than the seventeenth
century. The pillars at the sides . . . . are said to have been
taken from the Prior's House, and may be of the fifteenth century.'
—Note by Kemp in his edition of Pococke's *Tours*. " The mouldings
and detail of the archway are of very late date, probably fifteenth
century. The caps contain two shields : the one on the west side
may be blazoned, quarterly, 1st and 4th, a bend (for Vaus) ; 2nd
and 3rd, three covered cups (for Shaw) ; above the shield a mitre.
The shield on the east side bears the Vaus arms, a bend which i
divided into three rows of panes each diapered with a quatre-foi
ornament. Behind the shield is a crozier."—The *Inventory*.

[2] " A lion rampant within a double tressure flory counter-flory
above the shield, a crown of eight leaves (half shown) with supporters
two unicorns, gorged with similar crowns, and beneath the shiel
two thistles."—The *Inventory*.

are characteristic of late Norman work. There are indications that the doorway has been rebuilt in its present position. Several of the voussoirs have been replaced by rough substitutes. One has the chevron ornament inverted, another consists of a round boulder instead of a hewn stone. It is also noticeable that the horizontal joints in the masonry of the jambs are not in alignment, as might be expected in good Norman work. The carved work of the caps and corbel terminations is also singular. The flower-like ornament used for the outer caps on each side corresponds to that in the arch voussoirs. The second caps are decorated, each with a rough quatre-foil ornament, which has not the appearance of Norman work. Built into the wall at each side of the arch are three

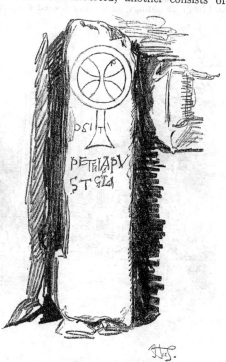

*The "Petri Apustoli" Cross at Whithorn Priory.*

carved stones which seem to have belonged to some earlier building, judging by the irregular way they are placed without reference to the design. A ridge or raggle is cut into the upper part of the wall and traversing the outer ring of the arch, clearly shows that a porch roof was built against this part of the nave at a late period."

The Museum in the lane beyond The Pend contains a remark-

able collection of sculptured stones.[1]   One of them is reckoned
among the most ancient monuments of British Christianity

[1] Besides those mentioned in the text, there are many cross-
shafts of green slate with interlaced work, bosses, incised crosses,
and bead mouldings, and many carved fragments.   Some of these

*Glasserton Church.*

are classed as Norse relics, shewing a "transition from Anglian
work to debased floral scrolls, hammer-head crosses, broken ring
plaits and ruder cutting, characteristic of the Viking period in
Cumberland and Yorkshire. . . . As Iona was the burial-place of
Hebridean chieftains, so Whithorn must have been the mausoleum
of the notables" of the Galloway coast.—W. G. Collingwood's
*Scandinavian Britain.*

and is described in the *Inventory* as " a rude pillar-stone, four feet high by one foot, three inches wide by nine and a quarter inches thick, inscribed on one face with the Chi-Rho monogram (in the unique form of a cross with expanded ends to the arms enclosed within a circular ring), and three horizontal lines of debased Latin capitals which read as follows :—LOC STI PETRI APVSTOLI—The place of S. Peter the Apostle. The first occurring S is a Gaelic form of that letter. This stone long stood at the roadside about a quarter of a mile south of Whithorn." It is referred to in the " Introduction " to the *Inventory* as shewing " characteristics found on similar monuments in France which date from the commencement of the sixth to the end of the seventh century. The inscription, LOC(US) S(ANC)TI PETRI APVSTOLI, is held to imply that it was a termon cross, marking the boundary of church lands or sanctuary girth. There is no similar monument now in Britain, though Fordun records one with an analogous inscription dug up at Peebles in 1261."

There is also " a rude pillar-stone of indurated claystone inscribed on one face with twelve horizontal lines of debased Latin capitals."

TE D(OM)INV
LAVDAMV(S)
LATINVS
ANNORVM
XXXV ET
FILIA SVA
ANNI V
IC SINVM
FECERVNT
NEPVS
BARROVA
DI

" We praise Thee, O Lord. Latinus aged thirty-five years and his daughter of five. Here the descendants of Barrovad made the monument (to them)." This stone bears no symbols of any kind. Certain characteristics of the inscription " common to pre-Christian epitaphs, and also to those of the very early Christian period in Britain and the Continent, indicate for it a fifth or sixth century date ". (*See* pages viii–ix.)

The most delightful short journey to be made from Whithorn keeps us still within the orbit of S. Ninian. It is to the cave [1] on

---

[1] The cave is railed in, and the key kept at Kidsdale farmhouse.

S. Ninian's Cave.

the shore of Glasserton Parish to which, according to an ancient belief, he used to go for devotional retreat. The tradition is supported by the discovery in recent times of incised crosses among the *débris* or carved on the rock. A low wall of dry-stone masonry stretches across the opening, and at the left end four steps descend to the floor, which is almost entirely covered with flagstones. A large water-worn boulder in which a circular basin had been cut was found when the paving was cleared. A trickle of water fell into it over the mouth of the cave, and the overflow was carried away by a drain. There is no reason to doubt that here by the margin of the sea the sometimes anxious evangelist and pastor sought the way of mystical peace.

> Troubled long with warring notions,
>   Long impatient of Thy rod,
> I resign my soul's emotions
>   Unto Thee, mysterious God !
>
> What avails the kindly shelter
>   Yielded by this craggy rent,
> If my spirit toss and welter
>   On the waves of discontent ?
>
> Parching Summer hath no warrant
>   To consume this crystal Well ;

Rains, that make each rill a torrent,
  Neither sully it nor swell.

Thus, dishonouring not her station,
  Would my Life present to Thee,
Gracious God, the pure oblation
  Of divine tranquillity !

*The View from S. Ninian's Cave.*

The fort at Rispain near Whithorn is usually described as
Roman ; but doubt is thrown on this attribution in the " Introduction " to the *Inventory*. " Though the appearance of the
Rispain fort does in some respects conform to the recognised
Roman plan, unlike such Roman forts as have been excavated,
it had only one entrance. The dimensions were, however,
small, a fact which might account for a departure from the
usual plan applicable to larger enclosures. The forms of
mediæval camps are frequently rectilinear, and the plan alone
is therefore not sufficient to establish its character. If Rispain
is Roman, it stands in singular isolation, supported by no other
fort, for the situation of the fort at Crows does not suggest a
Roman origin ; further, no Roman road traverses Galloway,
and the record of Roman relics found within the province is a
singularly scanty one. A landing on the coast near Whithorn,
and a very temporary occupation, are the only hypotheses that
may fit the circumstances."

*The White Loch of Myrton.*

## CHAPTER XV

### MONREITH

The Maxwells of Monreith—John Maxwell and the Pentland Rising
—The first baronet and some of his successors—The standing
stones of Drumtroddan—Cup-and-ring markings—Crannogs—
An ancient Celtic cross and its story—A lake sanctuary—The
garden—The Right Honourable Sir Herbert Maxwell, Baronet—
The house—Kirkmaiden-in-Fernis Church and the story of
S. Medana—Sir Herbert Maxwell's latter days.

THE lands of Myrton,[1] now a part of the territory belonging
to the Maxwells of Monreith, were previously in the hands of
the MacCullochs, and it was in the now ruined keep of Myrton,
distant less than half a mile from the modern house of Monreith,
that Sir Alexander MacCulloch, the most eminent member of
the family, entertained James the Fourth on more than one of
his journeys to and from Whithorn.

It was not until the seventeenth century that the later owners
of the lands of Myrton had a home beside the White Loch ;
but there were Maxwells of Monreith for centuries before that,
for the name of the estate belonged originally to a property

[1] Pronounced " Murrton." The full name is Myrton McCulloch,
the castle having been the chief residence of the McCulloch family.
A.S. *mere tun*, the dwelling beside the lake.—Maxwell.

conterminous with the old parish of Kirkmaiden-in-Fernis, which
is now incorporated in Glasserton Parish, and the Maxwells
were in possession so far back as the fifteenth century. They
were descended from the first Lord Maxwell and inter-married
with such families as the MacDoualls of Logan, the MacCullochs
of Myrton, and the Agnews of Lochnaw. John Maxwell,
younger of Monreith, who married Margaret, daughter of Andrew
Agnew, younger of Lochnaw, in 1656, was one of the Covenanters
who took part in the Pentland Rising and is said to have been
one of the three companions of Maclellan of Barscobe who had
to do with the initial *mêlée* at Dalry. He escaped from the battle-
field of Rullion Green, and his " good grey horse " is said to have
carried him without a halt to the old house of Monreith. As
a reward for its services the horse was never made to wear the
bridle again, but was kept in a large paddock and well cared for.
It is said to have lived to a green old age and to have become
the sire of a progeny long famous in The Shire for their mettle.
" As guid as Pentlan' " was, perhaps still is, a common expression
in the district in recommending a horse.

John Maxwell, to quote Sir Herbert Maxwell's account, " was
afterwards hotly pursued through various parts of the kingdom.
On a subsequent occasion, to escape from some soldiers in Edinburgh, he darted down a close and into a change-house, where
the landlady locked him into the meal-girnel. The soldiers
came and hunted every corner of the house in vain. They
vowed the fugitive had entered it ; but baffled in their pursuit,
they called for drink, and sat down to discuss it. One of them
sat on the top of the meal-chest within which Maxwell lay hid.
' I wadna say,' cried he, ' but yon bloody Whig is in this vera
kist. Gudewife, gie's the key till we see for oorsells.' The
landlady was equal to the occasion. Going to the foot of the
stairs, she called up, ' Jeanie, lass, rin awa' and ask the gudeman
for the key of the girnel, till we see if a Whig can lie in the meal
and no gie a hoast wi't.' The soldiers laughed, finished their
liquor, and went off." The session records of Glasserton Parish
state that " John Maxwell, brother to Sir William Maxwell of
Monreith, was forfeit in his estate for going to Pentland and not
joining with Prelacy. He was necessitated to hide himself
many a night and day, and to turn his back on all that he had,
and to flee to Ireland for the preservation of his life from bloody
persecutors, and died there."

William, the younger brother of John Maxwell, succeeded in 1671, and is an important figure in the family history. He was an Episcopalian and enjoyed the royal favour and became a

*The Old Tower and Mote of Myrton.*

baronet of Nova Scotia in 1681. Before this he had made large additions to the estates, and in 1683 purchased the lands of Myrton from Sir Godfrey MacCulloch. He obtained a charter from Queen Anne in 1703 constituting his property one barony to be called Monreith. He died in 1709 and was followed by his son, Alexander, who married a daughter of the ninth Earl

*Port William.*

of Eglinton. Sir Alexander is the subject of a charming chapter entitled " An Eighteenth Century Laird " in the fifth series of Sir Herbert Maxwell's *Memories of the Months*, wherein we are given glimpses into the intimate life of a Scots country house of the period. It was Sir William, the fourth baronet, who built and gave his name to Port William, the principal village and only seaport in the parish of Mochrum. His successor, Lieutenant-Colonel Sir William Maxwell, served in the Peninsular War and lost an arm at the battle of Coruña. The sixth baronet, also named William, was keenly interested in the history and antiquities of the Province and was able to supply Mr. P. H. MacKerlie with much information for his *History of Lands and their Owners in Galloway*. It fell to his son, who succeeded him in 1877, not only to share his historical and antiquarian bent, but also as a writer of unusual versatility and charm to make the name of Maxwell of Monreith widely known in the world of letters. He wrote many volumes of history, biography, and fiction and made numerous contributions to the literature of natural history, sport and archæology. A bibliography is given in *Who's Who*.

It was a happy circumstance that Monreith estate itself should be rich in antiquities, and that, when the proprietor discoursed of standing stones, crannogs, or cup-and-ring markings, he should be able to shew examples of all of these within a few minutes' walk of his house. The three standing stones on the farm of Drumtroddan[1] are, I think, the most impressive examples of this kind of relic in Galloway by reason of their great height, which is intermediate between that of the lower and that of the majority of the taller monoliths at Stonehenge. They are hidden in the midst of a dense thicket, and it would not be easy to find them without personal guidance or very minute instructions. The *Inventory* notes the site as being about a quarter of a mile north-east of the north lodge gate of Monreith House. Two of the stones are erect, and one has fallen. The height of the upright stones is a little over ten, and that of the prostrate one nine feet.

The cup-and-ring markings are in a neighbouring field. Their position and character are given thus in the *Inventory*: " In a grass field about half a mile north of the north lodge of Monreith House is a flat rock surface, on which is exposed, where the turf has been removed, several groups of cup and ring markings. . . . The markings occur at both ends of the rock, as well as near its centre, and may be divided into seven different groups. They consist of simple cups, or cups surrounded with

[1] Gaelic *druim trodain*, ridge of the quarrel.

varying numbers of concentric rings, from one to five. The circles are represented both with a radial groove from the central cup and without it : in group number two, five circular figures are connected by channels." The *Inventory* states also that " near the west side of Mid-Myrton plantation, which lies to

*Ancient Cross and the White Loch of Myrton.*

the west of Monreith Mains, on the exposed face of a rock, there is visible a single cup mark surrounded by four incised concentric rings. The greater part of the rock is covered with soil."

The oak piles of a crannog still rest in the midst of the area occupied formerly by the Black Loch of Myrton, and towards the southern end of the White Loch there is an island which has been found to be surrounded with oaken piles and constructed of materials similar to those in the crannogs of Dowalton Loch.

Besides these antiquities visible in their original situations, there is an ancient disc-headed Celtic cross standing on the lawn in front of Monreith House. It is said that when the first baronet purchased Myrton Castle and lands from Sir Godfrey MacCulloch, " he wished to take this old cross with him to his new castle, and that when he arrived with it at the march burn betwixt the baronies of Monreith and Myrtoun, flames burst out of the stone, the cart was upset, and the stone broken in two ; and on hearing from a wise woman that there never would be luck to the house of Monreith if the stone was carried away from the barony, the baronet ordered it to be taken back ". When the modern house was built in 1799, the cross was brought from its old place without misadventure. The following delineation is given in the *Inventory* : " In the grounds of Monreith House is a freestanding wheel-headed cross of greywacke measuring seven feet and six inches in height, one foot and six inches in diameter across the head, one foot and three inches in width across the shaft, and six inches in thickness, sculptured in relief on four faces thus :—*Front and Back*— On the circular head, an equal-armed cross with a boss in the centre, and four bosses in the circular interspaces between the arms, and on the shaft a single panel containing interlaced work. *Right and Left Sides*—On the shaft, a single panel containing interlaced work. The cross formerly stood on Court Hill at the Mower, the old Mansion House of the Barony of Monreith, and it has been surmised that its original site may have been Kirkmaiden."

The White Loch of Myrton has more than an archæological interest. It is a beautiful feature of the grounds of Monreith, for its sloping banks are covered with trees nearly all the way round, and the branches in many places overhang the water. Great clumps of rushes provide another ornamental detail, and here and there you will see a little bay brightened with rose-coloured and other hybrid water-lilies as well as the common kinds. The part of the bank where the continuity of the fringe of trees is broken is the end near the front of the house, so that from this point one looks down the vista afforded by the whole length of the loch. The Canadian pond-weed (*Elodea canadensis*) arrived here some time ago with its usual dis-

*Myrton Tower and the White Loch.*

astrous effect; but, wrote Sir Herbert, " although the appearance of this weed on a sheet of ornamental water is nothing short of a calamity, it is a calamity not without mitigation. The angler may weep or swear, according to temperament or sex ; but great is the gain to the wild-fowler and naturalist, for this succulent weed offers irresistible attraction to numberless aquatic birds. . . . Simultaneously with the outburst of *Elodea*, the widgeon arrived. This beautiful duck, though common on the adjacent sea-coast, was never seen, at least by me, on this lake till the autumn of 1893, when five of them spent the winter there and added their wild whistle to the familiar sounds of the place. The following year there were about a score, and at the moment of writing (1896) they may be seen in hundreds." After four years of the turbidity caused by diatoms and other micro-organisms the water recovered its transparency.

Another paragraph may be quoted from the first series of *Memories of the Months* for the list of waterfowl to be seen on it : " This lake is a never-failing source of interest to me. Occupying about one hundred acres, bosomed in sloping woods, and distant from the sea not more than a mile of bird-flight, it is resorted to by great numbers of waterfowl of many kinds. For more than half a century it has been treated as a sanctuary. No impious gun is allowed to be fired there—a regulation which, in my salad days, I used to denounce bitterly as quixotic and tyrannical. No doubt it appears in the same light to the rising generation ; but to the field naturalist it has afforded unusual opportunities of observation. Mallard, teal, coots, water-hens, water-herons, and snipe haunt it all the year round ; cormorants and seagulls fly in from the sea ; in autumn flights of widgeon, tufted duck, and pochards arrive, and a few scaup and goldeneyes drop in to tea, as it were ; wild swans and goosanders are among the rarer visitors, and four years ago a bittern condescended to take up his quarters in the reed-bed at the lower end." A few great crested grebes have nested here every season since 1897, and a visit from the Sclavonian grebe was recorded in January, 1901. A pair of purple waterhens (*Porphyrio coeruleus*) spent a summer here ; but when, it is supposed, they scented the harvest fields beyond the woods, they flew over to the stubbles, where they were murdered by young savages armed with catapults.

The Monreith garden and woods as well as the White Loch have a special interest for anyone who is already acquainted with that delightful series of seven volumes called *Memories of the Months*, wherein the author included many discourses on things seen and heard in the immediate neighbourhood of his own house; and here I may tell any reader who does not know them that no country house, or for that matter no town house where good literature and the amenities of country

*Monreith House.*

life are understood, should be without them. Three other volumes of a more or less similar kind from the same pen should be placed beside them—*Meridiana : Noontide Essays ; Post Meridiana : Afternoon Essays ;* and *Scottish Gardens.*

The garden at Monreith is primarily that of a botanist; yet it is full of interest and charm even for the uninitiated, so happily have the borders been laid out and the herbs within them disposed, there is such a profusion of unfamiliar flowering shrubs, and such a number of captivating scents. I remember being struck by this last detail on a warm forenoon in the latter part of June, when it seemed to me that there was a remarkable variety of fragrances greeting one in turn or subtly blending.

Sir Herbert held that a garden should have an individual character. The high surrounding walls that are so common in these northern latitudes may be needed sometimes; but surely nothing militates so much against the development of a distinctive appearance as confinement within such bonds. Fortunately they are rarely thought necessary in Galloway. One might transfer to Monreith what Sir Herbert wrote of another estate in his volume on *Scottish Gardens* : there is here " none of that tiresome affectation which thrusts the garden proper out of sight and prepares a few formal borders as a set-off to the architect's design. The garden here is part and parcel of the dwelling, a suite of roofless apartments, as it were, into which you can pass at any moment through a pretty gate of wrought iron, with no more trouble than going upstairs." This I should single out as the first attractive feature of this garden, that it is not shut off by itself within stone barriers, but comes up to the house like a besieging sea, breaking in a surf of blossoms against the very walls.

There is an isolated part immediately behind the house, a semi-circular terrace bounded by a low stone balustrade. This structure is decked with roses and other creepers, and within it runs a narrow grassy walk. A design wrought in clipped boxwood on a ground of shells—the Hebrew poet's aphorism, *Homo quasi flos egreditur et conteritur*—fills a concentric semicircle within the walk, and the rest of the space is occupied by little herbaceous plots with a boxwood edging. Half-way round, the balustrade gives way to a flight of stone steps leading down to a lawn broken here and there by clumps of rhododendrons, rose shrubs, and bamboo. This part of the grounds merges in, rather than is confined by, the surrounding woodland, for there has been a lengthwise clearance of the trees carried backwards for a considerable distance, so that, looking from the windows of the house or from the semi-circular terrace or from the lawn itself, one's eye travels down a woodland vista.

The main section of the formal garden flanks the house on the left and stretches up to the margin of the woods in that direction. The masses of exquisite flowering shrubs and the herbaceous

*A Corner in the Garden, Monreith.*

borders laid out in far-drawn curves provide a rich and varied feast for both sight and smell, while the scenic effect is helped by the observance of the precept implied in the statement that

" the columnar habit of such evergreens as the Lawson cypress, the incense cypress (*Libocedrus decurrens*), and the pencil cedar (*Juniperus virginianus*) is of priceless effect among flower-beds, providing those vertical lines which, as given by the Italian cypress, impart such a charming character to Mediterranean scenery ". Here also, as one looks up the length of the section, a narrow opening among the trees on a rising slope beyond gives at least the suggestion of another vista. The excellence of the trees as a background for the various borders and plots is apparent here also, and may be illustrated by this little picture from Sir Herbert's own pen : " No more splendid effect can be wrought with flowers than that which is before my eyes as I write. A large clump of torch lilies, occupying a circular bed on a slope of well-kept lawn, has thrown up more than a hundred spikes of vivid scarlet and yellow. Behind them is a dark wood ; the effect when the sun strikes the lilies is almost dazzling."

Sir Herbert Maxwell was one of the greatest authorities of his time on arboriculture and sylviculture. He urged upon the country through the medium of the leading reviews the need for the afforestation of national reserves and himself made experiments at Monreith with certain kinds of trees such as cypresses and araucarias to test their value for timber in this climate. He also made patient attempts to naturalize foreign species of birds and beasts; but, he wrote sadly, " the only permanent additions to the resident fauna for which I am responsible are three in number, and they are not examples of acclimatisation, but of restoration ", namely, badgers, jays, and squirrels. He exerted himself both within and outside of Parliament for the protection of wild birds and their eggs and was the author of a Bill which passed into law for the preservation of the S. Kilda wren. He acted as President of the Scottish Society of Antiquaries and was the first Chairman of the Royal Commission on the Ancient and Historical Monuments and Constructions of Scotland and furthered the bringing of numerous objects of archæological interest under the protection of His Majesty's Office of Works. The value of his books relating to Galloway is evidenced by the frequency of the references in these pages. Besides these various activities calling for special notice in a book of the scope of the present, Sir Herbert Maxwell was Parliamentary representative of Wigtonshire from 1880 till 1906, and a Lord of the Treasury from 1886 till 1892, was made a Privy Councillor in 1897, Lord-Lieutenant of The Shire in 1903, and a Knight of the Order of the Thistle in 1933.

In writing about country homes one does not find often that the interest of the personality of the proprietor overshadows that of the house in which he dwells. Sir Herbert, however, was a unique figure, not only among Scottish landlords, but among contemporary men of letters; and the surroundings of the house had absorbed so much of his thought and care, and their aspect been determined so largely by his taste, that in any account of Monreith the house itself was apt to receive scant consideration. It was inevitable that so keen an antiquarian should regret that the family deserted the old tower of Myrton,[1] which stands roofless now on a green height among trees near the east shore of the loch. The modern house, however, has a spaciousness and comfort far beyond what was possible in the former residence, and is, moreover, furnished and decorated with many of the old possessions of the family. The foundations of the noble collection of books were laid by Sir Alexander, the second baronet, who succeeded in 1710 and was " a great book-buyer ". His

*Sir Herbert Maxwell.*

dark mahogany dining-room table stands in one of the two large rooms forming the library, and a carved mahogany four-poster bed which he purchased in 1711 is still in use. There hangs on a wall of the ante-room and above the great stair a remarkable piece of *appliqué* work, on which Sir Herbert wrote at some length in *Scottish Gardens*. " This was the work of the wife of the third baronet (he died in 1771), who set herself to depict

---

[1] Myrton Tower is an instance of a keep erected on a mote.

in *appliqué* the flowers growing in the castle garden. They
were laid on a maroon ground to serve as a carpet—literally
a *parterre*—for the castle drawing-room. . . . A large basket
of flowers forms the centre ; smaller groups fill the four corners,
and round the carpet runs a continuous wreath looped with
ribbons."

Many of the objects of archæological value which came
into Sir Herbert's hands were given by him to the National
Museum of Antiquities in Edinburgh; but some which he
retained are arranged in cases in the library, while a cabinet
standing in another apartment contains war-medals received by
various members of the family. The walls of both the dining-
room and the drawing-room are hung with portraits including
King James the Seventh and Second, who is represented as a
very little boy ; Lady Jean Montgomerie, daughter of the ninth
Earl of Eglinton and wife of the second baronet of Monreith—
her portrait has been described as " a charming kit-cat of one
with soft brown eyes, a white skin, and abundant curling dark
hair " ; Eglintine Maxwell, daughter of the third baronet and
wife of Thomas Wallace of Lochryan, and her sister, Jean,
who was married to the fourth Duke of Gordon ; Sir Murray
Maxwell, K.C.B., the third son of Captain James Maxwell and
a grandson of Sir Alexander—he was born in 1775, entered the
Navy in 1790, became lieutenant in 1796 and commander in
1802, took part in the capture of Tobago and Demerara, became
Lieutenant-Governor of Prince Edward's Island, and died in
1831.

Of the losses suffered by Galloway in the Great War, none
was more widely and deeply regretted than that of Sir Herbert's
son, Colonel Aymer Maxwell. He commanded the " Collingwood " Battalion at Antwerp with the rank of lieutenant-
colonel, was struck on the head by a splinter of shell, and died
very soon in hospital. Commodore Henderson said in his de-
spatch : " His fine spirit animated his whole Battalion, and it is
to his example that I owe the fine and steady stand made by
the Collingwoods in their trenches." Colonel Maxwell was the
author of books on the grouse moors and pheasantries of
Britain.

On Monreith Bay, close under a steep, wooded slope, is one of
the oldest churches in Scotland, Kirkmaiden-in-Fernis. Its origin
is connected with the story of Medana, the beautiful daughter of

an Irish king. Among her many suitors there was a soldier—
*miles nobilis*—who was especially determined to win her. The
princess, however, had embraced the Christian faith and had
secretly taken the vow of celibacy. Rendered desperate by

*Kirkmaiden-in-Fernis.*

her suitor's persistence, she fled with two handmaids to Galloway
and landed at Portankill in The Rhinns, a place which took its
name from the chapel she built there, and led a life of poverty
and good works. One day she was startled by voices on the

shore. Her soldier rushed in and threw his arms about her.
She slipped from his grasp and, followed by her handmaids,
rushed into the surf and took refuge on a rock amid the water.
Her lover hastened after her ; but before he could reach her,
the rock floated off and carried its precious burden across to
Monreith Bay, where Medana found a short-lived peace. Her
lover discovered her new place of retreat. When he came into
sight, the lady promptly climbed a tree. " Why persecute me
thus ? " she exclaimed. " Those eyes compel me," her lover
began, and before he could say more, she tore them out and
threw them at his feet, saying, " Take them then ! " Distracted,
broken-hearted, and repentant, he went on his way. Medana
came down from her tree and asked her attendants for water to
bathe her aching face. Just as she was being told that there
was none at hand, a clear, healing stream broke out of the sloping
ground where her eyes had fallen. She washed with it and
recovered her sight. Her saintly life knew no further disturbance, and she was ultimately canonized. The chapels she had
built on the two sides of Luce Bay became the mother churches
of Kirkmaiden-in-Rhinns and Kirkmaiden-in-Fernis. If anyone doubt the details of the story, let him listen to Sir Herbert
Maxwell : " There, on the sweep of strand before the church,
lies the very rock which served Medana and her maids as a
ferry-boat, just where they left it on landing ; and there also is
the well bubbling cool and fresh from the rock, much venerated
at this day as a wishing-well by lovers and other afflicted persons.
To doubt the truth of the legend of St. Medana is to disregard
the plain evidence of one's senses."

The chancel of the old church is the burial-place of the Maxwells of Monreith. It was restored by Sir Herbert in the style
of the twelfth century, with a Norman arch and a round-
headed window. In one of the nameless graves in the churchyard
lies the body of Captain Thurot, a French naval officer, who
distinguished himself in the war between Britain and France
in 1760. He sailed into Belfast Lough with three vessels,
captured Carrickfergus Castle, and marched to Belfast, where he
requisitioned supplies. A little later, he was surprised in Luce
Bay by a superior British fleet, and he and three hundred other
Frenchmen were killed or drowned. His body came ashore in
Monreith Bay, and Sir William Maxwell gave it honourable
burial.

The memory of an earlier naval incident belonging to this coast is preserved in the name of a spit of shingle a few miles to the north, "Philip and Mary Point." It was called after a ship of the Spanish Armada that came aground there.

The succession to the Monreith baronetcy had continued from father to son from the time of the first holder of the title until Sir Herbert was followed by his grandson, Sir Aymer. Colonel Maxwell had married Lady Mary Percy, a daughter of the seventh Duke of Northumberland.

Sir Herbert was as remarkable a man in his latter years as he had been in his prime. When he was ninety years of age, he resigned the office of Lord-Lieutenant, and a little earlier gave up the chairmanship of the Royal Commission on Ancient Monuments; but for the most part he continued to carry the full burden of the many public and business responsibilities that he had undertaken, giving even to the affairs of The Province, The Shire, and the parish the scrupulous attention and ungrudging labour that he formerly gave to those of a Parliamentary committee, and with a geniality and charm that endeared him to all who were associated with him. He did not allow private sorrows to deflect him from the fulfilment of public duty, and in social relations permitted himself no relaxation of punctilio on account of his age. Even when he was in his ninety-third year, if he were escorting a departing guest to the railway station, he would insist on leaving the car and accompanying him to the platform, and then, when the train had come in, would follow him to his compartment and remain in talk until the train drew away. His interest in his favourite studies remained as strong as ever. A little more than a fortnight before he died, he wrote in a letter, "Among the early Christian structures in this county I reckon none more interesting than the 'Wells of the Rees' in Kirkcowan parish. . . . It is a very interesting spot, but I shall never see it again, for it can only be reached by a long and rough scramble." As he added year to year with lessening strength, his stature seemed rather to grow than to diminish in the eyes of his fellow-countrymen, and when it became known that after an illness of two days he had drawn his last breath on the 31st of October 1937, it seemed to many that "a whole wing of their palace of life had fallen".

*Glenluce.*

# CHAPTER XVI

## GLENLUCE AND NEW LUCE

The road to Glenluce—George Borrow's notes—The Devil of Glen
luce—A witch story—Glenluce Abbey—How " the landis o
Glenluse wes conqueist "—Story of Jock o' the Horn—The
Castle of Park—Stairhaven—Some smuggling incidents—The
Sands of Genoch—New Luce and Alexander Peden, " the
Prophet "—Laggangairn and Craigmoddie.

An excellent road runs from Monreith to Auchenmalg, a distance
of about eleven miles, keeping close to the shore almost all the
way. There are no old buildings to arrest one's attention, and
one will probably pass the slight remains of a chapel dedicated
to S. Finnian without noticing them. By scrambling up the
green heugh on the right, one would no doubt find the remains o
ancient forts, cairns, and circular huts ; but only a seriou
archæologist will wish to do so, and my duty to him is easily
discharged by referring him to the *Inventory of Monuments an*

*Constructions in Galloway.* On the left of the road is the rough
beach with occasional boulders where cormorants settle, and
the wide, shining surface of Luce Bay; on the right the great,
green slope. "That heugh, varying in height from sixty to a
hundred and twenty feet, marks the seaward end of the ancient
ice-field and consists from top to bottom of boulder clay, now
closely clad with kindly verdure and flowers of many hues.
It was the bed laid down by the ice-mantle, which, never resting,
crept forward irresistibly from the high grounds to the sea-level,
planing smooth the underlying rock strata, grinding the waste
into stiff clay, and carrying with it innumerable fragments of
harder material till it met the sea. There the ice-field broke
off into bergs, which floated away, leaving the tide to form its
beach by washing stones and boulders out of the underlying clay.
This is what is recognised all round the western Scottish shores
as the twenty-five foot beach, formed when the general level
of the land was that much lower than it is now."[1] The only
point at which the road leaves the shore is at Garheugh, and
there it does not veer inland, but climbs along the edge of the
precipices. Below are two or three fairly large caves often
occupied by tramps. After passing Craignarget[2]—"the Silver
Crag"—a trap dyke rising four hundred feet above the sea, it
winds inland over a great ridge and then descends into Glenluce.

George Borrow walked into Glenluce village on the 18th of
July, 1866. The following notes are found in his diary : " Capital

[1] Sir Herbert Maxwell's *Memories of the Months : Fourth Series.*
[2] The sculptured cross-slab found at Craignarget, now in the
National Museum of Antiquities, Edinburgh, is one of the most
remarkable monuments of the south of Scotland. It is an irregularly-
shaped slab of greywacke, three and a half feet in height, "sculptured
on one face with crosses, circles, and dots. Along each of the two
vertical edges is a rude border, composed of dots or cup-shaped
hollows and segments of concentric circles. The face of the stone is
divided into two panels by a horizontal line. Above this line is an
incised cross with a dot and ring in the centre of the head, a
transverse line at the bottom of the shaft forming a sort of base,
and cup-shaped depressions at the ends of the two horizontal arms.
On the background of the cross, to the left and right of the top arm,
are two circular rings; to the left and right of the shaft, a small
incised cross; and below the bottom of the shaft, a small incised
cross with three dots on each side of it. Below the horizontal line,
across the middle of the slab, is a Swastika cross, two intersecting
circles, a small cross, and a number of dots arranged in groups cf
threes and fours."—The *Inventory.*

dinner—salmon, mutton, and sweets ; first-rate water. Stroll behind the Inn. The glen, the little bridge, the rivulet and trees ; child playing in the water ; strong smell of turf smoke throughout the village ; cool, delightful evening ; stroll up and down. People in the street sitting or standing enjoying the cool." The turf has been supplanted by coal ; and the inhabitants, instead of sitting or standing in the street, congregate now around the bowling-green beside the stream in the cool of the evening ; but the tramp of to-day will remember, like Borrow, " the glen, the little bridge, the rivulet and trees ". He will agree also with him about the " very beautiful scenery " of the " upland dells lined with woods ".

Glenluce is famous for its Devil and its Abbey. " In this parish of Glenluce," says Symson, " there was a spirit, which for a long space molested the house of one Campbell, a weaver." The case was so notorious that it attracted the serious attention of the General Assembly of Divines in the days of the Common-wealth. The manifestations of the racketing-spirit, however, were the same as in the Rerwick and other instances all over the world, and we may share the opinion of Symson that " it would be tedious to give a full relation of all the stories concerning it." The record is given in George Sinclair's *Satan's Invisible World Discovered*, published in Edinburgh in 1685.

A Glenluce story illustrating the belief in witchcraft before the days of official witch-hunting began is given in *The Hereditary Sheriffs of Galloway*. " An ingleside story of the period, handed down as literally true, is that a labouring man's wife— a sensible, decent woman—having been detained late from home, was returning about the witching hour ; and

> When the gray howlet had three times hoo'ed,
> When the grimy cat had three times mewed,
> When the tod had yowled three times in the wood,

at a spot known as the ' Clay Slap,' she met face to face a troop of females, as to whose leader being cloven-footed she could not be mistaken. Her consternation was the greater as, one by one, she recognised them all, and among them the ladies of the manor. They stopped her, and in her terror she appealed to one of them by name. Enraged at being known, the party declared that she must die. She pleaded for mercy, and they agreed to spare her life on her taking an awful oath that she would never reveal the

names of any as long as they lived.  Fear prevented her from
breaking her pledge, but as one by one the dames paid the debt
of nature, she would mysteriously exclaim, ' There's anither o'
the gang gone ! '  She outlived them all and then divulged the
secret ; adding that on that dreadful night, after getting to her
bed, she lay entranced in an agony as if she had been roasting
between two fires.''

The Abbey is two miles up the glen.  It was founded by
Roland, Lord of Galloway, in 1190 and occupied by a colony of

*Glenluce Abbey.*

Cistercian monks from Melrose.  It was an extensive structure,
and, while it is not quite so large as Sweetheart Abbey, must
have resembled it closely.  The foundation of the nave, the gable
of the south transept, the cloisters, the court, and the vaulted
chapter-house, much the best-preserved part, remain.  The
description in the *Inventory* is too long for quotation ; but the
following details may be given from the account by Mr. David
Henry in *Archæological and Historical Collections relating to
Ayrshire and Galloway* : " The conventual buildings on the east

side of the Garth have been partially rebuilt, probably late in the fifteenth century—at least the chapter-house is about that date. . . . The entrance to the chapter-house is through a semi-circular-headed doorway, and by three descending steps the floor is reached, two feet below the level of the walk. . . . It is an exact square of twenty-four feet, and the central column composed of eight half-round shafts—four plain and four filleted—with small beads between, is eleven feet, two inches high to the top of the abacus and two feet in diameter. The whole height of the room to the points of the vaulting ribs is seventeen feet. The vaulting is quadripartite, the ribs resting on the central column and on corbels in the walls. The ' bosses ' at the intersections in the two eastmost compartments bear shields with coats of arms—one being the lion of Scotland within a tressure and surmounted by a crown, and the other the Crowned Lion of the Province of Galloway. The other intersections bear foliated flowers like roses on the bosses.

" The seat of the Abbot is indicated on the east wall, between the windows, by a kind of imitation stall, formed by a moulding raised on the ashlar facing of the wall and having a trefoil head ; but there is no recess, and the moulding—which still shows the chisel-marks of intentional defacement—has been of a poor and inartistic character. The stone seat bench which ran all round the walls has been removed. The builder—one hopes with the desire to prevent such spoliation—had built the slabs into the masonry ; but the spoilers have been too many for him, and have split them off by the wall line with chisels, the marks of which are still plainly visible ; perhaps they may be found doing duty as shelves in some dairy in the neighbourhood. The most prominent features in the windows are the large quatrefoils in their traceried heads ; the other forms are not elegant, nor are the sections of the mouldings good. Though very few of the details taken by themselves will bear to be tried by a high standard, the chapter-house as a whole is a very beautiful and finely proportioned room."

The story of how Gilbert, fourth Earl of Cassillis, secured possession of the Abbey lands after the Reformation is told in the *Historie of the Kennedyis.* "This last Gilbertt was ane particuler manne, and ane werry greidy manne, and cairitt nocht how he gatt land, sa that he culd cum be the samin." He entered into a conspiracy with the Abbot to obtain a lease of the property; but before the arrangements were completed the Abbot died. The Earl then found an ally in a monk of the abbey "quha culd counterfitt the Abbottis hand-writt, and all the haill Conventtis", and caused him to forge their signatures to the necessary document. When this had been done, the Earl feared that the monk might reveal the matter, and engaged

*Kitchen in the House of Park, near Glenluce.*

a knave to murder him. Then, fearing that his hireling might speak, he induced his uncle, Hew of Bargany, to accuse him of theft and hang him at Crossraguel. "And sa the landis of Glenluse wes conqueist."

Another tale of blood concerns one of the Hays of Park—Park Place, the castle standing high above the Luce Water

about a quarter of a mile from Glenluce, was their home.   There
was a wedding party near the abbey, and young Hay of Park
was one of the guests.   In the course of the feast a valuable
article of plate was missed from the table.   A blacksmith who
was also a guest was voluble in his indignation, and expressed
the wish that " cauld iron might be his hinner en' quhaever took
it ".   He became excited as the festivities went on, and rudely
called upon Hay to pay a sum he owed him for the shoeing
of a horse.   Hay was irritated by his insults, and at last drew
his sword and ran him through.   As the body was being raised
from the floor, the missing article fell from one of the dead man's
pockets.   The indignation of the company at the murder was
stayed for the moment by the thought that the smith had invoked
his own doom.   Hay was able to retire unhindered and fled the
country.

" A long while after, he returned to Glenluce, disguised as an
idiot pauper ; and, blowing a long horn, begged from house
to house, repeating a string of doggerel verses.   He was known as
Jock o' the Horn and visited all his old haunts, even venturing
to the House of Park.   Here he clamoured for alms, as elsewhere,
in jingling couplets.   He never, however, doffed his strange
disguise, though it was whispered in the neighbourhood of Park
that when the family were quite alone, the servants were sometimes kept out of the way, and that then poor ' Jock o' the Horn '
again took his proper place in the parlour and shared the family
meal."

> BLESSIT BE THE NAME OF THE LORD THIS
> VERK VAS BEGUN THE FIRST DAY OF MARCH
> 1590 BE THOMAS HAY OF PARK AND
> IONET MAKDOVEL HIS SPOVS.

This is the inscription carved on a panel above the doorway
of the castle.   The building belongs to the period when the
defensive motive was disappearing.   There is, however, a
gun-loop for the protection of the entrance.   The design follows
the L-shaped plan with four storeys and a garret, and is one of the
completest examples of its kind in Wigtonshire.   A two-storey
wing on the south-east and a wing of a single storey on the north-
east were added at a much later time than that to which the
original house belongs, probably in the eighteenth century.

Stairhaven is not widely known even in Galloway.   It would

not be difficult to give reasons for this. I was resolved to visit it nevertheless for these four reasons—I liked its name, George Borrow visited it, it has a practically disused harbour, and it was once a haunt of smugglers.

I have said I was resolved to see Stairhaven ; but the resolution involved no strenuous travelling. The distance is little more than two miles from Glenluce, the road is easy, and with a northerly wind one's bicycle almost takes one along of itself. The way lies along a raised beach and gives wide views westwards across the Bay of Luce to The Rhinns. The sand-flats on the north shore of the bay are broken by the final windings of the Luce Water and the Piltanton ; behind them stretch the sand-dunes of Genoch[1] ; and close at hand there is a noteworthy detail visible at low tide—the remains of the long, low walls stretching across the mouth of the Luce and containing the old " fish-yards " where the fish that delayed their retreat too long were easily captured.

" Stairhaven " is a modern name and has a simple etymology. It signifies " a haven built by the Earl of Stair." The older name is " The Craw's Nest " and is etymologically obscure. It has been suggested that it is a corruption of " Crossness ", " the headland of the cross." The place was known to Borrow as " The Craw's Nest ".

" A house by the sea side ; little pier ; a few fishing boats ; place seemingly deserted." These are the jottings entered by Borrow in his diary when he came to Stairhaven in July, 1866. He would have found nothing to add or subtract to-day. There is the one little house inhabited by a fisherman, and the little pier, a gigantic structure for so modest a port. It has survived from the days when Stairhaven was an outlet for the produce of the neighbouring farms and took in their lime and manure, and, although very few steamers come now to discharge and receive cargoes, it remained in perfect condition with not a stone out of place for many a year after its usefulness had almost entirely gone, contrasting strikingly, therefore, with the scattered fragments of the piers at Portpatrick and Port Logan, and pointing to the comparative protection afforded the waters of the bay by the colossal breakwater of The Rhinns. Yet the sands of Luce have buried many a wreck, disasters caused in some cases,

---

[1] Gaelic *gainmheach*, a sandy place. The Genoch Rocks in Kirkcolm surround a small bay with a sandy strand.—Maxwell.

not by storms, but through mariners sailing in here in the night when they thought that they were entering the Firth of Clyde. Near the head of the bay I saw the tops of a vessel's ribs appearing above the sand at low water. It might have been lost in just this way. Accidents from this miscalculation have been less frequent since the Mull of Galloway lighthouse was built.

Stairhaven without its pier would look very much like many another bit of the Galloway coast with a lonely fisherman's cottage, a range of stakes for drying nets, and boxes for packing fish lying around ; but that substantial, unused pier that might

*Stairhaven.*

have been a scene of busy trafficking and resounded to the clank of steam winches and the rattle of chains gives a curious sense of desolation in its apparent abandonment.

A microscopic scrutiny of Galloway literature has resulted in the discovery of one incident belonging to the history of Stairhaven. Since it is of the smuggling order, it may be regarded as representative. It happened that in the year 1771 when the place was at the height of its importance as a channel of furtive commerce, three luggers arrived from The Isle of Man ; but before the unloading of the contraband goods could be completed, the smugglers received an alarm and sailed away to dispose of the rest of their cargoes on the coast of Ireland. Enough tea, tobacco, and spirits, however, had been taken from

the ships to load a hundred and fifty horses, and so soon as the
caravan had been made up, it advanced into the interior.  Its
progress was not to be entirely uninterrupted.  The neighbouring
justices had learned that three vessels were to discharge valuable
cargoes at The Craw's Nest on this night, and a large party of
soldiers had been summoned from Stranraer and placed in
ambush while the excisemen watched, without disturbing, the
illicit enterprise.  The smugglers, on their part, had information of what was toward.  They unmasked the ambuscade
and scattered the soldiers before them.  Hearing musketry fire,
the excisemen, who had been following the caravan, rushed
forward, expecting to assist the military in making their capture ;
but were dismayed to find the smugglers marching on as if no
interruption had occurred, the soldiers nowhere to be seen, and
the caravan presenting too strong a rearguard for themselves
to attack.

That this was not an isolated instance of smugglers being
strong enough to overawe, defy, and defeat the forces of law and
order is attested by some reminiscences of an excise officer at
Wigton which he communicated to Joseph Train in 1840.  As a
boy he had seen a smuggling caravan of two hundred and ten
horses accompanied by about a hundred " lingtowmen " passing
within a mile of Wigton " in open defiance of the supervisor, two
excise officers, and about thirty soldiers stationed at Wigtown
to assist the revenue officers in the suppression of smuggling ".
The incident had been fixed in the boy's memory by the fact
that four of the smugglers' horses, overcome, it was supposed,
by the heat of the day and the strong smell of the tobacco, had
fallen dead on the road.

On another occasion, two luggers had arrived off Port William.
Both had a crew of about fifty men, and the one mounted
twenty-two guns, and the other fourteen.  They were about
to unload their cargoes when the excise officer stationed at
Wigton, the supervisor, and twenty-five soldiers appeared.
The commander of one of the luggers came ashore and told them
that if they did not retire immediately, he would cause a broadside to be fired on them and land a hundred armed men ; but
if they removed themselves and gave the smugglers a clear coast,
he would leave thirty or forty ankers of spirits for them on the
beach.  The excisemen's party went away, and the smuggler
kept his promise.

While I was staying at Glenluce, I observed on the map what seemed to be an odd bit of country subtending the north-west shore of Luce Bay. It bore the name, " Torrs Warren ", but so far as particular place-names were concerned was almost empty. Now, a blank on the map is full of invitation to the exploring spirit, and I went to see what that vacant space concealed. Within two miles from Glenluce a byway breaks off from the Stranraer road, passes the farm of Droughdool, a place that should surely have a ghost story connected with it, and crosses the Piltanton, a sluggish water in a deep, narrow channel with banks and bottom of mud. There had been feature-less stretches of open fields on both sides of the road hitherto ; but now the character of the country was changed. On the sea-ward side I saw the beginning of sand-dunes, and on the right almost continuous plantations—just the low-lying, rough and tumbled, desolate coast with a backing of woods that might have been the scene of *The Pavilion on the Links*.

I came once more to a dividing of the road, the one branch leading to Lochans and Portpatrick and the other to Sandhead and Drummore. The latter kept close to the sand-dunes and, like the scenery, presented a novel character, for it ran ahead quite straight and perfectly level for as far as the eye could follow it, like a causeway through the midst of a bit of marish land. The map shewed that it maintained this character for no less than three miles. The domain of the sand began not many yards away on the left. A faint cart-track leading towards it made me dismount after a furlong or two. The track dwindled away to a single footpath before it entered the sandy waste, and I followed it wondering greatly whither it might conduct and what kind of people used it. It undulated over heath-clad knowes and ridges and skirted the edge of deep hollows until I had the weird sense of having been drawn into the midst of a chaos that was neither of the kindly earth nor yet of the untamed sea, but shared, as it were, in both ; for here grew heather and bent in tufts and patches, but with no look of permanence in their tenure ; and those swell-ing billows, those deep troughs and far-drawn ridges of sand— were they not like a tormented sea arrested in its commotion ?

The path brought me in a little while to the skeleton of a cottage, a very old one that had plainly been deserted for a long time. When I looked in at a window, I saw lying on the earthen floor about a dozen rusted steel traps. The surrounding dunes are a great rabbit warren, and many rabbits are killed here. *The Statistical Account* of the parish written in 1839 said that about fifteen hundred dozen were killed annually.

Hector Boece places among these sandhills the scene of a battle between the Scots and the Northern Picts on the one hand and the Galloway Picts on the other. Many arrowheads, knives, spear-points, and other lethal weapons have been found on the farm of Torrs, so that perhaps he was right for once. I have a suspicion that some less public battles have been fought here. Gypsies and other tramps have often passed this way ; and cattle-drovers, a notoriously quarrelsome class, might, as they came from Port Logan, find this road more convenient than the one by Stranraer. I think that these sands must cover some unhallowed graves.

The road running up the valley of the Luce Water through what the writer of *The Statistical Account* calls " this dull country " reaches the village of New Luce after six miles. The church here is that in which Peden the Prophet ministered for three years. Peden was held in great honour among the Covenanters for his sainthood, his sufferings, and his prophecies. Like other ministers, he was ejected from his charge on the restoration of Episcopacy in 1662. He preached a farewell sermon to his congregation, and was often interrupted by their lamentations. He continued speaking until it was night, and ended by telling the people that they would never see his face in that place again. On leaving the pulpit, he closed the door, knocked upon it three times with his Bible, and said these words as often : " I arrest thee in my Master's name that none ever enter thee but such as come in by the door as I have done." The pulpit was not used again until after the Revolution, when a Presbyterian minister entered it. Peden wandered from place to place for a time, encouraging the faithful ; but was arrested and imprisoned on the Bass Rock. He was sentenced to be transported to Virginia ; but the captain of the ship which was to carry him and other prisoners across the Atlantic refused, according to one account, to take them beyond London. The prisoners were liberated there, and Peden made his way back to Scotland. He spent a Sunday in a Border village and was invited to preach, but replied, " Let the people go to their prayers. As for me, I neither can nor will preach this day, for our friends are fallen and fled before the enemy at Hamilton, and they are hashing and hagging them down, and their blood is running like water." This was on the 22nd of June, the day of the battle of Bothwell Bridge. On returning to Galloway, he prayed much for the prisoners who had been taken and declared that " the wild sea billows would be the winding sheet of many of them ". The vessel on which they were to be carried to the plantations was wrecked among the Orkney Islands, and many of the prisoners were drowned. When he married John Brown of Priesthill to Marion Weir, he said to the bride, " You have got a good man to be your husband, but you will not enjoy him long. Prize his company and keep linen by you to be his winding sheet for you will need it when you are not looking for it ; and it will be a bloody one." Nearly three years later, he spent a night at the house of Brown and his wife, and in the morning, when he was leaving, he muttered as if speaking to himself, " Poor woman, a fearful morning, a dark, misty morning, poor woman ! " The next morning Brown was shot by Claverhouse in the presence of his wife and children. Peden had been abroad all night and was then eleven or twelve miles away from the scene of Brown's death. Coming to a house in the morning, he gathered the family for prayer and used these words—" Lord, when wilt Thou avenge Brown's blood and let Brown's blood be precious in Thy sight ? " He was asked afterwards what he meant by this. " What do I mean ? " he replied. " Claverhouse has been at Priesthill this morning and has cruelly murdered John Brown. His corpse is lying at the end of the house, and his poor wife is weeping by it, and not a soul to speak comfort to her."

There is no reason to doubt that Peden had presentiments of coming events and telepathic impressions—if one admits telepathy—of contemporary ones, and that he gave them utterance in characteristic language. This provided an opportunity for those "designing persons " of whom Wodrow complains to " frame prophecies under Mr. Peden's name " for their own purposes. Peden's reputation as a prophet depends upon these inventions. There is no evidence that he claimed any " supernatural " gift as a foreteller.

He found refuge from his persecutors sometimes in Ireland and sometimes in Scotland until his death ended his suffering in 1686, when he was fifty-nine years of age.

If one likes to trudge for miles over rough moors or ha

enough interest in out-of-the-way antiquities to take a good deal of trouble to see them, one should certainly follow the by-way from New Luce to Balmurrie farmhouse, and then take a line a little east of north to the Standing Stones of Laggangairn.[1] Their position is a little north-east of the ruins of the old house of that name and close to the Tarf Water. The height above ground of the larger stone is a little over six feet, and the other is a foot shorter. " Each stone bears grooved on its west face a cross with arms expanding outwards, and in each of the angles formed by the intersection of the arms and the shaft, a small cross formed of single intersecting lines."[2] The reduplication of the crosses indicates a very early date. There is also a simple Latin cross incised on a slab leaning against the wall of the deserted garden.

The Wells of the Rees, that is, of the Sheepfolds, are on a slope of the moor a short distance beyond the standing stones —three wells, each covered with a dome-like structure about three feet in height built without mortar ; a little to the west of them is the site and the graveyard of the ancient church of Kilgallioch ; and on the north slope of Craigmoddie[3] stands a more recent monument of Christianity, the walled-in grave and slab where Alexander Linn, a Covenanter and one of Peden's parishioners, was buried. The stone was erected in 1827 in place of an older one, and bears the original epitaph : " Memento Mori. Here lies the Body of Alex[r] Linn who was surprised and instantly shot to death on this place by Lieu-General Drumand for his adherence to Scotland's reformation covenants national and solemn league 1685."

It is a long, rough trail from Balmurrie to Craigmoddie and back, and when you remount your bicycle, you feel as if you were sinking down into an easy-chair ; but it is a glorious moorland walk, and, whatever the weather may be, it will be strange if you do not find yourself repeating :

> Blows the wind to-day, and the sun and the rain are flying,
>   Blows the wind on the moors to-day and now,
> Where about the graves of the martyrs the whaups are crying,
>   My heart remembers how !

According to the plan of this book, the general movement is westwards from Maxwelltown to The Rhinns ; but the next chapter is given to a long digression eastwards.

[1] Gaelic *lagan g-carn*, hollow of the cairns.
[2] The *Inventory*.    [3] Gaelic *creag madaidh*, the dog's or wolf's crag.

# CHAPTER XVII

## FROM GLENLUCE TO NEWTON STEWART

A moor road—Cattle-droving—Barhapple Loch—The crannog—
 Dernaglaur Loch—Borrow's notes on the road—Rhododendrons
 at Craighlaw—Kirkcowan—The brownie—*The Brownie of
 Blednoch*—A pack-horse bridge.

MOORLAND roads like that between Glenluce and Newton Stewart
differ from others in that the impression made upon the traveller
depends so much on the weather. The reason of this is obvious
and may be illustrated from two experiences. The first time I
followed this road, it was a day of steady rain, and the broad,
flat stretches and curves of the moors, destitute of the contrast
of light and shade, looked their dullest and dreariest, and the
lonely cottages dotting the land at wide intervals might have
been the scenes of the most morbid crimes. The moisture, too,
shut out all distant views, confining one to the desolate road
running through the immediate moor. A journey of sixteen
miles in these circumstances does not arouse enthusiasm.

The second time, everything was different. It was a day of
sunshine with white, fleecy clouds floating high in the clear air,
and the undulating sky-line of the moorland heights led the eye
on continually to the distant range of the Monigaff hills. The
interest of the road lay partly in the fact that these were always
in front, disappearing now and then in the deeper hollows of
the moor or behind the infrequent plantations, but always coming
into view again a little nearer. The scattered homes were now
the shrines of ancient pieties and domestic peace.

When Robert Heron crossed these moors in 1792, travelling
westwards, he had a companion, he says, whose " conversation
was indeed necessary to raise my spirits above that depression

which they were naturally liable to suffer from the dreariness of the scenery upon which I now entered ". The road was used largely in those days by cattle-drovers bringing their herds from Ireland to England, and as Heron, alluding to them, enlivens his sententious comments for once with a scrap of vivid writing, I think that he must have passed a herd on the way. He says that as the drovers did not suspend their journeys on Sundays, they gave " great offence to the pious inhabitants of Galloway in those parts through which the highway runs. The appearance of the cattle on the highway, driven on irregularly, bellowing and straying ; their drivers running, hallooing, roaring, swearing:—This appearance alone cannot but be offensive to the piety of such as still respect the Lord's day. But this is not all. These cattle are to be brought off in the morning from those parks in which they have rested for the preceding night ; and the farmer or inn-keeper who has entertained them is, with his servants, necessarily engaged in the gathering and driving of them off. They are again to halt in the evening ; and now likewise occasion an indecent bustle and confusion in which they who receive them are unavoidably concerned."

Borrow saw nothing of cattle-droving in 1866, but agrees with Heron and every other traveller about the bleakness of the country. " The land ", he says, " seemed to be very poor and sterile." When, however, he fell into talk with a woman weeding a potato garden near Barhapple[1] Loch, he found it in his heart to praise the country, thinking no doubt of its beautiful aspect on that sunny July day ; but the woman differed from him, saying it was a " coorse country ". Borrow does not mention the usual name of the loch, but refers to it as " a kind of lake on my right hand, apparently about three hundred yards across." When he asked the woman its name, she told him, ' Dirskelvin ", the name of the farmhouse near at hand. He might have given the loch a less cursory regard had he known that it contained an ancient lake-dwelling. This, however, was not discovered until the loch was drained nearly twenty years after his visit.

A contributor to *The Times* who was present at the examination of the crannog says that it had taken about three thousand trees for its construction and that it measured a hundred and fifty-even yards in circumference. He says further : " The present

[1] Gaelic *barr chapeail*, chapel hill.

aspect of the surrounding country is bleak and treeless in the extreme. Low 'drums,' or sowbacks, so characteristic of a glacier-scraped country, rise out of vast tracts of peat-moss, the lakes themselves being probably but shallow basins scooped by the grounding of the land-ice of the later ice-fields out of the till or ground moraine laid down in the earlier glacial period. Nevertheless, when these crannoges were formed, a dense forest must have clothed the now desolate plain, consisting, as shown by the composition of the island, in this district principally of oak, birch, ash, hazel, and alder. The Scotch pine, largely employed in the construction of the Dowalton group, was not noticed in the Barhapple island. The structure of the wood is perfectly apparent, though all but the oak, which is very hard, cuts as soft now as Cheddar cheese."

Half a mile farther south, but not visible from the road, is another loch possessing a similar interest. Dr. Munro, the author of a chapter on the lake-dwellings of Wigtonshire, in the fifth volume of *Archæological and Historical Collections Relating to Ayrshire and Galloway*, writes : "From Barhapple we visited the neighbouring loch of Dernaglaur to see a small canoe that had been found near its margin in consequence of a partial drainage of its waters which had recently been effected. At the same time an artificial island just showed above the water, but not sufficiently to admit of being investigated. The canoe is kept buried in mud within a sort of natural harbour of stones on the eastern shore of the lake. It is a single-tree dug-out, having four ribs which divide its interior into three compartments. It measured eleven feet long, thirty-one inches wide, and eleven and a half inches deep, and had a groove, about nine inches from the end, for a stern board."

Besides its topographical interest, the following passage from Borrow is very likely a good example of the kind of notes he made for his travel books. "Came to a toll-bar, kept by one John Douglas, a little short fellow of seventy-three. Discourse —proceed. Afflicted woman by a cottage, asked me in ; Tarff river. Wretched country, came to groves. Half way house. Kirk Cowan on the right ; take wrong road. Written under the shade of trees whilst sitting on a stone near a house, after passing over the dreadful sunburnt moors. Discourse with old man mowing some grass by the road's side ; proceed ; no water ; at length came to a pleasant valley, pass under a rail road arch ,

asked a girl if there was any water near. She said that there
was none that she knew of. Presently saw a little rill under
some trees on the left hand side. Sat down. The horse and
cart with the women and children. ' Will it please you, sir, to
raise up in order that the mare may go down to drink ? ' When
they were gone I drank and drank. Woods. Sir John Dunbar's
place, proceed, drink, the man with the pails, discourse, Irish
and English. . . . On this journey I intended to have passed
through a place called Kirkcowan or something like it, but I
followed the main road and passed by a cross road which leads
to it, and afterwards entered the great road again near a river,
over which there were two bridges, an old and a new one. Kirk
Owen was the only place where I could have gotten refreshments
during a journey of 16 miles."

To the wayfarer over these moors, the plantations of the
Craighlaw estate—the " groves " near the " Half way house "—
are a pleasant interlude—the glowing blooms of the rhododendrons especially—as pleasant as the water of the little rill was to
Borrow after passing over " the dreadful sunburnt moors ".
I am always grateful to the proprietor who plants beautiful
shrubs near the public way, and am willing to believe that he has
in view the delectation of the passer-by. I remember being
delighted in the same way by the endless variety of blooms on
the thickly massed, colossal rhododendron shrubs bordering the
road in the Corsock estate in The Stewartry, and have pleasure
in giving it honourable mention also.

Borrow did not miss much when he left Kirkcowan[1] unvisited,
not even much in the way of a meal, so far as I have been able
to judge. It seems to me a dull village, and the writer of *The
Statistical Account* found remarkably little to say of the parish
as a whole. I remember the church at the north end of the
village street with its handsome square tower and an outside
stair leading to the gallery, and at the south end the ivy-covered
ruin of the old church built in 1658. Sir Andrew Agnew remarks
that " some of the old gravestones around it must go back to
about the same date. But owing to former neglect, and the
overcrowding of the churchyard, many of the oldest tombstones
have been removed from their places. A few of them have
recently been rescued, and built into the surrounding wall, to
ensure their future preservation."

[1] Church of Comgan.

The Tarf and Bladnoch streams, after wandering southwards through the moors for many miles, mingle their waters a little to the east of Kirkcowan. About a mile from the village the latter stream has a long, gradual fall, the Linn of Barhoise,[1] where the water breaks into continuous foam and spray among the rocks, and on the left bank there is the site of the old mill of Glashnoch. The Bladnoch, the Linn of Barhoise, and the

*Kirkcowan.*

Glashnoch Mill will be associated always with William Nicholson's poem, *The Brownie of Blednoch*, the greatest piece of vernacular literature that Galloway has ever produced. The brownie, that odd figure in the mythology of the wilderness

---

[1] Pronounced " Barhosh "; Gaelic *barr choise*, at the end of point of the foot of the hill.—Johnston.

freakish and friendly, coming suddenly to the neighbourhood of the farm-towns, and disappearing suddenly, has been traced to the Pict, the ancient inhabitant, dispossessed from the land, living in mountain retreats, but seen sometimes by the conquering race or finding employment among them. Heron, writing more than thirty years before Nicholson's poem was published, says, " Tales of ghosts, brownies, fairies, witches, are the frequent entertainment of a winter's evening among the native peasantry of Kirkcudbrightshire. . . . The brownie was a very obliging spirit who used to come into houses by night, and for a dish of cream to perform lustily any piece of work that might remain to be done. If old clothes were laid out for him, he took them in great distress and never more returned." Mactaggart says in his *The Scottish Gallovidian Encyclopædia*, " Brownies were nocturnal beings who thrashed farmers' corn, and did other laborious jobs, for which the *guid wifes*, as Milton says, ' had the cream bowl duly set.' They were seldom seen ; some think they were of no supernatural origin, but distressed persons, who were obliged to conceal themselves and wander about during some of the past turbulent ages." Mr. Harper gives a story of a brownie who " had undertaken to gather the sheep into the bught by an early hour, and so zealously did he perform his task that, not only was there not one sheep left on the hill, but he had also collected a number of hares, which were found fairly penned along with them. Upon being congratulated on his extraordinary success, Brownie exclaimed, ' Confound thae wee grey anes ! they cost me mair trouble than a' the lave o' them.' " I think I ought to insert the whole of the Galloway poem of which Dr. John Brown, the author of *Horae Subsecivae*, said, " Here is the indescribable, inestimable, unmistakable impress of genius. Chaucer, had he been a Galloway man, might have written it, only he would have been more garrulous, and less compact and stern. It is like *Tam o' Shanter* in its living union of the comic, the pathetic, and the terrible. Shrewdness, tenderness, imagination, fancy, humour, word-music, dramatic power, even wit, are all here."

## THE BROWNIE OF BLEDNOCH.

There cam' a strange wight to our town-en',
And the fient a body did him ken ;
He tirled na lang, but he glided ben
    Wi' a dreary, dreary hum.

His face did glare like the glow o' the west
When the drumlie cloud has it half o'ercast ;
Or the struggling moon when she's sair distrest—
    O sirs ! 'twas Aiken-drum.

I trow the bauldest stood aback,
Wi' a gape and a glower till their lugs did crack,
As the shapeless phantom mum'ling spak',
    " Ha'e ye wark for Aiken-drum ? "

O had ye seen the bairns' fright
As they stared at this wild and unyirthly wight
As he stauket in 'tween the dark and the light
    And graned out, " Aiken-drum ! "

" Sauf us ! " quoth Jock, " d'ye see sic een ; "
Cries Kate, " there's a hole where a nose should ha'e been,
And the mouth's like a gash which a horn had ri'en ;
    Wow ! keep's frae Aiken-drum ! "

The black dog growling cowered his tail,
The lassie swarfed, loot fa' the pail ;
Rob's lingle brak as he men't the flail
    At the sight o' Aiken-drum.

His matted head on his breast did rest,
A lang blue beard wan'ered down like a vest ;
But the glare o' his e'e nae bard hath exprest,
    Nor the skimes o' Aiken-drum.

Roun' his hairy form there was naething seen
But a philabeg o' the rashes green,
And his knotted knees played aye knoit between ;
    What a sight was Aiken-drum !

On his wauchie arms three claws did meet
As they trailed on the grun' by his taeless feet ;
E'en the auld gudeman himsel' did sweat
    To look at Aiken-drum.

But he drew a score, himsel' did sain ;
The auld wife tried, but her tongue was gane ;
While the young ane closer clasped her wean
    And turned frae Aiken-drum.

But the canny auld wife cam' till her breath,
And she deemed the Bible might ward aff scaith,
Be it benshee, bogle, ghaist or wraith—
    But it fear't na Aiken-drum.

" His presence protect us ! " quoth the auld gudeman ;
" What wad ye, where won ye—by sea or by lan' ?
  I conjure ye—speak—by the Beuk in my han' ! "
      What a grane ga'e Aiken-drum !

" I lived in a lan' where we saw nae sky,
  I dwalt in a spot where a burn rins na by ;
But I'se dwall now wi' you if ye like to try—
      Ha'e ye wark for Aiken-drum ?

" I'll shiel a' your sheep i' the mornin' sune,
I'll berry your crap by the light o' the moon,
And baa the bairns wi' an unken'd tune
      If ye'll keep puir Aiken-drum.

" I'll loup the linn when ye canna wade,
I'll kirn the kirn, and I'll turn the bread,
And the wildest fillie that ever ran rede
      I'se tame't," quoth Aiken-drum !

" To wear the tod frae the flock on the fell—
To gather the dew frae the heather bell—
And to look at my face in your clear crystal well
      Might gi'e pleasure to Aiken-drum.

" I'se seek nae guids, gear, bond nor mark ;
I use nae beddin', shoon nor sark ;
But a cogfu' o' brose 'tween the light and dark
      Is the wage o' Aiken-drum."

Quoth the wylie auld wife, " The thing speaks weel ;
Our workers are scant—we ha'e routh o' meal ;
Gif he'll do as he says—be he man, be he de'il,
      Wow ! we'll try this Aiken-drum."

But the wenches skirled, " He's no be here !
His eldritch look gars us swarf wi' fear,
And the fient a ane will the house come near
      If they think but o' Aiken-drum.

" For a foul and a stalwart ghaist is he,
Despair sits brooding aboon his e'e bree,
And unchancie to light o' a maiden's e'e
      Is the grim glower o' Aiken-drum."

" Puir slipmalabors ! ye ha'e little wit ;
Is't na hallowmas now, and the crap out yet ? "
Sae she silenced them a' wi' a stamp o' her fit ;
      "Sit yer wa's down, Aiken-drum."

Roun' a' that side what wark was dune
By the streamer's gleam or the glance o' the moon ;
A word or a wish—and the brownie cam' sune,
    Sae helpfu' was Aiken-drum.

But he slade aye awa' ere the sun was up ;
He ne'er could look straught on Macmillan's cup[1] ;
They watched—but nane saw him his brose ever sup
    Nor a spune sought Aiken-drum.

On Blednoch banks and on crystal Cree
For mony a day a toiled wight was he ;
While the bairns played harmless roun' his knee,
    Sae social was Aiken-drum.

But a new-made wife, fu' o' rippish freaks,
Fond o' a' things feat for the first five weeks
Laid a mouldy pair o' her ain man's breeks
    By the brose o' Aiken-drum.

Let the learned decide when they convene
What spell was him and the breeks between ;
For frae that day forth he was nae mair seen,
    And sair missed was Aiken-drum.

He was heard by a herd gaun by the *Thrieve*,[2]
Crying, " Lang, lang now may I greet and grieve ;
For alas ! I ha'e gotten baith fee and leave,
    O luckless Aiken-drum ! "

Awa' ! ye wrangling sceptic tribe !
Wi' your pros and your cons wad ye decide
'Gainst the 'sponsible voice o' a hale country-side
    On the facts 'bout Aiken-drum ?

Though the " Brownie o' Blednoch " lang be gane,
The mark o' his feet's left on mony a stane ;
And mony a wife and mony a wean
    Tell the feats o' Aiken-drum.

E'en now light loons that jibe and sneer
At spiritual guests and a' sic gear
At the Glashnoch mill ha'e swat wi' fear
    And looked roun' for Aiken-drum.

---

[1] A communion cup belonging to John Macmillan, minister of Balmaghie, and first minister of the Reformed Presbyterian Church. " This cup was treasured by a zealous disciple in the parish of Kirkcowan and long used as a test by which to ascertain the orthodoxy of suspected persons. If, on taking the precious relic into his hand, the person trembled or gave other symptoms of agitation, he was denounced."

[2] A farm in the parish of Penninghame.

And guidly folks ha'e gotten a fright
When the moon was set and the stars gi'ed nae light
At the roaring linn in the howe o' the night
    Wi' sughs like Aiken-drum.

*The Old Pack-horse Bridge near Kirkcowan.*

There is a story that the Rev. George Murray, minister of
Girthon and later of Balmaclellan, met the poet near the manse
gate and offered to give him some money if he would recite *The*

*Brownie of Blednoch*. Nicholson did this with much gesticulation and fervour. Mr. Murray, handing him a coin, said, "Now, William, I wish to know your own opinion of this wonderful poem." "It has ae faut," said the author, "an' that an ill ane : it has nae moral."

The road from Kirkcowan to Newton Stewart converges with that from Glenluce within two miles, and a little beyond their meeting one comes to the crossing of the Bladnoch and the "two bridges, an old and a new". The latter was built about 1800 and carries the modern road. The old one, about a stone-throw to the north, was a pack-horse bridge and is so narrow that no vehicle broader than a wheel-barrow could be taken along it. There are no parapets, and the surface is grass-covered with a single footpath running in the midst.

There are more plantations near the road in the later part of this journey than in the earlier, and I remember free-wheeling for long stretches as I descended towards the valley of the Cree and Newton Stewart.

The next chapter is also a departure from the general plan and approaches Glenluce through the northern moors.

*Head of Luce Bay.*

# CHAPTER XVIII

BARE fields, brimming waters, leafless coverts, hedgerows
where a close scrutiny can just detect budding points of green,
the bleating of lambs, the trilling of larks are constant features
of April in the wilds. It is usually a season, too, when cold
winds, blinks of sunshine, and short-lived storms of sleet and
rain sweep over a dim landscape ; but the week before Easter
in 1909 was notable for its summer-like warmth. I wished to
see The Moors of The Shire and took a road running in a south-
easterly direction from Barrhill.

The day presented an odd confusion of the seasons, there was
so much brightness and kindly heat over the land, and yet the
clumps of trees here and there looked grim and hopeless, and the
heather and bent wore the dull hues of winter. While I followed
the gradually ascending road, the distant Merrick group of
hills, veiled in haze, their summits still fields of snow with white
streaks stretching downwards and indicating the corries in their
sides, appeared as if rising slowly behind the undulations of the
moor. Yet the time was plainly spring, and at some places
it might have been thought that the year was still further
advanced. There was a suggestion of midsummer brilliance in
the blue waters of some wayside lochans as they gleamed in
the sun and danced with the wind, and great beds of rushes
growing in the shallows bent like cornfields under its impact.

One of the larger sheets of water near the road is called Loch Maberry.[1] A more desolate place could hardly be conceived. A broad expanse of chill-looking water is broken by one or two rocky islets, and on every side is the empty moor. In an old description of Galloway it is said of the river Bladnoch that " it runneth through Lochmabary (wherin ther is ane litle isle, with ane house upon it) ". The loch looks like a congenial abode of pike, and Sir Herbert Maxwell has told the story of a gamekeeper who confessed that on seeing a great fish of this kind here, he " gaed back frae the loch for fear o' him ". The dwellers on the " little isle with ane house upon it "[2], when they looked out of the window on a fine day, would see those evil-eyed creatures basking in the shallows all around them, and you can imagine them using them as bogeys to subdue the spirits of unruly children. A burn entering the loch on the west side rises some miles away near a place called Liberland (" leper-land "), a reminder of the time when leprosy had its victims in Scotland, and the sufferers were segregated in remote settlements.

After skirting the loch the road undulates over the moor of Kirkcalla. The name points to an ecclesiastical establishment. So does that of a neighbouring hill, Barneycleary (" hill of the clergy "). There are neither records nor remains of the kirk that stood long ago in this waste. There is still, however, a fragment of another ancient erection, The Deil's Dyke, a rampart extending across the whole of Galloway.

Joseph Train, who gave so much assistance to Chalmers, the author of that antiquarian work, *Caledonia*, as well as to Sir Walter Scott, traced the course of the dyke from end to end. His survey was made at intervals during several years ; but a few days' walking would take one along the whole distance. Anyone who inclined to seek his pleasure among the wide, silent moors and barren fells, following the dyke and lodging by night in some hospitable shepherd's cottage, would discover an agreeable departure from the ordinary walking tour. He would cross a road occasionally, but would never walk along one, and would leap or wade through many streams.

The Roman, The Picts', or The Deil's Dyke, as it is called

[1] Accent on second syllable ; loch of my dear S. Baire.
[2] For a description of the remains on the " Fortified Island, Loch Maberry," see the *Inventory*.

variously, begins on the farm of Beoch[1] on Loch Ryan. It
crosses the moorland farms of Cairnerzean, Kilfeather,[2] and
Derry,[3] takes the north side of Loch Maberry, and reaches the
Cree on the farm of Knockville.[4] It re-appears in Cardorcan
on the farther bank, and continues through the Camberwood
and Terregan and across the moor of Drannandow[5] between
the standing stones called The Thieves and The Nappers.[6]
" As it passes from Terregan to Dranandow," says Train, " it
runs through a bog, and is only perceptible by the heather
growing long and close on the top of it, whereas on each side
of it the soil only produces rushes and moss. Near the centre
of the bog, I caused the peat to be cleared away close to the dyke,
and thereby found the foundation to be several feet below the
surface, which appeared to me an indication of its great antiquity."    From Drannandow the course lies along the south
side of the hill of Garlick, passes through the farm of Auchinleck,[7] crosses the Palnure,[8] climbs Craignelder, and veers northwards to Craigencaillie on the Dee. It then traverses the foot-
hills and glens of the Kells range by way of the farms of Garrary,
Clenrie, Duckieston, and Knockreoch.[9]    Thence it continues
eastwards by the old bridge of Deugh between Carsphairn and
Dalry, crosses the farms of Muncaig and Auchenshinnoch,[10]
and passes through Glencairn, Tynron, and Penpont. In Train's
time the dyke was nearly entire on the farm of Southmains
on the Nith in the parish of Sanquhar. ·Train adds that " from
Southmains it is said to have taken an easterly direction till
it joined the large dyke, yet so entire at Thornithwaite, and at
Hightae Flow, in the parish of Lochmaben.    Thence it extended
to *Britton Wall*, in the parish of Annan, and ran into the Solway
Firth, nearly opposite Bowness, in Cumberland, where the great
wall of Adrian commenced."

He speaks of the rampart as being invariably eight feet

[1] Gaelic *beithach*, a place of birches.
[2] Gaelic *cill Phetir* or *Pheadair*, church of Peter.
[3] Gaelic and Irish, *daire, doire*, an oak or oak wood.
[4] Gaelic *cnoc bhile*, hill of the large tree.
[5] Gaelic *dronnan dubh*, black ridge.
[6] Norse *knappr*, hillocks.
[7] Gaelic *achadh na leac*, field of flat stones.
[8] Gaelic *pol n' iubhar*, stream of the yew trees.
[9] Gaelic *cnoc riabhach*, grey hill.
[10] Gaelic *achadh an sionnaich*, field of the fox.

broad and built of rough blocks of stone or, in the less mountainous parts of its course, of a mixture of stones and earth.
The generally accepted view is that it was erected in the time of
Hadrian by the *Novantae* or Niduarian Picts to check the
incursions of the people of Strathclyde; but, according to the
*Inventory*, " the nature of its construction and the situations
which it occupies raise serious doubts as to its defensive character,
and rather favour the idea that its purpose may have been the
demarcation of territory."

Whatever may have been the value of the dyke to the ancient
inhabitants of Galloway, one may look for little help in identifying it from those of the present day. A farmer of whom I
made inquiry near Kirkcalla told me that he had lived there
all his life and knew nothing about it, and a shepherd boy directed
my attention to what were manifestly the ruins of a modern
dry-stone wall. Although the superstructure of the old dyke
has disappeared, a section can be traced at a point east of the
south end of Loch Ochiltree and across Glenvernoch Fell about
a quarter of a mile south of the summit. At the highest level
Train found " the remains of a watch-tower made of very large
stones ", and " immediately above Glendochart ", he says,
" the line is interrupted by a circular stone wall one hundred
and ninety-two yards diameter. This is evidently a hill-fort
of large dimensions." These structures can be seen no longer,
for the stones have been used for fences. Nothing remains
but the curves and stretches of the dyke itself, covered all over
with moorland vegetation; and where once the moor may have
been filled with the clamour of the battles of mysterious races,
the black-faced sheep nibble, and moorfowl circle and cry.

About two miles south of Kirkcalla I came to the little village
of Knowe, or The Snap, as it is called sometimes, from the name
of the inn. It is entirely unremarkable save for the gaunt walls
of the ruined woollen mill overshadowing it. If you like to
explore such old deserted places, you will find water still trickling
along the lade, a wrecked mill-wheel, and rusty bits of machinery
lying among the grass.

Thenceforward I travelled through a sunlit wilderness, a
land of wide horizons and dim distances, and found presently
that I was in the midst of moorburn. At this time of the year
you are not likely to go far in Galloway without seeing smoke
rising from some hillside or from the slopes and level spaces of

the moors, and as your eyes sweep round the landscape, they will be arrested by other columns proceeding from invisible fires. If you were not in the secret, you might think that the devotees of some primeval cult were celebrating sacrificial rites on their high places.

John Mactaggart, the author of that queer miscellany, *The Scottish Gallovidian Encyclopædia*, has a good note on moorburn. He defines it as " the way they have in the moorlands of burning down the old heather, so that grass may arise to feed cattle and sheep ". He says nothing about grouse. The sportsman, however, gains by the process as much as the farmer, for as a writer in *Country Life* has said, " The young shoots of heather on which the grouse are dependent during the spring and early summer are slow in appearing if the heather is old and rank ", and " the tendency of young heather is to produce green vigorous shoots at an earlier period ". Mactaggart describes the sight in a happy way : " The work of *mureburn* goes on in the dry weather of spring, and blazes away with a rapid wildness, frightening hares and grouse from its neighbourhood. When viewed from the Lowlands on a fine night, it makes one fancy of the devastations of war, spreading so quickly when lighted and encircling the wild mountains in red flaming curves. It must also somewhat resemble that scene seen by some travellers in foreign countries, of forests set in flames by the natives to destroy serpents and scare away wild beasts." He adds that " when anything like bad news spreads fast, we say ' it goes like mureburn ' ".

The road now lay near the Bladnoch, the stream issuing from Loch Maberry. Near a house called Glassoch[1] I took a turning to the right, thus entering upon the Carseriggan Moor, and on reaching the highest part, looked back and had a wide view across the rolling country to the dim Monigaff hills crowded together like a herd of recumbent mammoths bathed in slumber. The heat of the day had made no perceptible difference to their snows, and the atmosphere was still full of haze.

From the crossing of the roads near the schoolhouse of Dirnow[2] I saw the smoke of a great conflagration rising beyond the Ink Moss, and approached it to get some photographic records. Coming nearer, I could distinguish the scattered

---

[1] Gaelic *glaiseachd*, a grassy place.
[2] Pronounced " Durnoo." Gaelic *dúr na' g-crodh*, burn of the cattle.

fires from which the smoke slanted upwards in parallel columns on a light wind ; nearer still, I saw the flames spurting and spreading as with a resolute deliberation and heard the heather crackle, the only sound in all that moor.

After a few more miles on the heights there came a sudden descent to Glenluce.

Before leaving the village, the admirer of John Ruskin should be told that that author was related to some old Galloway families, and that the tomb of one of his ancestors is in Glenluce Churchyard. The Rev. James Tweddell, minister of Old Luce, who was his great-grandfather, had married Miss Catharine Adair of Genoch, who was descended from the Agnews of Lochnaw and the Rosses of Balsarroch. Ruskin knew the coast from Dumfries to Whithorn, and has some characteristically fanciful observations in *Praeterita* and *Fors Clavigera*. These, however, scarcely demand quotation in a book dealing, not with Ruskin, but with Galloway.

*Praeterita* contains the story of how Thomas Carlyle, when he met Queen Victoria at Dean Stanley's house, described to Her Majesty the beauty of the province, and, asserting that " he believed there was no finer or more beautiful drive in her kingdom than the one round the shore of the Stewartry, by Gatehouse of Fleet ", became so much absorbed in his subject that, " in drawing his chair closer to the Queen, he at last became aware he had fixed it on her dress, and that she could not move till he withdrew it ! " Carlyle, of course, knew Galloway well. Craigenputtock is just outside the boundary.

Dunragit house, a mile and a half west of Glenluce, was the ancestral home of Admiral Sir John Dalrymple Hay, who was born in 1821 and lived to see the submarine. In his early years he was engaged in the suppression of the slave-trade on the African coast and of piracy in the China seas, and was Flag-Captain on the *Hannibal* at the siege of Sevastopol. He represented several constituencies in Parliament and became a Lord of the Admiralty and a Fellow of the Royal Society. Financial difficulties compelled him to part with the Dunragit estate in 1875, but later he was able to build a new home called Craigenveoch Castle on the shore of Whitefield Loch, near Glenluce. He published *Lines from my Log-Books* in 1898.

*North-West Castle, Stranraer.*

# CHAPTER XIX

## STRANRAER

Growth of Stranraer—A Norse ship-grave ?—The royal burgh—
John Livingstone—His remarkable courtship—Stranraer Castle
—Claverhouse at Stranraer—North-West Castle—A sanguinary
fishing-story—Sir John Ross—His first voyage in search of
a North-West Passage—His second voyage—Galloway-over-
Seas.

" A slight lowering of the land would constitute this peninsula
an island "—so writes Dr. Munro of the district called The
Rhinns, that is, The Headlands—" a condition which is proved
to have existed in former times by the abundant remains of
raised beaches still to be seen, especially on the west shore of
Luce Bay. When Loch Ryan and Luce Bay were thus united
and formed a continuous channel, the mainland from Finnart[1]
Point to Burrow Head was an exposed, rocky shore, affording
here and there points sufficiently sheltered to admit of the deposi-

---

[1] Gaelic *fionn ard*, white hill.

tion of permanently raised beaches—a good example of which may be seen in a section close to Dunragit railway station." If this former condition were restored, one of its most important consequences would be the submersion of Stranraer.

The town has grown from its obscure beginnings to its present position as the largest and busiest in Wigtonshire as a result of improvements in agriculture and communications. It is the market-town of a wide farming district yielding a large amount of dairy-produce, has direct railway connexion with Glasgow and Dumfries, and is the port for the shortest route between Britain and Ireland. In the middle of the eighteenth century the population numbered only six hundred and forty-nine souls. By 1831 the agricultural advance had increased it to three thousand, three hundred, and twenty-nine. There is a large Irish element in the town. " Of late years," says the writer of *The Statistical Account* of 1839, "a great many of the natives of the sister island, having left their country in quest of food and employment, have located themselves in hovels erected in the lanes and outskirts of the town, and depend, in a great measure, for subsistence, on the charity of the inhabitants." The population is now about six thousand.

There were two villages here in the seventeenth century, the one called The Chapel, and the other Stranrawer. They were separated by a burn which has been diverted and covered. " There is a chapel now ruinous," Symson writes in 1684, " from whence all on the east side of the bourn is called the Chapel." Symson records a curious discovery : " In this town the last year, while they were digging a water-gate for a mill, they lighted upon a ship, a considerable distance from the shore, unto which the sea at the highest spring-tide never comes. It was transversly under a little bourne, and wholly covered with earth a considerable depth ; for there was a good yard, with kale growing in it, upon the one end of it. By that part of it which was gotten out, my informers, who saw it, conjecture that the vessel had been pretty large ; they also tell me, that the boards were not joyn'd together, after the usual fashion of our present ships or barks, as also that it had nailes of copper." I venture the suggestion that this may have been a Norse ship-grave.

Stranraer was erected into a burgh of barony in 1596. In the charter the name is written " Stranrawer ", and this represents the correct pronunciation. It was doubtful for a time

whether " The Chapel " or " Stranrawer " was to be the leading
place-name; but the competition was finally decided in 1617,
when James the Sixth, " being of deliberate mind " that the
growing town should flourish, and " understanding that the said
Burgh and Harbourie of Stranraer, distant twenty-four miles
from any Burgh within this our Kingdom, is, and in a short time
by the large buildings and policie to be made within the same,
will not only be to the inhabitants frequenting, but also to all
others resorting thither, very convenient for the frequent trade
which will be there in buying and selling of all sorts of victuals,
merchandise, and other things necessary for the commodie
and sustentation of our leidges in the country about, tending
greatly to the publict utility of this our Kingdom ", created
the town " ane Free Burgh Royall " to be called the Burgh
of Stranraer, with all the liberties and privileges of a royal
burgh, and included in it the adjoining villages of Clayhole and
Hillhead in Leswalt Parish and Tradeston in Soulseat. The
Chapel appears to have been regarded as a part of Stranraer
already. The parish was constituted only a short time before
it became the seat of a Presbytery in 1638.

This was the year in which John Livingstone, one of the
most famous men who have been connected with the town, was
inducted as minister of the charge. He remained here for ten
years and says that " the people of Stranraer were very tractable
and respectful ". More than this, " the more serious persons
of his flock having, on his arrival, requested liberty to attend
family worship in his house, he offered to meet with them every
morning in the church. . . . They assembled daily, and after
singing a few verses of a psalm and reading a small portion of
scripture, on which he spoke ' only so long as a half hour glass
ran,' he concluded the meeting by prayer." Besides being a
devoted minister, Livingstone took an active part in public
affairs. He was one of the commissioners sent to The Hague to
treat with Charles the Second about the succession to the throne.
He was also a member of the deputation who went to Breda in
the following summer. " Livingstone had the discernment to
discover the vacillating and dissolute principles of Charles;
and when, after much hesitation and delay, he agreed to accept
the conditions offered him, and to subscribe the solemn league
and covenant, Livingstone, who presided and delivered a sermon
on the occasion, officiated with much reluctance, fully aware

that the king was insincere, and insisting that this solemn obligation ought not to be administered until a manifest change

*The Old Town Hall, Stranraer.*

had been effected in his principles, conduct, and councils."[1] He was one of the ministers who were banished in 1662, and spent

[1] *The Literary History of Galloway* by Thomas Murray.

the remaining ten years of his life in Rotterdam, where he died
in his seventieth year.

One of the most remarkable episodes in his life was the prelude
to his marriage. It cannot be given in other than his own words:
" Mr. Blair propounded to me that marriage; immediately
thereafter I was sent to London to have gone to New England,
and returned the June following. I had seen her several times
before in Scotland, and had the testimony of many of her gracious
disposition, yet I was for nine months seeking or I could get
direction from God anent that business, during which time I
did not offer to speak to her (who, I believe, had not heard anything of the matter), only for want of clearness in my mind:
although I was twice or thrice in the house, and saw her frequently
at communions and public meetings, and it's like I might have
been longer in such darkness, except the Lord had presented an
occasion of our conferring together; for, on November 10th,
1634, when I was going to the Friday meeting, at Antrim, I
foregathered with her, and some others, going thither, and propounded to them, by the way, to confer upon a text, whereon
I was to preach the day after at Antrim, wherein I found her
conference so judicious and spiritual, that I took that for some
answer to my prayer to have my mind cleared, and blamed
myself that I had not before taken occasion to confer with her.
Four or five days after, I proponed the matter, and desired her
to think upon it; and after a week or two, I went to her mother's
house, and being alone with her, desiring her answer, I went to
prayer, and urged her to pray, which at last she did; and in
that time I got abundant clearness, that it was the Lord's mind
that I should marry her, and then propounded the matter more
fully to her mother; and albeit, I was then fully cleared, I may
truly say, it was about a month after before I got marriage
affection to her, although she was, for personal endowments,
beyond many of her equals; and I got it not till I obtained it
by prayer, but thereafter, I had greater difficulty to moderate
it." The story baffles comment; but one is glad to know that
it ended well.

The only old building in Stranraer is the castle in the middle
of the town. Although it has been much altered, it is a good
example of a sixteenth-century keep of the L plan. It is said
to have been built by Adair of Kilhilt,[1] about the beginning of

[1] Gaelic *ceann na' eilde*, the hinds' hill.

*The Castle, Stranraer.*

the sixteenth century. It came into the possession of the
Kennedies and, later, of the Dalrymples of Stair. The structure
was heightened in the seventeenth century, and alterations

were made to adapt it for use as the town jail. The two upper floors were divided into cells which retain their iron doors and the bars in the windows. The wheel-stair continued to the original parapet-walk ; but this was built over with the addition made in the seventeenth century. " At the south-east and south-west angles the remains of two circular turrets still exist, and the continuous corbelling which supported the parapets is practically complete. The seventeenth-century work is curiously constructed. It is built in two distinct portions, the south part having a flat roof and battlemented cope, while the north part has raking side walls, finished with the same type of coping, evidently designed for a sloping roof. The building, which is now hemmed in and concealed by modern shops and houses, has been greatly abused within modern times. On the ground floor a pend has been slapped through under the stair to get access to adjoining property. A shed has also been erected against the west wall, and ten feet of this wall have been removed in forming an access to it. The building is not in good repair, but has been strongly built, and at present is in no danger of becoming a ruin."[1]

The castle is believed to have been the residence of Claverhouse in March, 1682. He wrote a letter from Stranraer in which he says, " I am just beginning to send out many parties, finding the rebels become secure, and the country so quiet in all appearance. I sent out a party with my brother Dave three nights ago. The first night he took Drumbui and one McLellan, and that great villain, McClorg, the smith at Moniegafe that made all the clikys, and after whom the forces have trotted so often. It cost me both pains and money to know how to find him : I am resolved to hang him ; for it is necessary I make some example of severity, lest rebellion be thought cheap here. There cannot be alive a more wicked fellow." There is evidence, however, that MacClurg escaped ; his name occurs in the list of fugitive outlaws proclaimed by the Government in 1684.

Another building in Stranraer is called " Castle ", but with only the slenderest pretensions to such a description—North-West Castle near the pier, once the home of Rear-Admiral Sir John Ross, the Arctic explorer. It might be called a curiosity house, for one cannot ramble through it without coming upon

---

[1] The *Inventory*.

reminders of seafaring such as are unusual even in the home of a sailor ; and of the exterior it may be said that, just as the name of the house points to one of the builder's Arctic quests, so the tall, grey, rough-cast front, buried in shadow all day long until the sun is low, gives a cold, severe effect, suggestive of dim, northern seascapes.

The most noteworthy feature of the house is the annexe built at the west end after Sir John's return from his second voyage into the far north. The whole area is occupied by the dining-room. In designing it Sir John took a ship's cabin as his model. The room is lighted only from above, the wall at one end is curved as in a ship's stern, and a continuous row of mirrors runs along one side. The denial of a view outwards is rather oppressive ; but this, with the subdued light, only helps the intended effect.

Voyages like those of Sir John Ross are interesting because of the contrast presented by their methods and instruments with those of more recent days. One difference is that the explorer of the early part of last century could not carry with him a battery of cameras such as have been used with valuable results on the expeditions of Bruce, Scott, and Shackleton. Sir John, however, used the pencil and the brush, and brought home some good and several very odd pictures. He had a few of them copied on a large scale by a scenic artist and arranged to run on rollers in front of a stage at the rectangular end of the dining-room. It was one of his pleasures in later life to exhibit them to his guests, supplying a commentary from his recollections. His sketches were used also to illustrate his books.

Sir John was descended from an old Galloway family who held some small estates in Wigtonshire. The Rosses were concerned in a curious fishing-story belonging to the early part of the seventeenth century. A family of small lairds called Lin, a turbulent race, occupied the house of Larg on the Water of Luce. They made a practice of fishing the whole course of the river in defiance of the rights of their neighbours, the Rosses and Hays. The trouble reached its climax when this disagreeable family dared their neighbours to fish in the debated waters at all ! The challenge was accepted, and the Rosses and Hays descended one day upon the river. They fished over several miles until they reached a bend of the stream near The Moor Kirk of Luce, that is, New Luce, when the Laird of Larg and his men came upon them " with invasive weapons ". A scrimmage followed, and three of the sportsmen were killed.

Sir John was a son of the Rev. Andrew Ross, minister of Inch near Stranraer, and was born on his grandfather's estate of Balsarroch in Kirkcolm Parish in 1777. He entered the Royal Navy at the age of nine, was made a lieutenant in 1801, distinguished himself in several engagements during the war with France, and, when peace was declared in 1815, was in full command of the sloop of war *Driver*.

It was as an Arctic explorer, however, that he was to win his chief distinction. His first voyage into northern latitudes was made in 1818 with the ships *Isabella* and *Alexander*. The expedition was fitted out by the Government and commanded by Ross. Lieutenant Parry was second in command and in charge of the *Alexander*. Ross's nephew, James Clark Ross, who gave his name in later years to the Ross Sea, sailed as a midshipman. The expedition did not, of course, find a North-West Passage, but Ross set at rest the doubts that had been entertained regarding the alleged discoveries of Baffin.

Ross stood on the border line between the era of the sailing vessel and the steamship, and deserves recognition as one of the earliest and most enthusiastic advocates of the use of steam in the Royal Navy as well as for the special purposes of Polar voyages. The Lords of the Admiralty were strongly opposed to the innovation. I have seen, through the kindness of Miss Cunningham, who was formerly proprietress of North-West Castle, Ross's own interleaved copy of his *Narrative of a Second Voyage in Search of a North-West Passage*. On some manuscript leaves he has placed on record some details which were not, or could not be, published in the text. He had written an article in *Blackwood's Magazine*[1] over the signature " ——, Captain, R.N. " on the possibilities of steam navigation and, later, a treatise on the tactics peculiar to it. This, he says, excited much attention except at the Admiralty, " where the powerful interest of my inveterate enemies, the two secretaries, not only excluded it from their patronage, but I was informed by high authority that, if the Admiralty had been able to prove that I was the

[1] April, 1827. Ross had a collaborator. The article is signed
*********
********* } Captains, R.N.

author of the article in *Blackwood's Magazine*, my name would have been taken off the list of captains !''

If Ross's efforts in regard to the Navy were fruitless so far, he was able at least to experiment in Arctic exploration. His project of a second voyage in search of the North-West Passage received no encouragement from the naval authorities. On the contrary, so soon as his plan was known, a Bill having the effect of cancelling the offer of £20,000 for the discovery was introduced into Parliament and passed. This, however, only meant the removal of one of Ross's difficulties ; for Sir Felix Booth, who financed the expedition to a very great extent, had been unwilling before this to be concerned in it, as he did not wish to appear in the *rôle* of a speculator. The ground of his reluctance existed no longer, and the names of the Boothia Gulf and the Boothia Peninsula commemorate his liberal assistance.

The *Victory* was fitted with a high pressure engine and paddle-wheels constructed so that they could be raised out of the water in a minute ; but Ross was served badly by his engine-builders —he speaks of '' their grossly negligent conduct ''—and in these days of perfected apparatus it is strange to read the record of his misadventures and disappointments. The voyage was begun on the 23rd of May, 1829 ; but before the *Victory* had left the Thames, delay was caused by a displacement of part of the machinery, and by the time that Margate was reached it appeared that the defects were very serious. The boilers leaked, one of the guide-wheels of the piston-rod on the starboard side was worn thin, and the connecting keys of the main shaft were loose. The makers had neither informed their client of these defects nor supplied any means to remedy them in the event of a breakdown. On the 30th of May the principal key of the main shaft on the starboard side broke, rendering the whole engine useless. It had been made of a bad piece of steel. It was replaced with an iron one, but this soon gave way. Some temporary repairs were contrived at Douglas Bay ; but on the 8th of June, when the *Victory* was nearing Port Logan in Galloway, the teeth by which the fly-wheel of the small bellows was turned '' gave way with a loud crash '', and it was reported that the boilers had burst. This was not true ; but the water was pouring out of the furnace door, and the engine was stopped by the putting out of the fire. The whole voyage to the Arctic regions was occupied very largely with repairs to the engine. Over and over again we seem to be reading that " the engine was at last set to work, but had not been half an hour in motion " when another accident occurred. Finally, on the 20th of October, when the ship had been stopped for the season, the engine was hoisted out and deposited on the ice, an event hailed with rapture by all.

The ship had sailed through Prince Regent Inlet into the Gulf of Boothia and it never came out. In May, 1832, the hope of extricating it was abandoned, and the company made their painful way over the ice with boats, sledges, and provisions to Fury Beach. They had to remain here over the following winter, and it was not until August, 1833, that they escaped in the boats, fell in with the whaling ship *Isabella*, formerly under Ross's command, and so returned home.

The fruits of the voyage included the discovery of the Gulf of Boothia, of the continent and isthmus of Boothia Felix, and of a great number of islands, lakes, and rivers, and the establishment of the facts that a North-West Passage must be sought farther north and that the north-east point of America extends to the seventy-fourth degree of north latitude ; the crowning achievement, however, was Commander James Clark Ross's discovery of the true position of the North Magnetic Pole.

It might seem as if this chapter had carried us far from Galloway. It has really taken us into Galloway-over-Seas. Look at a North Polar chart and behold the Galloway place and family names—Agnew River, Cape Carrick Moore, Cape Dalrymple Hay, Port Logan, Cape MacDouall, and Andrew Ross Land.

# CHAPTER XX

## LOCHINCH AND CASTLE KENNEDY

The White Loch of Inch—The heronry—Lochinch Castle—The grounds—The Kennedies—The Dalrymples of Stair—Viscount Stair—His family—The first Earl of Stair—The second Earl—Castle Kennedy—Soulseat Abbey.

AT a short distance from Stranraer, standing within the same grounds as the ruin of the famous Castle Kennedy—the property of the Earls of Cassillis until they lost their Wigtonshire estates—is the modern home of one of the most distinguished families in the annals of Scotland, and within the grounds one of the most remarkable examples of landscape gardening in the country.

Lochinch[1] is approached from Stranraer by what is known as the London Road. The explanation of its name is that there was a time when it formed part of the principal line of communication between London and Ireland. It was important as a military, and also as a trading, route. Cattle from Ireland were landed in great numbers at Port Logan and Portpatrick, and were then driven into England by way of Dumfries.

It is after a little more than two miles that the chief entrance to the stately demesne of Lord Stair is reached. Following the long carriage-drive leading to the castle, we have on the right hand the large White Loch, and by the wayside one of the antiquities of the estate, the ivy-clad ruin of the old church of Inch standing between the drive and the loch. Andrew Symson, minister of Kirkinner before the Revolution and author of *A Large Description of Galloway*, says of the loch that in it " there

---

[1] *Innse Crindaill*, Crindall's island, is a large crannog. *Loch innse Crindaill*, the loch of Crindall's isle.

are two several sorts of trouts ; the one blacker than the other, and each keep their own part of the loch ; so that, when they are in the dish at the table, those that are acquainted with the differences can easily tell in which part of the loch such and such a fish was taken ". He goes on to refer to " the parish kirk of the Inch, so call'd from a little island, call'd the Inch, situated in the loch, a little distance from the kirk ", and adds that

*In the grounds of Castle Kennedy.*

" within this little island, which is also planted with trees, is a little house built, into which the late Earl of Cassillis us'd to retire himselfe betwixt sermons, having a boat for that purpose, in which also he could be soon transported from Castle Kennedy to the church, and so back again ; the way from the kirk to the castle by land being about a mile on either side of the loch ".

The person to whom this note refers was John, sixth Earl of Cassillis, who attended the Westminster Assembly of Divines,

It has been supposed that his wife, a daughter of the Earl of Haddington, was the subject of the ballad of *Johnie Faa*[1] ; but there is no foundation for the belief, and there is strong evidence against it, for the countess died at Cassillis House, and was buried in the family vault at Maybole. There are no remains of the little house on the little island in the White Loch ; but we may note here an archæological detail of the neighbouring Black Loch—that it contains a crannog or lake-dwelling.

When I visited the island in 1911, I saw the places where the excavations had been made. It was more interesting, however, to watch the herons in the trees overhead. The Castle Kennedy heronry is believed to be centuries old. Until the year 1821 the birds nested on a small island in the White Loch, but in that year the largest trees were felled, and the birds took up their present abode. John MacDiarmid, author of *Sketches from Nature*, a book published in 1830, says, " The number of birds is considerable at present ; but it has often been remarked that they do not increase in anything like the proportion that the number of nests would lead you to suppose. Last year there were twenty-seven nests in the small island, and twenty-six this year, with two on a tree near the old Castle. Castle-Kennedy abounds with water as well as the grounds around Culhorn ; the sea-coast is within a little distance ; the burns that feed the loch are easily fished, and even the shallower parts of the lochs themselves ; still the herons, so far from increasing like rooks, appear to remain nearly stationary ; and, whether the young remove to other quarters, die early, or are shot while roaming along the extensive shores of Lochryan, during the herring fishing and other seasons, are points I have no means of determining. My own opinion is, that these birds are by no means so prolific as naturalists imagine." In 1911, about eighty years after MacDiarmid made his observations, the number of nests was just about the same. In answer to my inquiry on this point, one of the estate gamekeepers told me, " about thirty ".

A great park sweeps upwards from the northern margin of the White Loch, and the house occupies a commanding site at the summit of the slope. It is a little difficult, therefore, to understand how MacKerlie, the author of the *History of Lands and their Owners in Galloway*, came to think that the site " cannot

[1] See page 397.

be called a good one, being rather low ". It seems to be Mac
Kerlie's fate to be quoted for the purpose of expressing dis-
agreement, and it is easy to differ from him when he says further
that the house " does not present any attraction for special
notice ". It is really a magnificent mansion in the Scottish
baronial style, with a dignity proportionate to the extensive
possessions of the family, and is built of white freestone that
gives a very pleasing effect among the surrounding green slopes
and woods. The hall, the corridor, the dining-room, the drawing-
room, and other apartments on the ground floor are all planned
on a noble scale, furnished very handsomely, and decorated
richly with tapestries, paintings, and ornaments. More, perhaps,
than any other house in Galloway does this one give the impression of grandeur both without and within.

Of more general interest, however, are the famous dressed
grounds designed by Field-Marshal the second Earl of Stair.

Between Lochinch Castle and Castle Kennedy is a strip of
land about a mile in length, bounded on one side by the east
shore of the White Loch and on the other by the west shore of
the Black Loch. This was originally an island in Loch Inch,
and so it appears in Grose's drawing of Castle Kennedy made
in 1789. It was here that the second Earl exercised his skill
in landscape-gardening, transforming more or less the whole
area from its natural condition. The steep banks rising from
the two lochs have been broken throughout their entire length
into terraces and heights, " like miniature forts with bastions
and angles ", all clad with closely-mown grass ; a deep hollow
with terraced banks has in its centre a large round pond where
aquatic plants, including the lily of the Nile, thrive ; and at
the south end is a canal connecting the Black with the White
Loch and spanned by an ivy-covered bridge. The strip of
land between the lochs broadens and rises towards the south,
and at the highest point stands the ruin of Castle Kennedy,
with avenues of lofty trees radiating from it in almost every
direction. To trim and tend the original elaborate design
was a serious task, especially when some of the hedges had
reached the height of seventy feet. " Scarcely had the Marshal's
oaks cast their foliage a hundred times before a ruthless edict
of the seventh Earl . . . laid every stick of them low, and the
pleasure grounds went back to wilderness." The eighth Earl,
who succeeded in 1840, discovered a plan of the grounds in a

gardener's cottage, and decided to revive the former grandeur.
The alleys consisted at first of beeches and limes, but were
planted now with various kinds of conifer, so that the grounds
were converted into a great *pinetum*. The magnificent araucaria

*Castle Kennedy.*

avenue between the round pond and Lochinch Castle has survived undamaged the storms of nearly fifty years, but some of
the others have suffered more or less.

The artificiality of the grounds is one's first thought; yet
there is a charm about them that grows on one; and on a bright
windy day, when the lochs are broken into a wilderness of

foam-crested waves, when the long terraces are picked out in sunlight and shadow, and the great belts of conifers are full of movement, nothing more delightful of its kind could be conceived.

These grounds are one of the "show places" of Galloway and are open to visitors on a day in each week. George Borrow was a visitor in 1866, and made some jottings about the place: "Set off in the direction of Castle Kennedy. Fine view of mountains to the left. Plantations and old castle in the foreground. Most beautiful scene I ever saw—hot sun—far distant misty mountains—cattle in the water—stay to look at them."

The earliest notice of the Lochinch estate occurs in 1482, when John, Lord Kennedy, obtained extensive lands in the neighbouring parish of Leswalt, and was appointed keeper of the manor-place and loch of Inch, and bailie of regality of the Bishop of Galloway's lands on the water of Cree. It was his son who was created Earl of Cassillis.

It is believed that the lands acquired by the Kennedies in the parish of Inch belonged at that time to the monastery of Soulseat. The family added greatly to their Wigtonshire estates, and their influence became so important as to give rise to the rhyme:

> 'Twixt Wigton and the town of Air,
> Portpatrick and the Cruives of Cree,
> No man needs think for to bide there
> Unless he court with Kennedie.

John, seventh Earl of Cassillis, fell into financial difficulties. He was a strong supporter of the Covenanters, and was the only member of Parliament who voted in 1670 against the Act for punishing those who countenanced the holding of conventicles. He thus became obnoxious to the Government. In consequence of the quartering of the Highland Host on his estates, and losses incurred in other ways, his fortune was so much reduced that, like other landowners of the period in similar circumstances, he had to part with a great deal of his property. He sold his Wigtonshire lands to John, second Lord Bargany, in 1674; but he also became involved in money troubles, and the estates were purchased by an ancestor of the present owners.

The Dalrymples of Stair are an old Ayrshire family. They

owned a baronial estate in the parish of Dalrymple[1] in the fourteenth century, and from it apparently they took their name.
It was in the seventeenth and the earlier half of the eighteenth
century that the family rose to distinction, the heads of
three generations, namely, Viscount Stair and the first and the
second Earl, being among the most eminent men of their times.

James Dalrymple, created Viscount Stair, was born at
Drummurchie in the parish of Barr in 1619, was educated at
Mauchline Parish School and Glasgow University, and entered
the Army. After about two years of service he became, on the
suggestion of some of the professors, a candidate for the vacant
Chair of Logic in his *alma mater*, and was elected. Soon after
this he married Margaret, the eldest daughter of James Ross
of Balniel in Wigtonshire, who appears to have been a brilliant
figure. While discharging the duties of his chair, he gave himself
more and more to the study of Law, resigned his professorship
in 1647, and was admitted advocate in 1648. He made a
reputation at the Bar, and the opinion formed of his gifts is
indicated by the fact that in 1649 and also in 1650 he was
appointed Secretary to the Commissioners sent to treat with
Charles the Second at Breda, and, on the arrival of Charles in
Scotland, was one of the commissioners deputed to receive him.
Since his sympathies were Royalist, it was only with great
reluctance that he accepted office as Judge under Cromwell's
government, and he took his seat on the Bench in July, 1657,
under no other oath than that of fidelity to the duties of the
position. Shortly after the Restoration Charles knighted him,
and made him a Senator of the College of Justice ; but two years
later Dalrymple resigned his seat because he could not take the
" Declaration " oath denying the right of the nation to take
up arms against its sovereign. The resignation was not accepted,
and Dalrymple retained his office without taking the oath.
He was created a baronet presently, and was a member of the
Commission chosen in 1670 to consider the projected treaty
for the union of the kingdoms. He became in the following
year Lord President of the Court of Session. In 1681 he represented Wigtonshire in the Scottish Parliament. In the same
year the Test Oath was imposed, whereupon the Lord President
resigned all his offices. He was too good a Protestant and
Presbyterian for the government of that day, and had to retire

_____
[1] Gaelic *dal chruim puill*, land of the winding pool.

to Leyden in 1682 in order to place himself beyond danger. He came over with the Prince of Orange in 1688, was restored to the office of Lord President, and elevated to the peerage with the title of Viscount Stair. He was the author of the *Institutions of the Law of Scotland*, still a great text-book, and of other works. He died in 1695.

Lord Stair appears to have transmitted his legal aptitude to his sons. Before giving an outline of the career of his eldest son, who succeeded him, we may note that his second son, the Hon. Sir James Dalrymple of Borthwick, Bart., was a Principal Clerk of Session (Sir John Dalrymple, a Baron of Exchequer in Scotland, was one of his descendants); the third son was the Hon. Sir Hew Dalrymple of North Berwick, Bart., appointed President of the Court of Session in 1698; the fifth was the Hon. Sir David Dalrymple of Hailes, Bart., Lord Advocate from 1700 till 1720. (Sir David Dalrymple, a judge in the Court of Session, known best as Lord Hailes, the author of the *Annals of Scotland*, was his grandson.) The only son not mentioned already, the Hon. Thomas Dalrymple, entered the medical profession, and became Physician in Ordinary to the King in Scotland.

A literary interest attaches to Lord Stair's eldest daughter, Janet, whose sad love-story formed the groundwork of *The Bride of Lammermoor*.[1]

John Dalrymple, created Earl of Stair, was born in 1648, and admitted advocate in 1672. He was instrumental in preventing a British ship from being blown up by the Dutch in the Medway, and was knighted for this service by Charles the Second. Like his father, he had a share of Government persecution on account of his sympathy with the Covenanters. He was received to favour at Court, however, and became Lord Advocate in 1687 in succession to Sir George Mackenzie, who had been removed. Sir John was now called upon to prosecute persons who attended conventicles, and his lack of enthusiasm brought about the reappointment of Mackenzie in the next year. At the same time Sir John was nominated successor to Sir James Foulis of Colinton, both as Lord Justice Clerk and as an ordinary Lord. He was thus in office at the time of the Revolution, was a member of the Convention Parliament, and one of the three commissioners who conveyed the offer of the crown to William and Mary. He returned to the office of Lord Advocate after the Revolution,

---

[1] See page 200.

and became a Secretary of State in 1691 ; but as a result of the Parliamentary inquiry into the Massacre of Glencoe, in regard to which he had a grave responsibility, retired into private life in 1695. It was in this year that Viscount Stair died ; but his successor did not take his seat in Parliament for several years. His services to the nation, however, were not forgotten, and the earldom was conferred upon him in 1703.

The great question then agitating the two kingdoms was that of union. Lord Stair was one of the commissioners selected to arrange the Treaty of Union in 1705, and worked hard and usefully for the furthering of this measure both in Parliament and in the country. It was after a day of exciting debate in Parliament that he died suddenly on the 7th of January, 1707.

The first Earl of Stair was followed by his second son, John, who as a boy had had the misfortune to shoot his elder brother accidentally. He had a varied career, winning distinction as a soldier, as an agriculturist, and as an ambassador. After studying at Leyden and at Edinburgh he entered the Army, received his commission as lieutenant-colonel in the Scottish Regiment of Foot Guards in 1701, and served in Flanders as *aide-de-camp* to Lord Marlborough. He distinguished himself in Marlborough's campaigns, and became colonel of the Scots Greys in 1706. In the following year he succeeded to the earldom, and was elected one of the Representative Peers for Scotland. In 1708 he was once more at the seat of war, took part in the victory of Oudenarde, and brought home the Duke of Marlborough's despatches. He was sent as Envoy Extraordinary to Warsaw in 1709, and remained there until the next year, when he returned to service in the Army. On the fall of Marlborough in 1711, Lord Stair was deprived of his command, and retired to his estates for a time ; but on the accession of George the First in 1714 was made a Lord of the Bedchamber, a Privy Councillor, and Commander-in-Chief of the Forces in Scotland. In 1715 he went as ambassador to the Court of France, and remained there in that capacity for five years, counteracting the intrigues of the Jacobites ; but in consequence of his opposition to Law, the financier, " whose schemes for the restoration of the French credit excited such high hopes and ended in such dismal failure ", was virtually recalled about a month before the collapse of Law's Mississippi Scheme.

The next twenty years of his life were occupied principally

by such cares as tree-planting, agriculture, landscape gardening, cattle-breeding, and developing minerals on his Ayrshire property. He is said to have initiated the practice of planting turnips and cabbages in the open fields, and was a pioneer in other departments of agriculture, introducing new implements and machinery.

A day was coming, however, when he was to return to the public service of his country, little as he anticipated such an event. Even so late as 1741, when the power of Sir Robert Walpole, the Prime Minister, whose hostility had kept him in the background, was already waning, Lord Stair was writing in such a strain as this : " I am so thoroughly convinced that I can be of no use to my country or to my friends that I am going to set out this very day to take care of my little affairs as a farmer, where I shall hear very little of politics but what I learn from the newspapers " ; but in the following year Walpole resigned office, and Lord Stair, who was then in his seventieth year, was appointed Commander-in-Chief and Field-Marshal.

Europe was involved in war once more over the ordinance known as the Pragmatic Sanction, and the British Government sent sixteen thousand troops to Flanders under the command of Lord Stair to support the Austrian policy. Lord Stair combined with his military appointment that of Ambassador Extraordinary to the Dutch Court, and preceded the troops on his mission to The Hague. " Whilst there, he is reported to have obtained a social success over the minister of France, auguring well for the future. At a grand diplomatic banquet, according to the fashion of the day, toasts in the form of sentiments made their round, and the solar system had been selected as the field on which the envoys were to prove their wit. The French minister, jumping to his feet, beamingly proposed his master as ' the sun '. Lord Stair cordially accepted it. The glasses were drained, when the Austrian Ambassador gave the beautiful and chaste Empress Queen Maria Theresa as ' the moon '. Lord Stair drank that too. All eyes were turned upon him as he seemed to have been checkmated. After a short pause he rose smilingly and said, ' A bumper, gentlemen ; you shall drink to my master as Joshua, who bid the sun and moon stand still '."[1]

On the eve of the Battle of Dettingen George the Second

[1] *The Hereditary Sheriffs.*

arrived on the field and took over the supreme command. The battle, in which Lord Stair acted loyally, was a victory, but the partiality shewn by the King for his Hanoverian troops and for the advice of the Hanoverian generals led to Lord Stair's resignation of his post as Commander-in-Chief. The matter was discussed fiercely in Parliament ; but Lord Stair did nothing to inflame public opinion, nor did he pose as a martyr. On the contrary, in 1744, when there were rumours of an approaching French invasion, he offered his services to the King, and the unpleasantness was alleviated when His Majesty, "reposing special trust and confidence in your conduct and abilities", appointed Lord Stair to the command of the Forces in South Britain. He died at Queensberry House in 1747, and with him the succession of the Dalrymples in the direct line came to an end.

Castle Kennedy was his favourite residence until it was burned. It had been built in 1607 by the fifth Earl of Cassillis to take the place of the earlier stronghold of which John, Lord Kennedy, was appointed Keeper in 1482. It is " a good example of seventeenth-century symmetrical planning. . . . The main block has been four storeys in height above the vault, and the towers were carried considerably higher. The only architectural feature remaining is a portion of a fine dormer window in the north wall of the north tower."[1] Wings were added later on the north and the west.

The Countess-dowager announced the burning of the castle to Lord Stair's agent in London thus :

"Edinburgh, November 3, 1716.

". . . . Upon Saturday last the house of Castle Kennedy was burnt, of which I have no account of the way it was done, but only that the maid had put on a fire in the drawing-room for airing the room, and went to bed after she had put out the fire. However, in the night it broke out and burnt all, so as they had much difficulty to make their own escape, and could save nothing but my son's own picture and two more. I know he will be concerned, because Castle Kennedy was the favourite house he had in this country ; but we must all submit to the providence of God, and acknowledge His justice that orders all things well. And I desire you may transmit this letter to him, and observe his orders."

[1] The *Inventory*.

Thereafter Lord Stair lived at Culhorn [1] House when he was in this district.

In subsequent generations the succession has passed to descendants of the first Earl and of Viscount Stair, many of whom have served their country in the Army. An interesting account of the history of the family may be seen in Mr. William Robertson's *Ayrshire : its History and Historic Families*.

When Viscount Dalrymple succeeded his father, the eleventh Earl, in 1914, he had the misfortune to be a prisoner in the hands of the Germans, and was one of the officers selected for special ill-treatment in retaliation for the temporary refusal of the British Government to regard submarine pirates as ordinary prisoners of war. He was appointed Lord-Lieutenant of The Shire in 1935, on Sir Herbert Maxwell's resigning the office.

The monastery of Soulseat has been referred to already in connexion with the acquisition of the lands of Inch by the Kennedies. The site is on a peninsula running into Soulseat Loch, and is occupied now by the manse of the parish of Inch. The monastery was founded by Fergus, Lord of Galloway, as a home for monks of the Premonstratensian order, and was known as *Sedes Animarum* and *Monasterium Viridis Stagni*. The latter name is traceable to the green appearance of the water caused from time to time by the presence of spore-like vegetable growths. Symson says, " This Abbacy is commonly call'd Salsyde; by Speed Salsid, though by him misplac'd; *potius* Soul Seat, *Sedes Animarum* ; some say it should be Saul Seat, *Sedes Saulis*, one Saul being, as they say, Abbot or Monk thereat." [2] Chalmers says that " it was the mother of the more celebrated and opulent Priory of Whithorn, as well as the Abbey of Holywood, both of which were planted by monks of the same order. It appears to have been the original establishment of the Premonstratensian monks in Scotland ; and the abbots of Soulseat were the superiors of that order in this kingdom." Little is known of its history.

---

[1] Gaelic *cuil eòrna,* corner of the barley.
[2] Sir Herbert Maxwell traces the name to O.E. *sáwl sceot,* payment for the good of a dead person's soul.

# CHAPTER XXI

## FROM STRANRAER TO THE MULL OF GALLOWAY

The Rhinns—The murder of a minister of Stoneykirk—Ancient Christian monuments at Kirkmadrine Church—The Murder Stone—The MacDoualls—Logan House and the garden—The fish-pond—Port Logan and its pier—The coast between Port Logan and the Mull—The smugglers' cave at Breddock Bay—Drummore village and Kirkmaiden Church—S. Medana's Chapel and the Well of the Co'—The Double-dykes—The Mull of Galloway.

THE district known as The Rhinns of Galloway—a long, narrow, green ridge that would have been an island but for the low isthmus between Loch Ryan and Luce Bay—is a conspicuous feature in the map of Scotland. For the traveller—and no doubt for the resident also—it is in certain kinds of weather a very pleasant country in which to ramble or dwell. If it is to be seen at its best, bright weather is postulated, for, more than most landscapes, those smooth, green heights and tree-girt fields need the light and shade that sunshine gives. Let there be a brilliant day, drifts of highly-lighted cloud travelling between the blue of the sky and of the sea, a wind strong enough to break the water into foam along the shore, and that emerald peninsula will be a delight to the eyes.

A conventional guide-book conducting the reader from Stranraer to the Mull of Galloway might describe the scenery as " tame and uninteresting " ; and I remember a statement in a book of this kind that it was not worth while for the traveller to leave the main road. The pastoral uplands, however, are intersected by numerous byways ending usually in the yard of some remote dairy-farm or dropping down to the sandy shore of a bay—one of those little-visited bays where German submarines were reported to have been seen in 1915—and anyone exploring the district thoroughly and following a zig-zag course southwards by means of these tracks would be delighted continually by fresh views of the sea meeting him unexpectedly on the one hand or the other. He would also see what the traveller who took the advice of the guide-book would miss —some of the most ancient Christian monuments in Britain.

The main road itself has on the left the white sands and bright waters of Luce Bay and the dim coast of The Machars; on the right, pastures where great herds of cattle graze, and an occasional whitewashed farm-steading with its clump of trees; while now and again the road passes along a raised beach or through a quiet group of cottages.

The first village is Stoneykirk—S. Stephen's Kirk. I shall always associate it with a strange story of the murder of a minister of the parish. It was the custom here, as in some other places, that the minister on entering the pulpit at the hour of worship acknowledged the presence of the congregation by bowing towards the pew of the chief heritor. The families of MacDouall of Balgreggan and MacDouall of Garthland had an ancient dispute as to precedence in the representation of the line of the old Lords of Galloway. The Rev. Robert Campbell, who became minister of the parish in 1697, acknowledged the Garthland claim, and thus drew upon himself the hostility of the Laird of Balgreggan. He received friendly warnings that he must be on his guard and, although he continued to call at Balgreggan, was always careful not to eat or drink. One day, as he was leaving, the housekeeper, desiring some spiritual counsel, invited him into her room and incidentally offered him a glass of wine, which he drank, and presently he departed. It is said that when he crossed the Sand Mill Burn his body was already swelling, and that before he reached a farm half a mile farther on the buttons were bursting off his waistcoat. Some of the Balgreggan people followed him and saw him drop down dead near the village. They lifted the body, propped it up against the dyke with the help of the minister's walking-stick, rolled a log against the foot of the stick, and retired.

The first to come that way was the minister's man riding the horse to the water. The horse took fright and nearly threw his rider.

"Oh!" cried the man as he dismounted, "you might be doing better than near killing me!"

Seeing his master wrapped apparently in deep thought, he spoke again. Receiving no answer, he placed his foot on the log and so moved it. The walking-stick slipped, and the body collapsed on the ground.

There is no public record of the murder, nor does any attempt appear to have been made to arraign the criminals; but my informant referred me to the records of the Presbytery of Stranraer, which adopt an unusual phraseology in connexion with Campbell's death. It was the duty of every minister in turn to conduct the devotional exercises at the meetings of the Presbytery, and we find accordingly that "At Stranraer the 2 November 1709 years," *inter alia* the Presbytery "appoints Mr. Robert Campbell to have the presbiterial Excersise On i pet. 3. 16. against the next And Mr. Godefroy to writt to him Anent it" and "At Stranraer the 4th January 1710 years," *inter alia,* " Mr. Robert Campbell who was appointed to have the Excersise this Day being by the providence of God Removed by Death, Mr. Marshal at the Moderator's Desire preached from John ii. ii." The story suggests that the Laird of Balgreggan was able to inspire an extraordinary degree of timidity in his neighbours, and that the fallacy of singling out unusual events for association with "the providence of God" is more than two centuries old !

The byway leading to Kirkmadrine[1] Church, where there is an exceptionally important collection of inscribed monuments belonging to an early Christian century, begins a mile south of the village of Sandhead. After the half-private character of this road and the disused, grass-grown approach to the old church, one is startled to discover an oppressively new-looking structure. Kirkmadrine Church was the place of worship for the inhabitants of the ancient parish of Toskerton, merged long ago in Stoneykirk, and had become a mere heap of ruins when it was completely restored, with Cruggleton Church as a model, towards the end of the last century. Dean Stanley, who was here in 1871, the year before he published his *Lectures on the Church of Scotland*, says in one of his letters that "the name of Mathurinus is still distinct in its original characters " on one of the carved stones.

---

[1] Pronounced "Kirkmadreen". There was another parish of this name, now a part of Sorbie. "No authentic explanation of the dedication is forthcoming. The church in Stoneykirk . . . may be the church named Mothernin, mentioned among those held by the Chapter of Candida Casa."—Maxwell.

This was a misreading; but he was not far astray in saying that " nowhere in Great Britain is there a Christian record so ancient as the grey weatherbeaten column which now serves as a gate-post of the deserted churchyard of Kirk Madreen on the bleak hill in the centre of the Rinns of Galloway " [1]. He was unaware that the other gatepost shared in this singular interest. To

*Sandhead.*

bring his statement up to date, it must be added that both the " gateposts " are now safely housed in the porch of the church.

" The Kirkmadrine stones ", says the *Inventory*, " are long, narrow, undressed slabs, bearing each on one face and one of them

---

[1] See Preface to the Second Edition, p. viii, and p. 241 for an earlier monumental inscription. The Roman church at Silchester and some instances of the Chi-Rho monogram in mosaics, pave-ments, and building stones in Roman villas, and on some other objects are attributed to the fourth century.

on both faces an equal-armed cross within a circle, displaying at the side of the upper arms a small loop. This cross and loop are a modification of a symbol known as the Labarum or the Cross of Constantine, in reality a monogram derived from the first two letters of the word ΧΡΙΣΤΟΣ, adopted by the early Christians as a symbol of their faith. It has been found frequently in the catacombs enclosed within a circle (explained in an inscription at Milan to represent the name of the Almighty as being without beginning and without end), and it continued to be used on sarcophagi until about the end of the seventh century. Both stones at Kirkmadrine bear an inscription in Roman capitals, clearly cut, and carefully spaced, though not divided into words, but on neither do they show such distinctive characteristics as would indicate their date with any exactness. The inscription

*Ancient crosses at Kirkmadrine.*

on the more important of the two stones was originally preceded by the formula A et ω, now incomplete, and this formula Dr. Joseph Anderson has pointed out is not found in Gaul associated with the monogram later than the fifth century or the first half of the sixth. He further indicates that on these stones the loop is a modification of a Roman R and not of a Greek P, thus showing a step in the development towards the simple cross, a conclusion which was not attained in Gaul before the com-

mencement of the sixth century. From such considerations
it is held that it would be unsafe to assign an earlier date to
the inscriptions on these stones than somewhere in the second
half of the fifth century."

The inscription on one of the stones is :

> HICIACENT
> SCIETPRAE
> CIPVISACER
> DOTESIDES
> VIVENTIVS
> ETMAVORIVS

The words are not spaced, there is a mark of contraction over
the letters SCI, which stand for SANCTI, and a part of the stone
has been broken off after the letters IDES.  If these letters with
their supplement could be accepted as ID EST, the translation
would run : " Here lie holy and eminent bishops, namely,
Viventius and Mavorius " ; in an appendix, however, to Bishop
Dowden's *The Celtic Church in Scotland*, the Rev. Edmund
McClure writes : " Your Lordship's conjecture as to *Ides*
being part of a proper name, and not, as is generally assumed,
the remnant of *id est*, is doubtless right.  An eminent Cambridge
Epigraphist puts *idest* out of the question.  I would venture to
suggest that the name here intended was *Idesus*.  *Id* is a frequent element in early Cymric names . . . . and *Esus* is the
name of a Celtic deity . . . . The *et* coupling the last two of
three names is possible in late Latin."

*Viventius* and *Mavorius* are not Roman names, and the
authority just quoted suggests that the former may represent
an early British *Vevendi*, and that the latter may be a Latinized
form of some such name as *Maguor*.

*Sacerdos*, says Bishop Dowden, " was sometimes employed
with reference to both of the highest orders of the ministry—
those of Bishops and Presbyters."  " It was found necessary,
when it was sought to be precise, to use, when referring to Presbyters, such forms as *secundi sacerdotes*, or *secundi ordinis
sacerdotes*. . . ."

The legend on the other stone is in debased Latin capitals :

> SET
> FLOREN
> TIVS

M

and looks as if it were meant to be read in connexion with the previous inscription.

A third stone, discovered in 1916, bears the Chi-Rho monogram and, in lettering similar to that of the second stone,

INITIUM
ETFINIS

and may have formed the back of the second stone, which has been split off. The general inference is that within a generation or so of the death of S. Ninian Roman Christianity had established itself in The Rhinns.

After passing the end of the Kirkmadrine byway, the road to the Mull makes a descent to the shore, and runs near it until it reaches the little village of Ardwell. Just before entering it, it skirts the Murder Plantation on the grounds of the Ardwell property. Among the trees near the Ardwell gate lies a large boulder with the word MURDER carved on it, marking the place where one of the MacDoualls of Logan was killed in the sixteenth century. MacDouall wished to marry the daughter of MacKinna, the Laird of the estate of Barncorkrie,[1] which was then called "Portcorkerie"; but had a rival in Gordon of Clanyard,[2] whose property marched with MacKinna's. Gordon contrived to have the lady carried off and placed in the keeping of his kinsmen, the Gordons of Cardiness near Gatehouse-of-Fleet. The tradition says nothing about the lady's affections; but it is not likely that she made the journey to Cardiness willingly, as she appears not to have been married to Gordon, and it may be assumed that she favoured the suit of MacDouall, unless, indeed, she was disposed to invoke a plague on both their houses. MacDouall, at any rate, hearing that she was at Cardiness, thought it worth his while to follow her; but whether his intentions savoured of abduction or of rescue, he had no success. As he came past Ardwell on the way home, he was ambushed by a band of Gordon's vassals, dragged from his horse, and slain.

Although Gordon appears to have carried off the daughter

---

[1] Gaelic *barr an corcoraichdh*, hill-top of the ruddiness or (plur.) *barran chorcrai*, ruddy hill-tops. There is a mass of ruddy granite exposed here, where the cliff abuts on a bay called Portencorkrie.—Maxwell.

[2] Gaelic *claon àrd*, the sloping height.

of the Laird of Barncorkrie to no purpose, his relations with the family were not at an end. He proceeded next to abduct the father. If he could not have the lands with the daughter, he would have them without. He hung the laird by the thumbs over a high cliff and forced him to repeat the following words in the hearing of witnesses :

> From me and from mine,
> To thee and to thine,
> The lands of Portcorkerie
> I forever resign.

MacKerlie states that Alexander Gordon of Clanyard " had a charter of alienation, dated 1st June, 1551, confirming to him and his spouse, Janet Crawfurd, the five merk land of Porten-corkie ". Both Barncorkrie and Clanyard are now included in the Logan property.

The MacDouall family is remarkable if only because of the length of their tenure of their estates. According to Sir Herbert Maxwell, they are the only family of Pictish origin in Galloway who have remained in possession of their lands until the present day. They claim, moreover, to be descended from Fergus, Lord of Galloway. Mackenzie, the author of a work on the heraldry of Scotland, published in Edinburgh in 1680, has a curious note : " Macdowal is known to be amongst the ancientest Sirnames of Scotland, because he bears a Lyon collard, with a broken Crown about his neck, in remembrance of Dovallus, his Predecessour (as is alleg'd) killing Nothatus, who was a Tyrant, and who liv'd many years before Christ : which (if true) are the Ancientest Arms I ever saw belonging to any private family in Europe." Sir Herbert Maxwell, after weighing the evidence, concludes that " it seems reasonable to suppose that the collaterals of Fergus formed the clan MacDouall, and that the patronymic emerged as a surname when necessity for one arose ". In the latter part of the thirteenth century, when surnames came into common use, " MacDouall " is prominent in the records of Galloway affairs.

Even so late as the thirteenth and fourteenth centuries the Crown could not depend on the allegiance of the Galloway lords. They inclined sometimes to the Scottish, sometimes to the English King in the course of the international conflicts. At the battle of Largs in 1263 MacDouall and a large number of his followers contributed to the victory of the Scottish Army over the Norsemen; but when Edward the First entered Galloway in 1300 and halted at Cally near Gatehouse-of-Fleet, he sent a detachment into the west to secure the co-operation of Mac Douall, and rewarded him for his support by giving his son the heiress of Hugh de Champaigne in marriage.

When the greater part of the rest of Scotland had been won by Robert the Bruce, Galloway, where the influence of the MacDoualls and their sympathizers was supreme, still stood for the English King. Shortly after the death of Edward the First, Bruce invaded the Province, treating the inhabitants with great severity, but had to retire into Carrick on the approach of an English army under the Earl of Richmond. He went later into the north and won the successes that encouraged his brother Edward to make another attempt on Galloway. The Gallovidian forces, consisting of the adherents of MacDouall and some English troops, were defeated and scattered at the battle of Craignell on the Dee. The western part of Galloway still held out, however, and another battle had to be fought at Kirrouchtrie near the Cree river. The Gallovidian forces were broken again, MacDouall killed, and the inhabitants compelled to swear allegiance to King Robert.

In 1339 Duncan MacDouall renewed his fealty to the King of England and was pardoned for his late adherence to the Scots. The Scots prepared to make reprisals, and in 1342 MacDouall applied to Edward the Third for help. An English force was assembled on the Cumberland coast, and provisions were sent to MacDouall's castle on the " *Insula de Estholm in Galeway*". There is no island bearing the name of Estholm or Eastholm on the Galloway coast, and the use of it by a clerk in the fourteenth century is probably to be explained by his misreading or mis-hearing the Scandinavian *hestum ey*, " horse island," or Heston. The conclusion of this curious competition was that MacDouall had to surrender to his lawful sovereign.

It is not known when the MacDoualls came into possession of the Logan[1] estate. The old castle called Balzieland was destroyed by fire about the end of the fifteenth century, and the family documents are said to have been burned. A new charter obtained by Patrick MacDouall in 1504 states that the

[1] Gaelic *lagan*, a hollow.

lands had been held by the MacDoualls " beyond the memory
of man ". This, of course, is a common phrase in such instruments. Since that time the property seems to have descended
almost, if not quite, uniformly from father to son. The most
eminent member of the family was Andrew, a well-known lawyer
in the seventeenth century, who was raised to the bench with
the title of Lord Bankton and wrote a work on Scots Law.

The modern part of Logan House[1] dates from 1874 and is
built of red freestone. The three lofty storeys, with the tall
mullioned windows, the crow-step gables, the turrets, and the
large square tower, make one of the handsomest houses in
Galloway, and the venerable trees on the right and on the left,
the broad stretch of gravel immediately in front, and the wide
lawns upon which the windows look provide it with worthy
surroundings.

The mild climate of this corner of Wigtonshire favours the
growth of plants and shrubs such as few travellers expect to
see in any part of Scotland, and the neighbouring plantations
and the very high beech and other hedges dividing the garden
serve as wind-breaks. On coming round a corner, one beholds
almost with a shock of surprise a stately row of the Australian
palm-fern (*Cordyline Australis*) and a magnificent tree-fern
(*Dicksonia Antarctica*) ; in the more open part of the garden,
a long, unbroken row of well-established hydrangeas, several
eucalyptus trees—one of them about thirty feet high—a large
bamboo plant, and some very tall palms ; on the high wall
of the garden, the New Zealand parrot-tree (*Clianthus puniceus*)
and the passion-flower ; at one end of the terrace below the
wall, a bank of palms, and at the other, a large plant of Chilian
rhubarb, the leaves of which have attained in a favourable year
the diameter of nine-and-a-half feet ; and near the house a

---

[1] A bell preserved at Logan has " the following inscription in two
lines : NICOLAIVS RAMSA DOMINVS × DE DALHVISSI · ME ×
FIERI × FECIT · ANO · DNI · MILLESIMO × QVIGENTISIMO
XXXIIII × IHS · MARIA × IHONE × MORISON. The lettering
is chiefly Roman of early sixteenth-century type, but the D's, L's,
and H's are from a much older Lombardic alphabet. Above the
inscription is a rude frieze of short fleur-de-lys. The bell is remarkable in having no lines, rims, or mouldings, except those enclosing
the inscription. This bell is said to have been used at Clanyard
Castle about the end of the sixteenth century, and it was subsequently in use at the Parish Church of Kirkmaiden."—The *Inventory*.

Japanese umbrella-pine, which is said to be the best example in this country. The proprietor kindly allows visitors to enter the grounds and behold these treasures.

The making of the famous fish-pond on the north side of Port Logan Bay was begun in 1788 and completed in 1800 by

*Approach to Logan House.*

Colonel Andrew MacDouall. There is a basin, about thirty feet deep, blasted out of the rock, into which the sea flows at high tide through a narrow cleft. The pond itself is about eight feet in depth and is the abode of fish caught in the sea in summer. With the exception of the flounders, which hide themselves on the bottom, the fish become very tame in a few

weeks, and, when a visitor descends the stair to the edge of the
pond, come crowding to welcome him in the hope of being fed.
" Conceive ", says John MacDiarmid, " a lady feeding her poultry,
a knot of urchins scrambling for coppers, or a pack of fox-hounds
disputing the property of a solitary bone, and you will have some
idea of the ludicrous scramble " for the limpets and mussels
that are offered them. The cod are the most numerous fish
and the most confident, and allow themselves to be lifted out of
the water and stroked. " Some of the older ones are blind,"

*Port Logan.*

says a writer in *The Scottish Field*, " and for many years it was
imagined that the cause of this must be the comparative shallow-
ness of the water, the cod being a deep-sea fish and in his natural
state living about twenty-five to fifty fathoms below the surface.
This, however, is not the reason, for it has been lately ascertained
that when several fish together make a dash at the same morsel
of food, they often inadvertently scratch one another's eyes
with their needle-like teeth, thus injuring them, and ultimately
causing blindness." Besides the cod and flounders, there are
lythe, haddocks, blockans, and wrasse.

On the south side of the bay are the fishing village of Port

Logan and the ruined pier. The latter, like the fish-pond, was built by Colonel Andrew MacDouall, and was used largely by ships importing cattle from Ireland; with the extension of railways, however, its importance declined, the damage inflicted from time to time by storms was not repaired, and the greater part is now a mass of tumbled stones. Symson, who wrote in 1684, refers to an earlier pier made by Robert MacDouall, younger of Logan, who " hath been at great paines and expences to build a port for ships and barks cast in that way " and " hath lately procur'd an act of his Majesties privy Councill, for a voluntary contribution towards the building of an harbour there ".

When Colonel MacDouall made his pier, he wished the villagers to leave their houses on the shore and remove themselves to a new row which he erected on the slope behind; but they clung to their old homes. He built a sea-wall in front of their windows, expecting that this would drive them out. The villagers, however, valued it as a protection from western gales and were only confirmed in their determination to remain where they were. A second storey has been added to some of the cottages, so that from their upper windows the occupants can see the bay. In the case of one house a gangway stretches from the second storey to the top of the wall, where the road now runs.

Between Port Logan and the Mull the land fronts the sea with a great wall of rock. This is on the farther side of the peninsula from the main road, and few of the visitors who pass that way know that little more than two miles to the west there is some of the most impressive cliff scenery in Scotland. An occasional rambler who scorns to be confined to highways may stroll over the high moor to the edge and, throwing a stone seawards, wonder at the time that it takes to strike the water; but to behold the sea-washed crags in all their grandeur one must take a boat. On going down to the shore near Clanyard Castle, I was fortunate in finding a fisherman who would row me along towards Laggantulluch[1] Head. The water was calm, no other boat was in sight, and as we made our little voyage, I was conscious of two immensities—the smooth sea stretching to Ireland and the face of the cliffs reaching towards the clouds. There was no shore, and no breaking wavelets. The rocks ran down into the depths like the side of a pier, and the water rose and fell quietly along their face.

[1] Gaelic *lag an tulaich*, hollow of the hill.

I found at Breddock[1] Bay a steep beach of shingle and a cave
which I had hoped to see, and landed.   The cave is described
in Dr. Maxwell Wood's *Smuggling in the Solway and Around
the Galloway Sea-board* as a very large one, " from which the
tide never recedes and into which a pretty large boat can be
taken at high water.   Here again man's handiwork has improved
upon Nature, the rock all the way round the cave having been
levelled, so that one can walk right round.   At high water the
sea rises to within a few inches of the edge of the ledge, so that
goods could be easily discharged or embarked, as the case might
be.   As this cave was difficult to find for those not in the secret,
and in a rather sheltered position, it was very frequently used
by the smugglers."   I found that this description applied to
the cave no longer.   The stones forming the ledge have been
dislodged and now make a bank at the entrance, and the sea
does not enter unless with a very high tide and a gale.   Another
cave in this bay contains a large pool of fresh water filled by
the drip from the roof.

When Burns wrote the line

> Frae Maidenkirk to John o' Groats,

he was inverting the name of the southmost parish of
Scotland.   Drummore is near the latitude of Bishop Auckland.
Besides a little fishing fleet, it has a harbour where a coasting
steamer from Glasgow calls every fortnight.   Its church stands
on the top of a hill half a mile away, and is known popularly
as Kirk Covenant from the fact that it was built in 1639, the
year in which the National Covenant was signed throughout the
country.   It contains a triangular wooden panel said to have
been removed from the ruined Castle of Drummore and
bearing the crest of the Adairs and the following inscription :

P · A · D · R
O · GOD · MAK · ME · TO
HEIR · IN · FAITH · AND · PR
ACKTEIS · IN · LOVE · THY · HO
LY · WIRD · AND · CŌMĀDEMETIS
THOV · ART · ONLY · MY · SVPOIRT
GOD · MAK · ME · THANKFUL · 1618

P.A.D.R. stands for " Patrick Adair ".

[1] Gaelic *bràghadach*, place of the throat or gully.

From Kirkmaiden Church the road undulates for a mile or two over a high, treeless country until it reaches a point about three hundred and seventy feet above the sea and then descends in the next two miles and a half to the little isthmus connecting the Mull of Galloway with the mainland. On Mull farm, at the foot of a cliff facing Luce Bay, is the oldest remaining eccle-

*Drummore.*

siastical structure in Galloway, the Chapel of S. Medana, whose story is given at the end of the chapter on Monreith ; and about thirty yards to the south-east are the Chapel Wells, the largest of which is called The Well of the Co'. These are three natural cavities in the rock, and are filled by the sea at high tide. " To bathe in the well as the sun rose on the first Sunday, of May ", says *The Statistical Account*, " was considered an infallible cure for almost any disease, but was particularly efficacious in the recovery of 'back-gane bairns'. And till no very remote period, it was customary for almost the whole population of the parish to collect at this spot on the first Sabbath of May, which was called Co' Sunday, to bathe in the well, to leave their gifts in the cave, and to spend the day in gossiping or amusements."

Across the western end of the Mull runs an entrenchment called The Double-dykes, the last defence of the Picts, according to an ancient tradition, as they were driven southwards by the Scots of Ireland. Here took place the tragedy whereby the secret of the making of the heather ale was irrevocably lost. Robert Louis Stevenson made the story the subject of one of his *Ballads*, and Mr. Neil Munro used it in the volume of stories entitled *The Lost Pibroch*, and Sir Herbert Maxwell in *A Duke of Britain*.

" Mull " is from the Gaelic *maol*, " bare ", which is commonly used of headlands, through the Norse *muli*. Barbour has " Mullyr Snuk ", while Wyntoun gives " Mullyrryssnwk ". " It is to be noted ", says Dr. Watson, " that Wyntoun's— and Barbour's—expression means ' Mull *of* Rinn Snóc '; this suggests as a possible explanation that Rinn Snóc was the name of the double promontory from what is now Corsill Point southwards." Bellenden writes in 1536 of "ane gret snout of craggis callit be the peple the Mulis Nuk ". Not till 1564 do we find "the Mule of Galloway". The local pronunciation is " Moyle ".

The Mull itself is a high, bleak promontory a mile and a quarter long and a quarter of a mile broad, and when you go aside from the road running up to the lighthouse, you walk as carefully as if you were on a battle-ship with the deck-rails removed for action. It is really a hill of considerable height with sides almost perpendicular. One may differ from the writer of *The Statistical Account*, who thought that the erection of the lighthouse has " converted what before was merely grand into what is both grand and beautiful in a high degree "— perhaps he would have added to-day that the concussions of the fog-horn provide an impressive undertone for the cries of the wild-fowl !—but the balcony is a point of view three hundred and twenty-five feet above the sea whence one may behold on a clear day the peaks of Cumberland, The Isle of Man, a large part of the Irish coast, The Paps of Jura in Argyll, and the mountains of The Stewartry and Dumfriesshire.

To be here in a great storm one might endure cheerfully the
drenching spray and the buffeting winds.   Then, says John

*S. Medana's Chapel and the Mull of Galloway.*

MacDiarmid, " a great number of adverse tides which seem to
centre here, as well as the winds, contend for mastery in fearful

turmoil, hollowing, as they retreat, the sea into troughs that
might entomb a fleet in place of a ship, and spouting as they
advance with headlong fury against the solid land, till the giant
Mull, from its base to its summit, becomes enveloped in one
unbroken sheet of foam.  The shock is said to resemble the onset
of armies ; and as the howling blast dies away for an instant,
the noise of waters rising and rolling, heaving and dashing, is
heard as far off by mariners as the roar of the angry Corry-
vreckan itself.  Where the waves end, the spray begins and
descends around in such copious showers that the spectator,
though stationed at a considerable distance, gets as completely
drenched in a few minutes as he does when overtaken by a
thunder-storm.  To the westward are some tremendous cliffs ;
to the east, the shoals of the bay of Luce ; and the mariner,
during the stormy days of winter, cannot be too cautious in
avoiding dangers to which Scylla and Charybdis are poor in
comparison."

Even on a windless day, when the whole ocean seems to lie
in a perfect calm, there is no peace here.   If you scramble down
to Lagvag[1] Point at the north-east corner of the Mull, you will
find the sea, not making scarcely perceptible surges towards
the land, as you might expect, but racing past your feet ; and
will see a field of tumultuous foam where the currents meet and
clash a hundred yards beyond the end of the headland.[2]

There are some caves in the Mull that are accessible only from
the sea.  "One of these", says MacDiarmid, "is of ample
dimensions and is frequented by seals during calm weather,
when the phoca, after breakfasting heartily on fish, seeks the
sunny side of some ledge of rock, from which he can retreat
on the approach of danger.  The slightest noise, if he is awake
at the time, makes him leap or rather dive into the water, where
he is soon hid from observation ; but at other times the tribe
are surprised while quietly enjoying their wonted *siesta* and
either shot at or ensnared with ropes so as to become the fisherman's prey."

[1] Gaelic *lag bheag*, little hollow.
[2] " It is said ther is a place of the sea, close upon the Mule, wher
ships, if they enter, are quickly turned round and sunk down."—
*Description of the Sheriffdom of Wigtoun* by Sir Andrew Agnew
of Lochnaw and David Dunbar of Baldoon (Sibbald MSS. Adv.
Lib. Jac. 5th. i, 4), printed as an appendix to Symson's *Description.*

# CHAPTER XXII

## PORTPATRICK

Visitors to Portpatrick—Trade with Ireland—Sunday observance—
Colonel Gardiner—The Gretna Green for Ireland—Peter the
Great—Defoe—Bishop Pococke—Mrs. Siddons—Keats—The
old church—The harbour works—Incidents of war—Dunskey
Castle—Sandeel Bay—Sir William Brereton's notes.

IT may seem a staggering statement, but I believe it is true,
that there are people to whom Galloway means Portpatrick.
This is very much as if Canada were Vancouver City or Siberia
Vladivostok. These people travel in a comfortable, west-bound
express train from Dumfries, indifferent to Sweetheart Abbey,
the Colvend coast, Dundrennan, Kirkcudbright, and the shores
of Wigton Bay on the left, and the glories of The Glenkens and
the Galloway Highlands on the right, making by the most direct
route for the salt water, the sea-breezes, and a first-class hotel.
Besides these, there is a certain kind of visitor who comes to
Portpatrick, lodges at a hotel, plays golf, pays his bill, and goes
away, and does not know that he has been in Galloway. Finally,
there are the people who, when they are asked if they have been
in Galloway, answer without hesitation, " No ; but we have
been at Portpatrick."

Portpatrick is not a centre. It is on a circumference, and is
not, therefore, to be recommended to explorers. For holiday-
makers, however, who like a clean, quiet seaside village in a mild
climate with a golf-course, bowling green, tennis-courts, walks
along the cliffs, and a strand where sea-bathing is possible, it
serves very well.

It has been visited in the past by many people who were not
mere holiday-makers. The nearness of the Irish port of

Donaghadee—the distance is only twenty-one miles—caused
much trade, especially in livestock, to pass this way. The number of cattle and horses imported in 1790 was seventeen thousand,

*Portpatrick.*

two hundred and seventy-five ; in 1812 it was twenty thousand ;
but by 1837 it had fallen away to one thousand and eighty.
The decline was due to the invention of the steamship, which
made the short sea-route less urgent ; and cattle and horses

were sent thereafter to Glasgow or Liverpool. One of the secondary aspects of the traffic was " the troublesome confusion and indecency attending the landing of cattle on a Sunday " referred to by Robert Heron in the account of his tour through the western counties in 1792. Heron tells how the minister of the parish took firm hold of the nettle. Recognizing that it was useless to insist on the due observance of the Lord's Day if Irish cattle-dealers were allowed to profane it at their pleasure, he told his congregation that if any of them aided the dealers in bringing cattle ashore on a Sunday, he would proceed against them with the censures of the Church and every ecclesiastical penalty in his power unless the owners of the herds were able to state upon oath before the nearest magistrate that contrary winds were the only cause of their failure to reach Portpatrick on the Saturday evening. This measure had all the success that the minister desired.

Portpatrick was on the usual route for sending troops to Ireland, and there were permanent barracks here, a fact which accounts for the name of Barrack Street. The military were once called upon to render an unusual service to the parish. The minister had had occasion to reprove the Laird of Dunskey from the pulpit, and the Laird, thirsting for revenge, incited some of his people to remove and conceal the communion plate. The day for the observance of the sacrament approached, and the minister resolved to proceed as usual even if it were necessary to borrow vessels for the celebration from another parish. A disturbance was feared ; but a squadron of Lord Harrington's dragoons marched in unexpectedly on the Saturday evening with Major (afterwards the well-known Colonel) Gardiner at their head. The minister described the situation to Major Gardiner, who promptly sent a party of soldiers to compel the restoration of the plate. Early on the Sunday morning, patrols were on the watch against any untoward event. The whole squadron were present at divine service, and the Major remained to communicate. There is a reference in Doddridge's *Life and Correspondence of Colonel Gardiner*, under the date " 25 May 1725 ", to the pleasure with which he had attended a preparatory service on the Saturday, and he adds, " I took a walk upon the mountains that are over against Ireland ; and I persuade myself, that were I capable of giving you a description of what passed there, you would agree, that I had much better reason to remember my God from the hills of Port Patrick, than David from the land of Jordan, and of the Hermonites from the hill Mizar."

The village served for a long time as the Gretna Green for Ireland. People who were anxious for a hurried or a secret wedding and were able to satisfy the minister that there was no legal obstacle to their union had the proclamation made in the church immediately after their arrival, and the ceremony was completed without delay. Such marriages were registered by the kirk-session and attested by the minister and the witnesses.

*Portpatrick in 1815.*
(From William Daniell's engraving.)

The fees varied according to the rank and wealth of the contracting parties. At one time the lowest sum was £5, but it was raised latterly to £10 for the minister and £1 for the session-clerk. The Church Courts suppressed the practice in 1826. During the preceding period of about fifty years, the records shew the names of "one hundred and ninety-eight gentlemen, fifteen officers of the army or navy, and thirteen noblemen".

I have not succeeded in putting beyond doubt the tradition that Peter the Great rested for a night here. Peter came to England in 1698 to study naval construction, and spent most of his time working in the royal dockyards at Deptford. If he paid a visit to Ireland, his most convenient route would be by Portpatrick. The tradition is that he arrived in the evening at the inn which was known later as the Blair's Arms Hotel, and sailed in the morning with the Irish packet-boat. The room he slept in is known as the Emperor's room and is still used as a bedroom in the private house into which the old hotel has been turned.

Daniel Defoe made a succession of exhaustive journeys through the country and published in 1724 the first volume of *A Tour through the whole Island of Great Britain*, which was completed in the next two years. Doubts are entertained as to whether he really visited all the places of which he gives an account; but his notes on Galloway are those of a first-hand witness. His impressions of Portpatrick were not entirely agreeable. He says, " *Port Patrick*, which is the ordinary Place for the Ferry or Passage to Belfast, and other Ports in Ireland, has a tolerable good Harbour, and a safe Road ; but there is very little Use for it ; the Packet-boat, and a few Fishing vessels, are the Sum of its Navigation. There was nothing here to invite our Stay ; for it is a mean, dirty, homely Place : and as we had no business, but to see the Coast, we came away very ill satisfied with our Accommodation."

About forty years later Bishop Pococke described it as " a very poor place ". " Here ", he says, " they ship the horses from a rock, and when they land them from Ireland they help them out of the packet-boat into the sea, when they have brought the boat as near as they can to the shore."

Mrs. Siddons, accompanied by her husband, once spent a night here before crossing to Belfast to fulfil an engagement. In the morning, about the time for the sailing of the packet-boat, the villagers in the front street were startled by an eloquent outcry on the beach. Mrs. Siddons, who was about to go on board, had suddenly visualized a scene in one of her plays and was declaiming the lines :

> Methinks I stand upon some rugged beach,
> Sighing to winds, and to the waves complaining,
> While afar off the vessel sails away,
> On which my fortune and my hope's embarked !

Mr. Siddons, who was less imaginative, remarked, " Egad ! my dear, if we don't hurry, the vessel will be gone absolutely."

John Keats crossed to Ireland early in July, 1818, and returned two or three days later. Writing from Stranraer to his brother Thomas on the 9th, he says, " Having walked to Belfast one day and back to Donaghadee the next, we left Ireland with a fair breeze. We slept last night at Port Patrick, when I was gratified by a letter from you. . . . On calling for the letters at Port Patrick, the man snapped out, ' what Regiment ? ' "

The old church is cruciform in plan and " according to the

*Tower of the old church, Portpatrick.*

dates carved on the skew-puts was built between 1622 and 1629." The only feature of interest is the circular tower at the west end. It is " four storeys in height, terminating in a steep, slated roof, apparently modern, with a *flèche* at the apex. It is entered from the ground level by a doorway to the west, and on the first floor there is a door to the east, now built up. On each floor are several small windows. . . . The tower seems to have been erected originally as a watch-tower. . . . The stone-work is of a different colour and consistence from that of the church—the former being of soft red sandstone much decayed by the effects of weather, while the latter is of a grey-coloured hard stone and has resisted the effects of the weather excellently." There is a tradition that the tower was once used as a lighthouse, and " it is worthy of note ", say Messrs. McGibbon and Ross in *The Castellated and Domestic Architecture of Scotland,* " that a similar round tower at the church of Cockburnspath also occupies such a position as this looking out on the sea."

A tomb in the churchyard bears this inscription : " Hanc domum Gulielmus Donaldson extruxit, Anno Domini MDCCLI.

> ' I thank my God for Poverty,
> For Riches and for Gain ;
> For God can make a Rich man Poor,
> A Poor man Rich again.' "

The trade with Ireland, to which reference has been made, was not confined to livestock, and it was necessary to have a customs office here since many Irish products were contraband and others bore heavy duties. A weekly post between Scotland and Ireland by way of Portpatrick was established in 1662, and the letters from England also were sent through the village. The daily post was begun in 1790.

The first pier was built by the Post Office and was completed in 1774. In 1820 the Government decided to improve the harbour for the mail service, and the erection of the large piers on the south and north sides of the entrance was begun in the following year. John MacDiarmid, the Dumfries journalist, wrote a vivid account of the building operations and of the changes which they brought about in Portpatrick. He saw the freestone that had been conveyed from Dumbarton, the limestone from Wales, the iron from England, the wood from the Baltic shores, the diving-bells from London, the countless cartloads of whinstone poured into the sea to form breakwaters for the piers, the labourers—seven or eight hundred of them—digging, quarrying, building, or trundling barrows, the nightly effect when the work went on in the light of masses of blazing coals heaped up in cradle-grates and long lines of men could be seen toiling up or creeping down the narrow pathways, while " at every little interval the silence of night was left undisturbed till the quarrymen had retired beyond the reach of the mines they meant to spring ; and when the train was laid, the powder ignited, and the explosion heard, sounds resembling distant thunder reverberated among the cliffs, and then rolled along the level ocean, till even the sea-fowl left their midnight haunts, and wondering what the confusion meant, beat the air in fear and perplexity."

The south pier and the lighthouse at the end of it were finished in 1836. There was an unusually severe storm in January 1839, when the end of the pier was undermined and the lighthouse endangered. A sum of £13,000 which was to have been used for the completion of the work on the north side of the harbour was now spent on repairs, and nothing was ever done to carry the scheme any farther.

The two piers were designed to shelter the harbour. It was intended also that the one on the south should be used for the hauling out of sailing packets until they could clear the port; but when it was finished, steam had come into use, and haulage was necessary no longer.

The Irish mails were diverted to another route in 1849; but the harbour works were still kept in repair. Seven or eight years later the Government resolved to restore the mail service to Portpatrick, to make a new dock, and to deepen the channel. This was due to the simultaneous laying of the line from Castle Douglas and the County Down Railway. The dock was made, and the trains brought alongside it; but the Government departed from their undertaking to renew the mail service and gave the railway shareholders compensation in cash. It was not, however, until 1873, when the Harbour Acts were repealed, that the works were left to the ravages of the sea. It is a mistake to say that the wrecked piers are the evidence of a futile contest with the waves. They fell into ruin because no further care was taken of them.

During the war the port was used by larger craft than fishing-vessels. Patrols steamed in to send messages from the " wireless " station, and swiftly disappeared towards Ireland. Other incidents were that the steamers plying between Stranraer and Larne were convoyed sometimes by airships, and even in Galloway, trains halted and lay low at the warning of Zeppelin airships approaching Britain, as birds crouch in their coverts when a hawk appears on the horizon. In the early months of the war the province was racked with the fearful joy of an airplane scare. There were strong suspicions, amounting almost to imperturbable conviction, that the enemy had a base in the Monigaff hills. Over-strained eyes saw hostile airplanes above Glentrool, and there were even rumours of hydroplanes disporting themselves on the lochs. It was reported in Newton Stewart one forenoon that a discovery of " fifteen hundred tins " of petrol had been

*Dunskey Castle.*

made ; by the afternoon the quantity had reached " fifteen hundred tons "! Schoolboys neglected the works of Mr. Henty and Captain Brereton for more immediate thrills, and Mr. Buchan wrote *The Thirty-Nine Steps*.

Dunskey[1] Castle stands on a high promontory between two gullies about half a mile south of the village. If you walk round to the farther side of the gully beyond it, you will see how abruptly the precipices fall away to the water, and have the most striking view of the castle. " The main part of the building ", says the *Inventory*, " is an example of the L plan, that is, a square keep with a projecting wing at one angle containing the staircase, which in this case is exceptionally wide, with straight steps and intermediate plats—unusual features for the period. The main staircase leads to the great hall, and the upper floors have been served by a wheel-stair in the re-entering angle

[1] Perhaps *dùn sciathach,* the shielded fort.

above the main entrance—a very general plan during the
sixteenth century. The ground floor has, as usual, been vaulted
throughout. A long narrow wing to the north of the main
building has probably been a later addition. The castle is
entered by a vaulted passage under the north wing, leading
to a spacious courtyard bounded on three sides by the sea
cliffs. There seems to have been no means of defending the
castle from the walls, so that possibly its natural strength was
relied upon for security. Indications of domestic buildings
remain within the area of the courtyard, which no doubt included kitchen offices, stables, and servants' quarters." " There
appears to have been a castle of Dunskey from very early times,
though the present building probably dates no further back
than the beginning of the sixteenth century, and may have
been erected subsequent to an act of incendiarism ' by John
Makke of Myretoune ' and others, for which they received a
respite in 1503. It belonged at that date to the Adairs of
Kinhilt, and thereafter to the Montgomeries, Viscounts of Airds,
from whom it passed in the reign of Charles the Second to the
Rev. John Blair, minister of Portpatrick," and ancestor of a
line of proprietors.

Visitors go in a northerly direction to Port Mora or Sandeel
Bay for the bathing and to the wooded Dunskey Glen for the
pleasant walk, and may pass, without noticing, a little cave on
the south side of the bay with a stream of water pouring over
the entrance. It is referred to in the seventeenth-century
*Description of the Sheriffdom of Wigtoun* written by Sir Andrew
Agnew of Lochnaw and David Dunbar of Baldoon, who say
that near Portpatrick, " close by the sea, is a cave, called the
Cave of Uchtriemackean, accessible by six steps of a stair,
entering to a gate built with stone and lime, at the end of which
is a structur lyke ane altar. The people frequent this place
the first night of May, and wash deseased children with the water,
which runs from a spring over the cave." Even so late as
1791 this practice continued. " At the change of the quarter
(which is still considered with superstitious reverence)," says
the old *Statistical Account*, " it is usual to bring even from a great
distance, infirm persons, and, particularly, ricketty children,
whom they often suppose bewitched, to bathe in a stream which
pours from the hill, and then dry them in the cave." There
is a tradition that another cave near this one was once inhabited

by a monk. " If ", says the writer of the new *Account,* " the indulgence of bathing had been permitted to the hermit, he might here have enjoyed the benefit of a shower-bath with a dressing-room, besides the excellent plunge bath in the bay."

About a mile farther on is the Killantringan Lighthouse. Since it was erected, the lighthouse at Portpatrick has not been used.

Two roads connect the village with Stranraer, the one modern, good, and dull, the other old, precipitous, and delightful. The latter is the more direct. At its worst it must have been a great advance on the conditions in July, 1636, when Sir William Brereton, going from Stranraer to Portpatrick, followed a " foul winter way over the mossy moors ". His remarks on the port itself may be added to those given already. " We found only one boat, though yesternight there were fifteen boats here. We hired a boat of about ten ton for five horses of ours, and for five Yorkshiremen and horses; for this we paid £1 and conditioned that no more horses should come aboard save only two or three of an Irish laird's, who then stayed for a passage, and carried his wife and three horses. . . . Here we shipped our horses two hours before we went aboard. It is a most craggy, filthy passage, and very dangerous for horses to go in and out; a horse may easily be lamed, spoiled, and thrust into the sea; and when any horses land here, they are thrown into the sea, and swim out. Here was demanded from us by our host, Thos. Marshbanke, a custom of 2s. an horse, which I stumbled at, and answered that if he had authority to demand and receive it, I was bound to pay it, otherwise not; and therefore I demanded to see his authority, otherwise I was free to pay or refuse; herewith he was satisfied, and declined his further demand."

*Balsarroch.*

## CHAPTER XXIII

### LESWALT AND KIRKCOLM

Lochnaw Castle and the Hereditary Sheriffs of Galloway—Kempes'
    Graves and Kempes' Walks—Galdenoch Castle and its ghost—
    The byways of Kirkcolm—Salt Pans Bay—Smuggling story
    of Dally Bay—Balsarroch—Corsewall Castle—Portmullin—
    Celtic cross-slab at Corsewall House—S. Mary's Croft.

AFTER the three dull miles between Stranraer and Leswalt,
it is pleasant to follow the road that winds upwards among the
trees on the south bank of the Aldouran Glen[1], and pleasanter
still to reach the end of the ascent and cycle easily along through
the woods of the Lochnaw grounds. With a bend of the road
one has a glimpse of water, and in another minute the whole
loch appears, and beyond it the home of the Agnews of Lochnaw,
who were for some centuries Hereditary Sheriffs of Galloway.

The appointment to the sheriffship was made by James the
Second in 1451, and the office remained in the family until
1747, when hereditary jurisdictions were abolished. The only
break in the tenure began in January, 1682, when Sir Andrew
Agnew, the tenth Sheriff, who was considered too lenient in
administering the Acts against the Covenanters, and declined
the Test, was superseded by John Graham of Claverhouse.
He was restored to the office in April, 1689, after the Revolution.

---

[1] Gaelic *allt dobhran*, the otters' burn.

Lochnaw Castle is a long range of buildings belonging to four different periods—"a simple keep, seventeenth-century and eighteenth-century dwellings purely domestic in character,

*Lochnaw Castle.*

and a modern mansion-house". "There seems little doubt", says the *Inventory*, "that the keep now standing belongs to the sixteenth century." "The doorway has entered at the ground level, and communicates in the usual way with a vaulted basement and wheel-stair in one of the angles which gave direct access to the upper floors and parapet walk. The parapet is on three sides of the tower, supported by corbelling and having a machicolation at one point. Here the corbelling is in the form of a continuous moulding supporting the projecting parapet on each side. It is an interesting feature, showing clearly the development from the earlier type—a series of single moulded corbels of considerable projection, characteristic of the purely defensive castles." There is the following inscription on the south wall of the keep: DOM ANDREAS AGNEV 1426 NOMEN DOMINI FORTISSIMA TURRIS. "This inscription is said to have been re-cut in the time of the present proprietor's grandfather, but as neither the style of the building itself nor the character of the inscription synchronises with the date, the tablet is probably an insertion of a late period."

At one time the loch, which contributes so greatly to the charm of the situation, was drained away in order to add a fertile hayfield to the cattle-feeding resources of the estate. This was done by Sir James, the eleventh Sheriff, about 1700. Utilitarian motives appear to have been supreme with him, and he did not even spare an old castle that stood on the island. Requiring some freestone for an addition to his house, " he rent it to pieces, spoiling rybats, window-sills, and door-jambs, and blowing up the rubble-work to provide stones for fencing for his cattle." Since the loch had been drained, it was easy to remove the material. A hundred years later Sir James's great-grandson allowed the waters to re-occupy the area to the great satisfaction both of himself and of his descendants.

The grounds have been planted with many fine trees. There are the araucaria avenue on the Leswalt side of the house, and the grove of old beeches towards Portpatrick; and even from the public road there may be seen " many specimens of *Wellingtonia Gigantea,* the ' Big Trees ' of the Yosemite Valley; *Sequoia Sempervirens,* or Californian red-wood; *Cryptomeria Japonica,* which forms a great feature in Japanese landscapes; besides araucarias, yews, and many varieties of cypress ".

Most of these were planted by Sir Andrew Agnew, the eighth baronet, who died in 1892. We are indebted to him, not only for putting these excellent trees where the passer-by may see them, but also for writing a most entertaining book of Galloway history, tradition, and anecdote. *The Agnews of Lochnaw : a History of the Hereditary Sheriffs of Galloway, with Contemporary Anecdotes, Traditions, and Genealogical Notices of Old Families of the Sheriffdom, 1330 to 1747*, was published in 1864, and a re-written and much enlarged edition in two volumes appeared the year after the author's death under the title of *The Hereditary Sheriffs of Galloway, their "Forebears" and Friends, their Courts and Customs of their Times, with Notes of the Early History, Ecclesiastical Legends, the Baronage and Place-Names of the Province*. After quoting the titles in full, it is enough to add that this work is as readable as it is comprehensive.

There are two earthwork promontory forts near Lochnaw, one called Kempes' Graves on the north bank of Aldouran Glen at a point where the stream makes a sharp turn towards the east, and the other known as Kempes' Walks on the south side of Larbrax[1] Bay. The second is the largest work of the kind in The Shire. Of the fort in Aldouran Glen Sir Andrew Agnew says in the first edition of *The Hereditary Sheriffs* that " the remains of these earthen parapets, standing out in rounded hummocks, are called by the peasantry ' Kempes' Graves ; ' they being quite unconscious that this was a Danish camp, and that ' kempe,' a warrior or champion, is good old Norse. There is something in the traditionary phrase ; many of the warriors have probably been buried *near* the spot, but the old breastwork itself does not mark their tomb." In connexion with the camp at Larbrax Bay he says, " This bay was a favourable spot for navigators of early days to beach their boats, while they revelled on shore ; the entrenched camp above forming a citadel, by which the natives were kept at bay. There is no doubt that it was formed by the old Sea Kings. The spot is known as ' Kempes' Walks.' Here again, as in the case of the Camp of Aldouran, the name has been handed down from time immemorial ; and the present race of peasantry who use the word know nothing of its meaning. We ourselves have been told that ' Kempe ' meant fairies ! and that the said fairies dance sometimes here at night. This is an instance of how some fragments of truth underlie most genuine traditions. The extravagance of fairy revels at night is but the story, mystified by age, of the Norsemen carousing round their camp fires, whilst outside the entrenchment a grim ' kempe ' (or warrior) *walked*

[1] Gaelic *learg breac*, spotted, variegated hillside.

sentry the while—whence the ' Kempe's Walks ' which now
figures in the Ordnance Maps." When Sir Andrew wrote the
second edition of his book, he seems to have departed from one
detail of this theory, for he explains " Kempe's Walk " on the
map as an English surveyor's mistake for " Kempes' Wark,"
that is, " Work," ; but it is possible that in the main he is right.[1]

With Galdenoch[2] Castle standing in the open country on the
west of the Lochnaw woods and about half a mile from the sea
we come back to a comparatively modern structure. We see
here once more the familiar L plan ; but all the accessible
hewn work has been removed, the west wall has been broken
down to within eight feet of the ground at one point, and the ruin
is now used as a cattle-shed. The gables have crow-steps " of
the type peculiar to Galloway, made up of a number of small
stones covered over on the upper surface with one large slate-like
slab ". Galdenoch Castle is less interesting than the racketing
spirit by whom it was once haunted.

" The tenant's mother sat one morning at her spinning-wheel ;
an invisible power bore her along and plunged her in the Mill-
Isle burn, a voice mumbling the while, ' I'll dip thee, I'll draw
thee,' till the old dame became unconscious. Great was the
surprise of the family at dinner-time when grandmamma was
missed. Every corner of the buildings was searched ; the
goodman and his wife became alarmed, while the lads and
lassies ran madly about interrogating one another with, ' Where's
granny ? ' At last a well-known voice was heard, ' I've washed
granny in the burn and laid her on the dyke to dry ! ' Away
the whole party ran ; and sure enough the poor old woman lay
naked on the dyke, half dead with cold and fright."

Several ministers tried to lay the spirit by psalm-singing ;
but if they sang, the spirit out-sang them. A minister who was
considered an expert in spirit-laying was beaten like the rest,
and, annoyed at his failure, declared that he would never come
back. When the yard-gate had closed behind him, the voice
begged him to return, promising to tell him something he had not
heard before. Beguiled by curiosity, the minister did return,

[1] In the second edition of *The Hereditary Sheriffs* " Kempes' "
is given as " Kemp's ". This is probably to be explained by the
facts that the second edition was written from dictation and that
it could not undergo revision by the author.

[2] Prob. Gaelic *gall-daingneach*, stranger's castle.—Johnston.

but only to hear the cry, " Ha ! ha ! I hae gotten the minister to tell a lee ! "

" The farmer's family were now worse off than ever. The spinner's threads were broken short off ; peat clots fell into the porridge ; unsavoury materials were thrown into the kail-pot, when, after many years of trouble, a young man named Marshall, gifted with confidence and a stentorian voice, was ordained to the parish of Kirkcolm. He volunteered to try a bout with the Galdenoch ghost, and a large company assembled to assist. The minister hung up his hat, gave out a psalm, and led off the tune. The ghost sang, too ; the company endeavoured to drown his voice, but failed ; the fiend sang long and loud, and all had ceased but the minister, whose voice rose to a louder and louder pitch as he kept up the strains alone until the ' witching hour.' He called upon the wearied congregation to join once more. A burst of psalmody was the response ; and ' Bangor,' loud if not melodious, resounded through the castle-walls. Again all ceased exhausted, but Marshall undauntedly held on. Faint gleams of light streaked the eastern horizon, when an unearthly voice, husky and weak, whined, ' Roar awa', Marshall, I can roar nae mair ! ' Marshall still continued, determined to make assurance doubly sure ; but the ghost kept his word and was never heard again."[1]

To people who like to escape sometimes from high roads and commit themselves to a network of angular byways where a passing motor-car arouses a sensation not soon forgotten by the cottagers, and even a stranger on an ordinary bicycle is a grave distraction to field-labourers, the parish of Kirkcolm[2] is to be recommended. Look at the map, and it will appear as if in this ultimate protraction of the land the great western road that runs through Stranraer had broken into a delta of many streams. Thus one could go northwards from Lochnaw to Corsewall[3] Point by a dozen or more series of combinations of little cross-roads. Any resident in the district who was condemned to a bout of physical exercise for his health's sake might amuse as well as benefit himself by making the largest possible number of journeys between the starting and the turning point. Some pairs of routes would differ from each other only

---

[1] *The Hereditary Sheriffs.*
[2] Pronounced " Kirkúm " ; church of Columba.
[3] The cross well, dedicated to S. Columba in this instance.

to the extent of two or three hundred yards. If, however, one has the simple aim of reaching Corsewall Point, one will do well to take the roads near the shore, where the landscape is not impressive, but the seascape is wide. On the Irish coast, which runs from twenty to forty miles away, I remember seeing on a clear day the sunlit fields of Antrim like squares on a chessboard where the land slopes down to the sea. On the northwest is the ancient sea-path of the vikings who sailed their galleys round the Mull of Kintyre; and when you reach Corsewall Point and look up the Firth of Clyde, you are confronted by Ailsa Craig fifteen miles away and The Isle of Arran at the distance of thirty.

The names of Salt Pans Bay at Larbrax and Salt Pan Bay at Airies, like Salt Pans farther south in Stoneykirk Parish, have an obvious meaning. About 1640 Uchtred Agnew of Galdenoch entered into a contract with Alexander Ozborne for establishing salt-works on the Galdenoch shore. " This Ozborne paid him £240 as caution money that he would erect sufficient works, the laird stipulating when these were in operation to repay him this and £240 more, and give him a twenty-one years lease of the premises, an acre of ground to build on, grass for four horses, with liberty to cut and carry peats for his pan, at a silver rent of £480 and sixteen barrels of salt delivered at his mansion yearly. . . . . The venture proved an unlucky one. . . . The work seems to have been utilised for little more than home consumption ; its remains may, however, be traced upon the shore, and it gives the name of Salt Pans Bay to the creek where it was formed."

Even this exposed shore was used sometimes for smuggling operations. The following story illustrates the element of comedy that entered sometimes into the relations of smugglers and excisemen :

" Dally[1] Bay (where a beacon now warns the coasting craft of a sunken rock, beyond the Laggan, a natural pillar-stone) had been chosen as a rendezvous for a smuggler's landing, and a large cargo of the usual wares was lying in profusion on the beach. The custom-house officer at Stranraer had received information of their coming, and hurrying to the spot with a stalwart comrade, effected a seizure of the whole. The smugglers offered no resistance, but skulked off, and the tide-waiter, pluming himself not a little on his alacrity, seated himself on

---

[1] Gaelic *dealghe*, the thorns.

the confiscated goods, and sent off his A.D.C. to press men and horses in King George's name to remove them. His eyes gloated on the prey piled before him—wines, brandies, silks, tea from the East, tobacco from the West, Hollands from Schiedam. A gold-belted sabre hung to his belt, and he looked carefully at the priming of his pistols.

"Presently a weel-faured dame sauntered up, no less than Maggie McConnell (who, as a girl, had seen King William's fleets stand out of Lochryan), still fair though forty, and he, in the highest good humour, pleased at the chance of so pleasant a companion, preferred her the right hand of fellowship. How delusive are human hopes of happiness! Maggie's sonsy face gave no idea of the strength of her well-formed arms, which had the muscle of a prize-fighter, and, as locally expressed, 'could hauld up a two-year-old stirk like a wean.' Hardly had Maggie's right hand received the responsive squeeze of the exciseman when her left flew round his waist, and in a moment he measured his length upon the ground. Vainly he struggled in her embrace. She sat down coolly on her victim. Her next move was to tie her apron over his eyes, then to seize one of his pistols and cock it. In this ignominious position he coaxed and threatened by turns. Maggie was inexorable. He shouted for help in the king's name, and his hopes ran high as sounds of footsteps and horses drew near. Still she held him firmly, but by and by her grasp relaxed. Kindly kissing him, she undid the apron, and he looked up. Bales, boxes, casks had disappeared. Not a man was visible. A few cows, grazing quietly, were the only living creatures within the line of sight, excepting Maggie, who then slipped away also. Crestfallen and somewhat ashamed of having been vanquished and disarmed by an unarmed woman, it is believed he said very little about his deforcement, and it is probable that in due course some little reward was conveyed to his quarters by an unknown hand in acknowledgment of his silence." [1]

About a mile and a half inland from Dally, a plantation shewing the pressure of western gales runs along the roadside. Behind the trees there is the old house of Balsarroch, a little building of two storeys with small windows, crow-step gables, and thatched roof, once the property of the family from whom the explorers, Sir John Ross and Sir James Clark Ross, were

[1] *The Hereditary Sheriffs.*

sprung. Sir Andrew Noel Agnew refers to it in his guide-book to The Shire as " probably a good specimen of a small laird's house in this remote part of Scotland in the eighteenth century ". What is called the Marian Tower on a neighbouring hill is said to have been erected by a Ross in memory of his wife.

The oldest castellated and domestic building in The Shire of which any considerable part remains stands about a mile south-east of Corsewall Point. Corsewall Castle, says the *Inventory*, is " an interesting example of the few early fifteenth-century buildings in Wigtownshire ". " Only the ground floor now remains, containing a large vaulted chamber with an entrance on the ground level communicating with a wheel-stair in the thickness of the wall at one angle, which led to the great hall on the first floor. The upper floor would, no doubt, contain the usual arrangement of private apartments for the exclusive use of the owner and his family, while at the wall-head would be projecting battlements, supported upon stone corbels, with machicolations from which the garrison could defend the castle when attacked at close quarters."

The lighthouse at Corsewall Point is one of those built by Robert Stevenson. It was begun in 1815 and came into use the next year. The writer of *The Statistical Account* mentions two boat-creeks with roads leading to it. One of them, bearing the name of Portmullin, is about half a mile to the east of the light-house and has a dwarf pier. It was on a very still day that I found it. There were not even ripples on the water. I looked into the clear deeps and saw the πόντιον ἄλσος—the under-water forest, its long streamers " of crimson and russet and olive and gold " waving slowly with the gentle surge in " the liquid low twilight "—

> Soft blossomless frondage
> And foliage that gleams
> As to prisoners in bondage
> The light of their dreams,
> The desire of a dawn unbeholden, with hope on the wings
> of its beams.
>
> Through the subtle and tangible
> Gloom without form,
> Its branches, infrangible
> Ever of storm,
> Spread softer their sprays than the shoots of the woodland
> when April is warm.

N

There was a weird repulsiveness about it as if in its remoter depths it might be haunted by mysterious and horrific broods that were never caught in a fisherman's net. The thought of it came back to me in March, 1915, when I read that in these very waters the *Bayano* had been sunk by a German submarine.

As one follows the road running through the village of Kirkcolm and down the west shore of Loch Ryan to Stranraer, there are two subjects of ecclesiastical interest. In the garden at Corsewall House there stands a notable Celtic cross-slab. Its original site was at Kilmorie[1] Chapel two miles farther south, and when the old church of the parish was being restored about 1720, it was brought thence and used as the lintel for the principal entrance. The building was pulled down in 1820, and the slab was rescued by the proprietor of the estate. " It is sculptured on one face with incised lines," says the *Inventory*, " and on the other in relief, as follows :—*Front*—In the middle, but not extending to the top and bottom of the slab, is a cross with round hollow angles, having a very rudely drawn representation of the Crucifixion incised upon it ; the Saviour's limbs shown unbent, according to the ancient Byzantine fashion ; below the feet of Christ, the figure of a man or woman with two birds on the left, and a pair of pincers, and another object on the right : *Back*—Occupying nearly the whole of the slab is a cross similar in shape to that on the other face divided into three panels : the first, forming the head of the cross, has a small circular depression in the centre, within which there rises a boss, and the arms are filled with deeply carved foliaceous scrolls ; the second, below the head, is a small rectangular compartment within a double incised border, unornamented, but containing at one end a small incised Latin cross ; the third, which forms the shaft, shows two horns at the top with a coiled-up serpent between, while beneath are other two serpents forming interlacing designs."

The site of the ancient chapel of Kilmorie is on S. Mary's Croft. Not a stone of the structure remains. Symson, who wrote in 1684, says, " In this parish also, about a mile and a half from the kirk, in the way betwixt it and Stranrawer, there was of old a chapel, called Killemorie, but now wholy ruinous, within a little croft, of about fourty shillings sterling of yearly rent, possess'd by a countreyman, John McMeckin call'd

[1] Gaelic *cill Moire*, church of Mary.

ordinarly by the countrey people, the Laird, he and his prede-
cessours having enjoy'd the same for severall generations.   At
the side of this Chapel, in the croft, commonly called the Laird's
Croft, there is a well, to which people superstitiously resort,
to fetch water for sick persones to drink ; and they report, that
if the person's disease be deadly, the well will be so dry, that it
will be difficult to get water ; but if the person be recoverable,
then there will be water enough."   Sir Andrew N. Agnew
states that " John McMeikan's descendants still own the spot ;
and it is an interesting fact that this tiny holding should have
continued an independent property, in the hands of a single
family, for fully four hundred years.   When they received the
original grant is unknown ; but the grant was renewed as far
back as 1526."

*Gaidenoch Castle.*

*Loch Ryan.*

# CHAPTER XXIV

## FROM STRANRAER TO GIRVAN

The Mote of Innermessan—Craigcaffie Castle—The Deil's Dyke—
Lochryan House—Glen App—Carrick—Ballantrae—The War-
lock of Innermessan—The Stinchar Valley—Kirkdomine—The
martyr's grave in Barr Churchyard—The shore road from
Ballantrae to Girvan—The ballad of May Collean—Girvan—
Ailsa Craig—Its geology and history—Pennant's notes.

LOCH RYAN was known to the Romans as *Rherigonius sinus*,
and *Rherigonium*, a town assigned to the *Novantæ* by Ptolemy,
is supposed to have occupied the site of the later Innermessan,
the most considerable town in these parts, says Symson, until
Stranraer was built. The site, about two miles to the north-
east of Stranraer, is marked by a few cottages only ; but near
at hand is one of the antiquities of the neighbourhood, the Mote
of Innermessan, rising steeply to the height of thirty feet above
the bottom of the encircling ditch. A former minister of Inch
says, " On the 24th November, 1834, I caused a hole, three
feet deep, to be dug in the centre of the plain on the top. After
passing through a fine rich mould, we came to a stratum consisting of ashes, charred wood, and fragments of bone."

The road crosses the Kirkclachie Burn, twists to the right,

and brings Craigcaffie[1] Castle into view about a quarter of a mile away. We have in it an instance of an old castle that has been preserved almost undamaged. " Externally the keep is simple in appearance, the gable walls being finished with parapets and terminating in angle bartizans. There is no evidence to show that the parapet continued round the building. The entrance doorway in the north wall has a bold quirked bead on the angles of the jambs, and has evidently been surmounted by a pediment, of which little can now be traced. Over the doorway, and at some height from the ground, is a panel within a moulded architrave, divided into two parts ; the upper containing an inscription now illegible ; the lower two escutcheons. The dexter shield surmounted by the initials I N, for John Neilson, displays the Neilson arms : parted per chevron ; in chief, two sinister hands couped and erect ; and, in base, a dagger, point downwards : a star at fess point for difference. The sinister shield is surmounted by the initials M S, for Margaret Strang, his spouse. It is much weathered, but appears to have been charged with a chevron between three lozenges. The doorway is defended by a machicolation at the wall-head level carried upon two corbels. The windows have moulded jambs, and the architrave of the north-east window on the second floor has a late dog-tooth enrichment." The kitchen is a vaulted apartment and contained a well two feet in diameter, which is now filled up. The entrance to a small domically-vaulted chamber with a trap in the dome is almost in line with the well. The trap is now floored over, but " would probably be used for the haulage of water and other supplies from the kitchen to the principal floor ".[2]

The earliest notice of the property belongs to the beginning of the fourteenth century, when Robert the Bruce made a grant of the lands of " Kellechaffe " to John, son of Neil, Earl of Carrick. The castle was built in the sixteenth century, and the Neilsons were in possession until the latter half of the eighteenth.

About a mile and a half farther on, the road passes Lefnol[3] Point, where a fragment of the ancient rampart, usually called

---

[1] *Creag Chathbhaidh*, Cathbad's Rock. Cathbad is Irish. The Galloway name McHaffie or McCaffie is Cathbad's son, perhaps shortened from *Mac Gille Chathbhaidh*, son of S. Cathbad's servant, for Wodrow mentions John Mackilhaffy (*History* iv. 22).—Watson.

[2] The *Inventory*.

[3] Gaelic *leith pheighinn olainn*, halfpenny land of the wool.

The Deil's Dyke, can be detected on the north side of the
Beoch Burn. Eight feet broad at its base, with a ditch
on its north side, it wound across Galloway from Lefnol Point
to the Nith.[1]

It was on a bright, warm day in the middle of June that I
went along this shore-road. Little waves were rising under a
light breeze on the left, and a haze softened the view of the
upper part of The Rhinns beyond the loch.    Besides the works
of ancient dwellers in the land, there were signs of the changes
wrought by natural forces in the raised beaches at various points
on the right-hand side, picked out sharply in the strong light
and shadow of the day ; and the whitewashed cottages and
gardens, decked with roses and poppies, of the present inhabitants
of Cairnryan, shone out in their modest glory.

Behind the lighthouse at Cairn Point, just beyond the village,
are the wooded grounds of the Lochryan estate, and a short
avenue planted thickly on both sides leads up to the mansion.
At the end of the approach one's admiration is divided in a kind
of bewilderment between the charming quaint aspect of the
house itself and the wonderful, majestic clipped yews in front of
the court, towering above one in the midst of a little triangular
lawn. Here is unusual material for the etching pencil, sketch-
book, camera, or pen, if by any means one could do justice
to it, for the house has something of an exotic look, as if one
had wandered into some quiet corner of France or Flanders
and come face to face with an old *château* in the midst of its
carefully tended pleasaunce.    Just beyond the yews—they
stand on the lawn like colossal sentinels—is a high carved stone
balustrade with the entrance between pillars surmounted by
stone eagles ; behind this structure is the court, laid down with
turf and intersected by gravel paths ; and rising above the
farther end is the tall house front with its two wings projecting
along the sides of the court. The harled walls, the little windows
with sliding wooden shutters, the battlemented roof of the
centre, the roofs of the wings falling steeply away towards both
ends, the green hill called the Cairn rising abruptly behind the
pleasaunce, and the *hortus inclusus* effect produced by the lofty
masses of foliage impart a thrill of delight.

Among the contents of the large square hall, used in modern
fashion as a living-room, are an old brass-bound charter-chest,

[1] See page 288.

and the skins and heads of wild animals acquired by various owners of Lochryan. Some pieces of armour include a Toledo blade, and hanging in the staircase at the back of the hall are Marshal Ney's saddle, holsters, and stirrups, picked up by

*Approach to Lochryan House.*

General Alexander Wallace of Lochryan when Ney's horse was shot under him on the battlefield of Busaco.

The principal apartments on the second storey are the drawing-room and boudoir, with Queen Anne panelling painted in white and gold, and the dining-room with stained Queen Anne panelling and a collection of family portraits. One of the subjects is Frances Anna Wallace, an heiress of Lochryan, who was married to John Dunlop of Dunlop in 1748, and became famous as the friend and correspondent of Robert Burns. At a time of great distress caused by the death of her husband in 1785 she read and was delighted with " The Cottar's Saturday Night ". " Mrs. Dunlop ", says Gilbert Burns, " sent off a person express to Mossgiel, distant fifteen or sixteen miles,[1] with a very obliging letter to my brother, desiring him to send her half a dozen

*Lochryan House.*

copies of his *Poems*, if he had them to spare, and begging he would do her the pleasure of calling at Dunlop House as soon as convenient." Burns begins his answer to the letter by saying, " I am truly sorry I was not at home yesterday when I was so much honoured with your order for my copies, and incomparably more so by the handsome compliments you are pleased to pay my poetic abilities. I am fully persuaded that there is not any

[1] From Craigie House, near Ayr.

class of mankind so feelingly alive to the titillations of applause as the Sons of Parnassus ; nor is it easy to conceive how the heart of the poor Bard dances with rapture when those whose character in life gives them a right to be polite judges, honour him with their approbation." In the concluding paragraph he says, " I have only been able to find you five copies : they are all I can command. I am thinking to go to Edinburgh in a week or two at farthest, to throw off a second impression of my book ; but on my return, I shall certainly do myself the honour to wait on you, and thank you in person for the obliging notice you have been pleased to take of, Madam, your much indebted and very humble servt." This was the beginning of a friendship continuing throughout the poet's life, and described by Professor Nichol as one of " the most pleasing and permanent in literature ". A reproduction of Mrs. Dunlop's portrait is published as the frontispiece to Mr. William Wallace's *Robert Burns and Mrs. Dunlop* : *correspondence now published in full for the first time, with elucidations.* The dining-room furniture includes a small table which belonged originally to the Wallaces' house of Craigie and came into Burns's possession. After his death his son presented it to Miss Keith Dunlop, one of his friend's daughters.

At the same end of the room is a lively presentment of Eglintine, daughter of Sir William Maxwell of Monreith and wife of Thomas Wallace. It is said that when her sister Jean, the future Duchess of Gordon, diverted herself and the onlookers by riding a sow along the High Street of Edinburgh, she aided the enterprise by running behind, beating the animal with a stick ! She is said to have been " a favourite in the literary circles adorned by Hume, Adam Smith, and John Home ", and, looking at her portrait, one can readily believe the statement that she was " noted for her smart and humorous sallies ". She wrote two plays, *The Ton, or the Follies of Fashion*, produced at the Theatre Royal, Covent Garden, in April, 1788, but without success, and *The Whim*, a comedy in three acts, which was disallowed by the Lord Chancellor on account of its political allusions, but was printed in 1795.

Here are portraits also of General Alexander Wallace and his wife. He commanded the 88th Regiment, or Connaught Rangers, throughout the Peninsular War. Lord Wellington, having seen him lead his regiment in a gallant charge in the battle of Busaco, rode up, and, taking his hand, said, "Wallace, I never saw a more gallant charge than that just now made by your regiment." He distinguished himself also at Fuentes d'Onoro and Salamanca, was made a K.C.B., and rose to the rank of general in 1851.

The jessamine covering the east front of the house recalls the statement in an old charter that a certain amount of cloth was allowed the gardener annually " for ye jasmine on ye mansion house" to fasten it. Coming out by the door on this side, which may have been at one time the main entrance, one gets a general view of the dressed grounds filling the space between the house and the hill behind. To right and left the house is flanked by alleys of tall yews casting long shadows on a sunny day over the great lawns, and opposite the door, and running upwards to the wooded slope, is a wide raised alley of grass traversing the terraced lawns like a kind of causeway, and on both sides a row of sweet bays trimmed to resemble orange trees. Besides the trees and shrubs that are arranged formally, many magnificent conifers, including some examples of the blue pine, grow at intervals on the lawns. The grass-grown alley leading to the wooded lower slope of the hill ends under the shadow of two very old Spanish chestnuts with boles of enormous girth, and from this point a shaded path winds up the hill among firs, larches, and other trees, with here and there an araucaria or a clump of pampas grass. Among the trees and shrubs in the grounds are the bronze filbert, the yucca, the Japanese maple, the Chilian rhubarb, the eucalyptus, the bamboo, the myrtle, and the *cordyline australis*. This last plant was in flower when I saw it in June. One of Mr. Wallace's predecessors introduced many rare rhododendrons. These have now attained a gigantic size, and bloom luxuriantly for many months in succession. The grassy slopes, it may be said in passing, present a glorious display of daffodils and lilies in spring. The *anchusa*, the New Zealand flax, and the *clianthus,* are notable occupants of the flower garden.

On a square tower at the north end of the wall that separates the garden from the deer park an old equatorial sundial has been placed at such an angle that, on the one face or on the other, it indicates the time of day throughout the year. The upper face bears the date 1662, and is incised, in a series of concentric circles, with the signs of the Zodiac, the months of the year, and the names of twelve parts of the human body. All the available space is covered with a curious jumble of astronomical calculations, moral aphorisms, and Scripture texts.

A round tower at the other end of the wall is called the Pulpit because at a time when the nearest church was seven miles away the minister used to conduct open-air services here, preaching his sermon from this tower to a congregation seated on the grass below. It was not until 1841 that Cairnryan was made a *quoad sacra* parish, and the church built at the north end of the park.

The lands of the Lochryan estate bore the name of Croach[1] in ancient times, and the old house of Croach stood high on the edge of the Several[2] Moor, overlooking the Clady[3] Glen. The lands were a part of the estate of Innermessan, which the Agnews of Lochnaw acquired by charter in 1429. They were given by Sir Andrew Agnew, the second Hereditary Sheriff, to his second son, William. The Croach family intermarried with the Mac-Doualls of Logan and the Dunbars of Mochrum. In 1662 Alexander Agnew of Lochryan was fined six hundred pounds for his adherence to the Presbyterian form of church government. His son succeeded him in 1680, and married Margaret, daughter of Sir James Agnew of Lochnaw, in 1700. He rose to the rank of major in the Scots Greys, and also became a brevet lieutenant-colonel in the Army. It was he who built Lochryan House in 1701. The next proprietor was his son Thomas, with whom the male line of the Agnews of Lochryan ended. His sister Eleanor was married to Sir Thomas Wallace of Craigie in Ayrshire, who obtained the property in right of his wife.

The Wallaces of Craigie claimed kinship with both of the national heroes, Sir William Wallace of Elderslie and Robert the Bruce. One of the most distinguished members of the family was Sir Thomas, who became Lord Justice-Clerk. He was the father of Sir Thomas, who married Eleanor Agnew of Lochryan. Their only son, Thomas, died before his father, and the succession passed to their daughter, Frances Anna, who was married to John Dunlop of Dunlop, also the descendant of a very old Ayrshire family. Mr. and Mrs. Dunlop's youngest

---

[1] Guttural pronunciation ; Gaelic *cruach*, a stack or a hill.
[2] Separate land. " *Severale*, applied to landed property as possessed distinctly from that of others, or contrasted with a common." —Jamieson.
[3] Gaelic *cladach*, the shore.

daughter is mentioned by Burns as "the blooming Keith". She died unmarried.

Mrs. Dunlop does not appear to have lived at Lochryan after her marriage, and the house was allowed to fall into disrepair. Robert Heron, who passed this way in 1792, says of the house that "for these last forty years, it has been uninhabited. It contains some spacious rooms. Several fine paintings have been left to fade and moulder away, on the staircase. It has been by degrees disfurnished of almost everything else. The partitions still remain : and the roof although ruinous, is not yet entirely destroyed : but, the lapse of a few years will leave nothing but the bare walls."

Thomas Dunlop fell heir not only to the Lochryan estate, but also to the lands and barony of Craigie, and assumed the name of Wallace. He had to sell the Craigie property in 1783. It was he who married Eglintine Maxwell. They had two sons, Thomas, who died in infancy, and John Alexander Agnew, who succeeded to Lochryan. He was followed by his son, William Agnew, in 1857. On his death in 1892 the estate passed to a nephew, Mr. John Alexander Agnew Wallace. A claim to the baronetcy had been asserted by Mrs. Dunlop's son and his successors until 1892, but is maintained no longer.

It only remains to note that the famous ballad, *The Lass of Lochryan*, is not believed to have any historical foundation, and that Taliessin's phrase, " Between Caer Rian and Caer Rwyg ", used in connexion with The Deil's Dyke, refers to Cairn Ryan and Crawick on the Nith.

I have said the best that can be said of the journey from Stranraer to this point and have nothing to withdraw ; but it must be confessed that the road itself is in the main of a grovelling habit. Immediately after Cairnryan it changes its character and, as if tired of the close companionship of the salt waves, mounts and twists upwards in a spirited manner along a wooded hillside. The trees are not so closely set as to shut out the view on the left, and there comes at the same time the effect of greater spaciousness in the outlook, for the seascape begins to open out from the narrow bounds of Loch Ryan to the broad stretches of the Firth of Clyde. Far beyond Milleur [1] Point at the north end of The Rhinns the dim coast of Antrim be-

[1] Gaelic *maol odhar*, grey headland.

comes visible, and more to the right the little less faint line of
the Kintyre peninsula. As if designing a kaleidoscopic impression
for the traveller, the road then turns its back on the sea and
runs inland up an open glen where there is in summer a great
wealth of hawthorn and golden broom on the lower slopes,
while in autumn the tale of colour is taken up by large patches
of purple heather higher up. The road, after preparing itself
by a gentle ascent so far, takes a fancy to the other side of the
glen, crosses the burn, and makes a sudden attack on a steeper
hill than it has yet known. The hill is covered thickly with

*Glen App.*

long-established, towering pines forming a deep, continuous
shade, so that, although the traveller is climbing, he feels as if
he had plunged abruptly into a depth. On a hot day there is a
pleasing coolness here, and the moist rock-faces with their
colonies of ferns growing in pockets and crevices are a joy.
Besides the ferns there are many wild flowers, and the whole
of the left bank of the road makes a natural rock-garden. Such
are the delights of Glen App.

The name of the glen is traced to that ambitious monarch
of the eighth century, Alpyn, who proposed to add Galloway

to his dominions, overran the country with an army, was defeated
by a native chief near Kelton on the Dee, and as he was retiring
from this enterprise, was slain by a single assailant in the
neighbourhood of this glen. A pillar-stone called Leight-Alpyn
marks the place of his burial. This explanation of the name is
more credible than that of the philologist who maintained that
" Glen App " meant " glen of the ape ", adding that " at some
very remote period those animals, therefore, must have existed
in the south of Scotland, though they are long since extinct " !

*Bridge in Glen App.*

I found this road so alluring that I omitted to recall at the
moment the significance of a little stream of water plashing
down among rocks and trees shortly before the road turns away
from Loch Ryan. This falling streamlet bears the name of the
Galloway Burn, and marks the boundary between Galloway
proper and Galloway *Irredenta* or Carrick. Of Carrick, Kyle,
and Cunningham, the three ancient regalities into which Ayrshire was divided, the first was a part of Galloway until 1186.
It was the home of the royal line of Bruce and the scene of the
initial success of King Robert in the War of Independence.
Robert the Third included the lands of the earldom of Carrick

in the appanage of his eldest son in a charter of 1404, and it is in consequence thereof that the Prince of Wales takes the title of Earl of Carrick. This was the land of the Kennedies and the arena of one of the most virulent and sustained feuds in Scottish history. A house in Maybole, the capital of Carrick, echoed to some of the faithful contendings of John Knox. The Covenanters were strong in the district, and nearly every churchyard has its martyr's grave. A bold claim is made for Carrick in the popular rhyme :

> Carrick for a man,
>   Kyle for a coo,
> Cunningham for butter and cheese,
>   And Galloway for 'oo.

This does not mean that the soil of Carrick was unproductive. It yielded such plentiful harvests of grain in the seventeenth century, when Mr. William Abercrummie, Episcopal minister of Maybole, set down his observations, that " from hence are yearly transported considerable quantities of meal, both to GALLOWAY, and the *Fishing* in CLYDE ". " It affoords also store of cattle, so that great droves of cowes and bullocks are carried yearly hence, both into ENGLAND and other places of our own kingdome."

A mile or two after emerging from the top of Glen App, the road begins to descend into the valley of the Stinchar (the *ch* has the soft pronunciation), and two conspicuous features in the northward view arrest one, a hill on the land and a hill in the sea, the conical Knockdolian[1] rising eight hundred and sixty-nine feet on the other side of the Stinchar, and the rock-island of Ailsa towering out of the midst of the Firth of Clyde to the height of almost eleven hundred feet. From the sea in foggy weather the former is sometimes mistaken for the latter, and is known hence as " the false Ailsa Craig ".

Ballantrae, a widely-scattered village lying round the bay into which the Stinchar flows, depends on fishing and on summer visitors. The beach is stony, but there is a little sand where bathers disport themselves. A golf-course runs along the shore. There are pleasant inland walks, and the Stinchar has some

---

[1] Gaelic *cnoc*, a hill, and *dall*, to mislead ; the misleading hill, so called for the reason given in the text.

reputation as a fishing stream. If I were proposing a holiday residence on the Carrick coast, my choice would certainly fall on Ballantrae.

There are two literary facts about the place which the visitor ought to know. One is that the village is not the scene of Stevenson's romance, *The Master of Ballantrae*. I have given the truth of this matter in the chapter dealing with Borgue. The other is that Burns wrote a poem beginning, " Beyond yon hill where Stinchar flows ", and in deference to the judgment of some polite critics who thought " Stinchar "

*Ailsa Craig from the moors above Glen App.*

inelegant replaced this name with " Lugar ", the name of a tributary of the Water of Ayr. In Mr. Lang's edition the original reading is restored.

John Keats, writing at Ballantrae to his brother, on the 10th of July, 1818, says, " Yesterday we came 27 Miles from Stranraer—entered Ayrshire a little beyond Cairn, and had our path through a delightful Country . . . When we left Cairn our Road lay half way up the sides of a green mountainous shore, full of clefts of verdure and eternally varying—sometimes up sometimes down, and over little Bridges going across green chasms of moss, rock and trees—winding about everywhere. After two or three Miles of this we turned suddenly into a magnificent glen finely wooded in Parts—

seven Miles long—with a Mountain stream winding down
the Midst—full of cottages in the most happy situations—
the sides of the Hills covered with sheep—the effect of
cattle lowing I never had so finely.   At the end we had a
gradual ascent and got among the tops of the Mountains
whence in a little time I descried in the Sea Ailsa Rock 940
feet high—it was 15 Miles distant and seemed close upon us.

*Ballantrae.*

The effect of Ailsa with the peculiar perspective of the Sea in
connection with the ground we stood on, and the misty rain
then falling gave me a complete Idea of a deluge.   Ailsa struck
me very suddenly—really I was a little alarmed."
    The older name of Ballantrae was Kirkcudbright-inner-Tig,
arising from its association with the evangelist, S. Cuthbert,
and the situation of the church on a bank of the Tig, a confluent
of the Stinchar.   When a new church was erected early in the

seventeenth century, the name was changed to " Ballantrae ",
" the village on the shore ".

The ivy-clad ruin standing on a knoll beside the village
represents the castle where the Bargany[1] branch of the Kennedies
lived. Ardstinchar is said to have sheltered Mary, Queen of
Scots, on the night of the eighth of August, 1566. A carved
tomb in the churchyard is another memorial of the Bargany
Kennedies. There is the following inscription above the
entrance : " This Aisle contains a Burial Place of the Family
of Bargany and Ardstinchar Chief of the Name of Kennedy,
and a Monument raised over the remains of Gilbert the 16th
Baron who was slain in a feudal conflict with his cousin the
Earl of Cassillis at Maybole in 1601, at the early age of 25,
on which occasion, when overpowered by numbers, Bargany displayed the most consummate bravery. The Epitaph having
been defaced the Representative of the Family Hew F Kennedy
now of Bennane, mindful of their virtues, has considered it his duty
to erect this Tablet to the memory of his Ancestors." Some
account of the Carrick vendetta will be given in a later chapter.

The brothers Chambers, who wrote about 1832, have some
notes on the morals and manners of the inhabitants of Ballantrae in the smuggling period. The people in these parts were,
they say, " till within the last twenty or thirty years, almost as
wild and rude as the remote Highlanders of Ross-shire, though
no doubt a great deal wealthier. And what the natural circumstances of the district gave rise to was greatly influenced, at
one period, by the lawless state into which much of the population was thrown by smuggling. It is not yet more than forty
years since the immense bands of people who, in this district,
attend funerals would fall out on the road to the parish town,
where the churchyard is situated, and, without regard to the
sober character of their duty, set down the corpse and fight
out their quarrel with fists, sticks, and such other rustic weapons
as they happened to be possessed of, till, in the end, one party
had to quit the field discomfited, leaving the other to finish
the business of the funeral. Brandy from the French luggers
that were perpetually hovering on the coast was the grand
inspiration in these unseemly brawls."

If there is little serious history to be recorded about Ballantrae,

[1] The pronunciation is " Barginny " ; Gaelic *barr gaothanach*,
windy height.

there are one or two odd tales about Peter, the boat-builder and warlock of Innermessan, which have Ballantrae for their scene. Peter was once employed to build a boat for the fishermen of the village. " As he busily shaped the timbers, surrounded by many lookers-on, a rider was seen descending Drumconal at a tremendous pace and approaching the ford of the Stinchar. (This was many a day before the bridge was built.) ' The laddie goes hot-foot,' remarked one of the idlers. ' Does he ? ' rejoined the seer ; ' he'll just bide there a bit.' Peter then laid his enchantments upon him so effectually that the man's horse was arrested in his stride, his hind hoofs fixed in the ground, his forelegs curved in a semi-circle ; rider and steed were rooted to the spot in such an attitude as we have been accustomed to associate with another great Peter's statue on the Neva. Then Peter of Innermessan, having gratified his audience with this interesting tableau, coolly proceeded with his work until presently it pleased him, with a muttered ' Gang yer gate ! ' to allow the rider to proceed upon his journey."

The chronicler states further that " the fishermen of Ballantrae, superstitious like others of their calling, chuckled at the idea of the luck that must attend the boat built by so powerful an enchanter ; but their hopes were short-lived ; for as the wizard received the stipulated sum into his palm and turned to trudge homewards, he vouchsafed the unwelcome hint as to the future— ' That boat will droon her fu' ; ' and so it occurred in due course. One calm evening, the vessel, with an unusually large crew, was nearing the shore, when a sudden squall drove the party out to sea. Night coming on, no assistance could be given ; and neither boat nor fishermen were ever heard of after."

I do not suppose anyone could live at Ballantrae without being beguiled inland by the attractions of the Stinchar valley. As Abercrummie says, the Stinchar " makes a pleasant strath in all its course ". In particular there is the village of Colmonell,[1] which has a euphonic name, as well as a pretty aspect, and as one journeys up the glen, one begins to be impressed by something that is most noticeable throughout Carrick as a whole —the great number of old castles. The country fairly bristles with them. In the lower part of the valley between Ballantrae

<hr>

[1] "From St. Colmonella, died 611; called in *Adamnan*, Columbanus; Colum an Eala, ' Colum of the Eala' (name of stream in King's Co.)."—Johnston.

and Pinwherry[1] there are, for instance, besides Ardstinchar
Castle, the remains of the strongholds of Knockdolian, Kirkhill
at the entrance of Colmonell, Craigneil on the other side of the
glen, and Pinwherry at the meeting of the Stinchar and the
Duisk[2]—these five within the space of eight miles. Colmonell
has its memorial of the great persecution in the grave of Matthew

*Colmonell.*

MacIlwraith—" By Bloody Claverhouse I fell ". It has been
supposed that the martyr's name suggested " Mucklewrath "
to the author of *Old Mortality*.

Above Pinwherry the valley narrows, the hills on both sides
are steep and covered with woods, and at various points along

---

[1] Prob. " penny-land of the copse "; Gaelic *peighinn fhoithre*
(pron. whirry).—Johnston.

[2] Gaelic *dubh uisge*, black water.

the lower slopes there are many hawthorns and rhododendrons.
You pass here along one of the most delightful highways in
Carrick. Near Pinmore[1] the road climbs out of the Stinchar
valley, crosses a pass at the foot of the Dinvin[2] hill, and gives a
remarkable view of Girvan, the sea, and Ailsa Craig, all framed
within a setting of high hills. Also near Pinmore, a road breaks
off to the right, leading past the site of an old church, Kirkdomine,[3] to the upland village of Barr.

As the scene of well-known fairs, " Kirkdamnie, or as it is
now usually further corrupted Kirkdamdie, long had a celebrity
in the western shires quite equal to that of Donnybrook in the
sister isle."[4]

Of Barr there is little to say except that the churchyard
contains a martyr's grave and that the view of the Galloway
hills is of interest to the geologist.[5] The inscription on the
martyr's tombstone is as follows:

1685

HEAR · LYES · EDW
ARD · McKEEN · W
HO · WAS· ShoAT · IN
THIS · PARISh · BY · C
ORN: DOUGLLAS F
OF · ADheTaNCe · TO
THe· WOrD· OF · GOD
AND · SCOTLLANDS ·
COUeNATeD · WORK
OF · REFORmATION.

On the other side of the stone there is a sand-glass at the top,
and below it a hand holds a tablet bearing the words:

BE· FAITH
FUL · UNT
O · DEAT
H · &c.

---

[1] Gaelic *peighinn mòr*, big penny-land.—Johnston.
[2] Gaelic *dùn fionn*, white fort.
[3] The oldest form of the name seems to be that in a charter of 1404,
" Kildomine ", the Lord's church.
The remains of the church were removed in 1636, when the
Presbytery of Ayr decided that it was " necessary and expedient
that the materials of Kirkdomine as yet standing be taken down and
transported to the place where the new kirk is to be builded ", that
is, the kirk of Barr.          [4] *The Hereditary Sheriffs.*
[5] There is a drawing in Sir Archibald Geikie's *The Scenery of
Scotland viewed in Connexion with its Physical Geology*.

This was a case of shooting without trial. Wodrow tells how Cornet James Douglas with twenty-four soldiers " finding Edward Kyan a pious good man from Galloway, lately come thence to buy corn, who had fled in betwixt the gavel of one house, and the side-wall of another, they dragged him out, and took him through a yard. He was asked where he lived, and told them, upon the water of Menock. When one of the soldiers had him by the arm dragging him away, without any warning, further questions, or permitting him to pray, the said lieutenant, who was governor of the garrison at Balwhan, shot him through the head, and presently discharged his other pistol, and shot him again in the head, when lying on the ground struggling with death ; and one of the soldiers of the party coming up, pretended he saw some motion in him still, and shot him a third time. . . . He was but a youth, and could not have been at Bothwell, or any of the risings, and they had indeed nothing to charge him with but his hiding himself." Wodrow had before him " an attested account signed by persons present."

Apart from the section between Ballantrae and Girvan, the road along the Carrick coast is not likely to arouse enthusiasm. During these thirteen miles, however, it makes a bold bid for admiration, and the carriage-hirers of Girvan used to label it a " popular coach-drive ". It reminded me of another running along the east side of Luce Bay between Port William and Auchenmalg. I prefer the latter, partly because it is little-travelled, and the quietness is less likely to be shattered by crowded charabanc-loads of hilarious holiday-makers ; but have no hesitation in admitting that the road from Ballantrae to Girvan, running near the shingly beach, twisting round the bold Bennan[1] headland, rising at one point to a hundred and fifty feet above the sea, and commanding the whole width of the Firth of Clyde, the low line of Kintyre, The Isle of Arran with its lofty, jagged skyline, and Ailsa Craig, that colossal rock in the middle distance, will give the traveller much joy on a fine summer day.

About three and a half miles from Ballantrae, it passes near the mouth of a large cave which penetrates the Bennan Head for seventy feet. This is the nightly refuge of gypsies and other tramps. According to Carrick tradition, it was once the dwelling-place of that monstrous ogre, Sawny Bean, the cannibal,

[1] Gaelic *beinnan*, a little hill.

who has probably had something more than justice done him
in S. R. Crockett's romance, *The Grey Man*. Gamesloup, a
precipitous crag overhanging the sea a little farther on, was,
according to another legend, the scene of a different class of
villanies and of their appropriate conclusion. A laird of Carleton
amassed wealth by marrying heiresses and then throwing them
over this precipice into the sea. He was about to add one more
to the series of his matrimonial iniquities by drowning a lady
called May Collean or Culzean when he came by a violent end.
According to the ballad, however, he had not married the lady,
but had merely abducted her and was going to content himself
with robbing her of her personal belongings.

> Fause Sir John a-wooing came
>     To a maid of beauty rare ;
> May Collean was this lady's name,
>     Her father's only heir.
>
> He's courted her but, and he's courted her ben,
>     And courted her into the ha',
> Until he got the maid's consent
>     To mount and ride awa'.
>
> She's gane down to her father's stable,
>     Where a' the steeds did stand,
> And she has taken the best steed
>     That was in her father's land.
>
> He's got on, and she's got on,
>     And fast as they could flee,
> Until they come to a lonesome part—
>     A rock abune the sea.
>
> " Light down, light down," says fause Sir John,
>     " Your bridal bed you see ;
> Here have I drowned seven ladies fair,
>     The eighth one you shall be.
>
> " Cast off, cast off your jewels fine,
>     Cast off your silken gown,
> They are owre fine and owre costly
>     To rot in the salt sea foam."
>
> " O turn ye then about, Sir John,
>     And look to the leaf o' the tree,
> For it never became a gentleman
>     A naked woman to see."

He turned himself straight round about
  To look to the leaf o' the tree ;
She has twined her arms around his waist,
  And thrown *him* into the sea.

" Now lie you there, thou fause Sir John,
  Where ye thought to lay me ;
Although ye'd hae stripped *me* to the skin,
  *Your* claes ye hae gotten wi' thee."

" O help, O help now, May Collean,
  O help, or else I drown ;
I'll tak you hame to your father's gates,
  And safely set ye down."

" Nae help, nae help, thou fause Sir John,
  Nae help nor pity to thee ;
Ye lie not in a caulder bed
  Than the ane ye meant for me."

So she went on her father's steed
  As fast as she could gae,
And she cam' hame to her father's house
  Before it was break of day.

I went to Girvan feeling sure that I should not like it. It was obvious, however, from a study of the map, that it would be the most convenient point from which to explore the northern part of Carrick. There must be a considerable number of people who do like it, or there would not be so many rows of houses with the legend, " apartments to let ", displayed in the windows ; and for people to whom it does not matter much where they spend their holidays so long as there are a beach, a golf-course, and a railway station with a good service of trains to the nearest city, it may do very well. Against the dull, bleak streets, and the high winds and clouds of dust that prevailed during the days that I spent there, I must mention on the credit side the outlook across the Firth to Arran and Ailsa[1] Craig, the interest of the frequent atmospheric transformations, and the fact that a motor-boat goes from Girvan to the Rock. The voyage is worth making, for Ailsa Craig is not merely an island with a lighthouse, but has some remarkable features and several fragments of history, and gives, moreover, a novel standpoint from which to look at the main-

---

[1] Norse for " Ailsi's isle ".

land.  Indeed, a visit to it will stand out as the most notable
of one's Carrick experiences.

Geologists say that " like the rock of Dumbarton and the
Bass Rock, Ailsa Craig consists of igneous rock which once
filled the throat of a volcano, probably in carboniferous times.
This throat penetrated softer strata and may have been submarine, surmounted by a cone and crater.  The agents of
denudation have, however, subsequently removed the original
summit of the volcanic mass, together with much of the stratified
materials once enclosing it, and they have left the hard con-
solidated core, as we see it, rising from the sea-bed, and forming
an elongated dome." [1]  " The rock of Ailsa Craig is a light
greenish-gray, fine-grained micro-granite.  Examined in thin
slices under the microscope, it is seen to be composed essentially
of orthoclase-felspar quartz, and a dark-blue variety of horn-
blende known to mineralogists as riebeckite.  Zircon also occurs
sparingly as one of the rock-constituents.  The most interesting
of these minerals is riebeckite, which is of rare occurrence—the
only other locality in Britain from which it has been recorded
being the hill of Mynydd Mawr, some three miles west of
Snowdon.  Riebeckite was first discovered in granite from
Socotra in 1888.  Since then it has been detected in Corsica and
in Colorado.  It is this mineral which spots the Ailsa Craig
rock with the irregular dark-blue blotches. . . . During the
glacial period, Ailsa Craig was completely smothered in the
great stream of ice which poured down the Firth of Clyde
and made its way into the Irish Sea.  Fragments of the micro-
granite were thus detached and carried away by the ice, and
are now met with occasionally in the Isle of Man." [2]

Keats's sonnet is entitled *To Ailsa Rock*.

> Hearken, thou craggy ocean pyramid !
>     Give answer from thy voice, the sea-fowl's screams !
>     When were thy shoulders mantled in huge streams ?
> When, from the sun, was thy broad forehead hid ?
> How long is't since the mighty power bid
>     Thee heave to airy sleep from fathom dreams ?
>     Sleep in the lap of thunder or sun-beams,
> Or when grey clouds are thy cold cover-lid ?
> Thou answer'st not, for thou art dead asleep !
>     Thy life is but two dead eternities—

[1] Edward Hull, F.R.S., in *Ailsa Craig : its History and Natural
History* by the Rev. R. Lawson.
[2] James Geikie, F.R.S., *ibid.*

> The last in air, the former in the deep ;
> > First with the whales, last with the eagle-skies—
> Drown'd wast thou till an earthquake made thee steep,
> > Another cannot wake thy giant size.

Wordsworth's sonnet belongs to 1833 and bears the heading, IN THE FRITH OF CLYDE, AILSA CRAG. DURING AN ECLIPSE OF THE SUN, JULY 17.

> Since risen from ocean, ocean to defy,
> Appeared the Crag of Ailsa, ne'er did morn
> With gleaming lights more gracefully adorn
> His sides, or wreathe with mist his forehead high :
> Now, faintly darkening with the sun's eclipse,
> Still is he seen, in lone sublimity,
> Towering above the sea and little ships;
> For dwarfs the tallest seem while sailing by,
> Each for her haven.

The first documentary notice of Ailsa Craig occurs in a royal charter of 1404 confirming to Crossraguel Abbey the lands belonging to it, and naming among the rest *Insula de Ailsay, cum pertinenciis*. The Rev. Roderick Lawson, whose monograph on the island will be useful to visitors, epitomizes the history of its tenure thus : " The Earls of Carrick, previous to the endowment of Crossraguel Abbey ; the Abbots of Crossraguel Abbey, from that date to the Reformation in 1560 ; the Cassillis family from the Reformation to the present day."

The few historical incidents that have a link with Ailsa Craig are connected with the Spanish danger. Lord Maxwell, after the failure of his rising in support of the expected invasion, escaped down the Solway Firth and was pursued by a government vessel. He sailed into the Firth of Clyde, and finding when opposite Ballantrae that the pursuing ship still held after him, " withdrew himself, and passed with ane and himself in ane cokboit to *Ilshay*, and on the back of that ile, fand ane fischer boit, quhairin he cam to the land foranent the Abbey of Crosregale ", and there was captured.

" Becaus he could gett no entrance in the Abbey," says Calderwood, " he was forced to retire to an oastler hous in the toun, to gett his dinner. Whill he is at dinner, six or seven gentlemen were breaking up the doores of the hous. He fleeth to the wood, where he was taikin in a cave upon the fyft of June, by Sir William Stewart."

The next event in the history of Ailsa Craig arises out of the Spanish designs against Britain after the failure of the great Armada. Hew Barclay of Ladyland in Kilbirnie had become a Protestant, but had reverted to the old Church and been excommunicated. He went abroad and returned a few years later to plot with other Roman Catholics for the overthrow of the government.[1] In particular, he proposed to take possession of Ailsa Craig for the following purposes:—" to sett up and manteyne ane public Masse, quhilk should be patent to all distressed papists, wherefra so ever they shall come; to serve as ane place of releife and refreshment to the Spanyart or rather a port to them, on ther arryval in Ireland; to establish ane storehouse to keep furnishing and all things profytable to the use of the Erle of Tyrone, with the quhilk Erle, Ladyland by his commissioners had been buissy sen his last coming to Scotland."

His intention became known to Andrew Knox, " minister of God's Worde at Paseleye ", who informed the government. Finding the warning disregarded, the minister of Paisley, with a company of nineteen men, sailed to Ailsa Craig and took possession of the rock himself. Barclay arrived with thirteen supporters " to fortify the island, and victual the same for the ressett and comforte of the Spanishe armey, luiked for be him to have come and arryvit ". He found himself confronted suddenly by the minister and his army, who " forgadderit with him and his compleceis, tuke sum of his associatis, and desirit himselfe to rander and be takin with thaime, quha wer his awne freindis, meaning nawayes his hurte nor drawinge of his blude ". Barclay refused to surrender. He was driven backwards into deep water and so was " drownit and perisheit in his awne wilfull and desperat resolution ".[2] After this incident the Earl of Cassillis arranged for the proper custody of the island.

[1] " The Laird of Ladyland in Cunninghame, latelie come home out of Flanders, an apostat, reasoning against the truthe and blaspheming."—*Certan Greeves of the Generall Assemblie of Scotland assembled in Edinburgh, givin in to His Majestie the 20th of Februar* 1587.

[2] The minister of Paisley seems to have regarded the Firth of Clyde as a part of his parish. Nothing could happen there without his being on the spot at the opportune moment. In 1592, Calderwood tells us, " a certain young gentleman, named Mr. George Ker, brother to Marke Lord Newbottle, being readie to make for the saile out of Fairlie Raid, at the West Sea Banke, his speeches were taikin heed to, and he perceaved to be a Papist passing to Spaine, to traffique betuixt the King of Spaine and some Scottish noblemen. Mr. Andrew Knox, minister at Paisley, accompanied with some schollers of Glasgow, gentlemen's sonnes, and other

Many people who never heard of Hew Barclay must have
thought what a splendid fortress Ailsa Craig would make; yet
no galleries have been driven into its mass, no guns wait to
spread a curtain of fire across the sea. On the outbreak of
war in 1914, however, certain less obvious means were adopted
for the defence of the Firth, and it is rumoured that some
German submarines came to a final rest on the sea-floor.

A nervous reader should be warned not to be startled and
lose his footing as he climbs if a passing steamer blows its horn
in order to raise the cloud of birds. In Pennant's opinion
"the walk is horrible, for the depth is alarming." He ascended,
however, to the castle, a square tower of three storeys, and
saw the view of the bays of Girvan and Campbeltown on either
side of the Firth, but did not go to the summit of the rock as
the day was very warm. He notes that the Earl of Cassillis
rents Ailsa Craig "for 33*l. per ann.* to people who come here to
take the young gannets for the table; and the other birds for
the sake of their feathers. . . . The fowler ascends the rocks
with great hazard, is provided with a long rod, furnished at the
end with a short hair line with a running noose. This he flings
round the neck of the bird, hawls it up and repeats it till he
takes ten or twelve dozen in an evening." Pennant was impressed
by the "stupendous and amazing assemblage of precipitous
columnar rocks of great height rising in wild series one above the
other" on the east side, and thought it wonderful that "throstles
exerted the same melody in this scene of horror as they do in
the groves of *Hertfordshire*". 1772 was the year of his visit.

freinds, apprehended him upon the 27th of December in the Yle
of Cumra, before Boote, when he was ready to embarke, searched
his coffers, found diverse letters and blankes directed from George
Erle of Huntlie, . . . and other practisers, some in Latine, some
in Frenche, together with their caschets and signets" with the result
that Mr. George Ker was lodged in the Tolbooth of Edinburgh.
Some of the documents found are known to history as the Spanish
blanks. On the 20th of October, 1596, the General Assembly
"entered in consideratioun of the dangers of the kirk, arising of
the forefaulted excommunicated erles within the realme, and what
remedeis might be devised for preventing therof" and appointed
a vigilance committee. As we might have expected, the minister
of Paisley was one of the commissioners for the west.

# CHAPTER XXV

## THE GIRVAN VALLEY

Castles and Covenanters—Old Dailly Church—The charter stone—
   The Baron's Stone of Killochan—Remarkable incident of an
   entombed miner—The Girvan Valley coal-field—The Sunday
   labour question in 1701—The Burning Pit—A pit that burned
   for a hundred years.

ALONG the Girvan Water, as in the Stinchar valley, there are
many castles. Ascending the stream, we find on the one or on
the other bank those of Killochan,[1] Bargany, Brounston, Dal-
quharran,[2] Drummochreen,[3] Kilkerran,[4] Cloncaird,[5] and Blairquhan,[6] and Penkill Castle in a tributary glen. Some of them
come into notice as the homes of actors in the Carrick vendetta,
and not a few have a place in the story of the persecution
of the Covenanters. From some hillside rising above the Girvan
Water one may look down upon a series of points the history of
which brings before us all the personal factors in that period of
terror, agony, woe, and stupidity : the faithful meeting secretly
to worship God according to the rites which Scotland had
received from the Reformers and to listen to the exhortations of
their " outed " ministers, the high and the low suffering alike
for their fidelity, the informer and the covetous anxious to make
what they could out of the suspicions of the times, the perverse

[1] Gaelic *cill, cille*, cell, church, or *coill*, a wood, and *lochan*, a little
loch.
[2] Perhaps Gaelic *dail charrain*, meadow of the scurvy-grass or
corn-weed.
[3] Gaelic *druim-a-chritheinn*, hill-ridge of the aspen tree, from
*crith*, trembling.
[4] Church of Kiaran.
[5] Gaelic *cluain ceàird*, meadow of the smith.
[6] Probably *blar bhan*, white-looking, fair plain.

and incompetent government attempting an impossible task, the armed savages who acted as its enthusiastic tools.[1] The present house of Bargany, for example, was built by John, Lord Bargany, who suffered in the cause of the Covenant. When "The Bond" was pressed on the noblemen and other landlords in 1678—"The Bond" was a document by which the signatories bound themselves to abstain from conventicles, to keep their tenants clear of "the rebels", and to do all in their power to crush the popular movement—he was one of those who refused to sign it. During the renewal of persecuting zeal which followed upon the battle of Bothwell Bridge, personal enemies of Bargany who coveted his lands secured his imprisonment on the charge of having been concerned in the rising. When he was brought to trial, however, no evidence was produced in support of the charges formulated against him on this and on other counts. Again, the dining-room of Killochan Castle was the scene of conventicles. Drummochreen, represented now by a bit of ivy-covered wall, was the abode of John Macalexander, a resolute Covenanter, who was forced to give free quarters to some of the Highland Host and was fined eighty pounds. Kilkerran was the home of Alexander Fergusson, a son-in-law of the Bishop of Galloway, who guided the dragoons to the house of James Semple, the martyr, whose body lies in Old Dailly Churchyard. It was at Blairquhan Castle that the dragoons were quartered.

The erection of the old church of Dailly [2] Parish, three miles east of Girvan, is attributed to a period not later than the four-

[1] " And now the Highland Host (as it was called) appear upon the stage. . . . After they past Stirling they carried as if they hade been in ane enemies countrey, living upon free quarter where ever they came. They spread themselves through the whole counties of Clidesdale, Renfrew, Cunninghame, Kyle, Carrick; Galloway they did not reach. . . . As for the oppressions, exactions, injuries, and cruelties committed by the Highlanders among the poor people of the west countrey, it is a bussiness above my reach to describe. . . . A thinking man may apprehend what a company of barbarous Highlanders would doe, when they were sent upon design to turn the innocent people of the west countrey mad by their oppressions, in which office indeed you may believe they were very faithfull. . . . When this goodly army retreated homeward, you would have thought by their baggage they hade been at the sack of a besieged city."—Kirkton's *History*.

[2] Gaelic *dealghe*, thorns.

teenth century. A former minister gives the following description : " Like all ancient churches, the building stands due east and west. In length it is about ninety-two feet, in breadth twenty-five feet, over the walls. Each of the two gables is surmounted by a belfry. A cross formerly stood on the eastern belfry, but it was knocked down by the branch of a tree during a storm about a century ago. The double belfry is a very unusual circumstance, and testifies to the ancient importance of our old church. The western bell was used in Roman Catholic times for summoning the people to worship, while the eastern or ' sanctus bell ' was only rung when the more solemn services of the Church were being performed. The ' piscina,' a stone basin in which the priests washed their hands and also rinsed the chalice at the celebration of the Mass is said still to remain in the wall, within the tomb of the Bargany family, in the east end of the building."

Two large blue stones lie within an enclosure built against the north wall. Their size, roundness, and smoothness make them difficult to lift, and the attempt to do so has been regarded in the parish as a test of strength. Scott refers to one of them as " a charter stone " in a note to *The Lord of the Isles.* It is believed that they lay originally beside the altar in the church and that they served as sanctuary stones for criminals who could make their way to them. An incident in the history of the charter stone is given thus in Scott's note : " The village of New Dailly being now larger than the old place of the same name, the inhabitants insisted that the Charter Stone should be removed from the old town to the new, but the people of Old Dailly were unwilling to part with their ancient right. Demands and remonstrances were made on each side without effect, till at last, man, woman, and child of both villages marched out and by one desperate engagement put an end to a war, the commencement of which no person then living remembered. Justice and victory, in this instance, being of the same party, the villagers of the old town of Dailly now enjoy the pleasure of keeping the ' blue stane ' unmolested."

There is another notable stone not far away. The lifting of it has never been suggested as an athletic test, nor has it been bandied about by rival communities struggling for its possession. It has been put in its present place by the stupendous forces of nature, and by them alone is it likely that it will ever be dis-

turbed. It is a great detached mass of granite measuring about
four hundred and eighty cubic feet and weighing therefore about
thirty-seven tons, and is known as The Baron's Stone of
Killochan. Resting on a gentle, green slope, it is a reminder,
of the glacier that once ground its way down the Girvan Valley
and bore fragments of granite, great and small, from the central
mass of the Galloway Highlands towards the Firth of Clyde.
The tradition is that the barons of Killochan used it as a
judgment-seat, as a place of execution, and as a centre where
they could muster their forces, hold their councils, and divide

*Dailly.*

the spoils of victory. Sir Archibald Geikie has make it the
subject of a fascinating discourse in his *Geological Sketches*.

The same writer devotes another chapter in that volume
to "The Colliers of Carrick", and includes a detailed account
of the remarkable incident of a miner remaining alive after
being buried in a coal-pit for twenty-three days. The facts
are recorded as follows on a tombstone in Dailly Churchyard :
" In memory of John Brown, Collier, who was enclosed in
Kilgrammie[1] Coal Pit, by a portion of it having fallen in,

[1] Doubtful. Perhaps Gaelic *coill gramachaidh*, the wood of the
clenching or the gripping fast.—Johnston.

Octr. 8th, 1835, and was taken out alive, and in full possession of his Mental faculties, but in a very exhausted state, Octr. 31st, having been twenty-three days in utter seclusion from the world, and without a particle of food. He lived for three days after, having quietly expired on the evening of Novr. 3d, aged 66 years." During his entombment he had been able to walk about at first and supply himself with water; but growing weaker, had stumbled and fallen into the position in which his rescuers found him.

The Girvan Valley is the only part of Carrick where coal is mined. We have here "a little bit of the great Scottish coal-field which by some ancient terrestrial revolution has got de-tached from the rest and become, as it were, jammed in between the two steep sides of the valley of the Girvan". There is evidence of coal having been wrought in this district so long ago as 1415, and "coal heuchs" and "coal pottis" are mentioned in charters of the following century. In 1701 the Kirk Session of Dailly Parish were exercised on the subject of Sunday labour at the Drummochreen colliery. The miners thought it necessary to keep the hand-pump going in order to prevent the water from flooding the pit, and the Session appointed a deputation to speak to the coal grieve "anent his drawing water out of the hough of Dramochrein on Sabbath day". The chronicler does not say if, as a result of the Session's re-monstrance, the water was allowed to accumulate.

A special interest attaches to what is known as The Burning Pit. Owing to miscalculations in excavating and propping the workings, the pillars began to break down in 1848. The subsequent history as it is told by a local authority has a curious fascination. "Men were employed to prop and build up the workings, but all their efforts were of no avail. The *creep* gradually extended away to the east and as far west as the whin dyke, which proved a barrier against it in this direction. From this point it gradually, day after day and week after week, travelled uphill, affecting all the seams in its course, until it became evident that a portion of the workings would entirely break down. A desperate effort was now made to save the incline by propping and building the workings on each side, but this had no effect in stopping the creep. At last on the 6th of December, 1849, the whole workings from the eastern extremity to the whin dyke came down with one crash, shaking the whole surface as with the shock of an earthquake. Notwithstanding the serious aspect of matters previously, nobody about the place anticipated such a catastrophe. But the worst remains to be told. On that night, the 6th of December, or on the morning of the 7th, in consequence of the coal falling amongst the red-hot bricks of the engine furnace, the workings took fire. At five o'clock in the morning the fire was so strong that the flames reached the top of the pit, a distance of two hundred feet, and set the pithead frame in a blaze.

"All the attempts to extinguish the fire were unsuccessful, and it continued to make rapid progress. It appeared to come direct from the pit to the surface and also to spread along west to the whin dyke above Wallacetown and east to another whin dyke beyond Craigieside. The whole brow of the hill between these two points was red-hot for years. These two dykes, however, proved to be effectual barriers to the spread of the fire east and west. After all the coals near the outcrop were burned, the fire gradually crept away down the workings, and the surface became cooler until, at the present day, the main evidence that the fire still exists is the constant discharge of gases from the cracks and rents on the surface."

Another pit in this neighbourhood, that of Dalzellowlie, took fire in 1749. It belonged partly to the Kilkerran and partly to the Culzean estate, and one version of the disaster is that either the Kilkerran or the Culzean colliers had been working a seam belonging to the other property, and in order to save themselves and their employers from discovery had ignited the coal. Another tradition is that two shepherd lads had crept down and amused themselves by making a fire in the dark and that the flames had spread from this source. It was impossible to subdue the conflagration by excluding the air, as the pit was wrought from the surface; the ground, moreover, cracked as the fire extended; and the coal continued to burn for about a hundred years! An effect of the subterranean heat was seen in the rapid growth of the trees planted on the hill.

The geological wonders of the coast between Girvan and Ballantrae, a mere catalogue of which would occupy considerable space, have provided material for many discourses and controversies in the Transactions of the Geological Societies and elsewhere.

*Girvan from Turnberry.*

# CHAPTER XXVI

## FROM GIRVAN TO THE DOON

Turnberry—Marjory, Countess of Carrick, and Robert Bruce—The
birth of the future king—King Robert lands at Turnberry—Culzean—What Sir William Brereton saw—The grounds—Dunure
—The roasting of Allan Stewart—Greenan—Mary Queen of
Scots in Carrick.

As one follows the coast between Girvan and the Doon, there
come into view one by one the castles of Turnberry [1], Culzean [2],
Dunure [3], and Greenan [4], standing each on a rocky promontory
or crowning a cliff. Of the road to Turnberry there is little to
be said except that there is a continuous series of potato fields
between it and the sea—this coast produces the earliest crops
of potatoes in Scotland—and that there is on the right the slope
of a raised beach. When Stevenson passed this way, he noted
an odd feature of the cottages—" a triangular porch projected

---

[1] " Prob. hybrid ; Nor. Fr. *tourne*, ' a feudal court ', and O.E.
*byrig* or *burg*, ' a fortified place, castle ', *cf*. Queensberry. *Turn*
may just mean ' turn ' or ' corner '."—Johnston.

[2] Doubtful. Perhaps from Gaelic *cùil gheinne* (*gh* mute), nook or
corner like a wedge.—Johnston.

[3] Gaelic *dùn odhar*, grey fort.

[4] Gaelic *grianan*, a sunny spot, summer-house, also a mountain
peak.

from above the door, supported at the apex by a single upright post ; a secondary door was hinged to the post, and could be hasped on either cheek of the real entrance ; so, whether the wind was north or south, the cotter could make himself a triangular bight of shelter where to set his chair and finish a pipe with comfort. . . . So far as I am aware, it is peculiar to the little corner of country about Girvan."

The roads in northern Carrick as a whole, with one or two exceptions, are disappointing, and I shall attempt little in the way of praise. Not only are the roads dull, but the undulating or merely flat look of the country palls on one who has beheld the various glories of the coasts and mountains of Galloway and southern Carrick, and it is only when one turns to old tales that one realizes that this is still a country where the sentimental traveller may journey with something more than patience.

An accidental but important meeting occurred in this district in 1271. The persons were Marjory, Countess of Carrick, and Robert Bruce, son of the Lord of Annandale and Cleveland. The Countess was the daughter and heiress of Neil, second Earl of Carrick, and a granddaughter of Duncan, to whom the earldom had been awarded in 1186 on his resigning his claim to the lordship of Galloway. Before her meeting with Robert Bruce she had been married to Adam of Kilconcath, who had gone to Palestine in 1269 in the army of Louis the Eleventh of France to fight for the Holy Sepulchre and had died at Acre in the following year.

She was riding over her ancestral estate, followed by her attendants, when a knight who had been hunting crossed her path. His appearance and bearing produced on her mind an instantaneous and deep impression. It was doubtless in accordance with the etiquette of the period that she should send her attendants to offer him the hospitality of her castle of Turnberry. The stranger, knowing that his would-be hostess was a ward of the crown, did not wish to incur the royal displeasure, and refused the invitation. The Countess, after the manner of her sex, was the more determined to have her way, ordered her company to surround him, and led him with gentle but firm constraint to her castle. After a few days of her society, Bruce resolved to brave the King's wrath and married the Countess forthwith. The King, in his anger at this infringement

of his rights, seized the castle and estates, but was pacified
ultimately with a substantial fine. Thus it came about that
the earldom of Carrick passed to the Bruce family. The Earl
and Countess had twelve children. Their eldest son was Robert,
the future King of Scotland.

There is no record of the place of his birth, but it is quite
likely that he was born at Turnberry, and the shore and links
near the castle were doubtless his earliest playground. They
were the scene also of the beginning of his struggle for a kingdom. After his coronation at Scone in 1306 and his reverse
at Methven, he is said to have retired with his brother, Edward,
Sir James Douglas, Sir Robert Boyd, and other supporters to
the Isle of Rathlin near the coast of Ireland ; but there are
reasons for thinking that he found refuge in some part of the
Norwegian dominions.[1] In the spring of 1307 Douglas and Boyd
landed on Arran with some followers, intending to drive the
English out of the castle at Brodick, and hid themselves in
a wood. Their opportunity came when three ships sailed into
Brodick Bay and began to discharge stores for the enemy.
A large part of the garrison went down to the beach to assist
the sailors in unloading, and as they were climbing the slope
with their burdens, Douglas came upon them with his men,
killed some, put others to flight, and made a very welcome
capture of provisions, clothing, and arms.

The King came to Arran presently with a fleet of thirty-three
boats and three hundred men and looked often across the Firth
to the flat lands of Ayrshire, not hoping to win his kingdom
with so small a force, but trusting that the men of Carrick and
Annandale and many others throughout Scotland, whose interest did not lie with the English oppressor, would rise in answer
to a bold lead. A scout named Cuthbert was sent over to the
mainland to discover what prospect there might be of a rising
in strength. If the outlook seemed favourable, a lighted beacon
on the Carrick coast was to be the signal for Bruce to bring his
men over. Cuthbert found little encouragement, and it was
plain to him that he must not give that signal to the watching
eyes across the water.

The day when the signal was to be expected arrived. Bruce
looked over the Firth to the other shore and saw what he had
hoped to see. The wish was not father to the vision. There

[1] See Bain's *The Edwards in Scotland.*

was no doubt about that column of smoke, and he set sail with his men from King's Cross Point.

The wind was contrary and the passage slow. Before the little fleet could reach the Carrick shore darkness had fallen, and now instead of the column of smoke floating skywards the voyagers saw the glare of the fire itself. The boats were grounded near Turnberry Castle, and there Cuthbert met them, dismayed at this misadventure. He told the King that he had lit no signal

*Turnberry Castle and Lighthouse.*

fire, that the people of the country had been burning whins that day, and that it was vain to look for a rising in the King's favour. He was able, however, to give some useful information about Turnberry Castle, and the King, supported by his brother, Edward, resolved on a forward movement. An assault on the castle itself was impracticable; but the greater part of the garrison, two hundred men, were quartered, not within it, but at the small village of Clachanton a short distance away. A surprise attack was made here, and only one of the enemy escaped. Bruce retired thereafter into the wilds of Carrick and Galloway and drew to himself gradually the support of his fellow countrymen.

At Turnberry one may see little more than the ditch on the landward side, the courtyard occupied now by a lighthouse and a fragment of wall facing the Firth. A great contrast to this ruin is presented by the stately modern castle of Culzean spread over the edge of the land where it falls away to the sea in a steep cliff a little farther north. There is a similar contrast between the low, bare promontory where Turnberry Castle stands and the beautiful wooded grounds of Culzean. From the landward side, Culzean Castle gives more of the impression of palatial grandeur than any other building in the district ; from the seaward side, where it has less appearance of height

*Turnberry Golf-links.*

on account of the cliff below, it strikes one as finer than anything like it on the Rhine.

This is the seat of the Marquess of Ailsa, who is the chief of the Kennedy family. It was built in 1777. An old house called The Cove stood here before that date, and it is believed that its tower was incorporated in the new building, forming the central part of the south-east front. The Cove took its name from the coves or caves running into the rock below. It belonged to a branch of the Kennedy family; and if the May Collean of the ballad who eloped with and then drowned " the fause Sir John " had a dwelling-place outside the ballad-writer's imagination, it was here. This was the home also of Sir Thomas Kennedy, who rode into an ambuscade in the wood of S. Leonard's near Ayr in 1602, and was slain in revenge for the death of the Laird of Bargany in the previous year. Later in the same century it belonged to Sir Archibald Kennedy, whose name has an unenviable place in the inscription over the grave of Gilbert MacAdam, the Covenanter, in Kirkmichael Churchyard.

Sir William Brereton, who travelled down this coast in 1636, visited both the house and the caves. " We went ", he says, " to the cave of Carick, which is about eight miles from Aire, where there dwells a laird, Sir Alexander Kendrick of Cullen, who hath a pretty pleasant seated house or castle, which looks full upon the main sea ; hereinto we went, and there found no hall, only a dining-room or hall, a fair room, and almost as large as the whole pile, but very sluttishly kept, unswept, dishes, trenchers and wooden cups thrown up and down, and the room very nasty and unsavoury. Here we were not entertained with a cup of beer or ale ; only one of his sons, servants and others, took a candle, and conducted us to the cave, where there is either a notable imposture, or most strange and much to be admired footsteps and impressions which are here to be seen of men, children, dogs, coneys, and divers other creatures. These here conceived to be Spirits, and if there be no such thing, but an elaborate practice to deceive, they do most impudently betray the truth ; for one of this knight's sons and another Galloway gentleman affirmed unto me that all the footsteps have been put out and buried in sand over night, and have been observed to be renewed next morning."

The present-day visitor will be impressed by the noble grounds and gardens. These contain many interesting exotic shrubs and trees, upon which Sir Herbert Maxwell has discoursed with his customary felicity in a chapter of *Scottish Gardens*. It is long since the horticultural resources of Culzean were known, for Abercrummie speaks of The Cove as " standing upon a rock above the Sea, flanked on the South with very pretty gardens and orchards, adorned with excellent Tarrases, and the walls loaden with peaches, apricotes, cherries, and other fruit and these gardens are so well sheltered from the North and East winds, and ly so open to the South, that the fruits and herbage are more early than any other place in Carrict."

In the case of Dunure Castle, we come again to a ruin, but one much better preserved than that of Turnberry. The most famous event in its history is the roasting of Allan Stewart, Commen

dator of Crossraguel Abbey, in " the black vault ". The office
of Commendator had been created when the property of the
Church was secularized at the Reformation, and was held by a
layman appointed by the Crown. Gilbert, Earl of Cassillis,

*Dunure Castle.*

was made Commendator of Crossraguel Abbey by his uncle,
Quentin Kennedy, the last Abbot; but this arrangement,
lacking royal confirmation, did not hold good. The King
appointed Allan Stewart, who had married a sister-in-law
of the Laird of Bargany. According to the *Historie of
the Kennedyis*, the Earl was " ane particuler manne,

and ane werry greidy manne, and cairitt nocht how he gatt land, sa that he culd cum be the samin ". Diplomatic attempts to make the Commendator surrender his rights failed, and the Earl then resorted to the procedure of which the victim gives such a minute and gruesome account in his appeal to the Privy Council. The Earl carried Stewart to Dunure Castle and into " the black vault " and caused him to be stripped, bound to a spit, and roasted before a great fire, and, says Bannatyne, " that the rost suld not burne, but that it might rost in soppe, they spared not flambing with oyle (Lord luik thou to sic crueltie !). . . . In that torment they held the poore man, whill that oftymes he cryed for Godis saik to dispatche him ; for he had alsmeikle gold in his awin purse as wald bye poulder aneugh to schorten his paine." After prolonged torture, Stewart signed a paper renouncing the lands of the abbey. This was on the 1st of September. On the 7th the Earl returned with a confirmatory document and required Stewart to sign it ; but he said that he would rather die. The Earl ordered the fire to be relit for his captive as before. Then, says Stewart, " being in so grit paine as I truste never man was in with his life, I cried, ' Fye upon you ! Will ye ding whingaris in me and put me of this world ! Or elis put a barrell of poulder under me, rather nor to be demaned in this unmercifull maner.' The said Erle, hearing me cry, bade his servant Alexander Richard put ane serviat in my throat, whilk he obeyed ; the samin being performed at xi houris of the nyght ; wha then seing I was in danger of my lyfe, my flesch consumed and brunt to the bones, and that I wald not condescend to thair purpose, I was releivit of that paine, whairthrow I will never be able nor weill in my lyfetyme."

The Earl escaped with a very light punishment, being ordered by the Privy Council to find security for £2000 to keep the peace towards the Commendator. He might very well do this since he was allowed to keep the Commendator's lands ! The ordinary justice of the county was under the Earl's control, and in such a matter the Council declined to interfere. We learn also that Stewart survived his tortures and enjoyed a pension from the Earl, but " was ewer thairefter onabill of his leggis ". The threatened torture of Isaac the Jew in *Ivanhoe* appears to have been based on this narrative.

Of Greenan Castle Abercrummie says that it is " a high

house upon the top of a rock, hanging over upon the sea, with some lower new work lately added to it, but never finished. It is too open to the cold and moisture, arysing from the Sea, to be a desyreable habitation ; and has been designed to be the owner's security against a surprize, rather than a constant residence." Sir Thomas Kennedy of Culzean spent the night of the 11th of May, 1602, here, and rode forth in the morning to be murdered in the wood near Ayr.

The following notes by Sir Herbert Maxwell on Queen Mary's progress through the south-west in 1563 are based on her French equerry's roll of expenses. " On Sunday, 1st August, the Queen lay at Eglinton, where her host was her devoted adherent, Hugh, 3rd Earl of Eglinton. The next two days and nights she spent at the Monastery of St. John the Baptist at Ayr [*a St. Jean d'era*] proceeding on 4th August to Dunure, where she was entertained until Saturday, 7th, by Gilbert, 4th Earl of Cassillis [*a Duneura chez le Conte de Casel*]. That night she lay at Ardmillan, the house of Thomas Kennedy, a cadet of the powerful house of Cassillis [*soupper et coucher a Ermelan*], and on the following day she moved to another stronghold of the Kennedys', Ardstinchar [*Arstinchel*], whereof the ruined tower still stands conspicuous on a bluff overhanging the Stinchar at Ballantrae."

*Culzean Bay from Turnberry Castle.*

# CHAPTER XXVII

## CASSILLIS AND AUCHENDRAYNE

Cassillis—The ballad of *Johnie Faa*—Auchendrayne—The beginning of the Carrick vendetta—The fourth Earl of Cassillis *versus* the Laird of Bargany—Sir Thomas Kennedy of Culzean *versus* the Earl—Continuance of the vendetta between the fifth Earl and the young Laird of Bargany—The young Bargany and John Mure of Auchendrayne *versus* Culzean—The Earl *versus* Bargany—The Earl's design against Ardstinchar Castle—First attempt on the life of Culzean—The King intervenes—The Earl and his Galloway vassals—Bargany goes to his aid—Bargany's new grievance against the Earl—A treaty of peace—Fresh trouble between the Earl and Bargany—Culzean causes a plot against the Earl's life to miscarry—Consequent plot against Culzean betrayed by Auchendrayne—The King intervenes again—The vendetta receives fresh fuel—The Earl compasses Bargany's death—Culzean murdered by the Bargany faction—First prosecution of the Mures—The murder of William Dalrymple—Second prosecution of the Mures—Their execution

IN an earlier chapter I have promised the reader some account of the Carrick vendetta ; but when I think of its many successive phases, its cold-blooded schemings, its plots within plots, its hot-blooded deeds, its legal incidents, and the multitude of persons involved, I feel tempted to let the matter go by saying simply that the whole of Carrick was agitated in the latter part of the sixteenth century and the early years of the seventeenth by a feud between the Cassillis and the Bargany branch of the Kennedies as to whether the Earl of Cassillis, the chief of the family, was to be " King of Carrick " in fact as well as in name. Yet this would be inadequate treatment of a story which formed the theme of Sir Walter Scott's *Auchendrayne, or the Ayrshire Tragedy*, and supplied

S. R. Crockett with the material for one of his best romances,
*The Grey Man*. An excellent account will be found in Mr.
William Robertson's *Ayrshire : its History and Historic Families*,
where it occupies about thirty octavo pages. This chapter
must be confined to a brief outline. The principal sources
are the anonymous *Historie of the Kennedyis* and the records
of the High Court of Justiciary.

The houses of Cassillis[1] and Auchendrayne,[2] the homes
of two of the leading actors in the vendetta, stood a few miles
apart in the valley of the Doon. The old tower of Cassillis
still forms the principal part of the house, and the Dule Tree,
or Tree of Sorrow, where the Earls hanged those whom they
thought it well to hang, grows beside it. Here, the author
of the ballad, *Johnie Faa*, would have had us believe, the sixth
Earl hanged fifteen gypsies who had carried off his lady ; but
there is no foundation for the tradition embodied in the ballad.

> The gypsies cam to our gude lord's yett,
>   And oh but they sang sweetly ;
> They sang sae sweet and sae very complete,
>   That down cam our fair lady.
>
> And she cam tripping down the stair,
>   And all her maids before her ;
> As sune as they saw her weel-faur'd face,
>   They cuist the glaumourye ower her.
>
> " Oh come with me," says Johnie Faa ;
>   " Oh come with me, my dearie ;
> For I vow and I swear by the hilt of my sword
>   That your lord shall nae mair come near ye ! "
>
> .     .     .     .     .     .
>
> And when our lord cam hame at e'en,
>   And speired for his fair lady,
> The tane she cried, and the other replied,
>   " She's away wi' the gypsy laddie."
>
> " Gae saddle to me the black, black steed,
>   Gae saddle and mak him ready ;
> Before that I either eat or sleep
>   I'll gae seek my fair lady."

---

[1] " Prob. Gaelic and Irish *caiseal*, ' a wall, a castle ', with the
Eng. pl. *s*."—Johnston.
[2] Gaelic *achadh an draigheann*, field of the blackthorns.

And we were fifteen weel-made men,
    Although we were na bonnie ;
And we were a' put down for ane,
    A fair young wanton lady.

The trouble began in the time of Gilbert, the fourth Earl of Cassillis, and was occasioned by his cruelties practised on Allan Stewart, Commendator of Crossraguel Abbey. In these outrages he was leaving some of his own relatives out of account. The author of the *Historie of the Kennedyis,* referring to Stewart as " the Abott," says that " this Abott had mareyitt ane sister of the Lady Barganyis ; and for that respect, the Abott wsitt with the Laird of Bargany, and followitt his opinione in all his adois." The Laird of Bargany besieged the Castle of Dunure, took it by storm, and carried Stewart off, " brunt as he was, to Air ". " The King of Carrick " was infuriated by this mingled insult and injury, but Bargany had strong sympathizers and supporters both in Carrick and in the rest of Ayrshire, and was able to hold his own. Peace was made after a time : the Earl kept his ill-gotten gains, and allowed Stewart a pension. Soon after this the Earl died of a fall from his horse.

Carrick was once more convulsed by an open feud, for in appointing a tutor or guardian to his son and heir, the Earl had passed over his brother, Sir Thomas Kennedy of Culzean, and given the office to Lord Glamis, Lord Chancellor of Scotland. The Earl had had a good reason for doing so. One dark night some years earlier, Culzean had surrounded and fusilladed Dunure Castle, intending that the assault should be credited to the Laird of Carse, who was then at feud with the Earl. His purpose in making the attack was to cause the Countess, who was at that time *enceinte,* to miscarry, and thus secure his own succession. The Earl had learned the truth of this matter.

When Lord Glamis came into Carrick as guardian of the fifth Earl, Culzean and the Laird of Bargany resisted him in arms. Shortly thereafter Lord Glamis, attending a Convention of Peers at Stirling, was killed by a shot which was said to have been fired by one of Bargany's men. Culzean at once assumed the guardianship of his nephew. About this time the Laird of Bargany died and was succeeded by his son.

It is now to be shewn how Culzean ranged against him the

young Laird of Bargany and John Mure of Auchendrayne. A certain lady known as Black Bessie Kennedy had been infefted in the Brounston lands by her third husband, William Kennedy of Brounston—lands previously infefted in the Earl of Cassillis. In the course of a dispute that arose, she transferred her rights to the Laird of Bargany, who put her in possession of the six-pound land of Newark. She took up her abode in the house of her ally, but yielded presently to the influence of Culzean and took her departure, whereby the Laird of Bargany was grievously offended. The other quarrel was caused by the fact that Culzean, who had secured for Mure his appointment as Bailie of Carrick, used his influence with the Earl later to have him removed from the office.

A new issue concerning the Earl and Bargany followed on the death of John Baird of Kilhenzie,[1] who had married Bargany's sister. Baird had a son by a former wife, who succeeded him. The young Laird forcibly dispossessed his stepmother of some stores which had been left her by her husband. Bargany, anxious to avenge his sister, raided Kilhenzie and carried off an equal quantity of goods. The Laird of Kilhenzie was one of the Earl's dependants and appealed to him for remedy. The Earl would have marched upon Bargany, but was warned that the Laird would not be taken by surprise and decided to wait for a more convenient season.

Thus far we have as protagonists in these various quarrels Sir Thomas Kennedy of Culzean and his nephew, the Earl of Cassillis, on the one hand, and, on the other, the Laird of Bargany and John Mure of Auchendrayne. The anonymous *Historie of the Kennedyis* is written from the Bargany standpoint, and has been attributed to Mure of Auchendrayne himself. Although it may have been coloured by partisan feeling, there is nothing incredible in its statement that the Earl was resolved to crush the House of Bargany out of existence. It is said that he intended to begin by obtaining a treacherous entrance to Ardstinchar Castle and blowing it up, but that when he conferred with his uncle, he was dissuaded on the ground that the death of the young Laird and his wife, whom he had married out of the King's house—she was a sister of Lord Ochiltree and had been one of the Queen's Maids of Honour—would be

---

[1] Church or wood of Kenneth, Gaelic *Coinneach*.

thought much of by the King and the Queen, and that the destruction of so many innocent persons as would be involved in the blowing up of the castle would be a matter of general lamentation. Culzean advised the Earl to lie in wait for Bargany and his brother when they were abroad hunting, and the Earl accepted his advice. Bargany got wind of the plot against his life and accused Culzean of being a party to it. Culzean assured him that he had given his advice to the Earl merely in order to turn him from his more ruthless purpose. The prospect of peace was not improved by this explanation, nor by a legal victory won by the Earl in an action against Bargany upon the " assignation which he had got from Black Bessie of the lands of Newark ". Bargany took counsel with the Lairds of Auchendrayne and Dunduff and with the Master of Cassillis, the Earl's brother, who had a quarrel of his own with his uncle, and the sequel was an attempt on the life of Culzean.

According to the indictment, the accused had gone to Maybole on the 3rd of January, 1597, armed with hagbuts and pistols, and tied up their horses at the gate of the goodwife of Knockdai. They had then concealed themselves in Thomas Nasmyth's yard, which adjoined Culzean's house in Maybole. Presently Culzean, accompanied by his wife, his eldest son, and his two daughters, came along between the hedges in the yard, and the accused fired eight shots at him. Culzean and his family escaped without hurt.

The leading conspirators were Auchendrayne and Dunduff, and they had become sureties for the appearance of the others before the Court of Justiciary. Dunduff alone appeared. He was fined nine hundred merks for the non-appearance of the rest of the accused, was imprisoned in Edinburgh Castle, and set at liberty on his finding security for the payment of a thousand merks for his share in the outrage and of the other fine. Auchendrayne and the others implicated were now " put to the horn ", that is, outlawed, and their movable goods and gear " escheat ", that is, forfeited to the Crown. Culzean, by way of signifying his approval of the sentence, went to the Tower of Auchendrayne, destroyed all the plenishing, and wrecked the yarding. Mure and his colleagues were the more determined to compass his death. The Earl, on his part, brought an action at law against Bargany for the payment of arrears of teinds and obtained a decreet for forty thousand merks.

The King intervened in the hope of making peace between Cassillis and Bargany. He summoned them to his presence and " gart thame schaik handis ; and also the laird of Colzeone in sum missour : bot not with thair hairttis, because thair particular wes not sett doun at the agreanse ".

The Earl decided at this time to deal more hardly with his Galloway vassals in the matter of rents, and obtained a decreet to break their leases. When he summoned them to a court at Glenluce, they came in such force that they were able to besiege him in his house of Inch. He bethought him of Bargany as a possible source of succour. The minister of Colmonell was with him and became his ambassador, being allowed to pass through the line of the besiegers on the understanding that he was going to his kirk. The minister reached Ardstinchar in the evening and gave Bargany the Earl's message that if he would come to his relief, he would mend all the ill he had done him in the past and value him above all his other kindred to his life's end. Bargany at once " lapp on with forty horse ", ordered reinforcements to follow, and, riding all through the night, relieved the Earl at daybreak. He also acted as arbiter between the Earl and the lairds and effected a compromise. Then " my Lord drew on his bwittis and raid with the Laird to Ardstinchar, being convoyit be the Galloway menne to Glenapp, quhair the Laird of Barganyis frendis and seruandis mett him." He rested that night in the house which he had once intended to blow up ; but when the Laird called upon him some days later to carry out his recent undertakings, the Earl, influenced by Culzean, " geff na ansuer, bot lat the samin pass ouer with silense." Bargany thus acquired a new grievance.

Auchendrayne, who ever appears in the *rôle* of the cool and clever plotter, thought that endeavours should be made to restore peace to Carrick, and it is likely that the thoughts of others were tending the same way. The leaders of the rival factions agreed that there should be a general oblivion of the past quarrels ; Auchendrayne was allowed to return to the King's peace ; and to signalize the brighter day that was supposed to be dawning, Culzean's daughter was married to John Mure, younger of Auchendrayne. Mure did not prove himself a desirable husband or an agreeable son-in-law, and in entering into the marriage Helen Kennedy may have been immolating herself in the interests of conciliation. If this was so, her sacrifice was in vain.

There was soon a fresh outbreak of trouble between Bargany and the Earl. The former maintained a claim to the teinds, or tithe crop, of the lands of Girvanmains although the Earl had obtained a decreet against them on account of a debt owed him by Bargany. Bargany forestalled the Earl's intention of seizing the crop by occupying the stackyard at Girvanmains in such force that the Earl was balked. The Earl, however, had a similar decreet against the lands of Dungarth, and, determined not to be beaten there, sent his servants to reap the corn. Bargany descended on the farm, seized the grain that had been cut, and carried it off to Ardstinchar, justifying himself on the plea that the decreet against the land did not include the crop. Two days later the Earl arrived at Dungarth with a little army to reap the corn that was still uncut. Bargany appeared with nine hundred men. The Earl's force was larger, but not so well armed. A bloody contest was averted through the mediation of Lord Cathcart, whose wife was related to the Earl, and whose son had married Bargany's sister. In the end Bargany took the corn, agreeing to find security for the payment to the Earl of the duty on the land.

The Earl considered that Bargany had become inconveniently strong and sought to depress him by vexatious legal proceedings until the Laird's heart grew hotter than ever against his chief. The *Historie* states that he designed the Earl's death and that it was arranged that Girvanmains and the young Laird of Blairquhan should lie in wait for him near Ardstinchar Castle as he was riding from Carrick into Galloway. The scheme miscarried, however, for as he approached the ambuscade, the conspirators saw that he was accompanied by Culzean. According to the *Historie,* Culzean was privy to the plot, and it had been understood by Bargany and Auchendrayne that he was not to ride with the Earl so that he might not be implicated in the affair. Mure went to Castle Kennedy to upbraid him for his deceit. The Earl learned of his presence, confronted him, and charged him with being concerned in Bargany's design to murder him. Although Mure vehemently denied the charge, the Earl meant to keep him a prisoner; but Mure contrived to escape. The Earl thereafter took action upon a decreet which he had obtained against the Laird of Blairquhan and deprived him of Kelly Castle and Killenhow. Blairquhan retaliated by sending his son to be in Bargany's immediate following and to foment strife between him and the Earl.

It appeared to the conspirators that Culzean must have revealed their plot to the Earl, and they resolved to be avenged. Learning that he was about to go into Galloway, they arranged to entrap and slay him at Ardmillan Hill. It happened that Auchendrayne was about to have a meeting with him, and it was obvious that if the plot succeeded, he might be supposed to have had a hand in it. He therefore sent a letter to warn him of his danger, and Culzean kept a servant riding in front of him to spring any ambush. The conspirators seized the servant, and Culzean turned back, rode to Edinburgh, and made a complaint to the King. Bargany was summoned to the royal presence. He denied any knowledge of the affair, and when Culzean asserted that he had witnesses to support his accusation and these were produced, their evidence cleared Bargany. Once more the King sought to make peace between him and the Earl, and " gart thaim drink togidder and schaik handis." New dissensions soon arose ; there was a fresh plot against the life of the Earl ; and he decided that the time had come to put a period to Bargany's activities.

In the month of December, 1601, Bargany had business in Ayr, and although he knew that it was now dangerous for him to pass through the Earl's country, he rode thither with about a dozen horsemen. The Earl heard of this and sent spies to Ayr in order that when Bargany began his return journey, he might have instant knowledge of it. Meanwhile he gathered a force of twenty musketeers and two hundred horsemen armed with pikes. Auchendrayne rode to Ayr to warn Bargany of the Earl's preparations and besought him to remain in the burgh as he had not enough men to protect him. The Laird laughed at Auchendrayne's forebodings, but found eighty men among the burghers of Ayr to strengthen his company.

Thick snow was falling when he led his men out into the open country. They crossed the Doon by the old bridge and then halted while Auchendrayne once more urged the Laird to turn back as his men were still too few. Bargany, however, would not be discouraged. Addressing his followers, he said, " Sirs, I am heir to protest befoir God, I am nocht to seik the bluid of me Lord, nor his dishonour, in na sortt ; bot ryd hame to my Hous, in peace, giff he will lat me. And giff me Lord be to persew me, I hoip ye will all do your dewitteis, as becumis menne ; and he that will not be willing to do this, for my luiff and kyndnes, he will ather say he will tairy with me to the end, or leaff me now at this present ! " They all shouted that they would go on with him whatever befell, and advanced in two companies, Bargany leading the one, and Cathcart, the young Laird of Carleton, the other. The snow was still falling so thickly that " nane cud seine the lenthe of ane lanse befoir him " ; but as they approached Maybole, it cleared, and they saw against the white background of the slope beyond the Brockloch[1] Burn the dark figures of their enemies. Bargany was anxious to avoid a conflict. " I will nocht persew me lord," he said, " bot I will eschew all cummer, alse far as I may " ; and to this end he made to pass Maybole without entering it. The Earl ordered his men to attack, and his musketeers opened fire. Bargany was riding at the head of his company with a few other lairds. The fire brought down Knockdaw's horse and shot the bridle out of the hand of Bargany's brother, Drummurchie,[2] who fell and dislocated his shoulder. The burghers of Ayr broke away and fled. " Gude sir," cried Bargany, " we ar ouer few ! " With three other lairds and his page Bargany charged the Earl's horsemen " in sik sortt as the young laird of Grinak was strukin throw the chin, and he and horse baith strukin to the eird, and Row Cuninghame, Pochquhairnis broder, was strukin in at the knie with ane lanse and out at the buttok", and the Earl's steward was killed. Bargany's page also lay dead, two others of his few followers were unhorsed, Auchendrayne lay in the snow, seriously wounded in the thigh, and while Bargany was engaged with two spearmen, a third, whom he was not watching, " ane fellow callitt Johne Dik ", drove a lance into his throat. He could fight no more, and when he had turned his horse from the fray, fell to the ground. His friends carried him back to Ayr, where he died in a few days. " He was the brawest manne that was to be gottin in ony land ; " says the historian of the Kennedies, " of hiche statour and weill maid ; his hair blak, bott of ane cumlie feace ; the brawest horsmanne and the ebest of mony at all pastymis, for he was feirse and feirry and winder

---

[1] Gaelic *broclach*, a badger warren.
[2] Gaelic *druim Murcha*, hill-ridge of Murdoch.

nembill. He was bot about the aige of 25 yeair quhane he was
slayne, bot of his aige the maist wyise he might be, for gif he
had tyme to add experience to his witt, he hed been by his
marrowis." The Earl escaped any penalty for his death on the
ground that Bargany's force had included certain outlaws whom
he had been authorized to pursue with fire and sword. He had
recovered an undisputed supremacy in Carrick.

This did not mean, however, that there was an end of plottings
and deeds of blood. Bargany had been devoted friends who
would have considered themselves disloyal to his memory if
they had allowed matters to rest. His death cried out for
expiation.[1] Thomas Kennedy of Drummurchie, Bargany's
brother, and Walter Mure, the Laird of Cloncaird, were the
leading spirits of the faction, and there was always the sinister
figure of Auchendrayne in the background, usually in the
confidence of both parties. The recollection of old grudges
caused them to turn their thoughts to Sir Thomas Kennedy of
Culzean, and circumstances arose to give them an opportunity
of singling him out for a blow. Culzean had occasion to go to
Edinburgh, and before setting out sent a messenger to ask Mure
to meet him on the following day near the town of Ayr that they
might confer on some business matters. The messenger did
not find Mure in Maybole, and therefore asked the schoolmaster
to write down the request in a letter which was sent to Mure
at his house of Auchendrayne by the hand of " ane puir scholar,
quha beggit his leirning, callit William Dalrumpill ". The lad
brought the letter back and asserted that Mure was not at
Auchendrayne.

A chapel called S. Leonard's stood in a clump of trees among
sandhills about a mile south of Ayr. As Culzean rode this way
with his servant, expecting to meet Mure and anticipating no
danger, Drummurchie, Cloncaird, and four others broke from

[1] "At this tyme, me Lord of Abercorne, and the haill freindis,
concluditt that the buryiall of the Laird of Bargany . . . suld be on
the xv day off September . . . in the New Kirk of Ballantry; quhilk
the Lady had caussit build for hir husband, quhair scho had
gartt sett wp ane glorieous towme . . . His sister-sone, Young
Auchindrayne, beirand the Banner of Rewendge, quhairin was
payntitt his portratour, with all his wondis, with his sone sittand at
his knevis, and this deattone writtine betuix his handis, JUDGE
AND REWENDGE MY CAUS, O LORD!"
—*Historie of the Kennedyis.*

among the trees and slew him " with shots and strokes ". The
murderers were put to the horn, but evaded all endeavours to
bring them to justice.

Mure had taken care to be at home on the day of the murder ;
but the Earl believed that he had been a party to the plot, and
resolved that he should be punished. As Justiciary of the district he would, no doubt, have been satisfied to have this done
by ordinary process of law ; as head of the Kennedy family, he
was prepared to use cruder methods and entered into the following agreement : " We, JOHNE EARLE OF CASSILLIS, Lord
Kennedy, &c., Bindis and Oblissis ws, that howsovne our
broder HEW KENNEDY of Brounstoun, with his complices,
taikis THE LAIRD OF AUCHINDRANEIS lyf, that we sall mak guid
and thankfull payment to him and thame of the sowme of
tuelff hundreth merkis, zeirlie, togidder with corne to sex horsis,
ay and quhill we ressaw thame in houshold with our self :
Beginning the first payment immediatlie after thair committing
of the said deid. ATTOUR, howsovne we ressaw thame in
houshold, we sall pay to the twa serwing gentillmen the feis,
zeirlie, as our awin houshald serwandis. And heirto we Obliss
ws, vpoun our honour. SUBSCRYVIT with our hand, AT
MAYBOLE, the ferd day of September, 1602.

" JOHNE ERLE OFF CASSILLIS."

Common rumour likewise connected Mure with the murder
of Culzean. Mure was aware of an atmosphere of suspicion,
and it became a primary object with him to conceal the fact
that he had been cognizant of Culzean's intended journey to
Edinburgh. It appeared subsequently that he had really
received the letter sent by the hand of the " puir schollar ",
William Dalrymple ; that after reading it he had closed it
again, returned it to the lad, and instructed him to tell the
schoolmaster and Culzean's servant that when he had gone to
Auchendrayne, he had not found the Laird at home. Besides
this, he had sent a message to Drummurchie informing him of
the journey Culzean was to make the next day and shewing
how Bargany's death might be avenged. It was important,
therefore, to ensure the silence of Dalrymple. Mure had him
carried off to Auchendrayne, where he kept him for two or three
months. Meanwhile Mure had to answer a summons to appear
at the bar of the Privy Council on the charge of being art and

part of the murder of Sir Thomas Kennedy. As the essential witness was not forthcoming, the prosecution failed; but the Court ordered Mure to find caution in a thousand pounds for his subsequent appearance if he were summoned. Auchendrayne now considered that he would be safer if Dalrymple were removed from Ayrshire, and contrived to send him to the care of a friend in Arran, Montgomerie, the Laird of Skelmorlie; but Dalrymple did not like his new home and came back. Auchendrayne now designed a longer journey for him, and had him shipped to Flanders as a recruit for the Scottish Horse. If Dalrymple died for his country, Auchendrayne's mind would be at rest. Two or three years passed, and then, to Mure's dismay, Dalrymple, just returned from the wars, was seen in the district. It appeared to Auchendrayne and the younger Mure, who had also been concerned in the plot against Culzean, that more effectual measures must be used for ending an obvious risk.

They lodged Dalrymple with James Bannatyne, one of Mure's tenants, at the farm of Chapeldonan near Girvan, and purchased Bannatyne's aid in the carrying out of their design with "ane Lyfrent Tak of his rowme of Chapel-Donane, all writtin with Young Auchindranes awin hand". It was arranged that Bannatyne should bring the intended victim "to the Sandis of Girvan" on a certain night at ten o'clock. As the Mures rode to the place of meeting, they carried spades. At first some confer- ence took place among the conspirators. Bannatyne recoiled from the idea of murder and suggested that Dalrymple should be sent to Ireland. The elder Mure seemed to incline to this plan; but hesitation was dispelled by his son, who rushed suddenly at Dalrymple, threw him on the sand, and did not let him go until, assisted by his father, he had strangled him. They proposed to bury the body on the shore, where the rising tide would wipe out all signs of the deed, but found that whenever they dug a hole, it was filled immediately with water. They then drew the corpse out into the sea so far as they could wade, and committed it to the deep, hoping that an off-shore wind would take it to the Irish coast. The wind did not blow; the body rested all the next day where they had left it; and they waited in a fever of anxiety. At night they decided to bring the body ashore and bury it on land, but could not find it. They rode away uneasily from the scene of their vigil. The body had at last been carried seawards by the wind. It was tossed about for the space of five days and was then borne back to the place where it had begun its aimless voyaging. Some peasants saw it butting the shore among the foam and carried it to the nearest churchyard, where it was buried.

The report of the discovery spread abroad, and the Earl of Cassillis thought it desirable that an opportunity should be given for identifying the body. The mother and sister of Dalrymple asserted that he was the murdered man. Suspicion was directed upon Mure by a story that his little granddaughter had wandered into Girvan Church, where the body was exhibited, and that as she stood looking at it, blood had flowed.

Mure now devised measures to clear his tracks. As formerly Dalrymple, so now Bannatyne was the source of danger. He was sent to Ireland, and when the Earl of Abercorn caused him to return to Ayrshire, Auchendrayne hired James Pennicuik to murder him. Before this could be done, the Earl of Cassillis had induced Bannatyne to make confession before the Privy Council. This cleared the way for the trial of the Mures, and on the 17th of July, 1611, they, with Bannatyne, were placed at the bar of the High Court. Auchendrayne was charged with being art and part of the murder of Sir Thomas Kennedy of Culzean, and all three with the murder of William Dalrymple. They were found guilty and sentenced to death. Bannatyne, however, received the royal pardon and was set at liberty.

Reference has been made already to the theory that the *Historie of the Kennedyis* was written by the elder Mure. It is supported by the fact that the *Historie* breaks off thus : " Now, wpone malice for this caus, the Eirle of Caissillis and his (freindis) raissitt ane bruitt on Auchindrayne and his sone, and this manne of his, that thay suld haue forgadderitt with this boy William Dalrumpill, quha, as thay allegitt, was the cairreyar off this letter to Auchindrayne fra Colzeone ; and that thay, for to hyd the same letter, thay thrie had slayne him. . . ."

## CHAPTER XXVIII

A FORMER minister of Maybole, the Rev. Roderick Lawson,
has written some pleasant notes on the town and its neighbourhood, and is excellent on the subject of its name. "Be the
etymology what it may, the name itself in its modern form is
one of which any town may well feel proud. What a fine, mouth-
filling sound it has! There is no name of a town along the whole
line of the Glasgow and South-Western Railway which is for
a moment to be compared with it. Ayr, for instance, is plainly
too short, and Kilmarnock too long. Troon and Beith are
insignificant. Girvan and Greenock want sound, and Paisley
wants strength. Kilwinning is too smooth, and Ardrossan too
rough. Even Glasgow is no better than it should be. But
Maybole is simply perfect." It is a great thing when a minister
can be thoroughly enthusiastic about the name of his parish
if about nothing else! The name probably means " the town
by the marsh ". A bit of land, formerly a swamp, but now
drained and cultivated, is still called The Bog.

I entered Maybole from the north and should advise anyone
else to do otherwise. After surmounting the last of the undulations stretching between the river Doon and the town,
I came upon some ugly factory buildings and heard the grinding
and humming of machinery within. It might have been a
fragment of the Kingston district of Glasgow! Maybole, I
may explain in passing, has a large bootmaking industry and

also makes agricultural implements. One may congratulate
Maybole on the enterprise and wealth represented by its chimney-
stalks and pass on to more attractive subjects.

The old castle in High Street arrests one. Look at its narrow
tower, its crow-stepped gables, its mouldings, the quaint head-

*Maybole.*

ings of the little windows, the antique turrets, the oriel window
overhanging the old front, and feel grateful for its preservation !

It is believed to have been built about the middle of the seventeenth century, and was formerly the town house of the Earls
of Cassillis, for if Maybole could not be the county town of
Ayrshire, it was at least the capital of Carrick. At one time

there were twenty-eight " gentlemen's houses " here. No
doubt, the Earl's was the grandest; but if some of the
others even approached it in beauty, it would have been
worth while to thread one's way through several miles of factories to see them. The building which has served as the Tolbooth for nearly two centuries and a half is known to have been
originally the town house of the Lairds of Blairquhan; the
modern Town Buildings, however, have been built against it,
and it is now impossible to infer its aspect as a domestic structure.

The Collegiate Church, founded in 1371 by Sir John Kennedy
of Dunure in order that daily services might be celebrated for
the happy state of himself, his wife Mary, and their children,
is the oldest building of all. It was served by a provost and
three other priests. Most of the windows have been built up;
but it is still possible to admire their tracery and an elaborately-
carved doorway. After the Reformation the church fell into
disrepair and became a mere place of burial for the Cassillis
and one or two other families. A tablet at the east end of the
church gives the names of members of the Cassillis family who
were laid here between 1701 and 1832. It is quite likely, however, that the whole line of the former " Kings of Carrick "
were buried here—David, the first Earl, who fell at Flodden;
Gilbert, the second Earl, who was killed at Prestwick by Hugh
Campbell of Loudoun; Gilbert, the third Earl, who died at
Dieppe, it was supposed of poison; Gilbert, the fourth Earl,
who roasted Allan Stewart; John, the fifth Earl, who
caused the Laird of Bargany to be killed; and John, " the
grave and solemn Earl ", who represented the Church of Scotland at the Westminster Assembly. A tombstone in another
part of the interior bears the following statement within inverted commas : " He cannot return to us, but with God's
help we hope to go to Him "—surely a remarkable instance
of careless quotation !

The way from High Street to the Auld College, as the church
is called, lies down a very steep lane known formerly as the
Back Vennal, but now named John Knox Street ; and on the
right-hand side there is the old residence of the Provost of the
College. It is labelled " John Knox's House " because it was
the scene of a great disputation between the Reformer and
the last Abbot of Crossraguel on the question whether the bread
and wine brought forth by Melchizedek to Abraham were a

type of the Mass or not. The debate took place in September, 1562, and lasted for three days. The Abbot could not prove the affirmative, nor Knox the negative; so the logomachy ended where it began.

The story of the six Maybole men who lost their lives on

*Doorway of the Collegiate Church, Maybole.*

account of their fidelity to the Covenant differs from the normal types of martyrdom. The men were among the twelve hundred prisoners who were taken at Bothwell Bridge in 1679 and confined in Greyfriars Churchyard in Edinburgh. They were also among the two hundred and fifty-seven who were shipped at Leith for the American plantations. The prisoners were shut up in a hold that was much too small for them, and endured twelve days of its horrors before the ship set sail. The voyage to the Orkney Islands took a whole fortnight. Anchor had been cast off the Mainland of Orkney on the 10th of December when a storm arose, the ship broke from its moorings, and drove upon the Moul Head of Deerness. The crew scrambled ashore, but the hatches had been battened down upon the prisoners, and the master of the vessel refused to lift them. As the ship went to pieces on the rocks, forty-eight men struggled to land, but the remaining two hundred and nine were drowned, and among them were the six from Maybole. These men surely deserve to be remembered along with those who perished by the bullet or the sword. The names of the Maybole martyrs were Mungo Eccles, Thomas Horne, Robert MacGarron, John MacHarrie, John MacWhirter, and William Rodger. Their memorial stands in a corner of a field near the town.

A scrutiny of the names on the map makes it plain that, however many of the roads radiating from Maybole be left untravelled, the one leading to Kirkoswald must not ; for this is the way to Crossraguel Abbey, the greatest of the old ecclesiastical institutions in Carrick and the best preserved of the monastic buildings of Scotland.[1]

As I followed the road, it was interesting to recall what Stevenson had written about it.[2] It is on the whole a dull one, and he did not say much. Yet it is a little surprising that he

[1] The Order to which Crossraguel Abbey belonged had its headquarters at Cluny in Burgundy, and French influence appears in the architecture, " noticeably in the apsidal termination of the choir, a distinctly Continental feature and one rare in Scotland, as distinguished from the square end more peculiar to this country ". The apse is polygonal. The recurring damages and repairs to which the abbey has been subjected make it impossible to assign it to any one period. An attempt to reconstruct its architectural history has been made by Mr. James A. Morris in *Charters of the Abbey of Crosraguel*. The abbey was fortified with strong towers.

[2] Stevenson's essay, *A Winter's Walk in Carrick and Galloway*, is belied by its title. It was left a fragment unfortunately and contains nothing of the Galloway part of the tour. In a letter written in February, 1876, Stevenson says, " I went to Ayr, Maybole, Girvan, Ballantrae, Stranraer, Glenluce, and Wigton. I shall make an article of it some day soon, ' A Winter's Walk in Carrick and Galloway '. I had a good time."

considered the phrase, "dilapidated castles and monasteries", enough for Baltersan[1] Castle and Crossraguel[2] Abbey. There is, indeed, little to detain the fancy about the keep; but in the case of one who wrote so much about the monastery of Our Lady of the Snows we might have looked to hear something of the convent. It is true, Our Lady of the Snows was the

*Crossraguel Abbey.*

home of a living piety and a hospitable lodging-place as well, while this is a deserted ruin; but, as the local writer whom I have quoted already says, "the sacristy and the chapter-house, the cloisters and the cellars, the scriptorium and the gatehouse tower are all nearly intact, and one almost expects as one

[1] Gaelic *bail tarsuinn*, village set obliquely.
[2] Pron. Crossráygel, 1225-65 Cros- and Corsragmol. *Circa* 1560 Corsragvell. Prob. Gaelic *crois ràthaig mhaoil*, cross beside the bare or towerless fort.—Johnston.

wanders among the ruins to see a monk coming round the corner with his bare feet and shaven crown ", a suggestion that might have come from Stevenson himself.  Moreover, the reader who turns to the two magnificent quarto volumes of the Abbey Charters will find some very lively matter.  He will also learn the outstanding facts about the convent : that it was one of the few Clugniac settlements in Scotland, that its founder was Duncan, the first Earl of Carrick, that it had the Kings and Queens of Scotland, both of the Bruce and of the Stewart line, for its benefactors—Robert the First may have been educated here—that it held temporal sway over nearly the whole of Carrick, and that it maintained its witness to the things of the spirit for three centuries and a half until, when its life was thought to be gone, the eagles were gathered together.  The explanation of Stevenson's silence—the sufficient explanation— doubtless is that he did not happen to be in the mood for monasteries that winter morning.

He thought the village of Kirkoswald " Highland-looking ". Had his acquaintance with Carrick and Galloway been longer and more intimate, I am sure he would have joined the ranks of those who protest against this kind of description when it is applied to the south-western counties, who think it a superficial sort of appreciation which says of Galloway that it is as fine, or nearly as fine, as the Highlands, that its hills, its moors, its rivers, its lochs, its villages are " Highland looking ", for to know Galloway intimately is to have for it an affection that can be given to no other part of the earth—there are some people who fall in love with it at sight—and to bear about with one a treasury of visions of glorious bog-myrtle-scented moors stretching to the skirts of most memorable hills, of weird mountain desolations with no associated sounds save the croak of the raven, the screech of the hawk, and the whisper of the wind in the heath, of wooded glens where pellucid floods swirl over smooth rock or are shattered into dazzling foam among silvery boulders, of shining pastoral villages where peat-reek floats from the chimneys and its smell is carried on the air, of a far-drawn sea-board broken by little bays and estuaries, where woods embowering old-world homes come down to the edge of the waters, and one would no more say that Galloway was Highland-looking than one would say that the lady who commands one's heart's devotion was as adorable as Helen of Troy.

The ruined church of S. Oswald is very old. It was within its walls that Quentin Kennedy, the Abbot of Crossraguel, preached those sermons against the Reformation which involved him in his debate with John Knox. It was in this church also that Robert Burns worshipped in the summer of 1776, when he "learned to look unconcernedly on a large tavern bill", made love to Peggy Thomson, and studied trigonometry in the parish school. The churchyard is the most carefully kept that I have seen in these parts. There is no rank growth of grass and weeds a yard in height, but a smooth sward of a rich green such as one may find in a College court. Visitors come to see the graves of Burns's maternal ancestors, of his schoolmaster, Hugh Rodger, and of Douglas Graham, the original of "Tam o' Shanter".

There is more than one way of going from Maybole to the moorland village of Straiton. The most direct runs through Crosshill; but it is better to leave it about a mile and a half from Maybole and take a short byway running north-east and bringing you in a few minutes to a road leading through Kirkmichael. The churchyards of Kirkmichael and Straiton both have martyrs' graves. Gilbert MacAdam was attending a prayer-meeting near the House of Kirkmichael when he was made a prisoner by Sir Alexander Kennedy of Culzean, who was in command of a company of militia. He attempted to escape, and the soldiers shot him. The inscription on the memorial stone has had something of a history. The lines conferring an undesirable notoriety on his persecutor were at one time obliterated. "Old Mortality" carved the lettering afresh on a narrow block and inserted it in the stone. The epitaph runs thus :

> HERE · LYES · GILLBERT ·
> MᶜADAM    ·    WHO    ·    WAS ·
> SHOT · IN ·: THIS · PARISH ·
> BY · THE · LAIRD · OF · CO
> LZEAN · AND· BALLOCHMIL
> FOR · HIS · ADHERANCE · TO
> THE ·WORD · OF · GOD ·AND ·
> SCOTLANDS      ·      COVENAN
> TED · WORK · OF · REFORM
> 1685                    · ATION

*(marginal: JULY)*

I have referred to the poverty of northern Carrick in the matter of delectable roads. For a few miles beyond Kirk-

michael as you go towards Straiton, however, the way is enclosed among trees and runs high on the left bank of the
Girvan Water, winding and doubling with surprises that fairly
take your breath away, and giving now a lengthwise and now
a broadside glimpse of quiet pools and little cascades in the
river. If the time of your travelling be early summer, when
the leaves are most delicate and the greens most vivid and the
waters abundant, and if the day be one of strong sunshine,
your journey will stand out among your memories of " sweet
wayfaring."

Straiton Church has a pre-Reformation aisle with a Gothic
window and an outside staircase. No attempt was made to
build the modern part of the church in harmony with it. Indeed,
the former could scarcely be balder than it is. The aisle looks
as if it would gladly shake its unnatural companion into well-
merited ruin.

The martyr's grave is that of Thomas MacHaffie, the son
of a farmer in the parish. He was hiding in a glen on the farm
of Linfern about three miles south of Straiton when the dragoons
who were scouring the country caught sight of him. He was
suffering from a fever brought on by his fugitive life in the
wilds, but fled to the house of a friend. He was so weak that
on arriving he threw himself down on a bed. Here the soldiers
made an easy capture, and on his declining to take the Abjuration Oath led him out and shot him. The inscription is :

```
          HERE  ·  LYES  ·  THOMAS
          MᶜHAFFIE · MARTYR · 1686.
          THO · I · WAS · SICK · AND
          LIKE      ·   TO    ·    DIE
          YET · BLOODY · BRUCE
          DID    ·   MURDER   ·  ME
          CAUSE  ·  I  ·  ADHERED
          IN    ·   MY   ·   STATION
          TO  ·  OUR  ·  COVENANT
          ED      ·      REFORMATION
          MY · BLOOD · FOR · VENG
          ANCE · YET · DOTH · CALL
          UPON  ·  ZIONS  ·  HATERS
          ALL
```

Two memorable roads run from Straiton, one east and
another south. The former crosses an undulating moor till it
reaches Dalmellington, which is about seven miles away.

Sometimes, when the hills are out of sight, you might think you were in the heart of the Russian steppes. The latter climbs at first through a wild and grim hill-country that might be a miniature Caucasus and then leads you on a long trail through the desolate moors that lie at the feet of the mountain giants of Shalloch on Minnoch, Tarriefessock, Kirriereoch, and The Merrick towards Newton Stewart.

Before leaving Carrick we may note that, of the castles that have been named, Penkill in Dailly parish is one of the few that have been kept continuously in repair. It was built in the sixteenth century by Adam Boyd, first laird of Penkill and a grandson of the first Lord Boyd, who was one of the Regents and Great Chamberlain of Scotland during the minority of James the Third. It is the subject of William Bell Scott's sonnet-sequence published, with two short poems in the ballad form, under the title, *The Old Scotch House*. The great circular staircase in the modern addition was decorated by Scott with a set of mural paintings illustrating *The King's Quhair*. Dante Gabriel Rossetti was also a visitor here in 1869. Mr. William Sharp states that the Penwhapple Burn, which flows through the castle grounds, is the " wandering water, ever whispering " of *The Stream's Secret*.

Of the members of the Boyd family, one of the most famous was Zachary, who was born in 1585 and in 1623 was appointed minister of the Barony parish in Glasgow. His chief prose work was *The last Batell of the Soule in Death*, but he is better known by *Zion's Flowers*, a collection of metrical versions of Bible narratives. This work, devout in spirit, sometimes comical in expression, is very readable and was long known popularly as " Zachary Boyd's Bible ". He was still minister of the Barony parish when he died in 1653.

It is said that when he was making his will, his wife suggested that he should leave something to their common friend, Mr. James Durham. " Na, na, Margaret," he said; " I'll lea' him naething but thy bonnie sel' ! " Another version credits him with " I'll lea' him what I canna keep frae him ". When he died Mrs. Boyd became Mrs. James Durham. In his will he had divided his estate between his widow and the University of Glasgow.

Robert Boyd (1578–1627), Principal of Glasgow University, was the son of James Boyd of Trochrig and a cousin of Zachary.

*The Foot of Loch Doon.*

# CHAPTER XXIX

### TO THE DUNGEON BY LOCH DOON

Loch Doon—The story of The Murder Hole—Tradition of Loch
Doon Castle—Ancient canoes—John Stevenson, Covenanter—
King Robert and the miller's wife of Polmaddy.

THE head of Loch Doon is distant from Dalmellington about
ten miles, and there is a road nearly all the way. On leaving the
highway to Carsphairn, you cross some heights that are thinly
wooded with remains of the ancient forest, and then descend
to the point where the river Doon issues from the loch and
goes tossing down its rocky bed through the narrow, wooded
Ness [1] Glen. I remember the unusual beauty that the place
wore on a day early in January. For two or three days before,
heavy rain had been falling. The links of the Doon near Dalmellington were hidden beneath the far-spreading overflow of
Bogton Loch and every hillside burn was roaring. This
morning, however, the rain had ceased, and the sky cleared.
Mist never looks so beautiful as when it is drifting among pines
and the sun is shining. It swathed those low, wooded hills
at the foot of Loch Doon, so that one could not have told whether

---

[1] Gaelic *an eas*, the cataract.

they were low or great. Below them spread the blue waters,
rippling under the light breeze.

On the west of the loch there rises a broad tract of moor in
long sweeps and curves, and in the lower parts are some small,

*Ness Glen.*

rarely-visited sheets of water. A place called Rowantree on
the farther side was the scene of one of the traditional tales
of Galloway, the story of The Murder Hole.[1]  No travellers
came that way for pleasure, few came on business, and these

became fewer as rumours of unexplained horrors enacted in that waste spread through distant villages in the surrounding country. It was said that several persons who were known to have entered the moor had not been seen again. Officers of justice came to investigate, but left the mystery as it was. Other persons disappeared, and terror fell upon the few inhabitants. Some spoke of strange cries heard in the dark of the night. A shepherd who had lost his way in that quarter reported that he had seen three men struggling violently at a considerable distance, and that the struggle had ended with the sudden vanishing of one. The people of the moor began to leave it for less alarming neighbourhoods, until there remained only an old woman and her two sons, who complained bitterly of the poverty that hindered them from following so natural a course.

You are now to imagine a pedlar youth crossing the moor in haste amid the darkness of a night in November. Following the path among those lochs and mosses, he sees before him a light. He is more than half regretting his hardihood in making the journey when he remembers, with a feeling of relief, an old woman's cottage at which he had lodged for a night in the previous year along with a considerable company of travellers. He recalls also some eagerness on the part of his hosts to retain his company when the other travellers were going on their way, and looks now for a kindly reception. He comes close up to the cottage and knocks. The door is not opened, but an instant hubbub arises within. The youth steps aside to a window and looks into the lighted interior. The woman is hastily sprinkling sand on the floor. The men are crushing something large into a great chest.

A mischievous whim seizes the youth, and he taps on the window. All start round with such obvious dismay that he begins to be afraid ; but before he can retreat one of the men appears suddenly at the door, and, gripping him by the arm, hustles him into the cottage.

" I am the pedlar who came to you last year," he cried.

" Are you alone ? " inquired the woman.

" Yes," said the boy.

" Then you are welcome," said one of the men.

The pedlar was made to seat himself by the fire, and was not reassured as he furtively studied the dwellers in the cottage.

Almost immediately he was taken to a little room, where he was to pass the night. Everything here was in disarray. The curtains which were meant to screen the bed appeared to have been torn down violently. There was a table that had been broken. A stool lay on its side. The fastening of the door had been wrenched, and was now useless. The youth lay down on the bed and remained awake for a long time, imagining unnumbered possibilities and listening anxiously; but as no new cause of alarm arose, fell presently into an uneasy sleep. He was startled broad awake by a cry close at hand. He raised himself on the bed, looked around, and noticed a stream of blood creeping under the door. He stepped down silently, moved across the room, and put his eye to a chink, and almost smiled at his fears when he saw that it was a goat that had been killed; but, before he stepped back, heard that which renewed them a thousand-fold.

"An easier job than yesterday's," said the man who held the goat. "I wish all the throats were cut as easily. Did ever you hear such a noise as was made last night?"

"The Murder Hole is the thing for me. It makes a cleaner job. You have them dead and buried to your hand at once, and no signs left."

"Which is it to be for him?" asked the woman.

The elder son drew across his throat the knife that was wet with the goat's blood.

In three steps the listener was at the window of his room. He wrenched back the casement and scrambled into the darkness, but not apparently unheard. From the inside of the cottage came the sudden cry, "Loose the bloodhound!" The boy ran in a frenzy of fear, stumbling over embedded stones and slipping among moss-hags. The baying of the bloodhound soon broke the quiet of the dark moor, and along with it were heard the voices of the men as they urged it on to the pursuit. The pedlar stumbled once more and fell this time with violence upon a heap of stones. Wearing nothing but the shirt in which he had fled, he was badly cut, and lay there dazed and bleeding. His pursuers were now so near that he felt as if the edge of that knife, stained with the goat's blood, were already at his throat. He staggered to his feet, and again rushed onwards. The hound came to the place where he had fallen. It found blood there, regarded its work as done, and could not be persuaded to take up the scent again. The pedlar continued his terrified flight until the morning, when he came to a village. The indignation aroused by his story was none the less great that several of the inhabitants had lost relatives or friends in the manner that had been unaccountable hitherto. The male population set out immediately to seize the authors of the outrages, and on reaching their abode, nearly tore them limb from limb before hanging them on gibbets. Before their execution the criminals confessed to the destruction of nearly fifty persons in The Murder Hole, a narrow pool of enormous depth hid among the long grass of the moor. When the cottage was ransacked, there was found in the great chest the body of their last victim.

A pleasanter tradition concerns Loch Doon Castle, which stood until 1935 on a now submerged island near the head of the loch. During the wars of the fourteenth century the stronghold was besieged by the English, who, having failed to take it by assault, proposed to flood it by raising the waters of the loch. At the point where the river begins they built a barrier of earth and stones, and for additional security lined it with raw hides. As the water crept up the castle walls one of the besieged soldiers, named MacNab, volunteered to cut the dam. In the dark of midnight he slipped into the water with a large " bonnet sword " folded in his cap, swam down the middle of the loch, and reached the embankment unnoticed. He broke it at several points, but before he could escape, the pent-up waters swept away the obstruction and him along with it, so that he was battered to death as the liberated flood raged through the Ness Glen. It is said that, in recognition of the service he had rendered his country, a grant of land was conferred on his son. It still bears the name of Macnabston,[1] and is now a part of the farm of Beoch. It may have been just after this incident that the defenders of the castle landed on the Carrick shore of the loch and, meeting the English on a moorland height, which is still called the Brucean Hill, defeated them.

A discovery made in 1826 may take one back to a much earlier century than that of the War of Independence. In the dry summer of that year some fishers observed several canoes lying on the bottom near the Castle Island. These were raised from

---

[1] According to another version it was the reward of a traitor who yielded the castle to the English when it was held for Bruce by Sir Christopher de Seton after the battle of Methven.

their immemorial resting-place and were found to have been hollowed out of oak trees. Some of them were placed in a pond at the foot of the loch, but were removed when the loch was made a war-time hydroplane base.

The southward-stretching moor lies between two series of hills that seem to meet on the horizon. It is now as if you were in the midst of a colossal kind of avenue sweeping upwards to the north side of Craigtarson and the brink of The Cauldron. It was probably up this avenue that John of Lorn led his Highlanders in quest of the Bruce in 1307 ; but, except that some of the persecuted Covenanters sought refuge in these wilds, nothing of any note has happened here since then.

*The Head of Loch Doon, as it was.*

The hills were usually shrouded in mist when John Stevenson, the author of *A Rare Soul-Strengthening and Comforting Cordial for Old and Young Christians*, had occasion to travel this way. Stevenson is described on the title-page of his book as " Land-labourer in the Parish of Daily in Carrick, who died in the year 1728 ", and he includes an account of " what strange and remarkable providences he was trysted with". " I must own to His praise and glory that God dealt well with my soul when He led me into the wilderness, and as I escaped the sword of the enemy, so I found grace in the wilderness ; yea, during my nine years' suffering, I was much filled with joy and peace in believing. I was made to take joyfully the spoiling of my goods, and with pleasure for His name's sake wandered in deserts and in mountains, in dens and caves of the earth. I lay four months in the coldest season of the year in a hay-stack in my father's garden, and a whole February in the open fields not far from Camragen, and this I did without the least prejudice from the night air: one night, when lying in the fields near to the Carrick-Miln, I was all covered with snow in the morning. Many nights have I lain with pleasure in the churchyard of Old Daily, and made a grave my pillow; frequently have I resorted to the old walls above the glen, near to Camragen, and there sweetly rested." In the later part of his life he suffered from scrofula and " found

*The Castle Island, Loch Doon, as it was.*

an inclination to go to Moffat, though my circumstances were so low at the time, I knew not well how to get there ; but having asked counsel of the Lord, I said I would go, and make use of the water in faith, as a mean appointed, and frequently made useful by God."

He had been present at the battle of Bothwell Bridge and escaped unhurt. " When our forces fled from before the enemy, and all took what way to go they judged most proper for their safety, I rode not through Hamilton with the rest, but went about the town, and having got over a glen, when I got to the other side of it, I espied a party of the enemy just below me, and in the very way by which I behoved to ride. I could not turn back without alarming them, and therefore rode on. My comrade was riding just before me, with his head-piece and other pieces of armour which he had provided for his safety. I saw him dismayed, and that he could not well sit his horse through slavish fear ; on which, I whispered to him to go on composedly ; and I went before him with my carbine over my arm, and my sword drawn in my hand. The enemy came so close up to the way, and all standing under arms, that I could not ride past without touching clothes with them ; on which their commander, in a threatening way, asked me the word. I had resolved not to speak, whatever they asked of this nature, because I knew not their word, and thought it would irritate them the more if I told them what was not their word. As I spoke nothing, but rode on, depending entirely on the God whom I had chosen for my covering in the day of battle, I got past them unmolested ; but whenever my comrade came up, I heard the officer ask him, The word, dog ; on which, through fear, he told him what was not their word, which so provoked the commander, that he struck him over the head with his broad-sword, which, by reason of my comrade's head-piece, broke in two. This so enraged the commander, that he ordered some of his men to fire, which they did, and killed him on the spot. I still stepped on without the least hurry or confusion, and they never in the least molested me. Just as I passed them, I saw Colonel Burns lying in his blood, whom they had shot a little before, so that I must own the Lord was my safety, and the covering of my head in the day of battle : he hid me as in the hollow of his hand, and set remarkable bounds to the remainder of the wrath of the enemy, so the snare was broken, ' and I escaped as a bird out of the snare of the fowler ' ; and my sure and all-sufficient help was in Jehovah's name, who made the heavens and the earth.''

He tells his experiences among the hills of the Dungeon district thus : " The kind providence of God had provided a nursing for my wife in Craigdarroch, Ferguson, in Nithsdale. . . . Some months after I left Carrick to go and see my wife, but not knowing the way, I got a lad who had been in that country to be my guide. Accordingly we set off, but durst not keep the common road for fear of the enemy, it being now like the days of Jael, when the highways were unoccupied, and no peace to honest people when they went out or when they came in.    Being obliged, then, to go by the mountains, there came on a frightful mist and fog, so that we wandered in a desert and pathless way, and knew not whither we were going.    I told my guide that we were surely wandering, and therefore I would sit down and pray, as I usually did and do when in such a case. . . . Before I had done, the Lord had carried off the mist, so that we saw we had wandered, and afterwards were directed into the right way. . . .

" About a year and four months after this, I carried my daughter Elizabeth to Craigdarroch. . . . I got a horse and a woman to carry the child, and came to the same mountain, where I wandered by the mist before ; it is commonly known by the name of Kells-rhins : when we came to go up the mountain, there came on a great rain, which as we thought was the occasion of the child's weeping, and she wept so bitterly, that all we could do could not divert her from it, so that she was ready to burst. When we got to the top of the mountain, where the Lord had been formerly kind to my soul in prayer, and showed me the way where I was to go, I looked round me for a stone, and espying one, I went and brought it.    When the woman with me saw me set down the stone, she smiled, and asked what I was going to do with it.    I told her I was going to set it up as my Ebenezer, because hitherto and in that place the Lord had formerly helped, and I hoped would yet help.    The rain still continuing, and the child weeping bitterly, I went to prayer, and no sooner did I cry to God, but the child gave over weeping, and when we got up from prayer, the rain was pouring down on every side, but in the way where we were to go there fell not one drop, the place not rained on was as big as an ordinary avenue."

A monument in honour of " John Stevenson, of Camregan," was set up in Old Dailly churchyard in 1886, so that his memory appears to flourish in the district.    The tombstone reads—

> HERE · LYES · THE
> CORPS · OF · JOHN
> STIvnson · WHO
> DIED · MERCH · 17
> 1729 · AGE · 73.

The hills on either hand increase in height as you go onwards. The highest points of the lofty range on the left are Meaul and

The Carlin's Cairn, a name which brings you once more into touch with the Bruce traditions of Galloway. On the other side of these hills some streams converge and form the Polmaddy Burn, where there lived a miller whose wife helped the King in his need. She sheltered him for several days and misled his enemies when they came that way searching for him in every glen. In later days, when the King was able to reward his friends, he gave her a bit of land in the Polmaddy Glen, and she in turn, desiring to commemorate this royal gratitude, caused her friends to carry stones to one of the highest points overlooking the glen.

While stating that little reliance can be placed on the tradition of the origin of The Carlin's Cairn, the *Inventory* points out that " its very remote situation renders its sepulchral character doubtful."

*In a Galloway wood.*

# CHAPTER XXX

## CARSPHAIRN

The road from Dalmellington to Carsphairn—A story of the
Covenanters—Inscriptions in the churchyard—Antiquarian
rambles—A deserted mining village—Knockgray—Captain
Clark Kennedy's notes on the wild life of the district—Two
roads to Dalry.

WHEN Lord Cockburn went on the South-Western Circuit in
the autumn of 1844, he entered Galloway by Dalmellington
and Carsphairn[1] and was impressed by the " extensive inland
views, bounded and varied, not by wide plains, which, because
they are high above the sea, are said to be hills, but by real,
plainly marked, sticking-up mountains. There are a great
many beautiful places, and the whole country is alive with
streams." Beginning at Dalmellington, the road runs for
nearly four miles up a narrow defile with a stony water-course
at the side—no doubt it is its length and narrowness that always
make me think of a miniature Ampezzo-thal—and at the end
of the ascent one comes out suddenly on a high moor giving
some of those " extensive inland views ". At the foot of the
heathery slopes falling away to the west the continuity of the
moors is broken by a bit of Loch Doon; farther to the west
the sunshine on a clear day will pick out from its dark moorland
setting a little sheet of water called Loch Finlas; and farther
still in the same direction rise the hills near Rowantree, the
site of The Murder Hole. On the south you have the large
hills of the Kells range, and parallel with them the more imposing
and rugged, " plainly marked, sticking-up mountains " of the
Merrick group; and between the two ranges a long moor over
which the eye travels into a hazy distance filled by The Dungeon.

[1] Carse of the alders; Gaelic *fearna*.

The road undulates now along the valley of the Deugh with moors on the left and the steep, grassy sides of the Kells hills on the other bank of the stream until it reaches the little, clean, wind-swept village of Carsphairn.

Nowhere so inevitably as here does one recall these lines of Stevenson :

> Blows the wind to-day, and the sun and the rain are flying,
>   Blows the wind on the moors to-day and now,
> Where about the graves of the martyrs the whaups are crying,
>   My heart remembers how !
>
> Grey recumbent tombs of the dead in desert places,
>   Standing-stones on the vacant wine-red moor,
> Hills of sheep, and the howes of the silent vanished races,
>   And winds austere and pure :
>
> Be it granted me to behold you again in dying,
>   Hills of home ! and to hear again the call ;
> Hear about the graves of the martyrs the peewees crying,
>   And hear no more at all.

Carsphairn abounds in hills of sheep and has its circle of standing stones, but is the only parish in The Glenkens—the district including the parishes in the valley of the Ken, namely, Carsphairn, Dalry, Balmaclellan, and Kells—where there is no martyr's grave. The village, however, has its story of the Killing Time. Pierson, the Episcopal minister, maintained a persecuting policy towards the Covenanters in the parish, and kept Lagg informed of those who absented themselves from church. The people were not cowed, but merely exasperated, and, led by James MacMichael, proposed to make some sort of treaty with the minister to secure peace in the parish. Pierson received a deputation in the manse, but on learning their errand was enraged, would listen to none of their remonstrances, barred the door, and drew out his pistol. Companions of the deputies, who had remained outside, hearing cries from within, broke down the door with MacMichael at their head. He, seeing the pistol outstretched and conceiving his friends to be in imminent danger, shot Pierson dead.

His act was not approved by the Societies of the Covenanters, who removed his name from the roll of membership ; but, says the author of *The Martyr Graves of Scotland* naively, " he loved freedom in spiritual things as much as ever, only in the future he had to be more careful in his movements, and to keep more away from the busy haunts of men." The shot had other consequences. Claverhouse came into the district, and MacMichael and some others of his way of thinking sought concealment on Auchencloy Hill near Loch Skerrow. Claverhouse contrived to come upon them by surprise. Two of the men fled unnoticed, but the six who remained had to fight. Claverhouse became involved in a duel with MacMichael and was pressed so hardly that he called for help. MacMichael then said, "You dare not abide the issue of a single combat; and had your helmet been, like mine, a soft bonnet, your carcase had now found a bed upon the heath." While he was speaking, a dragoon had been approaching quietly from behind and the next moment split his skull with his sword. Of the other Covenanters, Robert Ferguson, John Grier, and Robert Stewart were shot, and William Hunter and Robert Smith were taken to Kirkcudbright, where they were hanged and beheaded.

The following atrocious incident is related of John Semple, who was the first minister of Carsphairn and died about 1677. It is an illustration of how the " saints of the Covenant " shared abundantly in, and even fomented, the delusions of the time. " His painful endeavours were blessed with no small success, especially on sacramental occasions. This the devil envied very much, and particularly one time, among many, when Semple designed to administer the Lord's Supper; before which he assured the people of a great communion, by a gracious and remarkable down-pouring of the Spirit, but that the devil would be envious about this good work, and that he was afraid he would be permitted to raise a storm or speat of rain, designing to drown some of them. 'But,' said he, 'it shall not be in his power to drown any of you—no, not so much as a dog.' Accordingly, it came to pass on Monday, that, when he was dismissing the people, they saw a man all in black entering the water a little above them, at which they were amazed, as the stream was very large. He lost his feet, as they apprehended, and came down on his back, waving his hand; the people ran and got ropes, and threw them to him, and there were ten or twelve men upon the ropes, yet they were in danger of being all drawn into the water and drowned. Semple looking on, cried, 'Quit the rope, and let him go; I see who it is, it is the devil ; he will burn, but not drown ; and by drowning of you would have God dishonoured, because He hath got some glory to His free grace in being king to many of your souls at this time.' All search was made in that country to find if any man was lost, but none was heard of, which made them to conclude it to be the devil." [1]

If the angler who comes to Carsphairn to fish the Water of Deugh[2] should be interrupted by a day when the attempt to beguile trout is manifestly foolish, he may go to the church-yard and see some old tombstones in the western part and ponder the epitaphs of men who, it is very likely, were anglers too since they lived in Carsphairn. There are three of these old inscriptions—

YOU TRAVLERS AS YOU
PASS BY COME READ AND
DO NOT FEAR FOR DO
UN BELOV THIS STON DO
TH LY TRUTH CHAMPION
BVRIED HERE ALTHOUG
H HIS BONS BELO THIS
STON DO PICE AND PICE
DECAY HIS SOUL IN
HEAVEN OF GLORY SHAL
ANE DEDM VEAR FOR AYE.

R · G · G · G
faithful · Robert · Grierson
Doth · ly · beside · this · stone
Who · in · his · life · tyme · was
Repute · ane · honest · one
Religeon · he · did · AWN
When · Few · it · countenancd
Eternity · is · come
Where · he · is · high · advancd
WHO · DIED · THE · II · OF · JVNE
1 6 9 9 · A G E D · 50

[1] *The Scots Worthies.*
[2] Gaelic *dubh uisge*, black water.

> This · monument · doo · now
> the · tell · wher · old · lochhead
> intered · was · his · nams · David
> m<sup>c</sup>lnay · who · nou · doth · pras · and
> not · pre · useful · church · milatnt
> and · the · church · traphant
>                    1 6 9 6

At a first reading this last inscription seems to lack lucidity.
The point is that the deceased, being now a member of the
Church Triumphant, has no further occasion for prayer.
While he was still in the ranks of the Church Militant, he was
probably tenant of Loch Head farm at the south end of Loch
Doon.

If, again, the visitor is curious about other memorials of
bygone generations or of vanished races, he should go to Holm
of Daltallochan farm, where he will see a cairn, a stone circle,
a standing stone, and a cross-slab; and to Lamford, where there
is a well-preserved cairn about half a mile east of the shepherd's
cottage, and " a small group of cairn-like mounds, probably
the ruins of small circular stone huts ", about a quarter of a
mile east of the cairn. In the course of a walk to the south
of the village he may come upon the site of a long chambered cairn
on Carnavel farm, two cross-slabs about three hundred yards
south of the summit of Braidenoch Hill, a cross carved in relief
at the entrance to the Dalshangan[1] grounds, the remains of
Dundeugh Castle a short distance north of the point where the
Deugh falls into the Ken, and a fort in an angle of the Deugh
on the farm of Carminnow about three-quarters of a mile west
of the High Bridge of Ken. Ascending the upper valley of the
Ken, he will find about three-quarters of a mile west-south-west
of Craigengillan " a large circular cairn, over the top of which
two walls have been erected at right angles to form a sheep
shelter ", and at Nether Holm of Dalquhairn[2] " a large circular
cairn with a diameter of about eighty-four feet, but now consisting merely of a ring of loose stones around the line of
the circumference. An oblong depression near the centre

---

[1] Gaelic *dail seangan*, field of the ants.
[2] Gaelic *dail chàirn*, field of the cairn.

possibly marks the position of a cist which has long since been opened."

Near Carsphairn are the remains of Lagwine Castle, once the home of the Macadams, ancestors of the famous road-maker ; and high on the side of the Coran of Portmark, about two miles distant, is a small cluster of cottages, the deserted mining village of Woodhead, where the schoolhouse has been turned into a summer lodging by a family who must surely share the tastes of the Silverado Squatters. Lord Cockburn remarks of Woodhead that "the lately detected lead-mines near Carsphairn, instead of marring, to my mind improve the scene, and even increase its wildness. It looks like a colony of solitary strangers who were trying to discover subterranean treasures in a remote land." Since the village was deserted, it has made the place look wilder still.

Leaving Carsphairn by the road on the left bank of the Deugh, one arrives in a few hundred yards at the gate of the shooting-lodge of Knockgray[1]. The avenue running up the slope at right angles to the road is lined on both sides with conifers of several kinds and an undergrowth of large rhododendrons with blossoms of wonderful, delicate hues, and it is delightful to leave the dusty road on a hot day and turn into the midst of its coolness and fragrance. Two or three generations ago Knockgray was a lonely house on the face of a moor ; but the aspect of the place has been so altered by planting that it looks now like a garden in a wilderness. Herons nest near the house, and tame turtle-doves perching on the branches of the pines or alighting sometimes on the sundial make the air musical.

Knockgray glories in its situation on the windy heights and in its view of the Kells range. Cairnsmore, one of the highest hills in Galloway, rises immediately behind it. An old rhyme runs :

> There's Cairnsmore of Fleet,
>   And there's Cairnsmore of Dee ;
> But Cairnsmore of Carsphairn's
>   The highest of the three.

It is unlike many high mountains in that its summit gives a wide outlook in several directions. This is due, of course, to

[1] Gaelic *cnoc gréaich*, hill of the elevated flat.

its isolation from other heights on all sides but one. Its immediate neighbours stand huddled to the east towards Cumnock ;
but in the north-west one can see the peaks of Arran, in the
south the Solway and the Cumberland hills, and between these
directions the great mountain masses of the Galloway Highlands.

Knockgray has a literary association with that hill country
on the south-west. Its late proprietor, Captain Clark Kennedy,
made the adventures of Robert the Bruce in Galloway the
subject of a spirited work reminiscent in its style and its episodic
method of the romantic poems of Scott. *Robert the Bruce, a
Poem, Historical and Romantic,* was published in 1884. For
those who share its author's minute knowledge of the Galloway wilderness, the recurrence of the names of remote hills,
crags, lochs, and burns that are known to few but the shepherds
who dwell among them and the occasional sportsman who comes
with rod or gun gives it a special interest. The poem is followed
by a large body of notes full of the lore of the hills. There is a
long note, for example, on the sundew, a little bog-plant especially common in Galloway. Referring to the eagle and other
wild creatures, he says, " Often have I seen it in the forest
of Buchan, winging its way to some high crag over the Loch of
Dee or Doon. The buzzard, the peregrine falcon, the raven,
the badger or ' brock,' as the folk of the country call it (as they
do in the north of Ireland also), the otter and the mountain-
fox are still common, and a few real wild cats (nearly extinct
in Scotland now) still hold their own in wilds where of old the
savage wolf wandered over the mountains, the red deer made
his abode in the forest, and the wild boar was numerous in the
marshes. The osprey or ' fishing-eagle ' is also still to be met
with, and still, I believe, breeds annually in Ayrshire and Galloway ; at all events, it did so since 1871, and is often to be
seen by the sea-shore, and sometimes also inland, by the more
sequestered of the many mountain lakes."  " Even to the
present time there are some goats in a state of wildness in
the mountains around Loch Dee and Trool and especially on the
farm of Craigencallie, amongst whose precipices I have occasionally observed the wild goats with their shaggy beards
and long horns. They are very hard to approach, but can sometimes be killed with the rifle. Many of those so-called ' wild
goats ' were originally tame, but have become shy by reason

of their wild habits and the ease with which they find their sustenance, even in heavy snow." Captain Clark Kennedy was a keen sportsman and hunted his own pack of otter-hounds.

I do not suppose that, even if one had to travel every day over the roads between Carsphairn and Dalry, one would ever grow tired of them. To the cyclist certainly the road on the east side of the Deugh and the Ken is difficult in a contrary wind, for it runs high above the river levels and has many ups and downs; but it is a good road to follow. It was even better when, about three miles south-east of Carsphairn, you could turn into a deeply shaded byway and reach in a minute or two a little bridge spanning a very narrow gorge where the river Deugh made an abrupt fall of over forty feet and a great turmoil in the linn below, while close above rose another kind of gorge formed by the thick plantations on both sides. The cascade was hidden from the road by the trees, but announced its presence to the traveller by the roaring of the water and lured him into the byway; and this was a part of its charm, that it was a little off the highroad and did not obtrude itself. When once you had been there, you would always return when making a journey between Carsphairn and Dalry.

At a time before the bridge was built, a tinker once leaped across the ravine. He had been suspected of a theft, and a party of dragoons had been sent to capture him. He had eluded them for some days; but they caught sight of him lying there asleep. They came at him with a shout. Awakened thereby, he rose and rushed at the narrowest part of the chasm and cleared it. Hence came the popular name, " The Tinkler's Loup."

I regret the disappearance of the precipices of blue-grey rock, the shining waterfall, the turbulent linn, and the enclosing trees, not for the sake of the tinker and his "loup", but for the sheer natural enchantment of that nook. I should think that the promoters of the Galloway Water Power Company must have had an uneasy conscience as the water crept up the walls of the gorge and submerged all. Perhaps a time will come when the people of this country will say that in such places such works shall no longer be permitted merely because water happens to be cheaper than coal.

A mile nearer Dalry there is the High Bridge of Ken and the College waterfall. Thereafter your attention is distracted from wayside details by the noble range of mountains some miles away on the opposite side of the valley. Thus you may overlook a new village made by the Water Power Company and bearing the trade-name of Kendoon. The obvious name for a village placed here was Dundeugh; but if you are inviting English capital to support your projects, it appears to be advisable to have place-names that do not overstrain the guttural powers of those to whom you appeal.

The gradients on the other road are less formidable. Just after leaving Carsphairn and crossing the Deugh, you ascend for a mile over Bardennoch Hill; but thenceforward, especially if you are helped by a north wind, you can go on an ordinary bicycle almost as easily as if you were sitting in a motor-car. In the case of such roads as these the bicycle is the most rapid means of travel that one ought to allow oneself. One really ought to walk.

This road, like the other, gives for a time an impressive view of the mountains, and in happier days one could reach The Tinkler's Loup by making a digression of a little more than a mile. I shall not try to catalogue the other attractions of the route, but leave them for the reader to discover for himself, warning him, however, that his satisfaction will be chequered from time to time by the works of the Galloway Water Power Company, of which something more will be said later.

Happy is the traveller who takes either of these roads, and happier still is he who has time for both.

# CHAPTER XXXI

## DALRY

The approach to Dalry—The mountains of Kells—The village—
Earlston Linn—The Gordons of Earlston—Mossroddick—
Lochinvar—The Holy Linn—The path to Balmaclellan—The
roads to New Galloway—The Glenlee ghosts—Inscriptions in
Kells Churchyard—The Garroch Glen—A pilgrims' way—The
Pentland Rising—The martyrs' grave—The Kenmure burial
aisle—The church—Names of the village—How to address
letters—The Pulharrow Glen—Loch Dungeon—The Cauldron
of The Dungeon—A winter sunset—Winter perils of The
Cauldron.

I HAVE tried to be sparing of superlatives in previous chapters,
remembering that I had still to deal with Dalry[1] and that if
I could not hope to rise to the lyrical eloquence that it deserves,
I must at least refrain from squandering prematurely the language at my command. In undertaking such a subject as this,
one sympathizes with the poets who, conscious of their inade-
quacy, appeal to the Muse to inspire them.

How best to approach the village presents no problem to
one who has never been there before—it is simply a question
of convenience ; but for the devotee it is one of propriety. The
south road from New Galloway and the east road from Moniaive scarcely let you see the village until you are actually
within it, and this means too unceremonious an entrance. I give
my verdict, therefore, in favour of the low road from Carsphairn
in the north, which allows you to throw a preliminary salutation
from a little distance. You come to a part of the way where
it makes a series of undulations, and at the top of every rise,
as you look across the masses of foliage embowering the river
in the depths of the glen, you see the cottages and gardens of

[1] Popularly supposed to be *dál righ*, the king's field, but *righ* is
pronounced *ree*.—Maxwell.

Dalry climbing skywards about a mile away.  If it is late on a
summer evening, you will notice also how the little white walls
retain the light of the dying day while all surrounding details
are sunk in shade.  Even when one is on the top of the Kells
range, seven or eight miles away, a small splash of white on the
east side of the Ken valley enables one to say, " There is Dalry ".

Close at hand the village has a dazzling effect in full sunshine,
for the inhabitants vie with one another in glorifying their
dwellings, not only growing flowers in strips of soil and training
creepers up the fronts, but painting or whitewashing the walls

*The Kells Range from the road between Dalry and New Galloway.*

every year, and your eye is constrained to seek relief sometimes
in the meadows and plantations on the other side of the glen.

I must not write another sentence without referring to the
view of the mountains of Kells.  Their grand masses with their
far-drawn skyline are a constant joy.  If you lodge on the north
side of the street, you can see them from the back windows,
and as you stroll about the village—along The Throughgate,
up Kirkland Street, or down the upper part of the main street—
they loom up before you, not, indeed, with the overpowering
imminence of the mountains around Innsbruck, but with a very
satisfying degree of grandeur, and compel you to look at them
often whether the sunshine of the morning and the forenoon is
lighting up the green and brown slopes of Millyea and Corserine

and the rocky corries in the sides of Milldown and Millfire ; or has given place, with the advance of the hours, to great masses of black shadow—to be exchanged for purple-grey as the evening comes on ; or mist, having covered the top of Corserine, is surging down upon the other heights ; or stormy-looking clouds are disposed along the whole range, each like an Ossa crowning a Pelion, while the sun, setting behind them, stabs their darkness with shafts of gold, making a picture of commingled shadows and brightness that affects you like a portent.

People who chatter and shout hilariously at popular watering-places would not be likely, one would think, to raise their voices foolishly in view of such majestic hills, and those who like quietness can count on finding it here. The men of the village are out of sight by day, following their trades or labouring on the neighbouring estates and farms, and it is not until the evening that they present themselves, sitting on garden seats in front of their cottages and smoking and talking or reading a newspaper. When I first knew Dalry, the only apparent stir was caused by the arrival of the horse-drawn coach from the station in the evening. Motor traffic means more liveliness, and the hotels[1] and the houses that let rooms are occupied fully in the summer months, but there is not enough space to admit of a crowd. The visitors, therefore, are never sufficiently numerous to spoil the quiet for one another. There is no bandstand nor anything in the nature of a promenade to tempt them to congregate, and negro minstrels and pierrots are unknown. The people who come to Dalry are usually of the kind who can amuse themselves and, therefore, do not need to be amused. Those whose happiness is incomplete without golf are pacified with a nine-hole course ; but this is not a noisy game. The occasional " click " from the nearest tee-ing ground, almost the only sound you will hear sometimes, serves rather to accentuate the quiet.

Then there is the air, dry and rich with moorland scents. On one of those rare nights when mist has come down on the village, I have gone out into the dark street and noticed that the air smelled just as if one were in the midst of an odorous moor on a wet day.

---

[1] The principal one is *The Lochinvar Hotel*, facing the Garroch Glen. *The Commercial Hotel* is quiet and comfortable. Motor-buses running between Glasgow and Castle Douglas pass the doors of both.

It is in The Glenkens, as the district drained by the Ken river is called, that the works of the Galloway Water Power Company

*Dalry and the Kells Range.*

had the most destructive effect on the aspect of the country. Reference has been made in the previous chapter to the ruin wrought at The Tinkler's Loup. I am constrained to unburden

my spirit by recalling also some of those details of the Dalry
neighbourhood on which I dwelt in the first edition, so that
another generation, educated to value the beauty of Scotland,
may know something of what has been lost—but could be
rediscovered more easily than the Lost Atlantis !

I wrote formerly that it was worth while to go to the Earlston
Waterfall, not only for its sake, but for every inch of the way.
Now, however, great concrete dams stretch across the valley
every few miles between Dalry and Carsphairn, holding up
extensive reservoirs and overhanging each its own power-house.
Instead of the natural river rippling through a pastoral and
wooded glen and full of delightful incidents we behold a chain of
artificial lochs leaving some tantalizing bits of the stream as it
was, while the pylons of the grid-line that conveys electric power
to central Scotland and the north-west of England bestride the
hills and moors.

On reaching the Allangibbon Bridge, about half a mile from
Dalry, one is confronted by a dam seventy feet high and more
than an eighth of a mile long, a grievous interference with the
allurement of that gorge where it was so good to linger on a
hot day among the firs and larches that shade the grey, lichen-
clad rocks and the now nearly-empty pools—a place of more
varied charm than Sandra Belloni's pine-wood.

Behind the dam and hidden in the depths of the reservoir
is the island that bore the clump of firs. There also is the shelf
of the dainty waterfall that spread like a curtain of white
lace across the stream. A little farther up the river was the
gorge of Earlston, its light-grey crags reflected in the long
linn where the water settled after the plunge. It is now nearly
brim-full, and the river an ordinary stream with rocky edges.
The reservoir-level begins just where the whole river used to
dash through a very narrow cleft and spread out fan-wise over
the rocks into a deep pool. Submerged also, except for a few
inches, is the rock where, from a ledge just above the surging
water, one could photograph the leaping salmon.

Within sight of Dalry itself is the Glenlee power-house at the
end of a concrete-lined tunnel more than three miles and a half
long and eleven and a half feet in diameter into which the
Black Water of Dee was diverted. That river formerly received
the water of Loch Ken ten miles farther south, beside the
railway viaduct. (Loch Ken was extended by making a barrage

near Glenlochar Bridge.) In order to store the Black Water the Company erected a dam considerably more than a quarter of a mile long and seventy-five feet high just above the Upper Bridge of Dee. Approached from the east, the reservoir looks like a natural loch; but when one comes from the Newton Stewart direction, one gets a shock on beholding that long dam stretching like a pallid weal across the landscape.

Before the water gathered, the King's Stone was removed to a new site. Another change is that the Upper Bridge shewn in the drawing on page 471 is no longer in use. The parapets have been taken away, but the arches remain—pathetic memorials of a place of much happy idling, whence one lifted one's eyes to a spacious moor through which the Black Water meandered, while just below the bridge the river swirled deep over smooth granite, broke over rock-faces in flashing falls, and surged over submerged boulders. A slight diversion of the road has been made and a new bridge built, the third to span the river here. The remains of the first, mentioned on page 470, are now buried in water.

Earlston Linn took its name from the old castle near the river, the home of the Gordons, a family who were strongly attached to the principles of the Reformation and the Scottish Covenants, and suffered many things for their faith.

In 1635 Sydserff, Bishop of Galloway, appointed a minister to the parish of Dalry. The appointment was not acceptable to the people, and Alexander Gordon of Earlston led the opposition. He was summoned to appear before the diocesan Commission Court, but did not obey and was fined and banished to Montrose. He was one of the elders sent by the Presbytery of Kirkcudbright to the General Assembly of 1638, served as one of the Commissioners for The Stewartry in the Parliament of 1641, and acted as a member of the Covenanters' War Committee for The Stewartry. He died in 1654 and was succeeded by his son, William.

William Gordon had been educated for the ministry, but when the Civil War broke out, was in command of a company under General Leslie. His persecutions began in 1663, when the Privy Council sent a Committee consisting of the Earls of Linlithgow, Galloway, and Annandale, Lord Drumlanrig, and Sir John Wauchope, of Niddry, to inquire into the riots that

had taken place at Kirkcudbright and Irongray over the introduction of Episcopal ministers. When the Commissioners were
at Kirkcudbright, they tried to induce Gordon to sanction the
ordination of an Episcopal minister to the parish of which he
was patron, but he refused and was cited to appear before the
Council. In the Act which the Council passed against him they
narrated " that they had considered several accusations exhibited
against Mr. Gordon of Earlstoun, for keeping of private meetings
and conventicles, contrary to the laws and acts of Parliament,
with his own judicial confession that he had been at three
several conventicles, where Mr. Gabriel Semple, a deposed
minister, did preach, viz., one in Corsack wood, and the other
two in the wood of Airds, at which there were great numbers
of people ; and that he did hear Mr. Robert Paton, a deposed
minister, expound a text of scripture, and perform other acts
of worship in his mother's house ; and that Mr. Thomas Thomson,
another deposed minister, did lecture in his own house to his
family on a Sabbath-day ; and that, being required to enact
himself to abstain from all such meetings in time coming, and to
live peaceably and orderly conform to law, he refused to do the
same. They did therefore order the said Mr. William Gordon
of Earlstoun to be banished, and to depart forth of the kingdom
within a month, and not return under pain of death, and that
he enact himself to live peaceably and orderly during the said
month, under pain of ten thousand pounds, or otherways to
enter his person in prison." The fines he incurred on account of
his adherence to the Covenanters amounted to £3,500.

After the failure of the Pentland Rising, Sir William Bannatyne was sent into Galloway with a party of soldiers to terrify
the people, and Earlston Castle became one of the garrisons.
Special attention was given to the parishes from which the rebels
came, and the atrocities that ensued lose little by comparison
with those of the Spaniards in the Netherlands or the Germans
in Poland. Wodrow's stories are corroborated by the Government's subsequent proceedings against Bannatyne on account
of the outrages and excesses which he had committed or allowed.
He suffered the absurdly inadequate penalties of a fine of £200
and banishment from Scotland.

Gordon, who had returned from exile after the Pentland
Rising, is heard of next and finally in connexion with the
battle of Bothwell Bridge. He was hurrying to join the insur-

gents, when a company of English cavalry met him and killed him. His son, Alexander, fought in the battle, narrowly escaped being made a prisoner, and had to live in concealment for several years.

Like the Pentland Rising, the rebellion that was broken at Bothwell Bridge was followed by an outburst of vindictiveness on the part of the Government. The landed proprietors of Galloway were the first to be struck. On the 18th of February, 1680, MacDouall of Freugh; William Gordon of Earlston and his son, Alexander; Gordon, younger of Craighlaw; Gordon of Culvennan; Dunbar of Machermore; and MacKie of Larg were called before the Justiciary Court. Hired witnesses deposed to their having been accessory to the rebellion, and they were found guilty and ordered to be executed when they were captured and to have their property confiscated. William Gordon, as we have seen, had been killed. His prosecution was conducted nevertheless in order that his estates might be forfeited. Further criminal processes were begun in June, and the ordinary sentence was execution and confiscation of property. Graham of Claverhouse received a commission from the Privy Council to seize the movable effects of all persons in Galloway who had been concerned in the rebellion or had fled from persecution. His brother, Cornet Graham, was one of his deputies and held a court at New Galloway, where all persons between the ages of sixteen and sixty were ordered, under the threat of the severest penalties, to appear and declare upon oath how many conventicles they had attended, who had preached, who had been present, and whose children had been baptized. Another court was held at Dalry.

Alexander Gordon was present as a Commissioner from Galloway at a general meeting of the Covenanters' societies at Ayr in March, 1682, when it was resolved to send him to the Continent to make known the unhappy state of the Reformed Church in Scotland. He went on such missions more than once, and it was as he was sailing from Newcastle for the Low Countries in the summer of 1683 that he was arrested. He was sent to Edinburgh, where the Council examined him in order to discover if he had had any connexion with the Ryehouse Plot, but nothing was established against him. As he had been sentenced to death after the battle of Bothwell Bridge, it only remained to appoint the day for his execution. When the Council had decided on the 21st of August that he should be beheaded

at the Cross of Edinburgh on the 28th, it occurred to them that
torture might succeed where mere examination had failed, but
they were doubtful if this were legal in the case of a criminal
sentenced to death, and sought guidance from London. They
received an answer that although the criminal might not be
subjected to torture in connexion with the cause for which
he was sentenced, he might undergo it in respect of plots,
conspiracies, and combinations that had taken place subsequently. Gordon was examined again on the 25th of September,
when the Council contented themselves with placing the instrument of torture beside him ; but he could not be led into
admitting that he had been concerned in any plot to assassinate
the King and the Duke of York. On the 23rd of November
there came a letter from the King ordering the Council to put
Earlston under torture. When his guards brought him into
the council-chamber, and the boot was about to be applied,
he was seized with fury, tossed the soldiers from him—he was
called The Bull of Earlston—and cowed the Council. They
thought that he was feigning madness, but four physicians
certified that he was suffering from *alienatio mentis, furore
latente laborans,* and advised that, instead of being taken back
to the Tolbooth, he should be removed to the fresh air of the
Castle Rock. He was kept there until April, when he was brought
down to the unwholesome Tolbooth. He petitioned the Council
to remove him again to " the air of the rock ", and they sent
him to the Bass Rock for a fortnight in August. On being
brought back to the Tolbooth he made an unsuccessful attempt
to escape and was loaded with irons. He was transferred to
the damp fortress of Blackness in September and lay there until
January, 1689, when he was set free. His lands were restored
to him in the following year. He became commander of the
Kirkcudbright Militia and Commissioner of Supply for The
Stewartry and lived until after 1726.

The little journey to Earlston is only one of many to be made
from Dalry. One cannot stay here without wishing to know
what becomes of the road after it leaves the top of the village.
The slender effort involved in walking the half-mile to the summit of the ridge meets with a most abundant reward, for on
looking back you are confronted with the whole of the mountains from the Bennan above the south end of Loch Ken to the
Coran of Portmark beyond Carsphairn. Close to the road is

the little loch to which Mr. Andrew Lang obviously refers
in the following passage in his *Angling Sketches* : " In a county
of south-western Scotland there is a large village populated by
a keenly devoted set of anglers, who miss no opportunity.
Within a quarter of a mile of the village is a small tarn, very
picturesquely situated among low hills, and provided with the
very tiniest feeder and outflow.  There is a sluice at the outflow, and, for some reason, the farmer used to let most of the
water out, in the summer of every year.  In winter the tarn is
used by the curling club.  It is not deep, has rather a marshy
bottom, and many ducks, snipe, and wild-fowl generally dwell
among the reeds and marish plants of its sides.  Nobody ever
dreamed of fishing here, but one day a rustic, ' glowering '
idly over the wall of the adjacent road, saw fish rising.  He
mentioned his discovery to an angler, who is said to have caught
some large trout, but tradition varies about everything, except
that the fish are very ' dour.'  One evening in August, a warm,
still evening, I happened to visit the tarn.  As soon as the sun
fell below the hills, it was literally alive with large trout rising.
As far as one could estimate from the brief view of heads and
shoulders, they were sometimes two or three pounds in
weight. . . .  The fish were rising actually at our feet, but they
seemed to move about very much, never, or seldom, rising
exactly at the same place.  The hypothesis was started that
there were but few of them, and that they ran round and round
like a stage army, to give an appearance of multitude.  But
this appears improbable.  What is certain was our utter in-
ability ever to get a rise from the provoking creatures."

Many moral and mental obliquities have been attributed to
trout by anglers as well as to anglers by other mortals ; but
Mr. Lang must be the first to credit them even for a moment
with the tricks of the stage.  No doubt he is right in discarding
the theory.  The loch is really full of large fish, but they are
very rarely caught.  I can bear witness, however, that it is
possible to catch them with the fly.  They are of a startlingly
brilliant colouring, and the flesh is a rich pink.

Whether one catch fish or not, Mossroddick is a fascinating
place.  No sounds rise to it from the village.  The grouse cries,
the whaup wails, and

> sometimes doth a leaping fish
> Send through the tarn a lonely cheer.

But for these there is silence unless it be the wind rustling the
reeds and grasses. On hot, still summer days when it is useless
to fish, it is good to sit here with a book and look often at the
glorious landscape. Then the loch, which includes the inverted
images of the distant hills and of the clouds overhead, reminds
one of the picture in *The Book of The Revelation* of the "sea of
glass mingled with fire".

A much larger loch with a famous name, Lochinvar,[1] lies
three miles across the moors on the north-east. It can be reached
by a path beginning at the head of the village or by side-tracks

*Lochinvar.*

branching from the high Carsphairn and Moniaive roads. A
few trees grow behind the gamekeeper's cottage on the west
shore, but all around are undulating moors. The country was
at one time covered with forest, and the loch would look more
beautiful then. Now it has the charm belonging to all open
moorland waters, and in legendary associations is richer than
most.

On the larger of the two islands there once stood a castle
owned by the Gordons of Lochinvar. Only a few stones remain.
It must have been a *domus angusta* in the literal sense ; but
there is excellent fishing round the island, and it would have been

[1] Gaelic *loch an bharra*, loch on the height (700 feet above sea-level).

possible to drop a baited hook from a window into the water with good hope of success—an agreeable diversion for an idle, rainy day. Perhaps "the lost bride of Netherby" beguiled some of her leisure in this fashion. Causeways connected the island with the shore, and in a dry summer, when the loch has shrunk, one's boat sometimes grates on the submerged cobbles.

In the reign of Alexander the Third a wild boar scared the countryside, destroying both men and cattle. Its notoriety spread far and wide, and the King offered knighthood and an estate to the man who should bring him its head. The Laird of Lochinvar waylaid and slew the beast. Tired out with the combat, he lay down to rest after cutting out and pocketing the boar's tongue and fell asleep beside its carcase. A man named Maxwell happened to ride past the place, and seeing what had occurred, resolved to make the most of it. He quietly cut off the boar's head and rode off to Edinburgh.

When Lochinvar awoke, he was astonished to find the animal lying headless. Suspecting a trick to forestall him, he mounted his swiftest horse and hastened to the capital. Maxwell was in the royal presence and was presenting the head.

"Wait, sire," cried Lochinvar, "the reward must be mine!"

"How so?" asked Maxwell.

"Because I killed the boar."

"How comes it that you have not the head?" asked the King.

"Because while I slept, this fellow stole it."

"But how am I to decide the truth of the matter?"

"Let this decide!" cried Lochinvar, throwing down the boar's tongue.

"Open the tusks," said the King to an attendant.

When the boar's mouth was opened, it was found to be tongueless.

"If that tongue does not fit the head, I claim no meed," said Lochinvar.

When the tongue was found to fit the root, the King admitted Lochinvar's claim and asked him how he had overcome the boar.

"I thrust my stout sword into his mouth and gored him down."

"Have you any surname?"

"None. I am Adam of Lochinvar."

" Kneel," said Alexander ; then, striking his sword on Lochin-var's shoulder, " Rise, Sir Adam Gordown of Lochinvar ! Be thy surname Gordown."

This may be the story of the winning of the lands on the east of Lochinvar, but it is not that of the origin of the name, " Gordon ". The family came from the district of Gordon in Berwickshire.

Besides Lochinvar there are several other lochs between Dalry and Moniaive where excellent sport may be had by those who have obtained permission to fish. They are approached in the first instance by the tortuous, hilly road running east from Dalry. The use of a bicycle is to be recommended strongly. It does not, indeed, greatly expedite the uphill journey in the morning, but is of very great use on the return. It can be left anywhere, stowed in the shed of some cottage or concealed among the heath. It has, moreover, the supreme advantage that when you have reached your loch after the tramp across the moor, you can fish with an easy mind, knowing that you do not risk having to tear yourself away just when the best sport of the day may be beginning, and that you can remain until midnight or early morning or the next day if you like. The high moor at the watershed is a weird place in the dark. Stand-ing there at dead of night, you will recall Browning's lines :

> The place is silent and aware ;
>    It has had its scenes, its joys and crimes,
> But that is its own affair.

The outpost of Galloway in that direction is Craigmuie, a moorland estate stretching up to the shore of Loch Urr, whence the Water of Urr flows. The property belonged for a time to Lieutenant-General James Douglas, brother of the Duke of Queensberry, whose name appears on a tombstone in Kells Churchyard in connexion with the shooting of a Covenanter. It was sold to Edward Goldie in 1679, and remains in the hands of his descendants. John Goldie, who succeeded in 1711, was appointed Commissary of Dumfriesshire[1] in 1734 and held the office for more than forty years. His daughter-in-law was one of Sir Walter Scott's correspondents,[2] and we must regret that her daughter's *Recollections*[3] were not published.

Two walks from Dalry deserve a brief note. The Holy Linn is reached most easily from the Moniaive road. A little beyond

---

[1] See page 69.    [2] See pages 19 and 21.    [3] See pages 22 and 69.

the byway leading to Lochinvar you can see on the right the wood that fills the deep glen of the Garpol,[1] and when you have crossed the intervening pasture, the sound of falling water will lead you to the end of your quest. The burn makes a sudden leap over a rock in the shade of the trees. Congregations of Covenanters assembled here for worship during the Persecution, and the " outed " minister of Balmaclellan baptized children at a natural font.

The path to Balmaclellan follows the line of the old road from Dalry to Dumfries, winding over the Mullach,[2] formerly crowned with a plantation of pines, crossing the Garpol by a bridge that is still intact, and climbing the steep slope where the houses of Balmaclellan are scattered.

I should not be able to forgive myself if I did not make some reference to the path beginning at the Allangibbon Bridge, winding over the Waterside Hill, and leading you to a foot-bridge near a little timber-mill, where the humming of the saw makes a strident note amid the sound of the breaking water and the rustling trees. Here you enter the elysium of the Garroch Glen, where you may wander in a maze of birches, oaks, and pines and spend uncounted hours idling at a little stone bridge or, following the road ascending among the trees, admire the infinite variety of wild flowers by the wayside, and perhaps go on to the meadows of the upper part of the glen that come between the woodland and the high moors.

Of the roads to New Galloway, the more direct runs down the left bank of the Ken and skirts a meadow with a tall monolith standing in the midst. The field is called Dalarran Holm, and is said to have been the scene of a battle between Scots and Danes, while the stone is believed to mark the burial-place of a Danish King. The more roundabout route crosses the Ken by the Allangibbon Bridge and passes the grounds of the Glenlee[3] estate.

Glenlee House is haunted. The following account of the ghost is given by a writer in the eighth number of *The Gallovidian* : " Mrs. S——, who is still alive, tells how the grey lady appeared to her one evening as she was sitting in front of her dressing-glass, waiting on her maid to come and do up her hair. While looking into the mirror, she became aware of some one

---

[1] Gaelic *garbh pol*, rough water.      [2] Gaelic *mullach*, a hill.
[3] Gaelic *gleann liath*, grey glen.

or something behind her, and then saw a lady enter by the door of her room, pass across the floor, and disappear through a door which communicated with a dressing-room. As the house was full of company at the time, she wondered whether some of the strangers had mistaken the way to her room, but she waited in vain for her return, and just as she was thinking of going to explore the mystery, it occurred to her that there had been no sound of doors opening or of footfalls on the floor, nor was there any sound in the direction in which the lady had disappeared, and finally it struck her that the lady was not dressed like anyone in the house. All this passed through her mind in less time than it takes to tell it, and when examination was made for this strange and unaccountable lady, she was nowhere to be found.

"Meanwhile, I must inform the reader that Mrs. S—— at this time knew nothing of the ghost story connected with the Park, and so she said nothing of the apparition which had disturbed her for fear of being laughed at, but she could not get the affair out of her mind. Some time afterwards she was calling at K—— Castle, and inquired of the lady of the house whether there was any story of Glenlee being haunted, or whether anything had ever been seen there of recent years. Lady G—— replied that Lady Ashburton was said to walk about in a grey silk dress, and that some even reported that they had heard the rustle of it as she passed on her ghostly way. . . . On another occasion Mrs. S—— was sitting up with Mr. S—— , who was seriously ill, and during the night a kind of rap was heard on the door or about the door which roused her to go and see what it was. Upon opening the door a face stared at her, but spoke not, and passed silently along the dimly-lighted corridor out of sight.

"While C—pt—n C—k K——dy was a guest at Glenlee, before going off to some entertainment one evening he ran up to his bedroom for something or other, and to his surprise there was a lady standing at his dressing-table putting some finishing touches to her toilette. The gallant C—pt—n withdrew, thinking that some of the ladies in the hurry of the moment had gone into the wrong bedroom. When he came down again, they were all upon the point of departure, and called to him to come along, but before getting into the carriage he said, 'You have forgotten one of the ladies.' 'Oh, no!' they said, 'every-

one is here, and but for your lingering we should have been off.'
' Are you sure ? ' he queried, and when they replied again that
everyone was there, he told them what he had seen.　But again
that strange lady whom the C—pt—n found so unexpectedly
at his dressing-table was never accounted for."

When another visitor awoke in the night, " something seemed
to be between him and the fire-place.　He could not see the fire,
and rousing himself, he distinguished in the faint light the form
of a lady as if bending over the embers, and whether it was his
motion or what he never knew, but she suddenly turned round
as if something had attracted her notice towards the bed, and
making a step or two forward, she glared at him with such a
distorted countenance which once might have been beautiful,
but was hideous now with the expression of all the evil passions
personified . . . . that he lost consciousness, and when next he
awoke, to his great relief the sun was shining through the blinds,
and some birds were twittering in the eaves, most welcome
sounds."

The writer whom I have quoted refers to Blacklock's *Twenty
Years' Holidaying in the Glenkens* for the statement that Lady
Ashburton was said to have poisoned her husband, who was
afflicted with *morbus pedicularis*, and mentions another tradition
that her butler poisoned her in order to possess himself of some
valuables.

There appears to be another ghost of a less virulent type.
" A gentleman who was visiting at Glenlee, on looking over
some family photographs, picked out one and said, ' This gentleman came into my room this morning before I was up and dressed
his hair with my brush and comb.'　They replied that that was
impossible, because he had been dead for some time.　The
gentleman, however, persisted in his statement, saying, ' I could
not be mistaken, as it was broad daylight, and I wondered at
him doing it, but said nothing, and he soon retired.　I saw him
so distinctly that I should know him again anywhere '."

After this place of ghosts, one feels more at ease among the
quiet dead in the churchyard of Kells, two miles farther on.　A
table stone tells of John Gordon of Largmore, WHO · DYED ·
JANUARY · 6 · 1667 · OF · HIS · UOUNDS · GOT · AT · PENTLAND · IN ·
DEFENCE · OF · THE · COVENANTED · REFORMATION, and an upright monument with an inscription covering both sides records
the martyrdom of another Covenanter.

```
          HERE LYES            MEN
     ADAM MACQWHAN      ME ( Skull and )  TO
     WHO BEING SICK     MO ( Cross-bones ) RI
     OF A FEVER WAS
     TAKEN OUT OF HIS    GENERAL  IAMES
     BED AND CARRIED     DOUGLAS BROTHER
     TO   NEUTOUN  OF    TO THE DUKE OF
     GALLOWAY AND THE    QUEENS BERRY FOR
     NEXT DAY MOST       HIS  ADHERENCE
     CRUELLY AND UN=     TO  SCOTLANDS
     JUSTLY SHOT TO      REFORMATION CO=
     DEATH BY THE COM    VENANTS NATION
     MAND OF LIEVTENAN   AL AND SOLEMN
                         LEAGUE 1685
```

The stone is small and has been placed for its better preservation
within a tall granite framework.

A sculptured stone bears this inscription : 1707 HERE · LY'S
THE · CORPS · OF · AGNES · HERESE · SPOVS · TO · ROBERT · CORSON
ALSO   MARY · AGNES : & · MARION · MARGRAT · AT · ONE · BIRTH
ROBT. · ANDREV · IAMES · AT · ONE · BIRTH · IOHN · ALEXR · COR-
SONS · CHILDREN · TO · ROT · CORSON· BVRGES · IN · NEVTOVN · OF
GALLAVAY · & · AGNES · M°BVRNY · HIS · SPOVS.    Although this
is not very lucid, the representation of Adam and Eve on the
other side of the stone does not seem inappropriate.  Another
sculptured stone shews a fishing-rod, a gun and a powder-flask,
a dog and a partridge, and marks the grave of John Murray, a
gamekeeper on the Kenmure estate, who died in 1777.  A prize
of a guinea which had been offered for the most suitable epitaph
was awarded to the Rev. John Gillespie, the minister of the
parish, who wrote :

> Ah John ! what changes since I saw thee last ?
> Thy fishing, and thy shooting days are past.
> Bagpipes, and hautboys, thou canst sound no more :
> Thy nods, grimaces, winks, and pranks, are o'er.
> Thy harmless, queerish, incoherent talk ;
> Thy wild vivacity, and trudging walk,
> Will soon be quite forgot.  Thy joys on earth,
> A snuff, a glass, riddles, and noisy mirth,
> Are vanished all.  Yet blest, I hope, thou art,
> For, in thy station, weell thou play'dst thy part.

The proprietor of Kenmure said one day to Murray that he
did not believe that there was anything but minnows in Loch
Ken.  Soon after this Murray saw some ducklings on the water
disappearing one by one.  He took a duck as a bait, and began
to angle with a strong rope.  The duck went under, the line

was taut and quivering, and it was plain that there was something powerful at the other end. As Murray drew back from
the edge, he saw a mighty pike lashing the placid surface of the
loch. He landed and killed it and carried it on his back to
the castle. As he did so, its head was above his, and its tail
was trailing on the ground. He threw it down before his
employer, saying " Ca' that a mennin ! " The fish weighed
seventy-two pounds. Its head is preserved in the castle.

Some historical notes fall to be made about Dalry. Kirkland
Street was a part of one of the old routes between Edinburgh
and the south-west, and was trodden by pilgrims on their way
to Whithorn. James the Fourth sometimes came this way.
The Lord High Treasurer's Accounts for a pilgrimage in 1497
include these details :

Item, to tua pur men be the way..........................xvij*d*.
Item, at Sanct Johnis Kirk of Dalrye, to the preist...xiiij*d*.
Item, to pure folkis thare.......................................ij*s*.
Item, to ane woman with the grantgore thare, be Kingis
    command  ...............................................iij*s* vj*d*.

When the King passed through the village in 1501, he paid
eighteen shillings for " belchair " and five shillings for the use
of the ferry over the Ken. Pilgrims and other travellers in those
days did not go round by New Galloway, but after crossing the
river at Dalry climbed the steep road rising from the foot of
the Garroch Glen and skirting the Glenlee woods. There are
more than two miles of continuous ascent, and the pilgrims
would be glad when they looked down at last on the broad valley
of the Black Water of Dee.

Queen Mary may have been here when the estate of Earlston
was in the hands of the Earl of Bothwell, and no doubt Bothwell
rode down the village street sometimes. The Regent Murray
was at Dalry on the 15th of June, 1568, " staieing there", says
Hollinshed, " in trust of the laird of Louchinware's coming unto
him, but he came not, whereupon the next day, being the 16th
of June, they razed the house of Kenmure, and another house
also, for that the owners were friends of the said Louchinware."
The " other house " was probably Shirmers Tower on the left
bank of Loch Ken.

Dalry's chief claim to a place in history is that the affair
called the Pentland Rising began here. The atrocities of the
Killing Time were still nearly twenty years distant ; but the

Covenanters of Galloway were being made desperate already
by the oppression of the Government and its agents. The
Restoration Government, despising the prejudices of the people,
had set itself to the task—difficult in the days of James the
Sixth, but still less practicable after the country had enjoyed
the ecclesiastical liberty of the Commonwealth—of establishing
Episcopacy, although, to quote the " Declaration " of the
insurgents, " it is known to all, that the king's majesty, at his
coronation, did engage to rule the nation according to the
revealed will of God in scripture ; to prosecute the ends of
' National and Solemn League and Covenants ' ; and fully to
establish Presbyterian government, with the Directory for
Worship ; and to approve all acts of parliament establishing
the same ; and thereupon the nobility, and others of his subjects,
did swear allegiance ; and so religion was committed unto him
as a matter of trust, secured by most solemn indenture betwixt
him and his people." It is the fact that the King had pledged
himself as a Covenanter that accounts for the frequent charges
of perjury brought against him.[1]

The people's attitude was not modified by the character of
the new incumbents who displaced the Presbyterian ministers.
On the contrary, their antipathy was "out of measure increased",
says Bishop Burnet, by the hurriedly-procured clergy, who
" were generally very mean and despicable in all respects.
They were the worst preachers I ever heard : They were ignorant
to a reproach : And many of them were openly vitious. They
. . . . were indeed the dreg and refuse of the northern parts.
Those of them who arose above contempt or scandal were men
of such violent tempers that they were as much hated as the
others were despised. This was the fatal beginning of restoring
Episcopacy in *Scotland*, of which few of the Bishops seemed to
have any sense."

The Government was not content to have its creatures conduct
services in empty churches, and insisted on conformity, imposing
fines on absentees. As the fine was levied for each Sunday of
absence, many of the parishioners were labouring before long
under hopeless burdens of debt. This was not the only kind of
pecuniary infliction, for the landlord was fined for the absence of
his tenants, and the tenant for that of his landlord, and so with
masters and servants. A person who was regular in attendance

[1] See page 23 n.

himself was not absolved from this exasperating class of fines. When the people were unable to discharge the debts that were accumulated upon them, they either saw their property confiscated and carried away or were compelled to give board and lodging to a number of rough and drunken soldiers.[1] It does not require a very vivid imagination to conceive the misery introduced into decent homes by the presence and insults of these unwelcome guests.[2] There was an additional injury, that their host, besides hospitality, had to provide them with pocket-money—three shillings sterling a day—and he was called upon often to pay for a larger number of men than were quartered on him. It is no matter for wonder that many fled from their ruined homes and sought refuge among the wild mountains and moors.

Such was the posture of affairs when the smouldering and ill-repressed fire leapt into sudden flame. On the morning of Tuesday, the 13th of November, 1666, John Maclellan, the Laird of Barscobe in Balmaclellan Parish, and three other hillmen, as the fugitive Covenanters were called, came down from their retreat to seek a meal in Dalry. As they approached the village, they met a number of the inhabitants attended by four of the military, and were told that an old farmer called Grier had refused or was unable to pay his church-fines and that in lieu of these the soldiers were compelling his neighbours to thresh his corn. While the hillmen were breaking their fast in the ale-house, the village was filled with the rumour that the soldiers had seized Grier and were about to roast him naked on his gridiron " because he could not pay ". The hillmen went immediately to the scene of this projected cruelty and urged the soldiers to release their victim. "Two of the soldiers were with the man himself," says Wodrow, " and refused the countrymen's desire, and some

[1] " They quartered sometimes in the houses of a man that kept the church, because another man who kept it not dwelt there before."—Kirkton.

[2] The character of the soldiers is illustrated in *Naphtali* : " In the Parish of *Carsphairn*, in an Inn at the Bridge of *Deugh*, on the Sabbath day, some of them being quartered there, they most prophanely and atheistically mocked at all preaching of the Gospel, saing, *let us go preach*, and then read their text out of the *Cherry and the Slae* (an old Scotch Amorous Poem) counterfeiting a form of divine worship, and as it is informed did sing another part of the same Poem in stead of the Psalms, and used all other mocking modes, as if they had been serious at God's worship."

high words passed betwixt them : upon the hearing of which, the other two rush out of another room where they were, with drawn swords, and make at the countrymen, and had almost killed two of them." Maclellan had his pistol filled with bits of a tobacco-pipe for lack of bullets. He fired at the corporal in command and wounded him. The other soldiers were overpowered, and the hillmen realized that they had begun a rebellion.

A congregation of Covenanters were holding a conventicle at Balmaclellan at this time. When the news of the Dalry incident reached them, they feared that they might be credited with a share of the responsibility and resolved on a bold step. They attacked the local garrison of sixteen men, killed one, and made the rest prisoners. It appeared now that the only course was to capture " Bloody Bite-the-Sheep ", as they called Sir James Turner, the lieutenant-colonel commanding the troops in the neighbourhood, and hold him a hostage for the redress of their grievances. Messengers were sent through adjacent parishes to summon the faithful to convene at Irongray Church that evening. Wild weather and deep darkness delayed their assembling until the next morning. The company, numbering about two hundred men, over fifty of whom were on horseback, then advanced to Dumfries, succeeded in their design of capturing Turner, and marched back to Dalry.

The rebels' first intention seems to have been to treat with the authorities so soon as they had Turner in their hands. It was later that they conceived the unfortunate plan of marching on Edinburgh and presenting their demands there. Looking for the recruits who did not come or who came in handfuls instead of the expected thousands, they made their discouraging progress in the worst of weather through Carsphairn, Dalmellington, Ayr, Cumnock, Muirkirk, Lanark, and Bathgate to the inevitable disaster at Rullion Green among the Pentlands. Many of the prisoners were executed ; to assist, supply, or correspond with any of those who had risen in arms was proclaimed treason ; and the unsupported charge of having been concerned in the rebellion was used freely as a means of oppression. Sir William Bannatyne's doings have been referred to earlier in this chapter.

Dalry Churchyard has no inscription relating to the Pentland Rising, but contains the grave of two of the Auchencloy martyrs. The stone bears the epitaph on the opposite page.

ROBERT STEWART OF ARDOCH AND JOHN GRIERSON WHO WERE MURDERED BY GRAHAM OF CLAVER

HOUSE ANNO 1684 FOR THEIR ADHERENCE

MEMENTO MORI

TO SCOTLANDS REFORMATION AND COVENANTS NATIONAL AND SOLEMN LEAGUE

BEHOLD! BEHOLD! A STONE'S HERE FORCED TO CRY
COME SEE TWO MARTYRS UNDER ME THAT LY!
AT WATER OF DEE WHO SLAIN WERE BY THE HAND
OF CRUEL CLAVERHOUSE AND'S BLOODIE BAND
NO S'OONER HAD HE DONE THIS HORRID THING
BUT'S FORCED TO CRY STEWART'S SOUL IN HEAVEN DOTH SING
YET STRANGE! HIS RAGE PURSUED EVEN SUCH WHEN DEAD
AND IN THE TOMBS OF THEIR ANCESTORS LAID
CAUSING THEIR CORPS BE RAIS'D OUT OF THE SAME
DISCHARGING IN CHURCHYARD TO BURY THEM
ALL THIS THEY DID 'CAUSE THEY WOULD NOT PERJURE
OUR COVENANTS AND REFORMATION PURE
BECAUSE LIKE FAITHFUL MARTYRS FOR TO DY
THEY RATHER CHUSE THAN TREACHEROUSLIE COMPLY
WITH CURSED PRELACIE THE NATIONS BANE
AND WITH INDULGENCIE OUR CHURCHES STAIN
PERJURED INTELLIGENCERS WERE SO RIFE
SHEWD THEIR CURSED LOYALTY TO TAKE THEIR LIFE.

HERE LYETH ROBERT STEWART SON TO MAJOR

The writer of these lines appears to have thought that when Claverhouse said, " Stewart's soul in heaven doth sing ", he was speaking under the influence of some power outside of himself making for veracity, and not in mere flippancy. There is no obscurity about his implication that Claverhouse had caused the remains of his victims to be raised from their first resting-place and re-interred in the northern part of the churchyard, the quarter reserved usually for criminals.

A ruined fragment of the old church stands beside the modern building—the Kenmure burial aisle, built as an annexe to the chancel, but separated from the present church by a narrow passage. The massive grille in the window seems to have been put into its place while the masonry was being erected. A moulded panel above the window bears the arms of Gordon and a lion rampant and a date not very legible, but believed to be 1546. How the cognizance of the Province of Galloway came to be impaled with a family coat of arms is not certain ; but it has been suggested that it was done by John Gordon, who was Justiciar of The Stewartry from 1555 and son of James Gordon, Chamberlain of Galloway. He may have considered that his father's office and his own, held by him for a very long time, justified him in combining the provincial with the family arms. Moreover, his first wife was a Home of Wedderburn, and the undifferenced arms of the Home family were the lion rampant. There would be, therefore, a double ground for the combination.

Some stones of an earlier church are visible in the walls of its successor. Unlike the polished red-freestone pilasters on the south front, those on the north side, says an architectural expert, " are built of massive blocks of strong grained silurian grit, so extensively used in ancient times in all buildings of any pretensions, civil or ecclesiastical, throughout the province of Galloway. They have all, without exception, been carefully hewn for other purposes than they now serve. One shews a glass groove with the leaden plug for a rivet or stanchion-end still in its place. Others are hewn with six-inch margins, and so in various ways indicate use in a previous building."

The village used to be called S. John's Clachan because the Knights Templars, who owned land here, dedicated the church to their patron saint, John the Baptist. It is spoken of sometimes as S. John's Town of Dalry ; but the name of the parish has come to be used commonly as that of the village. If, however,

you direct a letter to " Dalry " *simpliciter*, it will go to a place
of that name in Ayrshire, and if you address it to " Dalry,
Galloway ", it may, especially if you are writing from England,
go to Galway in Ireland.　The Post Office recommends " Dalry,
Kirkcudbrightshire ".　The latter word, of course, is inexact.
The proper form is " The Stewartry of Kirkcudbright ".

Not letters only, but travellers even, go astray sometimes,
not, indeed, to Galway, but to the Ayrshire Dalry.　I have
nothing to say against that place with its coal-pits, brick-fields,
and woollen and other factories ; but I wish to guard against

*Cairnsmore of Carsphairn from the mouth of the Pulharrow.*

any reader's going thither and then announcing that this book is
full of misleading information.

When you are at Dalry, the Kells mountains arouse in you
the desire to see what is on the other side.　This desire ought to
be satisfied.　You will look upon places that you will remember
all your days.

The best plan is to begin by yielding to the invitation of the
Pulharrow Glen.[1]　The road winds towards the mountains

---

[1] The valley of the Pulharrow " exhibits in a small compass, and
in the best condition, all the peculiar phenomena of glacial action . . .
scratchings, polishings, striations, glacier *débris*, moraine mounds,
and old lake basins. . . . There is one point of interest in this
valley specially worthy of attention.　Just before the Pulharrow

with much variety, in part through a thick wood, in part along open slopes sparsely clad with birches, and elsewhere over a level moor where Highland cattle wander. In summer the stream is hidden for the greater part of its course by the trees and bushes growing about it, but in winter its gleaming water can be seen through the trelliswork of bare branches. This wooded glen is a fine prelude to the barren moors and austere hills by which you are to fare presently. Meanwhile, with the rising and falling of the road, there has been shooting into view and again vanishing

*Loch Minnoch and Millfire.*

from sight the mountain range which forms the eastern wall of The Cauldron of The Dungeon—the rocky, precipitous sides of Milldown and Millfire and the great, green slopes of Corserine.

The road ends in the yard of a sheep-farm. One of the

enters the Ken, it turns round sharply towards the north, so sharply that the glacier mass that filled the glen could not take the turn, but climbed the hills at the angle, and joined the Ken glacier right over at the other side, thus rising three hundred feet from its level in the valley of the Pulharrow. This is indisputably proved by the direction of the *striae* on the sandstone at the part of the valley thus ascended, which are here very numerous and clear."—" On the Evidences of Glacier Action in Galloway " by William Jolly, in *The Transactions of the Edinburgh Geological Society* (1867–8).

attractions of walking in Galloway is that one so often comes to places where the road ends and the wilderness begins. From this point you ascend by low hills to Loch Minnoch and then cross a great stretch of moor till you are abreast of Loch Dungeon. The name seems to be a transformation of a Gaelic word meaning " rocky ", and describes the place exactly, for the part of the Kells range towering above the loch is simply a wall of rock with well-marked corries worn by the rains of millenniums. At some points there is no shore at all. The precipices run straight down into unfathomed, watery abysses, like those around the

*Loch Dungeon.*

Königsee, and as one scrambles along the steep rock-face at the height of perhaps twenty feet, one realizes that the name in its English meaning is equally appropriate, for if one fell into the loch, it would not be easy to escape. This is true even of the north side, where the water is shallow. The bottom is a dangerously soft, peaty soil, giving way readily under one's foot.

Many years ago a fight between an eagle and an otter was witnessed here. It is not said that they were fighting over a fish ; but perhaps they regarded each other as rival claimants of the fishing rights, and in any case the eagle would look upon the otter as his natural prey. The anglers who observed the contest said that as they were eating their luncheon on the shore, an eagle swooped down to the margin at a little distance. They moved nearer to see what was toward and found that an otter ,was being attacked. The animal tried at first to reach the loch, uttering cries of distress. Failing in this, it threw itself into strange postures to keep its enemy off. With the coming of a second eagle, however, it made another attempt and gained the water with the first assailant apparently digging its talons into its fur. The otter tried to dive, but the buoyancy of its tenacious foe made this impossible. A long struggle followed. If the one could not dive, the other could not soar. Sometimes the bird was thrown on its side with one wing in the water and one flapping in the air. Presently it seemed to become as frightened as its prey, for so soon as it could disentangle its talons, it retreated to the cliffs above to reflect on this surprising adventure.

The overseer of the sheep-farm once saw two eagles attack a wild drake as it swam in the loch. They acted in concert, the one swooping as the other rose, while at each threatening descent of its enemies the drake dived and swam along under the surface, to come up at as great a distance as possible. The eagles became tired of the unpromising contest and flew off.

In the earlier part of last century eagles were very numerous here. A farmer whose flocks had suffered seriously from their depredations resolved to try to clear them from the neighbourhood. There were several eyries on the cliffs above Loch Dungeon, but in places so perilous to approach that no shepherd would undertake the work of destruction. Climbing to the top of the cliffs and using a rude sort of crane, the farmer dangled a lighted tar-barrel in front of the nests. The startled birds flew out and back and forth over the loch, filling the air with their screams. Their terror overcame their reluctance to desert their young, and they fled the district, never to return in such numbers. The angler, however, must regret their complete disappearance, for it would be a pleasant interlude in his operations to watch the doings of those lordly birds, and give a further wildness to the scene to hear their cries echoing among the rocks.

After passing Loch Dungeon, you go up the glen of the Hawse Burn. A final stiff climb brings you to the summit of the range, and then The Cauldron of The Dungeon is before you. If it were not so large, you would say it was at your feet. No one will ever forget the first view of it from this point. I had spent the night at one of the sheep-farms at the head of the Pulharrow Glen. The shepherd awakened me at four o'clock and by six we were looking into The Cauldron. It was amid the impressive quiet of a sunny morning in June. A green slope ran down from our feet to the broken moor forming the floor of the abyss. Rather more than a mile away was the series of hills that make the other wall—Mullwharchar, The Dungeon, and Craignaw—and behind them the greater heights of Ben-yellary, The Merrick, and Kirriereoch, their summits wreathed in mist. Close under The Dungeon lay three small, ink-black lochs, scowling, you would think, at any attempt to penetrate the secrets of the place. It was almost as if you were looking from the clerestorey into the ruins of some vast, roofless cathedral.

Even more memorable was a winter visit. Frost had hardened the moor, and a cold December breeze was blowing, so that the going had been easy and rapid. It must have been between two and three o'clock in the afternoon when I reached the top of the ridge. I then turned northwards and tramped over ice and crisp snow on the summit of Corserine until, with the changing perspective of the confronting heights, I could look into and beyond the high glen between The Dungeon and Mull-wharchar, and thus, as I went along the hill, there opened out above that glen the waters of Loch Enoch lying under the deep shadow of The Merrick.. The sun shone on Luce Bay thirty miles away; but clouds overhung the land. Suddenly my eyes were arrested by a glory that was beginning to descend upon the wilderness. The clouds were massed to the west, and the sun was going down behind them. The radiance struck them, shot through them, turned them to a dazzling riot of colour, and sent long shafts of gold to search the bleak hills round Loch Dee. That swift effulgence breaking over the rocky hills and chill waters of The Cauldron filled one with a kind of awe.

In the wilder sorts of weather The Cauldron is a dangerous place, and many lives have been lost in it. It must be a wonderful sight under a snowstorm, but it would be well to be within the shepherd's cottage at The Back Hill of The Bush. Many years ago a shepherd who lived there was visited on a winter afternoon by another shepherd from a distant shieling. The visitor was late in departing, and when he began his journey, night was coming on and snow falling. The snow thickened, the darkness

grew deeper, and he had soon lost his way hopelessly. The wind
came in changeful gusts, now from one point and again from
another, so that he could get no guidance from it. He blundered
on for hours in a deepening desperation, seeking for some recog-
nizable landmark, a bend in a stream or a large boulder, but in
vain. At last, confused and baffled, exhausted and benumbed,
he dropped down on the snow and slept.

In the morning the sun rose in a clear sky and shone upon a
radiant world. The shepherd in the cottage under the hill came
to the door and looked abroad. He saw the outline of an unfamiliar object lying under the snow about ten yards away.
He went up to it, found it was the body of a man, removed the
snow from the face, and recognized his friend.

In the spring of a recent year there was found in The Cauldron
the body of a tramp who had there ended his vagrancy. It
was supposed that it had lain for about three months. The
inclement heavens under which the man had doubtless spent
many nights of his life could hardly have crowned their in-
hospitality in a more fitting place.[1]

[1] See Chapter XI.

*Loch Ken from New Galloway Golf-course.*

## CHAPTER XXXII

### NEW GALLOWAY TO THE DUNGEON

New Galloway—Kenmure Castle—The Upper Bridge of Dee—King
  Robert and the widow of Craigencaillie and her three sons—
  The battle of Moss Raploch—Battles of Edward Bruce—Craigen-
  caillie—Loch Dee—Dargall Lane—A byway from Newton
  Stewart.

VISITORS who fail to secure lodgings at Dalry will do well to
stay at New Galloway.[1] If the village cannot claim all the
attractions of Dalry, it possesses others of its own ; has a good
nine-hole golf-course commanding a delightful view of Loch
Ken with Kenmure Castle, surrounded by trees, in the foreground ; and can, moreover, boast of being a royal burgh.

  The existing volumes of the records begin with the year
1799. They contain little of general interest ; but the ordinary
matters dealt with by the authorities are diversified with a few
incidents such as these : " New Galloway 15 Decr. 1804. Com-
peared before the Magistrates & a part of the Councell, Baillie
John Heron to ansuer at the Instance of Jean Coltard in

---

[1] *The Kenmure Arms* combines the excellences of the Dalry hotels.
*The Cross Keys* is smaller, but said to be good.

Greenhead for a Trespass & Damages sustained by her from
the said Baillie Heron's Swine when the Magistrates after
hearing Parties Decern the said Baillie John Heron to make
good the loss sustained by the said Jean Coltart by the said
Baillies Swine riving her Cloak & the Magistrates having
sworn Baillies Thos. McCandlish & James Muir Directed them
to bring in a Verdict of said Damages & they having carefully
Inspected the Cloak find that the Damage amounts to six
shillings sterg. for which sum they Decern with Expences
reserving liberty to the said Baillie Heron to take the whole of
the Cloak at the Sum of Eleven shillings if he so Incline." On
the 27th of October, 1832, it was " unanimously agreed to that
in consequence of the spread of that dreadful Disease called
Cholera That the Fair held in the Month of November commonly called the Hallow Fair should this year be put a stop to
and the Magistrates and Counsellors hereby empower William
Candlish their Depute Clerk to advertise the same in both of
the Dumfries Newspapers the week previous to the usual time
of the holding of the said Hallow Fair."

The burgh was erected by a charter of Charles the First on
the petition of Sir John Gordon of Lochinvar ; but the " universal
Privileges and Immunities of the same " have not led to any
remarkable industrial results. If there is any part of Galloway
for which one should quote Robert Heron, it is this burgh, for
he was a native. Although he thought that " a connected
manufacture of boots and shoes, of saddles, of gloves might have
been formed here " ; that " a small manufacture of coarse
hats might be profitably enough tried at New Galloway " ;
that " the manufacture of linens might succeed here " ; and that
cotton-manufacture " may perhaps be tried at New Galloway " ;
one is thankful for " some circumstances " which caused him to
" fear that no very flourishing manufacture will, for a long while
yet to come, be established at New Galloway ", and that most
of his description holds good : " A few slate-houses, rising to the
height of two storeys, or a storey and a half, are interspersed
among the lower and thatch-covered houses : The little gardens
of the citizens lie close behind their houses, above and below
the town : They are divided by hedges ; and trees rise around,
or here and there among them : the spire of the court-house is
a distinguished object in the groupe : And when the smoke
rises from the little chimnies : and the whole is viewed either

from an elevation above, or from below : no assemblage of objects can be conceived, more pleasing to the eye, and the imagination."

I should hesitate to call the spire of the court-house " a distinguished object ". Its character, of course, distinguishes it from the neighbouring buildings ; but among other structures of the same kind it could hardly be credited with distinction. Some such phrase might, however, be applied with truth to Kenmure Castle, which stands a quarter of a mile south of the burgh.   A part of the building may be sixteenth-century work,

*New Galloway.*

but the greater portion belongs to the seventeenth century. There has, however, been a Kenmure Castle from an early date, The land was owned by the Lords of Galloway of the line of Fergus, and the castle is said to have been a residence of Dervorgilla.  About the beginning of the fifteenth century the Gordons became the proprietors.  Sir John Gordon of Lochinvar. who secured the charter for New Galloway, was raised to the peerage with the titles of Viscount Kenmure and Lord Lochinvar. He was a strong supporter of the Church of Scotland, and many of Samuel Rutherford's letters were addressed to his wife.  William, sixth Viscount, adhered to the Pretender in 1715, was made a prisoner at Preston, and executed on Tower Hill.  His estates and titles were forfeited, but an Act of Parliament restored them

to his direct descendant, John Gordon, in 1824. On the death
of the succeeding peer in 1847 the titles became dormant.

One of the loneliest roads in Scotland runs from New Galloway
to Newton Stewart, passing at first over several miles of moor,
where one sees no living creatures but sheep and moor-fowl.
It is overshadowed on the left by the steep, dark side of the Black
Craig of Dee [1]—if you see the summit when sunshine falls upon
it after a shower of rain, you will remember how it glistens like
a diamond. After crossing the Black Water of Dee the road
ascends over another stretch of moor until it enters the long,
narrow, crag-bounded glen of the Palnure and so descends
gradually towards the Cree Valley. Turning aside from this
road at the Black Water, one can reach The Dungeon without
any climbing.

*On the Road to Newton Stewart.*

The ruins of a bridge built about 1703 are now hid by
Clatteringshaws reservoir. The negotiations for its erection
belong to a time when men were settling down into quiet ways
after the political and religious turmoils ended by the Revolution,
and were turning their attention to practical affairs. The old
bridge is all the more significant that it was built at the instance
of an ecclesiastical court. The ministers and other persons in
Galloway brought influence to bear on the Privy Council in
1695 to induce them to authorize a national contribution, and
when this was refused, the Synod of Galloway raised the funds

[1] It is also called Cairnsmore of Dee.

by ordering a house-to-house collection within its bounds. For once a Synod justified its existence.

About a mile over the slopes on which the byway runs, or perhaps now submerged by the reservoir, is the battlefield of Craignell, and two and a half miles farther on is Craigencaillie, snuggling close under the side of Cairngarroch. Craigencaillie and

*The Upper Bridge of Dee, as it was.*

the moor lying on the north of the Upper Bridge of Dee were the scenes of one of Bruce's adventures. Bruce and his men had barely escaped capture by two converging forces somewhere near Loch Enoch. They had scattered after appointing Craigencaillie as the place of meeting. The King was the first to arrive at this point, and was hospitably received in a widow's house. The tradition preserved in the Macfarlane MSS. in the Advocates' Library, tells how " she, observing some of his princely ornaments, suspected him to be a person of eminence, and modestly asked him in the morning if he was her Leidge Lord. He told her yes, and was come to pay her a visit; and asked her if she had any sons to serve him in his distress. Her answer was that she had three sons to three several husbands; and that, if she was confirmed in the truth of his being their sovereign, they should be at his service. He askt her farther, if she could give him anything to eat. Her answer was, there was little in the house but a grist of [1] meal and goat's milk, which

*The Valley of the Black Water of Dee, from above the Upper Bridge.*

should be prepared for him; and while it was making ready her three sons did appear, all lusty men. The King askt them if they wou'd chearfully engage in his service, which they willingly assented to; and when the King had done eating he askt them what weapons they had, and if they could use them. They told him they were used to none but bow and arrow. So, as the King went out to see what had become of his followers, all being beat from him but 300 men, who had lodged that night in a neighbouring glen, he askt them if they could make use of their bows. M'Kie, the eldest son, let fly an arrow at two ravens parching upon the pinacle of a rock above the house,

[1] The MS. reads *Agust; a grist of* is the emendation adopted by the writer of *The Statistical Account of the Parish of Minnigaff*.

and shot them through both their heads, at which the King smiled, saying, I would not wish he aimed at him. Murdoch, the second son, let fly at one upon the wing, and shot him through the body ; but M'Lurg, the third son, had not so good success.

"In the meantime the English, upon the pursuit of King Robert, were encamped in Moss Raploch, a great flow on the other side of Die. The King, observing them, makes the young men understand that his forces were much inferior. Upon which they advised the King to a stratagem, that they would gather all the horses, wild and tame, in the neighbourhood, with all the goats that could be found, and let them be surrounded and kept all in a body by his soldiers in the afternoon of the day, which accordingly was done. The neighing of the horses, with the horns of the goats, made the English, at so great a distance, apprehend them to be a great army, so durst not venture out of their camp that night ; and by the break of day the King, with his small army, attacked them with such fury that they fled precipitantly, a great number being killed ; and there is a very big stone in the centre of the flow, which is called the King's Stone to this day, to which he leaned his back till his men gather'd up the spoil ; and within these thirty years there were broken swords and heads of picks got in the flow as they were digging out peats."[1]

After the English had been driven from the country " the three brothers, who had stuck close to the King's interest, and followed him through all dangers, being askt by the King what reward they expected ? answered very modestly, that they never had a prospect of great things, but if his Majesty would bestow upon them the thirty pound land of the Hassock and Comloddan they would be very thankful, to which the King chearfully assented, and they kept it long in possession."

According to another version, which Sir Herbert Maxwell follows, the King asked the mother of the three followers how he could best reward her for her help, and she replied : " Just give me the wee bit hassock o' land atween Palnure and Penkiln." This version is obviously better informed, as there is no land bearing the name of Hassock, but the word might be used very well to describe the tract enclosed between the Penkill and Palnure burns. Barbour relates the above story, but speaks of only " twa sonnys ", and does not give the epilogue. With

---

[1] Andrew Heron's *Description*.

regard to the accounts of Bruce's adventures and exploits in Galloway, Lord Hailes says truly enough that " to separate what may be true, or probable, from what is exaggerated, incredible, or false would be a laborious task " ; but there is point also in the remark of Sir Herbert Maxwell that " it is in solitudes such as this, where life has changed little in its outward aspect from remote antiquity, that tradition lingers longest and is least likely to be deceptive."

The story of the sons of the widow at Craigencaillie is supported, moreover, by heraldry and family names. To the gift of the " bit hassock " is traced the origin of the families of MacKie of Larg, Murdoch of Cumloden, and MacClurg[1] of Kirrouchtrie. The armorial bearings of MacKie of Larg were two ravens proper, upon a field argent, with an arrow through their heads ; and of Murdoch of Cumloden, argent, on a chief gules, a raven volant, pierced by an arrow.

When in 1308 nearly all the rest of Scotland had been won by King Robert, Galloway still stood for the English King, and Edward Bruce was sent to subdue it. He met the Gallovidian forces, consisting partly of Scots and partly of English, at Craignell and defeated them. Tradition points to a stand made by the enemy at a ford in the Dee called The Grainy[2] Ford, where they were defeated again. Mackenzie says in *The History of Galloway*, published in 1841, that " in a field called Druim Cheate (in English, ' the place of meeting '), where this encounter took place, on the estate of Deebank, the fragments of many warlike instruments have been found. Not long ago a piece of gold, which in all probability had formed a part of the handle of a sword, was discovered and sold for £6."

This was the beginning of Edward Bruce's victorious career in Galloway. He gradually reduced the province to his brother's allegiance, and received the lordship as a reward for his services.

The byway has on the left rough pastures rising to Craignell and Cairngarroch. On an occasion when I was riding my bicycle this way, I saw a sheep lying apparently dead with its legs in the air. Then it occurred to me that this might be a case of having fallen " aval " and took the necessary action. John Mactaggart says in *The Scottish Gallovidian Encyclopædia* (1824), " When an animal lies down upon its back, in such a

---

[1] See page 152.    [2] Gaelic *greanach*, gravelly.

manner that it cannot bring its feet to bear up its body, so as
to rise again, we say, that animal is *aval*. Ewes with lamb are
often in this state, and must be set on their feet by the shepherd's
aid, if not, they soon become a prey to the *corbies* and *hoody-
craws*."

Almost as soon as one leaves the Newton Stewart road and
takes the byway leading to The Dungeon, one crosses the route
of the old Edinburgh Road, which was broken up many years ago,
and thenceforward the track lies over the broad stretch of moor
between the heights of Low Craignell and Darnaw on the one hand
and the reservoir on the other. The house of Craigencaillie, with
its little clump of trees at the end of a small enclosure, and the
steep rugged side of Cairngarroch rising so close behind it that
from the edge of the summit you could almost drop a stone
down the chimneys, is the terminus of the road. You now
follow a rough footpath winding among heather and imbedded
boulders along the lower slopes of Cairngarroch. After about a
mile one comes opposite the point where the Cornelloch Burn,
which rises in Meikle Millyea, falls into the Dee. In dry weather
it is a mere trickle of clear water purling down the midst of one
wide slab of granite after another. Here the bed of the river is
covered with great boulders, and at various points, by means of
a series of carefully calculated leaps, it is possible to arrive
dry-shod on the farther bank. You then begin a rough moorland
walk of about four miles to The Back Hill of The Bush, and have
all the width of the moor from which to choose your route.
When you have left the Cornelloch Burn behind, you are well
within that vast enclosure of the hills which is bounded on the
east by the green, swelling sides of the Kells heights, Millyea,
Milldown, Millfire, and Corserine ; on the west by the steep crags
of Craiglee, Craignaw, and The Dungeon ; on the north by Craigtarson (" the thwart crag "), a spur running out from the Kells
range ; and on the south by Cairngarroch and Curleywee.[1]

If the Dee were in heavy flood, this route would be impracticable. A season of rains, indeed, would not be a time for
visiting The Dungeon at all. But if, after coming by Craigencaillie, you were determined to reach The Back Hill of The
Bush, it would be necessary to make a wide circuit round Loch
Dee, hoping to avoid the bogs under The Dungeon, which would
then be in a dangerous state.

[1] Gaelic *cor na ghaeith*, windy peak.

Loch Dee is itself a delightful place. Its shores of silver
sand, its granite islets covered with heath, and its background

*Loch Dee.*

of dark, steep mountains make it one of the grandest scenes
in Galloway. If you have obtained permission to fish, you have

the possibility of great sport before you, for the average trout
weighs about two pounds. The fish are very game and need
strong tackle. A secondary recommendation of the loch is
that, although it lies so far in the wilds, there is comfortable
lodging close at hand in The Black Laggan, the shepherd's
cottage standing near the southmost corner in a little glen
between Cairngarroch and Curleywee.

The Dargall Lane entering the loch at the west end is
perhaps the most unwholesome sight in Galloway. If any
place could be said to wear a look of moral obliquity, it is the
patch of bog where it emerges and lurks. The water does not
come dancing gaily among glittering stones from the heights, or
coursing over clean sand, but is simply there like a nightmare
or a stealthy declaration of war. Its converging streams,
narrow, furtive, almost hidden by the grasses, are of a staggering depth and, swelling flush with the surface of the moss, are
a natural trap for man and beast. The shepherds have fenced
them round.

In a book dealing professedly with byways I must not omit
the most memorable one in my experience, the steep bridle-
path rising behind The Black Laggan. It brings you soon to
a narrow pass on the side of Curleywee and plunges down into
the grimmest glen in Galloway, that of the Pulnee.[1] With
the hopefulness of ignorance I once decided to approach Loch
Dee by this route. Intending to stay at The Black Laggan for
several days, I had more luggage than is usual on such expeditions
and had bestowed it in a bag attached to the rear of my
bicycle.

The road from Newton Stewart ends at the farmhouse of
Auchinleck, and from that point to Loch Dee is about five
miles. Of this distance I suppose that I may have ridden
about five hundred yards altogether. For the rest, it was a
most laborious and disheartening journey. The bicycle made
frantic attempts to bury itself in gravel. The pedals jarred
continually against great boulders. On some of the steeper
places progress ceased altogether for the moment, and the
bicycle and I slid pathetically backwards among loose stones.
Sometimes the front-wheel and handle-bars turned right round
and faced me reproachfully and even angrily. More than once

---

[1] Gaelic *poll na' fhiadh*, the deers' stream.

the bicycle gave up the whole business in despair and lay down on the rocks with a weary clatter. Two shepherds passed me, and I shall not forget their look of silent stupefaction.

I do not think that the Pulnee Glen is named in Mr. J. McBain's *The Merrick and the Neighbouring Hills : Tramps by Hill, Stream, and Loch ;*[1] but this must be a mere accident. He knows all this wild country as minutely as most people know their gardens. His delightful chapters recounting his rambles and exploits should not be neglected by anyone who has been captivated by these hills and glens.

[1] Ayr : Stephen & Pollock : 1929.

*Loch Dee from the south-east.*

# CHAPTER XXXIII

## BALMACLELLAN, CORSOCK, AND CROCKETFORD

Balmaclellan—Persecution of Covenanters—Elspeth MacEwen—
  Monument to " Old Mortality "—Covenanter's grave —The
  Headless Piper—Corsock—Sufferings of John Neilson.—Loch-
  enkit martyrs' grave—James Clerk Maxwell—Crocketford and
  the Buchanites—Elspeth Simpson and Hugh White—Tenets
  and practices—The Midnight Manifestation—The Great Fast
  —The Great Fiasco—Friend Mother dies at Auchengibbert—
  The Society at Crocketford—Andrew Innes.

BALMACLELLAN[1] lacks only one thing—lodging for visitors.
Lying in a steep fold of a hill, it is just under the edge of a plateau
where there are such richly scented bog-meadows and moors
as are rarely found outside of poetry books, waysides that
scintillate with flowers, little knolls where the black Galloway
cattle often stand silhouetted against the sky—knolls where
you can look down upon Loch Ken and New Galloway and
feel almost on terms of equality with the Kells mountains—
streams inhabited by red-fleshed trout, and just one or two
cottages where you may spend weeks of superlative blessedness
if your proud spirit can brook a camp-ceiled room with a skylight ! What sounds come in through that skylight !—the
deep-bass remonstrance of calves thirsting for the milk-pails ;
the plaintive, clamorous, sometimes enraged bleating of lambs ;
the vehement gug-gug-gug of the grouse making a prodigious
fuss about nothing ; the resignedly sad wail of the whaup,
tapering away gradually into silence and suggesting a loneliness
like that of one exiled from both Heaven and Hell ; the pee-

---

[1] Gaelic, Maclellan's village.

wit's patient reiteration of its name to an inattentive world.
What scents are wafted in from the honeysuckle in the cottage-
garden and from the richest of bog-meadows across the road !
Upon what a world of delicate beauty and quiet do you look
out from that skylight !—the wayside clump of willows overhanging the ditch blue with forget-me-not ; the bright-green
sea of the meadow spangled with crimson ragged-robin, butter-
cups, speedwell, and " purple orchises with spotted leaves " ;
the brown moors turning to purple where the ridges meet the
sky. Here you are outside of any community, clear even of the
small village, enisled in the country as the lonely cottar knows
it. Here is richness, here is sweetness, here is pastoral peace
like a river. If I had occasion to choose a site for a house in
Galloway, it should be here. It is indeed difficult to write of
it all without rushing off incontinently to revel in it.

It seems incongruous to-day that this quiet parish should
be associated with barbarities to Covenanters and the persecution of women alleged to be witches. Yet these are matters
of actual history. When Sir William Bannatyne came into
Galloway after the failure of the Pentland Rising, his soldiers
were ordered to search for David MacGill in this parish. MacGill
eluded them by disguising himself in woman's clothes. The
persecutors avenged themselves on his wife, whom they accused
of being accessory to his escape. They bound her, put burning
matches between her fingers, and kept her in torture for hours.
She was driven nearly mad with pain. One of her hands was
entirely destroyed, and she died in a few days.

Mackenzie gives the following account of Elspeth MacEwen,
who was brought to trial for witchcraft in 1698 : " Elspeth lived
in a solitary house in the farm of Cubbox, called Bogha'. As
appears from the evidence of two gentlemen who visited her
in the jail of Kirkcudbright, she was a person of superior education. Still, however, her neighbours were tormented with her,
and every calamity that befel themselves or their cattle was
attributed to Elspeth's witchcraft. If a cow fell ill, it was
Elspeth's doing. It was, also, currently reported and believed
that if eggs were wanted at New-Galloway, application had
only to be made to the old wife of Bogha', and the market
was well supplied. But the worst cantrip that she played on
the wights of Balmaclellan was the following. She had a
pin in the kipple-foot, and when she pleased, could, by taking

out that pin, draw milk from her neighbours' cows. At length complaint was made to the Session, and the beadel, M'Lambroch, was sent off with the minister's mare to bring her to the Session. Elspeth, after expressing great wonder at this usage from the minister, consented to go. Tradition states, that the mare was dreadfully frightened, and, at a rising hill near the manse, since called the ' Bluidy Brae,' sweat great drops of blood. After undergoing an examination, she was sent off to Kirkcudbright, and confined there for about two years. Her imprisonment was rendered so wretched by her tormentors, that the miserable woman implored them to terminate a life so full of suffering. She was condemned, taken from prison, and burnt to death in the neighbourhood of Kirkcudbright."

Balmaclellan Churchyard contains a monument to " Old Mortality " with this inscription : " To the Memory of Robert Paterson, Stone Engraver, well known as ' Old Mortality ', who died at Bankend of Carlaverock, 14th February 1800, aged 88." Paterson's wife supported the family by teaching a school in Balmaclellan while he went about the country with his white pony visiting the graves of the Covenanters, repairing the old inscriptions, and erecting new monuments. There is also in this churchyard the grave of " Robert Grierson, who was shot to death by command of Colanel James Douglase, at Inglestoun, in the paroch of Glencarn, Anno 1685." The table stone covering the grave bears the following epitaph :

```
THIS MONMENT TO PASSENGERS SHALL CRY
THAT GOODLY GRIERSON UNDER IT DOTH LY.
BETRAY'D BY KNAVISH WATSON TO HIS FOES
WHICH MADE THIS MARTYR'S DAYS BY MURTHER CLOSE
IF YE WOULD KNOW THE NATURE OF HIS CRIME
THEN READ THE STORY OF THAT KILLING TIME
WHEN BABEL'S BRATS WITH HELLISH PLOTS CONCEALD
DESIGN'D TO MAKE OUR SOUTH THEIR HUNTING FIELD
HERE'S ONE OF FIVE AT ONCE WERE LAID IN DUST
TO GRATIFY ROME'S EXECRABLE LUST.
IF CARABINES WITH MOLTEN BULLETS COULD
HAVE REACHED THEIR SOULS THESE MIGHTY NIMRODS WOULD
THEM HAVE CUT OF FOR THERE COULD NO REQUEST
THREE MINUTES GET TO PRAY FOR FUTUR REST.
```

This stone is of comparatively late date. Another monument about sixty feet west of the church bears no carving or inscription, and is said to mark the grave of a witch.

R

Moors stretch eastward from Balmaclellan to Corsock.[1] The two chief constituents of the landscapes are the wide sweeps of peat-moss rising to distant craggy knolls and exhaling the pungent scent of bog-myrtle, and the occasional plantations of fir and larch. At long intervals there is a whitewashed cottage with its little garden by the roadside. If you travel this way by night, you may suspect the presence of the ghosts of cattle-droves and drovers[2] and actually meet that of The Headless Piper.

" Many years ago a drover, while making his way north and crossing that wild and thinly populated district which lies between the head of the parish of Parton and the Moor of Corsock, had the following uncanny experience : He had left the Parton district late in the afternoon with the intention of reaching a farm-house some miles north of the village of Corsock. By the time he reached the path over Corsock Hill, however, it had become dark, and occasional flashes of lightning foretold that a storm was at hand. With loud peals of thunder, vivid flashes of lightning, and a downpour of rain the storm at last broke. The only shelter near at hand was some thorn bushes by the roadside, under which the drover crept and stayed for fully an hour, while the storm raged and the darkness increased. When the storm had somewhat abated, the drover set out once more, hurrying as fast as the darkness would allow him. He had reached a very desolate part of the moor when his collie gave a low whine and crept close to his master's heels. The

---

[1] " Welsh and Cornish *cors*, ' bog, fen ', +dimin. *oc*. or *og*. "—Johnston.

[2] " The droves of cattle coming from New Galloway to England come by Trowhen, Knockdoket, then a litle north of Lochinkit till they come to Gal'gate, and then follow it southward till within about half a mile of Easter Marwhirn, and so on to Larg, and then to Dunfreis, &c.

" The best way but somewhat longer from Dumfreis to New Galloway is by Lochruttongate near the church, Miltoun of Urr, Kilpatrick Church, Kilwhamedy, Parton, Shirmers, New Galloway.

" From Dumfreis to Kirkcudbright the way is by Miltoun, Grange, Bridge of Urr, Carlingwork, &c. But if the water be litle, the nearer way is by Miltoun, Haugt, Carlingwork, &c. This is most patent for coaches and carts, and nearer."—*Description of the Parish of Kilpatrick Durham* (Macfarlane MSS. Vol. I, p. 510. Adv. Lib. Jac. 5th. 4. 19), printed in *Geographical Collections Relating to Scotland.*

drover stood up for a moment to try to find a reason for the dog's behaviour, when down in the glen between the hills he heard what at first appeared the sound of bagpipes, which increased quickly to a shrill, piercing wailing that struck terror to his heart, the collie creeping closer and closer to his heel, whining in a way that shewed he was as much frightened as his master.

" As he stood irresolute, a blaze of blue light flashed right in front of him, in the centre of which appeared the figure of a piper, his pipes standing like horns against the background of blue light. The figure moved backwards and forwards, playing the wildest of music all the time. It next seemed to come nearer and nearer, and the drover, now transfixed to earth with terror, saw that the piper was headless, and his body so thin that surrounding hills and country could be seen right through it. A blinding flash of fire, followed by an ear-splitting clap of thunder, brought matters to a close for the time being, and the drover fell prostrate among the heather. When he recovered his senses, the strange light had gone, and with it the headless piper. The storm had cleared off, and in due time he reached the farm, where he was put up for the night. When he told his story, no one spoke for a moment or two ; then the farmer's aged father broke silence : ' Ay, ay, lad, ye hae seen the ghost o' the piper wha was murdered on his wey frae Patiesthorn. I hae had the same fearsome experience myself, though it's mair than saxty years syne.' "[1]

Shortly before passing through the village of Corsock, the road begins to descend towards the Water of Urr, and after leaving the village skirts the wooded grounds of the Corsock estate. Corsock House was the home of Alexander Murray Dunlop, who acted as legal adviser to the party in the Church who seceded in 1843 and formed The Free Church of Scotland. It was he who drew up the famous document embodying the " Claim, Declaration, and Protest " adopted by the General Assembly of the Church of Scotland " anent the Encroachments of the Court of Session " in 1842, and, when the Government refused to admit the claims of the Church, the " Protest "

---

[1] From a letter by Mr. John Copland in Dr. Maxwell Wood's *Witchcraft and Superstitious Record in the South-Western District of Scotland.*

which was laid on the table of the Assembly of 1843 by the seceders.

Memories of an older religious struggle belong to the remains of a castle on the neighbouring farm of Hallcroft, once the home of a notable Covenanter. When Gabriel Semple, minister of Kirkpatrick-Durham, was driven from his charge in 1662, he found a home with John Neilson at Corsock Castle and preached within its walls. As the congregations became too large for the castle, they assembled in the garden, and presently they were grown so great that nothing less than the open field would serve. This, according to Wodrow, was the beginning of the "field-preachings" which were so largely resorted to by the Covenanters in the days when the Church was in the Wilderness. Neilson became a target for the hostility of the ecclesiastical and Government authorities. He was fined; troops were quartered in his home until he and his tenants were brought to the verge of ruin; and it is not strange that he should have taken part in the Pentland Rising. He was one of the prisoners captured at Rullion Green, and was tortured with " the boot " in order to extract from him an admission that there had been a settled plan of rebellion. He was sentenced to death for his complicity in the Rising and hanged at the Market Cross of Edinburgh. The following inscription is on a monument in Kirkpatrick-Durham Churchyard : HERE LYES THE EMINENTLY GODLY MARY McLELLAN LADY OF CORSOCK WHO DIED SEP 28 1697 WHOSE HUSBAND IOHN NEILSONE LAIRD OF CORSOCK FOR APPEARING FOR THE COVENANTS AT PENTLAND SUFFERED MARTYRDOM AT EDR : DECR : 14 : 1666 AND IS BURIED THERE IN GRAYFRIERS AND IOHN NEILSONE OF CORSOCK SPOUSE TO ANNA GORDOUN WHO DIED THE 24 DCMR 1706 WHO WAS PIOUSLY DEVOTED WITH HEROICK COURAGE TO MANTINE THE WORK OF REFORMATION AS WAS HIS NOBLE PROGENITOR.

Another memorial of the Covenanters stands on the broad face of a moorland hill near Lochenkit,[1] about three miles east of the bridge at Corsock, and covers the grave of four martyrs.[2] For anyone going thither by way of Brooklands, a granite monument erected in 1843 serves as a guide-post. The grave itself is surrounded by a small clump of trees, and the stone is inscribed thus :

[1] Gaelic *loch an chait*, loch of the wild cat.
[2] See page 23.

HERE LIES
Four Martyrs, John Wallace, William
Heron, John Gordon, and William
Stewart, found out and shot dead
upon the place by Captain *Bruce*
and Captain *Lag* for their adhearing
to the word of GOD, CHRIST'S Kingly
Government in his House and the
Covenanted work of reformation
against Tyranny, Perjury, & Prelacy.
2nd March MDCLXXXV

Rev. Chap. XII ver. II.

Behold ! here in this wilderness we lie,
Four witnesses of hellish cruelty.
Our lives and blood did not their ire assuage,
But when we're dead they did against us rage
That match the like we think ye scarcly can
Except the *Turk* or *Duke de Alva's* men.

To the annoyance of every visitor, the stone has been profaned
with additional inscriptions stating that it had been repaired
at various times by means of money raised after the preaching
of sermons by certain persons who might have had the good
sense to inhibit this outrage.

The most famous name connected with the Corsock district
is that of the great physicist, James Clerk Maxwell, who was
the son of the proprietor of the Glenlair estate and succeeded
his father in 1856. He was born in 1831 and educated at
Edinburgh and Cambridge. He held in succession the chairs
of Natural Philosophy in Marischal College, Aberdeen, of
Physics and Astronomy in King's College, London, and of
Experimental Physics in Cambridge. It was under his direction
that the Cavendish Laboratory in Cambridge was built and
equipped. He won a world-wide reputation through his researches in electricity and magnetism. In the biography
written by Professor Lewis Campbell and William Garnett
there is a picture of his boyish days at Glenlair, when it was
his pleasure " to scramble up the bed of the eddying stream that
' flowed past the smiddy to the sea,' and mark the intricate
tracery of holes and grooves which, in rolling the shingle, it
had worn and carved in the hard rocks ; or to watch the same
river in a ' spate ' ; rushing and whirling over those ' pots '
which it had wrought, and piling up the foam into mimic towers
like the cumuli of the sky." Clerk Maxwell was a man of intense

Christian faith, and when one enters the parish church of Corsock and looks at the stained-glass window erected to his memory, one remembers his scientific achievement less than those wonderful letters to his wife which make one think of the epistles of S. Paul.

The village of Crocketford is about five miles farther on and stands at the junction of the road from Balmaclellan with the broad highway running between Castle Douglas and Maxwell-town. Its one claim to notice is that the sect known as the Buchanites[1] had their later settlements here and founded the village. Delusion, imposture, and fanaticism have produced many strange growths in the history of religion; but Scotland has been comparatively free from such excrescences as the Buchanite Society. The leading spirits were Mrs. Buchan and the Rev. Hugh White.

Elspeth Simpson, the founder of the sect, was the daughter of the proprietor of an inn near Banff, and was born in 1738. She became the wife of a potter named Robert Buchan. After some years she separated from him and settled with her children in Glasgow. Ignorance, hysteria, and a perusal of the apocalyptic books of the Bible led her to believe that she had a religious mission, and induced " divine visions " and " revelations ".

Hugh White had been a licentiate of the Church of Scotland who had failed to secure an ecclesiastical appointment and had gone to America, where he may have been in contact with " The Shakers ". He returned to his native land with a deceptive academic halo, having acted as a " Professor " in some sort of college in America, and when he became minister of the Relief congregation in Irvine, was supposed by the rabble to be some great one. His dupes were unable to test his academic pretensions for themselves; they were further impressed by his blatant self-assertion, his sanctimonious punctilios, and those noisy crudities with which

> The weak perhaps are moved, but are not taught;

and a success was scored for the sounding brass and the tinkling cymbal. The holy ministry, indeed, was become a

---

[1] See Joseph Train's *The Buchanites from First to Last* (1846) and *History of the Buchanite Delusion :* 1783–1846, by John Cameron (1904).

profession in which Mr. White might have a career; the ambassador for Christ, a trickster in gown and cassock; the pulpit, a stage to support his capers; the material of preaching, so far as he was acquainted with it, a set of balls to be juggled with to the best personal advantage. It is instructive that the one conspirator, for whom chicanery and humbug were the breath of life, should have been gulled by the other.

He went to preach in Glasgow on a sacramental occasion, and Mrs. Buchan, who had not only heard of his fame, but had already corresponded with him, was present. She was immediately convinced of their spiritual affinity—if one were to do justice to Mrs. Buchan's peculiar modes of thought, one would rather say, their spiritual consanguinity—and she wrote a letter[1] to White in which she said:

" Rev. Dear Sir, Whom I love in our sweet Lord Jesus.

" I write you as a friend, not after the flesh, but as a Child of another Family that has lain in the womb of the everlasting decree from all eternity—a promised seed born from above. . . . I have met with many disappointments from ministers who were neither strangers nor pilgrims on the earth, and I can say by sad experience that I have been more stumbled by ministers than by all the men in the world, or by all the devils in hell. But I have rejoiced many times by the eye of faith to see you before I saw you with the eyes of my body."

---

[1] It is a pity that Train thought it advisable to put the letters of Mrs. Buchan which he quotes into a more presentable form than the original. The following is an extract from a letter quoted by Mr. Cameron : " O that you would concidder that he that will com will com & will not tarey. The popel hear some of them sies and firmeley belives that we are the children of God & would joine with us chierfuley but the Devil and the world and espesealey the clargey is become so uneasey that it apeares that this place will not be abel to bear us much longer so we desire you to make all spead & leat be joined in one in all things, & indeed I rather see you hear then ten thousand leatters from you ; for I all moast can not writ, for this is not a time for writ, but speaking face to face. We have thouaht it fit to send the berar to speake face to face with you, and he will inform you of all things as they are. We are all well in loat and portion, being God who has seperat us from a world laying in wickedness, but our souls are wired because of murderers. Now I beche you com out from among them & be ye seperat, & I am shoure I long to see you bothe hear."

The idea of " wired souls " is puzzling until one realizes that the writer means " wearied ".

Here we have the first hint of the doctrine that Mrs. Buchan was the " woman clothed with the sun, and the moon under her feet, and upon her head a crown of twelve stars " of the twelfth chapter of *The Book of The Revelation*, and that White was the spiritual " man child ". When White was initiated, he was dazzled and succumbed. As Mrs. Buchan's ally, it seemed, he might rise to greater things than he had hitherto hoped.

Mrs. Buchan was an antinomian, although it is possible that she was unfamiliar with the term and ignorant of her kinship with the Valentinian Gnostics. The marriage laws of the Bible and of Britain, she considered, were not only useless, but hurtful, and her disciples were set free from their bondage. What was regarded as sin by " carnal and worldly people " could not, if done by her followers, be offensive in the sight of God.

She gave great prominence to her theory of the Last Things. White announced that she was an Incarnation of The Holy Ghost and that all who did not accept her as such and receive her teachings would be consumed in the approaching conflagration of the world, when the Lord would appear and translate her and her adherents bodily to heaven.

These doctrines had not been developed, or at least were not published, in their full enormity when Mrs. Buchan first came to Irvine on White's invitation ; but religious conferences were held, and the fame of Mrs. Buchan's exalted piety and of her wonderful interpretations of prophetic and mystical passages of the Scriptures spread abroad. Her extravagance was too much for some of her hearers, who began to entertain grave doubts of their minister's orthodoxy—he intervened sometimes to explain that Mrs. Buchan's statements did not mean what they meant—and urged that it was desirable that Mrs. Buchan's visit should end. When she had gone, a deputation of the more sober-minded of the congregation entreated their minister to renounce all connexion with her ; but he refused, declaring that he would rather resign his charge. He was taken on trial for heresy by the Presbytery and deposed from his office.

Thereafter Mrs. Buchan returned to Irvine with White, and meetings were held in his house. The number who came out of sympathy or curiosity grew, and a tent was erected in the garden. While the conferences were going on, the meeting-place was pelted with stones and plastered with filth by the irreverent. It was under the impulse of the opposition and persecution that ensued that Mrs. Buchan proclaimed publicly that she was The Woman Clothed with the Sun and that White was The Man-child, of whom she had been spiritually delivered and who was to " rule the nations with a rod of iron ". This did not serve to conciliate popular opinion. Some adherents were secured, however, and Mrs. Buchan was given the honorific title of " Friend Mother in the Lord ". She was known also as " Light and Love " and as " Mercy ". The Man-child was content to be called " Friend White ". The resentment aroused by the Buchanites led to riots, and the little sect were driven from the town. The mob of Irvine thus supported Mrs. Buchan's theory to the extent of acting the part of the dragon before whom " the woman fled into the wilderness."

After wandering in the wilderness for a time, the company, who numbered forty-six, settled on the farm of New Cample, about a mile south of Thornhill. " Here ", says Andrew Innes, one of Friend Mother in the Lord's most zealous followers, " our apostolic life commenced. ' All that believed were together and had all things common '." At meals " all sat at the same table, and partook alike of the same food, with the exception of Friend Mother, who either served those at table herself, or was employed in directing others to do so. When the meal was over, she always pointed to one of the men to stand up before her. to whom she directed the subject of her discourse, while we all listened ; after which, a hymn being sung, we separated, and she commonly went to take a walk in the fields with Mr. White." The men, women, and children all passed the night in one dormitory. Burns, who had some knowledge of the sect, says of them in a letter dated the 3rd of August, 1784, that is, four months after the exodus from Irvine, " Their tenets are a strange jumble of enthusiastic jargon. Among others, she (Mrs. Buchan) pretends to give them the Holy Ghost by breathing on them, which she does with postures and practices that are scandalously indecent. They likewise dispose of all their effects, and hold a community of goods, and live nearly an idle life,[1] carrying on

---

[1] This detail is not true of the later history of the Buchanites. They " lived frugal and industrious lives, worked as carpenters, constructed spinning wheels and articles of domestic use, spun wool, wove stockings and woollen garments."—*The Book of Kirk-*

a great farce of pretended devotion in barns and woods, where they lie and lodge together, and hold likewise a community of women, as it is another of their tenets that they can commit no moral sin. I am personally acquainted with most of them, and can assure you that the above-mentioned are facts."

The time spent in the wilderness by The Woman Clothed with the Sun was twelve hundred and sixty days ; when, therefore, nearly three years and a half had passed since Friend Mother in the Lord had been spiritually delivered of Man-child White, it was believed that the date for the translation of the company to heaven must be close at hand, and efforts were made to bring together all Friend Mother's adherents, some of whom had remained in Irvine, that they might not miss the great event. Altogether sixty persons were assembled, and Friend Mother did her utmost to arouse their enthusiastic anticipations. " One evening," says Innes, " when we were all as usual employed, on a sudden a loud voice was heard as if from the clouds. The children, assisted by our great Luminary, struck up the hymn beginning :

> Oh ! hasten translation and come resurrection,
> Oh ! hasten the coming of Christ in the air.

All the members below instantly started to their feet, and those in the garret hurried down as fast as they possibly could through the trap door. But it being about midnight, and no light in the house, Mr. Hunter in the agitation of the moment, tumbled headlong down the ladder. In an instant, however, he bounded from the ground and with a voice as loud as a trumpet joined in the general chorus. The bodily agitation became so great with the clapping of hands and singing, that it is out of my power to convey a just idea of the scene. Every one thought the blessed moment was arrived ; and every one singing, leaping, and clapping his hands, pressed forward to the kitchen, where Friend Mother sat with great composure, whilst her face shone so white with the glory of God as to dazzle the sight of those who beheld it, and her raiment was as white as snow !

*patrick-Durham, Kirkcudbrightshire*, by the Rev. William A. Stark. They introduced the two-handed spinning-wheel into Galloway and had no rivals in its use in the south of Scotland. " They frequently spun yarn to the fineness of seven dozen cuts to the pound for the neighbouring gentry."—*Castle-Douglas Miscellany.*

" The noise was so loud that the neighbourhood was alarmed. Thomas Davidson, our landlord, came to our door like a man out of his senses. He rapped and called at the door till he obtained admission ; and he too squeezed into the kitchen, beseeching her to save him and the multitude by which the house was surrounded from the pending destruction of the world. She told them, however, to be of good cheer, for no one would suffer damage that night, for she now saw her people were not sufficiently prepared for the mighty change she intended them to undergo.

" As the light passed from her countenance, she called for a tobacco pipe, and took a smoke."

This thaumaturgic event was remembered among the sect as The Midnight Manifestation. The next episode was The Great Fast ordered by Friend Mother for the purification of her followers. If they fasted for forty days, they might be sufficiently prepared to ascend into heaven. The rigour of the fast, however, was mitigated with doses of " treacle mixed with hot water and allowed to cool ". As the period of the fast drew to an end, " White began to dress himself regularly in full clerical costume, gown, bands, and white gloves, and strut about the fields, every now and then surveying the heavens as if in momentary expectation of some preliminary sign of the coming event, while groups of country people watched his absurd performances afar off ; some with superstitious awe, others with ill-concealed scorn."

A light platform had been erected on Templand Hill in preparation for the company's departure heavenwards, and thither they betook themselves before dawn when the fortieth day had run its course. " While they were shouting, singing, and wildly stretching forth their hands from their frail platform to the rising sun, and while their glorious Mother—sublimely exalted above the rest, her buxom beauty showing well against the morning sky, and her long hair streaming in the breeze in the ecstasy of the moment—seemed like some divine Hebe about to return to her native sphere amid her quiring worshippers, suddenly a gust of wind swept across the hilltop ; the slight erections on which they were frantically swaying about fell to pieces, and vanished in a mass of struggling humanity, including the arch-impostor ! "

Instead of flying up to heaven, they had come ignominiously to earth. The Society did not recover from the blow. Many of the members went away and returned to a more orderly life. A remnant, however, accepted Friend Mother's explanation of the failure, that it had been due to want of faith on the part of her followers. New persecutions arose,[1] and the attenuated Society found refuge at Auchengibbert[2] in the parish of Urr. There, in March, 1791, Friend Mother died. When her end was drawing near, she told her companions that she had received sure evidence that she was The Third Person in The Holy Trinity, and that, therefore, although she might appear to die, she would not do so really. If they had sufficient faith, they might count upon her reappearing in six days, or if not in six days, in ten years, or if not in ten years, in fifty.

Extraordinary in its beginning and in its development, the story of the Buchanite delusion was, if possible, still more extraordinary in its ending, for Friend Mother by her dying promise secured the lasting credulity of her dupes. They enclosed her body in a wooden coffin and bore it with them to a new residence on Larghill near Lochenkit. At this time the Society was further reduced by the departure of White and some other members for America, and only twelve remained when another change of abode became necessary, and the survivors settled at Newhouse, Crocketford. Perhaps Friend Mother did not expect that any of her adherents would survive her for half a century ; yet Andrew Innes, who had reverently watched over her body, was still living when the fiftieth anniversary came round, full of faith and hope that he would see the body reanimated and that the promise would come true for him. He became pathetically excited as the 29th of March, 1841, drew near. The day came, and the night fell, and hope was unfulfilled. Once more there was an explanation—he was unworthy of so great a boon ! A little more than four years

---

[1] White wrote hymns and odes. The following stanza is from one of his pæans :

> The people in Closeburn parish residing
>   Came often our sermons to hear,
> And rudely they questioned our words, tho' most pure ;
>   Our persons they threatened to tear.
> They often with batons and cudgels combined,
>   With billets of wood and with stones ;
> But He Who has power all men to control
>   Prevented them breaking our bones.

[2] Gaelic *achadh an tiobair*, the well field.

later Innes died and was buried along with the body of Friend
Mother in the yard behind Newhouse. In accordance with
his instructions, his coffin was laid above hers so that if she rose,
he would be sure to rise too !

Hence comes the sad fate of Crocketford, that no one can
take it seriously. It seems as if the waving cornfields whispered
Buchanite absurdities, as if fatuous aspirations were borne
about innocuously on the moorland winds. The stones of the
village shout "Chicanery !" as the carts trundle through it,
and its very burial-place provokes the laughter of the
generations.

*Thrieve Castle.*

# CHAPTER XXXIV

### CASTLE DOUGLAS AND ITS NEIGHBOURHOOD

Castle Douglas—Former names—Carlinwark Loch—Thrieve Castle
—Archibald the Grim—William Douglas—Archibald the Tineman—The Duchess of Touraine—The fifth Earl—The sixth
Earl—The black dinner—James the Gross—The eighth Earl
and The Fair Maid of Galloway—James, the ninth Earl—The
Douglas power is broken—Later history of the castle—Architectural features—The Levellers—Laurieston—Lochenbreck—The
road from Laurieston to New Galloway—John Macmillan,
minister of Balmaghie and first minister of The Reformed
Presbyterian Church—Tombstones in Balmaghie Churchyard.

THE road from New Galloway to Castle Douglas crosses the
river by a handsome bridge, runs down the east side of Loch
Ken, and passes through the villages of Parton,[1] a pretty row of
cottages ; Crossmichael, where there is a martyr's grave ;
and Greenlaw, where the cats seem to outnumber the other
inhabitants.

There was a time when people whose hearts leap up at the
thought of crossing a river by a ferry could know this thrill
by going down the west side of Loch Ken to New Galloway
Station and then following the byway running east on the
north side of the line until they reached the narrows where the
natural Loch Ken ended, committing its waters to the Dee.

---

1 " Preserved within the modern church at Parton is a small
fragment of an effigy of a priest sculptured in low relief.  A portion
of an inscription in black letter is still decipherable, and reads
QUI OBIIT.  What is left of the effigy shows a few inches of the
end of the chasuble, the two ends of the stole, and the skirt of the
albe.  The ornamentation of the vestments is unusually rich.
Probably it dates from the first half of the sixteenth century."—
The *Inventory*.

The Boat o' Rhone ferry was just below the viaduct. Here was the scene of one of S. R. Crockett's short stories, " A Cry across the Black Water ".[1]

When one has been living for, say, some weeks in the quiet of The Glenkens or touring for days among moors and little whitewashed villages, it is an abrupt change to enter the delightful, modern town of Castle Douglas, with its well-appointed hotels, good shops, and busy population—a place wearing an air of mingled dignity and liveliness. Here you may stroll along streets with concrete pavements, meet considerable numbers of your fellow-creatures, buy books, replenish your wardrobe, and, since Castle Douglas lies on the great road connecting Dumfries and Stranraer, see motor-buses running to and from the greater towns and many cars and lorries passing through.

Within a short period the place had its name changed twice. A little village taking its name from an old causeway running across a morass on the border of Carlinwark Loch was known as Causewayend until the eighteenth century. There were people living in 1844 who remembered a cluster of cottages with a population of no more than twenty. The level of the loch was lowered in 1765 in order to give access to the thick underlying deposit of marl—a calcareous clay used at that time as manure ; and the industry of digging and distributing it brought a large influx of labourers. The expanding village came to be called Carlinwark. William Douglas, the merchant and manufacturer (afterwards Sir William Douglas of Gelston), purchased the land in 1789, had the village erected into a burgh of barony in 1792, and named it Castle Douglas. The name of the burgh, therefore, has no connexion with the Douglases who were Lords of Galloway. *The Statistical Account* of 1844 mentions the fact that " Castle Douglas is the great mart, not only of the parish of Kelton, but of the whole stewartry ", and says that " this town, the suddenness of whose rise rivals the rapid growth of towns in America, has already attained an importance that, in most cases, is the growth of ages. In an agricultural point of view, it far surpasses any other town in Galloway ; and, with the exception of Dumfries, it is second to none in the south of Scotland." This statement still holds good.

[1] *Bog-Myrtle and Peat.*

The space allotted to places in this book is usually in inverse proportion to their size and commercial prominence, and if any reader desire information about the various churches and schools, the town hall, the town council, the public library and parks, the water supply, the lighting, the hospital, the post-office, the banks, and the auction-marts of Castle Douglas, let him turn to Mr. Harper's *Rambles in Galloway* or to Maxwell's

*Castle Douglas.*

*Guide Book to the Stewartry of Kirkcudbright,* where he will find rich pasture.

When I came to the southern end of the town, there opened before me the far-extended woody shores of Carlinwark Loch, and it appeared that this was the playground of Castle Douglas. It was about eight o'clock in the evening, and I found the people engaged in a variety of diversions. Two tennis-courts under the shadow of the great trees embosoming the parish church

were occupied by enthusiastic players. Nearer the loch, a
large number of men and boys were playing or watching a game
of quoits. Off the tree-covered promontory called The Isle,
boys were swimming, splashing, and shouting with much hilarity;
and boating parties scattered here and there over the loch broke
the calm surface with their oars. Seats shaded by ancient trees
stand at intervals along the margin and invite persons of more
sedentary habit. As I watched from one of them the actors
in the scene, I became aware of a new group—a multitude of
girls and young women on bicycles, most of them hatless and
wearing light blouses, who came and went in twos and threes,
turning the road behind me into a cycle parade. One or two
solitary boys stood on the shore angling with worms. A fish,
probably a perch, made a splash now and then as it rose at
one of the myriads of spinners revolving with frantic speed
near the surface. Swans and their young made slow processions
in happy family parties, and the amorous drake followed his
mate with much clamour. One would turn sometimes from
all these active creatures to the little, quiet islands full of willows,
the lower branches of which rested on the water and stirred
it feebly when a gentle wind moved them, or look beyond the
loch and the surrounding woods to the high ridge of Screel
and Bengairn deepening slowly into purple-grey.

I hired a rowing-boat at the landing-stage the next day and
admired the dexterity of a blind youth in charge as he found
a cable, drew a string of boats towards him, disengaged
the one that I wished, and supplied me with oars. His misfortune had disqualified him for many occupations, but I should
think that few blind men would attempt this. Too vigorous
a thrust as he managed his little fleet, a slippery board on the
jetty, a foot caught by a forgotten rope, and the poor fellow
might suffer another disaster.

Many a day before the Hydro-Electric Scheme began, this loch
was the plaything and servant of man. In its natural state it
covered its present area. At some unknown date its level was
raised six feet by the erection of dams. This became clear in
1765, when a canal was cut to connect the loch with the river
Dee, and the waters were reduced to the original area. The
purpose in making the canal was twofold. In the first place,
it laid bare about eighty acres of marl; in the second, it made
it possible to convey cargoes of it to parishes on the Dee and

the Ken.[1] Experience shewed that while this manure stimulated the soil, it resulted also in its rapid exhaustion, and its use was discontinued. The canal is largely filled up ; but its beginning can be seen at the small village called The Buchan.

Besides revealing the existence of the dams, the reduction of the loch brought to light two small artificial islands, the homes of ancient lake-dwellers. It also changed The Isle at the north end into a peninsula. The Fir Isle at the south end was connected with the shore by a causeway made of "stones secured by strong piles of oak". *The Statistical Account* says further that "close to the side of the island, this road had a deep opening, in which large beams of wood, the remains of a drawbridge, are still visible under the water. The road is now a marsh, having been destroyed by the action of the water ; and here we have an additional confirmation of what is stated above respecting the original depth and extent of the loch ; for with the six feet of water that were drained off in 1765, added to what the loch at present contains, the construction of these works would have been impracticable." The tradition that there is a town in the depths of the loch may have arisen from the submersion of a few cottages at the time when the level was raised.

Thrieve[2] Castle, the ancient stronghold of the Douglases, is within two miles of Castle Douglas ; yet I have never seen anyone near it on the several occasions when I have been there. I do not wonder at this. There are no omnibuses to carry enthusiastic bands of summer visitors ; indeed, there is no road. Another reason may be that people who have never been within a mile of it can say, nevertheless, that they have seen it, for it stands in the midst of so broad and open a valley as to be visible from many distant points. As one goes along the roads in the neighbouring parts of the parishes of Kelton, Crossmichael, and Balmaghie, it presents itself from time to time, now behind a level stretch of meadows, now through a break in some plantation, and always with the same forbidding aspect. It is a rude, square tower standing on an island of twenty acres in the chill,

---

[1] Chalmers says, " In 1802 an act of parliament was passed, for making a navigable canal, from the port of Kirkcudbright to the boat-pool of Dalry, in Glenken." The plan was not carried out. What a route for an inland voyage it would have made !

[2] Welsh *tref*, Erse *treamh*, a homestead.

sullen Black Water of Dee, and has a certain barbaric majesty
suggesting not so much a place of covert and defence as a centre
of rule. One might think that the people of the country stood
in awe of it to-day as in the times when the " gallows knob "
had its " human tassel " dangling in the wind.

After cycling for a little more than a mile along the Gatehouse
road, I came to a byway on the right leading to the farm-
steading of Kelton Mains. It became clear on passing through
the farmyard that the bicycle would be of no further service,
for there lay between me and the castle a series of trackless
pastures. It was a cold September evening, and when I reached

*Thrieve Castle and the Dee from a point near Balmaghie.*

the bank of the river and looked upon the repellent stream and
the severe walls of the keep, I thought that the hour was fit.

George Borrow practised some of his favourite antics here.
" There were stepping stones," he says. " I did not make
use of them, but took off my shoes and stockings and waded
across. The water is very deep on the other side. . . . Written
on the green grass behind the Castle after bathing in the Dee
in a deep hole seemingly about 16 feet deep; went to bottom
and brought up a flagstone, which I flung on the shore." With
this may be compared the following passage in *Wild Wales*:
" ' You should have learnt to swim when you were young ',

said I, " and to dive too. I know one who has brought up
stones from the bottom, I daresay, of deeper pools than either
[of these], but he was a Saxon, and at carnal things, you know,
none so clebber as the Saxons."

Archibald the Grim, the first Lord of Galloway of the Douglas
line and the builder of Thrieve Castle, was a natural son of the
Good Sir James, known also as the Black Douglas from his dark
complexion, who supported Robert the Bruce throughout his
career and was killed in Andalusia in 1330. The earliest known
incident in the life of Archibald the Grim is his presence at the
battle of Poitiers in 1356, when he was made a prisoner. After
holding the offices of Sheriff of Edinburgh, Constable of Edinburgh Castle, and Warden of the West Marches, he was appointed
by David the Second to govern Galloway, a province where
the line of Baliol was still strong in popular sympathy, and
received a charter of all the lands between the Nith and the Cree,
that is, the area known as The Stewartry. Three years later,
in 1372, he induced Thomas Fleming, Earl of Wigton, to convey
to him for £500 the lands and superiority of The Shire and also
his earldom. He brought the whole of Galloway under one
lordship by this transaction, restoring the unity which had been
broken on the death of Alan in 1234, and increased his power
further by marrying the heiress of Sir Thomas Moray, Lord of
Bothwell.

He was called " the Grim " not, one is glad to learn, because
he was a terror to his dependants. The epithet was given him
" be the Englismen becaus of his terrible countenance in weir-
fare ". Not that he was much given to raiding the English
Border, for he devoted himself with energy to the rule of his own
territory. When James, Earl of Douglas, fell at the battle of
Otterburn in 1388, Archibald succeeded to the earldom, and might
have been made a duke ten years later if he had cared. The
title of duke came into use in Scotland for the first time in 1398,
when Robert the Third made his son, David, Duke of Rothesay,
and his brother, the Earl of Fife, Duke of Albany. The Earl of
Douglas is said to have been offered this new dignity, but to
have thought little of it. When the heralds hailed him, " Sir
Duke ! Sir Duke ! " he answered scornfully, " Sir Drake ! Sir
Drake ! " and declined the honour. He was now the most
powerful subject of the King, a fact illustrated by his securing
the marriage of his daughter, Marjorie, to the Duke of Rothesay,

the heir-apparent. Rothesay had been betrothed early in 1399 to a daughter of the Earl of March, but without the consent of the Estates. When the Earl of Douglas heard of this, he made the omission a ground of protest, proposed his daughter as a bride for the Duke, and offered a larger sum for the alliance than March had given. The King was not strong enough to resist his importunity, and the marriage of Rothesay to Marjorie of Douglas took place in February, 1400. This transaction had unhappy consequences for Scotland, but Douglas did not live to see them, for his death occurred not many months after the marriage. His conduct in forcing the King to break his agreement with the Earl of March is the one blemish which the historian discovers in his honourable career ; but, as Sir Herbert Maxwell suggests, he " may have been guided by true patriotic policy in stopping the alliance of the royal house with a family of dubious loyalty. The whole tenor of Archibald the Grim's conduct was so lofty and statesmanlike that one would fain acquit him in this affair from the spirit of faction and self-interest which tarnished the shields of so many of his successors."

His natural son, William Douglas, deserves a brief narrative. He fought his way to knightly renown in Border warfare and won the heart of the Princess Gelis or Egidia, daughter of Robert the Second. The beauty of this lady was famous, and she was sought in marriage by the King of France ; but Douglas had forestalled him. He married her in 1387 and thus obtained possession of the lands of Nithsdale, and received from his father in the following year the estate of Herbertshire in the shire of Stirling. He led an expedition to the coast of Ireland to avenge the depredations of the Irish pirates on the Galloway coast, destroyed the town and castle of Carlingford, seized the ships in the harbour, loaded fifteen of them with plunder, and returned to Loch Ryan after ravaging The Isle of Man on the way. When there was no fighting between Scotland and England, he must needs go abroad and offer his services to the Teutonic Knights against the Turks. He came by a violent death at Dantzig.

Archibald the Tineman, the eldest legitimate son of Archibald the Grim, succeeded to the lordship of Galloway and the earldom of Douglas on the death of his father in 1400. " The Tineman " signifies " the Loser ". It is true that he lost a number of things including several battles, an eye, and his liberty for some years. On the other hand, he did not lessen, but rather increased, the Douglas power. His losses were due more or less directly to the circumstances of his sister's marriage to the Duke of Rothesay. The Earl of March had been enraged at the setting aside of his daughter in favour of Marjorie of Douglas, and had a further grievance in that the dowry paid to the King in anticipation of his daughter's marriage had not been returned when the contract was broken. The alienation of March played a considerable part in the relations of Scotland and England. He allied himself openly with the English and led several invasions of Scotland. His defeat of the Scots in the battle of Nisbet in 1402 provoked Douglas to raid Northumberland. Douglas wasted the country to Newcastle, but, as he returned, March and Percy Hotspur met and defeated him at Homildon Hill. The story of the eleven years of his imprisonment in England is told fully in Sir Herbert Maxwell's *A History of the House of Douglas*.

Charles the Seventh of France requested Douglas to come to his assistance against the English in 1423. Douglas went with his ten thousand men and was appointed Lieutenant-General of the French Army and created Duke of Touraine. He did not achieve any great success. He attempted, but failed, to relieve the siege of Ivry. He tricked the garrison of Verneuil into a surrender ; but the Duke of Bedford advanced upon the allied French and Scottish forces and broke them up. The defeat seems to have been caused by the mutinous and pre-cipitate tactics of the French general, Narbonne. Douglas was killed in the battle.

The next ruler of Galloway was the Duchess of Touraine. The lordship passed to her by a special grant. Her rule of fully twenty years was successful and undisturbed. She resigned the lordship in 1450. The date of her death is unknown. She was buried in the chancel of Lincluden College.

Meanwhile, the lordship had been held in fee by her son, Archibald, fifth Earl of Douglas. When James the First began his brief reign in 1424, the Douglas family had reached a power unattained hitherto by any subject of the realm. The chief of the family took the titles of Earl of Douglas, Earl of Wigton, Lord of Galloway, Lord of Bothwell, Lord of Annandale, Lord of Eskdale, Duke of Touraine, Lord of Longueville, and Marshal of France. The fifth Earl died of a fever in 1439 and was succeeded in his estates and honours by his son, William.

It came about thus that, when the Duchess of Touraine resigned the lordship of Galloway in 1450, she was succeeded by her grandson, the sixth Earl, who was a boy of fifteen. The power and magnificence of his heritage were a source of alarm to Crichton, the Chancellor of Scotland, and Livingstone, the guardian of the young King, James the Second. The Earl and his brother, David, were beguiled to the court and presented to the King. It is said that while the company sat at dinner, a black bull's head was placed suddenly upon the table, the signal for the outrage that was to follow. The young Earl and his brother were seized and subjected to a mock trial on some unknown charge, and condemned and beheaded immediately in the castleyard. Contemporary opinion was reflected no doubt in the words of the ballad,

> Edinburgh Castle, towne and toure,
>   God grant thou sink for sinne !
> And that even for the black dinoure
>   Erl Douglas gat therein.

The object of the murder was attained, the Douglas power was broken. The lordships of Galloway and Bothwell passed to the Lady Margaret, the only sister of the murdered boys. James the Gross, Earl of Avondale, came into possession of the estates of Douglasdale and other lands, and succeeded to the earldom of Douglas. He was the second son of Archibald the Grim. Annandale went to the Crown.

The Douglas lands were divided, but only for a time. The effects of Crichton's work were to be undone before long, the Douglas lands reunited, and the Douglas power concentrated once more in the hands of one man. James the Gross may have been too old to attempt to avenge his murdered relatives ; but his son, William, who succeeded him as eighth Earl, took up the task. He became the favourite of the King, and was appointed to the command of the royal forces when he was only eighteen years of age, harassed Crichton and reduced his influence, secured a Papal dispensation to enable him to marry his second cousin, the Lady Margaret, The Fair Maid of Galloway, and married her in 1444, to the chagrin doubtless of Crichton, who must have felt now that he had a well-intentioned, but profitless, murder to his discredit. Douglas governed his territory in peace for three years after this event. Then the old, smouldering feud between the houses of Douglas and Percy burst into flame. Percy seems to have been responsible for blowing upon the embers, for he and Sir Robert Ogle invaded the eastern counties and burned Dunbar in the month of May. The Earl of Salisbury treated Dumfries in like fashion in June. Douglas and his brother, the Earl of Ormond, retaliated by invading Northumberland and setting Alnwick in flames. They made another excursion a few weeks later and burned Warkworth. Up till November, 1450, when Douglas went on a journey to Rome to be present at the Papal Jubilee, he had enjoyed the favour of the King ; but the most powerful subject in the country could hardly be without political enemies. It is possible that Kennedy, Bishop of S. Andrew's, an influential and sinister figure in the history of the time, had something to do with the Earl's absence from the country. In any case the Earl had not been long in Rome before he learned that disturbances had broken out on his estates either through the influence of *agents provocateurs* or on account of mismanagement on the part of a brother whom he had left in charge of his affairs. The King, moved perhaps by the Kennedy faction, made this an occasion for warring against the Douglas power, and razed a castle in Yarrow. The Earl returned speedily from Rome, was restored to the royal favour, surrendered his lands to the King, and received a new grant of them. Even if Douglas was innocent of the atrocities attributed to him by chroniclers of later generations, he does not seem to have been either a model subject or a good ruler. The new charter contains a clause to the effect that he is to enjoy his lands as fully and freely as did his predecessors " notwithstanding all crimes committed by him or his uncle, the deceased Earl Archibald ". It became known, however, that there was a league for purposes defensive and offensive with the " Tiger " Earl of Crawford, and this might be regarded with reason as a danger to the Stewart dynasty. Douglas was summoned to attend the King at Stirling in February, 1452, and received a safe-conduct given under the King's hand in Council. He went, and after a banquet was invited by the King to confer with him in a private room. It is supposed that the secret treaty with the Earl of Crawford was the subject of discussion. The story is that the King urged Douglas to break the confederacy, that Douglas refused, that the King exclaimed angrily, " If you will not, I

will ! " and stabbed him twice with his dagger. Sir Patrick
Gray completed the work with a pole-axe. It is plain that the
removal of the eighth Earl, like that of the sixth, was regarded
as a political necessity. The power of Douglas had become so
great as to be a constant menace to the royal house.

The eighth Earl had no children, and was succeeded by his
brother, James, as ninth Earl of Douglas and Lord of Galloway.
This Earl was perhaps the most consistently disloyal of his line.
He stood in high favour at the English court, entered into
treasonable relations with Henry the Sixth, and rose in rebellion
on account of his brother's murder. The King was placed in
so difficult a situation that he thought of abdicating the throne
and withdrawing from the country. The policy, however, of
detaching or defeating in detail the supporters of Douglas was
adopted with success, and the Earl was compelled eventually
to submit to the King's authority, to renounce all leagues
against him, and to undertake to enter into no more.

The next incident is hardly credible, but its explanation is
to be found in the King's impulsive nature. It was no doubt
a generous reaction of feeling towards his defeated rebel that
led him to support Douglas's appeal for a Papal dispensation
to enable him to marry his brother's widow, The Fair Maid of
Galloway. The dispensation was granted, the marriage took
place, and the Douglas estates were reunited once more. The
King suspected presently that the Earl was ignoring his obliga-
tions and entertaining treasonable designs, and resolved apparently that the Douglas power must be suppressed finally. He
laid sudden siege to Douglas's castle of Inveravon near Linlithgow
and captured and dismantled it. The royal troops overran the
Earl's estates in Douglasdale, Annandale, and the Ettrick
Forest, and besieged the castle of Abercorn. Douglas went to
its relief, but was deserted on the eve of an engagement by his
most powerful supporter, Lord Hamilton of Cadzow. This
example was infectious, and Douglas was left with two or three
thousand followers to confront the royal army. He rode away
from the impracticable situation and crossed the Border with a
few attendants.

A subsequent rising of his three brothers ended with their
defeat in a battle at Arkinholm, the site of the town of Langholm,
in May, 1455. The Earl of Douglas was attainted by Act of
Parliament in the same year, and his estates and honours

forfeited. The lordships of Galloway and Eskdale were attached
to the Crown, and Annandale given to the King's second son,
Alexander, Duke of Albany. The other estates were distributed
among loyal vassals. Meanwhile Thrieve Castle still held out
for Douglas, and the King entered Galloway in the autumn
and, after a siege, captured this last stronghold.

It was to stand sieges again in the two following centuries.
After its reduction by James the Second, it became a royal
castle and formed a part of the jointure of the queens of Scotland
until it was vested in the Lords Maxwell as hereditary keepers
in 1526. After the defeat at Solway Moss, Lord Maxwell had
given a pledge to the English that he would surrender his castles
to them. The Regent Arran accordingly besieged Thrieve
Castle in 1545, and captured it after two or three days. In 1640
it was held by Robert, Lord Nithsdale, for King Charles the
First against the forces of the Scottish Committee of Estates,
and capitulated after thirteen weeks. The Covenanters then
ruined the interior.

The architectural and defensive details are set forth fully
in the *Inventory*. The following sentences are taken from the
" Introduction " : " One of the most interesting features in
connection with the defences of this castle is to be seen at the
level of the openings to the upper floor, where a double row of
sockets has been formed on the exterior of the north, south,
and west walls to hold the ends of a projecting and covered
timber platform—a *bretâche* or brattice—designed for the defence
of the keep at close quarters. Moreover, it gave more room and
wider range for the discharge of missiles than would be allowed
by the narrow windows, while assailants working at the base
of the tower would be exposed to interference from directly
above. The east side, with its outer loopholed wall and angle
towers and other defences, was evidently considered of such
strength that a continuous *bretâche* could be safely omitted.
The *bretâche* is a feature of the period of which there are many
indications throughout Scotland as well as in France and England.
During the fifteenth century this timber form of construction
was abandoned in favour of stone parapets supported on moulded
corbels of considerable projection with machicolations or interspaces between, which served the same purpose, but had the
great advantage of being proof against fire.

" Thrieve Castle is a typical example of the castle-building of its period. The keep is oblong on plan and of exceptional size. It forms the principal feature of the design, making both the outer defences of wall and angle towers appear insignificant as compared with the great central mass of masonry. There is to this extent a reversion in principle to the pre-Edwardian or Norman type of fortress ; the keep is the dominating feature. Upon the level ground to the east of the castle indications exist of an outer enclosure or barmkin of considerable extent, a feature characteristic of the fifteenth century which was frequently added to the earlier keeps."

After the wrecking of the castle there were few disturbances in the neighbourhood until about 1725, when we hear of the rising of the Levellers. The trouble was occasioned by the fencing of fields and other measures adopted for the improvement of their estates by the Galloway proprietors.[1] The former practice was that each tenant had the right of pasturage over the whole property of the landlord, and this provided employment for many herds. The erection of the dykes interfered with the ancient custom and consequently threw many men out of work. At the same time the grouping of small crofts into farms led to much hardship. The evicted families emigrated to America and else-where if they had the means ; otherwise they were thrown into great distress and sought desperately to obstruct the operations of the landlords. It was at Whitsunday, 1723, that the new measures began to take effect.

The ensuing bitterness is expressed in some rude lines which were long popular in Galloway :

> The lords and lairds they drive us out
> From maillings where we dwell ;
> The poor man says, " Where shall we go ? "
> The rich says, " Go to hell."

---

[1] " The lairds were no more of the people," says Mr. S. R. Crockett. " They had taken the side of what all Galloway considered as an alien and persecuting sect, during the reigns of the second Charles and James his brother. Thus in most cases they had been divorced in sympathy from the clan or sept with which they were lineally connected. Add to this that many of the original landlords had either been dispossessed as disloyal to one party or the other during the long troubles, or had been driven to sell their lands to strangers from a distance. Hardly ever had this property returned into the hands of a Galloway man of aboriginal stock."

> These words they spoke in jest and mocks ;
> But by their works we know
> That if they have their herds and flocks,
> They care not where we go.

> Against the poor they still prevail
> With all their wicked works,
> And will enclose both moor and dale
> And turn corn fields to parks.

The discontented, however, did more than compose or repeat lampoons. A great annual fair was held at Kelton[1] Hill in the month of June, and here the plan for a general levelling of the fences was devised. A company of Levellers might consist of about fifty men with a captain, and, according to the account in *The Castle Douglas Weekly Visitor,* " each man was furnished with a strong *kent* (or piece of wood) from six to eight feet in length, which he fixed into the dyke at the approved distance from the foundation and from his neighbour. After having ascertained that all was ready, the captain bawled out, ' Ow'r wi't, boys,'—and ow'r accordingly it tumbled, with a shout that might have been heard at the distance of miles." Dragoons had to be brought into Galloway to suppress the movement ; but they behaved with restraint, and only a few lives were sacrificed. The malcontents made their last stand at Duchrae in the parish of Balmaghie, where the military took over two hundred prisoners. As they were being marched to Kirkcud-bright, many of them were allowed to escape ; but the leaders were brought to trial. Some were punished with fines or im-prisonment, and others banished to the plantations.

Many delightful roads radiate from Castle Douglas—one run-ning low among hills clothed with aromatic woods to Auchen-cairn, and another passing through Keltonhill, climbing high above the Dee, and affording a distant prospect of the Galloway Highlands. Then there are the various routes to Laurieston, a pretty, quiet village, which I formerly recommended as a secondary centre, thinking of people who walk ; but the modest inn where I lodged has been closed. The name of the place does not savour of Galloway. It used to be " Clachanpluck ", which does. The change was made by an eighteenth-century

---

[1] Either Gaelic *coilltean,* woods, or *calltuinn,* a hazel.— Johnston.

proprietor called Laurie, who chose this method of signalizing for future generations his visit to this planet.

The road on the west climbs up from Laurieston for two miles, chiefly among woods, and then brings you out on a great moor about six hundred and fifty feet above the sea, the moor of

*Laurieston.*

Lochenbreck, where there is a loch, an old pump-room, and a deserted hotel. MacKerlie was at loss to understand the propriety of the name. He says, " Robertson in his Gaelic topography gives Lochenbreck as derived from the Gaelic lochan-breac, the small speckled loch. No doubt such is the meaning, but we have been on it, and around it, and did not observe anything to occasion such a name." If he was on the loch, he must not have been there as a fisher. Had he hooked a trout, it might have dawned on him that the speckles were to be looked for neither on nor around the loch, but in it ! The water of the well is described as possessing the character of " a mild carbonated chalybeate spring ", and *The Statistical Account* of 1844 says that it has been " resorted to from time imme- morial. . . . For the accommodation of visitors and invalids, an inn has been provided in the vicinity of the well ; but there is reason to believe that, were the accommodation more ex- tensive, the resort to it would be still greater than it is." Large additions were made, and the hotel drew visitors from other parts of Galloway and from the cities of Scotland and else- where until about the year 1905, when the doors were closed. Someone may yet undertake the revival of the Lochenbreck Spa. The properties of the water are said to be valuable ; the high moorland situation is splendid ; motor-cars make it accessible ; and the hotel may not be beyond repair.

From this point one should certainly go on to Gatehouse. The road is one of the most heaven-kissing in Galloway. For weather I recommend a day of April sunshine punctuated with scurrying showers of snow and hail. Cairnsmore of Fleet, the great mountain in the west, will then be wearing a white mantle with fringes trailing down the flanks, and the sunshine in the various glens will be excluded for a few minutes from time to time by the rapid passage of the storms.

Of the road running northwards from Laurieston to New Galloway it is difficult to write with brevity or sobriety. Many a time in these pages the enormous wealth of material lying to my hands has compelled me to give summary treatment to matters of which I would rather have written in a less literal fashion, and so, I am afraid, it must be now ; but I may say at least that the traveller has the luxury of Loch Grenoch[1] on the

[1] Gaelic *loch greanach*, gravelly loch. *Cf.* Grainy Ford on the Dee. Like Clachanpluck, Loch Grenoch has had its name changed. " Loch Grenoch ", says S. R. Crockett, " became Woodhall Loch (or in the folk speech of the Parish Wudha' Loch). Farther afield we have a crop, happily thin sown and soon fading away, of Summerhills, Parkhills, Willowbanks, and such like—of which that most to be regretted is the merging of the ancient name of the Duchrae estate in that of the mansion-house of Hensol, a word which has no historical connection with Galloway, but merely preserves a souvenir of the

left for the first part of the journey, and of Loch Ken on the right for the final, and between these an interval where the road winds among deep hazel thickets that open occasionally so as to give him such glimpses of green pastures and quiet waters framed among dark trees that he cannot but drop from his bicycle to stand still and gaze. The floral splendours of the wayside banks in summer and the almost cloying sweetness of the air are remembered by every passer-by. S. R. Crockett, who writes of Balmagnie [1] Parish with the minuteness to be expected

*Little Duchrae, Balmaghie, the birthplace of S. R. Crockett.*

of one who was born and spent his youth in the midst of it, will have it that the mile between Laurieston and beginning of Loch Grenoch is " reminiscent of some parts of central France —the valley of the Creuse, for instance, George Sand's country—

early youth of a late proprietor." Little Duchrae, Crockett's birthplace, retains its name.

The loch mentioned above must not be confused with the one called Grenoch, Grennoch, or Grannoch, in Girthon Parish. That loch lies far from roads and is full of very game trout. The Pullaugh Burn, which flows out of it and at the end of its course is led tamely by an aqueduct into Clatteringshaws reservoir, appeals to those who like to fish in moorland waters.

[1] MacGhie's village.

or some of the lower tributaries of the Tarn. The tall poplars in front of the ruined smithy, the little burn that trips and ambles for a few hundred paces beside the traveller and then is lost, hurrying off into the unknown again as if tired of being overlooked—all these are more French than Scottish."

The byway winding over the ridge between Loch Grenoch and the river Dee provides no thrills, but brings you down to one of the historic sanctuaries of Galloway.

The parish church of Balmaghie, where John Macmillan, the first minister of The Reformed Presbyterian Church,[1] preached for many years in defiance of ecclesiastical and civil powers, strong in the devotion of his parishioners, is on the bank of the Dee, two or three miles from Laurieston. Macmillan was a native of The Stewartry and before receiving ordination to the ministry of the Church of Scotland in 1701, was associated with the followers of Richard Cameron, who were known as Cameronians, Society men, and Hill-men. The Cameronians were the most extreme sect of the Covenanters, insisting that the Presbyterian polity should be imposed, not only on Scotland, but on all the three Kingdoms. They were, therefore, profoundly dissatisfied with the Revolution Settlement, which ignored the Covenant altogether. They formed a small minority of the nation, but still hoped by the resolute maintenance of their testimony to bring the rest of the country round to their point of view. In remaining outside the Church as established at the Revolution, they did not regard themselves as seceders. It was the Church that had seceded from them. Meanwhile, they did not form a regular ecclesiastical organization, nor had they any ordained ministers, but met as Societies for worship and maintained a vehement propaganda.[2] A few Cameronians who believed that they had a call to the ministry entered the Church with the intention of labouring for the restoration of the ecclesiastical order of 1638–1649, and Macmillan was one of them. The path of a Cameronian in the Established Church, however, could not be easy, and difficulties arose when the

---

[1] See *A Cameronian Apostle, being Some Account of John Macmillan of Balmaghie* by the Rev. H. M. B. Reid, D.D. (1896).
[2] A good example of the titles of their publications is seen in *The Protestation, Apologetic Declaration, and Admonitory Vindication of a Poor, Wasted, Misrepresented Remnant of the Suffering, Anti-Popish, Anti-Prelatic, Anti-Erastian, Anti-Sectarian, True Presbyterian Church in Scotland.*

Government of Queen Anne required the Oath of Allegiance and Bond of Assurance from parish ministers. Queen Anne was an uncovenanted ruler and, therefore, from the Cameronian point of view, could not be recognized. Macmillan's dissatisfaction with the Constitution, especially where the Church was concerned, deepened, and he ceased to attend the meetings of the Presbytery. When he, with two sympathizers, was cited to appear before that court to answer for his conduct, he presented a statement of " Grievances ", which was published in the following year under the title, *A true double of a Paper of Grievances given in to the Presbytery of Kirkcudbright, July 6th*, 1703, *by Mr. John Reid, minister of Carsphairn ; Mr. William Tod, minister of Buittle, and Mr. John Macmillan, minister of Balmaghie : To which generally the whole fore-mentioned parishes adhere, and the greatest part of the Godly in the land*. The " Grievances " are twelve, and the remaining eleven follow from the first, which is stated as follows : " It is a great grievance, that none of our Assemblies hath, by an Act in solemn and ample form, and in name of this National Church, asserted and declared Presbyterian Government to be of divine right, unto which the Church has adhered and given testimony by suffering ; and that the late Prelacy was a most wicked usurpation, and grievous encroachment upon the rights of the said Church. The necessity of such an Act is evident, in regard the late Prelacy was never ecclesiastically asserted, but only depended on the civil sanction. And now, for the Church to remain so long silent in asserting her own right, after she had been deprived of the exercise of Presbytery about thirty years, doth manifestly imply a holding of it by the same tenure, viz., *Erastian Supremacy*. Especially, considering the Act of Re-establishment goes as far back as the year 1592, there is cut off what the Church had attained unto in her purest time, viz., 1638–1649 inclusive." Macmillan's testimony, it will be seen, is not a mere side-issue of Scottish Church history, but only one of the many phases of a controversy which is still alive.

Macmillan was deposed from his office on the 30th of December, 1703. He was, however, deeply entrenched in the sympathy and affection of the people, and continued to occupy his church and manse, defending himself on the ground of irregularities in the Presbytery's proceedings against him. This anomalous situation lasted for twenty-four years. The Presbytery fulminated in vain. The General Assembly and the Sheriff attacked the position without success. William MacKie was ordained as minister of the parish; but the ceremony had to take place at Kirkcudbright, and when MacKie attempted to take possession of the parish, a riot occurred. Some of the heritors, however, befriended him, and he conducted services in a building called by some " The House of Rimmon ", where he gathered a small congregation. At length, in 1727, he obtained a decree of the Court of Session against Macmillan for the rent of the glebe for seventeen years reckoned at a hundred merks yearly, and this was the immediate cause of Macmillan's departure. His supporters were anxious to discharge the debt; but he was resolved to go. After his deposition he had renewed his connexion with the United Societies and had received from them in October, 1706, a " hearty and unanimous call to come forth and dispense the Gospel ordinances faithfully and freely to us ". The acceptance of this " call " meant much itinerant preaching. The *Register of the Rev. John Macmillan, Being a Record of Marriages and Baptisms solemnised by him among the Cameronian Societies* shews the names of members from Logie in Stirlingshire in the north to Cummertrees in the south, and from Hawick in the east to Colmonell in the west, and if it became necessary or advisable to choose between the parish of Balmaghie and the wider field of labour, there could be no doubt that the claims of the Societies would weigh more heavily with him. Besides, he was more than ever the strenuous idealist in an age of compromise; the generation that had upheld him in the early days at Balmaghie was disappearing; for many of the younger people the old battle-cries had lost their appeal; and the parish was left to the uncovenanted ministrations of MacKie.

Macmillan made his home in Lanarkshire, where most of the Societies were, and exercised his ministry among the Suffering Remnant until he died in 1753 in the eighty-fourth year of his age. In course of time other ministers were ordained, and the Societies were constituted as congregations of The Reformed Presbyterian Church.

Members of that communion who come to Balmaghie on pilgrimage, and other visitors who are not indifferent to the contribution made by the Covenanters to our national history, will look for the table stone commemorating two martyrs who bore the same name:

HERE LYES DAVID HALLIDAY PORTIONER OF MEIFEILD WHO
WAS SHOT UPON THE 21 OF FEBR 1685 AND OF
DAVID HALLIDAY ONCE IN GLENGAPE WHO WAS LIKEWISE
SHOT UPON THE 11 OF JUNY 1685 FOR THEIR ADHERENCE TO
THE PRINCIPLES OF SCOTLAND'S COVENANTED REFORMATIONE.

BENEATH THIS STONE TWO DAVIDS HALLIDAYS
DOE LY WHOSE SOULS NOU SING THEIR MASTERS PRAISE
TO KNOU IF CURIOUS PASSENGERS DESYRE
FOR WHAT BY WHOME AND HOU THEY DID EXPYRE
THEY DID OPPOSE THIS NATIONS PERJUREY
NOR COULD THEY JOYN WITH LORDLY PRELACY
INDULGING FAVOURS FROM CHRIST'S ENEMIES
QUENCH'D NOT THEIR ZEAL THIS MONUMENT THEN CRYES
THESE WERE THE CAUSES NOT TO BE FORGOT
WHY THEY BY LAG SO WICKEDLY WERE SHOT
ONE NAME ONE CAUSE ONE GRAVE ONE HEAVEN DO TY
THEIR SOULS TO THAT ONE GOD ETERNALLY

A small upright stone tells of another victim:

|  |  |
|---|---|
|  | (skull & cross-bones) |
| HERE LYES | MEMENTO MORI |
| GEORGE SHORT | AND THE EARLE |
| WHO WAS PURSUED | OF ANANDALE |
| AND TAKEN AND | BECAUSE OF HIS |
| INSTANTLY SHOT | ADHERENCE TO |
| TO DEATH UNDER | SCOTLANDS RE |
| CLOUD OF NIGHT | FORMTION COVE |
| IN THE PAROCH | NANTS NATIONAL |
| OF TONGUELAND | AND SOLEMN |
| BY GRIER OF LAG | LEAGUE 1685 |

The author of *The Raiders* thought the churchyard "a right
desirable place for any tired wanderer's resting-grave", and
here lies "SAMUEL RUTHERFORD CROCKETT, Minister of the
Gospel and Novelist, born at Duchrae in this parish, on
24th September, 1859, died at Tarascon, France, on 16th April,
1914."

According to *Who's Who* the year of his birth was 1860, and so
it is given in the inscription on the monument unveiled in 1932
at the north end of Laurieston: TO THE MEMORY OF SAMUEL
RUTHERFORD CROCKETT, AUTHOR OF "THE RAIDERS" AND OTHER
TALES OF GALLOWAY, A NATIVE OF THIS PARISH. 24TH SEPTEMBER
1860—16TH APRIL 1914. A FAITHFUL SON AND CONSTANT LOVER
OF THAT GREY GALLOWAY LAND "WHERE ABOUT THE GRAVES OF
THE MARTYRS THE WHAUPS ARE CRYING, HIS HEART REMEMBERS
HOW."

# CHAPTER XXXV

## FROM CASTLE DOUGLAS TO MAXWELLTOWN

Buittle Church—Buittle Castle—Craignair and Dalbeattie—The
Mote of Urr—The Old Bridge of Urr—Drumcoltran Castle—
Hills Tower—Loch Rutton—An echo of the Jacobite occupation
of Dumfries—Goldielea—Burns's friendship with Mrs. Riddell.

I AM sorry that in beginning this final chapter[1] I cannot promise
the reader a grand climax, and anticipate that the following
notes will seem like a *diminuendo* passage, for when one has
surmounted the hill where the church of Buittle[1] Parish stands,
descended into the town of Dalbeattie[2], and taken the road running past Kirkgunzeon to Maxwelltown, it seems as if the *aura*
of Galloway were departing. Yet the soil is still of the province,
and the names of places and persons ; and one is prone
to linger for a while before crossing the Nith and realizing that
all is at an end !

Recent pages have dealt so largely in religious and ecclesiastical matters that I hesitate to mention a church once more and
at the very beginning of a new chapter ; but some readers at
least will be pleased to be told that the remains of a church with
the unusual feature of a chancel wider than the nave stand near
the modern church of Buittle, that the chancel is attributed to
the former half of the fourteenth century, and that the greater
part of the nave is older.

The descent from the church to Buittle Bridge on the Water
of Urr is so easy and delightful that only a keen historical or
antiquarian enthusiasm or the execution of some task intended
to provide fuel for such enthusiasm in other people would induce
one to check one's course at the byway leading to the site of

[1] That is, of the first edition.
[2] O.E. *botl*, a house.
[3] Field of the birch trees, Gaelic *beath*, or from *biota*, a churn.—
Johnston.

Buittle Castle. Let not the visitor, after committing himself to this short digression, be deceived by the tower called Buittle Place. This building, constructed, it is very likely, with stones taken from the ancient castle, appears to belong to the end of

*Buittle Church.*

the sixteenth century. The stronghold of the Lords of Galloway of the line of Fergus stood a hundred yards to the south-east. Here Dervorgilla gave birth to John Baliol, who became King of Scotland in 1292, and here she dated the charter of Balliol

College in 1282.  During the War of Independence, the castle
came into the hands of the Bruces, and Robert the First bestowed
it on Sir James Douglas.  Edward Baliol recovered the estate
and made the castle his home ; but the Douglases came back,
and the property remained in their hands until the forfeiture
of their estates in 1455.

Soon after returning to the road and continuing the descent,
one sees an aerial ropeway among the trees and hears the clatter
and din of machinery, unusual sounds in Galloway.  The road
is now skirting the foot of Craignair,[1] a great granite quarry, and
the noise comes from the crushing-mills.  Craignair is being
gradually removed and distributed over the world.  The Thames
Embankment, the Liverpool Docks, the Birkenhead and Man-
chester Town Halls, Insurance Buildings in London, Liverpool,
and Leeds, the lower part of the Eddystone Lighthouse, the
Great Bassas and Little Bassas Lighthouses in Ceylon are some
of the structures for which Dalbeattie granite has been used.
When Robert Heron passed through the " small village " of
Dalbeattie in 1792, he thought it " rather surprising that a
situation so favourable has not before this time been occupied by
a town or village of considerable magnitude ", and said that
" if some suitable manufacture could be established at Dalbeattie,
I should expect to see it rise to rival the most considerable
towns in this part of Galloway."  The granite industry has
been the principal means of fulfilling this anticipation, and the
burghers of Dalbeattie look with equanimity at their disem-
bowelled mountain.

Craignair must go ; but fortunately no money is to be made by
tampering with the Mote of Urr.  No charges of dynamite
make it shudder and dissolve, and its worst enemies are the
burrowing rabbits.  Besides the rabbits, the sheep and cattle
that are allowed to graze on its slopes deserve dishonourable
mention.  Originally a natural hillock rising between two
channels of the Urr, it has been trenched along its sides so as
to demark a base-court and a citadel ; measures six hundred
and twenty-five feet in length, three hundred and forty-four
in breadth, and eighty-five in height ; and is the most notable
monument of its kind in Scotland.[2]  Such mote-hills were designed

---

[1] Gaelic *creag an air*, crag of the slaughter.
[2] For a full description see *The Parish of Urr*, by the Rev. David
Frew, D.D., LL.D. or the *Inventory*.

primarily for purposes of defence, and were strengthened with
ramparts and palisades around the base-court and citadel.
There is evidence that wooden houses were built within the
enclosures. Antiquarians used to describe mote-hills as prehistoric or Roman or Saxon ; but " these flat-topped mounds
of earth and stone, in part natural or wholly artificial, are now
generally recognised as the work of the Anglo-Normans, though
the question of the authorship of all such mounds cannot be
said yet to have passed entirely beyond the bounds of controversy. . . . The chief arguments adduced for their purely

*Bridge of Urr.*

Anglo-Norman origin are : *First*—The small size of the mounds,
clearly indicating private as opposed to collective occupation—
the private fortress having been first adopted by the Normans.
*Second*—The name ' motte ', which has no place in pre-Norman
English, but which was current in the twelfth century. *Third*—
Their association here with early baronies founded under David
the First, and as a corollary their connection with other feudal
holdings, circumstances which afford an explanation of the
constant recurrence of the motes as the baronial messuages
all over Scotland, and demonstrate how in many cases they
came to be the court hills, seats of judgment, and gathering-
point of their associated territories, long after the residential

character of the messuage had ceased."[1]  The distance of the Mote of Urr from Dalbeattie is two miles and a half.

Three miles farther on is The Old Bridge of Urr, which may date from the latter part of the sixteenth century.  The parapets were built in 1843, and it may have been at the same time that the roadway was widened on the north side.  " Over the central pier on the south side there is a panel containing two shields placed one over the other, each bearing arms, now much weather-worn and partially indecipherable.  The upper stone is said to bear a lion rampant and crown with the initials I ∶ R ∶, while the lower shield bore a dexter hand *appaumé* between the heads of three animals now almost obliterated.  According to local tradition, there was formerly a single initial on each side of this shield and, beneath, the date 1580."[2]

The inveterate explorer who dislikes the idea of following a perfectly straight course all the way from Dalbeattie to Maxwell-town will find an excuse for a deviation in Drumcoltran[3] Castle on the north of the village of Kirkgunzeon,[4] where the retention of certain defensive features such as a deep bar-hole for securing the entrance, a parapet walk, and narrow windows suggests that it is one of the earlier sixteenth-century castles.  A panel above the doorway bears this inscription in raised letters :

> CELA SECRETA ∶ LOQVERE
> PAUCA ∶ VERAX · ESTO ∶
> (Ā · V) ·INO CAVE ∶ MEMĒTO
> MORI ∶ MISERICORS ESTO[5]

Another excuse is provided by Hills Tower.  A byway crosses the railroad at Lochanhead Station and winds over a ridge to the hollow where Loch Rutton lies.  The tower stands on Mains of Hills farm.  It appears to belong to the middle of the sixteenth century.  " The gargoyles at the level of the

---

[1] " Introduction " to the *Inventory*, Vol. I.

[2] The *Inventory*.

[3] " *Druim Cultrain*, the ridge of Cultran.  In the 12th and 13th centuries this land belonged to the Abbey of Holm Cultran in Cumberland."—Maxwell.

[4] S. Finnan's Church.  *Wynnin* occurring in some forms is " a Welsh rendering of Finnan, a familiar name for Findbarr of Moyville, who was resident in Whithorn for a considerable time and died in 579 ".—Maxwell.

[5] " Keep secrets hidden; speak little; be truthful; avoid wine; be mindful of death; be pitiful."

parapet walk represent the cannon of the period, made in two pieces and secured by iron bands." " The most striking feature in the group of buildings ", says the *Inventory,* " is the unique and interesting gatehouse in the centre of the western wall of the courtyard." A two-storey house bearing the date 1721 has been built against the east wall of the tower. One of the four panels on the front of this house contains a shield with the arms of Sir John Maxwell, who was created fourth Lord Herries in right of his wife in 1566, and of Agnes Herries, his spouse. The tower came by marriage into the possession of the MacCullochs of Ardwall in 1730.

From the neighbourhood of the tower one looks over a wide tract of country in several directions. Some fir trees are silhouetted against the gleaming surface of Loch Rutton. On approaching the loch one sees a crannog in the middle. Various objects discovered in it suggest that it was occupied at an early date in the thirteenth century. The *Inventory* states also that " a peninsula somewhat north of the centre of the east shore of the loch has been severed from the mainland by an artificial ditch and rampart drawn across the neck, thus transforming it into an island of about one acre in extent. . . . No relics were found in the interior, but teeth of animals were plentiful along the water's edge, and in the material of the rampart were found fragments of bone, deers' horn, glass slag, and nondescript iron or iron slag."

The old highway through this part of Galloway ran past the north end of the loch. Towards the end of 1745 the inhabitants of the district were living in dread that they might see coming along it a force of predatory Jacobites. The diary of the Rev. George Duncan, who was ordained minister of Lochrutton Parish in 1728, contains an interesting reference under the date, Sunday, the 22nd of December, 1745 : " A melancholy day—the rebels in Drumfries—about 4000, with the Pretender's son at their head, in great rage at the town for carrying off their baggage from Annandale, and for raising volunteers, and calling out the militia of the Country in defence of the Government—demanded £2000 sterling of contributions, . . . and that they convey their carts, with their carriages after them, to their headquarters. They were most rude in the town—pillaged some shops—pulled shoes off gentlemen's feet in the streets. In most of the churches for some miles about Drumfries no

sermon. God be blessed ! we had public worship. I lectured
I Sam. IV ; Mr. John Scott, minister of Drumfries (there was
no sermon there) preached. Much confusion in all the neighbouring parishes—rebels robbing people's stables—pillaging some
houses. They came to the border of our parish, but, God be
thanked ! came no further, and we suffered no loose usage."

After passing Lochanhead Station the road runs through a
narrow defile between steep, wooded slopes and descends to
Goldielea, an estate about three miles from Maxwelltown.
This was the home of Andrew Crosbie, a prototype of Counsellor
Pleydell in *Guy Mannering*. He was born in 1736 and admitted
to the Faculty of Advocates in 1757, and was soon known as the
most eloquent and daring pleader at the Bar. " He became
Vice-Dean of Faculty, and would have been President of the
Court of Session but for his inveterate love of tavern-haunting."[1]
He built for himself what has been described as a " very expensive
and whimsical edifice " in S. Andrew Square, Edinburgh.
Robertson, the Principal of the University, said to him, " Crosbie,
were your town and country houses to meet, how they would
stare at each other ! " The Goldielea estate was called Holm
in those days, and the house consisted of a single storey and was
thatched. Crosbie died in 1785, leaving a widow who was
granted a small pension by the Faculty of Advocates " in consideration of her poverty-stricken circumstances ". The Holm
property was bought by Colonel (afterwards Major-General)
Goldie. His wife's maiden name was Leigh, and he renamed the
estate after himself and her. Early in 1792 Walter Riddell
became the owner and changed the name to Woodley Park
in honour of his wife, Maria Woodley, Burns's friend. In 1794
Colonel Goldie was again in possession. According to one
account of the matter Riddell had not paid the purchase money.
Since then the name of Goldielea has been retained.

Burns was a frequent visitor at Woodley Park. Lockhart
describes his hostess as " a beautiful and very accomplished
woman ", and Cunningham states that she was " beautiful ".
" young and accomplished ", that she owned a good library and
was in the habit of lending the poet books, that " she was an
elegant scholar, and sometimes translated, from French or
Italian or Latin, verse for his amusement ". He repaid the
debt with poetic epistles and epigrams and even an epitaph !

[1] *The Scott Originals* by W. S. Crockett.

But, alas! the friendship suffered a grievous intermission in 1794. Burns was a guest at a dinner-party, became very drunk, and gravely insulted his hostess, Mrs. Riddell. It has been assumed that the lady was Mrs. Riddell of Woodley Park; but there are reasons for concluding that it was her sister-in-law, Mrs. Riddell of Friars' Carse, who received the direct offence.[1] The consequence was that the Riddell family treated Burns with marked coldness thereafter. The poet's bitter contrition is revealed both in letters and in verses. He was especially hurt by the obvious estrangement of an intimate friend, and unhappily allowed himself to indulge in some vituperative epigrams. These, in turn, became an occasion of penitence.

The friendship was resumed gradually in the following year. Mrs. Riddell was probably touched by the poet's misfortunes. In the summer of 1796, when Burns had gone to the small village of Brow on the Dumfriesshire coast in the vain hope of recovering his broken health, Mrs. Riddell, who was staying in the neighbourhood, "exerted herself", says Lockhart, "to make him as comfortable as circumstances permitted". She sent her carriage to bring him to her residence. On meeting her he said, "Well, Madam, have you any commands for the other world?" He expressed regret for "letters and verses written with unguarded and improper freedom" and lamented "that he had written many epigrams on persons against whom he entertained no enmity, and whose characters he would be sorry to wound". This was their last meeting. Burns died within three weeks. Mrs. Riddell contributed a sympathetic estimate of his genius and character to *The Dumfries Journal*, and helped to bring about the answer to the prayer uttered in his last letter to his brother, Gilbert—"God keep my wife and children".

[1] "Maria Riddell, the Friend of Burns," by Hugh S. Gladstone, in *The Transactions of the Dumfriesshire and Galloway Natural History and Antiquarian Society* (1914-15).

*Approaching the Merrick Range from Barrhill.*

# CHAPTER XXXVI

## THE NICK OF THE BALLOCH ROAD, SHALLOCH ON MINNOCH AND THE MERRICK

The Dailly Martyrs—More about Barr—The Nick of the Balloch road—Rowantree—The Murder Hole—The descent from the Nick of the Balloch—The Nick of the Balloch road again—The Session Stone—The peewit a danger to the Covenanters—The ascent of Shalloch on Minnoch—The ascent of The Merrick—Igneous boulders on the summit—The Loch Doon 'granite' area—The Fang of The Merrick.

I HAVE to thank *The Galloway Gazette* for expressing surprise at the omission of any reference in the first edition to the Nick of the Balloch road in Carrick. I had classed it as similar in character to the more easterly and more important road running south from Straiton, but on scrutinizing old diaries found no record of having been on it. I decided to treat the village of Barr as a fresh base for exploration, settling down there for so long a time as it might be necessary to get suitable weather for my plans, for I should not fall back upon the motor-car unless the wet weather of early July 1937 were to continue beyond all likelihood.

The road running up the valley of the Girvan Water reaches, about three miles from Girvan, the Old Dailly churchyard.

Some of the experiences of John Stevenson, the author of *A Rare Soul-Strengthening and Comforting Cordial for Old and Young Christians*, were recorded in Chapter XXIX, and the inscription on his tombstone is reproduced on page 427. He was not, however, the only memorable Covenanter of the district. In the same churchyard there is a memorial of " George Martin, schoolmaster, Old Dailly, who after an imprisonment of four years and four months, suffered in the Grassmarket, Edinburgh, on 22nd. Feb., 1684, for his adherence to the Covenant, also of two other Covenanters (names unknown) one of whom, according to tradition, was shot dead, while herding his cow at Killoup, and the other was struck down on his own hearth, at Black Clauchrie, Barr, and is buried near this spot ". There is also a tombstone announcing that " here lies the corpse of John Semple, who was shot by Kilkerran, at command of Cornet James Douglas. Also here lies Thomas McClorgan who was shot uncertain by whom for their adherence to the word of God, and the covenanted work of Reformation 1685." In 1870 the practice began of holding a conventicle in the Old Dailly church-yard on a Sunday afternoon in July, when the memory of the Covenanters is celebrated and their example upheld.

I had little to say about Barr in Chapter XXIV, having gone thither mainly to photograph the stone on the martyr's grave and then returned to Girvan. I had not much to say about Girvan either, but should have mentioned, if I had noticed it, a little monument in the strip of dressed grounds near the harbour bearing the legend, KNOCKUSHION (HILL OF JUSTICE) FROM TIME IMMEMORIAL THE SEAT OF THE HEAD COURTS OF THE JURIS-DICTION OF CARRICK.

The road to Barr branches off the Girvan Valley road and after passing Penkill Castle climbs to the height of six hundred and ninety-five feet. Just beyond the summit there is a place called Peden's Pulpit on the left side of the road, where a stone marks the scene of some of the Prophet's preaching labours. The road then winds downward—this section is known locally as The Corkscrew—into the hollow where Barr lies among its trees and waters, three hundred feet below the pass.

A very few days in Barr are enough to make one aware of its rather unusual attractions, and I stayed there for almost a month. The place is in touch with civilization on the one hand and, on the other, is an outpost towards the wilds. A bus runs between it and Girvan, but there is no regular bus traffic passing through it. In half an hour one can board a train or bus at Girvan for the ends of the earth, while in less than this time one can be plunged deep in the lonely quiet of hills where the chief sounds are those of purling burns and bleating sheep and the calls of grouse, peewits and an occasional black-headed gull. The Stinchar flows past the end of the village between well-wooded banks, receiving up and down its course here and there a tributary rippling gently under the shade of trees or thrown violently down a rocky gully. Barr is indeed a beautiful nook among closely enfolding hills with tall larches, birches, ash-trees and other woodland giants shading the little streets, the grounds of the churches, and the banks of the Gregg Burn.

I had to wait only three days for a dry forenoon. Meanwhile I was very comfortably lodged in *The King's Arms Hotel*, and if there had been need for soporific aid at night, this would have been supplied by the murmur of the Gregg Burn coursing rapidly in those rainy days past the front of the house.

I set off on my bicycle under a dull sky, leaving the village by the road that runs up the Stinchar Glen to Pinvalley [1] farm. Four miles from the starting-point one turns sharply to the right where a finger-post announces that here is a road to Newton Stewart. Beside Pinvalley farm-house I had to open a gate where the road began to climb and made a note of that gate as a danger to be remembered if one should be descending from the Nick of the Balloch in the dark.

A disciple of Wordsworth wrote

> My heart leaps up when I behold
> A single Railway line.

How much more may a connoisseur in travel exult when he comes upon a road that is grass-grown between the wheel-tracks ! I remembered that this was the state of the more easterly road from Straiton at the beginning of the century, but scarcely expected to find grass on a public road in 1937.

The track is the narrowest possible shelf consistently with being a road at all and winds up steep pastoral slopes that descend on the right to ever greater depths as one mounts higher and higher.

---

[1] *Peighinn a' Bhealaigh*, penny-land of the Pass.

A strong wind blowing down the valley made riding the bicycle impossible. This was no loss. Walking gave one more leisure to observe the mountains on the other side and the little glittering cataracts converging to make the Balloch Burn. The steepness and depth of the hillsides reminded me of the great passes between the Clyde and the Nith. There was also a suggestion of spaciousness here from the vista provided by the upper valley out of which the Balloch Burn was descending between the Balloch Hill on my right and the Glengap Hill on my left with, highest of all, the Haggis Hill filling the distance. These hills present a memorable outline that arouses in one the wish to follow it on foot, the alluring features being the nick to which the Balloch Hill falls away on its south side, connecting it with the Haggis Hill, and the tremendous declivity by which this hill in turn falls away on the east and disappears behind the Glengap and Polmaddie hills, leaving one to picture a very deep, narrow ravine. Meanwhile on the road itself there were the incidents of the Shiel Bridge and the Witch's Bridge spanning narrow torrents fringed with ferns that nodded under the impact of the spray of the breaking water. A stone-throw away on the left, just before the former bridge is reached, a sheep-ree encloses a curious structure of great, unhewn stones called The Druid's Grave.

Soon the upper part of the Balloch Valley was shut out as I came abreast of the Glengap Hill rising on the other side of the Corrn Roy Burn, and my attention was now drawn to a cut in the sky-line before me that looked as if it might be the Nick at the head of this tributary glen. In a few minutes I mounted the bicycle and so reached and passed the summit, twelve hundred and eighty-one feet about sea-level; but as the descent towards the junction with the road from Straiton began, there was to be no free-wheeling, for the still contrary wind came swirling along the mountain with great force. The ground now ran down abruptly on the left as it had formerly done on the right, and then, after a wide hollow where amid the brown moor I traced the earliest silvery trickling feeders of the Minnoch Water, rose to a ridge on the other side of which was the glen of the road from Straiton; beyond that was the greater Rig of the Shalloch; while behind that, again, were the more northerly of the mountains that make the western front of the central mass of the Carrick and Galloway Highlands—Shalloch on Minnoch,

Tarriefessock, Kirriereoch and The Merrick. Those trickles made it plain that I had crossed the watershed between the Stinchar flowing to the Firth of Clyde and the Minnoch Water, which after receiving the Water of Trool and many a hillside and moorland burn goes to swell the Cree on its journey to the Bay of Wigton. " Minnoch " means " middle " and marks the course of this river between the Cree and the Water of Trool that converge respectively on the right and on the left. Similarly we find " Loch Minnoch " as the name of a sheet of water lying between Loch Harrow and Loch Dungeon on the east side of the Kells range.

I now saw what the wind that had been hindering me in the Balloch Valley was doing on a broader field—bearing an ever-flowing sea of clouds against the hillsides so that little more than their bases was visible; but I remembered those mountains as I had seen them from other points in better weather and could make a mental picture of the magnificent panorama presented from the Nick of the Balloch under a clear sky.

I soon saw below me the windings of the road from Straiton towards which the track that I was following was gently descending. A few yards short of their meeting-point, the Rowantree Burn passes under bridges on both of the roads, and on its left bank is a rowan tree, probably not the first to give its name to the place, and I hope that it will not be the last to support the name.

At the angle of the roads are the slight remains of the inn and toll-house. These were not coaching roads, and the only traveller's reference that I have found is in Sir Herbert Maxwell's *Evening Memories*, where he tells how when he was a boy of ten years, he was taken with his father and mother on some country house visits : " At that time there was no railway nearer than Ayr sixty miles on the north and Dumfries seventy miles on the east. We travelled post in our big yellow carriage, with luggage atop and boot and rumble filled, over the wild mountainous region between Newton Stewart and Straiton, through the lonely toll bars of Suie and Rowantree, and so to Ayr. My mother whiled away the time by telling me the gruesome story of the Murder Hole."

The building has long been derelict. Latterly the walls had become dangerous, and the County Council were allowed to remove most of the material for the re-making of the road that

was going on in 1937. It was stipulated, however, by the landlord that the front wall should be reduced only to road-level,
which meant that, owing to the slope of the ground, the back
wall should be four feet high, and thus the outline of the house is
preserved.

At the schoolhouse, a mile farther on, I got directions for
finding the Murder Hole of fact, which must not be confused
with the part of Loch Neldricken to which Mr. Crockett transferred the name. In an article contributed to *Good Words* by
Sir Herbert Maxwell is given the only eye-witness's description
that I have seen : " There was a natural pit of unknown depth,
with a narrow mouth, peering into which one might see—nay,
may see to this day, inky water lipping to the green moss growing around the orifice. This murder hole has never revealed the
full tale of its secrets, for it cannot be cleared out ; but it was
to its depths that the remains of the victims were one by one
committed." Since this was written the hole has been filled up
to prevent its being a danger to children and sheep ; but the
site can be seen in a hollow of the moor just below the sheep-rees
of Craigenreoch. " Into this hole," says Mr. John McBain,
" two tramps threw the body of a man they had murdered and
robbed, and they were afterwards hanged for the crime near the
spot." A fuller Murder Hole narrative is given in Chapter XXIX,
and Sir Herbert Maxwell gives the version that he received in
*Evening Memories*.

The powerful wind that had opposed my upward journey to
the Nick of the Balloch still held and, as I returned towards the
Nick, swept me before it. At the summit the depth of the glen
was abruptly revealed, and although I had come up that way a
few hours earlier, it gave me a shock of surprise, something like
the startling effect that John Keats knew on seeing Ailsa Craig
suddenly ; but the road is narrow enough and, after passing the
summit, steep enough to demand close attention on either
bicycle or car, and I found myself taking little note of the scenery.
I was merely aware of a great prospect in the north, lines of
hills ranged behind one another like ridges of a field. On another
visit a few days later I saw also, beyond the hills, the Isle of
Arran, the intervening Firth of Clyde, and the Peninsula of
Kintyre.

The brakes were in use during almost the whole of the descent,
for the wind that had hindered me so much in the forenoon was

now blowing me downhill; at an outward bend of the track it gave me a dangerous buffet. One of my most memorable bicycle-rides was from the capital of Venezuela to the port of La Guaira. Then it seemed as if my fingers must be permanently stretched through the strain of holding the brakes. The descent from the Nick of the Balloch is not nearly so long, nor is it so steep; but it brought vividly to mind that earlier adventure.

After once scrambling up by the Nick and coming out upon the high, windy spaces, I was allured to repeat the journey and cross the Minnoch Valley to the mountains. Especially attractive was the rarely-climbed Shalloch on Minnoch, its outline from easterly points of view, as I had hitherto seen it most often, is so striking, and it has the statistical interest of being the highest mountain belonging exclusively to Ayrshire.

Three days after the journey to Rowantree the sun was shining in the morning, and although the weather forecast was not encouraging, I took the Nick of the Balloch road again. At the house of Shalloch on Minnoch the herd's wife detailed one of her ten children to guide me to the Session Stone, a large slab on the edge of the right bank of the Shalloch Burn, where Covenant-ing preachers are said to have led the worship of congregations during the Persecution. It is easy to believe the tradition. On the other side of the burn is a level space with a curved bank behind it that would make a good auditorium on a still day or in a westerly breeze. The Stone can be easily identified from its size and the initials of visitors carved on its surface. Mr. Crockett made use of it in *The Men of the Moss-hags* : " Opposite the Session Stone was a wide heathery amphitheatre where, as on tiers of seats, rows of men and women could sit and listen to the preachers. The burnie's voice filled up the breaks in the speech as it ran, small and black with the drought, under the hollow of the bank."

We made our way up the glen under a darkening sky, the weather seeming to fit the pathetic associations of the place. As we tramped over heath and moss amid scattered boulders, I told my young companion that it had been a custom of the herds in these parts to trample on the peewits' eggs whenever they found them, and that it had arisen in the days when our Covenant-ing forefathers had been hunted on the hills by dragoons and had had to meet with the utmost secrecy when they wished to worship God as faithful sons of the reformed Church of Scotland. Their reason for the destruction was that the peewit, alarmed by their presence, was very apt by its outcry to betray them to their enemies. Even in the nineteenth century instances of the practice occurred on the part of herds who did not know its origin. My guide had not heard of it.

From the Session Stone I took a fairly direct course towards the summit of Shalloch on Minnoch. As I climbed the long, easy slope, the weather became gloomier, the threatening clouds that were being borne inland from the Atlantic making a grand, though not a welcome, spectacle. The threat was soon fulfilled in falling rain. As I turned and looked southward, the far-spread lowlands with an occasional clump of little hills and here and there a sullen-looking loch or a dark plantation were turned to a purple-grey that seemed to be verging on black, and there darted into my mind the Hebrew tradition about a darkness that once fell upon the land of Egypt. Through the twilight I could see a hazy appearance of Arran with the Holy Isle shewing some-what less dimly like a dwarf Ailsa Craig. On the south of the hills gathered about the Balloch Valley I saw in the distance Knockdolian, also with a look of Ailsa Craig, but nearer the size of that great rock, and in the remote south could just make out the Knock of Luce.

At three points during that dismal ascent the royal blue of the common milkwort peeping up through grass, heath or sphagnum moss was a refreshing sight. The really common flowers on these mountains are the tormentil, the bog-asphodel and the eye-bright. Like the tormentil and eye-bright, the blaeberry plant accompanied me all the way to the top.[1]

Meanwhile dense clouds were trailing long, ragged skirts low upon The Merrick, Kirriereoch, Tarriefessock and Shalloch on Minnoch itself, and I reminded myself that I had a compass. I was too far up the hill to think of turning back. Just before I entered the cloud zone, I got a glimpse past the north-east front of Kirriereoch of a large part of Loch Enoch on its high shelf, a sight that after an interval of many years was worth the endurance of much mist and rain. My flimsy waterproof did not save me from being pretty thoroughly soaked from the waist downwards ; but I knew that there was an abundant supply of

---

[1] Mr. McBain has a chapter on the wild plants found among the Galloway Highlands and numerous allusions elsewhere in his *The Merrick and the Neighbouring Hills.*

hot water in the bathroom of the hotel at Barr and was sure that the herd's wife at the bottom of the hill would give me as many cups of tea as I wished even if I had not complimented her on the handsome contribution that she had made to the population of the country !

When I reached the cairns on the summit, there was nothing

*The Merrick from Loch Enoch.*

to be seen but the bare surface with its scant vegetation, and I had to content myself once more with calling to mind haunts of former years, from Loch Doon in the north to the Black Water

of Dee, from the neighbourhood of which I had often looked up
to the majestic eastern front of this mountain.

Honour had been satisfied with two ascents to the Nick of
the Balloch under my own power. When at last, in the middle
of July, there came a fine day that I could devote to The
Merrick, I used a motor-car to save time on the preliminary
journey to the herd's house of Tarriefessock. The undulating
floor of the Minnoch Valley was saturated with the recent rains
and, wishing to keep my boots and stockings dry for at least the
first half of the day, I took them off and walked barefoot. The
only discomfort was caused by the hard stems of the frequent
bog-myrtle, and these could usually be avoided. This, however,
was a very slow way of crossing the country, and on reaching
some rising ground near the farther side of the valley, I made
better speed, with my boots in their proper place, to the con-
fluence of the Kirshinnoch and Cross Burns.

Wading through the latter and passing the sheep-rees of
Kirriereoch, I held on up the right bank of the Kirshinnoch Burn
with the grim northern front of The Merrick before me. From
this approach the mountain looks like a megatherium risen
from the primeval slime, but now well washed by the rains of
the milleniums and lying at rest with head averted from Goat-
fell as if in calm disapproval of that insular neighbour visible
across Ayrshire and the Firth of Clyde, who may queen it over
Arran if she likes, but must not put on airs because of some
superiority in the number of her inches and dispute the monarchy
of The Merrick, whose realm extends from the North Sea to the
Atlantic Ocean.

The Kirshinnoch Burn runs between high banks. On reaching a double bend that made a place of shelter from the wind
blowing up the glen, I had a bathe in the burn, a sun-bathe on
a rock in the midst of the singing water, and a light luncheon,
a programme that made a good preparation for the real ascent.
Crossing to the left bank, I climbed the fairly steep slope at the
east end of the Kirriemore[1] Hill abutting on The Merrick, in
the latter part following the line of a ruined dyke, where the
parsley fern abounded.

Thereafter the ascent of The Merrick was as easy as that of
Shalloch on Minnoch. The sky was now somewhat overcast, but

----

[1] *Coire mór*, great corrie. *Coire*, literally a cauldron, but used
figuratively to denote a great hollow in a hillside.—Maxwell.

there was abundance of diffused sunlight, and much more extensive views were opened up than from Shalloch on Minnoch on that day of gloom. The Argyll hills overhanging the lochs at the upper end of the Firth of Clyde; the Isle of Arran and the Peninsula of Kintyre; Luce Bay and the Rhinns of Galloway; the Isle of Man; Screel and Bengairn near Castle Douglas; the coast of Cumberland; the Criffel group of hills above Newabbey were more or less clear. One looked down upon the mountains that confine Glentrool and that, seen from the bottom of that glen, appear so high. Farther off was the great mass of Cairnsmore of Fleet. Loch Trool was hidden by the Buchan Hill, Benyellary and the Fell of Eschoncan; but the Lochs of Glenhead, Loch Valley, Loch Narroch, a bit of Loch Neldricken, and, ten miles away in the south-east, the reservoir at Clatteringshaws lay amid the sombre colours of the mountains like pools of light. The Kells range filled the easterly view leading the eye northwards to Loch Doon. Turning to the north-east one saw at a great depth that pool which is dignified with the name of Loch Twachtan and farther away, a little north of the latitude of Shalloch on Minnoch, Lochs Macaterick, Slochy and Recar,[1] and other waters beyond.

Scattered thinly over the broad summit of the Silurian mass of The Merrick are large igneous boulders. Some geologists have held that they consist of Cairnsmore of Fleet granite and that they have been carried to The Merrick on floating ice. This hill is about four hundred feet higher than Cairnsmore, and the explanation offered of the greater elevation of their resting-place is that Cairnsmore has lost much of its height through sub-aerial denudation. The opinion held at the Scottish Office of the Geological Survey of Great Britain is that the Cairnsmore of Fleet granite cannot be distinguished with certainty from that of the mass lying below The Merrick on the east and known as the Loch Doon granite, they are so similar in character, and their variations are of the same kind. The glacial *striae* recorded on the large-scale geological maps " indicate in general a dispersal of ice from The Merrick as centre, but also there is an indication of a drift from east to west along the shoulder of The Merrick, as if the centre of dispersal lay at one time somewhat

---

[1] Loch Recar, near Loch Doon, seems to be for *loch an reacaire*; the *reacaire* was the person in the train of a bard who recited the poem composed by the bard himself.—Watson.

east of the summit. The presence of granite boulders is noted
on The Merrick without comment, and the inference is that they
are of the same character as that of the large granite mass that
lies immediately east of The Merrick. Movement uphill in an
ice current is a not uncommon phenomenon." I am indebted
to Mr. John B. Simpson, D.Sc., of the Geological Survey for
the letter from which I have quoted. There are, it may be noted
here, some fascinating pages on the Galloway and Carrick hills
in Sir Archibald Geikie's *The Scenery of Scotland viewed in
Connexion with its Physical Geology*.

Recent researches[1] on the Loch Doon granite area shew
that it is composed of three varieties of igneous rock. " The
prevalent type is a quartz mica diorite or tonalite. The central
ridge ", of which Mullwharchar, The Dungeon and Craignaw
are the chief heights, " is formed of biotite granite, while the
southern and north-western ends of the mass are norite. Therefore only the central mass can be termed a granite." The area
occupied by this intrusive mass is rectangular, measuring eleven
and a half miles in length and at its greatest width six and a
half.[2] On the west are the shales, grits, cherts, and greywacke
of The Merrick, and on the east those of Corserine. On the
right and the left of the central ridge of granite is found a
transition rock between granite and tonalite ; then the tonalite [3]
on the extreme right and left.

The detailed study given to the geology of this area by Mr.
F. I. Gardiner and Professor S. H. Reynolds did not extend
to the boulders lying on the summit of The Merrick, a thousand
feet above their field of work. Their concern was with the
types of igneous rocks in the well-defined area of their choice
and with their inter-relations and the effect of their heat on the

[1] See page x.
[2] Mr. R. J. A. Eckford estimates the extent of the other granite
areas in Galloway thus : " The Loch Dee granite approximately
covers forty-seven square miles of country. It is the smallest of
the three large Galloway intrusions. The Criffel and Dalbeattie
mass has a surface area of seventy-five square miles, while that of
Cairnsmore of Fleet is fifty-seven square miles. In addition to these
major intrusions there are a large number of minor ones, the largest
of these being Cairnsmore of Carsphairn, Drumore, and Creetown."
—The chapter on " The Geology of the Merrick Region " in Mr.
Andrew McCormick's *Galloway : The Spell of its Hills and Glens*.
[3] Mr. Eckford gives a diagram of a section of the rocks between
The Merrick and Corserine *ibid*.

surrounding sedimentary rocks. It would be interesting to know what conclusions could be drawn from the application to the boulders of the methods of examination used by them on the area of igneous rocks below.

The deposits of granite boulders that have been dropped by the glacier in the neighbourhood of The Merrick provide homes for the foxes and the otters, who make their furtive journeys by night. Apart from a few sheep, there is no appearance of animal life by day. Conditions are much changed since Loch Neldricken was named. The hill near the loch that is known as Craig Neldricken would naturally bear the name before the loch received it, for Dr. Watson, Professor of Celtic Languages in Edinburgh University, tells us that the word means " the deer trap ". He also helps us to picture what it meant : " The *eileirg* was a defile, natural or artificial, wider at one end than at the other, into which the deer were driven, often in hundreds, and slain as they passed through. The slaughter at the *eileirg* was the last stage in the great deer hunts which were once so common in Scotland and which survived in the north till the eighteenth century." [1]

Among the greater birds that may be seen in this wilderness the golden eagle can still be named ; but he comes only as a visitor taking an occasional glance at an old home of the family.

I left the summit by The Fang of The Merrick, a very narrow spur falling northwards at the east end of the mountain. So narrow and so steep is the descent that it is almost like coming down a ladder. So one drops upon a ridge giving an outlook, as if from an elevated gallery, over Loch Enoch and the granite hills that slope away from its shores—Mullwharchar and The Dungeon.

The western half of Loch Enoch lies on tonalite, according to the map of the Loch Doon area that accompanies Messrs. Gardiner and Reynolds' dissertation, and the eastern on the transitional rock between tonalite and granite. The boundary line runs through the west end of the more easterly of the two bays on the north side of Loch Enoch, passes through the eastern edge of the promontory on the south side, follows the eastern shore of Loch Neldricken and the north-east shore of Loch Valley, cuts across the promontory, and leaves Loch Valley some yards on the west of its extreme east point, then makes a roughly semi-circular curve towards the Cooran Lane, which it

---

[1] *The History of the Celtic Place-Names of Scotland.* See footnote on page 168 *infra*.

crosses in a northerly direction at a point in the same latitude as the Long Loch of Glenhead.

A little lower I found a stream breaking from some stones and flanked by sheets of moss through which the brook rockfoil held up its white cups. Botanical authorities seem to assume that the only British home of this high Alpine or Arctic plant is in the northern Highlands.

Descending into the glen of the Kirshinnoch Burn, I took the right bank because I should thus get a better view of the mountain that I was leaving. Along the skirts of Kirriereoch I found among the Silurian debris an abundance of the parsley fern. There were also some common, but ever-beautiful, ferns sheltered among rocks ; and at two or three points the blue bell, known in England as the harebell, shewed that it was not altogether a stranger. On passing an accumulation of boulders it occurred to me that here was a likely home for foxes, and so it must have been for ages, for " Kirshinnoch " means " the foxes' crag ". But more noteworthy than these details was the northern front of The Merrick overhanging one in this narrow glen, almost vertical precipices alternating with driblets of scree as if the monster were baring his teeth and slavering at the thought of a victim.

*Loch-in-loch, Loch Enoch.*

Rockcliffe.

## NOTE ON PTOLEMY'S PLACE-NAMES

SOME readers will like to have the very words of Claudius
Ptolemaeus of Alexandria,[1] the earliest geographer to give any
details concerning the south-west of Scotland. The passages
occur in his ΓΕΩΓΡΑΦΙΚΗΣ ΥΦΗΓΗΣΕΩΣ (*Geographicæ
Enarrationis*) II, 2. I quote from F. G. Wilberg's edition,
omitting the figures for latitude and longitude. The chapter is
headed Ἀλουίωνος νήσου Βρεττανικῆς Εὐρώπης πίναξα (*Albionis
insulæ Britannicæ situs. Europæ tabula prima*).

(1) Ἀρκτικῆς πλευρᾶς περιγραφή, ἧς ὑπέρκειται Ὠκεανὸς καλού-
μενος Δουηκαληδόνιος. Νοουαντῶν χερσόνησος καὶ ὁμώνυμον
ἄκρον . . . Ῥεριγόνιος κόλπος . . . Οὐινδόγαρα κόλπος . . . Κλῶτα
εἴσχυσις . . . . . .

(2) Δυσμικῆς πλευρᾶς περιγραφή, ᾗ παράκειται ὅ τε Ἰουέρνιος
Ὠκεανὸς καὶ ὁ Οὐεργιουίος· μετὰ τὴν Νοουαντῶν χερσόνησον, ἣ
ἐπέχει . . . Ἀβραουάννου ποταμοῦ ἐκβολαί . . . Ἰηνᾶ εἴσχυσις . . .
Δηούα ποταμοῦ ἐκβολαί . . . Νοουίου ποταμοῦ ἐκβολαί . . . . . .

(3) Οἰκοῦσι δὲ τὰ μὲν παρὰ τὴν ἀρκτικὴν πλευρὰν ὑπὸ μὲν τὴν
ὁμώνυμον χερσόνησον Νοουάνται, παρ' οἷς εἰσι καὶ πόλεις αἵδε.
Λουκοπιβία . . . Ῥετιγόνιον [by mistake for Ῥεριγόνιον read by
some MSS.].

Ὑφ' οὓς Σελγουύαι, παρ' οἷς πόλεις Καρβαντόριγον . . .
Οὔξελλον . . . Κόρδα . . . Τριμόντιον . . .

In the Latin version these passages are as follows :

(1) *Septentrionalis lateris descriptio, supra quod est Oceanus*

[1] The last recorded incident in his life belongs to A.D. 151.

*qui dicitur Duecaledonius. Novantarum Chersonesus et ciusdem nominis promontorium . . . . Rerigonius sinus . . . . Vindogara sinus . . . . Clotæ æstuarium. . . . .*

(2) *Occidentalis lateris descriptio, cui adiacet et Hibernius Oceanus et Vergivius ; post Novantarum Chersonesum, quæ est . . . . Abravanni fluvii ostia . . . . Ienæ æstuarium . . . . Devæ fluvii ostia . . . . Novii fluvii ostia. . . . .*

(3) *Incolunt præter septentrionale latus infra eiusdem cognominis Chersonesum Novantæ, apud quos hæc sunt oppida : Lucopibia . . . . Rhetigonium. . . .*

*Infra quos Selgovæ, apud quos sunt oppida Carbantorigum . . . . Uxellum . . . . Corda . . . . Trimontium. . . . .*

Some of the identifications seem obvious—Νοουαντῶν χερσόνησος as The Rhinns, and the ἄκρον as the Mull of Galloway ; but Ptolemy's measurements point rather to the Mull of Kintyre or, as Mr. T. G. Rylands[1] concludes after an exhaustive analysis, to the Point of Aird in Skye. 'Ρεριγόνιος κόλπος is Loch Ryan, and 'Ρεριγόνιον, a town in its neighbourhood, perhaps on the site of Innermessan. A Grecized form of the Gaelic *aber aimhne*, " mouth of the river ", is seen in 'Αβραουάννος, denoting the Luce. 'Ιηνᾶ εἴσχυσις corresponds to the estuary of the Cree. Skene[2] points out that the early Latin editions have, instead of *Ienæ æstuarium, Fines æstus,* and thinks that this may be the correct reading, and that Wigton Bay may have marked the utmost limit to which the Roman troops penetrated in Agricola's second campaign. Δηούα is, of course, the Dee, and Νοουίος, the Nith.

Where the names themselves are not evidence, Ptolemy's figures make it impossible to be sure of his exact positions. The sites of Wigton and Whithorn have been suggested for Λουκοπιβία. Καρβαντόριγον is assigned by Ptolemy to the *Selgovæ,* but appears to have been within the territory of the *Novantæ,* and has been identified with sites on the Urr and the Dee.

[1] *The Geography of Ptolemy Elucidated.*
[2] *Celtic Scotland,* Vol. I., p. 66 n.

# NOTE ON THE GALLOWAY CHURCH WINDOW

THE Rev. Oliver S. Rankin, D.D., D.Litt., Professor of Old Testament Language, Literature, and Theology in Edinburgh University, who was minister of Sorbie Parish from 1912 till 1937, has kindly provided ·me with his commentary on the window erected in Sorbie Church in memory of Sir Malcolm McEacharn, who purchased the Galloway House estate from the Earl of Galloway in 1909. The main conception is illustrated so aptly with representations of the most important events in the founding of the Celtic Church in the Province that it deserves to be regarded as The Galloway Church Window and not merely as the treasure of a single parish.

Professor Rankin's notes (written for the parishioners of Sorbie) follow :—

The chief theme of the window is found in the Latin (Vulgate, Gen. i. 3) inscription under the great six-foil tracery—" Dixitque Deus : Fiat lux. Et facta est lux "—which in our English is, " And God said, Let there be light : and there was light." In accordance with this theme of light we have represented in the headpiece of the window the creation of light, the light moving over the dark waters and struggling with the darkness. A dove, the symbol of the Holy Spirit (see Matt. iii. 16), is seen hovering over all (" Et spiritus Dei ferebatur super aquas "— " and the Spirit of God moved [in Hebrew hovered] upon the face of the waters "), and the idea of the Spirit moving over the face of the deep is further expressed by the four winds as angels in passage over the ocean. From the wings of these angel-bearers of God's Spirit dart beams of light. There is the north wind with dark and clouded countenance, coming in the snow-storm and with all the treasures and brightness of the falling snow; the west wind, with the red glow of the setting sun ; the south wind, with sombre aspect of face, but yet milder than the north ; the east wind, with the radiance of the sun-rising and the glory of " rosy fingered Dawn ".

These winds, as carriers of the Spirit of God and of the Light which dispels darkness, are one of the finest features of the window, not only because the idea in itself is beautiful, but because throughout the thought of Scripture has been followed. For example, in Gen. iii. 8 (Heb. text), Adam and Eve heard " the voice of the Lord God going in the garden in the wind of the day ", and they were afraid and hid themselves. Daniel (vii. 2) says, " I saw in my vision by night, and, behold, the four winds of the heavens strove upon the great sea." In Psalm civ. 3–4, in the original text, God reveals Himself in the wind and the lightning ; it is He " who walketh upon the wings of the wind, who maketh winds His messengers, flaming fire His ministers ". New Testament illustrations of this thought are Rev. vii. 1, and the Greek of John iii. 8. In the Old Testament " wind " and " spirit " are both the same word, Ruach.

In the lower divisions of the window the subject is still God's Light and Spirit, but this time historical personages are the bearers, or we can say the angels, for the word " angel " means messenger. The theme is : the light of Christianity borne by the missionaries of the cross.

In the part of the window on the east side, we see St. Margaret landing in Scotland (about 1068 A.D.) (" Sancta Margarita in Scotiam agreditur "). We see her ship, with the dragon-shaped prow, approaching, and at the landing-stage she is being welcomed by a kindly figure in armour, Malcolm Canmore, King of Scotland, who was soon to make Margaret his wife. Queen and saint, she was " a woman of great beauty of character. Devout, learned, and munificent, she exercised a marvellous influence for good both upon king and court, clergy and people." She brought with her civilization and culture. " Her husband was awed by the spectacle of her devotion, and ' seeing that Christ dwelt in her heart was always ready to follow her counsels ; what she disliked he disliked, and what she loved he loved for the love of her.' " In those days, as in our day, there were many who would not come to Holy Communion because they were not " worthy ". " What," said the Queen, " shall no one that is a sinner taste that holy mystery ? If so, then it follows that no one at all should receive it, for no one is pure from sin—no, not the infant whose life is but one day upon the earth." Not going to Church had also become a very bad habit at that time in Scotland, and people followed their usual occupations on the

Lord's Day as on other days. On Margaret's remonstrance this was entirely changed, and the Sunday restored to its proper purpose. In 1093, when she was on her death-bed in Edinburgh Castle, word was brought her that her husband and eldest son were slain in battle with the English. Though the news was sadness, yet with words of praise she gave thanks to God, and with this prayer upon her lips, " O Lord Jesus Christ, who by the will of the Father and through the Holy Spirit by Thy death hast given life unto the world, deliver me," there passed away a beautiful and saintly lady, of whom Scotland may well be proud.

In the central division of the window St. Ninian is showing the plans for building the first church in Scotland, called Candida Casa, or the White House (built 402 A.D.), to a Roman master-builder on his right, and to the native people of the land, of the warrior and pastoral classes, on his left. The Latin under this is, " Sanctus Ninian aedificat templum candidam casam "— " St. Ninian builds the church of Candida Casa ".

Over the picture of St. Ninian showing his plan we see the door of the new church, on either side of which grows the Tree of Life. The church-door represents at the same time the gate of the city of Tours, the town of St. Martin, St. Ninian's teacher. In the gate-way St. Martin on horse-back is pictured in the act of dividing his robe and giving half to a naked beggar. St. Martin, according to the legend, dreamed that night that he saw Christ in heaven showing the robe which he had given to the beggar, as a gift that had been given to Himself. This scene of the heavenly Christ displaying the robe is depicted in the uppermost portion of the arch of the church (or city) entrance. The intention of this is doubtless to show that Charity is the key-stone of the Church—" Except the Lord build the house, they labour in vain that build it : except the Lord keep the city, the watchman waketh but in vain." Farther up we perceive the church in building, a scaffolding and workmen at work.

In connection with the centre picture of Ninian, which records his historical evangelical work, are two others, one in each side division of the window, which though legend are the vehicles of spiritual truths. The first is the legend that St. Ninian placed in the earth the staff of St. Martin, to the possession of which he credits his being saved from shipwreck, and there-upon the staff becomes a branching tree. This is the import of the writing underneath—" Juvenis e naufragio ereptus baculum quo servatus in terram imponit." The second subject, on the western part of the window, is a garden springing up miraculously at the prayer of Ninian and yielding vegetables and fruits (" Hortus mirabiliter Ninia rogante fructum effundit "). Both these legends are exceedingly well executed, and their meaning finds a beautiful commentary in that striking fifty-fifth chapter of Isaiah (*vv.* 8–10). They both show the fruitfulness of the labours of the missionary light-bearers, how under their care the cause of Christ prospered and spread like a tree planted near a river, and how the torch of the Faith has been carried by one emissary after another ever farther throughout the ages.

Lastly, in the window's western light, St. Columba is landing (563 A.D.) with his companions in Iona (" Sanctus Columba in Ionam escendit "), and various inhabitants go forth to greet him. The ship which bears him to these shores has for figure-head a pelican. From her breast, from self-inflicted wound, flows blood with which she nourishes her thirsting brood. Thus is symbolized the love, sacrifice and endurance of this missionary saint. In Iona St. Columba was occupied " in directing the affairs of the little community, in constructing simple buildings for dwelling and for worship, in manual toil, and in transcribing copies of the Holy Scriptures ". He worked in Scotland thirty-four years. One Saturday in the month of June 597 he said, " This day is in the Holy Scriptures called the Sabbath, which means rest. And this day is indeed a Sabbath to me, for it is the last of my laborious life ; and this night at midnight, which commenceth the solemn Lord's Day, I shall go the way of our fathers." The same day going back to his cell in the monastery, he resumed his work of writing out copies of the Scriptures. He had just written the words of the thirty-fourth Psalm, " They that seek the Lord shall not want any good thing ", when he stopped and said, " Here must I end ; what follows let Baithene write." At midnight, when the community went to prayer, he hastened to the altar and knelt down. There his strength failed him, and blessing by signs the brethren, who could no longer hear him, he breathed forth his soul.

God's Light, God's Word, God's Spirit, creative, active, is the story of our painted pane. We are happy in the possession of its story, and the work of those here honoured in our Church for their furtherance of the Gospel of Christ should cause the thought to rise in us that we too must be bearers of the light.

O. S. RANKIN.

The window was designed and executed by Mr. Christopher Whall (1849–1924), of whose work numerous examples are to be seen in England and America. According to *The Journal of the American Institute of Architects*, " his acknowledged masterpiece is the group of six great windows in the Lady Chapel of Gloucester Cathedral." His daughter and pupil, Miss Veronica Whall (of Messrs. Whall & Whall, Ltd., London), in a letter to Dr. Rankin dated February 12th, 1938, said, " I have always thought the window in Sorbie one of his best." The periodical quoted stated that " he may almost be credited with the discovery of white glass ". This appears in the snowflakes in the upper portion of the Sorbie window.

*The Road along the Urr Water.*

# NOTE ON THE GALLOWAY HYDRO-ELECTRIC SCHEME

I HAVE to thank the Galloway Water Power Company for putting into my hands a copy of a *brochure* giving an account of the Hydro-Electric Scheme. Their map has made it possible to bring mine up to date. The reservoirs are shewn, and these may be expected to add to the angling opportunities of The Glenkens. The Dee and the Doon are salmon rivers, and fish ladders or passes have been formed at the necessary points. The pass at Tongland near Kirkcudbright makes an ascent of seventy feet. " It consists of thirty-five pools, of which four are large resting pools. Each pool is connected to the next by a submerged orifice through which the water descends and the fish swim up. The pass is the highest in the British Isles and it has proved remarkably successful in practice, some sixty fish having been counted in the pass at one time when it has been closed at both ends for inspection."

Special interest attaches to the pass for the river Doon. The reservoir level at the Loch Doon dam can vary as much as forty feet. In order to provide easy access from the pass into the reservoir at all levels a unique design has been adopted. " The pools are arranged in an ascending spiral inside a circular tower, and whichever pool is at the level of the water in the reservoir outside will be connected with it by means of a small sluice-gate through which the fish can pass." It is further stated that " from the base of the circular tower a channel runs through the base of the dam to the river below, and 45 million gallons of compensation water are to be discharged down the river each day together with an artificial spate of 80 million gallons once every three weeks ". Similar compensation is made on the Dee.

Loch Doon naturally discharges its waters by the river of the same name into the Firth of Clyde ; but the construction of the dam has enabled the Company to over-ride the watershed and by means of a tunnel considerably more than a mile long divert its waters into the Ken valley so as to pass through the power-stations at Kendoon, Carsfad, Earlston and Tongland.

An inevitable result of the raising of the level of the loch has been the submersion of the small islands near the head. The remains of Loch Doon Castle, which is mentioned on page 423, stood on one of the islands; but before the scheme was carried out, the walls of the castle were photographed, the stones numbered, and the structure re-built on the west bank at the nearest possible point to the old site under the supervision of His Majesty's Office of Works during the winter of 1935–36.

An interesting peculiarity of the scheme is that Loch Doon is made to store water " not only from its own watershed, but also from the upper reaches of the Water of Deugh and the Bow Burn ", both of which belong to the Ken system. " In times of heavy rainfall surplus water from these two rivers is carried through the Deugh Tunnel, 7,400 feet long, which is connected by a steel pipe-line to the Loch Doon Tunnel, the flow in which is then reversed so that the surplus water is carried back to Loch Doon and stored there for use in drier periods."

Visitors who are not engineers may wish to know the part played by the circular buildings that rise beside the power-houses. These are known as surge towers. " When a machine is closed down suddenly," the surge tower " allows the water from the aqueduct to rise into it unchecked till it finds its own level and so avoids water hammer in the pipe-line and aqueduct." In the case of the Glenlee power-house a surge chamber has been excavated in the hillside near the outlet of the tunnel that brings the water from Clatteringshaws reservoir.

The history of the scheme has been briefly summarized thus : " Scheme in formulation by the engineers, 1923–1926 ; Parliamentary powers obtained, 1929 ; works begun, 1931 ; works put into service, 1935–1936."

The Company state that " the cost of the complete scheme, including costs of Parliamentary promotion and of capitalized interest, management, legal and general expenses during the construction period, is estimated at about £3,000,000, or approximately £29 per kilowatt. The cost of generation of current is estimated at about one-third of a penny per unit for 182,000,000 units per annum, with a peak-load of 103,000 kw. and an annual load factor of 20 per cent.

" Glenlee Power Station went into commercial operation in March 1935 and Tongland Station in May 1935. During the six months ended March 1936 these two Stations together generated 88·5 million units."

_"The Ken near Dalry, as it was."_

# INDEX